BH217Hm   +

Hecht.

Odd destiny , the life of
Alexander Hamilton.

1982

ODD DESTINY

Beyond the Presidency: The Residues of Power

John Quincy Adams: A Personal History of an Independent Man

Never Again: A President Runs for a Third Term (with Herbert S. Parmet)

Aaron Burr: Portrait of an Ambitious Man (with Herbert S. Parmet)

ODD DESTINY

THE LIFE OF

Alexander Hamilton

BY

MARIE B. HECHT

MACMILLAN PUBLISHING CO., INC.

NEW YORK

Copyright © 1982 by Marie B. Hecht

Macmillan Publishing Co., Inc.
866 Third Avenue, New York, N.Y. 10022
Collier Macmillan Canada, Inc.

Library of Congress Cataloging in Publication Data

Hecht, Marie B.
    Odd destiny, the life of Alexander Hamilton.

    Bibliography: p.
    Includes index.
        1. Hamilton, Alexander, 1757–1804. 2. United
States—Politics and government—1783–1809.
3. Statesmen—United States—Biography. I. Title.
E302.6.H2H42   973.4′092′4 [B]   81–18578
ISBN 0–02–550180–1   AACR2

10   9   8   7   6   5   4   3   2   1

Printed in the United States of America

For two modern Hamiltonians,

LAURENCE AND MARJORIE HECHT,

with my respect and love

For there is justice in the claim that steadfastness in his country's battles should be as a cloak to cover a man's other imperfections; since the good action has blotted out the bad, and his merit as a citizen more than outweighed his demerits as an individual.

—PERICLES

Contents

ODD DESTINY

The Price of Illegitimacy

WHEN URBANE, WITTY Gouverneur Morris was asked to deliver Alexander Hamilton's funeral oration, he confided to his diary the problems that the assignment presented. "The first point of his biography," Morris said, "is that he was a stranger of illegitimate birth; some plan must be contrived to pass over this handsomely."[1] It is clear, despite protestations of generations of Hamilton biographers, that his bar sinister did not interfere with his public or private image; the truth is to the contrary. Elementary acquaintance with human psychology leaves no doubt that a brilliant, sensitive youngster must have been profoundly affected by the irregularity of his birth. Add to Hamilton's illegitimacy: poverty, desertion by his father and the death of his mother, all by the age of twelve; and the enormity of his childhood burden becomes apparent.

Hamilton tried to obliterate or to rearrange his past when he became a man. He told his children almost nothing about his childhood but attempted, rather, to cultivate a connection with his father's aristocratic family. It took the efforts of two twentieth-century biographers, Gertrude Atherton and Broadus Mitchell, to unearth what moldering traces were left of Hamilton's ancestry and childhood. In the West Indian islands of Nevis, St. Croix and St. Kitts, they ferreted out the roots of America's most eminent and influential eighteenth-century immigrant.

Alexander Hamilton was born on Nevis, a small island of the Leeward group, east of St. Croix. Tradition attributes its name to Columbus, who mistook a white cloud that hung over its peak for snow and called it Neve (snow in Spanish). Green, lush, dominated by Columbus's cone-shaped volcanic mountain, and surrounded by the deep blue sparkling sea, the island was taken from Spain by the

British during the rule of Oliver Cromwell. Soon afterward, Charles-town, its main city, became an important, busy seaport.

Hamilton always boasted that he was part French. His maternal grandfather, John Fawcett—probably originally Faucette—was a doctor and planter, forced to flee France along with masses of other Huguenots after the revocation of the Edict of Nantes. He married Mary Uppington, an Englishwoman much younger than he, and they lived on an estate called Gingerland. The couple had two daughters, Ann and Rachel. Ann, the elder by some fifteen years, was married in about 1730 to a planter named James Lytton. Because of a severe drought on Nevis in 1737, the Lyttons moved to the Danish island of St. Croix, where they bought a plantation named the Grange #9.

The Fawcetts' marriage was very unhappy. Among their problems were the age difference between them and constant quarrels about money. In early 1740, a separation was arranged in which Mrs. Fawcett was awarded an annual payment of fifty-three pounds and custody of Rachel, in return for relinquishing all rights to her husband's property. Mary soon discovered that a young, pretty girl growing up alone with an aging mother was more of a responsibility than a comfort. She looked around for a suitable husband for Rachel and, like so many matchmaking mothers, engineered a domestic disaster.

Sometime in 1745, sixteen-year-old Rachel Fawcett married John Michael Lavien or Levine, a merchant and planter from St. Croix, at least thirty-eight years old and a friend of the Lyttons. According to Allen McLane Hamilton, Alexander's grandson, Lavien was a Danish Jew, but newer evidence supports his German origin.

John Fawcett's will throws some light on the marriage. Rachel was left all his estate and real property. The windfall improved the financial picture for both mother and daughter, who left Nevis and moved to St. Croix. Undoubtedly news of Rachel's inheritance spread to the Lyttons and their friends, so it is likely that Lavien thought he had snared an heiress. Rachel was equally deceived, because Mrs. Fawcett believed that Lavien, whose finances were never stable, was a prosperous man.

Apparently the Laviens were mismated, and their marriage was an almost immediate failure. Although Mrs. Fawcett was living on St. Croix, earning her livelihood by renting out her slaves, she was not able to help her daughter adjust to a foreign husband. Mary Fawcett had encouraged Rachel to marry an older man, although her own experience with a May-December alliance had ended in a separation.

Rachel had a son, Peter, born about a year after the marriage, but maternity did not improve her relationship with her husband. Perhaps the victim of physical as well as emotional abuse, she fled her household, leaving baby Peter behind.

Lavien, in a rage, ordered Rachel jailed in the grim fortress at Christiansted, but she was not held there for long. He relented, stating that he was certain her imprisonment would make her more malleable and cause "a change for the better." He was mistaken; once freed, Rachel fled the island for St. Kitts, where she would be safe from her tyrannical husband. She did not try to claim her small son, knowing full well that, under the law, fathers were the legal guardians of their children.

Rachel's family was not particularly sympathetic to her. Wives were expected to endure, and the desertion of one's child, no matter how vicious the behavior of his father, was a bad precedent for all wives and mothers. Even after the rift in the Lavien household, James Lytton, Rachel's brother-in-law, continued to have business dealings with John Michael.[2]

Mary Fawcett took Rachel in, and together they left St. Croix for either St. Kitts or St. Eustatius. Rachel never saw her eldest son again.

By 1752, two years after leaving Lavien, she was living on St. Kitts with James Hamilton. The fourth son of Alexander Hamilton, Laird of Grange, Ayrshire, Scotland, one of the Cambuskieth Hamiltons, and Elizabeth Pollock, eldest daughter of Sir Robert Pollock and Anabella Stuart, James Hamilton was born in 1718. Like many younger sons of large and usually impoverished Scottish families, James was forced to seek his fortune abroad. He chose to go to the West Indies, where, unfortunately, he proved over and over that he had no aptitude for business or commerce. He had a reputation for changing his employment often, shuttling back and forth between the islands without making a permanent home. His erratic behavior was demonstrated dramatically by his desertion of his common-law wife and their children and his evasive behavior toward Alexander, even after his younger son became a famous man.

Accurate dating of the events in Alexander Hamilton's life before he came to America is impossible. Modern scholarship insists that the date of Alexander's birth be moved back from January 11, 1757, to January 11, 1755. The basis for the new date is a record found in the probate court of Christiansted, St. Croix, dated February 22, 1768, in which Alexander's age is given as thirteen and that of his brother James as fifteen. These "bastard children," it states, were born "after the deceased person's [their mother] divorce from said Levine."[3] Uncle James Lytton supplied the boys' ages for the document.

Alexander Hamilton always referred to his age based on the 1757 date. Advocates of the 1755 date cite the probate document as their strongest support but also point out that it provides an explanation for the child Alexander's overwhelming, almost embarrassing precocity. Why then did Hamilton lie about his age? One explanation is that Hamilton started his formal schooling late and wanted to be the same age as the other students. Another, more unkind suggestion is that Hamilton consciously fostered the myth of himself as a child prodigy and a boy hero.

Since the document in question is neither a birth certificate nor a baptismal record, there is no conclusive certainty about the 1755 birth date. This author prefers to preserve the historic image of "the little lion" meeting tremendous odds at a very tender age and so accepts Hamilton's statement that he was born in 1757.

Rachel, her lover and their two sons lived together unchallenged by John Michael Lavien until 1759. Although the abandoned husband knew of his wife's whereabouts and activities, he let the long period of time elapse before he sued for divorce on the grounds that she had abandoned her legal family. The petition alleged that Rachel had forgotten her duty and given herself, "whoring with everyone." These facts were so well known, Lavien charged, that her own family and friends "must hate her for it." He was moved to action, he claimed, because of his concern for the abandoned legitimate child. If he died, still legally married to this "shameless, rude and ungodly woman, she might take all of his worldly goods from the rightful heir and bestow them on her bastards."[4]

In the divorce document, Lavien additonally cited Rachel's dubious conduct on the island of Barbados in 1756, from which arose the speculation that George Washington might have been Alexander Hamilton's father. This story does not hold up. Washington took his brother Laurence to Barbados for his health and stayed with him from September 1751 to February 1752.[5] Alexander was not born until at least 1755. Further, the best historical opinion today says that "it seems probable that, despite his [Washington's] natural reluctance to accept the fact . . . he was sterile."[6] Casting Washington as Hamilton's father is an example of wishful thinking that takes its place beside the legend that Martin Van Buren was Aaron Burr's son. Later it will be argued that Hamilton was the son of Washington's heart, not of his loins.

Rachel ignored the court summons for her divorce hearing, her husband won the uncontested suit and obtained the divorce he sought. "Rachael Lavien shall have no rights whatsoever as wife to either John Michael Lewin's person or means," it read, and her illegitimate children were denied them as well. Furthermore, as mandated by Danish law, Rachel was forbidden to remarry, although her former husband could do so at will.

Once again James Hamilton's conduct becomes controversial. He did not marry his common-law wife now that she was free, nor is there any evidence that he tried to do so under English law. John Church Hamilton, Alexander's son, wrote that, after the divorce, the couple was married at St. Kitts. His statement was nothing more than a son's pious wish to legitimize his father.

Inevitably, news of Hamilton's illegitimacy reached the mainland. Throughout his public career and afterwards, malicious anti-Hamiltonians exploited this fact. Hamilton may have confided the truth to his admiring, understanding father-in-law, Philip Schuyler, and perhaps even to his adoring wife and his beloved eldest son, but none of the Hamilton letters that are preserved mentions the subject. It is known that his widow destroyed some of Hamilton's correspondence; John Church Hamilton, whom his mother chose to write the official biography, asserted that his paternal grandparents were married, and all the other family members clung to the story. Hamilton biographers of the nineteenth and early twentieth centuries either glossed over the subject or repeated the official position. Illegitimacy did not suit the dignity of a Founding Father.

Rachel's involvement with James Hamilton embroiled her once more in a difficult relationship, though her family and friends did not ostracize her. There is a record of James and Rachel standing as godparents to Alexander Thornton, four months old, in 1758. But lack of money and James's inability to hold a steady job ate away at the precarious connection.

It is impossible even to speculate on James Hamilton as a father. It suited Alexander in later years to maintain a sporadic correspondence with his father and to offer him money and hospitality. The money was accepted, the hospitality refused with transparent excuses. What is known is that James left his family in 1765 and went to St. Kitts, presumably for business reasons, while Rachel and the boys stayed on St. Croix. He never saw any of them again, nor did he take any responsibility for their support.

Rachel was alone, without even her mother to turn to. The for-

tunes of the Lyttons had also worsened. James Lytton had sold his
Grange plantation and moved, with his wife Ann, to an apartment in
Christiansted. Though still reasonably comfortable financially, Lytton was depressed by his children's misfortunes. James Jr., Lytton's
younger son, suffered business losses and then disgraced the family
by stealing his deceased wife's slaves and departing with his second
wife to the Bay of Honduras. Lytton's oldest daughter's husband
died in poverty; she remarried, and then both she and her second
husband died. Ann Lytton, Alexander's favorite relative, left her
daughter with her aged parents and followed her husband, who had
declared bankruptcy, to another island. Ann's brother Peter, after the
death of his wife and the failure of his business enterprises, also left
the island. Eventually he returned and committed suicide. This succession of Greek tragedies that afflicted James Lytton made him a
kind of recluse, in no condition to succor a niece by marriage recently deserted by her lover.[7]

Rachel rented a house with a small connecting store and tried to
make a living by selling staples such as beef, pork, salted fish, rice,
flour and apples. She was not very successful. In 1767, she moved her
family's living quarters to No. 23, on the south side of Company
Street, a Capt. William Egan's house. A year later, she moved back to
her former house, possibly after a liaison with Captain Egan.

It was a dismal existence for the unfortunate young woman who,
tradition says, was beautiful, witty and brilliant. Circumstances
forced her to apprentice her son James Jr. to Thomas McNobeny, a
Christiansted carpenter, and her clever younger son Alexander to
Beekman and Cruger, a commercial firm that hired him as a clerk.
Before, and perhaps after, Alexander started to work, he helped his
mother in the store, thereby acquiring some idea of business.

In February 1768, Rachel fell ill with a fever that became progres-
sively worse. Anne McDonell took care of her for a week; then, seeing that the poor woman was not getting better, she called Dr.
Heering. He was unable to help; perhaps the hardships and disap-
pointments of her life had robbed Rachel of the will to fight for
life.

Alexander caught his mother's fever, and he too lay ill. On February 19, the doctor performed a bloodletting on the boy and ordered
"a clyster." Rachel's expense book for that day records "a chicken for
Elicks" and eggs, white bread and cakes for Rachel's funeral. She
died at nine o'clock in the evening.

Within an hour after Rachel's death, representatives of the probate court came and sealed up the room. The pathetic list of the dead woman's possessions was duly recorded: a trunk, pots and pans, six chairs, two tables and two porcelain basins. Among the other articles in the house and the outbuildings were seven silver teaspoons, one pair of sugar tongs, one red skirt, one white shirt, one black sun hat, one chest of drawers, one bed, one feather comforter, one pillow and, most interesting, thirty-four books. In the lumber room, which was also sealed up by the authorities, were such items as eight salted porks, three firkins of butter, six leather chairs, three different tables, eleven cups and saucers, three stone platters, two metal candleholders, one mirror in a brown frame and one goat. Also listed by the authorities were two slave boys and two sons, James Hamilton and Alexander Hamilton. It was said that the deceased had willed the slave boy named Ajax to her son Alexander and the other slave boy, Christian, to James.[8]

Peter Lytton took charge of the bereaved children and made the funeral arrangements. On February 20, Rachel Fawcett Lavien was buried in the churchyard of St. John's Anglican church, Christiansted. Her two young sons, wearing black veils, stood at her graveside.

James Hamilton did not come to the funeral, nor did he reclaim his children. He must have known about Rachel's death through the Lyttons, but he continued his wandering, feckless life, ignoring his natural responsibilities. Hence, though they still had a living father, James Jr. and Alexander Hamilton were now on their own.

The unfortunate youngsters were about to be dealt an additional blow. On August 3, John Michael Lavien stole the orphans' mite. He filed a claim for his ex-wife's estate, naming their son Peter as the sole heir. James and Alexander, the statement alleged, could not inherit because they were "born in whoredom." The court, faithful to the sacred laws of matrimony, sustained Lavien's claim.

In July of the following year, Peter Lytton committed suicide, leaving an old will that failed to provide for his wards. However, even if there had been a will, the king would have been entitled to the suicide's common property. Now James and Alexander were dependent on strangers.

The brothers were unable to stay together. James was taken in by Mr. McNobeny, the carpenter to whom he was apprenticed. Probably Alexander was taken in by Thomas Stevens, the father of his friend Edward. His childhood, in terms of parental or familial love and care, was ended.

His prospects were dismal. He had been taught to read and write by his mother and then was sent to a school run by a Jewess. Hamilton often told his children with great glee that his teacher would stand him up on a table next to her—otherwise he would have been too small to be seen—and have him recite the Ten Commandments in Hebrew.[9] The story still persists in the islands that the child Hamilton went to a Jewish school because his illegitimacy barred him from any other.

The thirty-four books in the list of Rachel's possessions must have constituted Alexander's gold mine of knowledge. The titles are unknown, but from his children's recollections Plutarch and Pope were Hamilton's favorites. There must have been other classics, religious books and some works in French.

The traditional belief that Dr. Hugh Knox, the Presbyterian minister, was Alexander's mentor, filling all the lacunae in his education so that he was prepared for college, has been disproved. Since Knox did not take up permanent residence on St. Croix until May 1772 and Hamilton left the island about five months later, Knox's influence on Alexander was, even if intense, of short duration.[10]

Hamilton's most vital education was acquired on the job, working for Beekman and Cruger. The firm was located on the colorful waterfront of Christiansted, fronted with buildings of seventeenth- and eighteenth-century Danish style, with colonnades to provide shade from the intense tropical sun. By 1769, the company was engaged in the export of raw sugar and other island products and in the importation of supplies for the plantations.

Alexander learned some accounting and bookkeeping, as well as the rudiments of trading, and proved a natural master at writing business letters. The young lad met and dealt with seamen who had traveled the world and was exposed to the horrors of the slave trade. Advertisements in the Christiansted newspapers of 1771 and 1772 reveal that slaves from the Gold Coast were frequently offered for sale in Cruger's yard.[11]

The most revealing account of Alexander's business education is available in a series of letters that he wrote from November 1771 to February 1772, when, at barely seventeen, he was left in charge of the company by Nicholas Cruger, who went to New York for his health.

Alexander's letters are so businesslike, intelligent and spirited that it has been suggested that the Hamilton family improved and changed them before publication. Since the surviving letters are not the originals but letterbook copies, doubters have suggested that Hamilton was only the amanuensis for David Beekman, Cruger's retired partner, was really in charge.

However, it is commonly accepted that Hamilton wrote the letters and that they were an early display of his amazing ability to make independent judgments and to shoulder responsibility. In his capacity as acting head of Cruger's, Hamilton wrote his remarkable letters, prepared commercial documents and kept the books. He told his children that his experience at Cruger's was the most useful part of his education; it increased his knowledge of mathematics and gave him a taste for chemistry that made him a champion of its study.[12]

The influence and importance of this brief flurry as an entrepreneur affected Hamilton's concept of himself and stirred up a restlessness that he revealed to his friend Edward Stevens. In a much quoted letter to Stevens, who was in New York studying medicine at King's College, Hamilton contradicted his latter-day glorification of his clerking career.

Dated November 11, 1769, the letter expresses an almost desperate frustration and a gloomy analysis of his progress. Stevens's projected visit to St. Croix would be very nice, Alexander wrote, but he might not be there to welcome him. "To confess my weakness, Ned, my Ambition is prevalent that I contemn the groveling and condition of a Clerk or the like to which my Fortune, etc., condemns me." He would "willingly risk my life tho' not my Character to exalt my Station," he added. Though he saw no hope for immediate promotion or change of status, "I mean to prepare the way for futurity. I am no philosopher you see and justly said to Build Castles in the Air . . . yet Neddy we have seen such Schemes successful when the Projector is Constant. I shall conclude saying I wish there was a war."[13]

Hamilton's detractors have pounced on this letter. Here, written plain and at a painfully young age, is Hamilton's raging ambition, his determination to claw his way to the top and his love of war. It is a curious twist of fate that this is the earliest Hamilton letter to survive. But, examined without prejudice or foreknowledge, it can be viewed as the outpouring of a gifted boy with few prospects who fears that his hopes for himself are idle dreams unless, as sometimes happens, "when the Projector is constant," the dreams can be made reality. As a reader of Plutarch, Hamilton knew that war was often the road to greatness.

The details in Alexander's letters to Nicholas Cruger and others during his brief reign as acting head of the company reveal much about trade in the West Indies, as well as insight into the writer's mind. Alexander, sick or well, was conscientious and diligent. "I am so unwell that it is with difficulty I make out to write these lines," he said. He then chided his ailing employer for dealing in inferior merchandise. The shipment of flour from Philadelphia was "very bad" because of its "most swarthy complexion." Consequently, it would be "highly necessary to lessen the price or probably I may be oblig'd in the end to sell at a much greater advantage."[14]

Danger from pirates on the West Indies run caused Alexander to warn Tileman Cruger, Nicholas's brother who carried on the family business in Curacao, that their ship should be armed there, since it was illegal to do so in St. Croix. He also told Tileman that the ship-master, Capt. William Newton, "seems rather to want experience in such voyages."

On November 16, 1771, Hamilton wrote commandingly to Newton that he had to "follow in every respect" the instructions given to him and to be very choice in the quality of mules he carried, to carry as many as the ship would hold and to take a large supply of provender for them. Three trips had to be made this season, Hamilton reminded Newton, and "unless you are very diligent" it will be too late because the crops were already in. Newton, Hamilton told his employers, talked of the difficulties and dangers on the coast but "no doubt exaggerates a good deal by way of stimulation."[15]

Hamilton did consult on major decisions. In a letter to Nicholas Cruger, he told him that in certain matters he had "the concurrence and advice" of both your attorneys and, in another letter, mentioned that he had not seen Mr. Kortwright yet about the lumber contract. The responsibility weighed on the lad, and he wrote, almost patheti-cally, to Cruger, "Believe me Sir I dun as hard as is proper." Cruger seemed to trust Alexander and was fond of him. In a letter, Hamilton acknowledged some baskets of apples that his employer had sent him from the mainland.[16]

Newton's voyage was unsuccessful. On February 1, 1772, Hamil-ton wrote to the captain, sharply ordering him to follow Mr. Tileman Cruger's direction about the cargo in every respect. "Reflect continu-ally on the unfortunate voyage you have just made and endeavour to make up for the considerable loss therefrom accruing to your owners," he chided. He then repeated instructions about caring for the mules and getting four guns before going on the homeward voyage.[17]

Newton returned to St. Croix with the ship undamaged, but the forty-one mules were in terrible condition. After putting them out to pasture, Hamilton predicted that a third of them would die. The *Thunderbolt*'s first voyage had been unfortunate, Alexander lamented, which did not stop him from trying again. Once more he tried to impress Tileman Cruger with the importance of arming the vessel with guns. It would be "a great pity" to lose the vessel for lack of them, he argued. He also urged Tileman to provide more mules and to set sail with "the utmost despatch" lest the *Thunderbolt*'s second voyage "miscarry like the first." Please send a statement of accounts "so that I may enter all things properly," the youthful businessman requested.[18]

Capt. Robert Gibb suited Hamilton as little as did Newton. "Believe me Sir nothing was neglected on my part to give him the utmost Despatch," Hamilton wrote to Henry Cruger, but his cargo was stored away very "Hicheldy-picheldy," which caused delay. Added to Gibb's lack of neatness, strong contrary winds detained him from sailing out of the harbor for two days. The prices he got for Gibb's cargo also annoyed Hamilton. The lumber was sold immediately for £16, which was lucky, Hamilton told Cruger, because the going price was less, due to the large amount that was being exported from the continent. The mahogany he brought was of "the very worst kind" and fit only for endwork, which was why the price obtained was low, Hamilton said.[19]

Hamilton wrote to Cruger, giving a graphic account of the "dissatisfactory occurrences" connected with the *Thunderbolt*'s February voyage. Captain Newton delivered "41 more skeletons. A worse parcel of mules never was." There were forty-eight of the poor beasts at first, but seven died in passage. This time Hamilton exonerated Captain Newton, explaining that the sloop took twenty-seven days to come from Curacao because of calms and little wind.

Blame was reserved for brother Tileman, who, because of illness, accomplished no sales or anything else. He refused to hire the guns as requested because, said Hamilton, "I only had mentioned the matter to him but that you had never said a word about it." He had asked the captain to hire four guns himself, Hamilton explained, because "one escape may not be followed by a second, neither do I see any reason to run the risque of it."[20]

A couple of weeks after the above letter was sent, Nicholas Cruger returned to St. Croix and took back his business. Alexander continued in the company's employ, and letters and parts of letters appear in his handwriting. One to Henry Cruger concerned a cargo of 250

Gold Coast slaves who arrived at the Cruger establishment "very indifferent indeed, sickly and thin, they average about 30 £."[21]

Hamilton had other than business talents that he was trying to develop. On April 7, 1771, he wrote to the *Royal Danish American Gazette*, enclosing a pastoral poem, which appeared in the *Gazette*, along with an introductory note that identified Alexander as "a youth about seventeen."

Though juvenile and amateurish, the poem is important for its insights into Hamilton's thoughts on love and marriage. The shepherd in the poem found his love asleep "Beside a murm'ring brook," stole "a silent kiss" and, when she awakened, boldly clasped her in "a fond embrace."

> Our panting hearts beat mutual love—
> A rosy-red o'er spread her face
> And brightened all her charms

Mutual love discovered, the shepherd and his lass immediately went to church where "Hymen join'd our hands."

> Believe me love is doubly sweet
> In wedlocks holy bands—

wrote the young poet. The couple then lived happily ever after, tending their flocks together.

> We fondly sport and fondly play,
> And love away the night.[22]

This early poem extolls married bliss; implied is a yearning for a love that is "doubly sweet" and a criticism of his parents for their failure to regularize their relationship. One can only speculate on the slings and arrows that were directed at the two Hamilton boys because of their bastardy.

Since it is unlikely that any other prominent American published as many important pieces in the country's newspapers as did Alexander Hamilton, it is interesting that it was a piece of journalism that was instrumental in changing Alexander's life.

On the night of August 31, 1772, "one of the most dreadful hurricanes that memory or any records whatever can trace" struck St. Croix without warning. It raged at the north from dusk until ten o'clock, then quieted for about an hour before it shifted to the southwest "and returned with redoubled fury," blowing until three in the morning.

The destruction was indescribable. Homes crashed to the ground while the piercing shrieks of the victims "were sufficient to strike astonishment into Angels." Most of the buildings on the island were leveled, almost all of them damaged. The agony of the homeless and the injured was increased by the roaring of the sea and wind and the strong smell of gunpowder that permeated the air.

The above description appeared in the *Royal Danish American Gazette* on October 3, 1772. It was written by an eyewitness described in the paper as "a youth of the Island," who addressed the article to his father. The author of the piece was Alexander Hamilton, whose father was probably residing on St. Vincent's at the time of the hurricane. There is no evidence that there had been any communication between father and son. Dr. Hugh Knox received the manuscript as acting editor of the *Gazette* while the regular editor was away, and he liked the pious tone of the work.

Young Hamilton began his "reflections" on the natural calamity by castigating mankind. "Where now, oh! vile worm, is all thy boasted fortitude and resolution? What is become of thine arrogance and self sufficiency? . . . . How humble, how helpless, how contemptible you appear." What then is the lesson of the "horrors of the night, the prospect of an immediate cruel death . . . of being crushed by the Almighty in his anger?" Hamilton answered: "Rejoice at thy deliverance, and humble thyself in the presence of thy deliverer."

With a show of compassion seldom seen in so young a man, Alexander exhorted the survivors and the more fortunate not to forget the dead, the wounded, the sick, the dispossessed. "See tender infancy pinched with hunger and hanging on the mother's knee for food! . . . Her poverty denied relief, her breast heaves with pangs of maternal pity, her heart's bursting, the tears run down her cheeks." Those who "revel in affluence" must bestow their "superfluity" on these victims. Whatever you have suffered, the youth begged, "do not withhold your compassion. . . . Act wisely. . . . Succour the miserable and lay up a treasure in heaven."

Though loaded with purple passages, Alexander's effusive letter impressed his readers, especially the wealthy ones to whom he turned for expressions of mercy and help. They also were impressed by his graceful bow to Ulrich Wilhelm Roepstorff, the governor general of St. Croix, to whom the closing lines of the hurricane letter were addressed. "Our General has issued several very salutary and humane regulations, and both in publick and private measures has shewn himself *the Man*."[23]

The gaudy, effusive letter was the catalyst that decided Dr. Hugh Knox, Nicholas Cruger and other sympathetic islanders to finance

Alexander Hamilton's education. It was decided to send the youngster to the mainland to study medicine. He would complete his studies and then return to St. Croix to supply the residents with much
needed medical care.[24]

In October 1772, Alexander Hamilton sailed for Boston, whence he
was to proceed to New York. It was a hazardous voyage; the ship on
which he sailed caught fire and was saved from destruction only
after heroic efforts by the passengers and crew.

Of Hamilton's reflections as he sailed north to a new life little more
is known than his terse statements about the fire, which he passed
on to his children. Once again, his reticence about his early years is
displayed. Very likely, Alexander sailed away from his tropical isle
without a backward glance; he left behind no fond parents and relatives, only the embarrassment of his illegitimacy, so well known to
those who lived there.

Hamilton escaped physically from the scenes of his childhood, but
the scars of his early experiences accompanied him. Despite his ability to mask the facts, to his in-laws and his children the truth appeared and reappeared in the gibes of his enemies. Eventually
everyone knew, but many tried to pretend that they didn't. The
Hamilton family steadfastly rejected the fact of Alexander's illegitimacy. Gertrude Atherton's search for the truth about Hamilton's
birth led her to the West Indies. Later she tried to discuss her findings with Dr. Allen McLane Hamilton, Alexander Hamilton's grandson, a distinguished psychiatrist, unable to deal with this personal
unpleasantness. When Atherton visited Dr. Hamilton, he was interested and helpful, anxious to show her the material he had gathered
to prove that his grandfather was the author of Washington's Farewell Address. "But when I approached the subject of Hamilton's
origin he was evasive."[25]

In his own book, Dr. Hamilton refuted the story that Alexander
had Negro blood, explaining that early authors, who had never seen
even a portrait of their subject, assumed that all West Indians would
be "swarthy," with black hair and piercing black eyes. On the contrary, Alexander was fair and blue-eyed with reddish brown hair, a
lock of which the doctor was proud to possess.[26]

Sailing to the American mainland, Alexander was enacting an
early version of the eager immigrant coming to the new land to seek
his fortune. Along with a passionate desire to succeed, he brought a
reserve of brilliance and energy that would eventually startle his new
countrymen.

2

Education for a Revolutionary

ALEXANDER HAMILTON'S SHIP docked in Boston. Arriving in a strange, cold town whose autumn-leaved trees bore little resemblance to his tropical palms, the young man must have felt lonely and homesick. Since his letters of introduction were to New Yorkers and New Jerseyites, he immediately booked passage to New York City by sea, the cheapest and fastest way to get there.

Nicholas Cruger had arranged with the New York merchant firm of Kartright & Co. to sell West Indian products and to put aside the profits for Hamilton's needs. The "Co." part of the firm was Hugh Mulligan, whose brother Hercules is the source of the few details known about Alexander's life in New York City and Elizabethtown, New Jersey, where he went to school. Unfortunately, the Mulligan narrative was written long after the events described and suffers from the usual defects of such disclosures—selectivity, inaccuracy and the need to be self-serving.[1]

The principal reason for Alexander's trip to the continent was to get an education. He was poorly prepared; lacked formal training, particularly in the classics; and was older than the other students on his level. Two of Reverend Knox's friends, William Livingston and Elias Boudinot, both residents of Elizabethtown, New Jersey, were charged by him to solve the problem of Hamilton's education. It was decided that he should attend the local preparatory school, which was run by Francis Barber, a young Princeton graduate. The academy, under Presbyterian control, offered a curriculum that was adaptable to Alexander's needs. All the college requirements were taught there: English composition and literature, geography, mathematics and Latin composition and translation of such Latin works as Cicero and Virgil.

In the winter and spring of 1733, Alexander attended the Elizabethtown Academy, paying tuition of five pounds a year, one pound
ten shillings for wood and cleaning costs and one pound for "Entrance light money." He carried a demanding schedule that often
required him to work until midnight. In the summertime, Hamilton
told his children, he would rise at dawn and go to the nearby ceme-
tery to find the quiet he needed for his studies.

William Livingston and Elias Boudinot often invited the lad to
their homes, where they enlightened him about revolutionary activities in Boston. Living so far from the turmoil, the two men held a
moderate, watchful-waiting position. Nevertheless, they were Whigs
and made their West Indian protégé aware of the troubles of the
mainland colonies.

Hamilton and Boudinot shared similar backgrounds; both had
French Huguenot forebears and parents who had lived in the West
Indies. The young man enjoyed being part of the Boudinot family,
which included two daughters, Susanna Vergereau, aged eight, and
Anna Maria, seven months, and provided warmth and affection for
the exiled youth. Later, after he left Elizabethtown for New York
City, Alexander returned for Anna Maria's funeral. He stayed up all
night with the little dead girl and then wrote an ode to "the sweet
Babe."

The poem reveals that Alexander had spent a lot of time with the
infant. His "doating heart / Did all a Mother's fondness feel," and he
speaks of Anna Maria's "pratling in my happy arms."

> No more the self important tale
> Some embryo meaning shall convey
> Which should thy imperfect accents fail
> Thy speaking looks would still display.[2]

Driven by ambition and the pursuit of excellence, Hamilton put
himself through a lightning course of study. He wanted to justify the
expectations of his sponsors and to catch up with his peers. At some
time during that year of preparation, inspired by the strict Presbyterian atmosphere, Alexander made extensive notes on the Book of
Genesis. He also gathered data, which miraculously survived, on the
geography of North and South America. At a much later date, these
notes were used as the basis of a brief that Hamilton prepared for
New York State during its land controversy with Massachusetts.[3]

During his residence at Barber's Academy, Hamilton made occasional trips to New York to attend to financial matters. While there, he

stayed with Hercules Mulligan, who served as liaison between Kartright & Co. and Hamilton. In less than a year after Alexander's entrance into the academy, Barber wrote to Mulligan to say that his charge was prepared to enter college. Hamilton then informed Mulligan that he preferred Princeton to King's College "because it was more republican."[4]

Boudinot and Livingston were trustees of Princeton, and Hugh Knox and Barber were alumni. Any contact that Alexander had with college men was with Brockholst Livingston and his friends, who were students at Princeton. Also, there were many boys from the West Indies there because Princeton made a special effort to attract the islanders to the school.

Hercules Mulligan sympathized with Hamilton's choice. He was "well acquainted" with Princeton's president, John Witherspoon, and willing to expedite matters by introducing Hamilton to him. They went together to Witherspoon's house, where Mulligan soon persuaded the president to examine Alexander. Witherspoon was entirely satisfied with the young man's performance. It was Hamilton who made problems when he presented Witherspoon with a modest proposal that was not well received. Alexander was willing to be placed at whatever level the president deemed proper, but he wanted to be allowed to progress from class to class as rapidly "as his exertions would enable him to do." Dr. Witherspoon, taken aback, replied that he could not accede to the request unilaterally and would have to submit it to the trustees.

About two weeks after the interview, Hamilton received a polite letter saying that the college could not accede to his request. It was "contrary to the usage of the college," but, Dr. Witherspoon added kindly, he was certain that "the young gentleman would do honor to any seminary at which he should be educated."[5]

The scanty material available on Hamilton's short but important residence in Elizabethtown tells nothing about his adjustment to America. Judged by its results it was a successful transition. He was instantly accepted and received with affection, a happy state of affairs that must be attributed to the youth's charm and affability. Alexander knew how to ingratiate himself with older people, a skill that had gained him such strong sponsors as Cruger and Knox. As a dependent, rootless boy he had no real claim on these people, so he had to earn and keep their goodwill. The shadow of the island counting house, the fear that he would have to return to eternal "clerkdom," provided adequate incentive for him to maintain the image of a bright, enterprising, promising young man. Also, Alexander felt genuine gratitude for being accepted in the best society as an equal in birth and breeding.

In the spring of 1773, New York City's King's College (now Columbia) admitted young Hamilton to the sophomore class on the terms that he had requested. Thus, a lack of flexibility on the part of Princeton's president and trustees lost to the college a most distinguished alumnus and prevented Hamilton and Aaron Burr, son of the first president of Princeton and grandson of its second, from having the same alma mater. However, the two future rivals would not have been at school at the same time; although a year younger than Hamilton, Burr had already graduated.

King's College, located on the edge of New York City, was an impressive three-story structure that sported four gables, four entrances, a balustrade on the roof and a graceful cupola topped by a steeple. The college's president, Rev. Myles Cooper, was a dedicated Loyalist and the leader of a circle of friends who shared his persuasion. Boudinot feared that Hamilton would succumb to Tory influence.

The blueprint for Hamilton when he left St. Croix called for his studying medicine. Not long after he started at King's College, he had to give it up. The medical course was very rigorous, and Hamilton's preparation did not provide him with the entrance requirements.[6]

Robert Troup, who became Hamilton's lifelong friend and supporter, is the main source for information about Alexander's college days. He, like Mulligan, wrote an account almost forty years after the events. There are no indications that Hamilton sowed any wild oats in college. King's "Book of Misdemeanours" mentions no infringement of the rules by the exemplary West Indian. Therefore, he must have conformed in the matter of morning, afternoon and evening prayers; attendance at two Sunday services; promptness in classes; and proper academic dress.

Troup's account presents a picture of Alexander as a most intense young man. He studied hard and made rapid progress in all subjects, especially languages. Among his close friends were Edward Stevens of St. Croix (his boyhood friend Neddy) and Samuel and Henry Nicoll. The coterie formed a Weekly Club to improve their skills in composition. Troup reported that at all the club's performances in debating, Hamilton "made extraordinary displays of richness of genius and energy." The little society lasted until war terminated Hamilton's college career and dispersed the members.

For some time while at King's College, Alexander shared a room and bed with Troup. Religion, his roommate said, was a very significant part of his friend's life. In addition to church attendance, Alexander prayed on his knees morning and night, apparently aloud, for Troup said that he was affected by the young man's "fervour and eloquence." Well read on religious subjects and a "zealous" believer in the fundamentals of Christian doctrine, Hamilton was also a bit of an evangelist. He argued forcibly to justify his beliefs, with the hope of promoting his roommate's enthusiasm for religion.[7]

Hamilton courted his muse while at King's. Troup spoke of a small manuscript of poetry that Hamilton gave him as a token of friendship. Unfortunately, it was lost with all of Troup's books and papers during the Revolution.

Despite the fact that as soon as he came to America, Hamilton was exposed to moderate Whig influence as exemplified by his Elizabethtown friends and despite his own assertion that he wanted to go to Princeton because of its republican bent, Troup insists that Hamilton was originally a monarchist. Troup may have based this belief on Hamilton's admiration for the principles of the English constitution and his knowledge of English history. However, Troup's story of Hamilton's conversion to the patriot cause is intriguing, though unsubstantiated. He says that "under his bias towards the British monarchy," Hamilton made a trip to Boston after their Tea Party, and, while there, Bostonians "listed him on the side of America," and so he returned to New York City "a warm Republican," ready to resist the claims of the British Parliament.[8] This journey seems unlikely for a young man without time or money. It was not necessary to visit Boston to become bitterly resentful against the mother country. In all the colonies, newspapers thundered against the "Intolerable Acts" that King George piled on Massachusetts.

Hamilton may have been the author of "A Defence of the Destruction of the Tea," published in Holt's paper, as Troup and others claimed. If not, it would be only a short time before he got started on his pamphleteering career.

There is no newspaper account or corroborative evidence of Alexander Hamilton's address at the meeting in the fields on July 6, 1774, but all his biographers, including this one, cling to the tradition. The meeting took place at what was then the site of the new liberty pole and is now City Hall Park. Its purpose was to persuade a hesitant New York to send delegates to the Continental Congress scheduled to meet in Philadelphia the following September.

A large crowd gathered at the 6 P.M. meeting. The chief attraction was Capt. Alexander McDougall, who had just been released from prison, where he had been held for publishing an address against the Townshend Acts.

At first the slight, sandy-haired student from the West Indies stood by, watching the people and listening to the reading of the nine resolutions. Friends urged him to add his persuasive words to the others. Hesitantly, Hamilton climbed up to the platform. At first he stumbled, then, inspired by his own words and the importance of the occasion, he started to speak earnestly and with confidence. Great principles were involved in this controversy, he said, and then painted "in glowing colors" the history of the oppressions of Mother England and the duty the colonies had to resist. Success was a certainty, the youth insisted; the "waves of rebellion sparkling with fire" would wash back "on the shores of England the wrecks of her power, her wealth and her glory."[9]

McDougall and other leading Whigs who were present, such as John Lamb, Marinus Willett and John Jay, may have sensed a nascent power in the young man's words, but little did they suspect that he would surpass everyone present that day. The business at hand was to choose delegates to go to the aid of stricken Boston and to agree to stop all importing and exporting until the British agreed to unfreeze the port of Boston. The purpose, perhaps due in some small part to Hamilton's forensic effort, was accomplished.

When Hamilton's first authenticated pamphlet was published, everyone attributed it to John Jay. It seemed inconceivable that the young, raw student, a new recruit to the cause, could be the "Friend to America" whose brilliant pamphlet refuted the Anglican clergyman Samuel Seabury's "A Westchester Farmer."

In a smooth, flowing prose that presented a tight argument, a style completely different from the turgid Hurricane letter, Hamilton argued that slavery would be the lot of the American colonies if Great Britain did not change her policies, and that only protesting congresses and economic sanctions would impress King George and the British House of Commons. The time for petitions to the Crown was past, he wrote; nonimportation was the only hope.

Hamilton asked: "What then is the subject of our controversy with the mother country? It is this, whether we shall preserve the security to our lives and properties which the law of nature, the genius of the British constitution, and our charters afford us, or whether we shall resign them into the hands of the British House of Commons, which is no more privileged to dispose of them than the Grand Mogul."[10]

In answer to aspersions against Congress made by the "Westchester Farmer," Hamilton reminded him that in the infancy of the present dispute "we used remonstrance and petition" and were met "with contempt and neglect." The Stamp Act was repealed and the Revenue Acts partially repealed only because the commercial interests of Great Britain were being harmed. Let Americans learn from Rome, who was celebrated for her justice and lenity but made her dependent provinces "the continual scene of rapine and cruelty."[11]

Hamilton was not daunted by the threat of war. Great Britain did not want "to enforce her despotic claims by fire and sword"; it would be "madness itself." Our numbers were great, our courage known, contests for liberty were always bloody and obstinate. It might well prove a hard and impracticable task. Besides, while at war Britain's commerce would be "in a state of decay," and she would be exposed to her enemies.

Seabury's warning that Great Britain would stop American trade was put aside by Hamilton. America could live without trade. She was self-sufficient in food and clothing and "by the necessity of the thing" would establish manufactures.

Hamilton concluded by appealing to the farmers to support New York. He assured them that they would benefit by nonimportation. Manufactures would flourish so that farmers would get a big price for their wool, hemp and flax. "And while you are supplying the wants of the community, you will be enriching yourselves." Judge for yourself, Hamilton advised, while insinuating that the "Westchester Farmer" was "an artful enemy" who was possibly a British spy. Do not forsake the plain path marked by congress, he begged all New Yorkers, lest by separating from the rest of America you "repent your folly as long as you live."[12]

"The Farmer" answered Hamilton several weeks later, and Hamilton responded with a lengthy pamphlet called *The Farmer Refuted*, which gave an analysis of natural-rights philosophy and a preview of the Fabian strategy that Washington would adopt in the war to come. In this polemic, Hamilton displayed a thorough, impressive knowledge of Hobbes, Locke, Grotius, Puffendorf, Burlamaqui and Montesquieu.

The "Westchester Farmer's" acceptance of the Hobbesian position that man in a state of nature was free from all restraint of law and government was, said Hamilton, an "absurd and impious doctrine" that denied the Deity's "eternal and immutable law which is . . . indispensably obligatory upon all mankind, prior to any institution whatever." This law of nature was the basis of the natural rights of mankind and therefore "all civil government, justly established, must be a voluntary compact between the rulers and the ruled . . . for what original title can any man, or set of men have to govern other except their own consent. . . . The idea of colony does not involve the idea of slavery," nor did it imply "subordination to our fellow subjects in the parent state while there is one common sovereign." Therefore, Parliament could not legislate for the American colonies. Every Englishman's birthright was to participate in framing laws that bound him or his property. Since he could not exercise this right in person, he gave his vote to "some person he chooses to confide in as his representative. . . . Abolish this privilege and the House of Commons is annihilated."[13]

The House of Commons did not want to favor the interests of the colonies but rather to increase oppressive legislation because it was jealous of "our dawning splendour" which portended approaching independence. The right of the colonists to exercise legislative power, Hamilton said, was an inherent right, founded upon man's right to freedom and happiness. No matter how rich or poor, how high or small an individual's rank, the individual in America was on a less favorable footing than any person in Great Britain. This was the fault of the British Parliament.

As an example of the unfairness of the British colonization policy, Hamilton cited the case of New York, which had no charter and therefore was excluded from one of the most important privileges granted to the others. "The sacred rights of mankind are not to be rummaged for among old parchments or musty records. They are written, as with a sunbeam, in the whole volume of human nature, by the hand of the Divinity itself, and can never be erased or obscured by mortal power."[14]

The Farmer warned that the outcome of a contest of arms with the disciplined troops of Great Britain would be inevitable defeat. Hamilton did not agree. "There is a certain enthusiasm in liberty, that makes human nature rise above itself in acts of bravery and heroism." America would not yield without a "bloody struggle."[15]

In later years, Hamilton was often accused of seeking a military solution to problems of state. Here, the youthful writer projected a military strategy that would make an American army victorious. The colonists had superior numbers, and the armies would take care not to meet the enemy on large plains. Instead, a pitched battle had to be avoided, while the British soldiery would be harassed and exhausted by frequent skirmishes. Americans, the West Indian said, were better adapted to such a form of fighting than regular troops. As for feeding, arming, clothing and paying troops, the American army "on the spot with us, will be much more easily maintained than those of Britain at such a distance." The countryside had abundant provisions. America had adequate materials to make necessary clothes, and already several colonies were pretty well stored with ammunition. England's enemies, France, Spain and Holland, despite agreements not to interfere in a family dispute, would supply America. "A more desirable object to France and Spain than the disunion of these colonies cannot be imagined." In addition, France and Spain needed the supplies they got from the American colonies and their islands in the West Indies, and would be in the greatest depression if deprived of the trade.

After these fiery words, Hamilton concluded on a conciliatory note, expressing hope for a speedy reconciliation of "the unnatural quarrel between the parent state and the colonies." With proper piety, Hamilton asserted that he was a warm advocate of limited monarchy and a well-wisher of the present royal family. As did the author of the Declaration of Independence a year and a half later, Hamilton heaped all blame on Parliament.[16]

The pamphlet, printed at the James Rivington Press in New York in February 1775, supports the claim of precocity for its author and foreshadows Hamilton's career as a polemicist and pamphleteer, as well as his interest in military affairs. Here, too, is first displayed Hamilton's use of primary sources and extensive documentation, as well as his intellectual courage. When accused of having opinions influenced by prejudice, he answered that he remembered when he had had strong feelings on the side he now opposed. It was the superior force of the arguments in favor of the American claims that changed his mind, Hamilton said.[17]

Hamilton's refutation of the arguments of the Westchester clergyman was a giant step in the direction of the extremists. No longer influenced by the Elizabethtown moderates, his reading of Blackstone and others swayed him toward a recognition of Britain's injustice to the American colonies. Hamilton became a separatist because he recognized that only if free could America develop into a productive society.

Hamilton's private life during this time was occupied with studies, writing and military drill. Maj. Edward Fleming, formerly an adjutant of a British regiment, had married a Miss De Peyster, settled in

New York and became a partisan of the American side. He formed a volunteer company made up of eager New York gentlemen, some of them college students, to teach them the manual of arms. Both Hamilton and Troup joined and met with the company every morning in the churchyard of St. George's Chapel to practice the drill.[18]

The embryo company wore short green coats and leather caps that bore the inscription "Freedom or Death." Hamilton told his son that the group was known as the "Hearts of Oak," but a list of independent foot companies of New York during this period describes the uniform as belonging to "The Corsicans."

Although by the beginning of hostilities at the battles of Lexington and Concord in April 1775, Hamilton was totally in agreement with the American cause and already serving as a volunteer, he abhorred the mindless violence of the mob, even when aroused by patriotic fervor. A fine example of his feeling was exhibited when he protected his Tory college president Myles Cooper, that "obnoxious man," from the mob's fury.

On May 10, a "great force" of liberty boys, aroused by a letter that had named Cooper as one of those responsible for New York City's Loyalist leanings, marched to King's College, shouting vengeance. Threats of tar and feathers and murder were heard in the mild spring night. When they reached Cooper's house, Hamilton, with Troup at his side, was there to receive them and, leaping onto the stoop, harangued the mob with fearless eloquence. While Cooper was hurried out his back door to the safety of a British ship anchored in the harbor, Hamilton lectured the bully boys on their disgraceful conduct, which brought shame on the cause of liberty.[19]

On the first anniversary of his dramatic escape, Cooper published a poem commemorating the incident in London's *Gentlemen's Magazine*, signed "An Exile from America." It paid tribute to "a heaven-directed youth/ Whom oft my lessons led to truth" coming to him and crying "Awake! Awake! . . . —this instant fly—/ The next may be too late."

Hatred of mob excesses did not stop Hamilton from participating in the war, nor did it still his pen. His next attack on England, published in June, was called *Remarks on the Quebec Bill*. Great Britain, mindful of her need for French-Canadian support against the rebellious colonies, passed legislation giving the right to the Canadians to remain Catholic and French. Anti-Catholic attacks in the colonial newspapers abounded, and Hamilton's was one of them.

"We may see an inquisition erected in Canada," and presently tyranny would find as propitious a soil in America as it had in Spain or Portugal, Hamilton warned. The province would be inhabited by "none but Papists." Attracted by the natural advantages of "this fertile infant Country," droves of emigrants from all of Europe's Roman Catholic countries would come, so that in time the thirteen American colonies would "find themselves encompassed with innumerable hosts of neighbors, disaffected to them, both because of difference in religion and government."[20]

Sentiments such as Hamilton's had an unfortunate effect on the Quebec campaign undertaken by the colonial army and accounted in part for the cold reception often given the troops when they arrived in Canada. There were some Canadians who would have been friendly to the cause but were frightened by these expressions of Protestant bigotry.

The Loyalist party, aware of Hamilton's skillful pamphleteering, tendered him a number of attractive offers to join the king's party. It was not an outlandish idea. Hamilton had been sympathetic to ideas of a monarchy and admired a well-structured society. He was always an uncomfortable ally of egalitarianism and never adjusted to any displays of populism. But he rejected any offers from the Tories. Frederick C. Oliver, a perceptive British biographer of Hamilton, commented that "the habitual ignorant Habit" of democratic historians to picture him as an adventurer was puzzling. Hamilton never, not even as a young man, sold his sword. "If we are in reach of an analogy," he suggested, it will be found "rather among the knights of the Round Table than among the soldiers of fortune."[21]

Hamilton was under fire for the first time on the night of August 23–24, 1775. The New York Committee of Safety, deciding that a score of cannon mounted at the Battery should be moved to a safer place, assigned the task to Captain Fleming's company. While the big guns were being hauled away, the *Asia*, a British man-of-war lying in the harbor, sent a punt with some soldiers toward the shore. The colonists fired on it, killing one man. The *Asia* returned the fire immediately. Troup, on shore at the time, retreated with the other rebels, leaving behind Hamilton's musket, which he had charge of while his friend was employed dragging the heavy cannon up Broadway. When he returned from his chore, Alexander met Troup and asked for his musket. Troup told him where he had left it, whereupon Hamilton went to retrieve it, ignoring the firing "with as much unconcern as if the vessel had not been there."[22]

Hamilton's formal entry into the war did not take place until 1776,

but before that he had started to study gunnery and was in correspondence with John Jay, a representative in the New York Provincial
Assembly, about some of the events going on in the city. Hamilton
was enraged when, under Isaac Sears, a New York leader of the Sons
of Liberty, a company of New England horsemen took away the
types of his former publisher, James Rivington. Though "fully sensible of how dangerous and pernicious Rivington's press had been and
how detestable the character of the man is in every respect," he
disapproved of the action. The multitude lacked the reason and
knowledge necessary to keep them from moving from opposition to
tyranny and from oppression to a disregard for all authority. He also
feared quarrels between New Yorkers and New Englanders.

There was a further danger in an episode such as the Sears attack
on Rivington. If men from neighboring provinces came in "to chastise the notorious friends of the Ministry" here, it would look as if
New Yorkers were disaffected from the American cause and required
the interference of their neighbors. On the whole, Hamilton said, all
cautious and prudent Whigs had to condemn the Sears raid. He
advised that troops raised in the Jerseys, Philadelphia or any province other than those of New England be stationed in the parts of
New York "most tainted with the ministerial infection." This was
warranted because the ministry might soon make a raid on New
York, and there should be some order and regularity.[23]

Jay liked Hamilton's letter so much that he asked him to send
regular reports on any important developments in the province.
Hamilton answered with the news that the Tories were getting ready
to elect a new assembly. He believed that the governor would soon
dissolve the old assembly and issue writs for the new one. The Tories'
assumption was that the people were so involved with their new
congresses, institutions and committees that they would dismiss the
assembly as of no importance, do nothing and so leave the Tories free
to elect their own creatures. To counter this, Hamilton told Jay, he
had circulated a handbill or two to raise the necessary alarm and
planned to send out others.

In order to keep the people focused on the assembly, Hamilton
proposed that four of the Continental Congress delegates present
themselves as candidates for the assembly, ideally Livingston, Alsop,
Lewis and Jay, who were also the Continental Congress delegates.
This show of strength would weaken the opposition by displaying
that the Whigs had a majority. And Hamilton advised Jay to come to
New York. "Absence you know is not very favorable to the influence
of any person no matter how great."[24]

The war changed Hamilton's plans or, in a sense, fulfilled them. Still relatively unknown, without any position in the world, not yet self-supporting, he thought about how he could best serve his adopted country. Opportunity knocked when the Provincial Congress ordered that an artillery company be raised to defend New York. Hamilton applied for the command. Though his youth and inexperience in warfare were against him, Alexander had some positive assets: the needed skills, some prominence as the author of strong Whig pamphlets and some acquaintance with such influential men as John Jay and Alexander McDougall. According to Troup, at McDougall's request, Jay obtained a commission from the Provincial Congress. But Hercules Mulligan wrote that Hamilton was promised the commission if he could recruit thirty men, and that he accompanied Alexander and helped him to enlist twenty-five men. Mulligan added that Hamilton was given the company and equipped the men from his own pocket. This seems unlikely, since Hamilton had no money.[25]

The records of Congress state that McDougall recommended Mr. Alexander Hamilton for captain of a company of artillery on February 23. Evidence of knowledge of the military science was demanded, for there is a certificate in the records that testifies to Hamilton's skill. He was examined in the presence of McDougall and found to be qualified. On March 4, Hamilton's appointment was delivered.

In the meantime, Elias Boudinot obtained a position for Alexander as aide-de-camp to Lord Stirling, who commanded New York City. This was a more prestigious post than a captain of artillery, but Hamilton wanted active service to achieve fame by deeds of arms and by his own valor.

Now in command of a company of sixty-nine officers and men, smartly uniformed in blue coats with buff cuffs and facings, Hamilton was ordered to Kingston, New York, to guard the colony's records, moved out of the city because of the expectation that the British would try to capture New York. This undemanding duty gave the young officer an opportunity to drill and train his men.

In May, Hamilton sent a detailed complaint to the Provincial Congress, saying that his company was the victim of breach of contract and unfair treatment. His men were not getting the same pay as the continental army, as promised. As a result, their captain was finding it difficult to attract recruits. Since the search for enlistees was a priority, Hamilton asked that Congress pay expenses for sending into the country for soldiers. He also wanted the smock that was given to other troops as a bounty to be issued to his company. It would be serviceable in summer while the men were doing fatigue work, and it would save their uniforms.[26]

Hamilton's fears about his men's discontent were real. Some had deserted and were on board a continental ship in the harbor. Hamilton was sent an order permitting him to go on board any vessel in the harbor to search for his deserters.[27]

Somewhat later, Hamilton complained to the New York Convention again. Contrary to their contract, his soldiers were receiving one third less provisions than the rest of the army. The committee appointed to examine the matter decided that since Captain Hamilton's company was now a part of Gen. John M. Scott's brigade, its provisions would be issued as part of the brigade.

The conventional structure of the army made an unbridgeable gulf between officers and enlisted men, without any provision for a non-commissioned man to become an officer. Hamilton proposed Thomas Thompson, his first sergeant, be promoted to lieutenant to fill a vacancy. "His advancement will be a great encouragement and benefit to my company . . . and will be an animating example to all men of merit to whose knowledge it come," Hamilton argued.

The innovative proposal was sent to Col. Peter Livingston, who, after consultation with Hamilton, approved Thompson's promotion. Hamilton could have arranged to give one of his friends the post, but he preferred to help a man for whom he had personal respect and to set a precedent for the recognition of outstanding ability.[28]

What Alexander Hamilton's thoughts were and where he was on the day that the Declaration of Independence was accepted by New York's Provincial Congress at a meeting held on July 9, 1776, are not known. Most likely he and his brigade were drawn up at their parade ground to hear the Declaration read as had been ordered by Congress. On that evening he might have witnessed the crowd's destruction of the leaden statue of King George III, which stood on Bowling Green. No doubt the mob action would have reawakened his worries about liberty and order. He would also have been profoundly disturbed about the uneasy position of the patriots in New York City. The British expedition had come down from Halifax with the largest force ever assembled by any European power outside of Europe. On June 19, the armada was sighted off Sandy Hook. By July 2, the ships had reached New York harbor.

Hamilton's company was involved in erecting the complicated fortifications that were to protect New York from the British invaders. By August 8, Washington announced that the large British transports were due to arrive and the warning would be sent out from the heptagonal fort constructed on Bayard's Hill (now Canal and Mulberry Streets). In the daytime a flag and three guns would give the alarm; at night a light with three quick shots. Hamilton and his men were stationed at Bayard's Hill, Manhattan's main earthworks.

On the morning of August 23, the British made a successful amphibious landing and encamped 15,000 men at Flatbush before the Americans realized what had happened. Four days later, the British army captured almost all the patriot outparties, Lord Stirling and his brigade and Gen. John Sullivan. Altogether, they took about a thousand rebel prisoners.

Washington and his generals held a hasty conference at which they decided to evacuate the army to New York City and place Alexander McDougall in charge. Under cover of the night, helped by heavy seas which kept Adm. Richard Howe's fleet from entering the bay, the colonial army was loaded into small boats and transported safely across the East River to the city.

Hercules Mulligan recalled that before the Long Island defeat, Captain Hamilton and Rev. John Mason dined at his house. After dinner the two men lamented the army's situation on Long Island and speculated on possible plans for its removal. Hamilton and Mason decided to write an anonymous letter to General Washington, outlining their plan for the best way to draw off the army. Mulligan saw Hamilton write the letter, heard it read after it was finished and then delivered it to Col. Samuel B. Webb, a member of Washington's family. Washington must have read the letter, Mulligan insisted, because the mode of drawing off the army which was later adopted was nearly the same as the one described in the Hamilton letter.

There was general agreement that it was impossible for the colonial army to hold New York City, but it was up to Congress to decide whether it should be burned before it was evacuated. Though Washington argued that providing the British with warm, elegant winter quarters was a mistake, Congress voted against destruction. Therefore, 5,000 soldiers were kept in the city and 8,000 on Harlem Heights while the evacuation was taking place.

General Howe landed on September 15, about two days before the colonial forces were able to complete the removal of their supplies, their sick and their wounded. The British general landed at Kip's Bay (now the East River and Thirty-fourth Street), directing an impres-

sive crossing that provided covering fire from the British frigates in
the river; almost no boats and few men were lost.

The colonial defenders, seeing the formidable force approaching,
ran away. Aaron Burr, General Putnam's aide, was ordered to move
all stragglers and lost brigades to Harlem Heights. If Alexander
Hamilton was stationed at Fort Bunker Hill during this retreat, as
Mulligan asserted, he would have met Burr and followed Major
Burr's instructions for conducting his exhausted artillery company to
Harlem Heights.[29]

A second momentous meeting is reported to have taken place on
Harlem Heights (present site of Columbia University). The story is
that General Washington, making his rounds of the battleground,
observed Hamilton directing his men in throwing up an earthwork.
Impressed with the young officer's command of his men and skill in
his work, he invited him to his tent. No evidence other than tradition
has been found for either the Burr or Washington meeting with
Hamilton.[30]

The Battle of Harlem Heights, a victory for the continental army,
restored American morale but did not convince Washington that he
could hold New York City. Instead, he moved north to Westchester
and then maneuvered a series of strategic retreats across New Jersey.
Hamilton's battery performed a major service at New Brunswick.
Somewhat in advance of Washington's army, Captain Hamilton
placed his battery on the high west bank a few hundred yards from
the Raritan River. Thus positioned, the guns covered General Washington's crossing to the west side of the Delaware and made it possible for him to proceed to Princeton. This action also delayed
Cornwallis in his pursuit of the elusive American army.

An eyewitness, identified only as a veteran officer, provided a description of Alexander Hamilton at this time. He was "a youth, a
mere stripling, small, slender, almost delicate in frame," standing,
"his cocked hat pulled down over his eyes, apparently lost in
thought, with his hand resting on a cannon, and every now and then
patting it as if it were a favorite horse or a pet plaything."[31]

Less certain than the New Brunswick battle role is the part that
Hamilton and his battery played in the battles of Trenton and
Princeton. One tale, probably spurious, has it that a stray British
company took refuge in Princeton College's Nassau Hall. Hamilton's
artillery company was ordered to fire on the building to force them
out, and a ball, fired by its captain, hit a portrait of George III
hanging on the wall.

The turning point in Hamilton's life occurred on March 1, 1777, when he was appointed an aide-de-camp to Gen. George Washington. The exact events are controversial but whatever called Hamilton to Washington's attention, the circumstance that precipitated the appointment was the illness of Robert Hanson Harrison, who had served as Washington's scribe. Hamilton, the author of partisan pamphlets against the "Westchester Farmer," as well as a courageous and skilled artillery officer, was a perfect candidate for the job. Washington wrote to Harrison to stay away from camp as long as was necessary to recover his health and to forward to Captain Hamilton an invitation to join the commander in chief's staff. At the same time, a colonel's commission was offered to Hamilton.

Hamilton realized the possibilities of this appointment. He hated to put aside dreams of military glory, but he was too intelligent to decline a connection with Washington. It would elevate him in the eyes of his friends and sponsors and increase his value to the New York congress. From student recruit to a position at the side of the chief of the patriot army was a great leap for a young unknown from the West Indies.

3

The Little Lion

ONCE HAMILTON AGREED to become an aide to General Washington, he suppressed his misgivings about sitting at a desk, writing letters and dispatches, or jumping to obey the orders of the commander in chief while battles were being waged far from the protected headquarters. The company of Washington's aides was made up of courageous, intelligent and energetic young men from the most distinguished families in the country. To be one of them was to rise in social position.

Hamilton's first priority was to be well accepted as a member of Washington's family. It was a band of lively officers, most of them in their twenties, with a sprinkling of thirty-year-olds such as Thomas Mifflin, Tench Tilghman and Robert Harrison. Hamilton exerted his charm and wit to gain acceptance as their equal. He won the friendship of Harrison at once. The Marylander, who had been Washington's lawyer and had served with him on a Virginia committee, immediately dubbed his young colleague "the little lion," a title that was used affectionately by Hamilton's friends all his life.

Before he arrived at Washington's headquarters to take up his duties, Hamilton was seriously ill, which delayed his arrangements for the dispersal of his company until early March. At that time he informed the New York Provincial Congress of his appointment to Washington's staff and of the sad dwindling away of his company, so that it numbered only twenty-five, "because of various reasons."[1] Congress decided to order the company to enlist in the service of the continental army and to inform Colonel Hamilton of the decision.

The word of Hamilton's strategic position with the top military command greatly interested New York's Committee of Correspondence, which asked that he convey army news. "With cheerfulness,"

Hamilton replied, but, he reminded the committee, any opinion that he conveyed would be his own, not Washington's. His first report from Morristown headquarters carried only reports of daily skirmishes designed to harass the enemy. It was encouraging to report that British deserters were coming into camp every day, complaining that they had not been paid for a long time and if they dared to complain, were "most barbarously Treated." George Washington had been quite seriously ill but was now recovered and had been joined by his wife.[2]

In April, a report from Hamilton allayed the New York committee's fears that the British were making the capture of the Hudson River their first objective, in order to destroy continental shipping and keep Washington's army from crossing to the New York side until the British army reached Albany, icebound at that time of year. Philadelphia attracted them, Hamilton predicted. If they went there, they knew that the city was surrounded by a large number of people "inimical to us" who would give them all their assistance. Hamilton encouraged the New York committee by telling them that Washington was very pleased by their zeal and abilities and, though a northward operation by the British seemed inconceivable, he had decided to station a large body of troops at Peekskill until the enemy moved away.[3]

The possibility of a British takeover of Philadelphia, the seat of the Continental Congress, continued to be Washington's primary consideration. There were problems with the New Jersey troops also. Disaffection had become so extensive that Washington wanted Governor William Livingston to take immediate action against "the most atrocious offenders" to serve as an example for the others. Hamilton favored doing something about the disaffected lest the friends of America "lose zeal," but he had strong reservations about a resolution passed by New York State's Congress that provided for the court-martial of people accused of spying, recruiting enlistments for the British or supplying them with provisions. The utmost care had to be exercised in punishing these offenders; otherwise they would become vindictive, Hamilton advised. "I would either disable them from doing us any injury, or I would endeavour to gain their friendship by clemency."[4]

Although involved with his headquarters duties, Hamilton was very interested in the new New York State constitution, being hammered out by his friends in the Provincial Congress. The constitution was being written under the most trying circumstances. The Provincial Congress, acting as the constitutional convention, met first at White Plains and then had to move northward ahead of the British, until it settled at Kingston. A committee of thirteen was chosen to draw it up, but the first draft was written by John Jay, aided by Robert R. Livingston and Gouverneur Morris.

Morris wrote to Hamilton on May 16, almost a month after the constitution was accepted, that he had some misgivings about it because it lacked a vigorous executive and "was unstable from the very nature of elective government."[5]

Hamilton agreed that the executive was too weak. To determine the proper qualifications for the chief executive "requires the deliberate wisdom of a select assembly and cannot be lodged with the people at large." He disputed with Morris about his statement that "instability is inherent in the nature of popular governments." On the contrary, "a representative democracy where the right of election is well secured & the exercise of the legislative, executive and judiciary authorities vested in select persons, chosen *really* and not *nominally* by the people, will in my opinion be most likely to be happy, regular and durable." Neither he nor Morris saw anything wrong with the very high property qualifications for voting required by the constitution; as late as 1790, only 1,303 of the 13,000–14,000 male residents of New York City could vote. Hamilton agreed with Jay's maxim that "those who own the country ought to govern it."[6]

Among Hamilton's other correspondents at this time was Hugh Knox, who followed his protégé's career with all the anxious interest of a patron. Knox wrote that he was filled with "high satisfaction" and rejoiced, along with Alexander's other island friends, at his "Good Character & Advancement" which, the clergyman observed piously, was the just reward of merit. Knox advised Hamilton to be "the Annalist & Biographer as well as the Aide de Camp of General Washington & the historiographer of the American War."[7]

Washington was famous for making excessive demands on his aides. "I give in to no kind of amusement myself; consequently those about me can have none, but are confined from morn to eve, hearing and answering applications and letters of one and another."[8] Nonetheless, the young men found time for recreation. The young ladies eyed the dashing officers at the commander in chief's headquarters with great interest, which was, of course, returned with enthusiasm. Hamilton knew the William Livingston family when he lived in Elizabethtown, and now William Livingston was New Jersey's first governor. When Suzanna Livingston, known as Miss Suky, suggested that Colonel Hamilton start a correspondence with her sister Catherine, who was interested in politics, he was more than cooperative. "Kitty," a charming, flirtatious young woman, was five years older than Alexander.

In the eighteenth century, letter writing was an exercise in grace and wit, especially when a man was writing to a lady. "You know, I am reknowned for gallantry, and shall always be able to entertain you with a choice collection of the prettiest things available," he told Kitty. "I fancy my knowledge of you affords me a tolerably just idea of your taste," he said, but he would like her to give him "intimations" about herself because "woman is not a *simple*, but a most complex, intricate and enigmatical being. . . . If you would choose to be a goddess . . . I will torture my imagination for the best arguments . . . to prove you so. . . . And, after your deification, I will call out of every poet . . . the choicest delicacies." Hamilton then reminded himself that amidst his "amorous transports" he had to be a politician and intelligencer. He told Kitty that though the enemy seemed to be brooding some mischief in Philadelphia, he assured her that the coming campaign would bring success. Among other good effects of the peace would be the removal of obstacles to "that most delectable thing called matrimony—a state, which, with a kind of magnetic force, attracts every breast to it, in which sensibility has a place."

Hamilton followed Kitty on her travels with his series of amorous letters. When the British occupied Elizabethtown in 1776, William Livingston moved his family from their estate, Liberty Hall, to Backing Ridge. And Kitty often visited her sister Sally, who was married to John Jay.

Banter filled the pages of Hamilton's letters until he turned to politics. "Your sentiments respecting war are perfectly just," he conceded. "Every finer feeling of a delicate mind revolts from the idea of shedding human blood."[9]

But the warrior's thoughts were really turned to the imminence of military activity at last. Howe seemed to have decided to evacuate Brunswick and to move by sea, either to Philadelphia or up the Hudson. Hamilton told the New York committee that the British army had to be prevented from getting any supplies in New York State. Their horses were in miserable condition, so that if they could not replace them, "they should not be able to penetrate any distance into the country."[10]

Acting on information obtained from spies, British prisoners of war and deserters, Washington moved from Morristown to Middle Brook,

New Jersey, less than seven miles from Howe's camp at Brunswick, and tried to anticipate the British general's next move. He did not let Howe force the Americans into battle until the last week in June, when the British general moved his army from Brunswick to Amboy. Howe's army came out of Amboy and tried to cut off the American left led by Lord Stirling, who had to retreat to Westfield, then Amboy and, finally, to the mountain pass. The British followed as far as Westfield and then withdrew to Amboy, plundering and burning all the way.

In defense of Washington's tactic of retreat and avoidance of the enemy in the field, Hamilton wrote: "I know that some people will accuse us of cowardice and weakness," but "The liberty of America is at stake and the loss of one general engagement could ruin us therefore it would be folly to hazard it unless our resources were at an end and some decisive blow was necessary or our strength was so great we would be sure of success. Neither situation exists. We must realize Howe will get no more from England and must make due [sic] with what he has while our army is growing in discipline, supplies and size. It is painful to leave some of our countrymen a prey to the British and wounding to a soldier's feelings to have to decline to fight."[11]

Howe gave up trying to entice the elusive Washington into battle and withdrew to Staten Island. On July 6, Hamilton informed Gouverneur Morris that Howe's designs were more of a mystery than ever. If he were sensible, he would remain on Staten Island, gather his forces, wait for reinforcements from Europe and generally bide his time until he could force the colonial army into action. However, all reports indicated that the British ships were being stocked with food and water for two months and preparations made to move the troops somewhere.[12]

Bad news—"heavy, unexpected & unaccountable"—arrived at Washington's headquarters. Gen. Johnny Burgoyne had taken Fort Ticonderoga. If it could not be held, Hamilton said angrily, why was so much expended on trying to defend it? "I wish to suspend judgment," he told John Jay, but it seemed that there had been "the most abandoned cowardice or treachery." The American army's plan now was to go to Peekskill as soon as the weather permitted because Howe's army had embarked and was probably going up the Hudson. If the American army arrived first, all would be well, the aide wrote encouragingly. The leaders had to appear hopeful so as to calm the people's fears.[13]

Hamilton's reports to the New York Committee of Correspondence served two purposes: information about the continental army for New York's leaders, and an opportunity for Washington to advise and influence the leaders of the besieged New York area. This made Hamilton a liaison between the two groups, but his deepest loyalties were with Washington and the continental army.

Hamilton deduced correctly what the British master plan was at this time. Burgoyne would march down from the north and Howe move up from New York. Howe bungled the plan by sailing to Philadelphia, the patriot capital. Burgoyne harassed the back settlements in New York State with the help of the Indians, but Hamilton did not think that he would be rash enough "to plunge into the bosom of the Country" without assurances that he would be met by Howe. It was, on the whole, better for the Americans for Howe to take Philadelphia rather than join Burgoyne, Hamilton believed, but the occupation of the capital might have the adverse effect of making American currency decline.[14]

Gouverneur Morris's gloomy report to Hamilton from Saratoga, pronouncing Fort Edward and other forts in the area indefensible, conflicted with information received at Washington's headquarters that Fort Edward would be an excellent post from which to stop Burgoyne's progress. Livingston was as pessimistic as Morris. He said that Hamilton's figures on the size of the British army were a "grand underestimation." Burgoyne's command, including the soldiers stationed in Canada, was at least 10,000 men, plus an indeterminate number of Indians. The continental army, according to New York estimates, had no more than 4,000 troops. By the last report, Burgoyne was at Fort Edward, and the American army had retreated as far as Saratoga already. To increase the problem, Tories and the warriors of the Six Nations were ready to join the British, thus cutting off the inhabitants of Tryon County from the rest of the state, the result being that New York will be "intirely Subjected."[15]

Hamilton, now at headquarters in Germantown, Pennsylvania, was sympathetic but firm. He, too, was anxious about New York, but the main problem was not the numbers of the enemy but "the panic in the army (I am afraid pretty high up) and the want of zeal in the Eastern States."[16]

The choice of a general for the critical northern command disappointed Hamilton. He favored Philip Schuyler, despite his recent failures, and was not overjoyed when Congress awarded the strategic command to Gen. Horatio Gates. He "is hardly the man," Hamilton said. He did endorse Jay's suggestion to send Governor Clinton and all the New York militia to the upper part of the state to help oppose Burgoyne.

By August 10, Livingston had an even gloomier report for Hamilton. The troops were so dispersed that they could not stop the enemy, and Boston refused help. Fort Schuyler was resisting but had only twenty days of supplies left. Only four of New York's fourteen counties remained in colonial hands. When Fort Schuyler fell, as inevitably it had to, universal despair might result in the state's surrender. If it did not happen, said Livingston, it would be due to the enemy's timidity, not American conduct.[17]

Hamilton was sorry to hear about New York's plight. Speaking for his chief, Hamilton said that the loss of New York would be greater than any blow struck by General Howe. Washington was giving all the assistance that he could to the northern army. Two regiments left Peekskill to move northward, and about 500 of Daniel Morgan's riflemen left Trenton for Peekskill, where sloops would pick them up and move them up the river. Morgan's men were used to rifles and wood fights and were commanded by officers of extraordinary bravery. They would soon chastise the Indians and force them to desert their British friends.[18]

From Washington's headquarters in Delaware, Hamilton rejoiced by letter with Governor Clinton over the relief of Fort Schuyler. Since Howe was now safely in the south, the eastern states were free to exert all their energies against Burgoyne.

Hamilton was ready for action in his sector also. On August 22, Howe's fleet had been sighted in Chesapeake Bay, which meant that Philadelphia was his objective. Washington ordered the troops to leave Germantown for Wilmington, Delaware, where they were placed in a position to overlook the city.

The British landed at Elkton, Maryland, in terrible condition. They had been six weeks at sea with only three weeks' supply of food for the horses; many of the poor beasts died or survived as skeletons. Since the army could not move until the horses were replaced, Hamilton favored attacking the enemy boldly before they entered Philadelphia. "I opine we ought to do it, and that we shall beat them soundly if we do. . . . I would not only fight them but I would attack them for I hold it an established maxim that there is three to one in favor of the party attacking."[19]

The longed-for attack took place at Brandywine Creek, but it was a defeat for Washington's army. Dr. Benjamin Rush, sent to treat the wounded American prisoners held in the British camp, was disdainful of the ragged, undisciplined, defeated colonial army and its leaders. He wrote: "The Commander-in-Chief, at this time the idol of America, is governed by General Greene, General Knox, and Colonel Hamilton, one of his aides, a young man of twenty-one years of age."[20]

After Brandywine, Washington moved to Warwick Furnace, a distance forty miles west and a little north of Philadelphia, in the foothills of the Alleghenies. From there, Washington sent Hamilton on a mission to destroy some mills on the Schuylkill River, used to supply the American army and now on the route of the British army and no doubt willing to serve the enemy.

Colonel Hamilton, with the assistance of Captain Lee and a small troop of horse, had to get to the mills before the enemy; it was necessary to descend a long hill leading to a bridge over the mill race. Hamilton posted two lookouts at the top of the hill and, as soon as he reached the mills, commandeered a flat-bottomed boat to carry his party across the river in case the British appeared suddenly. Shots rang out from the sentries; the enemy approached. Hamilton immediately ordered four dragoons into the boat and jumped in himself. The British horsemen could be seen chasing the sentries down the hill, so Captain Lee, with the two remaining Americans, decided to get back to the bridge, rather than detain the boat.

The recent storms that had proved so disastrous to Washington's hungry, tattered army had swollen the mill race, and the flood, coupled with a violent current, made the position of the boat perilous. Lee distracted the British for a few minutes with a wild ride to the bridge, hoping to give Hamilton a chance to get away. Lee and his men reached the bridge and crossed it, unharmed by enemy fire. Hamilton, however, was fired on by another contingent of British troops, and the boat was tossing so wildly on the angry water that it was impossible to return the fire. Lee, despairing for Hamilton's life, sent a dragoon ahead with a letter describing the tragic incident.

Washington had hardly finished reading the letter when Hamilton appeared in an extremely distressed state; he thought that Lee had been cut off and either captured or killed. Relieved to find that Lee and his dragoons had escaped unharmed, he was sorry to report two horsemen and one of the boatmen wounded.[21]

Immediately after this adventure, Hamilton wrote to John Hancock, president of the Continental Congress, advising him that if Congress had not yet left Philadelphia, it should do so immediately;

the enemy might enter the city that very night. At 9 P.M., Hamilton wrote to Hancock again, in case he had not received the first letter. He described the action at Deveser's Ferry, explaining that due to the preparations he had made for his escape and the sudden appearance of the British, two boats had been left behind that might have been commandeered by the enemy. By employing the boats, the British could carry fifty men at a time across the river, so that in a few hours they would have a large enough force to defeat the American militia blocking their entrance into Philadelphia. "This renders the situation of Congress extremely precarious if they are not on their guard; my apprehensions for them are great, though it is not improbable they may not be realized."[22]

Congress had already decided that if it became necessary to leave Philadelphia, the members would go to Lancaster, Pennsylvania. After receiving Hamilton's letter, some left at midnight of September 19.

John Adams, awakened at 3 A.M. to be informed of the flight, wrote to his wife Abigail: "In the morning of the 19th Inst., the Congress was all allarmed, in their Beds, by a Letter from Mr. Hamilton, one of General Washington's family, that the enemy were in possession of the Ford over the Schuylkill, and the Boats, so that they had it in their power to be in Philadelphia before morning." Adams was annoyed by "the false alarm" which occasioned the flight. "Not a soldier of Howes has crossed the Schuylkill," he grumbled to his diary on September 21. But six days later, the British occupied Philadelphia.[23]

Before Howe reached Philadelphia, Hamilton was sent there to get blankets and clothing for Washington's army. Washington was certain that his attractive young representative would use both charm and firmness to convince the Philadelphians to assist the soldiers, "whose sufferings they are bound to commiserate." On September 22, the day after Hamilton left Washington's camp on Reading Road, twenty-eight miles from Philadelphia, he received a letter from the chief; he was sending eight or ten additional men to assist him. Reports disclosed that three or four persons in the city had more than 3,000 pairs of shoes. As soon as the shoes and blankets were collected, Hamilton was to send them off by interior roads, but he was not to forget to obtain all the other supplies that were needed.[24]

Washington's star was in eclipse at this time. After the occupation of Philadelphia the following week, his army was defeated at Germantown. Up north, however, a victory was being celebrated. New

York was saved. General Gates had triumphed over the British army of Gen. "Gentleman Johnny" Burgoyne, who surrendered to him at Saratoga on the seventeenth of October, thus achieving what had been called the turning point of the war. Though not an unconditional surrender but an arrangement whereby the defeated British army agreed to return to England and not fight again in this war, it provided Washington's critics with a rival with whom to challenge him. Gates soon became the focus of an anti-Washington movement.

It was decided at a meeting of General Washington's Council of War that one of his family should be sent to General Gates to tell him that he must send troops from his northern army to reinforce the continental army at Philadelphia. On October 30, Hamilton was ordered by Washington to set out for Albany immediately, "at which place or so you will find Gates."[25]

Hamilton's new mission was one of great delicacy and significance. Washington was well aware of the victor of Saratoga's dislike and of Gates's support from military men such as Gen. Thomas Conway, members of Congress such as John Adams and other prominent figures such as Dr. Rush. By appointing Hamilton, Washington showed great confidence in his young aide's tact and loyalty, which Hamilton wished to justify. En route to Albany, he stopped at Fishkill, New York, where he met Colonel Morgan and his men and persuaded General Putnam to agree to send 4,000 men south. The energetic aide also found out from Putnam that General Wendt and 700 militiamen were about to cross Peekskill, so he sent orders for them to march to Red Bank, New Jersey. While Hamilton waited for some French horses before leaving for Albany, General Poore's brigade arrived, only to be redirected by Hamilton to join Washington. "So strongly am I impressed with the importance of endeavouring to crush Mr. Howe that I am apt to think it would be adviseable to draw off all the continental troops," he wrote to his commander.[26]

On November 5, Hamilton arrived in Albany, met with General Gates and was promised General Patterson's brigade. Although not really convinced, he yielded to Gates's opinion that two brigades should stay in the north, remembering Washington's counsel that he must "pay great deference" to General Gates's judgment. But in short order, having investigated further, Hamilton was disgusted by Gates's treachery and his own naïveté. He wrote to Gates that he had learned that Patterson's brigade was the weakest of the three, with no more than 600 soldiers fit for duty. Further, 200 men in the company had terms so near to expiration that they would no longer be in service by the time they reached their destination. Therefore, Hamilton said, his instructions from his Excellency General Washington required that one of the other brigades be substituted for the one assigned.[27]

Hamilton warned Washington about how powerful a rival Gates had become. Though he did not accept the victor of Saratoga's contention that to lessen the size of his army was to expose New York and New England "to the ravages and depredations of the enemy," Hamilton admitted that "I found insuperable inconveniences in acting diametrically opposite to the opinion of a Gentleman; whose successes have raised him into the highest importance. . . . General Gates has influence and interest elsewhere: he might use it." Hamilton defended his own action by explaining that he had insisted on sending troops from there without General Gates's approval, "should any accident or inconvenience happen in consequence of it, there would be too fair a pretext for censure, and many people are too well-disposed to lay hold of it." Hamilton apologized to his chief for not following his instructions, but, he said, "I ventured to do what I thought right, hoping that at least the goodness of my intention will excuse the error of my judgement."[28]

Either Hamilton proved more persuasive at a later meeting with Gates, or the general had second thoughts about defying Washington. Hamilton was able to prevail upon Gates to send Glover's brigade southward, along with Patterson's.

Hamilton's troubles were not over. When, on his return trip, he arrived at New Windsor, he found that General Putnam "had neglected and deranged everything." Poore's and Learned's brigades had not started their march to join Washington, and Colonel Warner's militia had been sent to Peekskill to aid in an expedition against New York City, "at this time the Hobby Horse with General Putnam," Hamilton fumed to Washington. He addressed himself with great severity to General Putnam, his senior by many years. "I now Sir, in the most explicit terms, by his Excellency's Authority, give it as a positive order from him, that all the Continental troops under your Command may be Immediately marched to Kings Ferry, there to Cross the River and hasten to Reinforce the Army." He added: "Attacking N. York out of the question for the moment."[29]

Hamilton reported to Washington that Putnam had defied orders and asked that he be sent instant directions to do what was asked of him. "I wish General Putnam was recalled from the command of this post and Governor Clinton would accept it," Hamilton said. His wish was soon answered. At the time neither Washington nor Hamilton knew that Congress had relieved Putnam of his command on November 4 and ordered him to join the commander in chief at White Marsh, Pennsylvania.[30]

Hamilton's instinctive dislike of Putnam was in contrast to Aaron Burr's fondness for the former Roger's Ranger of the French and Indian War, who had become a tavern keeper and was now a fifty-eight-year-old major general. A reluctant, unhappy aide to Washington, Burr had been grateful when John Hancock arranged an exchange with Samuel B. Webb, Putnam's aide. Burr liked being part of the hearty general's informal household and remained attached to his command through the New York and New Jersey campaigns. Burr left Putnam only when he was appointed a lieutenant colonel and given command of the regiment of Col. William Malcolm, a New York merchant who sponsored the regiment but left the fighting to his second in command.

Hamilton planned to accompany the troops back to main headquarters in Pennsylvania, but by November 10, still in New Windsor, he wrote that he was "very unwell but I shall not spare myself." Two days later he had to tell Washington that he had fever and violent rheumatic pains throughout his body, which did not prevent him from observing the shortcomings of General Putnam and his army. Every part of the old general's conduct was marked with blindness and negligence and gave "general disgust," Hamilton reported. As for the troops, they "have unfortunately imbibed an idea that they have done their part of the business of the campaign and are now entitled to repose. This & lack of pay makes them against a long march this late in the season."[31]

While at Fishkill, recovering very slowly from a severe respiratory illness, the young man informed Gates that General Howe now had reinforcements which increased his army to 6,000–7,000 men. General Washington had 5,000 at the most, and General Putnam had detained the militia under his command until too late. "I give you the present information that you may decide whether any further succour can with propriety come from you."[32]

On the night of November 14, Hamilton arrived at Denis Kennedy's house in Peekskill, too exhausted to go any farther. Governor Clinton was unable to keep the young man from attending to the march of troops as soon as he was back on his feet. Still very weak, he crossed the ferry to fall in with General Glover's brigade, which was traveling to Fishkill.

A letter from Washington, sent from his White Marsh, Pennsylvania, headquarters, relieved Hamilton of some of his feelings of failure. The commander in chief, who was quite capable of compassion especially when dealing with his favorite aide, wrote soothingly, "I approve intirely of all the steps you have taken, and have only to wish that the exertions of those which you have had to deal with had kept with your zeal and good intentions." He hoped that Hamilton's health had improved enough to permit him to accompany the rear of the troops marching south.

Hamilton was too weak to make the winter trek, but while recuperating, he observed the activities in the area and sent Governor Clinton an account of some illegal and reprehensible practices. Some officers, some of them high in command, had been taking the property of inhabitants and converting it to their own use without compensating the owners or the state, he wrote. Cattle were being seized and sold at a kind of mock auction by order of a general officer. A stop had to be made to this and the perpetrators punished. "I am studying this to place before Gen Washington for an enquiry."[33]

Clinton tried to excuse the practices on the ground that soldiers regarded as their lawful prize anything taken within the enemy lines, even when the property belonged to someone on the same side. He tried to placate Hamilton by ordering General Putnam to look into a case of the sort under attack. Putnam ignored the order.[34]

No bleaker place in the world could have been chosen for the tired, underfed, underclad American troops than the windy side of the hill where they were encamped at Valley Forge. Congress failed to provide them with the stores that Washington had pleaded for. Clothing, shoes and blankets as well as food were short, so that the prospect for the winter was starvation, bitter cold and inevitable illness and disease. A soldier wrote in January 1778 that "Twenty-six in one York regiment have been three weeks without a shirt; one fourth of our men now barefoot without blankets or breeches, now lying uncovered in the field—and believe me this is real." By mid-February, about 400 men lacked the most basic clothing to cover themselves; many could not leave their quarters. One day, while walking through a company street, Washington observed a soldier wrapped in a blanket dash from one hut to another. With horror, the commander realized that underneath his blanket the soldier was completely naked.[35]

Hamilton, who arrived at Valley Forge headquarters shortly before the New Year (1778), was shocked by the deprivation into which

Congress had allowed the army to sink. In a letter written on Washington's behalf to the quartermaster general, he authorized him to impress any wagons that he could lay his hands on. "For God's sake, my dear Sir," he implored, "exert yourself upon this occasion, our distress is infinite."[36]

Everyone blamed Congress for this "infinite distress." Hamilton told Clinton that many of its members were "fit for the trust," but this could not be said for the body as a whole. The colonel added wryly, shivering with the cold on that bleak February day, "You have not perhaps as many opportunities of knowing it as I have. Their conduct with respect to the army especially is feeble indecisive and improvident insomuch that we are reduced to a more terrible situation than you can conceive." Most of the great men in our councils were in the field or in state governments. "You should not beggar the councils of the United States to enrich the administration of the several members. . . . A Congress despised at home and abroad will not bring success to our European negotiations."[37]

Hamilton became involved in the curious and disgraceful comedy of errors that revealed the anti-Washington "plot" known as the Conway Cabal. Because of his closeness to Washington, he seemed a likely candidate for the person who was responsible for the leak to the commander in chief. Were it not for General Gates's phenomenal success at Saratoga and his gratitude to his twenty-year-old aide, James Wilkinson, who had worked very hard on the terms and the details of the surrender, the whole affair might never have been exposed. As it was, Gates rewarded Wilkinson with the mission of carrying the news of victory to Congress and then to the commander in chief. Included in the dispatches was a recommendation that Wilkinson be promoted to brigadier general.

Wilkinson took his time carrying the good news from Saratoga to York, Pennsylvania, where Congress was sitting. The first delay was due to Wilkinson's attack of "convulsive colic," which kept him from leaving camp until October 20. After he got started, he spent eleven days traveling the 285 miles from Albany to York, visiting George Clinton and Gouverneur Morris and then spending two days at Easton with his former mentor, Dr. William Shippen of Philadelphia, now director-general of hospitals. There he heard about Thomas Conway, a French officer of Irish parentage, who had wangled from Congress the rank of brigadier general and an appointment to Washington's command. Conway, who had an inflated opinion of his military talent, became dissatisfied and highly critical of Washington. He preferred General Gates, who had seen a lot of service in the British army, and started a correspondence with him distinguished by its indiscreet, hostile remarks about Washington's competence. Gates, with equal indiscretion, agreed with Conway. Wilkinson, as Gates's close confidential aide, knew of the contents of the correspondence.

Wilkinson left Easton reluctantly on October 27 because his fiancée, Ann Biddle, was there visiting the Shippens. His next stop was Reading, Pennsylvania, where he joined General Mifflin, another Gates admirer and Washington detractor, and two like-minded congressmen. The next day a heavy rain delayed Wilkinson's departure again. He dined with Lord Stirling and his aides, McWilliams and James Monroe. Later in the evening, his tongue loosened by liquor, Gates's aide revealed confidential information about the Conway-Gates correspondence and the plan to supplant Washington to Mc-Williams, who passed it on to Lord Stirling. Stirling revealed the plot to Washington.

More delays kept Wilkinson from delivering tidings of the Saratoga victory until October 30. Charles Thompson, acting president of the Continental Congress, knew about it already. Somewhat later, the slow-moving messenger reached the Washington camp at White Marsh to make the official report to the head of the army. He was received courteously by Washington, who concealed his anger over Gates's unforgivable delay.

It was not until December 3 that Gates learned that his private anti-Washington correspondence was known to his victim. Thomas Mifflin wrote: "An extract from General Conway's letter to you has been procured, and sent to headquarters. . . . General Washington enclosed it to General Conway without remark." Gates, shocked and apprehensive about his future, replied to Mifflin: "I entreat you, dear General, to let me know which of the letters was copied off. It is of the greatest importance that I should detect the person who has been guilty of that act of infidelity."[38] There was no reply.

After considerable reflection, Gates decided that Alexander Hamilton was the informer. When Wilkinson returned to Albany on December 8, Gates told him of his suspicion, explaining that Hamilton had visited him in early November to demand reinforcements for Washington's army and had been left alone in the room for about an hour, during which time he took the letter out of the closet and copied it, and the copy was furnished to Washington. Wilkinson, who realized to his dismay that he was the responsible party, decided to keep his involvement secret and offered another scapegoat.

He suggested that Col. Robert Troup, another of Gates's aides, was to blame. He insinuated that Troup, in an unguarded moment, disclosed the secret correspondence to Hamilton, who then, prompted by "various motives," mentioned it to Washington. This explanation seemed logical to Gates, since it was known that Troup and Hamilton had been close friends at college and that, while in Albany, Hamilton had spent more time with Troup than any other person.

The only problem was that Troup assured Gates that Wilkinson's accusation was "utterly unfounded in truth." It was not long before the true story of the party at Lord Stirling's and Wilkinson's indiscreet revelations emerged. As a result, there was a rift between Wilkinson and Gates that terminated in an abortive duel.

At the end of March 1778, Hamilton was ordered by Washington to work with a committee on the exchange of prisoners. He, William Grayson and Elias Boudinot were charged with the task of writing a treaty based on the principles of justice, humanity and mutual advantage. This was a difficult assignment because of the record of disgraceful treatment of American prisoners aboard the British prison ships anchored in New York harbor. The agony of the unfortunates crammed into the holds of the ships was worse than any experience on the battlefield, and men could be incarcerated in the floating hells for years. Though Americans sent food to the starving prisoners, the British kept most of it for themselves. "The air was so foul at times that a lamp could not be kept burning by reason of which three boys were not missed until they had been dead for ten days," one prisoner wrote.[39]

After the Battle of Saratoga the situation improved a little; the British realized that the Americans were in a position to retaliate. And, sad to state, Congress established prison ships that equaled in horror their British counterparts.

The negotiations at Germantown between Howe's commissioners and the Americans failed. Howe did not want a treaty that was binding on the nation or extended beyond his command. He wanted a limited arrangement, founded on mutual confidence between him and Washington. Hamilton explained to Washington that such an offer had to be turned down. "The private faith of an individual could not in the nature of things be a competent, or proper security for a treaty of public import." It would be unfair because "the public faith would be plighted for our engagements," and only General Howe would be bound to carry out those of the British. Howe's commissioners intimated that to deal with the Americans at all was to acknowledge them, which they did not want to do. The American commission concluded that the sort of treaty they could have obtained would have been temporary, would cease with Howe's command, could have been violated by public authority and hence would be "highly derogatory to the dignity of the United States."[40]

Though no treaty was made, in late May Congress accepted a proposal from General Howe for mutual exchange of prisoners. Washington asked Elias Boudinot, American commissary of prisoners, to come to Valley Forge at once to carry out the operation, but he failed to appear. When Sir Henry Clinton, Howe's replacement, was observed to be readying a departure from Philadelphia, Washington again sent for Boudinot. Before a reply could be received, Joshua Loring, the British commissary of prisoners, arrived, ready to negotiate the details. Washington appointed Hamilton to act in Boudinot's absence. As a result of the arrangements, on June 5, all American prisoners in Philadelphia were marched to the Lancaster Road, where they were met by the same number of British prisoners of equal rank, and the exchange took place.

Clinton had been ordered to leave Philadelphia because of the new French alliance that would give the American rebels the support of the French navy. Washington decided to leave Valley Forge, knowing that his army had been matured and tempered by its winter of suffering and improved by rigorous instruction in the manual of arms by the self-styled Baron von Steuben. Hamilton left camp with his commander.

At first, Hamilton was ambivalent about Von Steuben's value to the army. He wrote to his friend William Duer, "he has great fondness for power," a shortcoming that many were to attribute to Hamilton. Washington was granting him too much power, which was alarming other officers. The baron wanted to enforce discipline or subordination or obedience to orders, which was a power that should belong only to the commander in chief and would "inflame the army" if put in other hands.

There was some professional jealousy in these remarks. A plan for the change of the composition of the army was one of Hamilton's preoccupations during this time. At the end of January, Washington had submitted a lengthy report to Congress on ways to improve the army, based on letters Hamilton had written to the commander. Just before leaving Valley Forge, Hamilton repeated his ideas for remedying the poor discipline in the army. Reduce the number of regiments, he advised. Send the duplicate officers home. They might complain, but if put on half pay for a while as compensation, they would soon stop.[41]

Washington's new strategy was to follow the British across New Jersey, harassing them constantly. With the revitalized army, he was not averse to a proper battle. Acting on his wave of optimism, Washington sent his young French general, the Marquis de Lafayette, and Mad Anthony Wayne to seek out the enemy and to engage him if the situation was favorable. Hamilton, assigned to Lafayette partly because he spoke French, wrote to Washington at Cranberry, New Jersey, from a place about eight miles from Allentown that the enemy was four miles from this place and had passed the road that turned off toward South Amboy, which meant that they were heading for Shrewsbury. The Americans had to halt for lack of provisions. General Wayne's division was almost starving and unwilling to continue until they were fed. If they did not receive supplies immediately, Hamilton said, "the whole purpose of our detachment will be frustrated."

Somewhat later on that same day, June 26, Hamilton wrote to Washington again; the enemy's van was a little beyond Monmouth, their rear about seven miles from Allentown. Their baggage was in front, their flying army in the rear, with a rear guard of about a thousand men. It would be folly to attack them, Hamilton judged, but the Americans might try moving to a position near the British left flank, which would keep them from turning either flank. South Amboy was sure to be the enemy's next object. He was interrupted by a letter from Lafayette, ordering him to move to Englishtown the next morning with his men and to be wary of a surprise attack.[42]

The battle that followed near Monmouth Court House should have been an easy victory instead of a success "far inferior to what we, in all probability, should have had," Hamilton told Elias Boudinot, now a member of the Continental Congress from New Jersey. The blame, he stated firmly, was Gen. Charles Lee's, "either a driveler in the business of soldiership or something worse."

The puzzling events began with Lee's irritating vacillation over whether he should insist on the command of the advanced corps or decline in favor of Lafayette. Finally, Washington, "tired of such fickle behaviour," ignored Lee and ordered Lafayette to proceed.

The British, marching from Allentown, had thrown all their best troops in the rear, so that Washington detached two brigades to strike at them and sent General Lee to command the whole advanced corps of about 5,000 men. Lee's orders were to pursue and attack the enemy's rear as soon as he received intelligence that the British troops were on the march.

On the morning of the twenty-eighth, Lee received the news and started out with his troops, reaching the enemy's rear a mile or two beyond Monmouth Court House. Though the position was favorable, Lee did not attack. Instead, he changed his position about two or three times until the American advanced corps fell into a confused retreat. None of this was reported to Washington, but as the main body of Americans approached the supposed place of action, he saw troops retreating in great disorder, pursued by the British. Washington immediately regrouped his forces and finally beat the enemy, killing and wounding at least a thousand of the best British troops.

Hamilton had been in the thick of the battle himself. While assisting in forming the troops under Colonel Olney, his horse, wounded by a cannonball, caused him to fall. He was "considerably hurt" and had to retire from the field for a while, James McHenry wrote to Boudinot. After a brief rest, Hamilton was up again, rallying and charging and seeming to court death.[43]

The repercussions from the Battle of Monmouth started on June 30 with a series of three offensive and challenging letters from General Lee. The general complained of unjust treatment by Washington, "instigated by some of those dirty earwigs who will ever insinuate themselves near persons in high office." One of them being Alexander Hamilton, although his name was not mentioned in the correspondence. Lee arrogantly demanded that a court of inquiry hear his case. Washington agreed to a court-martial.[44]

Lee was charged with misbehavior before the enemy, making an unnecessary, disorderly and shameful defeat, and disrespect for the commander in chief in letters he had written. Since Hamilton was the officer who delivered Washington's orders to Lee, he was a star witness at the court-martial proceedings that took place on July 4 and 13 at New Brunswick, New Jersey. At the trial, Hamilton testified in a dignified and temperate manner, very different from the denunciatory tone of his letter to Boudinot: "I shall continue to believe and say—his conduct was monstrous and unpardonable."[45] He did state that although General Washington did not and could not give positive orders to General Lee to attack the enemy at all events, his intention "was fully to have that enemy attacked on their march and that the circumstances must be very extraordinary and unforseen, which, consistent with his wish, would justify the general not doing it." General Lee asked Hamilton whether, in a letter or conversation with him, he had communicated General Washington's intention as fully or as clearly as he did to the court. "I do not recollect that I ever did," Hamilton had to answer.

On the second day of the trial, Hamilton's evidence was more damaging. He said that he had heard Washington say to Lee that he should remain where he was and check the advance of the enemy, and that Lee had agreed to obey the order. "I was some little time after this near General Lee, during which, however, I heard no measure directed, nor saw any taken by him to answer the purpose above mentioned." General Lee then asked Hamilton a question, the answer to which made the two men eternal enemies. "Did you not express on the field an idea diametrically in reverse of my State of mind from what you have before mentioned in your testimony?" Hamilton answered firmly, "I did not," and added, "I said something to you in the field expressive of an opinion that there appeared in you no want of that degree of self-possession, which proceeds from a want of personal intrepidity. I did not change this in my evidence here but only said that there appeared a certain hurry of spirits, which may proceed from a temper not so calm and steady as is necessary to support a man in such critical circumstances."[46]

Lee responded in kind when he spoke in his own defense, saying that Hamilton was a man of sense and valor, "although it is not that sort of valour, unless by practice and philosophy he can correct, will ever be any great use to the community."

Though the court found Lee guilty on a number of charges, he was only suspended from his command for a year.

Hamilton squirmed under Lee's attack. He could not ignore it but felt impelled to justify his conduct to Lord Stirling, the president of the court-martial. What really went through his mind during the battle, Hamilton recalled, was that Lee lacked the self-possession requisite of a general who had to make decisions promptly. "A certain indecision, improvidence and hurry of spirits were apparent," he wrote. The purpose of his letter, Hamilton told Lord Stirling, was to explain his testimony and was founded on further reflections.[47]

Both factions remained angry. Lee continued to make anti-Washington remarks. Though the commander forbade duels, his aides would not be satisfied until they had avenged his honor. John Laurens succeeded in outmaneuvering Hamilton for the privilege of challenging Lee to a meeting. Hamilton was his second, and Maj. Evan Edwards acted for Lee. The four met at the edge of a woods near Philadelphia on the afternoon of December 24, 1778. As arranged, Lee and Laurens fired at each other at five or six paces. Lee was wounded slightly and wanted a second exchange, but both seconds opposed it. After Lee insisted, Laurens agreed to continue, until Hamilton said that unless Lee was motivated by personal enmity, he did not think that the affair should continue further. Once again, Lee insisted. Hamilton was ready to yield, but Edwards was adamant. Finally, the two seconds prevailed on the combatants to return to town.[48]

Aaron Burr was also at the Battle of Monmouth. He, too, had his horse shot from under him and was thrown to the ground but not injured. He, however, was a friend and supporter of General Lee, due, in part, to his dislike of Washington, which dated from an episode that had occurred at the Newburgh headquarters. Washington had surprised Burr surreptitiously reading his mail and delivered a "terrific reproof" to him. From that time on, Washington stood in the way of Burr's advancement in the army.[49]

The Lee episode provided Hamilton with some bad moments, but its effect on his career was a positive one. He was firmly established as an intrepid Washington partisan whose loyalty to his chief was almost feudal. Constancy was a trait that pleased the commander in chief and gave him the confidence to rely more and more on his brilliant young aide's talents. Hamilton was now a member in the highest standing of Washington's military family with first-class credentials for entrance into the best society, which would prove more than adequate for his next major step upward—matrimony.

4

The Fortunes of Love and War

Aғᴛᴇʀ ᴛʜᴇ Bᴀᴛᴛʟᴇ ᴏғ Mᴏɴᴍᴏᴜᴛʜ there was a lull in the military affairs of the colonial army. French naval aid, so eagerly awaited, proved a disappointment. Gens. John Sullivan and Nathanael Greene, backed by the French fleet under Comte d'Estaing, attempted to take Rhode Island from the British in a battle at Newport. It was a failure. The French fleet sailed north to Boston, leaving the disillusioned Americans to fend for themselves. Both Washington and Hamilton agreed that despite the understandable anger of the American officers, "prudence dictates that we should put the best face upon the matter to the World, attribute the removal to Boston, to necessity."[1]

During this quiet time, Hamilton wrote three letters that were published in the New York *Journal* in October and November 1778, exposing the activities of Samuel Chase, a congressman from Maryland. Hamilton, using the pseudonym "Publius," afterward made famous as the signature for the *Federalist Papers*, accused Chase of taking advantage of his knowledge that flour would be in great demand because of the needs of the French fleet by joining with businessmen to monopolize the staple, thus forcing up the price more than 100 percent.

Even this early in his career, Hamilton was disgusted by official misconduct, particularly when it involved making a profit from public position. He berated the Marylander, saying: "The love of money and the love of power are the predominating ingredients of your mind. . . . Your avarice will be fatal to your ambition." More interesting than the personal abuse directed at Chase was Hamilton's view of the status of a congressman. It is "the most illustrious and important of any I am able to conceive. He is to be regarded not only as a legislator, but as a founder of an empire."[2]

Confined to the sedentary task of being Washington's scribe and

sometimes his adviser, Hamilton allowed himself to become en-
meshed in a tempest in a teapot with Rev. William Gordon, a
Congregational minister from Jamaica Plain, Massachusetts. Gordon,
a dedicated gossip in the process of writing a history of the American
Revolution, was the source of an ill-advised statement uttered by
Francis Dana, a Massachusetts congressman, in a Philadelphia coffee
house. Col. John Brooks started the controversy on July 4, 1779,
when he quoted Dana's statement that Hamilton had said "it was
high time for the people to rise, join General Washington and turn
Congress out of doors." He also said that Hamilton was "in no way
interested in the defense of this country, and therefore was most
likely to pursue such a line as his great ambition dictates."[3] The
source of his information, Dana told Hamilton, was Dr. Gordon.

Usually tactful and apt at smoothing over difficulties in his role as
Washington's aide, Hamilton was riding his military high horse in
this case, which he believed concerned his honor. He asked his informant Brooks to dig deeper into his memory for the real author "of
this insinuation." Brooks's reply aggravated Hamilton further. He
admitted that he had omitted Dana's words, "desperate Fortune,"
and had played down Dana's "unfavorable representation of your
character" and charge that Hamilton's plan was "fatal to the liberties
of this country" and "pleasing to the Tories."[4]

Col. David Henley of Boston tried to smooth Hamilton's ruffled
feathers, telling him that Gordon had often occasioned quarrels of
this sort but had escaped the consequences because he was a clergyman. Hamilton immediately made Henley his messenger and gave
him a letter to deliver directly to Dr. Gordon. The clergyman answered at once that he was in touch with his source who "may probably make no objection to my giving you his name." Gordon offered
to lay the whole matter before Congress, and if Congress thought it
"a matter of sufficient consequence for them to take up—but not
otherwise," he would reveal the name.[5]

The Henley mission was in October. After a delay of two months,
Gordon sent another letter in which he said that his informer had
told him that his statements were confidential, motivated only by an
attachment to the public cause and were not made from personal
prejudice. If Hamilton wanted to pursue the matter further, Gordon
offered to transcribe the correspondence, send it to Congress and
reveal his informer, a man who was known to several delegates, he
hinted slyly.[6]

In mid-December, Hamilton wrote to Gordon that he knew and

had always suspected that the sole author of "the calumny" was Gordon himself. As for his threat to involve Congress in a business so little worthy of their attention, it was a mere trick. "I now put an end to the correspondence on my part."

Dr. Gordon wanted the last word. In the spring of 1779, he sent Washington a lengthy, rambling account of his dispute with Hamilton, enclosed one of the aide's letters and charged that Colonel Hamilton "hath reduced me to the necessity of taking measures for my own vindication." Unless Hamilton declared on his honor that "he will not represent me as the *author* of the report concerning him," Gordon threatened, he would communicate with several congressmen to bring the matter before that body.

After a delay of two months, Washington asked Hamilton to answer the points in Dr. Gordon's letter so that they might be conveyed to the clergyman. Washington also wrote to Gordon. If he wished to make any charges against Hamilton or any other officer, Washington said, he would have to present his case before a court-martial, otherwise he would best hold his peace.[7]

The foolish matter had some important implications that would haunt Hamilton in one way or another all his life: the accusation that he was a monarchist who favored a military dictatorship under Washington; and that all of his behavior was motivated by an insatiable ambition. The episode served as a warning to Hamilton to employ discretion at all times. Congress had been harsh in its action against military men who criticized their activities. Hamilton knew this and was particularly worried that the anti-Washington faction might delight in attacking the commander in chief through him. Very young and vulnerable at this time, he had been justifiably angered by the accusations of the gossiping clergyman, and though he had advised others to control their anger and act rationally, when he was the victim and his honor was questioned, he saw the situation quite differently.

The romantic nature of the camaraderie of the young officers in the Revolution, particularly in Washington's close-knit family, has been often noted. Allen McLane Hamilton called Hamilton, Lafayette and John Laurens an American Revolution version of the Three Musketeers. In the case of Hamilton and Laurens, there was a remarkable intensity in their feelings. Dr. Hamilton conceded that the expressions of friendship in their correspondence were "quite unusual even for those days," and said that Hamilton's most loyal friends were drawn to him by "his humorous and almost feminine traits, which were coupled with a fascinating culture and a flow of spirits that almost bubbled over."[8]

John Laurens, the son of Henry Laurens, a prominent South Carolina planter who became a president of the Continental Congress, was taken to Europe by his father, who decided that the young man's education would be improved by continental flavoring. Geneva was chosen, and young Laurens studied there, becoming part of its best society. After the Revolution started, John wanted to return home, but his father insisted that he go to London to study law. While there, he became involved with a Miss Manning, a young woman from a good family. Although John wanted to be free of any tie that would keep him in London, after his mistress became pregnant he had no choice but to marry her. He made an arrangement with her father that the forced marriage would take place, but it was understood that when Laurens returned to America, his wife and child would stay in England. Laurens explained to his own father that "pity obliged me to marry."[9]

Not long after the duel with Lee, Laurens went home to present the South Carolina congress with an original scheme to help his home state, which was being hard pressed by the British. Augusta, Florida, and Savannah, Georgia, had already been taken, and an invasion of South Carolina was expected. Laurens proposed that two to four battalions of Negro troops be raised by the government and financed by contributions from their owners. Hamilton, with whom this idea had been discussed, endorsed it enthusiastically, having seen similar units in the West Indies.

After Laurens went south, Hamilton wrote to John Jay, then president of the Continental Congress, in support of the proposal. Hamilton predicted that "with proper management" the Negroes would make "very excellent soldiers" and they could not be in better hands than those of Mr. Laurens. In answer to the common objection to using Negroes because "they are too stupid to make soldiers," Hamilton said, "I think their want of cultivation (for their natural faculties are as good as ours) joined to that habit of subordination that they acquire from a life of servitude will make them sooner become soldiers than our white inhabitants. . . ." The most radical aspect of the plan was that in return for their service, the slaves would receive their freedom and their muskets. Hamilton was writing to Jay, who shared with him a hatred of slavery and so felt free to add, "The dictate of humanity and true policy equally interest me in favour of this unfortunate class of men."[10]

In April 1779, Hamilton sent Laurens the first in a series of letters that abound in sentimental passages of unusual intensity. "I love you," he told John, but it was not until their separation that he realized "the value you had taught my heart to set upon you." Alexander said that because of his opinion of mankind, he had planned to keep his life free of "particular attachments." He reproached Laurens for taking advantage "of my sensibility to ste[al] into my affections without my consent."

"At the end of this letter, however, he asks John to find him a wife. "And now my Dear," he wrote, "as we are on the subject of a wife. . . . Such a wife as I want will, I know, be difficult to be found." His requirements were, among others, that she be "young, handsome (I lay more stress upon a good shape), sensible (a little learning will do), well bred . . . chaste and tender . . . of some good nature, a great deal of generosity."

Hamilton was devastatingly frank about his insistence that this hypothetical wife have money, "the larger the stock the better." Since he had not much of his own and little possibility of acquiring a great deal, his wife must have "a sufficiency to administer to her own extravagances." And he admonished Laurens that, when drawing a picture of him for the many competitors "for such a prize as I am," he should be "civil to your friend; mind you do justice to the length of my nose."[11] This was a bit of bawdy familiar at the time which equated the length of a man's nose with that of his penis.

Laurens remained at home as a member of the South Carolina legislature. Although Hamilton wrote to him regularly, Laurens was a poor correspondent. On September 11, 1779, Hamilton complained that he had received only one letter from John since his departure, and that one, dated July 14, "arrived just in time to appease a violent conflict between my friendship and my pride." He had written five or six letters and would have written more "had you made a proper return," Hamilton said. "But like a jealous lover, when I thought that you slighted my caresses, my affection was alarmed and my vanity piqued. . . . But you have now disarmed my resentment and by a single mark of attention made up the quarrel."[12]

The noble experiment to employ black troops with an eye to emancipation was rejected by the South Carolina legislature, not surprising to anyone but the two starry-eyed young revolutionaries who had devised it. Laurens was further disturbed by Charleston's offer to Sir Henry Clinton, who had the city under siege. If Clinton would withdraw his troops from South Carolina, the state would withdraw from the war and allow the peace treaty that would be made after the war to decide its eventual fate. Clinton refused.

John's letters were free of Alexander's penchant for overblown sentiment. He sent his love "to all our dear colleagues," not to Alexander in particular.[13]

Laurens did not forget Hamilton when he refused a congressional offer of an appointment as secretary to the American minister at Versailles. He went to Philadelphia and told the president and two other members of Congress that Alexander Hamilton was "equally qualified in point of integrity—and much better in point of ability." If Congress did not act on the suggestion, rather than cause a delay or the appointment of "a dangerous person," Laurens told Hamilton, he would accept the post.

Alexander answered modestly that although John had overrated his qualifications, "that partiality must endear you to me." He thought his chances were poor because "I am a stranger in this country. I have no property here, no connexions." His chronic frustration at having to remain the favored company clerk instead of earning military credits in the field spilled out. "I am chagrined and unhappy, but I submit. In short, Laurens, I am disgusted with everything in this world but yourself and *very* few more honest fellows and I have no other wish than as soon as possible to make a brilliant exit. Tis a weakness; but I feel I am not fit for this terrestrial Country."[14]

Despite the despairing tone of this letter, Hamilton was already planning to remedy his family and financial shortcomings. Legend has it that Alexander and Elizabeth Schuyler first met in the fall of 1777, when, during the Gates mission, Hamilton was invited to the Schuyler home by Gen. Philip Schuyler. This meeting, if it occurred, was unnoticed by either Alexander or Betsey. Col. Tench Tilghman, who met Betsey when she was eighteen, described her as a "brunette with the most good-natured dark, lively eyes that I ever saw, which threw a beam of good humour and benevolence over her entire countenance."[15]

During the winter of 1779–80, Betsey Schuyler visited her aunt, Mrs. John Cochran, wife of the surgeon-general of the Middle Department, in Morristown and soon became a part of the lively social circle that included the attractive young officers stationed at Washington's headquarters. She and Alexander met at parties, dances and sleigh rides. In a short time, Hamilton was monopolizing all her attention. In February, in a letter to Margarita Schuyler, Alexander described her older sister's charms and the "influence" she had gained over him. He wrote: "She is most unmercifully handsome. . . . Her good sense is destitute of . . . vanity and ostentation. . . . She has good nature, affability and vivacity. . . . In short . . . she possesses all the beauties, virtues and graces of her sex. . . . Cupid has in a trice metamorphosed me into the veriest inamorato you perhaps ever saw."[16]

By mid-March, while in Albany negotiating with the British about a prisoner-of-war exchange, Hamilton wrote to Betsey in such a confident and serious manner that there must have been an understanding between them. He called her "my dearest girl" and advised her to go to Philadelphia while she had the chance. "I wish you to see that city before your return [to Albany]. . . . You must always remember your best friend is where I am," he reminded her.[17]

Betsey and Alexander had known each other less than six months when Miss Schuyler accepted Hamilton's proposal of marriage, sometime around April.

Throughout his life, Hamilton was attractive to and attracted by women, but Betsey never wavered in her devotion to him while he lived or to his memory afterward. When she died at the age of ninety-four, a tiny bag was found hanging around her neck. In it was a piece of yellowed paper, so old that it had been stitched together with thread. On the paper was a poem that Alexander had written to her during the winter of his courtship.

Answer to the Inquiry Why I Sighed

Before no mortal ever knew
A love like mine so tender—true—
Completely wretched—you away—
And but half blessed e'en while you stay

If present love [illegible] face
Deny you to my fond embrace
No joy unmixed my bosom warms
But when my angel's in my arms[18]

Hamilton's letter to Philip Schuyler, asking for his daughter's hand in marriage, has not survived. Schuyler's consent arrived from Philadelphia, where he was serving as a delegate from New York to Congress, on April 8. The general asked only that the two young people have a proper family wedding. Angelica, Betsey's older sister, had eloped with John Barker Church, a wealthy Englishman living in the United States under the name of John Carter, forced to flee England because of an involvement in a duel. Schuyler would discuss wedding plans with his future son-in-law at Morristown, when he arrived there in a few days. The wedding was arranged for December. Hamilton wrote engagingly to Mrs. Schuyler: "I leave it to my conduct rather than expressions to testify the sincerity of my affection for her [Betsey], the respect I have for her parents, the desire I shall always feel to justify their confidence and merit their friendship."[19]

In discussions of the wedding, Alexander probably glossed over his parents and background, and definitely gave the impression that he was in touch with his father. In a letter to Betsey several months later, he told her that he had written to his father and invited him to come to America as soon as peace with Great Britain was established but had not yet received an answer.

James Hamilton's family connections were an asset. As the son of a Scottish laird, he was the social equal of descendants of Dutch patroons. The irregularity of Hamilton's birth, however, could become public knowledge at any time, yet unless Alexander was very unlucky, it would be after the marriage. But Hamilton wanted the recognition and affection of his lost father, a mirage that he pursued until the old man's death.

During that winter, John Laurens was with the American forces in South Carolina under Maj. Gen. Benjamin Lincoln. On February 1, Sir Henry Clinton began his attack on Charleston. Hamilton knew from reports delivered to headquarters that the situation was grave. In May, Charleston fell to the British, and Laurens was captured but granted a parole stipulating that he could not leave Pennsylvania.

Hamilton tried to arrange an exchange for Laurens, though the rest of Washington's family challenged the propriety of that because of Laurens's membership in the inner circle. "We all love you sincerely," Hamilton told John at the end of June, "but I have more of the infirmities of human nature than the others; and suspect myself of being bypassed by my partiality for you." In a light tone, Hamilton told his friend that he was "on the point of becoming a benedict. . . . Next fall completes my doom." The description of Betsey that followed was almost painfully accurate and in contrast to the passionate letters Alexander wrote to her. "She is a good hearted girl who I am sure will never play the termagant, though not a genius she has good sense enough to be agreeable, and though not a beauty, she has fine black eyes—is rather handsome and has every other requisite of the exterior to make a lover happy. And believe me, I am lover in earnest. . . ."

Unable to be exchanged, Laurens became very depressed and stopped writing to his friends at Washington's headquarters. Hamilton chided him gently: "Remember that you write to your friends, and that friends have the same interests, pains, pleasures, sympathies. . . . In spite of Schuyler's black eyes, I have still a part for the public and a part for you; so your impatience to have me married is misplaced; a strange CURE by the way, as if after matrimony I was to be less devoted than I am now."[20]

Earlier, in June, Hamilton had been hopeful for a brief moment that he would see some action. Washington sent him to observe the landing of the Hessian troops at Elizabethtown, about 3,000 men, Hamilton reported. The New Jersey militia was sent to stop the Hessians, an inadequate attempt, Hamilton judged correctly. By the end of the month, the British had raided and burned Springfield. Hamilton could hardly restrain his rage in a report of the disaster to Laurens. "Our countrymen have all the folly of the ass and all the passiveness of the sheep in their compositions," he fumed. "They are determined not to be free—If we are saved France and Spain must save us. . . . The States have the means within their power to seize this golden opportunity. They comply by halves though we try to rouse them."[21]

Added to his frustration, Hamilton was dejected over Betsey's absence in Albany. He wrote to her longingly; then, having praised her fatuously, he wanted to improve her. Employ your leisure in reading, Alexander advised. She excelled in all "the amiable qualities"; now excel in "the splendid one." If she would follow his suggestion, "I shall take pride in it." It would diversify their enjoyments and amusements and "fill all our moments to advantage."[22]

Hamilton cheered up a little when news came that Rochambeau's fleet would soon arrive at Newport, bringing "pleasing expectations of a successful campaign." Alexander assured his "angel" that she was seldom a moment absent from his mind. Until they were reunited he could not be happy, and he suffered even more because, perhaps, his Betsey was suffering "the keenest anxiety for the situation of her lover not only absent from her but exposed to a thousand imaginary dangers."[23]

Hamilton's hope of an attack on New York City by the French fleet was dashed when Thomas Graves and his English fleet sailed into New York harbor, giving the British superiority. Alexander informed Betsey and begged her to write more often and to be more open with him. The tide of war would soon turn, he predicted, and it was what he wanted. "A military life is now grown insupportable to me because it keeps me from all my soul holds dear."

After receiving three letters in succession from Betsey, Hamilton was ready to "discard forever" his fears that she did not love him. But he admitted other anxieties, which he raised in a lightly serious manner. "Do you soberly relish the pleasure of being a poor man's wife?" he asked the daughter of wealthy patroons on both sides of her family; Betsey's mother was a Van Rensselaer. He stated honestly that Betsey's "future rank in life," if married to him, "is a perfect lottery"; it might be exalted, or it might be humble. "The last is most probable; examine well your heart."[24]

Having decided to gamble on her fiancé's future, Betsey asked Alexander to visit her in Albany before the end of the campaign. He refused reluctantly, explaining that he disliked it when others had been so unmilitary as to be away during a campaign. Besides, Washington was "peculiarly averse" to this practice, and if this was to be his last military campaign he must be particularly constant and punctual. This is the first hint that Hamilton was considering leaving the service.[25]

War news continued to be bad, especially from the South. General Gates was beaten badly at Camden, South Carolina, and then retreated 180 miles in three and a half days. Hamilton, who took malicious pleasure in Gates's humiliation, observed that his action disgraced Washington and the army. But despite the rout, Hamilton had confidence that North Carolina and Virginia would not fall to the British.[26] He still saw the odds as favoring the Americans, but he admitted his doubts about the war's outcome to Laurens, who was certain to be exchanged in a few months. "We are in a dreadful situation," he observed. Apart from the military situation, the army was living on short rations with no hope of any change in the near future. The soldiers were soured; the officers disgruntled. "I hate Congress—I hate the Army—I hate the world—and I hate myself," he said.[27]

In mid-September, Washington, accompanied by Hamilton, went to Hartford to meet Rochambeau and the Chevalier de Ternay. The two Americans hoped to be told that the French admiral, the Comte de Guiche, was on his way from the West Indies, ready to defeat the British fleet and enter New York Harbor. Instead, bad news about the French fleet was awaiting their arrival. Hamilton acted as interpreter for Washington and Rochambeau, but the meetings accomplished very little. The next step on the itenerary was West Point, where Washington wanted to inspect the defenses.

West Point, the military post guarding the Hudson River, is situated on a natural promontory of rock at the point where the Hudson curves and narrows. Gen. Benedict Arnold was its commander. Discontented after the Battle of Saratoga, consistently denied the promotion that he felt he had earned, Arnold, claiming that a wound in his leg made him unfit for active service, insisted upon the West Point appointment. After receiving it, he moved into Beverly Robinson's house, on the eastern bank of the Hudson about two miles southeast of West Point.

General Washington, accompanied by Hamilton, Lafayette and General Knox, arrived at the Robinson house at 10:30 A.M. on September 25, 1780. After breakfast, Washington and a few other military men were rowed across the river to West Point, where they spent the day inspecting the fortifications. Hamilton stayed behind.

When Washington and the others returned a little after four o'clock, they found Hamilton "more shocked by the discovery of a treason of the deepest dye" than by anything he had met with before. He handed Washington a packet of letters taken from Maj. John André, a British officer, when he had been captured. The letters left no doubt that General Arnold was betraying West Point and that André was his British confederate.

Washington ordered Hamilton to pursue Arnold and catch him before he could reach asylum on a British warship anchored in the river. Hamilton rode as fast as he could to Verplanck's Point, but he was too late. Warned of André's capture, Arnold had escaped by water to the *Vulture* and had been taken aboard. The ship then sailed to New York City. Thwarted, Hamilton wrote to General Greene to detach a brigade and send it to West Point.

Upon his return from the wild-goose chase, Hamilton "saw an amiable woman frantic with distress for the loss of a husband she tenderly loved—a traitor to his country and to his fame." Alexander described his visit to Peggy Shippen Arnold as the most affecting scene he had ever witnessed. The young woman, daughter of Edward Shippen of Philadelphia, had just joined her husband at West Point. She told the American leaders that her first knowledge of Arnold's plan was when her husband informed her, just before his flight, that he had to leave his country and his family forever. When Washington arrived, Mrs. Arnold was completely distraught, one moment raving that there was a plot to murder her child and the next dissolved in tears.

By the following morning she was more composed. Hamilton visited her "to soothe her by every method in my power...." She feared that the enmity of the country would fall on her for her husband's crime. Acting as Washington's spokesman, Alexander tried to persuade Peggy that her fears were "ill founded."

In a letter to Betsey, Alexander wrote that Mrs. Arnold received her callers in bed "with every circumstance that could interest our sympathy. Her sufferings were so eloquent that I wished myself her brother to have a right to be her defender." He added smugly that he would never do anything "that would hazard your esteem. 'Tis to me a jewel of inestimable price & I think you may rely I shall never make you blush."[28]

If Betsy felt a twinge of jealousy over Alexander's excess of sympathy for Peggy Arnold, her suspicions about the lady's sincerity have been vindicated by history. When Hamilton arrived at Verplanck's his quarry was gone, but he found a letter for Washington that Arnold had sent from the *Vulture*. It contained an exoneration of his conduct, saying that he had acted on the principle of love for his country "however it may appear inconsistent to the world, who very seldom judge right of any man's actions," and a request for mercy for his wife. He begged that she be permitted to join him or go to her friends in Philadelphia. Washington, who wanted to believe that the attractive, charming young woman whose family was well known to him was innocent and who had probably been subdued by her extraordinary display of histrionics, arranged a safe-conduct for her.[29]

In 1838, Matthew Davis, Aaron Burr's friend and biographer, published a story that Burr had told him. En route to Philadelphia from West Point, Peggy Arnold stopped overnight at The Hermitage in Paramus, New Jersey, the home of Theodosia Prevost, a British officer's wife who later married Burr. At first, Peggy displayed her histrionics for the guests, but as soon as she and her hostess were alone, she confessed to Theodosia that she had corresponded with Major André, was disenchanted with the American cause and had convinced her husband to surrender West Point.[30]

Other stories confirm this. Sometime before Arnold's appointment to West Point, Mrs. Arnold dined at Robert Morris's house, where a friend congratulated her on a report that her husband would be given a more active command than that of the military fortress. The young woman, to the consternation of all present, went into a fit of hysterics and would not be comforted. After the treason was discovered, the Morrises were convinced that Peggy had known about the West Point conspiracy and might well have been the negotiator.[31]

Letters found in the Sir Henry Clinton papers expose Peggy Arnold's complicity beyond any doubt. She knew of the plot from the beginning, and corresponded with André and other conspirators, her motivation probably the promise of fame and fortune. Arnold was to be well paid for his treachery and rewarded with an important command.[32]

The Arnolds escaped, but Maj. John André of the British army, Arnold's intelligent, attractive co-conspirator, had been captured in disguise within the American lines with the damning evidence of the conspiracy concealed on his person. André wrote a dignified appeal to Washington, explaining that he had intended to meet a person for intelligence on neutral ground but had been betrayed within the American posts and forced to assume a disguise. Therefore, he hoped that he could be treated as an honorable person. But the verdict handed down was that he would be hanged, the death of a spy.[33]

Hamilton visited André several times during his imprisonment and was the bearer of a request to Washington to allow André to send an open letter to Sir Henry Clinton. André explained to a sympathetic Hamilton that Clinton had been very kind to him, and he did not want his benefactor to be reproached by others because it appeared that he had ordered André to run these risks. "I would not for the world leave a sting in his mind that should embitter his future days," André said, so filled with emotion that he could hardly finish the sentence. Hamilton took the letter and persuaded Washington to grant André's request to forward it to Clinton.

André's character, his aristocratic, gentlemanly behavior throughout his ordeal, appealed to Hamilton's love of romance. Hamilton wrote to Laurens:

To an excellent understanding well improved by education and travel, he united a pleasing elegance of mind and manners, and the advantage of a pleasing person. 'Tis said he possessed a pretty taste for the fine arts, and had himself attained some proficiency in poe[try] music and painting. His knowledge appeared without ostentation, and embellished by a diffidence, that rarely accompanies so many talents and accomplishments, which left you to suppose more than appeared. His sentiments were elevated and inspired esteem. They had a softness that conciliated affection. His elocution was handsome; his address easy, polite and insinuating.[34]

Hamilton watched over André, who was about to die as a common criminal, with sympathy and wonder. A last appeal to Washington to die a professional death was denied. André was not told of the harsh verdict so that he could still hope, but when he approached the place of execution he saw the cart and the other preparations, and he knew his fate. "Must I then die in this manner?" he said. Hamilton, much moved, wrote later: "He died universally esteemed and universally regretted."[35]

Hamilton had urged Washington and others to honor André's request to be shot like a gentleman instead of hanged. Washington had refused. In his letter to Laurens, Hamilton referred to a suggestion that Sir Henry Clinton might be induced to give up Arnold for André, and "a Gentleman did propose it to the English Major that he might propose this to Clinton." André refused, and, Hamilton added, "the moment he had been capable of such frailty, I should have ceased to esteem him." However, in a letter to Betsey, Hamilton stated that it had been proposed to him to speak to André about the exchange but that he had refused, feeling that such a suggestion would mean forfeiting André's esteem.[36]

These two protestations were a cover-up for a letter that Hamilton surreptitiously sent to Clinton on behalf of André. The letter, dated September 30, 1780, was written in a disguised hand, signed almost illegibly "A.B." The evidence that it was sent by Hamilton rests on the endorsement on the letter in Clinton's hand, found in his files, that said, "Hamilton W[ashington's] aid-de-camp. Received after A. death."

The anonymous letter said that everyone admired Major André's character, virtues and accomplishments, though he was an enemy. "Perhaps he might be released for General Arnold, delivered up without restriction or condition. . . . Arnold appears to have been the guilty author of the mischief; and ought more properly to be the victim, as there is great reason to believe he meditated a double treachery, and had arranged the interview in such a manner, that if discovered in the first instance, he might have it in his power to sacrifice Major André to his own safety." The language in this letter is very close to the phraseology in a Hamilton letter to Laurens.

Another piece of evidence that links the Clinton letter to Hamilton is the statement by John Graves Simcoe, André's friend, that "a paper was slid in without signature, but in the handwriting of Hamilton, Washington's Secretary, saying that the only way to save André was to give up Arnold."[37]

If Washington knew about the letter, it was typical of the sort of private negotiation in which he sometimes engaged. It is known that Lafayette, with or without Washington's knowledge, sent Aaron Ogden to Paulus Hook to suggest to the British that if Arnold were returned to the Americans, André might be released. Ogden reported that he dropped the hint to the post commandant, who relayed the proposal to Clinton. But Clinton could not yield Arnold because, from the British point of view, Arnold had done nothing wrong; rather, he had seen the error of his ways and had returned to king and country. To yield him would be to recognize the rebels as legitimate adversaries.[38]

In his long account of the Arnold-André affair, written to Laurens and later published in the New-York *Evening Post*, Hamilton expressed the feelings of most of his countrymen when he wrote that congratulations were in order "on our happy escape from the mischiefs with which the treason was big." In part this was a reference to the prevalent belief that Sir Henry Clinton had hoped to seize Washington and others, including Hamilton, who was usually with him, when he took West Point. This conjecture developed after the fact. At the time that the arrangements were made for Arnold's delivery of West Point, it was not known that Washington would be making an inspection tour.[39]

The drama did not distract Hamilton entirely from his interest in his coming marriage. In early October, while occupied with giving testimony in the trial of Joshua Hett Smith, accused of aiding Major André and General Arnold, Hamilton kept up a lively correspondence with Betsey. "You intrude on my sleep, I meet you in every dream. . . . 'Tis a pretty story indeed that I am to be thus monopolized by a little *nut brown* maid like you and from a soldier metamorphosed into a puny lover." He was also honest and intelligent enough to ask his fiancée to reflect seriously on the obligations of marriage. "I give you warning; don't blame me if you make an injudicious choice," and if she wished to change her mind, "don't give me the trouble of a journey to Albany and wait until the day before the marriage to find 'you can't take the man,' " as one of their acquaintances had done. Lest she fear that these cautions were a reflection of his own thoughts, he assured her that he believed their mutual affection would last and increase.[40]

After this letter there was silence from Betsey. Alexander worried that he had said too much. He did not understand that it was difficult for a simple girl, with neither education nor literary flair or events of any excitement to relate, to keep up a correspondence with a brilliant suitor. Nevertheless, her failure to acknowledge this provocative letter written so close to the wedding date was a genuine cause for alarm. Hamilton wrote again, repeating how happy he was at the thought of their approaching marriage, and described a dream that he had had several nights earlier.

In the dream, Alexander arrived in Albany and found Betsey

asleep on a green near her house; beside her, in an inclined posture, stood an unknown gentleman, who held Betsey's hand in his and watched her with silent admiration. "As you may imagine," he wrote, "I reproached him with his presumption and asserted my claim." The gentleman insisted that he had a prior right, and the dispute became heated. The argument awakened sleeping Betsey, who, "yielding to a sudden impulse of joy," flew into Alexander's arms and decided the quarrel with a kiss. Hamilton then woke up and lay the rest of the night "exulting in my good fortune." Who was his rival, Alexander asked Betsey, because "dreams you know are the messengers of Jove."[41]

As Freud discovered, the significance of the dream lies in what it means to the dreamer. The other man, "a gentleman," may have been the man the Schuylers would have chosen for Betsey, someone from her own set. The fear in this dream may have been Hamilton's dread that news of his illegitimacy would reach the Schuylers. Alexander's strong self-image saved him even in the dream, which was stimulated by Betsey's failure to write. The dream had a happy ending; Betsey awoke and chose him openly.

Alexander Hamilton and Elizabeth Schuyler were married on December 14, 1780. The wedding took place at The Pastures, the Schuyler home in Albany. The bride wore a white gown and a lace veil that had belonged to Angelica Van Rensselaer, her grandmother. At his fiancée's request, Alexander doffed his uniform for a black velvet coat, white satin breeches and a pair of rhinestone buckles, his wedding gift from Lafayette.

The ceremony took place in front of the fireplace in the blue drawing room in the presence of the entire Schuyler family. Hamilton was represented only by his friends and comrades in arms. Maj. James McHenry wrote a nuptial poem, which Hamilton enjoyed immensely. "The piece is a good one—your best," he wrote to the poet. "You know I have often told you, you wrote prose well but had no genius for poetry. I retract."[42]

George Washington was not present at the wedding but, from his headquarters at New Windsor, New York, sent the newlyweds congratulations.

Schuyler wrote to Hamilton shortly after the wedding that "you cannot my dear Sir be more happy at the connection with the family that I am."[43] Now Alexander had a family of his own, one as distinguished, wealthy and influential as could be desired. The Schuylers, descended from the earliest New York settlement, provided the

West Indian lad with deep American roots, a lovely, devoted wife and a father-in-law who accepted him wholeheartedly.

"I am the happiest of Women," Betsey wrote to her sister Peggy, "my dear Hamilton is fonder of me every day; get married I charge you." Hamilton added a postscript to his wife's letter, advising his sister-in-law not to become "matrimony-mad." It was good when their stars united two people who were compatible, "but it's a dog of a life when two dissonant tempers meet, and 'tis ten to one but this is the case."[44] This did not seem to be the case for the Hamiltons. Alexander's letters to his "dear Angel" were more loving and passionate than they had been before the wedding.

From New Windsor, where he was stationed, Hamilton summarized the military situation for Laurens, who was on his way to France as envoy extraordinary. Jersey and Pennsylvania troops were mutinying. Gen. Philip Schuyler wanted to invite several states to a convention to give Congress power to raise funds. "A loan of money is the *sine qua non*," Hamilton said.[45]

Discontent with his job as an aide gnawed at Hamilton even more painfully after his marriage. He was no longer dependent on the goodwill of his friends and patrons, or on the warmth and prestige offered by Washington's family. It took a very small episode to bring the discontent to a head—the famous quarrel between Hamilton and Washington.

Hamilton described the occurrence in a letter to Philip Schuyler. On February 16, when Washington passed Hamilton on the stairs, he said that he had business to discuss. Hamilton replied that he would wait upon him immediately, then continued downstairs to give Tench Tilghman a letter for the commissary containing a pressing order. On his way back to join Washington, Lafayette stopped Hamilton for about a minute. "He can testify how impatient I was to get back," Hamilton wrote, "and that I left him in a manner which but for our intimacy would have been more than abrupt." The general was not in his room but standing at the head of the stairs, where he accosted Alexander and said in a very angry tone: "Colonel Hamilton you have kept me waiting at the head of the stairs these ten minutes. I must tell you Sir you treat me with disrespect."

"I am not conscious of it Sir, but since you have thought it necessary to tell me so we must part," Hamilton answered, "without petulancy, but with decision," according to his account.

"Very well Sir if it be your choice," Washington answered, and they separated.

In less than an hour, Tilghman came to Hamilton, bringing a message from the general in which Washington said that he had great confidence in his aide's abilities, integrity and usefulness and wanted to engage in a "candid conversation" in order to "heal a difference which could not have happened but in a moment of passion." Hamilton, obdurate, sent back the answer that he could not change his mind. He was "determined to leave the family" but would not quit until he was replaced and in the meantime would conduct himself as before, so that it depended on Washington "to let our behaviour to each other be the same as if nothing had happened."

Hamilton told Schuyler that he had always disliked the office of aide-de-camp because of its having in it "a kind of personal dependence." Furthermore, he said, he was soon disillusioned about Washington's character, and, despite his place in the commander's councils for the past three years, "I have felt no friendship for him and have professed none. I wished to stand rather upon a footing of military confidence than of private attachment." Hamilton explained that he supported Washington because he was honest, and his competitors had "slender abilities and less integrity"; therefore, his popularity was essential to American safety.

Hamilton added that he contemplated entering the artillery or light infantry. A campaign command would leave him the winter to pursue studies for his future career. While an aide to Washington, he had to be on duty all the time.[46]

Schuyler was "surprized and afflicted" by the news of his son-in-law's break with General Washington. In a letter remarkable for its tact, good sense and affectionate concern, Schuyler tried to persuade Hamilton to make his peace with the commander by pointing out that he alone of all of Washington's family had the qualifications so essential "to aid and council a commanding General environed with difficulties of every kind." He alone could manage the correspondence that required such delicate judgment. Furthermore, if they separated, what would be the effect on the French minister, the French officers and even the French court? No one in Washington's entourage knew enough French to convey the general's ideas. Schuyler suggested that Washington had tried to heal the breach and regretted his hasty temper. He urged his angry son-in-law to make the sacrifice of his "maxims of conduct" and agree to a reconciliation.[47]

No effort of persuasion could change Hamilton's mind. He needed to break away from Washington much as an adolescent must break away from his father. That Washington had outbursts of temper was a reality, but Hamilton knew better than anyone the pressure and frustration that Washington had to live with. This petty episode served Alexander's purpose, an irrefutable fact in light of Washington's almost abject apology. Hamilton wanted to leave headquarters and seek military glory. He knew that the war was drawing to a close; the coming campaign might be the last one. He no longer needed Washington's patronage; he was a permanent member of the powerful Schuyler clan.

Two months after the break, Hamilton still had no definite prospects. It was awkward for him to approach his friends in the service, but he did write to Gen. Nathanael Greene, now head of the southern army. "I am about leaving [Washington] to be anything that fortune might cast up. I mean in the military line." He could not explain because the enemy might intercept the mails, but he wrote cryptically, "This, my dear General, is not an affair of calculation but of feeling." It was only in the postscript that Hamilton asked if there was anything worthwhile for him in the southern army.[48]

Lafayette, who knew about the quarrel, was greatly disturbed. "My dear friend, you would be more useful at Headquarters," he wrote. However, he would be glad to have Hamilton with him in "the southern wilderness," where he was stationed.[49]

Neither feeler resulted in an offer of a military assignment, so, in mid-April, Hamilton and Betsey moved to De Peyster's Point. From there, realizing that a command must come directly from Washington, Alexander applied to him for some employment in the coming campaign. Since he was not connected with any regiment, Hamilton asked for a command in the light infantry corps, reminding his chief that he had begun in the line in 1776.

Washington answered at length, refusing but with an explanation. If he sent another corps southward, it had to be composed entirely of eastern troops, and to add to the discontent of the officers of those lines "by the further appointment of an officer of your rank to the command of it" would involve difficulty and have serious results. Washington stressed that his refusal had no other motive than the one expressed.[50]

On April 30, Hamilton retired from the staff of the commander in chief without an assignment.

He pleaded his case again in early May. He summarized his qualifications: early entrance into the war; active participation in the campaign of '76, "the most disagreeable of the war," as head of a company of artillery; participation in all the subsequent battles while an aide.[51] This appeal also failed.

In mid-July, quite unexpectedly, the entire situation changed.

Hamilton went to Washington's encampment at Dobbs Ferry, where he was stationed with about 6,000 men, apparently expecting that some post would be waiting for him. When Alexander arrived nothing was said about a command, so he wrote a letter to Washington, enclosing his commission. To Hamilton's surprise, Tench Tilghman came to him as the great man's emissary, asked that he keep his commission and conveyed an assurance that some command would be found for him.

Hamilton's appointment arrived at the end of the month. It was exactly what he had hoped for; two light companies from New York regiments and two companies from York, Pennsylvania, were ordered to form a battalion under the command of Lt. Col. Alexander Hamilton and Maj. Nicholas Fish. The battalion would be attached to the advanced corps under Col. Alexander Scammel. Washington had been very generous, giving Hamilton a command equal to his rank and teaming him with Fish, whom he esteemed as an officer and a friend.

When Hamilton first arrived at Dobbs Ferry, Washington and Rochambeau were still debating whether to attack Sir Henry Clinton in New York or Cornwallis in Virginia. On August 24, news arrived that Admiral de Grasse had sailed his fleet of twenty-nine warships with troops aboard into Chesapeake Bay. Since he was not coming to New York, the decision was made. But De Grasse would stay on the American coast only until October 15, which meant that the French and American armies would have to be transported to Virginia at once.

Hamilton had been preparing Betsey gradually for his inevitable departure for the battlefield, but now that it was so close, he asked Schuyler to "intimate by degrees" and so protect her from too severe a surprise. By August 22, he had to tell her that he was departing with his troops for Virginia. He tried to reassure her that whatever happened, he was certain it would all be over by the end of October, when he would "fly to the arms of my Betsey . . . the only treasure I possess in the world whose love is the food of my hopes. . . ."

Philip Schuyler visited Alexander before the departure for Virginia, but Betsey was pregnant, and her parents thought a meeting with Alexander would be too emotional. "I charge you do not suffer your spirits to be too much agitated: remember that not only your health, but perhaps the existen[ce] of our babe depends upon the tranquillity of your mind. Any accident would affect me more than I can tell," Hamilton wrote to his wife. And from Head of the Elk,

Maryland, on September 6, he wrote to Betsey that on the following day he and his troops would embark for Yorktown. Certain of American success, he would surely meet her by early November. At that time, he promised, he would renounce public life and devote himself to her.

Preparing to enter battle for the first time as a married man, Hamilton was no longer the carefree knight errant of the 1776 campaign. "How chequered is human life! How precarious is happiness! How easily do we often part from it for a shadow!" he wrote to Betsey.[52]

Meanwhile, Philip Schuyler was making plans for Hamilton. He informed Alexander that when the New York State legislature convened at Poughkeepsie on the first of October, delegates would be chosen, and his friends would propose Colonel Hamilton. Betsey was well, he reported, but had been so affected by her husband's departure southward that for a while he feared the consequences. Angelica Church, his oldest daughter, had just given birth to a fine boy, and he hoped that "her sister would give me another."[53]

General Cornwallis, under Clinton's orders, had established his troops at Yorktown, Virginia. There he waited for the arrival of the British navy and, in the meantime, fortified Yorktown and Gloucester Point, a town on the other side of the York River.[54]

Washington, improvising because his plans had been centered on a siege of New York City, was fortunate that Sir Henry Clinton still believed New York to be the main target of the French and American forces. Not until too late did he realize that Washington was on his way south, or that De Grasse had sailed to the Chesapeake, landing 4,000 French troops to help Lafayette cut off any attempt by Cornwallis to beat a retreat to the Carolinas. Washington and Rochambeau, after a hazardous march over terrible roads with a shortage of food, joined the French.

Restless and anxious about Betsey while he waited at the camp before Yorktown, Alexander mused about his approaching fatherhood. "You shall engage shortly to present me with a *boy*," he ordered his young wife. A girl would not answer the purpose, for with her mother's charms and her father's caprices she would "enslave, tantalize and plague one half the sex." With great tenderness, he wrote: "The idea of a smiling infant in my Betsey's arms calls up all the father in me."[55]

The chance to perform a glorious deed that Hamilton had awaited since boyhood fell to him on October 14. Washington assigned to Lafayette the assault on two British redoubts, Nos. 9 and 10, located

near the York River, which were firing on the second parallel
(trench) that the American army had been building. These redoubts
had to be captured in order to complete the second parallel without
endangering the lives of those working on the entrenchments, and to
clear the way eventually for the capture of the British army. The
allied batteries pounded at the two redoubts, until, on the afternoon
of the fourteenth, it was decided that they were ready to be stormed.

Lafayette assigned his former aide, Lt. Col. Gimat, to lead the
American light infantry in the attack on redoubt No. 10. As soon as
Hamilton, who was the officer of the day and Gimat's senior, heard
about the decision, he went to Lafayette and demanded his prior
right to the command. The Frenchman, ambivalent, appealed to
Washington for a decision, as did Hamilton, with such eloquence
that he emerged from the conference shouting to Major Fish, "We
have it, we have it."[56]

Washington handed down a Solomonesque solution. Gimat's battalion led the van with Hamilton in command, Major Fish following
after and Col. John Laurens, with eighty men taking care of the left
column, ready to surround the rear of the redoubt to cut off retreat.
Colonel Barber's battalion was delegated to act as a supporting
column.

At nightfall the signal was given by the French guns, and, with
unloaded muskets so as to make no noise, Hamilton led his men over
parapets and all obstacles, ignoring the heavy enemy fire. He was the
first to storm the parapet, closely followed by the officers of Gimat's
battery, with Laurens bringing up the rear.

When reporting his successful exploit to Lafayette, Hamilton gen-
erously praised all the officers and men. "There was not an officer nor
soldier whose behaviour, if it could be particularized, would not
have claim of the warmest approbation." With admirable good taste,
he also commended the French officers. Even the enemy was com-
plimented for "an honorable defense."

At the time it was said that Lafayette, with Washington's approval, had ordered Hamilton to put to death all of the enemy taken
on the redoubt in retaliation for British atrocities, but that Hamilton
did not execute the order for humane reasons. Years later Hamilton
refuted the story.[57]

Washington acknowledged to General Greene that the capture of
the redoubts "will prove of almost infinite importance to our Ap-
proaches." Cornwallis admitted to Clinton that with the loss of the
advanced redoubts, "my situation now becomes . . . critical."[58] And

in a few days, Cornwallis asked for surrender terms. For the Americans, the Yorktown victory was the last major foray of the war, which was to continue for some time. For Hamilton, Yorktown was the splendid conclusion of his military career.

John Trumbull's painting *The Surrender of Cornwallis at Yorktown* shows Washington on a black horse, with a number of his officers, also mounted, next to him. Hamilton, in a position of honor, is the nearest standing figure to Washington and the others, with Laurens at his side. "I wish there was a war," young Hamilton had written from St. Croix to Neddy Stevens. He dreamed that such a cataclysm would rescue him from monotony and obscurity. It had. Now, with excellent connections including a great commander in chief, a marriage into one of the most distinguished families of his adopted country, a noble deed to culminate his war record, Alexander Hamilton had laid the foundation for a spectacular postwar career.

Rehearsal for Greatness

ONE OF THE MOST ENGAGING ATTRIBUTES of Alexander Hamilton was his precocity. His genius manifested itself while he was a very young man, and matured and developed with him. While function- ing as Washington's right hand, this astounding youngster found time to diagnose and prescribe for the nation's political ills and to expound his economic system in letters that are forerunners of his great papers. Many of his ideas appear in embryo in these early drafts. Notes from Postlethwayt's weighty tome, *Universal Diction- ary of Trade and Commerce, Demosthenes' Orations* and Plutarch's *Lives* were sprinkled through the pages of his military pay books, testifying that he engaged in serious reading during the war.

Hamilton never talked about the genesis of his passion for finance to his children or his friends. As a boy, he worked in his mother's store; as a lad, at Cruger & Co.; but in his early letters he scorned the role of clerk and yearned for a military career. James Hamilton's pathetic failures might have made his son shy away from commerce and finance; instead, Hamilton was drawn to a study of these sub- jects, analyzing his country's ills as being, in a large part, economic and linking the power of a country with its financial stability.

Hamilton detected the dangers inherent in the confederation sys- tem that attempted to govern the nation during the war years and after. Lack of congressional power was the fundamental defect, Hamilton urged over and over. The states were zealous of their power, Congress indifferent to its lack of power, which made it inde- cisive. Since the states, not Congress, were responsible for financing the army, Hamilton had been confronted constantly by Congress's weaknesses.

In October 1780, Hamilton wrote to Isaac Sears, a former leader of the Sons of Liberty and a privateer owner during the war, that "we must have a Government with more power. We must have a Tax in kind. We must have a foreign Loan. We must have a Bank on the true Principles of a Bank. We must have an Administration distinct from Congress and in the hands of Single Men under their orders." In this brief paragraph, all of the elements of what became known as the Hamiltonian system were presented in their simplest form.[1]

A month earlier, in a long communication to James Duane, a New York congressman who favored congressional reform, Hamilton coupled his economic position with his continental position. The states' "jealousy of all power not in their own hand" left Congress with hardly the shadow of power. Congress offended when it tried to play the impossible role of executive. Congress was too small, and its fluctuating membership was complicated further by the tendency of the old members to misinform the new ones in order to promote their own side.

Hamilton offered solutions. Congress should be given the necessary powers: either by assuming discretionary powers that can be implied to have been vested in the body for the safety of the states; or by immediately calling a convention of all the states to meet on November 1, for the purpose of establishing a general confederation with power and authority to handle the war. Six years later, the Annapolis convention would meet for just such a purpose.

As a second step, Congress should instantly appoint a secretary of foreign affairs, a president of war, a president of marine and a president of trade, with functions like those of their counterparts in France. Taxation and the erection of a bank were essential steps. In defense of his system, Hamilton wrote: "There are epochs in human affairs, when *novelty* even is useful. If a general opinion prevails that the old way is bad, whether true or false, and this obstructs or relaxes the operation of the public service a change is necessary if it be but for the sake of change."[2]

Laying down his sword and doffing his uniform in the summer of 1781, Hamilton plunged into private life with ardor. He joined Betsey at her parents' Albany estate, where the young couple quietly awaited the birth of their first child. Philip, born on January 22, 1782, was named after his paternal grandfather. "You cannot imagine how entirely domestic I am growing," the new father wrote to a friend. "I lose all taste for the pursuits of ambition. I sigh for nothing but the company of my wife and baby."

This bucolic contentment was only a delusion. Hamilton admitted that a sense of duty kept him from renouncing public life entirely. It was only "delicacy" that stopped him from trying to get a command in the current campaign. In a letter to Washington, he renounced any future claim for compensations from his commission during the war or after, but, since "the most promising appearances are often reversed by unforeseen disasters," he would retain his rank while permitted to do so. Hamilton assured Washington that his zeal for the common cause had not abated and that he would be ready at any time, in any capacity, civil or military, "consistent with what I owe myself." Washington did not take the bait, so Hamilton remained in private life for the time being.[3]

The profession he chose was the law. In his petition to come under the New York State Supreme Court ruling of 1778, which waived the three-year clerkship requirement for war veterans who had started their law studies before the Revolution, Hamilton claimed that he qualified. Though he had neither served in a law office nor taken formal college courses, Hamilton said that he had acquired the foundation of legal studies through his own extensive reading. He pointed out that he had studied such philosophers and authors of international law as Locke, Burlamaqui, Grotius, Montesquieu and Pufendorf. Blackstone was known to him, as were Coke's reports and the texts of English Statutes.[4] The ruling was due to expire in April, too soon for him to be ready for the examination, so Alexander also asked for an extension until October. Both requests were granted.

Hamilton, ill and bedridden off and on from the time he returned to Albany until the beginning of the New Year, was unable to start his law studies until January 1782. The young couple and Philip moved into a modest house in Albany and lived on half the arrears of Hamilton's army pay, for he refused help from his father-in-law. Robert Troup, who was just beginning his law practice, moved into the house to help his friend with his preparation for the bar and the rent.

Although Troup was a neophyte at the law himself, he could, at least, advise Alexander about what to study and what kinds of questions he would be asked. While studying, Hamilton compiled his notes into a manual, which he called *Practical Proceedings in the Supreme Court of the State of New York*, a compendium of 177 pages. It is the first treatise in the field of private law written after the separation from Great Britain. The small book lacks organization and is a haphazard compilation of notes on whatever book Alexander happened to be reading. With all its shortcomings, it was the only available comparative legal study that included English, colonial and state law.[5]

Robert Troup praised Hamilton's manual effusively, claiming that it served as a grammar for future students and the basis for subsequent enlarged practical treatises. It must have been used by other students; the only copy that has survived was written in a handwriting other than Alexander's, suggesting that a later student copied it.

Hamilton could not blot out the larger world. When he heard about the position that Washington had taken on the Asgill case, he could not restrain himself from expressing his opinion. The case arose from the hanging of Captain Huddy, an American army officer, by a band of Loyalists retaliating for the killing of Philip White, a Loyalist who tried to escape from his colonial captors. Huddy was found with a message attached to his corpse that read, "Up goes Huddy for Philip White." Washington called a war council, which decided that Captain Lippincott, the commander of the Loyalist band that had hanged Huddy, had to be executed, or a British officer of equal rank held as a prisoner die in his place. Washington accepted the council's decision and wrote to Sir Henry Clinton, explaining the sentence. Clinton refused to give up Lippincott. A captive British officer was chosen by lot. Captain Asgill, aged nineteen, became the scapegoat.

Hamilton was horrified when he heard about the case. "An ill timed proceeding," he protested to General Knox, and one that would be "derogatory to the national character . . . so solemn and deliberate a sacrifice of the innocent for the guilty must be condemned on the present received notions of humanity and encourage an opinion that we are in a certain degree in a State of barbarism." Washington took the position that the determination had been made, so there was no turning back. Hamilton protested that "pretexts may be found and will be readily admitted in favor of Humanity." Washington then tried to delay by passing the buck to Congress, which body, in its usual ineffective manner, refused to take action. The situation was saved when Lady Asgill, the unfortunate youth's mother, appealed so touchingly to the French king and queen that they intervened through their representatives in America, who approached Washington. He immediately referred them to Congress, and, since French money was essential to America, the plea was heeded. Congress passed a resolution to release young Asgill.[6]

Even before his legal studies were completed, Hamilton allowed himself to be persuaded back into public service. Robert Morris, now superintendent of finance, remembered his young friend's enthusiastic, brilliant letters on finance and offered Hamilton the post of receiver of taxes for New York. His task would be to collect New York's share of the $8 million that Congress wanted from the states. At first, Hamilton was told that he would be paid 25 percent of taxes received; when he protested that the yield would be no more than £100 a year, Morris agreed to a salary based on the amount of taxes assigned the state, not the amount collected. Still, Hamilton felt uncomfortable; he would then be taking money for no work. The whole system of taxation in New York State, he judged, "is radically vicious, bothersome to the people and unproductive to the government."[7] Hence, there was little for a continental receiver to do unless he might address the legislature. Morris was attracted by the idea. By all means, Morris said, Hamilton should exert his talents in persuading the state assembly. On that basis, as a press agent for his financial system and a one-man lobby in the legislature, Hamilton accepted the appointment.

True to his word, Hamilton went to Poughkeepsie in July when the state legislature met. He presented his credentials as receiver of the continental taxes to Governor Clinton and requested a conference with a committee of the two houses. During the next six days, Hamilton explained to several committees the army's overwhelming need for money so that the war could be brought to a speedy conclusion. As usual, the legislature was reluctant to part with the required funds, but there was a dawning recognition that the Articles of Confederation needed amending and that a general convention should be called. A resolution was sent to the Continental Congress on August 15, 1782, where it met with aggravating delays and postponements.

Hamilton's Poughkeepsie appearance netted an unexpected prize. He was appointed a delegate to the Continental Congress for one year, starting that November, which meant that he would have to give up his receivership. It was small loss; there was little more that he could do in that capacity to further his principles. He did have the satisfaction of having persuaded the legislature to appoint a committee to work during the recess to devise a more effective system of taxation and to communicate their findings to him.[8]

His experience as receiver of taxes added to Hamilton's doubts about political men. His report to Robert Morris on New York's finances was unflattering, but he suspected that a "true picture" of other states would reveal similar problems. The general fault, he suggested, was that the government sought popularity, to please rather than to benefit the people. Instead of assessing taxes on the basis of ownership of property, persons chosen by the people would "determine the ability of each citizen to pay." The true reason for this, Hamilton opined, was to discriminate against the Tories and favor the Whigs.[9]

Hamilton's lengthy report to Morris included an analysis of the opinions and influence of New York's leading public men, delivered with unsparing sharpness. Governor Clinton was "a man of integrity and passes with his particular friends for a statesman . . . his passions are much warmer than his judgement is enlightened." Schuyler carried more weight in the legislature than the governor, his son-in-law judged, but sometimes his measures miscarried.[10]

Hamilton's often repeated judgment on the worthlessness of the human race made his affection for the few for whom he cared seem more intense. In an endearing description of "our little stranger," he drew a portrait of his seven-month-old son. "He is a truly fine young gentleman, the most agreeable in his conversation and manners of any I ever knew—nor less remarkable for his intelligence and sweetness of temper . . . his features are good, his eye is not only sprightly and expressive but it is full of benignity. . . . If he has any fault in manners, he laughs too much."[11]

John Laurens had returned from France in September 1781 and resumed active duty in the Southern army in early 1782. With peace imminent, Hamilton hoped to entice Laurens into a political partnership. He urged Laurens to quit the army, "put on the *toga*, come to Congress. We know each others sentiments, our views are the same, we have fought side by side to make America free, let us hand in hand struggle to make her happy." The letter, dated August 15, was signed "Yrs for ever." Before it arrived at its destination, John Laurens was dead, killed in a minor skirmish with a British foraging expedition.[12]

Laurens's death brought to a close the romantic era in Hamilton's life. "I feel the loss of a friend I truly and most tenderly loved, and one of a small number," Hamilton wrote to General Greene.[13] At the time of their early acquaintance, Laurens provided Hamilton with a model wherein grace and refinement, charm and intellect were tempered with diffidence and a flair for self-criticism. Hamilton, who had a tendency toward sharpness, was impressed with these qualities. The friendship with Laurens had smoothed some of Alexander's rough edges.

At about this same time, Hamilton learned that his half-brother Peter Lavien had died in South Carolina. A letter from the executor of his estate indicated that there was some small inheritance for Hamilton, which, apparently, he never collected. He had never met the brother for whom he was disinherited by his mother's divorce decree, but he needed to cling to even this tenuous and painful relationship. When informing Betsey of Peter's death, he wrote: "You know the circumstances that abate my distress, yet my heart acknowledges the rights of a brother. He dies rich, but has disposed of the bulk of his fortune to strangers." Dr. Knox wrote to Hamilton about Peter's will, regretting that "no justice seems to be done . . . and that as things are situated and perplexed I fear little will come out of it for any of the heirs."[14]

Hamilton was admitted as counsel before the New York State Supreme Court at the end of October. His preparation for the bar had been erratic, interrupted by public duties. He cannot have studied law intensively for more than a few months.

He was in a contradictory mood at this time. He was due in Philadelphia to take his seat in Congress on November 4, but he did not arrive until three weeks later. A letter to Lafayette, written in cipher, reveals some of his feelings—melancholy over Laurens's death and reluctance to leave Betsey and baby Philip. "I am already tired" of public life, he told Lafayette. He would serve his year in Congress and then retire "a simple citizen and a good paterfamilias." Part of Alexander's disgust was with the states' refusal to continue their exertions if the war lasted. The peace treaty was essential unless France continued to help, he wrote. As for Lafayette's idea that he should be one of the peace commissioners, Hamilton protested, "It is a thing I do not desire myself and which I imagine other people will not desire."[15]

Despite his misgivings, Hamilton set out for Philadelphia, aware that, for the first time, he would be among those who made national policy. Instead of having his ideas presented through an intermediary such as General Washington or Robert Morris, his own voice would be heard in the hall of the lawmakers. He was well fitted for his new position. As Washington put it to General Sullivan, a delegate from New Hampshire: "I can venture to advance, from a thorough knowledge of him [Hamilton], there are few men to be found of his age who have a more general knowledge than he possesses; and none whose soul is more firmly engaged in the cause, or who exceeds him in probity or in sterling virtue."[16]

On November 25, 1782, when Hamilton formally took his seat in the nation's ruling body of thirty members, Elias Boudinot, his New

Jersey mentor, was president. Among the more distinguished members were John Rutledge of South Carolina, Oliver Ellsworth of Connecticut, James Wilson and Richard Peters of Pennsylvania, Nathaniel Gorham of Massachusetts, James McHenry of Maryland and James Madison of Virginia. It was a small body when everyone was present, and seldom were there more than twenty members present at one time, of which only a handful was actively involved.

The only record of Hamilton's speeches during his eight months in attendance in the Congress is found in Madison's notes. That indefatigable record keeper made daily entries, describing the proceedings of the sessions on 4- by 6-inch pages that were then bound into booklets.

Almost immediately a partnership arose between Hamilton and tiny James Madison, five years his senior and a member of Congress since March 1780, based on the similarity of their political positions. They both wanted to ensure a successful end to the war, and they both wanted the United States to rest on a firm national foundation. Eventually, these two men would become political opponents, but during this critical period they worked together, although not without some differences of opinion and reservations. They represented different worlds. Madison was a southern planter; Hamilton an embryo lawyer allied with financial and urban interests.

Full of energy and ideas, twenty-five-year-old Hamilton plunged into controversy over every issue that presented itself. Unfortunately, the inherent weaknesses of the confederation doomed all of his attempts to failure. It was painfully ironic that the most important matter in contention, the question of finance, Hamilton's forte, could not benefit from his genius; the impotence of the Articles of Confederation left no opportunity for any worthwhile solution. Nevertheless, Hamilton tried.

In order to pay its debts at home, abroad and to the army, Congress had proposed an impost of 5 percent on all foreign goods. Rhode Island, the Congress was informed unofficially, was adamant in its refusal to go along with the scheme, which meant its defeat, since there had to be unanimous agreement among the states. Rhode Island's chief objection to the impost was that tax collectors not accountable to the state would be brought in, and Congress would be permitted to use the money collected from Rhode Island's commerce without her consent.

Hamilton's proposal to appoint a delegation of three congressmen to go to Rhode Island and appeal to Gov. William Greene for ratification of the impost was accepted. He then drafted the letter to be presented to Greene, which pleaded for the impost as "indispensable for the prosecution of the war." Greene was warned that if the scheme was rejected, "calamities of a most menacing nature" could be anticipated.[17]

The delegation was proposed too late. William Bradford, speaker of the Rhode Island assembly, wrote that Rhode Island had decided against the impost. Congress decided to name a committee, including Hamilton, Madison and Thomas Fitzsimmons, to answer Bradford. Hamilton, the chief writer, employed his best polemical style. "The conduct of the war is intrusted to Congress," he reminded the speaker, and that body "after full and solemn deliberation" recommended the impost, which appeared to them to be the "cornerstone of public safety." He concluded that Congress was "harassed, the national character suffering and the national safety at the mercy of events."

Hamilton's eloquence was wasted on Rhode Island; unexpectedly, Madison's own state, Virginia, did an about-face by repealing its approval of the impost. Despite Virginia's action, the committee, with Hamilton as the chairman, continued to work on a modified plan. At the same time, another problem threatened the sorely tried ruling body. With peace in the offing, the American army, unpaid as yet, wanted its money before it disbanded. The two problems would soon melt into one.

Added to Hamilton's frustration over the congressional problems was his resentment at having to live a bachelor's life. Betsey had agreed to write to him at least once a week and to join him as soon as possible. By December 18, he was hopeful that she was ready to start. She should be very careful of the child on the journey, "I am apprehensive on his account," wrote the doting father. Governor Clinton should give her the money owed him for his congressional service, and when she reached Poughkeepsie, if she needed money, she should borrow from a Mr. Barry. Hamilton was firm in his resolve to take no money from his father-in-law.

Christmas came and went, and still no Betsey. Impatiently but lovingly, Hamilton wrote to her on January 8 that he would be miserable if his letter still found her in Albany. "Every hour of the day," the young husband wrote, "I feel a severe pang . . . and half my nights are sleepless. Come my charmer and relieve me. Bring my darling baby boy to my bosom."[18] Soon afterward, Betsey and Philip joined Alexander and stayed until summer.

A potentially dangerous situation was developing as it became known that the treaty of peace would soon be signed. The soldiers and officers of the continental army grew more and more suspicious that they would become the victims of the peace. They worried that Congress would dismiss them without their back pay or pensions as soon as the war was over. Many of them decided that they would not lay down their arms until they were paid.

Hamilton, whose close connection with the military made him their natural spokesman, expressed concern but played his own hand cannily. He saw that the army situation might serve his major interest, the well-being of the United States. The impost, he calculated, could pay all the country's debts, including those of the military. The question he asked himself was whether he was willing to risk the possibility of violence on the part of the disgruntled army in order to get the impost passed. The event that pulled the entire situation together was known as the Newburgh conspiracy.

At the end of December 1782, a three-man delegation representing the army—headed by General McDougall, a former sponsor of Hamilton, and including his friend Col. John Brooks—arrived in Philadelphia to present to Congress the army's demands for their pay and pensions. The petition was ominous. "The uneasiness of the soldiers for want of pay is great and dangerous; further experiments in their patience may have fatal effects. . . . We beg leave to urge an immediate adjustment of all dues."[19] Included in the petition was a scheme of payment for officers called commutation, which substituted full pay for half of an officer's average life expectancy, instead of half pay for life.

During the interval between the arrival of the military delegation and January 6, when the petition was received by Congress, the army advocates were persuaded by the nationalists, prominent among them Hamilton and Robert and Gouverneur Morris, that the success of their mission was closely linked with the proposed funding system. McDougall wrote to General Knox, who remained in camp, that "the influence of Congress with that of the army and the public creditors to obtain permanent funds for the United States" would promise the "most ultimate Security to the Army." Hamilton wrote to Gov. George Clinton. "We have now here a deputation from the army, and feel a mortification of a total disability to comply with their just expectations. If, however, the matter is taken up in the proper manner, I think their application may be turned to a good account. Every day proves more & more the insufficiency of the confederation."[20]

Congress, aware of the seriousness of the army petition, referred the matter to a grand committee, which included Hamilton and Madison. After some conversations with the army delegates, during which there was plain speaking about the intensity of army resentment in Newburgh and whispers of mutiny, the grand committee appointed Hamilton, Madison and John Rutledge to compose a report on army claims, including in it a financial report on the confederation's resources.

On January 22, the grand committee's report, written by Hamilton, was submitted to Congress and then debated for three days. In the midst of the deliberations, Robert Morris caused general consternation by sending Congress a letter of resignation. If some provision for paying the public debts was not made by the end of May, he could not stay on. Congress, upset, decided to leave the problems of current army pay and back payments to Morris and to exert every effort to get from the states "substantial funds" in order to pay the entire debt of the United States. The nationalists had won a round. But, as yet, no headway had been made on the key provision, commutation, which would provide the retired officers with full pay for six years, based on an average life expectancy of twelve years after retirement.

Once again, Congress formed a committee that included Hamilton. And again, largely due to New England's consistent opposition to commutation, when Hamilton resubmitted the measure on February 4, it failed. Hamilton was discouraged and angry.

A few days after the failure of the bill, Brooks returned to Newburgh with letters for Knox that revealed the rejection of commutation. Using the pseudonym "Brutus," McDougall wrote that the army might be forced to declare that it would not disband without its pay and commutation, and might even mutiny. Hamilton, who hated and feared mob action, would not have supported the army instigators unless he had a strong countervailing force in mind. It was George Washington.

Hamilton wrote to his former chief, with whom he had been out of touch for over a year, marking the letter "confidential." Whether we continued to have war or peace came, we would have "an embarrassing scene," he wrote. The best policy would be to urge the army's claims with moderation but firmness. The problem would be to keep "a *complaining* and *suffering army* within the bounds of moderation." The solution, Hamilton stated firmly, was for the commander in chief "to *take the direction of them*."

There had been a subtle change in the positions of Washington and Hamilton, of which Hamilton was quick to take advantage. He told the commander that he had to know the truth because many in the army felt "that delicacy carried to an extreme prevents your espousing its interests with sufficient warmth." Assuring Washington that he knew the "falsehood of this opinion," Hamilton twisted the knife a little. The perception was not "less mischievous by being false," and its tendency was "to impair that influence which you may exert with advantage" to moderate any commotions. The "great desideratum," Hamilton told Washington, was the establishment of general funds "which alone can do justice to the Creditors of the United States (of whom the Army forms the most meritorious), restore public credit and supply the future wants of government."[21]

This letter was the seeding of the great collaboration of Washington and Hamilton, which was to have a profound effect on the course of the new American republic. For this brief moment, Hamilton was the instigator and the driving force. But if he thought that he could persuade the older man to follow blindly, he had forgotten his apprenticeship. Washington, at his headquarters in Newburgh, was concerned with the immediate army problem and not ready to see so general and far-reaching a national solution.

In his answer to Hamilton several weeks later, the commander-in-chief emphasized his opinion that if there were a "political dissolution" of the army because of Congress's inability to pay, it would be productive of Civil commotions & end in blood." If the army was not taken care of, "the distresses we have encountered, the expenses we have incurred and the blood we have spilt in the course of our Eight Years war, will avail us nothing."[22] Washington avoided Hamilton's trap, refusing to connect his obligation to moderate the army with the promotion of Hamilton's scheme for continental finance.

The Newburgh conspiracy must now be examined for clues to any Hamilton involvement. During the long Revolutionary War, a group of fiery young officers had become critical of Washington's Fabian tactics and, regarding themselves as the future career officers of the United States Army, looked elsewhere for leadership. They associated themselves with General Gates, whose star was in eclipse at the moment but who still had some following among certain anti-Washington congressmen.

Hamilton loathed Gates for his behavior to him after Saratoga and his shabby treatment of Philip Schuyler at an earlier date. The question is: Was Hamilton capable of using Gates to accelerate the nationalist cause, particularly since the plan included arousing the army to mutiny but keeping it from taking over—a dangerous game?

The nationalist congressmen who worked for the impost often met privately to discuss their progress, and on the evening of February 20, Hamilton revealed that he had written to Washington. Asserting that Washington's patriotism and firmness were so great that he would allow himself to be cut in pieces before yielding to dishonorable or disloyal plans, he wanted the general to be "the conductor of the army in their plans for redress, in order that they might be moderated & directed to proper objects." Hamilton then made a statement that answers any supposition of his support of Gates or anyone else who would head a mutiny. He said that he wanted Washington to assume leadership in order "to exclude some other leader who might foment and misguide their [the army's] councils."[23]

Congress received the preliminary peace treaty on March 12, which relieved anxieties about the continuation of the war but intensified the need to solve the army problems. Though the treaty was generally regarded as favorable, information that much of it had been negotiated by the American commissioners without the participation of France, contrary to the orders of Congress, disturbed the congressmen. Hamilton took a middle position. He disapproved of the commissioners' action on the separate articles but maintained that they were to be commended for the terms of the treaty. He was appointed to a committee of five to study the problem, but, in short order, the so-called secret provisions were printed in the newspapers and became known to all. Consequently, the committee decided that the commissioners' misconduct toward France should be acknowledged but that it was too late for a formal censure. In truth, Hamilton had been opposed to the original instructions to the commissioners: that all preliminary, intermediate and final negotiations had to be revealed to France. He appreciated France's contribution to the American fight for freedom but considered "the preponderance of foreign influence as the natural disease of popular governments."

Hamilton praised John Adams for his fortitude in insisting upon "the two cardinal points of the fisheries and the navigation of the Mississippi." To John Jay, Hamilton wrote that the peace was not only glorious but timely. "The New England people talk of making you an annual fish-offering as an acknowledgement of your exertions in preserving the fisheries."[24]

The imminence of peace was consoling, but it only exacerbated the army crisis. The activist wing of the army started to circulate the Newburgh Addresses, which proposed changing "the milk-and-water style" of their last petition to Congress and developing an entirely new approach to redress of their grievances. To Washington's distress, copies of the addresses were circulated throughout the camp.

Washington told Hamilton that he well understood the predicament in which he stood; "as a citizen and as a soldier, it has been the subject of many contemplative hours."[25] So, as the propaganda spread and the officers became more militant, Washington took the offensive. On March 11, he issued general orders that included a blanket denunciation of the officers' behavior and his endorsement of an officers' meeting to be held in five days, to discuss the army situation. He was well aware that such a meeting would be presided over by the senior officer, General Gates.

On Saturday morning, March 16, the officers met in their "new building," a sort of officers' club, which Washington had ordered to be built to encourage sociability. Gates opened the meeting, but, before any business could take place, Washington entered and asked to speak to the assembly. He delivered a vigorous attack on the anonymous addresses that had aroused the camp. "What can this writer have in view?" Washington asked. "Can he be a friend to the army? Can he be a friend to this country? Rather is he not an insidious foe?"[26]

Urging the officers not to tarnish the army's reputation for courage and patriotism, the commander in chief showed a flair for the dramatic not usually associated with the austere American monument. He started to read a letter from Joseph Jones, to prove that Congress was well intentioned toward the army, and then paused. He searched in his vest for his spectacles and put them on, murmuring apologetically that he had "grown grey in the service of his country and now found himself going blind." At those affecting words, the audience dissolved into transports of emotion, some weeping openly. Plans for a revolt were forgotten.[27]

Washington left the meeting, now safely in the hands of his supporters. Meekly, Knox proposed resolutions that requested Washington to renew the army's pleas to Congress. The proposals that had inflamed the assembly just a few days earlier were proclaimed abhorrent.

A few days later, Congress received a communication from Washington in behalf of his officers and men. The nationalists immediately reintroduced a motion for the acceptance of commutation. A committee, which included Hamilton, recommended five years' full pay for all officers who had been eligible for half pay for life. Convinced finally of the seriousness of the army's potential threat, even such a constant opponent as Arthur Lee capitulated.

In April, the impost amendment was also accepted by Congress. It was a hollow victory for Hamilton, who refused to vote for the mangled remains of his original bold plan. The emasculated version limited the operation of the impost to a twenty-five-year period and, worse, provided that its revenues could be used only for paying debts. Furthermore, its effectiveness was questionable, for the tax collectors would be appointed by the states and not the national government.

Hamilton has been charged, without reason, with fostering a coup in order to get his impost tax. The military arm would have been led by Gates, a man whom Hamilton detested. He hated mob violence and could have tolerated it least if led by men in uniform. Most conclusively, he would not have alerted Washington to the danger, had he wished to see a coup succeed. And he knew that once stung into action, the commander in chief would prevail.

Now that contact was reestablished, Washington and Hamilton had much to say to one another. But first, Washington wanted to know whether his former aide had used the army (and therefore himself) "as mere Puppets to establish the Continental funds." Tactfully, the commander wrote that "the Financier [Robert Morris] is suspected to be at the bottom of this scheme."[28] He knew very well that Hamilton and Morris thought alike on financial matters and had been working together.

Hamilton defended himself by saying that he was not surprised by such suspicions "inferred, nor should I be surprised to hear that I have been pointed out as one of the persons concerned in playing the game described." There were two classes of men in Congress, Hamilton explained, "one attached to state, the other to continental politics." It was the "advocates for Continental" who had "blended the interests of the army with other Creditors." No matter what had been said, the men against whom the suspicions had been directed were "the most sensible, the most liberal, the most independent and the most unequivocal friends to the army. In a word they are the men who think continentally."[29]

Within a week, Washington replied, agreeing that the new peace treaty was "upon the *whole* . . . a more advantageous Peace than we could possibly have expected." And, placating his young friend, he accepted Hamilton's innocence. The army considered him "a friend" who was "zealous to serve them" and represented their interests in Congress "upon every occasion."[30]

Hamilton wrote the draft of the ratification of the preliminary peace treaty for Congress on April 15. His mind was on his own needs. "Having no future view in public life, I owe myself without delay to enter upon the care of private concerns in earnest," he wrote to Governor Clinton. Two other delegates had to be sent as soon as possible. "It would be injurious to me to remain any longer."[31]

Though the threat of a serious army rebellion had been averted by Washington, Congress was startled to hear in mid-June that eighty "mutineers" were on their way from Lancaster to Philadelphia to assert their demands. As the hastily appointed spokesman for the ruling body, Hamilton advised Maj. William Jackson to meet the rebellious soldiers and "by every prudent method" persuade them to return to their posts and assure them that Congress would do them justice.[32] Jackson was unsuccessful; the angry soldiers entered Philadelphia, without incident, and quietly joined their colleagues who were stationed in the city.

Congress's president, Elias Boudinot, greatly alarmed, called the members into special session. The fifteen congressmen then in Philadelphia had hardly gathered in the State House early in the afternoon when they realized that the building was surrounded by about 500 mutineers, many of them intoxicated, all of them flourishing their muskets and shouting their demands. Hamilton was infuriated and helpless. He and the other congressmen could do nothing but sit in their chamber and await rescue, which did not come. Instead, the Supreme Executive Council of Pennsylvania, meeting in the State House at the same time, agreed to the mutineers' request for a committee of their own officers to present their grievances. The soldiers then had the audacity to ask Congress to approve their action. Congress did so, expecting that the mutineers would disperse and go home. Instead, the jeering crowd continued to protest. After three hours of a barrage of insults, the congressmen closed their meeting and, with whatever dignity they could muster, walked out to face the dissidents. They were completely ignored.

Hamilton added this episode to his list of grievances against the mob. He resented passionately that he had no power to strike back at them but had to endure their insolence. Later that day, at a meeting of the congressmen in Carpenter's Hall, Hamilton proposed that Congress leave Philadelphia in protest. Pennsylvania had to be pun-

ished for her "weak and disgusting" unwillingness to call out the
militia to defend the Congress of the United States, Hamilton declaimed, and suggested that they move either to Trenton or Princeton, New Jersey. While the meeting was going on, the rebellious
soldiers dispersed without incident and returned to their barracks.

Subsequent meetings with the Pennsylvania Council failed to calm
Hamilton's outrage. He was deaf to arguments that the mutineers
had been entirely peaceful, and that the public would not have accepted spilling the blood of the men who had won the war for them,
just to avenge an insult to congressional pride.

On June 24, Hamilton presented his committee's report on their
meetings with the state authorities. The conclusion reached was that
the governor of Pennsylvania could not be depended upon to act
against the rebellious troops in any way; therefore, the president of
Congress should call a meeting to take place in Trenton or Princeton
that very Thursday.[33]

Since the abortive mutiny had evaporated, the flight of Congress
to New Jersey was regarded by many as ludicrous. Hamilton was
charged with deliberately engineering the exodus from Philadelphia
in order to gradually move the capital to New York. Disturbed by the
attack, Hamilton asked Madison, "as a witness to my conduct and
opinions," to testify that he had manifested "a strong disposition to
postpone the removal from Philadelphia," even against "the general
current of opinion."[34] Madison supported his colleague loyally, but
the national capital was eventually moved to New York City.

Before severing his relations, now somewhat uncomfortable, with
Congress, Hamilton prepared a long resolution in which he analyzed
the shortcomings of the Articles of Confederation and proposed that
a general convention be called to revise them. He scored the weaknesses of the central government, especially the lack of an executive
and an effective federal judiciary. He warned that the federal government would now have to deal with foreign nations and, still
without power, "pass all general laws in aid and support of the laws
of nations." Hamilton, whose stock was low, whose patience was
ebbing and whose eyes were now on his personal future, marked his
resolution "abandoned for want of support."

Betsey and Philip had left Philadelphia for Albany in May, another reason for Hamilton's shortness of temper. Soon after their
departure, Hamilton made several attempts to escape from his duties,
but there were so few members of Congress in attendance that he felt
obliged to stay. Finally, he decided that he would wait for the arrival

of the definitive treaty of peace, stay a few days for discussion of it and then join the family. In a letter to his wife, Hamilton summed up his mood. "I give you joy my angel of the happy conclusion of the important work in which your country has been engaged. Now in a very short time I hope we shall be happily settled in New York."[35]

6

A Private Interval

NEW YORK CITY, just emerging from wartime occupation by the British, somewhat shabby, parts of it burned out from the fighting and unpaved except for Wall Street and Broadway, was a wise choice for a rising lawyer. Alexander Hamilton installed his family in a brick house on the corner of Broad and Wall Streets and opened his law office.

Hamilton had no personal fortune, but he had excellent connections. The Schuylers were related to the four other leading Dutch families: the Van Rensselaers, Livingstons, Van Cortlandts and Beekmans. John B. Church, Hamilton's brother-in-law, for whom he was agent as well as attorney, and his partner, Jeremiah Wadsworth of Hartford, Connecticut, were two of the wealthiest men in the country. Robert Morris and Gouverneur Morris were friends, as were army comrades such as Tench Tilghman of Maryland. Most important of all, he had a close friend and protector in the nation's hero, Gen. George Washington, a connection that Hamilton, more mature now, carefully fostered. Complimenting him on his Farewell Address to the army, Hamilton told Washington that it would not be "without effect," but it would have had more if it had included Washington's opinion of the present government and of "the absolute necessity for change." Nonetheless, the address would ultimately "do you honor" with "the people at large—when the present epidemic phrenzy has subsided."[1]

While condemning the "phrenzy," Hamilton was able to reap a handsome profit from one phase of it. He became an active defender of Tories who were being victimized in the liberated city. The clauses in the British-American peace treaty that guaranteed the Tories restitution and compensation for their destroyed or sequestered properties were cavalierly ignored. Once the bill that provided for confiscation of Loyalist estates was passed, Gov. George Clinton sold at auction Tory land that would have an approximate value today of about $2 million. To aid the lagging finances of New York, the land was sold in large blocs to ensure its purchase by rich speculators, who would then invest their profits in business.

Hamilton reasoned that to drive the wealthy British and Loyalist merchants out of New York City was to drive their buying power and their gold out with them. He observed that reports of violence upstate and in Albany itself had already caused an exodus of Loyalist merchants from the state. First, he pointed out, they dumped their goods on the market.[2]

The most harmful of the New York State anti-Loyalist laws was the Trespass Act, passed on March 17, 1783, when it was already known that the preliminary articles of peace had been signed. The law stated that any American citizen whose property had been occupied by a Loyalist during the war had the right to sue for damages, regardless of any British order that had allowed such an occupancy.

The famous case of *Rutgers* v. *Waddington*, which Hamilton argued, established his reputation as a lawyer and fixed his position on judicial review. Elizabeth Rutgers, a widow, and her son Robert owned a house and brewery on Maiden Lane in New York City. The two left the city after the retreat of the American army in September 1776. The British seized the brewery and held it until June 1778, at which time it was rented to two British merchants, Benjamin Waddington and Evelyn Pierrepont, whose agent was Joshua Waddington. The broken-down brewery, which the tenants restored to working order, spending £700 in repairs, commanded an annual rent of £150, starting in May 1780 for a period of three years. When, in June 1783, it became certain that New York would be evacuated, the British commandant ordered that the rent be paid to the owner's agent, Anthony Rutgers. There was confusion about the sum that was owed and about back rent, and then, two days before the British evacuation, on November 23, 1783, a fire destroyed the brewery. In December, Waddington and Pierrepont gave possession of the buildings that were left, the storehouse and the stable, to Rutgers, but they could not agree on the rent owed. A suit for £8,000 for back rent was then filed by Elizabeth Rutgers against Joshua Waddington (the agent) under the Trespass Act.[3]

The case became a prototype for the Whig-Tory conflict. The

public was disapproving when Hamilton joined Brockholst Livingston and Morgan Lewis as counsels for the defense. His action reinforced his advocacy of the rights of the hated Tories, already expressed in his first *Letter of Phocion*, which asserted that the power of the peace treaty was supreme over a state law.

An alien bill, passed by the state legislature in 1783, that threatened the civil rights of all men who had lived within the British lines during the Revolution was the subject of Hamilton's *A Letter from Phocion to the Considerate Citizens of New York on the Politics of the Times in Consequence of the Peace*. In support of civil liberties, Hamilton's pamphlet asked the question: "What shall we do to perpetuate our liberties and secure our happiness?" The answer was: "Govern well." The golden mean was the young lawyer's advice. "Abuse not the power you possess," he cautioned, "and you need never apprehend its diminution or loss. But if you make wanton use of it . . . you, like others that have acted the same part, will experience that licentiousness is the forerunner to slavery."[4]

Hamilton castigated the populace for the false spirit of Whiggism that inculcated "revenge, cruelty, persecutions and perfidy;" rather than the true spirit of Whiggism, which was "generous, humane, beneficent and just." It was not in the interest of the community to expel those who had supported the king in the late war, he insisted; their capital leaving the city would only weaken its economic stability.[5]

In a private letter to Gouverneur Morris, Hamilton pointed out the irony of the New York Tory hunt. "This legislative folly," he said, had been "so plentiful a harvest to us lawyers that we have scarcely a moment to spare from the substantial business of reaping." Instead of passing "wholesome" regulations for improving government and politics, "we are laboring to continue methods to mortify and punish Tories and to explain away treaties."[6]

In Europe, the attitude toward Tories was one of pity. John Jay wrote to Hamilton from Paris that "an undue severity towards them" would be "impolitic, as it would be unjustifiable." But the public took the short view, indulging the lust for revenge. In answer to Jay, Hamilton could only call New York's actions "strange doings." And "the only dishes that suit the public palate now," were "discrimination bills, partial taxes, and schemes to help those with public power."[7]

The first Phocion letter was answered by *Mentor*, which elicited a second letter from Hamilton. Elevating the issue to one far loftier than the question of the welfare of the New York Tories or even the validity of the Trespass Act, the young lawyer linked it boldly with the survival of the nation.

He wrote that "those who are at present entrusted with power, in all these infant republics, hold the most sacred deposit that ever was confided to human hands. With governments as with people first impressions and early habits give a lasting bias to the temper and character." Our governments had had no habits. Therefore, "how important to the happiness not of America alone, but of mankind that they should acquire good ones." If the United States had shaken off tyranny and really "asserted the cause of human happiness," then the world "will bless and imitate." But if the United States proved unfit to govern herself and despotism trampled liberty, "we shall have betrayed the cause of human nature." He asked, "Is the sacrifice of a few mistaken or criminal individuals an object worthy of the shifts we are reduced to to evade the constitution and the national engagements?"[8]

The case of Elizabeth Rutgers versus Joshua Waddington came to trial before the Mayor's Court in New York City in February 1784. Hamilton prepared at least five briefs for the controversial case, pouring into them a vast knowledge of international law and studding them with many references to Grotius, Pufendorf, Burlamaqui, Vattel and others. His attempt to paint this case on a large canvas was challenged by the attorney for the plaintiff, who tried to diminish the display of scholarship by stating, simply, that the war waged against the American colonies was "an *unjust* war" and that, therefore, the "*unjust* party acquires no right." The law of nations stated as a maxim that "no right can be derived from an injury."[9]

Hamilton worked just as zealously to keep his arguments away from any examination of British behavior in the city during the occupation. Instead, he pointed out that the law of nations did not concern itself with the justice of the war, and, as Grotius said, "The fruits *during the possession* belong to the conqueror."[10]

The enemy had the right to use the plaintiff's property, as argued above, and having exercised that right and paid for it, could not be made answerable to another without injustice and in violation of universal society. And it could not be done "without a violation of the Treaty of Peace." It must not be said that Congress had no right to bind a state by the treaty, for then "the confederation is the shadow of a shade." Here Hamilton expressed his genuine opinion of the status of the United States Congress; his main task, very shortly,

would be to change its nature. Foreign nations only recognized the
sovereignty and independence of the United States based on the
Union and the Declaration of Independence, which all states accepted. It was on that basis that the United States had the power to
conclude a peace. Therefore, the union's constitutional powers were
not "controulable by any State!"[11]

This assertion was the earliest effort to demonstrate that the courts
had the right to judicial review. Quietly, as if he were not suggesting
an original concept, Hamilton advised the court to declare the Trespass Act null and void because it was in conflict with the peace
treaty with Great Britain. In a letter to Washington, written about
ten years later, Hamilton reflected on his stand in *Rutgers* v. *Waddington.* "I was for a long time the only practiser who . . . opposed
the treaty to the Act [Trespass Act] . . . and produced delays till the
exceptionable part of the act was repealed . . . there ought never to
have existed so critical a conflict between the treaty and the Statute
law of a State."[12]

Although the Mayor's Court took note of Hamilton's charge—to
act on the principle that a state law was superseded by a treaty—the
body declined to be identified with such a disturbing concept. The
judges could not elevate themselves above the legislature, "which
would be subversive of all government." Politics was at the root of
this pious assertion, for the legislature, completely dominated by
Governor Clinton, criticized the Mayor's Court for its exceedingly
mild stand and reasserted its endorsement of the Trespass Act.

The Mayor's Court decided, more or less, in favor of Hamilton's
client. Mrs. Rutgers was awarded rent for the period of time when
the merchants held her property under civilian orders, but not while
the property was handled by the British occupation authorities.
Robert Troup and Egbert Benson, Mrs. Rutgers's attorneys, decided
to appeal the case, at which point Hamilton urged Waddington to
settle out of court. The State Supreme Court, Hamilton knew, was
even more under the governor's thumb than the Mayor's court.

Hamilton defended several Loyalists and Englishmen who sued
Americans, which did not endear him to the superpatriots who regarded him as a rampant anglophile. But the cases paid the family
bills and enhanced Hamilton's reputation as a successful lawyer.
Chancellor Kent, who, many years later, tried to characterize the
members of the New York post-revolutionary bar, reserved his greatest praise for Hamilton. He was superior for his "profound penetration, his power of analysis, the comprehensive grasp and strength of

his understanding, and the firmness, frankness and integrity of his character."[13]

Hamilton's greatest rival at the time was another young lawyer and former military officer, Col. Aaron Burr. That gentleman had retired from the army earlier than Hamilton because of ill health and then had studied with Judge William Paterson, attorney general of New Jersey, and afterward with Thomas Smith, a former New York lawyer who had fled to Haverstraw from the beleaguered city with his excellent library. Burr, as did Hamilton later, tried to circumvent the three-year preparation time required by the New York Supreme Court. With a letter of introduction from General McDougall to Gen. Philip Schuyler, Burr was able to persuade Hamilton's father-in-law to give him a letter to the court in Albany. Armed with his letters of recommendation and credentials stating that he had studied before the war at his brother-in-law Tapping Reeve's law school in Litchfield, Connecticut, Burr presented himself to Chief Justice Richard Morris, who agreed to listen to his plea. Burr's application failed to win the court's acceptance until he appeared in court to plead his own case. Impressed by the charismatic young man, the court, composed of some of the most distinguished jurors of the day, agreed to allow him to take the examination. It was a severe one, but Burr passed it and was admitted to the bar in April 1782. At first, he practiced in Albany, where he lived with his new wife, the former Mrs. Theodosia Prevost, and his brood of stepchildren. When the British evacuated New York City, Burr moved south and bought a house in Wall Street, where, eventually, he became a neighbor of the Alexander Hamiltons.

Although not a legal scholar, Burr had strong assets that made him a leading lawyer. Kent said that he was "acute, quick, terse, polished, sententious and somewhat sarcastic in his forensic discussions. He seemed to disdain illustrations and expansion and confined himself with stringency to the point in the debate." Further, he had the happy reputation of seldom losing a case. However, Matthew L. Davis, Burr's biographer and close friend, said, "Colonel Burr accorded the palm of eloquence to General Hamilton whom he frequently characterized as a man of strong and fertile imagination, of rhetorical and even political genius and a powerful declaimer."[14]

Burr and Hamilton had much in common in those days. Physically, they were both short, slight men, handsome, well dressed and elegant. Hamilton was sandy-haired and blue-eyed, while Burr was noted for his piercing black eyes. Both had a passion for military glory and used their military titles throughout their lives. Both were exceedingly attractive to women and soon gained reputations for dalliance. Like Hamilton, Burr had forsworn public entanglement for private advancement, and for the same reasons—the demands of a growing family. Hamilton had served a term in Congress; Burr, in the spring of 1784, was elected a member of the state legislature. It is significant to note that Burr, the descendant of privileged and prominent forebears, the product of a strict Calvinist upbringing, was elected by the radical wing of the Whig party, the most anti-British and the most pro-democratic. Hamilton, on the other hand, the poor boy who was an aristocrat only by marriage and inclination, was already regarded as a stubborn Federalist.[15]

Hamilton continued to be accepted with enthusiasm by the Schuylers. He took full charge of the family interests and had the general's entire confidence. Although Hamilton had a flourishing law practice, he was often short of cash. General Schuyler would have liked to give him substantial help, but his son-in-law was too proud to consider it. However, the hams, fruits and cheeses that arrived from the Schuyler farm were gratefully accepted.

John B. Church, Angelica Schuyler's husband, was Hamilton's wealthiest client. The responsibility for his interests and those of his partner, Jeremiah Wadsworth of Hartford, Connecticut, became even greater at this time because the Churches had returned to Europe. A fondness, or perhaps more, has been attributed to Alexander for his very attractive, vivacious sister-in-law. Her letters to him were always affectionate and sometimes suggestive.

Hamilton was recognized, even by Americans abroad, as a man to be reckoned with. From Paris, Angelica Church wrote to Betsey that "Mr. Franklin has the gravel" and wants to return to America. "They talk of Papa or Col Hamilton as his successor." Angelica asked to have Hamilton's writings sent to her and then wrote: "Adieu, my dear, embrace your *master* for me, and tell him that I envy you the fame of so clever a husband, one who writes so well. God bless him." A postscript followed: "Tell Colonel Hamilton if he does not write to me, I shall be very angry."[16]

In the same letter, Angelica asked: "Is your lord a Knight of the Cincinnati? It has made a wonderful noise here." She referred to the Society of the Cincinnati, which had been founded in 1783 by Revolutionary War officers. Its membership was open to American army officers who had served honorably for three years or more. It was divided into state societies; Hamilton was on the New York State

Committee, and George Washington was its first president-general.

The Cincinnati was fiercely criticized from its inception as an undemocratic institution whose aim and direction were to form the nucleus of an American aristocracy. The outcry against the bylaw that made membership in the organization hereditary caused the national committee to consider reform. Hamilton, as a member of the New York Committee of Correspondence, wrote a defense of one of the organization's principles under fire: "To promote and cherish between the respective States that Union and national honor so essentially necessary to their Happiness and the future dignity of the American empire." For nationalist Hamilton, this was one of the prime virtues of the Cincinnati. In impassioned prose, he wrote that the members of the Society reverenced the sentiment as "the only sure foundation of the tranquillity and happiness of this country. To such men it can never appear criminal . . . to support . . . That noble Fabric of United Independence, which at so much hazard, and with so many sacrifices they have contributed to erect; a Fabric on the Solidity and duration of which the value of all they have done must depend!"[17]

In a report for the Society of the Cincinnati written in 1786, Hamilton expressed his opinion on the controversial hereditary clause. "An *hereditary succession* by right of primogeniture, is liable to this objection—*that it refers to birth what ought to belong to merit only*: a principle inconsistent with the genius of the society founded on friendship and patriotism."[18]

The euphoria engendered by the success of the Revolution and the promise it held for all Americans, politically and financially, lasted only a short while. Americans were tired of wartime austerity and anxious for all the luxuries that only European goods could provide. Republican simplicity in dress gave way to Parisian finery. Continental paper money was worthless and being driven out by gold and silver. The infant industries, started during the war by necessity, faltered, while European goods were dumped on the consumer-hungry citizenry. France and Spain closed their West Indian ports to American vessels, while Great Britain, having lost the war, worked on winning the peace by stopping all commerce with her islands that had commodities needed by the United States.

Hamilton watched these developments with a sense of despair, knowing that unless nationalism could be made acceptable to the American people, their experiment in freedom would fail. From the start of his career, Hamilton was scorned as no true democrat because he believed that a sense of property developed in a man the will to create, develop and expand production, to build his own wealth, which in turn would build the nation's wealth. Like John Locke, he believed that man had given up freedom in a state of nature to protect his property, so that private property, not government, came first.

Hamilton and the propertied classes supported a strong central government in order to create a climate for financial development. During his brief tenure in Congress, Hamilton tried to promote his financial program, and when it misfired, he retired to private life and concentrated on finding a nonpolitical way to further economic stability. He decided that the way was to establish a bank for New York.

At this time, only Philadelphia had a bank, the Bank of North America, and several New Yorkers wanted the bustling city of New York, now out of British hands, to establish its own bank. Robert R. Livingston proposed setting up a land bank with a capital of $750,000, one-third of it to be contributed in cash and two-thirds in landed security. Most of the city's merchants objected that land had backed the inadequate note issues during the colonial period, while others objected that such a bank would form the basis of a landed aristocracy. Hamilton, who also opposed the project, wanted "to convince the projectors themselves of the impracticality of their scheme," he wrote to John B. Church. But "the Chancellor [Robert R. Livingston] had taken so much pains with the country members, that they all began to be persuaded that the land bank was the true philosopher's stone that was to turn all their rocks and trees into gold."[19]

In the past, Hamilton had advocated competition in banking because he believed that it benefited the community. But the "strange doings" he was observing in New York changed his mind. If people were "paid to counteract the prosperity of the State they could not take more effectual measures than they do," Hamilton observed to Gouverneur Morris. Anti-Tory legislation to place public property in the hands of those in power and partial taxes were being employed to "banish the real wealth of the State and substitute paper bubbles . . . the only dishes that suit the public palate at this time."[20] Therefore, a bank based on specie was essential.

Much of Hamilton's time during 1784 was dedicated to the founding of the Bank of New York. He entered into the discussions of policy late as the representative of Church and Wadsworth, but his views prevailed. He wanted "to have the bank founded on such principles as would give you a proper weight," he wrote to his brother-in-law. One of the proposals agreed upon before Hamilton's arrival was unacceptable to him. It stated that no stockholder, no matter how large his holdings, would have more than seven votes, the same number to which the holder of ten shares was entitled. At a meeting with "some of the most influential characters," Hamilton was able to persuade them to change the rule to allow one vote for every five shares over ten. Hamilton was appointed a director of the bank, a position that he accepted, he told Church, until he or Wadsworth could take it over.[21]

Gen. Alexander McDougall, Hamilton's old military friend, became the first president of the bank, located originally in the Walton House at 67 George's Square, also known as 156 Queen Street, and then later in Pearl Street. In 1787, it moved to 11 Hanover Square. Hamilton did not yield his seat to his clients and remained a director until 1788. At the time of the bank's incorporation, in 1791, he held eleven and a half shares at $500 per share, while Aaron Burr held twice as many shares.

Hamilton wrote the constitution of the bank and its charter, which became a standard model for other bank charters. However, strong political opposition to the bank, led by Governor Clinton, who thought the bank oppressive to the people, endangered acceptance of the charter. Undismayed by the state's refusal of a charter, the officers of the bank decided to open without it and ordered their subscribers to pay for half of their shares. For the next five years, knowing that the bank was being blamed for all kinds of financial problems and that its directors were being accused of favoring the rich when giving loans, the bank did not reapply for a charter. It was not until 1791 that a bill was passed chartering the bank, partly because of Hamilton's appointment as secretary of the treasury.

Among Hamilton's public activities at this time was membership in the Society for the Manumission of Slaves. John Jay, recently returned from Europe and his work as a peace commissioner, was its president. At a meeting held at the Coffee House in New York City, attended by thirty-two prominent men, Hamilton was appointed chairman of a committee to develop "a line of conduct" in relation to the slaves owned by the members. Hamilton's proposal that the members of the society free their own slaves was promptly turned down.

The Manumission Society engaged in such activities as registering the names and ages of freed slaves to protect them from attempts at reenslavement, sponsorship of petitions to the state legislature calling for the gradual abolition of slavery and the publication of anti-slavery tracts.

Aaron Burr, also a member of the Manumission Society, became the leading advocate of manumission in the state assembly. He proposed the immediate abolition of slavery in New York State, as well as granting freedmen suffrage; the right to hold office; and the right to intermarry with whites. No part of his bold program was adopted. It was not until 1799 that an act was passed providing that all females born after July 4, 1799, were to be free on reaching the age of twenty-five, and all males on reaching their twenty-eighth birthday. The number of slaves in New York was reduced to 15,000 in 1808, but it was 1841 before all vestiges of slave ownership disappeared.[22]

Hamilton served on the board of the Manumission Society all of his life, although he held slaves as long as he lived. In 1796, an entry in his expense books reads: "cash to N. Low 2 negro servants purchased by him for me $250."[23] The size of Hamilton's family, which eventually expanded to eight children, and his constant struggle to make ends meet suggest that domestic help of this kind eased the expenses.

Hamilton's home life prospered. His first daughter, Angelica, was born in 1784. Since Alexander's law practice often took him to Albany and other remote parts of the state, Betsey had to manage the household without him. From Westchester, Alexander wrote that Colonel Burr, who was also trying a case there, had heard that the house Hamilton was renting was being offered for sale for £2,100. If this was so, Betsey should purchase it. If better arrangements could not be made, she could agree to payment in three installments, but it would be more advantageous if half could be paid in a short time and the rest in a year. Money was always a pressing problem. In 1783, Hamilton had petitioned the New York legislature to assume the $2,820 debt that Congress owed him, for which he had a certificate from the United States treasury.[24]

The personal relationship between Alexander and Betsey was affectionate. Letters from Hamilton were liberally sprinkled with endearments such as "my beloved" and "my angel." Yet Hamilton had a reputation for philandering. Betsey was not a belle like her sister Angelica, and gossip about the relationship between Hamilton and his lovely sister-in-law persisted throughout the years.

The St. Croix community watched their favorite son's rise to fame and fortune with pride and, perhaps, a touch of envy. Hugh Knox,

Hamilton's sponsor, wrote with affection but also with some asperity. He talked of his protégé's "laudable ambition to Excel"; then he added, "Your matrimonial connection I should think might enable you to live at your ease." Reverend Knox was in touch with Hamilton's older brother James. Apprenticed to a carpenter in St. Croix while still a boy, James never prospered. He wrote to his successful brother, describing his difficulties and asking for money. In a typical delaying action used by families to evade such requests, Hamilton said that he would send as much money as he could afford at present. He begged his brother to exert himself to stay at St. Croix for two more years, and then he would invite him to the United States. Apparently Hamilton had not heard from James in a long time, because he asked him if he was married or single. Advice flowed from Alexander's pen. James must avoid getting into debt, and "it is my wish" that if married, "he should stay that way."

His words about his father were genuine, although difficult to understand. "What has become of our dear father? I have written to him but have not heard. Perhaps he is no more." If their father was dead, Hamilton wrote, "I shall not have the pleasing opportunity of contributing to render the close of his life more happy than the progress of it." He often worried that his father was "suffering poverty. I entreat you if you can to relieve me of my doubts and let me know how or where he is, if alive, if dead how and where he died. Should he be alive inform him of my inquiries, beg him to write to me, and tell him how ready I shall be to devote myself and all I have to his accommodation and happiness." This tenderness for the lost father contrasts strangely with Alexander's hard-line treatment of his brother. "Do not come to this country now," Alexander warned James, "it is all out of order because of war and people in business having a hard time. My object in future to get you started on a farm."[25]

This letter is important in fathoming Alexander Hamilton's feelings. Far from seeking revenge, Hamilton wanted a father, even a bad one, and most of all he wanted that father's recognition of his success. Hamilton was never to have that satisfaction. Brother James died a year after this letter was written. James Sr., as well as the story can be pieced together, returned to St. Kitts after deserting his family and then drifted around the southern islands until sometime before June 1793, when he settled on St. Vincent. There the unreconstructed profligate remained for the rest of his life.

Hamilton had to content himself with the Schuylers, who were only too happy to be his surrogate family. His relationship with all of them was cordial and affectionate. As an early Burr biographer put it in characterizing New York politics: "The Clintons had *power*, the Livingstons had *numbers*, the Schuylers had *Hamilton*."[26] With the Churches, Hamilton was involved financially as well as emotionally. When they sailed for Europe after the Revolution, it was supposed to be a temporary absence. By 1785, it looked as if they would remain there permanently. In a letter to Angelica, Hamilton tried to persuade her "not to wed yourselves to a soil less propitious to you than will be that of America. You will not indeed want friends wherever you are. . . . But go where you will you will find no *such* friends as those you have left behind." In a more personal and suggestive sentence, Alexander wrote that his apprehensions were confirmed that if he did not see his "dear sister" in Europe, he would not see her again; therefore, "judge the bitterness it gives to those who love you with the love of *nature* and to me who feel an attachment to you not less lively. I confess for my own part I see one great source of happiness snatched away."[27]

The absence of Church dumped tremendous responsibilities on Hamilton's shoulders. He held Church's power of attorney and had to make decisions about his brother-in-law's large holdings in business and real estate. When Pennsylvania canceled the charter of the Bank of North America, in which Church and Wadsworth were large shareholders, it became Hamilton's problem. The matter was complicated because the bank was still chartered by the Congress of the United States. Wadsworth, who wanted to get his money out of the bank, asked Hamilton to prepare a letter summarizing the position he, Church and four other large stockholders held. Hamilton wrote that "if the Bank of North America no longer had any solid foundation because the State of Pennsylvania, despite the United States charter, refused to allow it to carry on its operation either the bank should remove to another state where it would be legally protected or those shareholders who wish to be released should be at liberty to withdraw their shares."[28]

The letter precipitated a bitter stockholders' meeting, which revealed some questionable bank practices. Wadsworth pressed Morris and the other insiders until they agreed to Hamilton's plan of legal disintegration. But Hamilton and his group were outfoxed. The bank involved itself in a friendly suit that dragged on in the courts, allowing a delay of several years. In the meantime, Morris tried to force Pennsylvania to recharter the bank, getting himself and several friends elected to the Pennsylvania legislature. They were elected, but there was not a pro-bank majority, so the bank was not rechartered.[29]

The bank fiasco was only an example of the current disarray. Congress was almost nonfunctioning. From October 1, 1785, to April 30, 1786, Congress was able to conduct business on only three days; it did not have a quorum of members present on the other days. The situation was serious.

Hamilton was not really satisfied to bury himself in private life. His expressions of domestic contentment were excessive. He was driven by a fear of being left behind. The country needed his fierce nationalistic spirit, and he needed to display his prodigious talent on a larger screen than a law practice offered. The desperate, critical events that were shaping up would give the nationalist cause a chance. The states were at commercial war with each other. The nation's fiscal picture was dismal. The particular nature of Hamilton's genius was needed for the preservation of the new nation. The prologue would take place at Annapolis, Maryland.

7

A Necessary Interval

ALEXANDER HAMILTON'S RISE to national prominence could not
have occurred without the support of the electorate of New York
State. He recognized that if he hoped to further national interests,
which coincided with those of the merchant class in the city and
the large landholders in the north, he would have to confront Governor Clinton in his own lair. The Clintonites, mostly farmers and
frontiersmen, feared that a strong central government would increase
their taxes; support the peace treaty, and thus the rights of the
Tories; and force the payment of debts. So far, they had been able
to keep control of the assembly, the state's lower house, because
there was a broad-based suffrage for the assembly. The upper house,
the senate, had more rigid voting requirements and so was a bastion
of the rich.

To achieve more anti-Clinton representation in the assembly,
Hamilton united the merchants, bankers, large landholders and others with similar interests. The first foray yielded victory with the
election of such loyal personal and political friends as William Duer,
Robert Troup and William Malcolm. However, though, as Robert
Troup admitted candidly, he and the other two knew that they were
sent to the state legislature "to make every effort to accomplish Hamilton's objects," it was not enough for Hamilton to pull the strings
from behind the scenes.[1] Hamilton's own aggressive, resourceful
presence was needed to defeat the popular New York governor.

Hamilton's election to the assembly was accomplished with difficulty. He was elected but was only fourth among the nine designated
to go to the assembly. The people did not support Hamilton unless
pressured by their employers.[2]

Two issues concerned Hamilton enough to overcome his reluctance and motivate him to try for a seat in the legislature. One was old business; the other a new problem. At this time, all the states except Georgia and New York had endorsed the impost duty that Congress had recommended in April 1783, and Georgia was about to sign. New York was still holding out; her taxes on imports provided a large percentage of her revenue. Hamilton circulated a petition favoring the impost, which recapitulated his earlier arguments: the need for compliance with all the other states, the national government's need for revenue and the fact that "the mode provided in the confederation for supplying the treasury of the United States has in experiment been found inadequate." The petition asserted that the "interests and liberties" of the citizens of New York State were as safe in the hands of their fellow citizens representing them for one year in Congress as with their fellow citizens representing them for one or four years in the state senate or assembly. "Government implies trust." Without it, Hamilton repeated, "the ends for which it is constituted" could not be attained, and instead there would be "insult from abroad and convulsion and confusion at home."[3]

Many signatures were obtained for Hamilton's petition, and other petitions were circulated through the state. Public meetings were arranged, as well as endorsements of well-known figures from other states, but all efforts to obtain New York's approval of the impost failed.

On April 13, 1786, Assemblyman John Lansing succeeded in getting an amendment to the impost passed by a vote of 33–22, providing for the collection of the tax by state, not federal, collectors. The nationalists were crushed by the defeat. A compromise amendment, in which New York agreed to Congress's set of regulations in the interest of conformity, lost by a vote of 31–21. Schuyler failed with a similar tactic in the Senate later that month.[4]

New York State was willing to accept the impost bill only if the collectors were employed by the state and the state's paper money was accepted. Congress asked the New York State legislature to reconsider its decision and change the unacceptable revisions. Since the legislature had already disbanded, Clinton would have to call a special session, which he refused to do. The Federalists were infuriated by Clinton's arrogant, narrow interpretation.

The new issue that influenced Hamilton's decision to run for office was a major one, and he was to make it the prelude to the most important change in the United States since the Revolution.

James Madison, once again to become Hamilton's partner in the struggle for a stronger union, was the prime mover of the events that culminated in the miracle at Philadelphia. Rivalry between the states over mutual waterways and the need for commercial regulations had spoiled state relationships from the beginning. In early 1785, the efforts of Madison and Washington had resulted in the amicable regulation of the Chesapeake and the Potomac by Maryland and Virginia. At a meeting at Mount Vernon, Maryland invited her neighbors Delaware and Pennsylvania to attend. Madison spoke of "the present anarchy of our commerce," blaming the postwar depression on it. For example, New York required any ship from New Jersey weighing more than twelve tons to clear customs as if it had come from a foreign port. In retaliation, New Jersey taxed New York City £30 a month for the use of the Sandy Hook lighthouse. This kind of tit-for-tat was practiced all along the Atlantic seaboard.

Inspired by the Virginia-Maryland commercial conference, Madison drafted a resolution, which, for political reasons, he had John Tyler introduce into the Virginia legislature. It called for a conference with "the other states in the union at a time and place to be agreed on to take into consideration the trade of the United States . . . and to consider how far a uniform system in their commercial regulations may be necessary to their common interest and their permanent harmony."[5] The resolution was accepted, and Annapolis, Maryland, was chosen for the site. The date was set for the first Monday in September 1786. Gov. Patrick Henry of Virginia was delegated to ask his fellow governors to send representatives to the Annapolis meeting.

George Clinton submitted the call for delegates to the New York legislature on March 16, 1786. The Hamiltonians bent all their strength to get the proposal accepted. They succeeded and were also responsible for the choice of delegates. However, when the time came, only Egbert Benson and Alexander Hamilton went to Annapolis.

There, they lodged with most of the other delegates at George Mann's City Tavern, a fine establishment of one hundred beds with stables for fifty horses, known for its elegant food.

Hamilton was disappointed, although not surprised, that only twelve delegates representing five states arrived for the convention. After some thought, however, he saw the paucity of delegates as an asset. The nationalist cause could be better served because there would be fewer in opposition, since, as he surmised correctly, states refused cooperation and delegates stayed home suspecting that "political objects are intended to be combined with commercial," if they did not dominate completely.[6]

New York, New Jersey, Pennsylvania, Delaware and Virginia sent delegates. Maryland, the host state, and the others had not appointed any. Trade discussions would be fruitless with so many absentees. Consequently, rallying Madison and relying on the New Jersey commissioners' authority to discuss important matters other than trade and to return with an agreement that provided for "the exigencies of the Union," Hamilton swayed the delegates to issue a call for a conference with wider powers.

Hamilton's first address to the miniature convention was deemed too strong by Virginia's Gov. Edmund Randolph. Madison warned Hamilton that if he lost Randolph's support, he lost Virginia; the speech was "toned down" to become digestible to "tender stomachs." The modified address was sent to the legislatures of the five participating states, to Congress and to all the state governors. Even watered down, its thrust was bold, emphasizing that the reasons for a future convention with "more enlarged powers" were "of a nature so serious as . . . to render the situation of the United States delicate and critical." The states were to appoint commissioners to meet in Philadelphia "on the second Monday in May next" to "render the Constitution of the Federal Government adequate to the exigencies of the Union."[7] The issue now rested with the state legislatures to participate or let the matter stand.

Hamilton was seated in the New York assembly on January 12, 1787. According to Troup, Hamilton wanted to be a member of the legislature to "render the next session subservient to the change meditated." His term "proved to be one of the links in the great chain of events, which produced the general convention at Philadelphia."[8]

Philosophically, Hamilton was in an adversary position to Governor Clinton and so took over the leadership of the opposition as soon as he entered the assembly, complementing Philip Schuyler, who was well entrenched in the opposition role in the senate. The matter of the impost and Clinton's refusal to call a special session of the legislature came up at the start of the session. In his annual message to the newly seated legislature, Clinton presented his reasons for turning down the congressional mandate. Hamilton was appointed to a committee to prepare a reply to Clinton's message. When the draft was submitted to the assembly, there was surprise and consternation that there was no mention of the governor's action.

The Clintonites, led by Samuel Jones, a Long Island lawyer who represented Queens County, insisted that the assembly endorse Clinton's position. A fiery debate ensued, and Hamilton used the assembly as a forum in which to criticize the governor's contention that a special session would have impaired "the right of free deliberation on matters not stipulated by the [Articles] of Confederation." Clinton should have complied, Hamilton declared, "from motives of respect to the union and to avoid any further degradation of its authority, already at too low an ebb," adding, "Powers must be granted, or Civil Society cannot exist; the possibility of abuse is no argument against the *thing*; this possibility is incident to every species of power however placed and modified."[9]

Jones replied that approval of Clinton's message was not a constitutional issue and emphasized the dangers of congressional interference in local government. Hamilton riposted. If we failed to respect federal decisions, we "add these embarrassments. . . . You see us the laughing stock, the sport of foreign nations and what may this lead to? I dread, Sir, to think. . . . There is more involved in this measure than what presents itself to your view." Hamilton was preparing the groundwork for the call to the constitutional convention. But he lost the first round. The assembly voted to compliment Clinton on his message.

Hamilton achieved some victories during the session, opposing certain provisions contained in an act regulating state elections. One article proposed giving inspectors at elections the right to question illiterate voters on their preferences. Hamilton declared that such an arrangement would be "contrary to the very genius and intention of balloting; which means that a man's vote should be secret and known but to himself."[10] The vote supported his position; the clause was struck out.

Another triumph, connected with the same bill, affected Hamilton himself. The proposal was made that "no person receiving a pension from or holding any office or place under the United States of America shall at any time hereafter have a seat in, or sit or vote as a member of the Senate or Assembly of this State." Hamilton argued that the constitution gave every citizen a right to a seat in the assembly, and that it was unconstitutional for any man to be deprived of any of his constitutional rights, except for some offense for which he has been convicted. The clause was removed, as was another that would have disqualified anyone from holding state office who had "committed hostilities against vessels or property" of any citizen of the state. Hamilton's argument against this anti-Loyalist amendment

was that disqualifying citizens "by general description was a dangerous practice that subverted the liberty of the people."[11]

A bill was introduced requiring that a woman who was secretly
delivered of a child, and whose child then died or was stillborn, had
to produce, within a month, a witness before a magistrate to prove
that she had not murdered the child. If the mother did not comply,
she would be considered guilty of murder. Hamilton argued that it
was neither "politic or just," and had to be deleted. This law forced a
woman delivered of a stillborn child in such circumstances to "publish her shame," thereby closing the door to her ever being admitted
"to virtuous society." Therefore, she might well prefer "the danger of
punishment from concealment to the avowal of her guilt." Such a law
would place the courts in a "delicate dilemma," and the law itself
would have no good effect because it would be evaded.[12] The clause,
which was dropped, must have reawakened feelings about his own
young abandoned, unwed mother.

However, Hamilton supported a piece of legislation that would
have operated against her. The Council of Revision challenged a bill
that forbade the party in a divorce adjudged guilty of adultery to
remarry. Hamilton certainly saw in this the tragedy of Rachel
Lavien, forbidden by Danish law to remarry and so condemned to live
out of wedlock with James Hamilton. Her son voted with the majority against the council's effort at reform. But if Rachel had not
chosen to ignore convention and law, Alexander would never have
been born, and, in the future, his own admitted adultery would have
brought such a law into action against himself. Hamilton loved many
women, was charming and gallant, but underneath were suspicion
and rejection, a reflection of resentment against the mother who
made him illegitimate and then, while he still needed her, died and
left him to the care of strangers.

The impost question was revived when William Malcolm introduced an act to grant Congress the authority to collect the tax in
order to pay off the debts of the United States contracted during the
war. The bill, a reasonable compromise, allowed duties on certain
importations and a 5 percent ad valorem duty on all other goods. The
collectors, who would be appointed by New York State but accountable to and removable by the Congress of the United States, would
be empowered to make the rules necessary to levy and collect taxes.
The first part of the proposal passed by one vote, but the section
granting Congress power over the collectors lost by nineteen votes.

Hamilton made a long, impassioned speech in support of granting

Congress power to levy and collect the impost, but to no avail. "Can the union subsist without revenue?" he asked. If the states were not united, "they will infallibly have wars with each other and their divisions will subject them to all the mischiefs of foreign influence and intrigue." The phrase "wars with each other" referred to Vermont's desire to be independent of New York, an issue not yet resolved and one that, over the years, often erupted into violence.[13]

In mid-March, Hamilton introduced a bill that would acknowledge the independence of Vermont, thereby once more challenging Governor Clinton, who could not tolerate the loss of territory or the financial loss; he had a heavy investment in land claimed by Vermonters.

The story of Vermont's struggle for independence goes back to 1749, when New Hampshire's Governor Wentworth, completely blind to New York's claims to the area west of the Connecticut River, granted huge areas their freedom. The liberated territory became known as the Hampshire grants, and in time Ethan Allen became the leader of its cause. New York continued to maintain stoutly that the land was hers.

When Ethan Allen captured Fort Ticonderoga from the British in 1775, thereby becoming a war hero, he expected that his reward would be congressional recognition of Vermont as a state. However, Congress equivocated, even after Vermont declared its own independence and started a civil war with New York. In May 1779, Ethan Allen and his troops raided Brattleboro, capturing several New York officers and wounding several New Yorkers. Congress sent a delegation to the Grants to try to make a settlement. Nothing came of it. Clinton, irate, threatened to withdraw the New York delegation from Congress.

Clinton was even angrier when, in 1781, the New York senate passed a resolution for the appointment of commissioners to settle with Vermont, declaring he would prorogue the legislative body if it endorsed an action "so ruinous to this State" and "destructive to the general peace and interest of the whole confederacy."[14]

Ethan Allen, like Clinton, had private interests at stake; he, too, was heavily invested in land in the disputed area, but he had a Vermont title to it. Clinton maintained that in his zeal for his state's independence, Allen was in treasonable correspondence with the British, a view that Allen himself encouraged when, in an attempt to put pressure on Congress, he wrote frankly that he believed Vermont had "an indubitable right to agree on terms of cessation of hostilities with Great Britain" if the United States kept on refusing statehood. The people of Vermont would be "most miserable" if they had to defend the independence of the other states while those states were "at full liberty to overturn and ruin the independence of Vermont."[15]

Border violence continued between the Yankees (Vermonters) and the New Yorkers throughout this time. In 1782, Ethan Allen took prisoner and locked up all the New York party leaders he could seize. He also threatened to make the houses of the recusants "as desolate as Sodom and Gomorrah."[16]

On March 14, 1787, Hamilton introduced a motion for leave to bring in a bill on the independence of Vermont, recognizing that Vermont was a de facto state with its independence "fixed and inevitable." He emphasized that Vermont, for her own safety, sought connections elsewhere, "and who that hears me doubts but that these connections have *already* been formed with the British in Canada." Vermont is "useless to us now, and if they continue as they are, they will be formidable to us hereafter."[17]

Ten days later, a petition was presented by several New Yorkers who owned land in Vermont in which they asked for the protection of their property under the social compact.

Hamilton answered that in January 1777, when Vermont declared its independence, it was during the war and could not have been challenged. By the time of the declaration of peace, Vermont had enjoyed freedom for several years. Was New York in a situation in which it could undertake the reduction of Vermont? Where were its resources or public credit for an offensive war? There was no doubt that British officers were in secret intercourse with Vermont leaders. Hence, Hamilton concluded, he preferred that Vermont stay as it was.[18]

The senate voted down Hamilton's bill, but this temporary Clintonite victory did not stop Hamilton, who believed in the necessity and inevitablity of the renegade state's freedom.

In the spring of 1788, Nathaniel Chipman and other Vermont leaders met to find a means to avoid unfavorable decisions for Vermont in cases brought by New York landowners for compensation. They decided to approach prominent nationalist leaders from New York who they hoped would cooperate in settling the differences and achieving statehood for Vermont. An express was sent to Hamilton's residence in Poughkeepsie, where he was attending the ratification conference. With the help of Schuyler, Benson and others, Hamilton composed a reply that stated their position. The following winter, Hamilton met with Chipman in Albany to work out a plan of action. Finally, in the summer of 1789, over the protests of Governor Clinton, New York appointed commissioners empowered to accept Vermont's statehood. Chipman served on the Vermont commission. Hamilton witnessed the signatures of the New York members to the agreement and inspired Chipman's speech to the Vermont convention at Bennington in January 1791, in which he begged the state to seek admission to the Union. The following month, after sixteen years of existing in limbo, Vermont entered the Union.[19]

Although the power of the nationalists in the New York legislature was weakening, an event that was shaking the nation influenced the attitude of many toward the need for a constitutional convention. The event was a rebellion by the desperate, debt-ridden farmers of western Massachusetts under the leadership of Capt. Daniel Shays, who, like most of his followers, had served in the continental army.

Armed mobs of penniless farmers had already stopped the courts from sitting in Northhampton, Worcester, Concord and Great Barrington in an effort to prevent mortgage foreclosures. However, in December 1786, when Daniel Shays led 1,200 men on a march against the arsenal at Springfield, Massachusetts, a shudder of fear went through the United States. This was armed revolution. In reality, it was a sad crowd; the fierce revolutionists were armed mostly with pitchforks and staves. Gen. Benjamin Lincoln, with the militia, hunted the disorganized rabble into the hills. By the end of February, Lincoln had captured 150 insurgents and dispersed the rest, including Shays, who escaped to Vermont. Eventually all the participants, and Shays, were pardoned, but the fear that the uprising stirred served the cause of the nationalists and the constitutional convention.

Hamilton's commitment to the participation of New York in the proposed constitutional convention was still powerful, but the strength of his partisans was weakening. Of the five delegates to Congress whom Hamilton nominated, only Egbert Benson was accepted by the assembly. Clintonite strength was displayed again when Philip Schuyler, nominated for Congress by the senate, was defeated by John Lansing, Jr. And the antinationalist majority was successful in reducing the number of delegates to be sent to the constitutional convention from five to three. Only one vote saved the delegation from being restricted by a charge that it could not agree to any changes in the Articles of Confederation that conflicted with the provisions in the New York State constitution.

In March, the selection of delegates to Philadelphia eroded Hamilton's hopes for a strong nationalist contingent. His effectiveness as a proponent of a strong central government was crippled by the presence of two loyal states'-righters, Robert Yates and John Lansing, Jr., as his colleagues. The New York triumvirate was informed by the legislature that it was elected "for the sole purpose of revising the Articles of Confederation" so as to "render the Federal Constitution adequate to the exigencies of government."[20]

At this time Hamilton's personal life was tranquil. His financial records show that his wine bills were high, which indicates that he entertained a lot, because he was a moderate drinker. While still in the army, James McHenry, who had studied medicine before the war, prescribed a regimen for the young man, who suffered from chronic constipation. McHenry recommended a fat-free diet, lean beef rather than mutton or ham, and few vegetables. Water was advised as "the best insistence in the process of digestion." As for wine, "never go beyond three glasses—but by no means every day." In time, Hamilton would be the best "councellor in diet" because "a man who has had ten years experience in eating and its consequence is a fool if he does not know how to choose his dishes better than his Doctor."[21]

Although the Hamiltons had three children of their own at this time, Philip, Angelica and Alexander, they adopted a little girl. She was the daughter of Colonel Antil of the Canadian Corps of the continental army, who had retired from the service penniless and unable to collect his military claims. An unsuccessful farmer and desperate after the death of his wife, he came to New York with his small daughter to ask help of the Society of the Cincinnati. While in the city, ill and despondent, he died. Hamilton took the little orphan home and brought her up with his own children. Later, she married Arthur Tappan, a successful New York merchant.[22]

Having achieved his goal by election to the constitutional convention, Hamilton had no further interest in serving in the New York legislature, especially since it would not meet in New York City the following year. In late April he declined candidacy. Instead, he readied himself for the trip to Philadelphia. The convention was scheduled to meet on May 14, but Hamilton did not arrive until May 25, the first day on which a quorum of members was present.

8

"An Assembly of Demigods"

THE DELEGATES Alexander Hamilton joined in the Philadelphia State House on May 25, 1787, included the two most distinguished Americans of the time, George Washington and Benjamin Franklin, as well as many other prominent patriots. James Madison and other nationalist friends were also at the convention.

Disputes of historians over the motivations of members of the historic convention have continued since 1913, when Charles Beard presented his shocking thesis that the founding fathers were unrepresentative opportunists seeking to write a document to serve their own economic and class interests. But even Beard found it difficult to fit Hamilton into his mold. In 1787, Hamilton owned only "a petty amount of public securities which might appreciate under a new system" and some western land. The worst Beard could say about Hamilton was that his principles of government were "no mere abstract political science. He knew at first hand the stuff of which government is made."[1]

While in Philadelphia, Hamilton lived at The Indian Queen, located at Third Street between Market and Chestnut streets, with other members, or at The Hills, the country estate of Robert Morris. His pattern of attendance at the convention was a subject of conjecture and reproof. From May 25 to June 29 he attended regularly but then left for New York and, except for a brief appearance on August 13, did not return to Philadelphia until September 6. He then stayed until the last day, September 17, the sole New Yorker present at the completion of the convention's task.

Instead of being a prime mover of the convention, Hamilton behaved in a restrained, even eccentric manner, particularly on June 18, when he took a whole day of the convention's working time to unravel a plan for the United States that everyone, including himself, knew would be unacceptable. Madison, who had arrived in Philadelphia early and had spent the previous winter preparing for the convention, offered an explanation for Hamilton's behavior. The New Yorker kept quiet, said Madison, out of respect for those of superior age and experience, and an unwillingness to "bring forward ideas dissimilar to theirs." Also, he was in "a delicate situation" in relation to his own state, "to whose sentiments as expressed by his colleagues, he could by no means accede." Finally, realizing the crisis "which now marked our affairs," namely, the intense disagreements that were taking place in the convention, he felt obliged to present his own ideas, which were unfriendly to both the Virginia and New Jersey plans, particularly the latter.[2]

On May 25, the first meeting day, George Washington was unanimously elected president of the convention. The undoubted hero of the American Revolution, his austere and noble presence would add stature to the convention and unite it. He wrote to Thomas Jefferson, the American minister in Paris, "My wish is that the Convention may adopt no temporizing expedient, but probe the defects of the Constitution to the bottom, and provide radical cures whether they are agreed to or not."[3]

The Pennsylvania delegation proposed the motion to elect Washington, a graceful gesture since Benjamin Franklin was the only possible contender for the post. After General Washington was conducted to the president's chair, James Wilson of Pennsylvania proposed Temple Franklin for convention secretary. Hamilton then nominated Major William Jackson, chancellor of Virginia, who was elected. Later in the day, Hamilton, George Wythe and Charles Pinckney were appointed to a committee to prepare the standing rules and orders.

The rules committee proposed and the convention accepted "that nothing spoken in the House be printed, or otherwise published or communicated without leave" and that no copy be taken of any entry on the journal during the sitting of the House without leave of the House, and that members only be permitted to inspect the journal.[4] Full secrecy as to the proceedings was imposed on all the members, the purpose to ensure freedom of debate without outside pressure or fear of reprisal or criticism by a hostile press.

Jefferson, writing from Paris to John Adams, who was in London as minister to England, reported of the federal convention: "I am sorry they began their deliberations by so abominable a precedent as that of tying up the tongues of their members. Nothing can justify this example but the innocence of their intentions and ignorance of the value of public discussions." Nonetheless, he was certain that their decisions would be good and wise, for "it is really an assembly of demigods."[5]

At a later date, Hamilton defended the restrictions: "Had the deliberations been open while going on," he said, "the clamors of faction would have prevented any satisfactory result. . . . Propositions made without due reflection, and perhaps abandoned by the proposers themselves on more mature reflection, would have been handles for a profusion of ill-natured accusations."[6]

Despite the strictures, there are records of the proceedings. The most complete account is in Madison's notes, published in 1840 after his death. The Jackson journal, written by the official secretary, was made available in 1819 and included the notes of Luther Martin, delegate from Maryland. Later, the records of Robert Yates, William Pierce, Rufus King, William Paterson, James McHenry, John Lansing and Alexander Hamilton appeared. Hamilton's notes, unlike the others, were not transcripts of the events but random, free-style jottings written in response to the speeches he heard, meant to help him develop his rebuttals.

Hamilton's first recorded convention statement was made on May 29 after Virginia's Gov. Edmund Randolph presented the Virginia plan, a comprehensive proposal written by James Madison that called for a new constitution of the United States. Hamilton said that a necessary and preliminary inquiry into Virginia's propositions needed to be made: "Whether the United States were susceptible of one government or required a separate existence connected only by leagues offensive and defensive and treaties of commerce."[7] His was a penetrating question, albeit a cynical one, from a confirmed nationalist whose own belief was that a new constitution was long overdue.

Looking at the Articles of Confederation from the distance of two centuries, it is obvious that the unicameral Congress without an executive accomplished a great deal. The United States was independent, an admirable peace had been arranged, the states had willingly ceded much of their western territory which was being settled and an impressive pattern for the admission of new states had been designed, a unique accomplishment never attained by any other society. Yet the most brilliant and prescient thinkers of the day, among them Hamilton, believed that continuation under the Articles meant doom for the new republic; either the quarreling states or outside predators would consume the infant nation.

On June 18, Hamilton presented his astounding constitutional plan for the United States to the convention. The gathering received it without reaction. It was blacked out because it struck at the sacred federal system. No persuasion, no appeal to historical precedent, no eloquence could eliminate the existence of the thirteen states. Hamilton only emphasized his foreignness when he failed to empathize with the other men at the assembly. They were Virginians, South Carolinians, Pennsylvanians, New Yorkers, Georgians, New Englanders whose roots were in the lands of their fathers, and no philosophical, amorphous entity such as a central government could sever them from their bonds of affection for their native states.

Hamilton observed that both the Virginia and New Jersey plans had "essential defects" because they continued the federal system. As long as the states existed, "all the passions . . . of avarice, ambition, interest which govern most individuals and all public bodies, fall into the current of the states, and do not flow in the stream of the Genl Govt." His solution was only "by such a compleat sovereignty in the general Government as will turn all the strong principles & passions above mentioned on its side."[8]

Another unpopular note that Hamilton kept sounding was his admiration for the British government. In his private opinion, the British government was "the best in the world," and he doubted whether anything short of it would do in America. In speaking his mind on the executive, Hamilton laid the groundwork for accusations that he supported a monarchy in the United States that followed him all of his life. Could there be a good government without a good executive? Hamilton's answer was that the English model was the only good one because the "Hereditary interest of the King was so interwoven with that of the Nation, and his personal emoluments so great, that he was placed above the danger of being corrupted from abroad—and at the same time was both sufficiently independent and sufficiently controuled, to answer the purpose of the institution at home." A republic's weakness was its liability to foreign influence and corruption and men of little character acquiring great power and "becoming easily the tools of intermeddling Neibors [*sic*]." Therefore, rather than an executive for seven years as had been proposed, Hamilton wanted an executive for life, who would not have the "Motive for forgetting his fidelity and will therefore be a safe depository for power."[9]

After these introductory comments, Hamilton announced that he would read a sketch of his plan, although he was aware that "it went beyond the ideas of most members." This paper, he warned, was not to be regarded as a proposal to the assembly. It was meant only "to give a more correct view of his ideas" and to suggest amendments to Randolph's plan. Hamilton's plan recommended a bicameral legislature, made up of an assembly and a senate, with the power to pass all laws in every area, subject to a veto described below. Members of the assembly would be elected by the people for a three-year term. The members of the Senate would be elected by electors chosen by the people from election districts into which the states would be divided, and would serve during good behavior. When there was a vacancy in the Senate, it would be filled from outside the district.

The executive would be a "gouverneur" who would serve, like the Senate, during good behavior, elected by electors chosen by the people from the above-mentioned election districts. His powers and duties would be: execution of all laws and a veto on all laws about to be passed; direction of war; treaty-making power; sole appointment of the heads of departments of finance, war and foreign affairs; nomination of ambassadors with the advice and consent of the Senate; and the power of pardon, except for treason. On the gouverneur's death, removal from office or resignation, the president of the Senate would fulfill his duties until a successor was appointed.

The Senate would have the sole power to declare war, approval of all treaties, and advice and consent in the appointment of all officers except chiefs of finance, war and foreign affairs.

The supreme judicial authority would be held by judges, who would retain their offices during good behavior and would be paid "adequate and permanent salaries." The court would have original jurisdiction in all cases of capture, and appellate jurisdiction in cases in which the revenues of the national government or citizens of foreign nations were concerned. The United States legislature would institute courts in each state.

The gouverneur, senators and all officers of the United States would be liable to impeachment for corrupt conduct and, if convicted, would be removed from office and disqualified from holding another.

All laws of the individual states or of the federal government contrary to the constitution would be void. In order to avoid passage of such laws, the governor of each state would be appointed by the general government and would have a veto on all laws passed in his state. No state would be permitted an army or a navy, the militia of all the states to be under the sole and exclusive direction of the United States.

After the outline of his plan was presented, Hamilton explained its provisions, delivering his remarkable discourse, quietly and coolly. The house then adjourned. At a later date, Madison showed his transcript of the speech to Hamilton, who accepted it, adding only one or two changes.

Judge Yates's account of the speech was memorable only for some pungent remarks that he attributed to Hamilton. The one most often repeated was that "the people are gradually ripening in their opinion of government, they begin to be tired of an excess of democracy, and what even is the Virginia plan but pork still, with a little change of the sauce." Yates also recorded a clear statement of Hamilton's basic view of democracy. "The voice of the people has been said to be the voice of God and, however generally this maxim has been quoted and believed, it is not true in fact. The people are turbulent and changing; they seldom judge or determine right." Therefore, Hamilton advised, give the rich and well born "a distinct permanent share in the government. . . . Nothing but a permanent body can check the imprudence of democracy." According to Lansing, Hamilton said that "the principal citizens of every state are tired of democracy," not the people. Hamilton's own notes suggest a third version. Government ought to be in the hands of both the few and of the many, or whoever had the power would tyrannize over the other. They should be separated, but representation alone would not do it. "Demagogues will generally prevail. And if separated, they will need a mutual check. This check is a monarch." When he presented his speech to the convention, Hamilton substituted "gouverneur" for the dreaded word "monarch."[10]

The reception of the speech was as unusual as its content. Hamilton, elegantly dressed, spoke without interruption. No outraged egalitarian challenged him. The company was surprised, perhaps absorbed and certainly amazed. Gouverneur Morris declared that it was "the most able and impressive speech he had ever heard." But everyone took Hamilton at his word when he said that he was not making a proposal. They all went home and the next day resumed the business of the convention as if Hamilton's June 18 speech had never been made. Though the speech may have been too radical a departure from the spirit of the convention, it was an honest expression of Hamilton's fears that in a democracy there was a need for a permanent body such as he conceived his lifetime senate to be. His proposal was modeled on the classical theory of a mixed constitution.[11]

Hamilton's alleged pessimism was a recognition of the economic needs of the American people and the belief that it was the duty of government to respond to the people's needs. In this he was far ahead of his time. He implied realities about human nature and the nature of government that many preferred to leave unsaid. Hamilton, wiser, if less idealistic, pointed out that to persuade a man to be a public servant, the government must arouse his passions for the general welfare.[12]

Hamilton's plan, motivated by his admiration for the British system, substituted for a monarchy a permanent president and a permanent senate. It took some of the arrogance of youth to speak so long and so freely, knowing how unpopular his words were. Some delegates resented the tone of the presentation more than its content, calling it smug and pompous. But his admirers marveled at the breadth of political knowledge displayed by "one of the most remarkable geniuses of the Age."

Though the protection of secrecy had been adopted by the members, much of what Hamilton said that day, of monarchy in particular, would be recalled and distorted then and later. The June 18 speech was a brave gesture and, as Gouverneur Morris put it, "a generous indiscretion."

Many nationalists regarded Hamilton's day-long speech as a mixed blessing. Madison and Wilson worried that the delegates would react very unfavorably to Hamilton's intimation that the states be abolished; such a bizarre idea might destroy their cause. His friends told Hamilton that he had carried candor to a dangerous point, and the next day, somewhat chastened, Hamilton tried to deny his assault on America's sacred cow, the sanctity of the states.

He said that he had not been understood. When he spoke of abolition of the states, he meant only that the national legislature should have indefinite authority, else rivalry between the states would be too formidable an obstacle for the national government.

In order to appease the anxieties of the small states, Hamilton explained that there were two circumstances that would guarantee their security under a national government. One was the geographical position of the three largest states, Virginia, Massachusetts and Pennsylvania. Separated as they were by distance and by the diversity of their interests, "no combination therefore could be dreaded." Secondly, from Virginia to the smallest state, Delaware, "ambitious combinations" of groups of states would be counteracted by "defensive combinations" of others. There was no evidence of combinations simply on the basis of the larger against the smaller. Hamilton's second thoughts were ignored by most of the antinationalist members. They agreed with Dr. Johnson's statement that "one gentleman alone (Col Hamilton)" in his remarks against the New Jersey plan "boldly and decisively contended for an abolition of the State Govts."[13]

Every time Hamilton spoke at the convention, he returned to his fear of a weak central government. The three great objects of government, he said on June 19, were agriculture, commerce and revenue. These could be attained only by a "general government." And two days later, he opposed General Pinckney's proposal that the legislature of each state, rather than the people, elect the members of Congress. This would increase state influence, "which could not be too watchfully guarded against," Hamilton argued. Further, "all" had to admit the possibility that state governments might "dwindle into nothing," and so the new system "shd not be engrafted on what might possibly fail." As for the length of term for representatives, Hamilton preferred three years rather than less, in order that there might be "neither too much nor too little dependence on the popular sentiments." Too frequent elections, he maintained, tended to make the people listless and to encourage the success of factions.[14] The suggestion failed; the motion for a two-year term for members of the House of Representatives carried.

On the following day, the convention discussed the payment of stipends to the members of the national government. Hamilton felt that fixing the wages would be inconvenient and strenuously opposed the payment of legislators out of their state treasuries. "Those who pay are the masters of those who are paid," he warned. The cost to the states would be unequal, and the distant states would have to pay for more days of traveling. The state governments would be "the rivals" of the central government and therefore ought not to be the paymasters.[15]

There was considerable debate that day on the resolution to make members of the legislature ineligible for other offices during their term and for one year after. Those who favored it pointed to many instances of venality and abuse by the members of the British Parliament. Hamilton answered: "We must take man as we find him, and if we expect him to serve the public must interest his passions in doing so. A reliance on pure patriotism has been the source of many of our errors." He added that "there may be in every government a few choice spirits, who may act from more worthy motives. One great error is that we suppose mankind more honest than they are . . . when a member takes his seat, he should vacate every other office." The United States Constitution reads: "No person holding any Office under the United States, shall be a Member of either House during his Continuance in Office."[16]

On June 26, Hamilton spoke briefly during the discussion of the length of term of senators. He had already given his opinion that senators should have life tenure, so that when he rose to speak he said that he did not want to "enter particularity into the subject." He agreed with James Madison that the fate of republican government was being decided forever, and "if we did not give to that form stability and wisdom, it would be disgraced & lost to mankind forever." Though he did not think favorably of republican government, he spoke to those who did "in order to prevail on them to tone the Government as high as possible." Though he differed with Madison and the others as to the best form of government, he was as zealous an advocate of liberty as any man and as willing a martyr to it."[17] The assembly decided on a six-year term for senators.

By this time the delegates had been in session about five weeks. Addressing President Washington, venerable Dr. Franklin reflected his own and others' increasing impatience with the lack of unanimity in the proceedings, "a melancholy proof of the imperfections of the Human Understanding." Though they had gone back to ancient history and viewed modern constitutions, nothing seemed "suitable to our circumstances," Franklin observed regretfully. He suggested that prayers, seeking divine help, be held in the assembly every morning before the business of the day started and that the clergy of the city take turns officiating.

Madison recorded in his notes that Hamilton and several others agreed that such a resolution might have been proper at the start of the convention but were apprehensive about its adoption "at this late day." They argued that it might lead the public to believe "that the embarassments and dissensions within the Convention, had suggested this measure." Franklin answered that "the past omission of a duty could not justify a further omission," and the proposal was made that a service be preached on the Fourth of July and prayers offered every morning. The meeting adjourned without taking a vote on the measure.

Years later, Jonathan Dayton's account of Hamilton's response to Franklin's proposal was related by a William Steele in a letter to his son. According to this, Franklin proposed a three-day adjournment for the convention as a cooling-off period during which the members should discuss each other's sentiments and a chaplain be appointed to start each day with prayers. Washington and all the others except for one man were delighted and affected by Franklin's proposal. "Mr. H—[Hamilton] rose and said that he agreed with the first proposal but opposed the appointment of a Chaplain. He was confident that the assembly was competent to transact their business and therefore he saw no necessity to call in foreign aid." The others ignored the speaker and carried the motion.[18] Though in conflict with Madison's notes, this is an interesting example of the persistence of animosity against Hamilton, even long after his death.

Throughout the convention, Hamilton suffered from being odd man out in his own delegation, a perpetual minority of one. Since the unit rule was employed for voting, New York would almost inevitably vote contrary to Hamilton's beliefs. His deserted law practice, his abandoned family and the discomfiture of his position were pulling Hamilton in the direction of New York.

On June 29, Hamilton spoke in opposition to the equality of states in the House of Representatives. He said that it was absurd to think that if the smaller states renounced their equality, they also renounced their liberty. The state would lose power, but the people would be just as free. Again Hamilton cautioned against the dissolution of the Union and the establishment of partial confederacies. Alliances would immediately be formed with rival and hostile European nations who would "foment disturbances among ourselves, and make us parties to all their own quarrels." This was a critical moment for forming a responsible government. "We should run every risk in trusting to future amendments. As yet we retain the habits of union. . . . Henceforward the motives will become feebler, and the difficulties greater. It is a miracle that we are now here expressing our tranquil and free deliberations. . . . It would be madness to trust to future miracles. A thousand causes must obstruct a reproduction of them."[19] Hamilton then left the constitutional convention.

Hamilton's opponents judged that he retired from the Philadelphia battlefield in defeat. George Mason wrote: "Yates and Lansing never voted *in one single instance* with Hamilton who was so much mortified at it that he went home." Six years later, Roger Baldwin told a large group of people that Hamilton left the convention after his proposal failed and declared he would "intermeddle no further in the matter."[20]

Hamilton fled the convention because he was overwhelmed with a

sense of alienation. He was different from the others, a foreign visionary who foresaw a great nation dominant in commerce and
industry. The others, practical, solid citizens, were not yet ready for
his soaring ideas.

But Hamilton was a fighter who might withdraw from the field in
order to rearm, but he would return. Not even the cold reception of
his master plan stopped his ardor for a vigorous constitution. While
traveling north through New Jersey on his way home, Hamilton
talked to many people to get their reactions to the convention. In a
letter to Washington, he wrote that men from all over the state
thought that the convention had "a critical opportunity for establishing the prosperity of this country on a solid foundation." The chief
fear expressed by "thinking men" was that the convention would not
go far enough, lest it shock popular opinion. While reluctantly admitting that the people were not yet ripe for his own plan, Hamilton
thought them ready for one "equally energetic." Although the men in
office in his own state, Clinton and his followers, were working at
giving "an unfavourable impression of the convention, the current of
opinion seemed to be running strongly against them."[21]

It was not Hamilton's intention to be absent from Philadelphia
indefinitely. He told Washington on July 3 that he would stay in
New York "of necessity" for ten or twelve days, and then, "if I have
reason to believe that my attendance at Philadelphia will not be
mere waste of time," he would return. Washington's reply gave a
depressing picture of what had been going on in Hamilton's absence.
"I *almost* despair of seeing a favourable issue to the proceedings of
the Convention, and do therefore repent having had any urgency in
the business," he wrote. The antinationalists, he believed, were behaving like narrowminded politicians. "I am sorry you went away,"
the president of the convention wrote, "I wish you were back."

The convention recessed for two weeks on July 26, which gave
Hamilton a fortnight's grace for his private business.

While in New York, Hamilton succumbed to his anger at Yates,
Lansing and Clinton and tried to discredit Clinton in a move that
only injured himself and his cause. He wrote an unsigned article that
appeared in the New York *Daily Advertiser* on July 21 in which he
alleged that Clinton "reprobated the appointment of the Convention
and predicted a mischievous issue of that measure." After giving
reasons why the convention was necessary, Hamilton wrote that

however justifiable it might be in the governor to oppose the appointment
of a convention . . . the general voice of America having decided in its

favour, it is *unwarrantable and culpable in any man*, in so serious a posture of our national affairs to endeavour to prepossess the public mind against the hitherto undetermined and unknown measures of a body to whose councils America has . . . entrusted its future fate . . . such conduct in a man high in office argues greater attachment to his *own power* than to the public good.

This harsh personal attack on their leader aroused the Clintonians to answer it. Hamilton, in his response, revealed his authorship of the piece in question and that he had left his name with the printer, available to anyone who asked. The governor could have answered him, Hamilton told the readers of the *Daily Advertiser*. The apologists, he wrote, "in the intemperate ardour of zeal for his character seem to forget another *right*, very precious to the citizens of a free country, *that* of examining the conduct of their rulers."[22]

During the New York interlude, Hamilton avoided involvement as a second in a duel. John Auldjo, a partner in a British mercantile house based in the United States, was challenged by Maj. William Pierce, a former aide to Gen. Nathaneal Greene and now head of a Savannah, Georgia, business, because of an alleged insult regarding the payment of some accounts. Auldjo asked Hamilton to be his second.

Hamilton wrote to Nathaniel Mitchell, Pierce's second, urging that they work together to keep "extremities" from taking place. He also wrote to Pierce, pointing out that Pierce and Auldjo had no real enmity between them, only a difference, advising him "to be content with *enough* for *more* ought not to be expected." The strategy worked. In a letter to Auldjo, Hamilton stated that Pierce seemed to be satisfied, "and I presume that we are to hear nothing farther of the matter."[23]

On August 13, Hamilton was in Philadelphia again. The question on the floor was the number of years of citizenship required to qualify for the House of Representatives. The delegates proposed four, seven or nine years. Elbridge Gerry wanted eligibility in the future to be limited to native-born Americans. Hamilton was, in general, against "embarrassing" the government with minute restrictions. There might be a danger, but there was also an advantage in encouraging foreigners. Europeans of moderate fortune would be attracted here if they were treated as equal citizens. Hamilton moved that the requirement for eligibility be merely American citizenship. The legislature should have the discretion to determine the rule of naturalization. Madison seconded the motion, and Wilson withdrew his motion in favor of Hamilton's. But the assembly voted a seven-year citizenship requirement.[24]

Hamilton stayed in Philadelphia for only a few days. On August 20, he wrote to Rufus King from New York that he had informed his colleagues Robert Yates and John Lansing, who had left the convention on July 10 in opposition to the formation of a national government, that "if either of them would come down," he would accompany him to Philadelphia. In the meantime, if anything unexpected happened in the plan before the convention, King should let him know. He also wanted to be informed "when your *conclusion* is at hand," for he would return at that time.[25]

At this time, Hamilton received a copy of a letter that had appeared in a Fairfield, Connecticut, paper, revealing a scheme, said to be favorably received at the British court, to invite Frederick, Duke of York, second son of George III and secular Bishop of Osnaburgh, to become king of the United States. The letter, Hamilton wrote to Jeremiah Wadsworth, had been sent by "one Whitmore of Stratford [Connecticut] formerly in the Paymaster General's office to James Reynolds of this City." Hamilton wanted Wadsworth to find out the letter's author, and the political connections of Whitmore and the others who were circulating the letter. "Be so good as to attend to this inquiry somewhat particularly, as I have different reasons of some moment [for] setting it on foot," Hamilton wrote.[26]

Wadsworth answered late in August that the letter appeared to have been written "to secure the antifederal party to comply to the convention," lest worse befall. Whitmore was identified as a man named Wetmore, who had always stood for good government. Col. David Humphreys was going to New Haven where Wetmore lived and would talk to him.

In September, Humphreys reported to Hamilton that Loyalists were circulating the rumor. Whether they had fabricated the story, Humphreys did not know, but he thought that it was either a hoax or an attempt to feel out the public on royalty. Loyalists did hope for the advent of the Bishop of Osnaburgh, Humphreys maintained. Yesterday where he had dined, "half in jest and half in earnest" the king's son was given as the first toast.[27]

For the first time, the name of James Reynolds came to Hamilton's attention. Much later, Reynolds tried to ruin Hamilton's reputation. In John Church Hamilton's collection of his father's letters, Hamilton's letter to Wadsworth was included, but Reynolds's name was deleted.

Hamilton resumed his seat in the constitutional convention at the beginning of September. While in New York, he had made a major decision about his attitude toward the new constitution. Despite his general "dislike of the scheme of government" that was being shaped, Hamilton "meant to support the plan to be recommended as better than nothing." He would accept any system that would save America from the danger threatening her.[28] Since the other two delegates from New York had deserted their posts, Hamilton realized that he, as the sole survivor, would be acting as an individual, rather than as part of a state delegation. This freed him to break his silence and to comment on the final controversial issues.

The committee of eleven chosen on August 31 to work on all unfinished business brought up the important question of how to choose the president, proposing that electors, selected in whatever way the individual state legislatures wished, should elect the president. Each state would have as many electors as they had representatives and senators in Congress. If there was a tie or no candidate won the majority of the votes, the Senate would decide the election. The president would serve a four-year term and be eligible for unlimited reelection.

The committee's plan, Hamilton observed, had a dangerous flaw. Since there were so many different views in the different states, it would be difficult to achieve a majority for one plan, so the choice would devolve on the Senate. The remedy would be to let the highest number of ballots, a majority or not, decide who would be president. To the objection that too small a number might appoint the president, Hamilton pointed out that as the plan stood, the Senate was free to make the candidate with the smallest number of votes the president.[29] Eventually, the committee's plan was adopted, with the change that if no candidate received the majority of the votes, the election would go into the House of Representatives, the people's body.

On September 8, Hamilton spoke a number of times. He showed a vigor in the closing days of the convention that had been absent before. The final days also gave him a chance to display his organizational skills. He was elected to a committee that included Johnson, Gouverneur Morris, Madison and Rufus King to review the style of the articles and to arrange them. Although there was no resentment against him because of his lengthy absence, Hamilton's preferences were seldom adopted. He supported the proposal of Williamson of North Carolina to increase the membership of the House of Representatives. The popular branch of the Congress should be on "a very broad foundation," he argued, rather than on so narrow a scale that the people would be "jealous of their liberties." The close connection between the Senate and the president would tend to perpetuate him by corrupt influence, so that a large representation in the other branch of the legislature should be established. Williamson's motion was defeated.

Elbridge Gerry reopened the subject of the method of amending the Constitution. Hamilton observed that it was desirable that there be an easy way to remedy the defects "which will probably appear in the New System." However, he felt that the state legislatures would originate changes only if the change increased their power. It was the national legislature that would be "most sensible to the necessity of amendment" and should be empowered to call a convention whenever two-thirds of each branch concurred. Madison found the phrase, "call a Convention for the purpose," vague and proposed a fuller clause, which Hamilton accepted.[30]

During this last phase of the convention Hamilton did some amazing turnabouts, and from one of its most obstreperous members he became an appeaser. Suddenly worried about legitimacy, first he agreed with Gerry that it was bad taste not to require Congress's approval of the new Constitution. Then he objected to the provision that the acceptance of the document by nine states would institute the new government. He proposed that Congress be sent the plan, and if it was approved it should be sent to the governors of all the states, who would then submit it to their legislatures. If nine of them ratified it, it would take effect. Some of the members feared that the proposal would give Congress a chance to sabotage the new Constitution, either by not submitting it to the states or refusing to dissolve itself. The proposal also prepared the way for Randolph to threaten that he might reject the whole plan and propose that state conventions be allowed to offer amendments to be submitted to a second convention empowered to "settle the constitution finally." Wilson, with good sense, answered that "after spending four or five months in the laborious & arduous task of forming a Government for our country, we are ourselves at the close throwing insuperable obstacles in the way of its success."[31] Again, Hamilton's proposal was rejected.

Dr. Johnson and the committee on style submitted the Constitution to the convention on Wednesday, September 12. At this last moment, Williamson moved to reconsider the clause that required three-quarters of each house to override the veto of the president and to substitute two-thirds of each house. Hamilton agreed, and Madison went along with him. The proposal passed.

For several more days minor changes were proposed and debated, until on Saturday, the fifteenth, all agreed to accept the Constitution as amended. The task was almost completed when the delegates went home to rest on Sunday. On Monday, September 17, Benjamin Franklin, feeble but determined, rose with a written speech, which he gave to James Wilson to read for him. It was a plea to all members who still had objections to the new Constitution to do what he was doing, ". . . doubt a little of his own infallibility, and to make manifest our unanimity, put his name to this instrument."[32]

Hamilton also expressed his wish that every member should sign, lest refusal "kindle the latent sparks which lurk under an enthusiasm in favor of the constitution which may soon subside." Once again he reminded all that no man's ideas were more remote from the plan than his, but one could not "deliberate between anarchy on the one side and the chance of good on the other."[33]

Pleas for unanimity went unheard. Randolph, Mason and Gerry refused to sign, but all the members who were present did so. Alexander Hamilton, the only New York representative present at the close of the convention, signed for his state.

While the last members were putting their signatures on the document, Franklin looked at the president's chair, whose back was painted with a sun coming over the horizon. He said quietly to the few members near him that painters had difficulty distinguishing between a rising and a setting sun. Often during the session, the old man said, he had looked at the painted sun and wondered whether it was rising or setting. "But now," he remarked, "at length I have the happiness to know that it is a rising and not a setting sun."[34]

Supporters and critics of Alexander Hamilton alike have lamented his uneven, uninspired performance at the grand convention. Neither his minority position on the New York delegation nor his extremely individual plan for a powerful elitist government quite exonerate him from the charges. His role in the convention was bizarre and undistinguished. He missed opportunities to shine. He was absent during weeks of important debates. But, granted that Hamilton was a lesser light in Philadelphia, he became the sun, moon and stars in the cause of ratification. There is no more striking example in history of passionate commitment to a cause that its defender distrusted than Hamilton's to the United States Constitution.

As a final gesture of defiance, just before he left the convention,

Hamilton handed to Madison a constitution that he had developed during the meetings. It differed somewhat from the June 18 plan, but its greatest significance was that, although it was never offered to the members, its author was unwilling to throw it on the scrap heap or bury it among his own papers. It was the fruit of his frustration.

After he left Philadelphia, Hamilton appointed himself the conscience of New York, prime defender of the Constitution, which he saw as the one chance for uniting the country. In the process of accomplishing this crusade, Hamilton would win the fame that he had sought from boyhood. The rising sun that Franklin saw would be both Washington's and Hamilton's.

9

Hamilton as "Publius"

HAMILTON HAD STARTLED THE CONVENTION with so fervent an endorsement of the flawed Constitution that there was now no turning back. His colleagues, Yates and Lansing, explained their opposition in a letter to sympathetic Governor Clinton. The measures about to be accepted by "the body of respectable men" to whom their constituents had given "the most unequivocal proofs of confidence" were "destructive to the political happiness of the citizens of the United States," they said. The proposed Constitution consolidated the United States "into one government," whereas Yates and Lansing believed in the "preservation of the individual states and in their uncontrolled rights." Such a general government as the convention proposed would be destructive of the civil liberty of the citizens, unable to maintain obedience to the laws in the extremities of the United States, intolerably expensive to support, and unable to know or respond to the great majority of the inhabitants.[1]

The public became aware of the contents of the secretly composed Constitution as quickly as newspapers throughout the country could obtain copies and publish them. The document became the immediate object of passionate controversy, particularly since, to most, a completely rewritten, original Constitution was a total surprise. The newspapers filled their columns with debate in an outpouring of print. Were the people, after having fought for many years to free their thirteen states from British rule, now being asked to yield to another distant tyrant called the Union? It was obvious that ratification would not be simply a rubber stamp applied to the work of the demigods.

The part that Hamilton chose to play as defender of the Constitution made him the instant recipient of abuse from Clinton's Antifed-

eralists. The most caustic insults appeared in the *New-York Journal*
in September and October 1787, under the byline "Inspector." That
pseudonymous critic referred to Hamilton as "Tom S**T," "an
upstart attorney," "a blockhead" and "superficial self-conceited
coxcomb."[2]

Among the Clintonians' "many contemptible artifices" was "an insinuation that I *palmed* myself upon you and that you *dismissed* me
from your family," Hamilton wrote to Washington. He asked the
general to "put the matter in its true light." By return post, Washington declared that the charges against Hamilton were "entirely unfounded." Gratified, Hamilton assured Washington that the only use
he would make of the letter would be to put it in the hands of a few
friends.[3]

The two men exchanged information on the prospects for ratification in their respective states. In New York City, the new Constitution was as popular as it was possible for anything to be, Hamilton
told Washington. It even had favorable prospects throughout the
state, but once "the flood of official influence is let loose against it,"
the result became unpredictable. Washington, who had just returned
from Philadelphia, said that he had little information on the new
Constitution's general reception. It seemed to be popular in Alex-
andria and a few of the adjacent counties, but some of the most
important people in Virginia were in violent opposition to it. He was
referring to such prominent men as Patrick Henry, Richard Henry
Lee, James Monroe and Governor Randolph.[4]

The precise moment at which Hamilton conceived the idea of publishing a series of articles that would explain in detail the articles in
the Constitution and try to persuade people to support it is not
known. James Madison recorded that the idea for the essays was
Hamilton's and that he approached him, John Jay, William Duer and
Gouverneur Morris as collaborators. Madison and Jay accepted.
Morris was unwilling because he was too busy, and William Duer
submitted some sample efforts that were "intelligent and sprightly,"
Madison said, but not suitable for Publius's serious purpose.

Tradition tells that Alexander Hamilton composed the first Federalist paper in the cabin of a sloop sailing down the Hudson River
from Albany, where he had attended the fall session of the Supreme
Court. Whether true or not, neither the pressure of his legal practice
nor any other obstacle stopped Hamilton from producing a series of
brilliant political tracts, starting in October 1787 and continuing,
except for a break from April 2 to early May 1788, until his final
effort on May 28, 1788.

Publius, the pseudonym that the triumvirate used, was inspired by the life of Publius Valerius, founder of the Roman republic. Publius was known for his eloquence, which, Plutarch said, he employed in the service of justice. When Publius instituted the Roman republic, he resolved to introduce a government that would be "instead of terrible, familiar and pleasant to the people."[5]

A theory has been forwarded that Hamilton wrote the Federalist papers as a second thought, and his first thoughts on the new Constitution appeared under the signatuare of "Caesar" in answer to the letters of "Cato," to refute Cato's opposition to the Constitution. One reason for ready acceptance of Hamilton's authorship is that the Caesar letters corroborate his position of June 18 and reinforce the popular conception of Hamilton as a monarchist. Cato has been convincingly identified as George Clinton, although that identification has also been challenged. Hamilton himself did not suspect that Clinton was Cato; in a letter to Washington, written after the publication of the second Cato letter, he said that the governor had not publicly declared himself.[6]

A comparison of the style of Caesar and Publius reveals a marked difference. Caesar uses denunciatory invective, while Publius is full of sweet reason. Hamilton had not written in the style of Caesar since he was a fiery young Revolutionary answering the Farmer tracts. Further, the Caesar letters lack the rich lode of historical references and citations from the philosophers always present in Hamilton's work.

Evidence purporting to prove that Hamilton wrote the Caesar letters is derived from two documents uncovered by Paul Leicester Ford in 1892, both of which are no longer available. One is a letter supposedly written by Hamilton to an unknown on October 18, 1787.

Since my last the chief of the state party has declared his opposition to the government proposed, both in private conversation and in print. That you may judge of the *reason* and *fairness* of his views, I send you the two essays with a reply by Caesar. On further consideration it was concluded to abandon this personal form, and to take up the principles of the whole subject. These will be sent you as published and might with advantage be republished in your gazettes.

A. Hamilton[7]

According to Ford, the letter was in the handwriting of John Lamb, a Clintonian who was collector of customs for the Port of New York. As far as is known, no other scholar saw the letter, which was destroyed in 1911 in a fire that incinerated many priceless documents kept in the New York State Library. At first, the letter seems to clinch Ford's identification of Hamilton as Caesar, but more careful reading raises doubts.

Ford's second piece of evidence is even more questionable, since the significant phrases were written in the third person. He quoted, without a date, a notice that he alleged appeared in *The New-York Journal*.

A writer in the state of New-York, under the signature of *Cesar*, came forward against the the patriotic *Cato* and endeavoured to frighten him from starting any objections and threatened that '*Cato* would be followed by *Cesar* in all his marches;' but we find that as soon as ever *Cato* came freely to discuss the merit of the constitution *Cesar* retreated and disappeared: and since that a publication under the signature of Publius . . . has appeared in that state.[8]

Here, too, the meaning is not entirely clear. It is not stated, but rather suggested, that Caesar and Publius are the same person, and the name Hamilton is not used. The omission in the last line could alter the meaning of the whole notice, and what is very puzzling is that even after extensive research in the *Journal* and other contemporary newspapers, the notice was not found.

There are other indications that Hamilton did not write the Caesar letters. Both were obviously composed by the same person, but Hamilton was in Albany when the second letter was written. When, on October 19, 1780, "A Man of No Party" published "Remarks On Some Late Writings," in which he identified, in his own cryptic way, those who had been using pen names, he did not connect Hamilton with Caesar. On the contrary, he said that Hamilton should defend the Constitution himself, rather than depend on others to do it for him. In the same piece, Cato was revealed as "undoubted some little state sovereign," a not very subtle reference to Clinton. As Jacob E. Cooke said, ". . . without certain knowledge of the identity of the man who *did* write the Caesar letters," it is not impossible that Hamilton was the author, but he is "no more likely a candidate than other New York Federalists."[9]

The authorship of some of the Federalist papers is also controversial. Both Hamilton and Madison were reported to have made lists of their own contributions, but their claims are contradictory in the case of fifteen essays, leaving seventy properly assigned.* The

---

* Note: Hamilton wrote Numbers 1–6; 11–13; 15–17; 21–36; 59–61; 65–85. Madison wrote Numbers 10; 14; 37–48. Jay wrote Numbers 2–5 and 64.

essays in which authorship is in dispute are Numbers 18–20, 49–58 and 62–63.

There are four Madison lists available. The earliest was supplied by an anonymous author who signed himself "Corrector" to an article that appeared in *The National Intelligencer*, March 29, 1817, claiming that his list was copied "from a pencilled memorandum in the hands of Madison." Richard Rush, a Madison cabinet member, reported he had a list in his copy of *The Federalist*, for which he had a statement of authorship signed by Madison. And an article in the *City of Washington Gazette* of December 15, 1817, printed a list said to have been furnished by Madison himself. There is no evidence that Madison had anything to do with these three lists, but a fourth appears to be genuine. Jacob Gideon published an edition of *The Federalist* in 1818, based on "the copy of the work which that gentleman [James Madison] had preserved for himself," correctly assigning each essay to its rightful author.

The problem persists, however, because the authors themselves disagreed about which of the disputed pieces each had written. There are only three Hamilton lists that can be considered seriously: the Benson list, the Kent list and the list that Hamilton was said to have preserved in his own copy of *The Federalist*.

The Benson list is based on a romantic story. Reported by Hamilton's close friend and self-appointed apologist, William Coleman, in March 1817, it states that about two days before Hamilton's death, he visited his old friend, Judge Egbert Benson, at his office. Robert Benson, Jr., the judge's nephew and clerk, regretted that his uncle and Rufus King had gone to Massachusetts. Hamilton, while talking to the young man, almost surreptitiously toyed with a volume from the law office's shelves. After the fatal duel, Robert Benson remembered Hamilton's action on that day and, searching through the book he had handled, found inside it an unsigned paper in Hamilton's handwriting, listing the Federalist papers that he had written. Judge Benson reputedly pasted the list in his copy of *The Federalist*. Later, the book was given to the New York Society Library for safekeeping, but it disappeared with the list pasted in it in about 1818.

Coleman was not able to substantiate the story, and Robert Benson added only the recollection that the memorandum had been thrust by Hamilton into a volume of Pliny's *Letters*.

Why did Hamilton conceal the list in that curious manner? Perhaps he would have given it openly to Benson had he been in his office. Hamilton's real reason for visiting the judge was, very likely, to discuss the approaching duel. Although the existence of the list may be doubted, the visit did occur. Hiding the list would be consistent with the aura of secrecy with which both Burr and Hamilton enveloped their approaching encounter. Still, the evidence is thin for accepting the Benson list.

A more promising possibility rests on a notice published in the *Port Folio* on November 14, 1807, announcing that Hamilton's executors had deposited in the New York Public Library his copy of *The Federalist* "in which he has designated in his own handwriting, the parts of the celebrated work written by himself, as well as those contributed by Mr. *Jay* and Mr. *Madison*." Unfortunately, no one can attest to having seen the copy or to its existence. The list, as presented in the *Port Folio*, was the same as the Benson list.

Chancellor Kent, a devoted admirer of Hamilton, confused the controversy further by providing lists discovered on the inside covers of his copy of *The Federalist*. However, differences exists in the ink and pen that the chancellor used, and, even more puzzling, some of the numbers were written over, although not by Kent because the handwriting is not his. The editors of the Hamilton papers, after careful handwriting analysis, found strong indications that the changes in the numbers were made by Hamilton, thus making the Kent list the only evidence available in Hamilton's own hand. According to Kent's notes, Hamilton told him which papers he had written, but Kent confessed that he was not sure he remembered what Hamilton had told him, nor was he certain that Hamilton himself could remember accurately without looking at a copy of *The Federalist*. Further, the conversation took place after 1800 because Hamilton is referred to as "General," a rank he did not achieve until 1798, and the meeting took place in Albany, where Hamilton went after he resumed his law practice. It is reasonable to accept Hamilton's approval of Kent's list and equally reasonable to doubt Hamilton's memory. Consequently, no conclusion can be reached about authorship of the disputed papers based on the lists.[10]

Since both Hamilton and Madison employed similar arguments and, in fact, discussed many of the essays with each other, deducing authorship from internal evidence is also futile. Each historian tends to line up on the side of his favorite. John C. Hamilton awarded authorship of all the disputed papers to his father. The Madison supporters acquired a nonhuman ally, a computer. The computer analysis was based on the frequency with which certain words were used by each writer, and on a study of the words that one man used and not the other. Madison supporters accepted the study; Madison won the authorship of all the disputed papers. Hamiltonians remained unconvinced. After reading the eighty-five papers, what emerges is the realization that both authors wrote in much the same eighteenth-century style and followed the same line of reasoning, which they based on similar arguments. Mechanical evidence, programmed by man, is inconclusive in the light of serious, scholarly study.[11]

As for the mystery of the conflicting lists, Hamiltonians are at a disadvantage because Hamilton did not think about the matter until, if one accepts Benson's list, he was on the threshold of eternity. Others had to come to his defense later, when the question of authorship developed into controversy. Madison, still alive, was able to defend himself and marshal aid. As to the credibility of the two men, time dims the keenest memory. Even when Hamilton made his July 1804 list, if he did, the collaboration was already sixteen or seventeen years old.

The most judicious resolution of the dispute is to grant Madison Federalist 18, 19 and 20, based on the marginal note in his own copy of *The Federalist*. Madison wrote that although he and Hamilton had taken up the subject matter (ancient and modern confederacies), Hamilton had entered "more briefly into the subject." They agreed, therefore, that the subject be left to Madison. In these papers the size of Hamilton's contribution cannot be defined, but he did collaborate on them.[12]

The rest of the disputed papers cannot be awarded to Madison conclusively. Edward G. Bourne, who analyzed them carefully, attributed them to Madison. On the other hand, the claim of John C. Hamilton, who spent a lifetime exhaustively studying Hamilton's writings, that his father wrote them cannot be dismissed on filial grounds. Jacob E. Cooke's criteria—that Madison's claim was "definite" and Hamilton's "carefully made"—make the most sense. There it must rest, a fascinating enigma, and yield to a consideration of the contents of the Hamilton numbers.

"My Countrymen, I own to you, that, after having given it an attentive consideration, I am clearly of the opinion, it is your interest to adopt [the new Constitution]. I am convinced, that this is the safest course for your liberty, your dignity and your happiness. . . . I frankly acknowledge to you my convictions, and I will freely lay before you the reasons on which they are founded," Hamilton as Publius wrote in the first Federalist paper, which greeted the New

York public in the pages of its *Independent Journal* or the *General Advertiser*. The scope of Publius's work was carefully outlined: how the Union would promote political prosperity, the inability of the confederation to preserve the Union, the necessity for an "energetic" government to preserve the Union, the Constitution's conformity to "the true principles of republican government," the Constitution's analogy to the New York State constitution and the "additional security its adoption would give to the preservation of liberty and property.[13]

Hamilton and Madison believed that Publius's purpose was to convince, influence and enlighten. Since the Constitution had to be accepted in order to save the United States, their presentation had to explain the contents of the document in the most positive manner, while anticipating the arguments and reservations of the Antifederalists. They knew as experienced lawyers that they had to argue from a position of strength; to be effective, therefore, they sometimes soft-pedaled their extreme nationalism and emphasized the provisions that protected the power of the states. Though a polemic, in the sense that its chief purpose was to persuade, the tone of *The Federalist* is dignified and quiet.

Hamilton, the essays made clear, had not changed his perception of man. He spoke again of the capriciousness of the human mind and the tendency for men to be swayed by their passions, rather than by reason. In Federalist 35, he developed his social analysis and answered his opponents, the Antifederalists, who questioned the right of the rich and powerful merchants and landholders to represent the artisan and poor tenant. "It is said to be necessary that all classes of citizens should have some of their own number in the representative body, in order that their feelings and intents may be better understood and attended to." Hamilton argued that the merchant was the natural representative of the artisan, the landholder of the poorest tenant and the members of the learned professions, being impartial, the object of confidence to all. The lower classes, so to speak, "are sensible that their habits in life have not been such as to give them those acquired endowments, without which in deliberative assembly, the greatest natural abilities are for the most part useless."[14]

Elitism was widely accepted in the eighteenth century. To have actual representation of all classes would have been, as Hamilton said, "altogether visionary."[15]

In Federalist 15, Hamilton declared his nationalist credo. "If we adhere to the design of a national government . . . we must extend the authority of the union to the persons of the citizens—the only proper objects of government." If this was not done, the states, "thirteen distinct sovereign wills," would prevent the "complete execution of every important measure that proceeds from the Union. . . . Congress at this time scarcely possesses the means of keeping up the forms of administration."[16]

In speaking of the executive, Hamilton used his favorite word, "energy." Executive energy, he said, was a leading character in the definition of good government. The ingredients that constituted this priceless attribute were unity, duration, an adequate provision for support and competent powers. The executive should be personally responsible for his behavior in office. The longer the duration of his office the better, since "it is a general principle of human nature that a man will be interested in whatever he possesses, in proportion to the firmness or precariousness of the tenure, by which he holds it." The republican principle, Hamilton said, demanded that the executive have a sense of what the people want, but "it does not require an unqualified complaisance to every sudden breeze of passion, or to every transient impulse which the people may receive from the acts of men, who flatter their prejudices to betray their interests." The people usually "*intend* the PUBLIC GOOD," but they sometimes were mistaken. Therefore, those who had been appointed the guardians of their interests had to withstand their "temporary delusions" and give them time for cooler reflection. This concept of stewardship was an aristocratic principle derived from the British crown.[17]

In Federalist 78, Hamilton presented the concept of judicial review, which became, at a later date under Supreme Court Justice John Marshall, one of the unique contributions of the American constitutional system. Reinforcing the doctrine of separation of powers, Hamilton granted to the judiciary the final word on the constitutionality of laws passed by Congress. The courts, said Hamilton, were designed "to be an intermediate body between the people and the legislature . . . in order . . . to keep the latter within the limits assigned to their authority. . . . A constitution is in fact and must be, regarded by the judges as a fundamental law." The judges had to ascertain its meaning and the meaning of any act passed by the legislature. Therefore, "if there should happen to be an irreconcilable variance between the two, the Constitution ought to be preferred to the statute. The intention of the people to the intention of their agents."[18] Otherwise, the people's rights and privileges would amount to nothing and be subject to the acts of the particular legislature, so that judicial review was an implied if unspoken part of the Constitution.

Hamilton had defended the need for a strong judiciary in an earlier essay. He pointed out that the lack of a judiciary had been a major defect of the Articles of Confederation. "Laws are a dead letter without courts to expound and define their true meaning and operation," he wrote. The courts were to be a bulwark of the Constitution and a protection against legislative invasions of the Constitution. Judges had life terms so that they might be "a safeguard against the effects of occasional ill humours in the society." They not only served to moderate "the immediate mischiefs" of such laws but also served as a "check upon the legislative body in passing them."[19]

The bitter ideological clash between Hamilton and Thomas Jefferson was foreshadowed in Federalist 84, in which Hamilton explained the absence of a bill of rights in the new Constitution. In a letter to Madison in December 1787, the American minister to France wrote: "A bill of rights is what the people are entitled to against every government on earth, general or particular, and what no just government should refuse or rest on inference."[20]

The Constitution contained such rights, Hamilton argued. Among them was the privilege of habeas corpus, which, Blackstone said, was "the *Bulwark* of the British constitution" and guaranteed against bills of attainder and ex post facto laws. The guarantee of trial by jury and a defined, limited treason law were included, as well as a prohibition against titles of nobility, "the cornerstone of republican government; for so long as they are excluded, there can never be serious danger that the government will be any other than that of the people."[21]

Hamilton dismissed the need for a bill of rights with a few terse statements. Bills of rights were "stipulations between kings and their subjects," such as the British Magna Carta and Petition of Rights. They had no application to a Constitution founded upon the power of the people. "The people surrender nothing, and they retain everything, they have no need of particular reservations." A bill of rights might be dangerous. "For why declare that things shall not be done which there is no power to do?" As to liberty of the press, a much discussed topic, Hamilton wrote with some asperity: What was the liberty of the press? It could have no definition without "latitude for evasion." Its security, therefore, "must altogether depend on public opinion, and on the general spirit of the people and of the government," which was "the only solid basis of all of our rights." In conclusion, Hamilton asserted, "the constitution is itself in every rational sense, and to every useful purpose, A Bill of Rights."[22]

Hamilton's final appeal for ratification said: "A *Nation* without a *National Government* is, in my view, an awful spectacle. The establishment of a constitution, in time of profound peace, by the voluntary consent of a whole people is a *Prodigy*, to the completion of which I look forward with trembling anxiety."

The publication of the essays in the newspapers required meeting deadlines so stringent that there was seldom time for the authors to read their own copy. Since, in March 1788, Madison had to leave New York to prepare for the ratification fight in the Virginia convention, Hamilton had to take full charge of publication details. Archibald McLean, the printer, said that Hamilton had at first contracted for twenty to twenty-five numbers, so that when the essays were published as a book, instead of one slim volume, there were two volumes of more than 600 pages. The set, costing six shillings, did not at first have a large sale but later went into several editions and was translated into many languages.

The influence of *The Federalist* on the ratification of the Constitution is debatable. After the first number appeared in the *New-York Independent Journal* on October 27, 1787, other numbers appeared there at various intervals, and in the *New-York Daily Advertiser* and the *New-York Journal and Daily Patriotic Register*. There were seven New York City newspapers publishing at the time, of which four carried the Federalist essays. In the rest of New York State, twenty-three numbers appeared in Albany papers, eleven in the *Hudson Weekly Gazette* and seven in the Poughkeepsie *Country Journal*. Only sixteen newspapers and one magazine outside of New York City printed numbers of *The Federalist*: four each in Massachusetts, New York and Virginia; two in Pennsylvania; and one each in Rhode Island and New Hampshire. And no more than twenty-four of the eighty-five papers were printed outside of New York City, mostly the earlier ones.[23]

Not only was the audience for the papers distressingly small, but in some states the essays did not appear until after ratification. The consensus was that they were too abstruse and complex for general consumption. One contemporary writer commented that Publius was not "intelligible to the common reader." Louis Otto, the French chargé in New York, was very harsh in his denunciation of the work. It was "of no use to learned people and too sophisticated and too long for the ignorant."[24]

For the most part, the general public was not aware of Publius, but the papers were read and discussed by many of the delegates to the state conventions. Madison requested Hamilton to send forty trade copies of Volume One of the printed edition of *The Federalist* and twelve finer copies to Governor Randolph for circulation among the Virginia delegates. Hamilton sent Benjamin Rush, who with James Wilson spearheaded the movement for adoption in the Pennsylvania ratifying convention, copies of the early numbers. In his cover letter, he wrote that they might have a good effect on some of the Quaker members and, if he did not want them, to forward them to some southern members.[25]

Local leaders were influenced by the Federalist essays because the New York papers circulated throughout the United States. Therefore, it is likely that Federalist leaders, whether in Boston or Richmond, "took their cues from Publius as he made his way up and down the eastern seaboard."[26]

George Washington forecast the destiny of Publius's work. "When the transient circumstances & fugitive performances which attended the *crisis* shall have disappeared, that work [the Federalist Papers] will merit the notice of Posterity; because in it are candidly discussed the principles of freedom & the topics of government, which will always be interesting to mankind so long as they shall be connected in Civil Society."[27]

Hamilton must be given the lion's share of credit for the work of Publius. He conceived the idea, wrote the greatest number of the papers and saw to their publication. While the identity of Publius was still secret, James Kent wrote that he must be Alexander Hamilton, "who in genius and political research is not inferior to Gibbon, Hume and Montesquieu."

The task of turning out the Federalist papers would pale beside Hamilton's next project. New York had not yet ratified when the last Federalist paper was published, and there was a likelihood that the Empire State would reject the document. No greater challenge ever faced Hamilton. He was the acknowledged leader of the Federalists in a hostile state and about to attend a convention in which his side was outnumbered. Poughkeepsie would be the scene of a great triumph or a great defeat for him, as well as for the Constitution. Hamilton cared deeply about the future success of the country, but he realized that his own future was at a crossroads as well. If there was to be a new government and if New York was among its supporters, there would assuredly be an important place in it for Alexander Hamilton.

10

"The Political Porcupine"

PUBLIUS HAD DONE what he could to publicize and explain the new Constitution. Madison was concerned about opposition in Virginia, but that state's Federalists had the support of General Washington and Governor Randolph, both of whom had been present in Philadelphia. New York, on the other hand, had Governor Clinton, who pretended to be undecided but was immovably hostile to ratification.

It was not until January 11, 1788, that the New York State legislature met to discuss the Philadelphia convention's call for a state ratifying convention. By that time, Delaware, Pennsylvania, New Jersey, Georgia and Connecticut had ratified. In his opening address to the legislature, Clinton casually mentioned the congressional act that called for transmitting the proceedings of the Philadelphia convention to the legislatures of the states. At the same time, he submitted the Yates and Lansing letter, which gave their reasons for withdrawing from the constitutional convention. Clinton said piously, "From the nature of my office you will easily perceive it would be improper for me to have any other agency in this business than that of laying the papers respecting it before you for your information."[1]

Clinton's strategy all along had been to make no public statements against the Philadelphia convention, but Hamilton was convinced that his real foe was George Clinton. Hamilton wrote to Gouverneur Morris and to Madison of word received through secret channels that Clinton believed the Union to be unnecessary. The governor was a power-hungry despot who had a closed mind to the new Constitution because it would limit his power, Hamilton said.[2] He had gauged his enemy correctly. The governor would emerge, finally, as an Antifederalist par excellence.

The Antifederalists were just as wary of Hamilton as he was of
Clinton. Melancton Smith worried that the Antifederalist majority in
both houses of the legislature might represent less control than the
numbers indicated. At the beginning of the session, the assembly
chose only one Antifederalist, Abraham Yates, for the new state delegation to the Continental Congress. The other delegates, Egbert
Benson, Leonard Gansevoort, Ezra L'Hommedieu and Alexander
Hamilton, were all Federalists. Smith reflected on the superior skill
of the Federalists and the need to watch Hamilton and Schuyler
carefully. "The *better sort* have means of *convincing* those who differ
from them. . . . And how prevalent these means may be, I cannot
pretend to say, I confess I fear their power."[3]

Hamilton's appointment to the Continental Congress was a political
victory but otherwise a nuisance. As the number of state ratifications
increased, Congress became increasingly reluctant to undertake serious business. Consequently, Hamilton did not take his seat in the
ruling body until February 25, 1788, and between then and October
attended irregularly. The New York State ratifying convention
needed his full attention. When he and his colleagues were elected to
Congress, the Antis hoped that the strong Federalist quartet would
be removed from the state scene, but the Federalists had planned
their strategy carefully.

Egbert Benson opened consideration of the Philadelphia resolutions by offering a startling motion to the assembly. He proposed that
the number of delegates to the ratifying convention equal the number of assemblymen in the state legislature and that they be elected
by "all free male citizens of the age of twenty-one and upwards." The
meeting, he suggested, should be held on the third Thursday in June
at the Poughkeepsie courthouse. To the surprise of Benson and his colleagues, the resolution was adopted.

The provision for universal manhood suffrage was unique among
the states; most restricted the ballot to those usually qualified to vote
for members of the lower house of the state legislature. Since the
resolution passed with no debate in the assembly and very little
opposition in the senate, it appears that most of the legislators
thought that the decision on ratification of the new Constitution
should be made by the vote of the people. But the New York electorate was already broad-based, and "in practice men were rarely
turned away from the polls even if they did not qualify under the
suffrage law." Furthermore, many were annoyed that the subject of
ratification took up so much space in the newspapers. Intelligent

voting on the issue was handicapped by illiteracy, as high as 50 percent in some areas of New York State. "Timolean" in the *New-York Journal* said: "At this crisis . . . the minds of men are *on one side violently agitated and active,* on the other and the greater part, *a sleepy indolence and inattention seems to prevail.*"[4]

Abraham Yates, the Antifederalist leader in the senate, tried to attach a statement to the assembly resolution to censure the Philadelphia convention. The people should know that the delegates "went beyond their powers," he argued. He would propose rejecting it forever, except that the other states let it go to the people. Philip Schuyler let Yates's harangue continue to the end. Then he arose and observed quietly that Yates had provided the legislators with no new information and that everyone on the continent was well acquainted with the resolutions upon which the constitutional convention had been called. At the final vote, Yates was ignored, and the Benson resolution passed by a majority of four.[5]

The decision of the New York State legislature, to delay election of members to the Poughkeepsie convention until April and the meeting until June, was seen as advantageous by both sides. The Federalists predicted that a number of other states would have ratified by then, making New York State ratification more compelling. The Antis, on the other hand, viewed delay as an opportunity to mount a vigorous campaign of seven months.

The paper war started as soon as the date for elections of delegates to the Poughkeepsie convention was revealed. Newspapers and broadsides were the mass media at the time, with broadsides more effective; they were much cheaper to produce and more easily distributed. Outside the cities there were few newspapers, but handbills could be distributed at meetings and in country stores or just nailed up on trees and fences along public roads. Dame rumor was another effective propaganda tool. The Antifederalists played on the people's fear of royalty by whispering that George III's son, Prince William Henry, was on his way from Canada to mount the American throne, or that the American army was about to leave for France to pay off the congressional debt.

The Federalists spread their own propaganda, emphasizing Washington's enthusiastic support of the proposed Constitution. Less admirable were the tactics of an enthusiast such as Judge William Cooper. He admitted freely that he "went around to the people and told them that they owed him, and that unless they voted for Mr. Jay, he would ruin them."[6]

The situation in New York was complicated by the split in allegiance of the leading families. The Livingstons fell out, causing a schism between the manor and the Clermont branches. Philip Schuyler tried to persaude Henry Livingston not to run for the Poughkeepsie convention and to yield to Edward Livingston, the chancellor's popular younger brother, but Henry refused. Furthermore, the manor lords had enemies among their own tenantry who resented them and were glad of the opportunity to vote against them.[7]

By April, tension over the election was so great that the New York delegates to Congress returned home to campaign. Both the Federalist and Antifederalist candidates rode around the countryside, speaking to any audiences that could be rounded up and handing out a storm of handbills. The Federalists hired outriders "to collect the freeholders and freemen of the quarter to meet them at a certain place *to confer on the constitution.*" The Antifederalists would follow after, wait their turn and then speak to the crowd, getting in the last word. A week before the election, John Jay could only lament that the outcome was "problematical."[8]

The election results were so devastating to the Federalists that silence was their only response. Albany, where the Feds had made a major effort, did not elect one of them to their delegation. Of the sixty-five delegates to be sent to Poughkeepsie, only nineteen were Federalists. New York City elected nine; two came from Kings County and two from Richmond County. There were six unexpected seats from Westchester, but the northern counties were unanimously Antifederalist; it was a complete rejection of the Dutch patroons. Hamilton had written to Madison several weeks before the election of a gradual swing on the part of the people toward acceptance of the Constitution. It was coming too late to influence the election, but it had to be cultivated. An analysis of the voting results bears out Hamilton's perception. The Antis' margin of victory was not as large as was assumed at the time. They had won only 56 percent of the votes.[9]

The election awarded forty-six seats from nine counties to the Antifederalists. The one faint hope that Hamilton discerned was that some of the delegates were not completely committed. Though chosen because of their position on the new Constitution, they were not expected to be mere rubber stamps; they were expected to go to Poughkeepsie to debate their opinions with their opponents and to come to a final decision after due deliberation.

Poughkeepsie was a busy port on the Hudson River with a population of nearly 3,000, the most frequently used state capital since Kingston had been burned by the British in 1777. Hamilton was thoroughly familiar with it; he often went there to try his law cases.

On June 14, the Federalist contingent embarked from New York City, attended by a madly cheering throng. Hamilton was probably among the delegates who set out on the eighty-mile sail up the river. On the same day, the Antifederalist delegation, led by Governor Clinton, arrived at the dockyard to board a vessel bound for Poughkeepsie. All was quiet. Throughout the convention period, the New York City Federalists, by word and deed, supported their representatives in the struggle for ratification.

The Federalists were at a numerical disadvantage going into the convention, but Hamilton had planned the battle as carefully as a war campaign. The arrows in the Federalist quiver were the hope for previous ratification by nine states, the requirement for adoption of the new Constitution and a change in the sentiments of the people. "We shall leave nothing undone to cultivate a favorable disposition in the citizens at large," Hamilton said.[10]

Particularly significant to the success of Hamilton's plan was ratification by New Hampshire and Virginia. Early in June, Hamilton had written to John Sullivan, president of the New Hampshire ratifying convention, that knowledge of his state's ratification would be of great help to the cause in New York. Once a favorable vote had been obtained, Hamilton asked Sullivan to send the news by express rider to Poughkeepsie. "Let him take the *shortest route* to that place, change horses on the road, and use all possible diligence. I shall with pleasure defray all expenses, and give a liberal reward to the person."[11]

Virginia was still not decided, an ominous threat, Hamilton believed. He prayed that she would accede, for her example "will have a vast influence on our politics." He arranged for prompt receipt of news from Virginia.

As time went on, Hamilton had hopeful tidings about New Hampshire ratification. Rufus King wrote from Boston that he had arranged for an express to carry the New Hampshire results to Springfield, Massachusetts, and from there, General Knox had engaged a conveyance to bring word to Poughkeepsie. The decision will be "as we wish," and New Hampshire's acceptance will put "your Convention in a new and indeed an extraordinary light." As added encouragement, King declared that the people of Massachusetts were entirely satisfied with ratification, which had been achieved in February.[12]

In Virginia, the policy was to spin out the session to find out what
New York was doing or "to weary members into adjournment," Madison informed Hamilton. The two parties in Virginia were balanced
almost equally, but if the Antis should win, it would be because of
Kentucky, which was unanimously against the Constitution. Henry
Lee, another Virginia Federalist, wrote that the Feds' majority, if
they had one, was very small; still, he was pretty certain that the
outcome was safe unless adjournment became the issue, in which
case, "love of home may move some of our friends to abandon their
principles."[13]

If necessary, Hamilton was prepared to try to convince the Antifederalists that New York's failure to accept the new system would
rend the Union into northern and southern factions. When he tried
out this ploy on Yates, that gentleman declared to Abraham Lansing
that it had no effect on him.

The first gathering of the New York delegation took place at the
newly completed courthouse situated on the west side of Market
Place between Main and Union streets. The two-story-high building
was made of stone and crowned by a graceful cupola. The sixty-five
members of the convention were easily accommodated in the large
courtroom, which was spacious enough to hold about two hundred
visitors as well.

After the delegates assembled at the courthouse on June 17, they
elected Gov. George Clinton president of the convention by a
unanimous vote. The Antifederalists were pleased that their leader
was so recognized, and the Federalists preferred their most distinguished opponent in a position where he could not easily enter the
debate. Unlike the Philadelphia convention, the New York delegates
decided to keep their doors open to the public and to start their daily
sessions with a prayer. The only other business of the day was to
appoint two Federalists, James Duane and Richard Morris, and three
Antifederalists, Samuel Jones, John Lansing and John Haring, to
prepare the rules to be presented to the group on the following day.

Twelve rules were prepared and adopted on the eighteenth, and
the entire Constitution was read to the delegates. It was decided that
the debate would begin the next day.

On Thursday, June 19, at 10 A.M., the convention got down to
business, to debate the pros and cons of the proposed Constitution.
Though Hamilton had the greatest claim to the keynote speech, as
the only man in the state to have signed the Constitution and the
instigator of the Annapolis convention, he had not been asked. Once
again he was reminded that he was a foreigner, a newcomer and a

member of the aristocracy only by marriage. The opening speech was delivered by Robert R. Livingston, the chancellor of New York State, a noted orator and, above all, a Livingston.

Directing his attention particularly to "those gentlemen present, who have yet formed no decided opinion," he told them that New York was already unpopular for her wealth, and were she outside the Union, her position would be dangerous.

Although the speech provided a flow of vivid imagery, it was flawed by tactlessness and a certain condescending air. The conclusion was unfortunate. "Many of us, Sir," the chancellor said, addressing Clinton, "are officers of government, many of us have seats in the Senate and the Assembly—let us on this solemn occasion forget the pride of office. . . . As magistrates we may be unwilling to sacrifice any portion of the power of the State—as citizens we have no interest in advancing the powers of the State at the expense of the Union."[14]

After completing his address, Livingston handed a resolution to the chair. In the handwriting of both Livingston and Hamilton, it proposed that no vote be taken on the new Constitution until it had been considered clause by clause. Oddly enough, the Antifederalists went along with the proposal, thereby winning precious time for their opponents during which Virginia or New Hampshire could become the essential ninth pillar to the "Grand Foederal Edifice." Livingston's speech was pompous and antagonistic, but he achieved a coup with his proposition—at least three weeks of debate.

The Antis were quite prepared to go through the charade of a reasonable, thoughtful convention. The *Country Journal* (Poughkeepsie) wrote that the hundred or two hundred spectators who had come to Poughkeepsie to attend the convention were enjoying "a mental feast exquisite as uncommon. The first geniuses of the country have here a field on which their powers have ample room."[15] Governor Clinton was providing his people with an edifying spectacle, while satisfying the requirements of Congress and demonstrating that New York was not going to issue an unconsidered negative vote.

Hamilton spent the early days of the convention talking incessantly to anyone who would listen. Philip Schuyler, at his son-in-law's request, stayed in town. Although anxious to aid the cause, he was not hopeful about the result. New Hampshire's acceptance of the Constitution, he believed, would bring New York into the Union, but he expected that acceptance would be conditional, either quid pro quo amendments or an adjournment "under pretense of taking the sense of the constituents."[16]

On Friday, June 20, Hamilton gave his first major speech to the convention. His most formidable opponent at the Poughkeepsie convention was Melancton Smith, a Long Islander and a successful lawyer and merchant. Smith had served as a captain in the Dutchess County militia during the Revolution and had been for some months a member of the Continental Congress. Before moving to New York City, he had lived in Poughkeepsie, where he served as sheriff. Smith was called the most responsible and prominent of the Antifederalist speakers, incomparable in his powers of "acute and logical discussion," with a style that was "dry, plain and syllogistic." He had the ability to "entice his opponent into a subtle web from which it was difficult to extricate himself."

Smith's first argument presented the theme he repeated throughout the debates. He doubted frankly whether the new Constitution was a good one. At the moment, he objected to the three-fifths compromise that allowed slaves to be included in apportionment of congressional seats, although they were excluded from any participation in the government. He also wanted an increase in the total number of representatives in the House of Representatives.

The *Country Journal*, in a burst of effusive rhetoric, characterized Hamilton's impact on the convention: "He stands the political porcupine, armed at all points, and brandishes a shaft to every opposer. A shaft, powerful to repel and keen to wound."[17] Hamilton shot his first quill at Smith, using the principles of the Union as his theme.

In part one of the speech of June 20, Hamilton maintained that the old confederation could not become the basis of a new system. "Will any man who entertains a wish for the safety of his country, trust the sword and the purse with a single Assembly organized on principles so defective—so rotten? . . . A government totally different must be instituted." There had to be two branches with divided powers to check each other. "This was the result of their [the constitutional convention's] wisdom; and I presume that every reasonable man will agree to it."[18]

The next morning, John Williams, an Antifederalist from Clinton county, and Melancton Smith replied to Hamilton's speech. When Hamilton was recognized again, he went on with his arguments in a carefully considered manner. He flattered his audience deliberately by avoiding rhetoric and depending on reason. "Sir, we hear constantly a great deal which is rather calculated to awaken our passions and create prejudice, than to conduct us to the truth and treat us to our real interests."[19]

In answer to the Antifederalist proposal to increase the size of the

House of Representatives so that each congressman would represent 20,000 instead of the proposed 30,000, Hamilton appealed to his opponents' common sense. Understanding fully their wish for adequate representation of the many groups in American society, he asked, by what rule of reasoning was it determined "that one man is a better representative for twenty than for thirty thousand?" Yes, a very small number of representatives would give some "colour for suspicion"; ten would be unsafe, one thousand too numerous. "But I ask him why will not ninety-one be an adequate and safe representation?" Again, he rehearsed the argument of adequate checks and balances by the president on Congress, by the two houses of Congress on each other. By these means and the "obvious and powerful protection in their own State governments" there is no danger from "the madness of tyranny. . . . Sir, the danger is too distant, it is beyond all rational calculations."[20]

An honorable gentleman observed that a pure democracy, if practical, would be the most practical government. Hamilton answered that "experience has proved that no position in politics is more false than this." Later, he asked why an aristocracy was often mentioned. "For my part, I hardly know the meaning of this word as it is applied. . . . But who are the aristocracy among us? Where do we find men elevated to a perpetual rank above their fellow citizens; and possessing powers entirely independent of them? The arguments of the gentlemen only go to prove that there are men who are rich, men who are poor, some who are wise, and others who are not—That indeed every distinguished man is an aristocrat."[21]

The immediate result of Hamilton's speech was inconclusive. Its eloquence was appreciated by even so prejudiced a listener as De Witt Clinton, the governor's nephew. But George Clinton had not succumbed to the oratory. He continued to believe that there was more safety in the state than in a strong federal government. Hamilton answered that "from New Hampshire to Georgia, the people of America are as uniform in their interests and manners as those of any established in Europe." Though at first there might be some difficulty because of difference in interests, these varying interests "will be constantly assimilating, till they embrace each other and assume the same complexion."[22]

Hamilton was tireless in his battle for ratification. After holding the floor most of the day, he reported the progress to Madison, who was fighting a similar battle in Virginia. "The only good information I can give you is that we shall be some time together and take the chance

of events," Hamilton told Madison. The objective of the Antifederalists, he realized, was to force conditional amendments through the
convention. Good news could come only from outside Poughkeepsie.
Virginia was still not entirely certain, and Madison's "indisposition"
was also a worry. He did, however, agree with the Virginian that
adoption by New Hampshire was certain.[23]

On June 23, when the convention met again, the debate became
acrimonious. Jay, sensing danger, made a conciliatory speech that
was much admired. "My earnest wish is, that we may go home attended with the pleasing consciousness that we have industriously
and candidly sought the truth, and have done our duty." A spectator
commented on Jay's speechmaking, saying that though a stranger to
passion and all the other tricks of the orator, yet no one heard Jay
but was pleased by him "and captivated beyond expression."[24]

The next day, Gilbert Livingston attacked the proposed Senate as
a potentially dangerous body of men being given an excess of power.
He offered an amendment. "No person shall be eligible for more than
six years in any term of twelve years"; the state legislatures would
have the power to recall a senator and to replace him for the rest of
the term. Eventually, Hamilton got the floor and delivered a major
address on the powers of the Senate.

Instability had been a defective feature of most republican systems, he argued. The Senate, under the new constitution, would
avoid this malady by achieving continuity. The proposed amendment, on the other hand, "will render the senator a slave to all the
capricious humours among the people." State legislatures were "the
image of the multitude," so that the same prejudices and factions
would prevail. The purposes of the Senate had to be realized. In
foreign affairs, for example, "the knowledge is not soon acquired. . . .
Is it desirable then that new and unqualified members should be
continually thrown into that body?"[25]

On June 25, while Hamilton was hammering away at Livingston's
amendment, good news was on its way. Under this amendment, Hamilton stressed, the senators would be constantly "attended with a
reflection that their future existence is absolutely in the power of the
States. Will this not form a powerful check?" Furthermore, a constant rotation would produce many disadvantages fatal to the prosperity of the country.[26] The speech failed in its purpose. The
Clintonians could not be dissuaded from their fixed belief that the proposed Senate would become an entrenched power, far removed from
the needs and interests of the people of New York.

That day Hamilton received a letter from John Langdon of Concord, New Hampshire, informing him that on June 21, New Hampshire had adopted the federal Constitution by a majority of eleven votes. Fifty-seven had voted yes; forty-six had voted no. Chancellor Livingston announced the news to the convention, pointing out that ratification of New Hampshire, the ninth state, had dissolved the confederation and established the new government under the Constitution.

Melancton Smith allowed the Federalists no joy from the news. He said that the change in circumstances had not altered his feelings on the subject. He had long been convinced that nine states would accept the Constitution. It should not influence deliberations, said Lansing, for "it is still our duty to maintain our rights." New York's dissent could not prevent the operation of the government since nine states acceded, but "let them make the experiment."[27]

Now Hamilton and his friends had to assess the possibility that New York might choose to stay outside the Union. Hamilton felt the responsibility for achieving New York ratification even more heavily.

"The Antis are firm and I hope and believe will remain so to the End," Governor Clinton wrote to Abraham Yates, who was in New York City attending the Continental Congress. Yates wrote back with equal firmness: "Even if all twelve of the other states ratify the Constitution, New York ought not to."[28]

The will of the convention was to continue as before with the paragraph-by-paragraph reading. There were no objections until Section 8, Article 1 was reached. John Williams spoke at great length against the power given to Congress to lay and collect taxes, duties and imposts, and offered an amendment that would greatly curtail federal taxing power. Melancton Smith endorsed the proposal, believing that without restraint on Congress, in no time individual states would not be allowed to raise any money at all. Williams agreed and stated further that extending such taxing power to Congress would "annihilate the state government."[29]

Hamilton tried to persuade his listeners to shed their passions on the subject of the impost and give the matter "cool examination. . . . It is more easy for the human mind to calculate the evils than the advantages of a measure; and vastly more natural to apprehend the danger than to see the necessity of giving power to our rulers." He tried to calm the Antis with the assurance that "the Authority of Congress to make laws which were to be the Supreme Law of the Land, did not imply that State Laws where they have concurrent Jurisdiction should not also be Supreme."[30]

While keeping up his spirits during the meetings by orating

fiercely, in the evenings Hamilton often fell into a depression. Madison became his confidant. "Our only chance of success depends on you," he wrote on June 27. The adoption of the Constitution by New Hampshire was not enough to sway New York. "There are some slight symptoms of relaxation in some of the leaders; which authorises a gleam of hope, if you do well; but certainly I think not otherwise."[31]

Hamilton's arguments were a repetition of his utterances as Publius, but his eloquence was inspired in part by animosity against Clinton and his former colleagues, Lansing and Yates. The memory of his position at the federal convention as a minority member of the New York State delegation still rankled.

The Clintonites hoped to trap Hamilton by recalling his strong statements against the states, made in Philadelphia. The Federalists then read excerpts from official state papers and speeches of Governor Clinton's, made during the Revolutionary War, in which he deplored the weakness of the Continental Congress, particularly its inability to meet costs, thereby passing the burden on to the state.

In a peroration directed to the sympathies of the audience, Hamilton declared that the long speeches he had been making had exhausted him and perhaps made him too vehement in the warmth of his feelings. For this he wanted to apologize. His candor won so much sympathy from the audience that Hamilton let down his reserve in a rare moment of self-revelation in his reply to the accusation that he would benefit from the new system by acquiring rank and power. "If, today I am among the favored few, my children, tomorrow, may be among the oppressed many. . . . The changes in the human condition are uncertain and frequent. Many on whom fortune has bestowed their favors, may trace their family to a more unprosperous station; and many who are now in obscurity may look back upon the affluent and exalted rank of their ancestors." It was unfair to look on the advocates of the Constitution as influenced by "ambitious views," he charged.[32]

Angered by the Federalist attack on Clinton, Lansing recalled Hamilton's assertion during the Philadelphia convention that state governments ought to be subverted or reduced to mere corporations. Now, said Lansing, Hamilton says that state governments are necessary to the preservation of liberty. Hamilton disputed Lansing vigorously, maintaining that his ideas had been the same during both conventions.

The two opponents became irate. Hamilton called Lansing's insinuation "improper, unbecoming and uncandid." Lansing rose to deny the imputation and to appeal to Yates, who had taken notes at the Philadelphia convention, for proof of the accuracy of his report on Hamilton's words. Angry shouts met Yates's remarks. The chairman had to call for order. Further unpleasantness was avoided by a motion to adjourn.

At three o'clock in the morning of July 2, Colonel Henley rode into New York City, carrying the news that Virginia had ratified the Constitution. The bells rang out and continued their pealing until dawn, when ten volleys were fired to commemorate the ten states that had ratified the Constitution.

Anxious that the embattled Federalists in Poughkeepsie receive the good tidings as quickly as possible, William Livingston mounted his spirited bay horse and started out for the convention city. About nine hours later, the exhausted horse and rider arrived at the courthouse with the fateful packet, which Livingston handed to the doorkeeper.

George Clinton was speaking when Livingston was spotted standing in the doorway. All eyes turned to him, and the news traveled so quickly through the room that the buzz drowned out the governor's voice. The Federalists gave a loud cheer, while outside the building a procession of townspeople circled the courthouse to the accompaniment of fife and drum.

Still, the Antis, relying on their numerical superiority, continued the clause-by-clause reading, with an eye to making amendments. Hamilton commented to Madison that "our arguments confound but do not convince. Some of the leaders [Antifederalist] however appear to me to be convinced *by circumstances* and to be desirous of retreat. This does not apply to the Chief who wishes to establish *Clintonism* on the basis of Antifoederalism."[33]

New tactics had to be devised. Antifederalist Nathaniel Lawrence wrote to John Lamb that the information from Virginia had no effect on us, but "they have quietly suffered us to propose our amendments without a word in opposition to them. What their object is I know not." Fortunately for the Federalists, there was a Fourth of July adjournment. The two opposing factions did not let their differences spoil the annual day of rejoicing. Members of both parties dined together and toasted the twelfth birthday of the United States. One participant said that the spirit of the convention had changed from "angry debate" to "cool reasoning" and that matters were likely "to take a favorable turn."[34]

The holiday amiability of the delegates was not sufficient to soothe

the impatience of the citizenry, who had had enough of the convention's delay. In Albany, a violent confrontation took place between the two factions in which bayonets, swords, clubs and stones were used. One person was killed, and eighteen were injured. "The Antifederalists were the aggressors and the Foederalists the victors," Hamilton told Madison.[35]

The resumption of debate resulted in tedious sessions on technicalities. Since they could no longer defeat the new Constitution, the Antifederalists decided to reform it. They became convinced that their amendments, now five in number, would result in "a nearly perfect system."

The Federalists were wary of the road to amendment. Madison had written to Hamilton, enclosing the Virginia act of ratification, which had appended to it a number of recommendations and, he felt, highly objectionable amendments. Before the end of the Virginia meeting, Patrick Henry and George Mason had introduced a Bill of Rights, consisting of twenty articles plus two other amendments. "My conjecture is that exertions will be made to engage two thirds of the Legislature in the task of regularly undermining the government," Madison warned. "This hint may not be unworthy of your attention."[36]

Hamilton answered Madison with felicitations and his own misgivings about "the business of amendment making." The system "will be wounded in some of its vital parts" in that way, particularly in the power of taxation.

On July 12, Hamilton gave an impassioned address. The day before, Jay had argued forcibly for a resolution to adopt the Constitution. It was part of the plan to capitalize on the certain knowledge of a moderate wing among the Antis that favored adoption of the Constitution with conditions.

Again using the personal approach, Hamilton touched on the efforts to prejudice the convention against him. He pointed out that rumors had been circulated stating that he was an ambitious man, "unattached to the interests and insensible to the feelings of the people," without integrity or virtue. In a "pathetic appeal" that "fixed the silent sympathetic gaze of the spectators, and made them all his own," Hamilton said that in no instance "had he ever deviated from the line of public or private duty."

He pointed out that the convention's proposal to accept the Constitution only on its own terms was unacceptable. A partial rejection was a total rejection; the other states would not tolerate New York's conditions but would consider her action a means of exerting a kind of commercial tyranny. Once again, Hamilton went over his arguments for the Constitution and, finally, entreated the assembly "in a pathetic strain to make a solemn pause, and weigh well what they were about to do." A pro-Federalist newspaper noted that the "unprejudiced spectator" applauded and admired the speech, while opponents remained embittered and obstinate.[37]

A struggle for power between the two rival factions ensued for the next few days. The Federalists were willing to risk adjournment to bring the matter to their constituencies, and Judge Hobart, on July 16, made such a motion. Abraham Yates feared that since the Antis were scattered, the newspapers would cause a Federalist victory. In truth, public opinion had switched so that now ratification was widely favored.[38]

When Hamilton rose to speak on July 17, he made another stab at persuading the convention to adopt the Constitution. If adoption took place as proposed, he asserted, New York was out of the Union. Some might think that then New York could enjoy her revenues and wealth, but, he predicted, "the Union will not permit us to remain so because their interests & safety will not permit it."[39]

He read a letter from James Madison, that the Antifederalists in the Virginia convention had rejected the idea of restricted ratification and left the matter of amendments in the hands of the new government. Once again Hamilton dwelt on what would happen to New York if she stayed out of the Union. "What can be hoped for from the other States? Can we compare our strength against the whole? Who will help us—France or Great Britain? France is the United States' ally. What would Britain gain from it? Will she take the weaker by the hand to oppose the stronger?" New York State was divided; the southern part favored the new government, and even if the northern section could force the southern districts, the Union would help the latter. Hamilton did not want to see such a division, but "it will take place if we reject the Constitution." Many patriots had agreed to the Constitution, he argued, naming Hancock, Adams, Franklin and Washington, who came forward after the war and "hazarded his harvest of glory" because he saw that his work was but half done. "Let us take care not to oppose the whole country," Hamilton said.[40]

The amendment to adjourn lost, as Hamilton wished, and the Federalists remained firm in their refusal to accept conditional ratification. At this point, Melancton Smith presented a compromise that he hoped "will avoid the objections on both sides." It proposed that the Constitution be ratified without conditions, but with the reservation that New York could secede from the Union if the amendments were not considered by the new government within a certain number of years, possibly two or seven. The Antifederalists, startled, reacted to Smith's capitulation with a vote to adjourn and meet among themselves.

When the convention reopened on the eighteenth of July, there was only silence. John Jay told Washington that the Antis were "embarrassed," afraid of division, and yet a considerable number were opposed to the new plan. After a desultory debate, the meeting adjourned; once more, the Antis met to find a way to resolve their dilemma.

Now back in New York City attending the moribund Continental Congress, Hamilton wrote to Madison to ask his opinion about the possibility of New York's admission into the Union with Smith's amendment. If it could be done, Hamilton said, "I do not fear any further consequences." Since, certainly, Congress would recommend amendments "to render *the structure* of the government secure . . . the more considerate and honest opposers" would be satisfied, and thus, in time, "the party of the center would break up."[41]

From the nineteenth to the twenty-second, the convention went through the motions of reviewing the proposed amendments. At the same time, at Clinton's suggestion, a committee of four, made up of Federalists Harison and Duane and Antifederalists Yates and Smith, worked on the arrangement of the amendments. Even at this time, the final verdict could not be predicted. Hamilton reported to Madison that there was "a great diversity" in the views of their opponents, but "upon the whole," however, "our fears diminish."[42]

While Poughkeepsie held its breath, New York City Federalists decided to mark ratification of the new Constitution with an elaborate celebration, postponed from the Fourth of July to July 23, with the hope that either New York would then be in the acceptance column or the celebration itself would sway the obstinate delegates. Preparations for the gala event under the direction of talented Pierre L'Enfant occupied the capital city.

The most imposing float in the glorious pageant was the Federal ship *Hamilton*, named in honor of New York's defender of the Constitution. The ship, built for the occasion by ship carpenters as their contribution to the festivities, had a seven-foot keel and a ten-foot beam. Completely rigged, it was equipped with thirty-two guns and manned by thirty sailors and a full complement of officers under the command of Commodore James Nicholson. Mounted on a wooden trailer and drawn by ten magnificent horses, it received the maximum attention from the eager crowd.

Every effort was made to display unity and splendor, as well as artistic flavor. There were ten divisions in the pageant, representing the ten states that had ratified, and the emphasis was on the city's trades and crafts. The parade, led by trumpeters and a body of artillery drawing a fieldpiece, followed by dignitaries escorted by a company of light horse, included amazingly elaborate floats as each trade tried to outdo the others.

The Society of the Cincinnati turned out in full military uniform, headed by Anthony Walton White riding a gray horse, led by two black men in white oriental dress and turbans, and holding a sculpture of the arms of the United States.

All manner of men participated in the parade. After the succession of artisans, tradesmen and merchants, judges and lawyers, the sheriff and the coroner followed. Then came ten law students carrying the ratifications of the ten states, and Robert Troup, John Lawrence and John Cozine carrying the new Constitution. The administration, professors and students of Columbia College, all in academic dress, marched, carrying a banner with a device representing science. The Chamber of Commerce was next in the line of march, including in its number William Maxwell, vice-president of the Bank of New York. Clergymen and physicians were the last civilian group, followed by an artillery detachment.

It was an unprecedented spectacle, both beautiful and moving because it represented a peaceful transfer of power. More than 5,000 people participated in the parade, which extended for a mile and a half. The marchers wound their way to the Bayard County seat near Grand Street. Here, a banquet had been set up in a design arranged by L'Enfant. A canopy of canvas covered the feast of bullocks, mutton and ham served at tables spread for 6,000 guests. Over the tables was a dome surmounted by a figure representing Fame, holding a scroll with the words "Independence, Alliance with France, and Peace."

An ode composed for the occasion paid tribute to the Constitution and three men: Washington, Franklin and Hamilton. Of Hamilton, the author wrote:

> ... And thou,
> Our City's boast, to whom so much we owe

In whom, tho' last and youngest of the three,
No common share of excellence we see:
In every greatful heart thou hast a place,
Nor Time, nor Circumstance can e'er erase.

It was a glorious occasion. Thomas Greenleaf in the New York *Journal* wrote that "the poor Antis" who watched "looked as sour as the Devil."[43]

While New York City celebrated Hamilton and ratification, the Poughkeepsie convention continued its debate. As time started to run out, factions were developing among the Antis. Governor Clinton was the leader of the largest bloc, whose primary purpose was to keep control of the state. Lansing was their spokesman and supported their interests by proposing conditional ratification. There was no hope for the Federalists in that quarter. But Melancton Smith and a following from Dutchess County and Long Island, despite their dislike of the new Constitution, were beginning to like even less the idea of the dissension that would arise if New York was expelled from the Union. There was also a small group, made up of Samuel Jones and a few others, who seemed to have "capitulated to the Federalist side."[44]

July 23 was the beginning of the end of the Poughkeepsie convention. Smith's motion of July 14, calling for the adoption of the Constitution "on condition" until the amendments "shall have been submitted to and determined upon by a general convention," was changed by Samuel Jones. He proposed that " '*upon condition*' be stricken out and 'in full confidence' inserted."[45] The proposal was passed by thirty-one votes to twenty-nine.

The Antis had not yet surrendered. The next day, a motion was made by Lansing, providing that New York might withdraw from the Union if a second federal convention were not called within a specified number of years. Hamilton spoke against the motion.

His strongest argument was a letter from James Madison, which answered the question of whether New York State might become a member of the new Union if her ratification was conditional. No, said Madison. "The Constitution requires an adoption *in toto* and *for ever.*" The other states had done so. "An adoption for a limited time would be as defective as an adoption of some of the articles only. In short any *condition* whatever must viciate the ratification."[46] Hamilton asked that, instead of the proposal, a circular letter stating the defects of the Constitution be written and sent to the other states.

Finally, on July 25, by a vote of 30–27, the Poughkeepsie convention as a committee of the whole turned down the secession motion and then, by the same vote, agreed to ratify the Constitution "in full confidence" that their proposed amendments would be adopted. They accepted unanimously a circular letter that Jay had written, with some changes made by Hamilton, to be sent to their sister states. The gist of the letter was that "the majority of us" objected to several articles, but "an invincible reluctance" to separate from the others prevailed upon "a sufficient number" to ratify without "previous amendments. We all unite in the opinion that such a revision will be necessary to recommend it to the approbation and support of numerous Body of our constituents."

Hamilton was recognized as the champion of ratification by the people of the state, as the federal ship *Hamilton* had made clear. He captured the imagination of the convention and turned it around. His eloquence moved the delegates and the citizenry, and his persistence and clever strategy kept the convention from ending earlier and as an Antifederalist victory.

For Hamilton the future was brighter than it had ever been. His party was triumphant nationally, if not in New York State, and the national government that he had nurtured and defended was soon to come into existence. In the meantime, he was a delegate to the "lame duck" Continental Congress, with the self-imposed mission to keep the seat of government in his own city.

Federalist Politics

Though New York's ratification of the Constitution was not a perfect triumph because of the annoying circular letter that sought a second convention, it was, nonetheless, the achievement for which Hamilton and the other Federalists had worked. It came just in time to save New York from losing her position as host to the new government. Hamilton wanted the capital located in his city for many reasons. It would boost Federalist prestige in the state, and, personally, it would be convenient if there were a place in the new government for Hamilton. Further, having to endure the seat of the government under the Constitution would be a satisfying irritant to Governor Clinton.

The New York Federalists, Madison confided to Washington, had agreed to the circular letter "to purchase an immediate ratification in any form and at any price, rather than disappoint this city of a chance for the New Congress." General Webb agreed and spoke of "the rage of the inhabitants" of New York City against the delay in adoption that would lose the capital to Philadelphia, "a fatal stroke to our Commerce." If this happened, Webb predicted, the life of Clinton and his party "would not be safe in the City."[1]

Hamilton, who resumed his seat in the Continental Congress upon his return from Poughkeepsie, tried to enlist the support of other Federalist members. He realized that New York City would not be the final choice because it was located too far north, but he hoped that its initial selection would keep the capital from being located any farther south than Philadelphia.

The chief contenders for the capital city were Philadelphia, Baltimore, the Potomac region and New York City. Though there was general agreement in the Continental Congress to appoint presidential electors in January 1789, have them cast their ballots in February and convene the new government in March, the question of where was moot.

On August 4, Madison, who did not want New York to win lest that make it difficult later to establish the capital on the Potomac, voted for Baltimore. His motion, surprisingly, carried. But in two days, Baltimore was out of the running. Rhode Island, which had not yet ratified the Constitution, caused a distraction by disputing participation in setting up a government that she did not accept.

When discussion on the site was resumed, the New York Federalists were concerned that New Jersey would get the temporary capital or would lend her support to Philadelphia. Hamilton wrote to William Livingston, Governor of New Jersey, that his state would be better off with New York City as the seat of the government rather than Philadelphia. "The South wants to carry the government further South," he warned.

Finally, Hamilton offered a workable compromise: The temporary seat would remain in New York City, and the new Congress would make future decisions about a permanent capital.

As did most people in the United States, Hamilton assumed that George Washington would be the new nation's first president. In August 1778, he wrote to his former chief enclosing a set of Publius's papers, identifying himself and Madison as their chief writers with some aid from Jay. "I take it for granted, Sir, you have concluded to comply with what will no doubt be the general call of your country in relation to the new government," he wrote. "You will permit me to say that it is indispensable you should lend yourself to its first operations." Without him, Hamilton declared, the system would not have the "*firm establishment*" it required at the outset.[2]

But Washington was reluctant, preferring to stay at Mount Vernon and tend his acres. He also had sincere doubts; the possibility that people might think him self-seeking or overambitious troubled him. May "the great Searcher of Human Hearts" be "witness that I have no wish which aspires beyond the humble and happy lot of living and dying a private citizen on my own farm," he lamented.[3]

Neither modesty nor indifference could have shielded the former commander in chief from the tributes offered him during and after the constitutional period. The Pennsylvania *Packet*, an exceedingly influential paper, mentioned Washington often as the president-to-be. At the Fourth of July celebrations all over the country in the summer of 1788, toasts expressed the feelings of the people for their hero. A new Federal song said: "Great Washington shall rule the land."[4]

Hamilton had not forgotten how to handle the eminent Virginian. In September, he wrote once again to Washington. The success of the new government depended on his accepting the office of the president, Hamilton insisted. "The point of light in which you stand at home and abroad will make an infinite difference in the respectability with which the government will begin its operations in the alternative of your being or not being the head of it."

But John C. Hamilton wrote that his father had had some misgivings about the Washington presidency, regretting that a precedent would be set for awarding the presidency to a soldier.[5] This reservation suggests once more the ambivalence that Hamilton felt for Washington. He admired him and yet resented him, particularly for the ease with which he stood by while greatness was thrust upon him.

The second letter argued that Washington had come "into public view" again at the convention; thereby, in effect, he had pledged himself to take part in the government that would be established as a result of it. Feigning humility, Hamilton wrote that he hoped his "frankness" would not annoy his recipient. "It has been prompted by motives which you would not disapprove."[6]

The problem of who would be the first vice-president was not as easily solved. Sectionalism was an important consideration; the certitude of the top office being filled by a southerner mandated that a northerner get the second office. John Adams, John Hancock, John Jay and George Clinton were the most frequently mentioned.

Information that Adams was unfriendly to Washington gave Hamilton some misgivings; he feared that Adams and Richard Henry Lee, with whom Adams was "in the habit of uniting," might start a cabal that would prove embarrassing to the chief executive. "Consider this," Hamilton cautioned Theodore Sedgwick; "sound the reality of it and let me hear from you." Sedgwick answered that Adams was "less democratical" now and "of unconquerable intrepidity & incorruptible integrity." Sedgwick, the speaker of the Massachusetts house of representatives, observed that men's minds were focused on either Adams or Hancock.[7]

When General Knox visited John Adams in Braintree, the two men discussed the Society of the Cincinnati, and Knox relieved Adams's fears about it. The former minister to England had no suspicion that Knox was there at Hamilton's request to sound him out about the vice-presidency and, if possible, to dampen any desire for the job. Knox hinted broadly that Adams was too important to take second place to the Virginian. He also suggested that Adams was too candid to have to adjust his beliefs to Washington's. All subtlety was lost on Adams, who wanted to be vice-president, although he would not seek the office but rather expected it to be bestowed upon him.

In early November 1778, Hamilton resigned himself to the Adams candidacy. After mature consideration, "I had but one scruple" about him, he wrote to Sedgwick. "I have relinquished it." Though Hamilton conceded that Adams had "an ardent love for the public good," his jealousies were a continual fault. But, Hamilton wrote, if, as Sedgwick said, they were no longer present, nothing should disturb "the harmony of the administration."[8]

After writing to Washington again and reminding him that his acceptance of the presidency was "indispensable," Hamilton informed Madison that he was supporting Adams for the vice-presidency. With a decided lack of enthusiasm, Hamilton pointed out that Adams was an important character in the eastern states and if he were not vice-president, he would have to be nominated for another important office, or he would become a malcontent who would work against the government.[9]

The concern now was to ensure Washington's election. Because of the way that the Constitution was written, the candidate was not designated as running for president or vice-president, and it was possible to have "a man treading close upon the heels of the person we wish as president." A few votes withheld from Washington might elect Adams president.

In a letter to Pennsylvanian James Wilson, Hamilton outlined his formula for dealing with the possibility that the electors who favored John Rutledge and George Clinton would redirect their votes to Adams. The only safe strategy was "to throw away a few votes, say seven or eight, giving them to persons not otherwise thought of." Having already proposed to friends in Connecticut and New Jersey to throw away two from each of these states, Hamilton told Wilson, "I submit to you whether it will not be well to lose three or four in Pennsylvania." Adams should have a plurality of the votes for vice-president, but if there was to be a risk run it could not be Washington's. Wilson was asked to write to friends in Maryland to join in the plan.[10]

Washington was agreeable to the selection of Adams as vice-president. While still ostensibly making up his mind about the presidency, he wrote to Benjamin Lincoln that he would give Adams his "full confidence" and cooperate with him for "the national prosperity."[11]

The presidential electors met on February 4, 1789, and cast their votes according to the Hamiltonian plan. Washington was elected unanimously. Col. Jeremiah Wadsworth informed Hamilton that Connecticut had "given her vote agreeable to his wishes," namely a full vote for Washington and two less for Adams. Maryland threw away her votes on Colonel Harrison, and South Carolina on Rutledge. South of Pennsylvania, the only votes that Adams received were five from Virginia. Clinton received three. When Congress convened on April 6, the final returns revealed sixty-nine votes for Washington and thirty-four for Adams.[12]

John Adams received the news that he had been elected by a plurality, not even a majority, with bitter anger. For a few days he considered refusing the office. He accepted only after deciding that otherwise he might be doing "a great mischief" and be responsible for the "final failure" of the government.[13]

The new vice-president had no suspicion that the architect of his humiliation was Alexander Hamilton. Abigail Adams wrote to her husband that she had no doubts about Hamilton's goodwill toward him. Hamilton had shown William Smith, their son-in-law, a letter from James Madison in which he had written: "We consider your reasons conclusive, the gentleman you have named [Adams] will certainly have all our votes and interest for Vice-President." However, when Adams arrived in New York to take office, he learned of the election plot against him. At first, he was inclined to dismiss the suggestion that Hamilton was involved. He admired Hamilton's success. Then, as more evidence accumulated proving that Hamilton was responsible for his loss of so many electoral votes, Adams became less complimentary, and referred to Hamilton's "high-minded ambition" and "great penetration." There was nothing more dangerous than throwing away votes, Adams declared. It was "betraying a trust, it is a breach of honor, it is perjury. . . . If a repetition takes place I will drag out to public infamy both dupers and dupes, let who will be among the Number." The seeds were sown for a future harvest of discord between the two men.[14]

Hamilton had succeeded in electing his candidates to national office, but he had not established Federalism firmly in New York State. Governor Clinton remained a formidable power who would be very difficult to defeat in the coming gubernatorial election. Hamilton and his friends decided to back Judge Robert Yates, now a moderate and a supporter of the Constitution who the Federalists believed could pull in votes from all factions. Yates's dramatic exit from the Philadelphia convention to illustrate his dissent was now forgotten. The Federalists remembered only his conciliatory position at Poughkeepsie. Yates was esteemed as a man and as a judge. His opposition to the Constitution, Hamilton wrote, "was such as its friends cannot but disapprove," but since its adoption, he had been moderate with "a regard for peace and decorum."[15]

A committee of correspondence, set up to support Yates, included Hamilton and a dozen others, one of whom was Aaron Burr. At this time, Hamilton and Burr were rivals at the bar but otherwise friends and neighbors who traveled in the same social circles. Burr was uncommitted politically but wanted to help Yates, who had facilitated his admission to the bar.

The campaign that Hamilton and his friends launched was assiduous, using broadsides, speeches in every part of the state, correspondence to all who could help. Hamilton was chairman of the committee of correspondence, which included Burr, Troup, William Duer, Richard Platt and John Murray. Hamilton's major effort in the compaign was a series of sixteen letters published between February and April 1789, attacking Governor Clinton as incurably opposed to the federal government. The authorship of the papers was thinly concealed under the pseudonym H.G., which suggests Hamilton Grange.

The H.G. letters, addressed to a mythical resident of Suffolk County, examined George Clinton's personal and public life with complete lack of charity. The first letter characterized Clinton as a man who "very early" got the reputation of being "a very artful man." Clinton's skill as a soldier was a myth, said H.G. He was in combat only once, at Fort Montgomery, where he made a well-timed retreat. Philip Schuyler, said his loyal son-in-law, was defeated by Clinton in the first election for governor of New York State only because of the votes of a considerable body of militia under Clinton.[16]

Although given credit for the good order in the city upon the evacuation of British troops, H.G. observed that there had been no problem to deal with. And Clinton had favored the anti-Tory laws, which were passed by the New York legislature contrary to the peace treaty, and he did nothing to mitigate or abrogate them.[17]

The most serious count against Clinton, Hamilton declared, was his enmity against the American Union. He opposed the new Constitution before it was framed and after it appeared with "unreasonable obstinacy." He opposed its adoption by the state and was even un-friendly to the residence of the Continental Congress in New York City. And Hamilton claimed to have evidence proving that Clinton used "personal influence" with the members of the legislature to prejudice them against the impost.[18]

Harping on the theme of Clinton's rudeness to Congress while it was housed in New York, H.G. charged that the governor had not visited either of its two presidents, nor had any hospitality been extended to the members. Having rejected the idea of the Annapolis convention, prejudged the Philadelphia convention, even after ten states had ratified the new Constitution, the governor persisted "*to the last in his negative*." He ignored the hazards of resistance "to the general sense of America"; he was unwilling "*to sacrifice the pride of opinion to a spirit of accommodation*."[19]

Governor Clinton had made clear that he would keep up the spirit of opposition in the people until "the *amendments proposed* or an-other convention (I am not sure which) could be obtained." This was unjustifiable. The system needed improvement, H.G. admitted, but "I reprobate the idea of one State giving law to the rest." The governor said that it was disadvantageous to New York to have the seat of the government; it would promote luxury and dissipation. Everyone knew it would bring wealth to the state. What it added up to was that Clinton "has entertained a project for erecting a system of *State Power* unconnected with, and in subversion of the Union." Hamilton cautioned, "I conceive a man capable of adopting such views as too dangerous to be trusted at the head of a State."[20]

Governor Clinton's supporters denied that H.G.'s "scurrilous" let-ters would do their candidate any harm. But H.G. was answered by "Wm. Tell," who accused his opponent of being "puffed up . . . by an expecting band of sycophants, a train of ambitious relations and a few rich men." The anonymous "Wm. Tell" claimed that he knew H.G.'s identity and was the first to accuse Hamilton, in print, of being a womanizer. "Your private character is still worse than your public one, and it will yet be exposed by your own works, for [you] will not be bound by *the most solemn of all* obligations *******" Broadus Mitchell believes that the seven asterisks conceal the word "wedlock."[21]

As Election Day neared, the campaign was stepped up. A Federal-ist broadside, circulated in New York City, answered the Clintonian accusation that the ancient families and respectable citizens favored Governor Clinton, while strangers, adventurers and bankrupts opposed him. On the contrary, the broadside asserted, supporters of Judge Yates are "a respectable proportion of all classes of citizens." On April 28, just as the polls opened, Hamilton issued a last call for support of Yates. "Let every man, who believes a change necessary, step forward with the *Independence* of a *Freeman* and lend his aid!"[22]

Despite the efforts of the Federalists, the aging governor was re-elected. The final vote was close: 6,391–5,962. Though a victory, it showed diminishing power for Clinton, and his party lost its majority in the lower house and some seats in the senate. It was a disappointment for Hamilton, although political observers termed his management of a near victory over the powerful Clintonians "the work of a genius." The Federalists elected all nine of their candidates from New York City to the assembly, and, to Hamilton's satisfaction, Philip Schuyler was reelected to the senate. The New York Federalists also elected three of the five national congressmen, two of them Hamilton's close friends, Egbert Benson and John Lawrence.

The next battle for the Federalists was over the method of choosing the United States senators from New York State. Due to Clinton's negligence, New York State was not represented at the first session of the first Congress; the legislature had been convened too late to designate representatives. At the special session of the state legislature in July, Schuyler proposed that the assembly and the senate each nominate two men for the United States Senate. If the selections were not the same, the assembly would vote for one of the senate's candidates and the senate for one of the assembly's. Foolishly, since the Federalists now dominated both houses, the Clintonians turned down the idea. After several days of debate, the assembly proposed Schuyler and James Duane, who was married to a Livingston. The senate supported Ezra L'Hommedieu, who was unacceptable to the assembly. Instead, that body proposed Rufus King, who had left Massachusetts and recently settled in New York. The senate accepted him.

Behind the scenes, a caucus of Federalist leaders agreed to Schuyler unanimously but preferred James Duane to King by a vote of twenty-four to twenty. King refused to oppose Duane. Then L'Hommedieu and Lewis Morris, both state senators, announced that they were not bound by the balloting. Hamilton, who received the news from Troup, immediately informed King. The efforts of the two insurgents were doomed; the assembly rejected both and then unanimously voted for King. The senate approved him by a vote of

eleven to eight. Although Hamilton was influential in the final outcome, it was King's own popularity that defeated the others. Hamilton wrote to King, saying that he had circulated an "idea" that it
would be injurious to the city to have Duane elected "as probably
some unfit character would be his successor."[23]

The election of Schuyler and King was regarded as another indication of Hamilton's growing political power, but he was disappointed
that the newcomer drew the six-year term, while Schuyler had to be
satisfied with a two-year tenure.

On April 30, George Washington was inaugurated President of the
United States in a ceremony that was the culmination of six days of
festivities, beginning with the great hero's arrival in New York City.
People from all over the country converged on the city. Every house,
public and private, was overflowing with guests.

Church bells rang out at nine in the morning to call the citizens to
church, and all business was closed for the day. At noon the procession formed in Cherry Street opposite the president's house. First
came the soldiery; then the sheriffs; then the Senate committee,
made up of Ralph Izard, Tristram Dalton and Richard Henry Lee;
after them, George Washington, followed by the House committee
which included Egbert Benson, Charles Carroll and Fisher Ames.
Chancellor Robert R. Livingston, John Jay, Henry Knox and distinguished citizens followed. The line of march was from Pearl and
Broad streets to Wall Street. In front of the refurbished Federal
Hall, the soldiers formed a lane through which the president-elect
walked to the door of the building, where John Adams welcomed
him and conducted him to the Senate chamber. Adams then solemnly
introduced Washington to the members of Congress and invited him
to take the required oath to be given by Chancellor Livingston.

With dignity, his bearing erect and soldierly, the incoming president moved to the center of the group of attending dignitaries. His
thinning brown hair powdered and clubbed behind, he was dressed
in a suit of black velvet, a dress sword at his side. In deep, tremulous
tones, he repeated the words of the oath, after which he kissed the
Bible. Livingston then cried loudly, "Long live George Washington,
President of the United States." The crowd echoed the chancellor's
cry enthusiastically.

Washington's inaugural address covered no new issues and avoided
anything controversial. It contained only the recommendation that
Congress assume the responsibility of advocating constitutional amendments in order to meet objections and "to relieve inquietude." He

referred delicately to the matter of his compensation by asking, as he did when appointed commander in chief, that it be limited "to such actual expenditures as the public may be thought to require." After calling on "the benign parent of the human race" to favor the American people and their government, the new president bowed and sat down. The audience was moved by Washington's dignity and grace. "He had the soul, look and figure of a hero united in him," the French minister wrote home.[24]

Since Hamilton was not a member of the new government, he watched all the proceedings from the sidelines. However, his house at 57 Wall Street, next door to his office, was located very near the Federal building, and he was the constant host to many influential members of the government. One lady remembered seeing Hamilton and Madison talking together often. On one occasion, she said, as the two men spoke animatedly to each other, they would turn and laugh and play with a monkey that was climbing around in a neighbor's yard.[25]

Washington conferred with Hamilton frequently and dined occasionally at the Hamilton dinner table. In May, a few days after the inauguration, the first president asked Hamilton's advice on the etiquette he should observe in office. Hamilton answered at great length.

The public good required that the dignity of the office of president be upheld, Hamilton stated as the basic axiom. The important consideration, however, was "to steer clear of extremes." The president was not a monarch but had to establish the respect of his own countrymen and the representatives of monarchs. A levee day once a week for receiving visits, at which the president would stay a half an hour, was suggested. He would return no visits, accept no invitations, but give formal entertainments two to four times a year. He would invite members of the legislature and other officials to family dinners at which he would "never remain long at table."

Officially, for business, the heads of departments and foreign ministers would be given access to the president. Senators should have individual access "on matters relative to the *public administration* . . . it will be considered as a safeguard against secret combinations to deceive him." Discrimination against representatives was permissible in this case, since the Senate, under the Constitution, was "coupled with the president in certain executive functions treaties and appointments."[26]

Washington thanked Hamilton for his advice. "It is my wish to act

right: if I err; the head & not the heart, with *justice* be chargeable."
Washington appointed Tuesday afternoon from three to four o'clock
as his reception time. "At their first entrance they salute me, and I
them, and as many as I can, I talk to," Washington said.[27]

If the hero of New York ratification and the champion of nationalism felt betrayed at being only an adviser but not a participant at the
commencement of the new government, no record of his feelings
exists. On the Fourth of July, 1789, Hamilton held the spotlight
when he delivered the funeral oration for General Nathanael Greene.
The Society of the Cincinnati, Baron von Steuben in the lead,
marched to St. Paul's chapel, where Mrs. Washington, Vice-President
Adams and other dignitaries were already seated. The president was
too ill to attend. Hamilton's speech was eloquent and suitably lauda-
tory. Senator Maclay, always a dyspeptic observer, granted that the
speech was well delivered and the content good but added, "I thgt he
should have given us some acct of his virtue as a citizen as well as a
warrior, for I supposed he possessed them, and he lived some time
after the war, and, I believe, commenced farming."[28]

A few weeks later, John Adams asked Hamilton to take his son
Charles into his law office, which Hamilton agreed to do. In the same
letter, Adams hinted at the possibility of a Hamilton appointment.

During the summer, Washington, recovered from a painful abscess
on his thigh, was in the city. Congress was debating the establishment of the executive department with anger and division of opinion.

Applications for all sorts of positions had to wait while the president followed his rule that, in matters requiring congressional involvement, he would not take "a single step" until that body acted.
Meanwhile, the chief executive rode around New York City on a
white horse with a leopard-skin housing and a saddlecloth trimmed
in gold binding. He talked with Hamilton often, but there is no
evidence that he discussed or hinted at any position. Hamilton had to
practice patience and hope a little longer.

12

Mr. Secretary of the Treasury I

THE PRESIDENT APPOINTED Alexander Hamilton secretary of the treasury on September 11, 1789; the Senate approved the appointment the same day.

Bishop William White, Robert Morris's brother-in-law, told Hamilton's son that Washington asked Morris, "What are we to do with this heavy debt?" Morris answered: "There is but one man in the United States who can tell you; that is Alexander Hamilton. I am glad that you have given me this opportunity to declare to you the extent of the obligations I am under to him."[1]

Robert Troup, in his *Memoir*, said that Washington called on Hamilton, informing him of the nomination to the financial department as soon as it was organized. The following day, Hamilton asked Troup to wind up his law practice if he received the appointment. Troup acquiesced, observing that accepting a government post would be a hardship for the expanding Hamilton family. The future secretary of the treasury agreed but explained that having urged Washington to accept public office, he could do no less. Further, he believed that he would promote "the welfare of the country" by restoring public credit.[2]

During the congressional debate over the establishment of the executive departments, one of the most controversial issues was whether the president needed the consent of the Senate to dismiss an appointee. In Federalist 77, Hamilton said that consent would be necessary "to displace as well as appoint." This would safeguard the country when there was a change in president and "would not occasion so violent or so general a revolution in the officers of the government." A new president, Hamilton argued, must retain the former's cabinet officers as long as they gave evidence of "fitness" for their offices. The first Congress struck down Hamilton's principle, asserting that the president had the power of removal. John Adams, the second president, did not at first exercise his prerogative, of which Hamilton took advantage.

Washington waited for Congress to conclude its deliberations before he made any official appointments. Gossip said that Madison had already masterminded the presidential selections, and that Madison thought Hamilton "best qualified" for the office of secretary of the treasury and told Washington that all those who knew him preferred him for the job.[3]

The formation of the Treasury Department elicited some surprising proposals from the lawmakers. Jealous of its power of the purse, some members of the House of Representatives did not want to yield to a presidential appointee. Elbridge Gerry proposed that, instead of a single individual, a board be established to head the controversial department. Madison again prevailed when he proposed that the Treasury, as well as the other departments, each have one man at its head, removable, he added, by the president.

Still, Congress was not willing to treat the Treasury the same as the other two departments, which, they decided, would be answerable directly to the president. The act creating the Treasury Department provided that it would be under the control of the president but directly responsible to Congress.

On September 21, ten days after Hamilton's appointment, Congress acted on this principle. Declaring that since one of the reasons for the creation of the new government was the failure of the Confederation to establish a fiscally sound economy, Congress intended to see to it that the country's debts were paid and its credit restored. Adequate provisions for these needs was of "high importance to the national honor and prosperity," and the secretary of the treasury was ordered to "prepare a plan for that purpose."

Hamilton was pleased to be so charged. Until January 14, when he submitted his report, the secretary of the treasury worked on it with dedicated zeal, but not to the exclusion of all else.

Hamilton was often in the House during the fall session, and, not content with exerting his influence in the legislature, he also wanted the primary place in Washington's confidence. Up to this time, Madison had been closest to the presidential ear. He had strongly advised important positions for fellow Virginians Jefferson and Randolph, about whose appointments Hamilton was not told until the day before the two names were sent to the Senate for confirmation.

With a confidence more ingenuous than arrogant, Hamilton was optimistic about his ability to fulfill his gargantuan task in the allotted time. In a letter to Lafayette about his cabinet appointment, he said there was "a reasonable expectation" to satisfy the public if "I am properly supported by the Legislature, and in this respect I stand at present in the most encouraging footing." The debt due to France "will be among the first objects of my attention." He would prefer it if the installments on the principal of the debt could be suspended for a few years, "a valuable accommodation for the United States," Hamilton urged. Of course, the arrears of interest and future interest would be paid punctually. "It would be best if the offer came unsolicited from France as a fresh mark of good will," the new secretary suggested.[4]

At this time, neither Hamilton nor Madison realized consciously that their friendship was beginning to sour. Madison had been behind the plan to subjugate Hamilton to the power of the House of Representatives by forcing him to present a program for the restoration of the economic health of the nation directly to that body. And when Hamilton was in office about a month, he had the opportunity to challenge Madison's position as Washington's chief adviser.

Under the leadership of Madison, Congress had retaliated against Great Britain for a series of unfriendly acts, including limiting American trade with the West Indies and refusing to evacuate the western forts. Hamilton, acting independently, talked to George Beckwith, England's unofficial representative, about these problems.

Washington, much perturbed over the state of Anglo-American commercial relations and the failure of England to send a minister to the United States, decided to send a special envoy to Great Britain. Both Madison and Jay, then acting as secretary of foreign affairs, were asked to recommend someone. Madison responded with a barrage of arguments that delayed the president's decision for a week. Hamilton, who approved the Washington plan, suggested Gouverneur Morris, an anglophile and a Hamiltonian.

Washington should wait until Jefferson's return from France before appointing an agent for the English mission, Madison maintained. Delaying just long enough to appease Madison, Washington appointed Morris to the post. Nonetheless, appearances were maintained. Hamilton wrote to Madison in October, asking him what taxes would be "*least* unpopular." Madison blamed the tardiness of his reply—not until November—on a long illness from which he had just recovered. He recommended: a tax on home stills, an increase in duty on imported liquors, a land tax and a stamp tax on the proceedings of the federal courts.[5] This was one of the last pleasant exchanges between the two men.

During the three months that Congress was absent from New York, Hamilton devoted himself to organizing his department, acquainting his staff with the standards of excellence he demande. from them and building a structure for the Treasury Department that would stand during his tenure and afterward. No detail was too small for his attention. His goal was a sound economy that would restore the floundering young nation permanently to financial stability.

"Tomorrow I open the budget & you may imagine that today I am very busy and very anxious," Hamilton wrote on January 7, 1790, to his sympathetic, affectionate sister-in-law, Angelica Church, who had returned to England in November. The secretary of the treasury had labored arduously, employing his amazing powers of concentration. He was aware that his enemies were ready to stop him before he got started; his friends were counting on him; and the speculators, foreign and domestic, were waiting to benefit from the plan. Even Hamilton's friends were kept in the dark about the system being developed. To Henry Lee, who had inquired about it prematurely, Hamilton wrote politely that he must be as discreet as Caesar's wife, as must "every man concerned in the adminstration of the finances of a Country...."[6]

Though Congress had ruled that department heads could not appear before them in person, some efforts were made by Hamilton's friends to make an exception for him. Elias Boudinot suggested that the secretary of the treasury be present in the House in order to answer questions on a subject that was "so intricate" it would not be easily comprehended "without oral illustration."[7] Congress refused to change its mind.

Hamilton wrote that the document he was presenting was "the result of his enquiries and reflections" on making "an adequate provision for the support of Public Credit," as requested. The debt of the United States, "the price of liberty," had not been settled in the first seven years since independence due to "the embarrassment of a defective constitution." Now the obligation would be taken care of, and it would be seen that the benefits of public credit were various and obvious. Hamilton listed several: the extension of trade; promotion of agriculture and manufactures; and the lowering of the interest rate, which would make borrowing easier and cheaper.

These desirable effects could be achieved only when the public debt was funded. Therefore, the debt had to be converted into interest-bearing bonds that would come to maturity at a prescribed period of time. Permanent funds had to be provided to pay the debt; eventually, he promised, funding would increase the value of land.

Hamilton did not fear opposition to his proposal that the foreign debt be paid as contracted. He expected controversy over the domestic part of the debt, so in order to forestall the objections, he explained his position on discrimination between the original holders of the public securities and the present possessors, many of whom had purchased them at a very low price because of the misfortunes of the original owners. The former, some maintained, should receive full value for their securities; the latter only the cost and the interest, with the difference going to the original owners. Hamilton rejected this idea. Such a plan would be difficult to carry out and would constitute unfairness to some who bought in good faith. It would be contrary to the constitutional principle that the rights of original owners and assignees must be considered equal. The Constitution provided that "all debts contracted and engagements entered into before the adoption of the Constitution shall be as valid against the United States under it, as against the Constitution."

An even more controversial issue was tackled next. The secretary proclaimed that it was his "full conviction that an assumption of the debts of the particular States by the union . . . will be a measure of sound policy and substantial justice" and that it would contribute to "an orderly, stable and satisfactory arrangement of the national finances." If all the public creditors received their payments from one source, equally, at the same interest, "they will unite in the support of the fiscal arrangements of the government."[8]

Hamilton calculated the foreign debt at $11,710,378.12 and the domestic debt at $40,414,085.94. By way of encouragement, he promised that the establishment of American credit in Europe would cause the interest rate to fall because no other country would have such good security. The natural resources and unsettled land in the United States far exceeded that of any other country.

As to how the debt could be liquidated, Hamilton proposed that $2,239,163.09 be paid annually to retire the foreign debt and that the domestic debt be paid off at the rate of 4 percent per year on the total. Payment of the foreign debt would require further loans from abroad; otherwise, the United States would suffer a cash drain and a balance-of-payments deficit. The rest of the needed money would be obtained from present duties on imports; wines and spirits, including those distilled within the United States; tea and coffee and tonnage (a duty on vessels). These taxes should be high in order to avoid the need for direct taxation. Those articles carrying high duties, Hamilton pointed out, were luxuries, "even pernicious luxuries," if overused. A decrease in the consumption of distilled spirits "would encourage the substitution of cyder and malt liquors, benefit agriculture and open a new and productive source of revenue."[9]

To sugarcoat the pill, Hamilton gave assurances that "the most scrupulous care" would be taken to protect those affected by the plan from "every species of injury by the conduct of the officers to be employed."[10]

The duties on liquor would be used, first, to pay the interest on the foreign debt. Out of the residue, $600,000 would be reserved for the cost of the current service of the United States. The surplus and money from the other duties would be used to pay the interest on the new loan. The revenue from the post office, estimated at not less than $100,000, should go for a sinking fund, which subject would be discussed in a later report.

"The proper funding of the present debt will render it a national blessing," Hamilton said, although, he added quickly, he believed in the eventual "extinguishment" of the debt. In the meantime, commissioners, consisting of the Vice-President of the United States, the Speaker of the House of Representatives, the chief justice, the secretary of the treasury and the attorney general of the United States— either all or any three of them—would supervise the discharge of the debt. With the approval of the president, they would be authorized to pay the interest and installments on the foreign debt and purchase the public debt "at the price it shall bear in the market, while it continues below its true value." This favored the public creditors, since it tended to raise the value of the stock. In this way, the government would be in competition with foreigners, which would accelerate the rise of the stock. In Hamilton's opinion, when the stock reached its true value, foreign speculators would become beneficial. Their money used for American agriculture, commerce and manufactures would help the United States. Hamilton touched briefly on founding a national bank and promised to submit a plan during the session.

The procedure for the assumption of the state debts, Hamilton's most startling proposal, he saved for the end of the report. Assumption would be made on equal terms with the public securities, although interest payments would not start until January 1792. In conclusion, the secretary of the treasury repeated that the establishment of public credit by payment of the public debt was "the desideratum toward relief from individual and national embarrassment." It was his "anxious wish" that an effectual plan would be implemented this present session, so that a better impression of the good faith of the country be given and the creditors relieved.

Although Hamilton's detractors accused him of taking his financial theories from Gouverneur and Robert Morris, his own letters, to James Duane in 1779 and to Robert Morris in 1781, contain the outlines of these ideas. His financial views were on record in his "Continentalist" articles and in his replies to Rhode Island when the impost was rejected. It was Hamilton's genius that created the brilliant arrangement of ideas that became the Hamiltonian system. It was a splendid proposal, long-range and courageous.

The House ordered the secretary's report printed for the benefit of the members and gave them two weeks to study and digest it before submitting it to debate. The interim gave speculators, who had been hounding the members for information about the contents of the report, time to intensify their siege. Deducing that assumption of the state debts was part of the plan and that, consequently, securities would increase in value, some enterprising speculators sent agents or went themselves to the Carolinas and Georgia to purchase any state securities they could put their hands on. During the debate in Congress, Georgia's James Jackson declared: "My soul arises indignant at the avaricious and immoral turpitude which so vile a conduct displays."[11]

Hamilton expected serious opposition to his report but was shocked when he was told that its chief critic was James Madison. Later, Hamilton said that when he accepted the office of secretary of the treasury, he assumed that he would have "the firm support of Mr. Madison. . . . I do not believe that I should have accepted under a different supposition." The two men, Hamilton recalled, enjoyed "a similarity of thinking," both on the general principles of national policy and government and on the administration of finances. Madison justified his change of opinion on the grounds that "the very considerable alienation of the debt, subsequent to the periods at which he had opposed discrimination, had essentially changed the state of the question—and that as to assumption, he had contemplated it to take place *as matters stood at the peace*." Hamilton thought about Madison's point that the assumption of the states' debts should be as they stood at the peace but, on further reflection, concluded that it would be impractical and liable to immense difficulties.[12]

The debate over Hamilton's report occupied the first Congress from early February to August 1790. The provision for the foreign debt, interest and principal was easily accepted, but the congressmen divided over a motion introduced by Aedanus Burke. He proposed that a discrimination should be made between the original holders of the public securities and their assignees and that a scale of depreciation be prepared accordingly. Madison supported the proposal even after Burke withdrew it, waxing emotional over it and refusing to allow it to die.

Fisher Ames described Madison during these debates. His person was little and ordinary. He spoke low, but his language was to the point, "a little too much of a book politician." He was a Virginian who thought his state "the land of promise" but was afraid for his popularity there. He was cool "with a grave and self sufficient air, a good and able man," but "he had rather too much theory and wants that discretion which men of business commonly have. He is also very timid and seems evidently to want manly firmness and energy of character."[13]

No matter how often he was assailed by the arguments of the Hamiltonians, Madison clung to his notion of fairness. Defenders of the report pointed out that the debts were transferable and that those who had sold them, for however small a price, had done so freely and for their own needs. Those who had bought them ran the risk that they would become worthless. It was conceded that some of the original owners were soldiers and other worthy people, but the responsibility of Congress was to those who actually held the securities.

Senator William Maclay of Pennsylvania, whose biased comments added spice to all the parliamentary struggles of the day, was equally offensive about the two chief protagonists. He offered Madison a plan to slash all interest to 3 percent and pay everything by making debt certificates payable only in public land. After being handed the plan, Maclay related, "his Littleness" returned the resolutions without reading them. "The obstinacy of this man has ruined the opposition," he said. About Hamilton, Maclay observed that his scheme was "a movement of political absurdity," and he himself had "a very boyish, giddy manner, and Scotch-Irish people could well call him a 'skite.' "[14]

On February 22, after a week of debate, Madison's motion was defeated by a humiliating vote of 36–13. Only nine Virginians and four other southerners supported him. Hamilton was relieved that the first hurdle had been cleared.

As the debate continued, it became clear that the division was, essentially, over the new Constitution itself. How strong should the central government be? The supporters of states' rights did not want the nation to be economically unstable, but the price was too high if such stability meant a national taxation as outlined by the secretary of the treasury. They choked on the assumption of state debts.

Those states that had been paying off their debts were reluctant to accept being taxed for their delinquent sisters, such as Massachusetts and South Carolina. Madison suggested that the national government reimburse the states for the part of the debt that had been paid, a gesture to his own Virginia, whose citizens were righteously indignant about paying the debts of other states. Madison's proposal was defeated 31–29, a narrow margin this time.

On March 3, the opponents of assumption tried a diversionary tactic. They suggested that further discussion be postponed until the secretary supplied a report on the funds that might be raised and applied toward the payment of interest on the debts of the individual states, if the debts were to be assumed by Congress. Hamilton displayed his remarkable ability to meet impossible deadlines in record time. The next day, to the amazement of his friends as well as his enemies, the report was delivered to the House, complete with a list of taxable items and the expected revenue from each of them. But Hamilton's champions were unsuccessful against the strong bloc that opposed assumption. On April 12, the bill was defeated 31–21. Tench Coxe had written to Hamilton in March from Philadelphia that all the public creditors in his state were against assumption. The Antis opposed it because it would mean consolidation of the country, and many of the Feds and "principal country gentlemen" did not like it because Pennsylvania owed so little and possessed government securities to a greater amount.[15]

Hamilton, resourceful and resilient, cast about for another way to save his plan. The means presented itself with the renewal of interest in the matter of the placement of the national capital. The catalyst was Thomas Jefferson, who had just returned from Paris to assume the office of secretary of state.

Though well known to each other by reputation, Hamilton and Jefferson had not met before they became colleagues in the Washington cabinet. The strongest link between them had been James Madison, Jefferson's intimate friend and neighbor. Hamilton and Jefferson were a study in contrasts. Jefferson was tall, rangy, somewhat awkward in manner and sloppy in dress. Hamilton was short, and slight, but erect, gracefully made and elegantly dressed. Jefferson had the natural confidence of his aristocratic background. Hamilton could be arrogant to enforce his importance and thus betray an insecurity behind his proud façade.

Jefferson admired Washington, whom he did not know well. The two men had served together twenty years before in the Virginia House of Burgesses, but during the Revolution, Jefferson had been governor of Virginia, while Washington was in the field as commander in chief. After the war, Jefferson had gone to France. Washington received his new secretary with cordiality, without a glimmer of foreboding that there was to be a violent clash between Jefferson and the secretary of the treasury.

During the financial controversy that raged in Congress, Washington took no public stand. He saw his proper position as that of a neutral bystander because Congress had ordered his secretary of the treasury to report directly to it. Washington was not as interested in financial affairs as he was in foreign relations and the problems of the War Department. However, it was accepted at the time that he agreed with Hamilton.

Washington's diary reveals that he read Hamilton's report on January 2, 1790, but he did not leave a record of his reaction. In private letters to his friend, David Stuart, he revealed his feelings. "The Cause in which the expenses of the War was incurred, was a Common Cause," but, he added, he had not made his sentiment known. Although Washington had felt anger and grief at having to dismiss his army with only promise of payment, he did not support Madison's discrimination proposal.[16]

Jefferson's arrival added another question mark to the success of Hamilton's system. The secretary of state was known to be an agrarian, scornful of commerce and speculation. Jefferson seemed cooperative at first, but Hamilton knew that he could not depend upon him as an enthusiastic ally. The Virginian's interests were elsewhere. He wanted the capital of the United States located in the South on the Potomac. The two issues became entwined in Jefferson's plans.

Neither Hamilton nor his friends recorded a version of the grand bargain made between Jefferson and Hamilton, which was to save the assumption plan and place the capital of the United States on the banks of the Potomac River. All accounts of the deal are from Jefferson's pen or the reports of other Antis. In his *Anas*, which combined an account of the bargain written three years later with one written twenty-five years after the event, Jefferson recalled that the pact was proposed after the assumption bill had been defeated by the House and Congress so disturbed by the conflict that the two parties were "too much out of temper to do business together."

Jefferson hated the bill as fiercely as anyone. Then, as he was going to the president's house "some day" (between June 12 and June 20), Jefferson met Hamilton on the street, "looking sombre, haggard & dejected beyond description even his dress uncouth and neglected."

Hamilton asked to talk to him, which Jefferson agreed to, very disturbed about his colleague's agitation. They either stood and talked, or, in the later version, Hamilton walked Jefferson back and forth for half an hour. The secretary of the treasury expounded on the necessity for assumption to save the nation's financial structure and the new danger that the creditor states would secede if his plan was not passed. If the plan failed, Hamilton warned, he would resign from the administration. Since assumption had failed by only a small majority, Hamilton entreated Jefferson to appeal to his friends, who might set the machinery in motion again. Jefferson suggested that Hamilton dine with him and Madison the following evening.

After dinner at Jefferson's house, the three men discussed the problem. Hamilton and Madison worked out a compromise in which it was agreed that the assumption bill would be reintroduced into the house. Madison could not bring himself to vote for it but agreed to allow two other Antifederalists, Congressmen Alexander White and Richard Lee, to be persuaded to change their votes in its favor, thus easing its passage. Since the bill "would be a bitter one to the Southern states," it would be sweetened by "the removal of the Seat of Government to the Potowmac," after ten years in Philadelphia, which Hamilton agreed to support.[17]

This story, constantly retold, displays Hamilton in a poor light, sick with despair, turning to the noble pair of Virginians to resuscitate his program. Probably the meeting occurred, but it is certain that the author of the *Anas* exaggerated its importance. The two congressmen delegated to switch their votes would not have made the difference, and, further, the critical resolution of both problems took place in the Senate, not the House. Self-interest on the part of the states influenced their position. Those that stood to gain from assumption, Massachusetts and South Carolina, supported it. Such states as Virginia, Connecticut, Maryland, Georgia and North Carolina, almost out of debt, opposed Hamilton's plan. New York, New Hampshire, Pennsylvania and Delaware took no position, but Pennsylvania was thought to be the swing state.[18]

The residence issue had been discussed a great deal in caucuses and private meetings. Pennsylvania wanted the capital so intensely that her delegates were willing to make an arrangement with the southerners in which Philadelphia would be the temporary capital and the Potomac site the permanent one. Once the capital was firmly established in Philadelphia, many believed it would never be moved. There were reports of frequent negotiations among the congressmen and speculation that the issues of assumption and residence were linked together. Early in June, Fisher Ames noted that Pennsylvania congressmen had bargained with three Virginia counterparts to obtain approval for Philadelphia as the temporary capital, in return for the defeat of assumption. William Smith of South Carolina, who wanted the capital to remain in New York, wrote that the residence bill "was the offspring of a political cohabitation . . . between Pennsylvania and Virginia . . . having forced its way through the Senate [to which it was first introduced] by a large majority, it was ushered into the House of Representatives, where it underwent the solemn farce of a discussion."[19]

On June 28, Butler of South Carolina introduced the residence bill into the Senate. After Baltimore lost out, the Potomac site was selected as the permanent capital by a vote of 16–9. The next day, a close race developed between the supporters of New York City and of Philadelphia as the temporary site. At this critical stage in the dispute, New York's Sen. Rufus King said that Hamilton was responsible for the final outcome. The funding system, which had to include assumption, was the critical national achievement whose attainment must encompass every sacrifice, including residence. "The project of Philadelphia and Potomack is bad," Hamilton conceded, but Massachusetts would give up New York and Baltimore "because her object is assumption." If Hamilton made any arrangement, it did not work; Massachusetts continued to vote against the pairing of Philadelphia and the Potomac. King's accusation proved only that even his friends considered Hamilton capable of almost any bargain to achieve his system.

After many attempts to find a solution, a tie of 13–13 was achieved.

Vice-President Adams broke the tie by voting against Philadelphia, and then South Carolina's Butler, formerly a New York advocate, disgusted as were many of his colleagues with the amount of time being spent on the issue, voted for Philadelphia. The others jumped on the bandwagon, and on June 30, the Philadelphia-Potomac arrangement won.

In the House, many congressmen, such as Benjamin Goodhue of Massachusetts, saw the time spent on the residence issue as a delaying tactic, preventing the decision on public credit, "the great business the public had justly expected from us." Hamilton's former enemy Aedanus Burke asserted that the residence bill was "calculated . . . to arrest the funding system, and throw everything into confusion." Thus, the alleged influence of the two secretaries' bargain fades into a romantic myth. The passage of the residence bill in the House was necessary to clear the way for a decision on Hamilton's funding measure, which, it must be remembered, had been requested by the House. Consequently, the House passed the Senate's residence bill.[20]

The House supporters of the Hamiltonian system had not let it be forgotten after its April defeat, but now that it was almost summer and the probability of adjournment neared, no further delay was permitted. On June 2, a funding bill was adopted by the House that ignored the section on the assumption of states' debts. In that form, the bill went to the Senate. On June 14, the Senate committee reported on the funding bill with a recommendation that the assumption of state debts be added to it. On the following day, the last phase of the long battle for part one of the Hamiltonian system started. The conflict contracted into an argument over whether debts should be funded at 6 percent, as promised by the Continental Congress, or 4 percent, as Hamilton recommended. The secretary of the treasury, amazed that his father-in-law and other friends opposed him on this issue, fearful of a last minute defeat of his plan, offered a compromise. The principal of the public debt would be paid at 6 percent, the arrears of interest on the debt at 3 percent. In addition, the hostile states were placated by an increase of credits, as, for example, a $500,000 increase for Virginia and $800,000 for North Carolina.

On July 16, the Senate voted 15–11 to add assumption to funding and to make it one system. Hamilton estimated that five votes were needed to reverse the April 12 House negative. Jefferson's bargain provided for only two, those of Representatives White and Lee. The final count on July 26 was 34–28 for the Senate bill. Hence, the bargain was not responsible for its passage, any more than it could be given credit for the passage of the residence bill. Congressional factions grouped and regrouped around the issues, as is their custom. The acceptance of both funding and assumption was achieved in the Senate. The great bargain, so dear to Jefferson, was only another ploy in the struggle for acceptance to the secretary of the treasury. He never mentioned his dinner with Jefferson and Madison.[21]

In justice to Madison and Jefferson, it must be admitted that, despite their personal feelings, they realized the importance of establishing financial stability for the United States. Assumption was necessary, but they deplored the gains that irresponsible speculators were reaping. Hamilton ignored the speculators, regarding them as an inevitable but minor evil.

Hamilton's enemies have tried to implicate him in schemes to benefit himself and his friends from foreknowledge of the details of his public credit plan. No evidence has been found to support these accusations. He was, perhaps, at fault in his judgment when he selected William Duer as assistant secretary of the treasury, since he knew him to be an ardent speculator. Duer was chosen for the post in September 1789, and three months later he made an agreement with William Constable, a prominent New York financier, "to purchase on time as many continental securities as can be obtained" and to use the money from them to invest immediately in the debts of North Carolina and South Carolina, "to the extent of sixteen thousand specie dollars."[22]

Hamilton did not make one cent from such dealings, but, it must be acknowledged, he had a curious indifference to Duer's dealings that is hard to fathom. In Hamilton's defense, it must be remembered that during this time he was working night and day on the organization of the department, as well as on the preparation of his report. Even if he entertained the idea of exposing or dismissing Duer, the scandal would have resulted in a popular reaction against Hamilton's policies.

Duer resigned from office in April 1790, giving as his reasons the removal of the seat of government from New York to Philadelphia and the pressure of his business interests. "I interest myself in your happiness too sincerely not to acquiesce in whatever may redound to your advantage," Hamilton wrote diplomatically to Duer. Then he hinted at the truth, saying, "I confess, too, that *upon reflection* I cannot help thinking you have decided rightly.[23] The two men remained close friends, and Hamilton was loyal to Duer even after the speculator's dramatic change of fortune.

During the most critical period of congressional debate over Hamilton's plans, his enemies acted. At the end of March, Aedanus Burke of South Carolina suddenly launched a raucous and irrelevant attack on Hamilton, charging him with having insulted the Revolutionary War record of the militia of South Carolina in remarks made in his eulogy of General Greene, delivered on the Fourth of July, 1789. Hamilton was quoted as saying that Greene succeeded despite being "embarrassed by small fugitive bodies of volunteer militia, the *mimicry of soldiership*." After a flowery, impassioned defense of southern soldiers, Burke faced the crowded gallery of the House and declaimed the falseness of the assertion and of the person who had expressed it. He was called to order by many members, but he was not subdued. He then turned to the gallery again, where he erroneously thought Hamilton was sitting, and said loudly, "I throw the lie in Hamilton's face."

Hamilton replied to Burke's histrionics in a restrained manner, refusing to allow the provocation to distract him from his serious mission, the passage of the public credit program. He did not direct his words in the Greene eulogy "To the militia of *South Carolina* in particular, nor to the *Militia* in general but merely to *small fugitive* bodies of *volunteer militia*," Hamilton said. Then he tossed the matter into Burke's lap "to judge what conduct, in consequence of the explanation will be proper on your part."[24]

On April 1, the same day that he received the letter from the secretary of the treasury, Burke replied. He had suffered torture from the insult inflicted on him, but he did not call on Hamilton that day for it "would have been downright madness in me; you, on the full tide of popularity, in your own city: I, a stranger. . . . Had I called you to Account, and hurt a hair of your head, I knew too well the Spectre of Antifederalism would have been conjured up to hunt me down."[25]

According to Burke's account, three days later Hamilton sent his friend Rufus King to offer accommodations honorable to both men. As a result, a committee of congressmen was formed to arbitrate between the two adversaries. In a letter to Hamilton of April 6, the committee said that although Hamilton's disavowal did not convince Burke, it was apparent that his intention was "to make a disavowal"; therefore, they suggested that to resolve the conflict, Hamilton write another letter to Burke, making an explicit declaration of his intention. In return, Burke would write a letter in which he would make "a full and satisfactory" apology to Hamilton on the subject of whatever took place that was offensive to him. The two disputants acted accordingly, and the matter was ended.

Although the political overtones of this absurd episode are obvious, in a history of Hamilton's life any confrontation in which his honor was involved must be considered seriously in light of future events. The timing of Burke's explosion of hostility was significant. If it had succeeded in touching off a physical confrontation, it would have imperiled the Hamiltonian system, perhaps destroyed it at its start, along with its author. Whether the idea was Burke's alone or he was encouraged in his folly by others is speculative. Wiser minds prevailed, and this time the recipient of the insult refused to be made a victim of his overdelicate sense of honor.

13

Mr. Secretary of the Treasury II

THE GOVERNMENT'S MOVE from New York would be inconvenient for the family, but it was the price that had to be paid for Hamilton's beloved financial system. In August, he wrote to Gen. Walter Steward, asking him to find a house in the new capital. Steward should first learn where the Treasury Department was to be located and then look for a residence as near the offices as possible. "A cool situation & exposure will be a very material point," Hamilton wrote. The house had to have at least six rooms, particularly good dining and drawing rooms, and "I like elbow room in a yard." As to the rent, "the lower the better consistently with the acquisition of a proper house. But I must leave that to what is practicable."[1]

Hamilton asked other friends as well to be on the lookout for a house in Philadelphia. Finally, Congressman Thomas Fitzsimmons located one on Walnut Street with sufficient rooms and a reasonable rent. Fitzsimmons was asked to inform General Steward of his find, lest he too engage a house. "I leave it to you & him to do as you think fit for me," Hamilton said.[2]

Shortly before the Philadelphia house was secured, Elizabeth Hamilton and the children left New York City for Albany to visit the Schuylers. Mrs. Hamilton had not improved as a letter writer; her husband complained on September 11 that the post had arrived "and not a line from my dear Betsey." In a day or two he received her letter, asking him to join the family. As tired as he was of living alone, he had to stay in the city because "I am the only one of the Administration now here and . . . it might be very awkward for me to be absent also." Either she could come down to New York with her father, who was due on the twenty-seventh, or he would try to return to Albany with her father.

During the summer and fall of 1790, the Nootka Sound incident and the plan for a national bank occupied the secretary of the treasury. Washington was concerned with what was happening "on the other side of the water." Misunderstandings with Great Britain over the western posts and commerce persisted, and the continued absence of an official British representative in the United States made communication almost impossible. Gouverneur Morris's mission was not yielding clear results. Furthermore, there was a probability of war between Great Britain and Spain over Nootka Sound on Vancouver Island. British traders had set up trading posts at Nootka Sound in defiance of Spain's claim to a trade monopoly with the Pacific Coast Indians. Recently, Spanish forces had sailed from Mexico, attacked the British settlements and captured the settlers.

In May 1790, Lord Dorchester, governor of Quebec, was informed by Lord Grenville, the British home secretary, that there might be war with Spain; it was possible that the United States might decide to support Spain in return for help in ousting the British from the Northwest. To counter this, George Beckwith was assigned to the United States to assess the American position and convince the former colony of the feasibility of an Anglo-American alliance against Spain.[3]

Committed Jefferson scholar Julian Boyd, in his book, *Number 7*, accused Hamilton, who had several private conversations with Beckwith at this time, of deliberately misrepresenting what Beckwith said to him in his reports to Washington. According to Boyd, Hamilton provided the term "alliance" with Great Britain, whereas there was "no trace" of such a British proposal in Beckwith's discussions with him. Hamilton wanted a British alliance so desperately, Boyd maintained, that he was willing to hazard a "bold deception" to get it.

Gilbert Lycan, in his study of Hamilton and foreign policy, exonerates Hamilton ethically as well as diplomatically. "Historians have never taken very seriously the old idea that the minister of foreign affairs expects each of his ambassadors to report every trend and every conversation with the unerring accuracy of a barometer," he wrote.[4]

When Washington heard that the British were making preparations for war with Spain in Canada, he wondered if Canadian troops would expect to be allowed to march across United States territory on the way to fight the Spanish in New Orleans. As was his custom, the president asked his cabinet members, Vice-President Adams and Chief Justice Jay for their opinions. Jefferson recommended silence.

Jay and Adams recommended refusal but were unwilling to go to war over the issue. Secretary of War Knox and Secretary of the Treasury Hamilton favored granting passage with conditions.

Options should be kept open, Hamilton advised. The president should call Congress into special session and make war preparations and, at the same time, discreetly carry on talks with Spain and Great Britain. Preferring an agreement with Great Britain, Hamilton wanted the United States to do nothing unless certain of receiving territorial gains if she entered the war. If there had to be an alliance with either country, it should be temporary, because commerce with the world was the nation's best policy and therefore neutrality its best position.

Hamilton hedged on the question of a British request to march her troops through American territory. It would be a disagreeable situation, he said; a refusal might be ignored, and "our concurrence might expose us to the imputation either of want of foresight to discover a danger or of vigor to withstand it."[5]

In making a choice between Spain and Britain, Great Britain might make concessions in return for our future neutrality, he pointed out. "An explicit recognition of our right to navigate the Mississippi to and from the Ocean with the possession of New Orleans would greatly mitigate the causes of apprehension from the conquest of the Floridas from the British."[6]

Conflicting predictions of war and peace traveled across the ocean in the fall of 1790. Hamilton's own overseas correspondent, John B. Church, was pessimistic. He wrote from London in November that everyone there was in "awful Suspence" awaiting the messenger from Mr. Fizherbert, the British minister to Spain, as to Spain's answer to Britain. Meanwhile, a tremendous naval force was gathered and ready to sail. Church predicted that war would not come, for even the most successful war would leave Great Britain in terrible debt. Notwithstanding, "a mad Credulity prevails here just as it did at the Commencement of the American War, we despise our Enemy, and dream of nought but Victory, and the Capture of Spanish Wealth, the Mines of Mexico and Peru are already ideally in our possession."[7]

Church's wish that Spain would consent to peace came true. The Nootka Convention provided that Spain would free the captured British ships and men, and grant Britain the right to settlement and trade at certain points along the Pacific coast. This arrangement became the basis of British claims to the Oregon territory. The result for the United States was favorable. A weaker Spain improved the likelihood of the continuance of free navigation of the Mississippi. And the fact that the United States did not help Spain improved relations with the former mother country. Hamilton had supported the right side.

The second phase of Hamilton's economic plan for the new nation was presented to the House of Representatives on December 14, 1790. The report was a fully realized blueprint for a national bank, which enumerated its benefits, described the problems it would generate, analyzed its shortcomings, presented arguments why the Bank of North America would not be adequate to the country's needs and described the structure of the proposed bank.

The principal advantages of a bank, Hamilton said, were threefold. First, a bank would augment the use of gold and silver, and those banks "in good credit can circulate a greater sum than the actual quantum of their capital in Gold and Silver. The extent of the possible excess seems indeterminate." Of course, this ability of a bank "to circulate a greater sum than its actual capital in coin . . . must be gradual; and must be preceded by a firm establishment of confidence." Banks increased the active capital of a country. "By contributing to enlarge the mass of industrious and commercial enterprise, banks become nurseries of national wealth."[8] A second advantage of a national bank was the greater ease with which the government could obtain pecuniary aid in sudden emergencies. Thirdly, the payment of taxes was facilitated through the bank's ability to increase and quicken the quantity of money being circulated.

Hamilton then reviewed the "real or supposed" disadvantages of banks. With admirable tact, he admitted that "in the infancy of an institution," banks might be somewhat imprudent in their lending policies, but in a short time, "the *interest* will make it the *policy* of a Bank, to succour the wary and industrious; to discredit the rash and unthrifty; to discountenance both usurious lenders and usurious borrowers."[9]

To the accusation that bank lending stopped other kinds of lending, Hamilton replied that there would always be those who preferred to invest their funds in real estate mortgages rather than in bank stock, "which they are apt to consider as a more precarious security." The capital of every public bank would be restricted within a defined limit, "which the legislature will adjust. Once this is done there is no longer room for the investment of any additional capital."[10]

There might be overtrading on occasion, Hamilton said, but the new and increased energies that commercial enterprise would enjoy from the bank greatly outweighed "the partial ills of the overtrading of a few individuals, at particular times, or numbers in particular conjunctures." The practice of giving credit to adventurers and fraudulent traders had to be regarded in the same spirit. Banks would take all precautions, but if, in spite of care, they are "sometimes betrayed into giving false credit to such persons, it must be remembered that, more frequently, banks aid men of little or no capital to go into business."[11]

Hamilton left for last the "heaviest charge," that banks tended to banish the gold and silver of the country. The permanent increase or decrease of the precious metals in a country "can hardly ever be a matter of indifference," he admitted. A nation without mines of its own had to have a favorable balance of trade, which depended on the "State of its agriculture and manufactures, the quantity and *quality* of its labor and industry." Granted the truth of this, banks increased the amount of precious metals, because by augmenting the active capital of the country they generated employment, which expanded labor and industry. The resulting products, which might be exported, produced the favorable balance of trade that increased gold and silver.[12]

Hamilton then discussed whether any existing bank could serve the purpose. Of the three banks in the United States, only the Bank of North America in Philadelphia had had a direct relationship with the government of the United States. But its new charter from the state of Pennsylvania restricted its activities so as to "render it an incompetent basis for the extensive purpose of a National Bank."[13] The Bank of North America's capital was restricted to $2 million, too small an amount to service the needs of the government.

Hamilton explored the principles upon which a national bank should be organized. He rejected the establishment of a land bank rather than a money bank. The bank should not be structured so that the profits benefited the state. It should be "under a *private* not a *public* Direction, under the guidance of *individual interest*, not of *public policy*." The dangers of government control would be overwhelming. "What nation was ever blessed with a constant succession of upright and wise Administrators?" he asked. "The state ought not to own the whole or a principal part of the stock of the bank. It should, however, take care to know the soundness of the bank at all times since the bank's paper would be allowed "to insinuate itself into all the revenues and receipts of the country."[14]

Finally, Hamilton respectfully submitted rules for a national bank. The capital stock should be no more than $10 million, divided into 25,000 shares at $400 per share. Subscription to the bank should continue until the public debt was redeemed. No loan should be made by the bank for the use of the United States in excess of $50,000 unless authorized by United States law. The bank should be managed by twenty-five directors, all of whom had to be citizens of the United States and one of them the president. No similar institution should be established while this bank was in existence. The directors of the bank could establish offices within the United States, but only for discount and deposit. Lastly, the President of the United States should authorize a subscription of no more than $2 million for the capital stock in order to enlarge the specie fund of the bank and give it an immediate extension to its operations. The $2 million should be paid out of monies borrowed under congressional acts and should be reimbursed in ten years by equal annual installments, or sooner, if possible. "Though it is proposed to borrow with one hand what is lent by the other," Hamilton admitted, bank notes would be put into circulation instead of gold and silver, and, since the dividend on the stock would exceed the interest paid on the loan, there would be a profit. Hamilton concluded with an appeal to the Bank of North America to cooperate in facilitating the accomplishment of "the great object," the founding of a Bank of the United States.[15]

On December 23, when the House conveyed the report to the Senate, Senator Maclay responded with a sense of resignation. His attitude, shared by others, explains the unexpected ease with which the Senate accepted the Hamiltonian bank plan. He was certain of its acceptance, Maclay declared, although he had "no great predilection for banks." They were antirepublican and operated like "a tax in favor of the rich, against the poor." He deplored the possibility that the bank might become "a machine for the mischievous purposes of bad ministers; and this must depend more on the vigilance of future legislators than on either the virtue or foresight of the present ones."[16]

The Senate committee appointed to prepare the bank bill delivered it on January 3. Its opponents did not hope to defeat the bill, only to make some changes. Maclay proposed to make it of some benefit to the public "which reaps none from the existing banks." This was the gist of debate in the Senate.

Hamilton observed the proceedings in the Senate with some anxiety. He had briefed Schuyler and emphasized that his plan must not be altered. The debate centered around the preservation of the interests of the public and the length of time for which the bank should be chartered. Attempts to limit the life of the bank to seven or ten years failed. Finally, a twenty-year charter with an expiration date of March 4, 1811, was agreed upon.

The House did not start its debate on the Senate bank bill until February 1, 1791. Hamilton's plan, now more than six weeks old, had to face wide-ranging, bitter recrimination from House members. It was accused of being antifarmer; "an endless labyrinth of perplexities," beneficial only to moneymen; certain to plunge the nation into debt; and unconstitutional. Madison emphasized the unconstitutionality argument. After the debate on the bill, he emerged as a strict constructionist of the Constitution, an apostate from nationalism. The break with Hamilton was complete, his new alliance with Virginia politics and Jefferson an accomplished fact.

The two Virginians were now close friends and allies. In September 1790, they had traveled home together, taking three weeks to make the trip. They visited the site of the new national city, called on Washington at Mount Vernon and visited mutual friends. Jefferson asked Madison to share his large new house on Market Street in Philadelphia when they returned, but Madison refused, lest residence with Jefferson be interpreted as collusion between the executive and legislative branches of the government.

In November, Jefferson arrived at Montpelier, Madison's mountaintop plantation, to pick him up for the return to Philadelphia. Their leisurely fifteen-day trip provided ample opportunity for discussion of the emerging Jefferson party, to be further strengthened by the addition of two young, ambitious Virginians, both congressional replacements. James Monroe was to go to the Senate and William Branch Giles to the House of Representatives.

Once back in Philadelphia, Madison drafted Washington's State of the Union speech, with Hamilton's assistance, and then wrote the House of Representatives' reply. He had been quiescent until Hamilton's national bank proposal roused him to vigorous dissent.

Madison's argument against the bank's constitutionality centered on his opposition to a broad interpretation of the Constitution, which would stretch the "necessary and proper" clause into a "chain" that would "reach every object of legislation within the whole compass of political economy." A national bank would make borrowing money convenient, as Hamilton asserted, but there was too much danger in

using convenience as a justification for Congress approving legislation that was not included in the enumerated powers granted in the
Constitution. Not convenience but necessity must be the yardstick
for using the elastic clause, and the national bank was not necessary,
Madison said.[17]

The constitutional issue was argued by other congressmen as well.
William Branch Giles of Virginia eloquently urged that while in its
infancy, the new government should ensure the affections of the
people by keeping within the known boundaries of the Constitution,
rather than "increase the previously existing jealousies." Elbridge
Gerry of Massachusetts answered Giles spiritedly in defense of the
use of the "necessary and proper" clause. Shall this Constitution
have no more "energy than the old? Shall we thus unnerve the
Government, leave the Union, as it was under the Confederation,
defenceless . . . ?"[18]

On February 8, the House passed the bill by a vote of 39–20. The
lines upon which the vote split were sectional; northern commercial
interests versus southern agrarianism. All but six of the affirmative
votes were from the northern states; fifteen of the twenty negative
votes were from the southern states.[19]

"The constitutionality of it [the bank bill] is objected to," Washington wrote to Hamilton on February 16. He had asked Attorney
General Edmund Randolph for his opinion. Randolph replied that
"the Constitution does not warrant the Act." The secretary of state
concurred with Randolph. Having received these two opinions,
Washington requested Hamilton's judgment on "the validity & propriety" of the bill "as soon as is convenient."[20]

Jefferson's reply to Washington was a short, closely argued brief
that limited its attention to a narrow analysis of the subject and
avoided the broader issues. As a tactic, this proved to be a mistake,
and Hamilton's lengthy, carefully reasoned presentation eclipsed his
rival's in the art of persuasion.

It is likely that Jefferson and Randolph discussed their opinions,
since several of their arguments were the same. Both asked whether
"the specified powers of legislation involve the power of granting
charters of incorporation," as Randolph phrased it. Both said no.
Jefferson was particularly concerned that the establishment of a bank
would expand the delegated powers granted to the legislature by the
Constitution. He quoted the Tenth Amendment. "All powers not delegated to the United States by the Constitution, nor prohibited by it
to the states, are reserved to the states, or to the people." Therefore,

"to take a single step beyond the boundaries thus specially drawn around the powers of Congress, is to take possession of a boundless field of power, no longer susceptible of any definition." The enumerated powers granted to Congress to lay taxes, borrow money and regulate commerce with foreign nations, among the states and with the Indian tribes did not justify the establishment of a national bank, Jefferson said. Nor did the "general welfare" clause at the end of the power, "to lay taxes for the purpose of providing for the general welfare," cover the matter. Congress, he judged, could not use the general welfare clause "to do any act they please" lest the Constitution be reduced to a single phrase, "that of instituting a Congress with power to do whatever would be for the good of the United States; and as they would be the sole judge of the good or evil, it would be also a power to do whatever evil they pleased."[21]

The elastic clause of the Constitution, which provided that Congress "may make all laws *necessary* and proper for carrying into execution the enumerated powers," did not apply to the bank. All these powers could be carried out without a bank; therefore, a bank "is not *necessary*" and so not "authorized" by the phrase. The bank bill might make it more convenient to collect taxes, and a bank bill might be "a more *convenient* vehicle" than treasury orders, "but convenience does not constitute necessity," Jefferson said. "Can it be thought that the Constitution intended that for a shade or two of *convenience*, more or less, Congress should be authorized to break down the most ancient and fundamental laws of the several States?" he asked.[22]

Finally, Jefferson reminded Washington that the presidential veto was a constitutional "shield" against the legislative invasion of the right of the executive, the judiciary or the states. The present bill invaded the rights of the states, Jefferson believed, but, he conceded, if the president had any doubts about the bill's constitutionality, "just respect for the wisdom of the legislature would naturally decide the balance in favor of their opinion."[23]

The mildness of Jefferson's conclusion was consistent with his republican hesitation to advocate the use of presidential power over the power of the representatives of the people. He was ambivalent about his feelings because he felt that the legislature had been manipulated by one man—Alexander Hamilton. Jefferson was almost resigned to the inevitability that the secretary of the treasury would have his way with Washington, although he knew that Madison had been asked to draft a veto message.

A week after he received the president's request for his opinion on
the constitutionality of the bank bill, Hamilton put it into his hands. It
had occupied him "the greatest part of last night," he told Washington on February 23. In her account of that night, told when in her
nineties to Arthur Latham Perry, Betsey Hamilton said that Jefferson
thought that we ought not to have a bank but that "my husband said,
we must have a bank. I sat up all night, copied out his writing, and
the next morning he carried it to President Washington and we had a
Bank."[24]

Hamilton introduced his defense of the bank with engaging frankness. "It will naturally have been anticipated that, in performing this
task he would feel uncommon solicitude," Hamilton wrote in the
third person. Just the fact that the measure originated with him
would produce that feeling. But his chief concern arose from his
"firm persuasion" that the principles forwarded by the secretary of
state and the attorney general would be "fatal to the just & indispensable authority of the United States."[25]

Hamilton lost no time in refuting the arguments of his colleagues
in the cabinet on the authority of the United States to erect corporations. It was "unquestionably incident to *sovereign power* to erect
corporations," and therefore to the power of the United States "in
relation to the objects intrusted to the management of the government. Under the constitution there are *implied* as well as *express*
powers, and the former are as effectually delegated as the latter,"
Hamilton stated boldly. He conceded that implied powers were delegated equally with expressed ones. A corporation could be erected
by Congress "as an *instrument* or *mean* of carrying into execution
any of the specified powers, the only question being if the corporation has a natural relation to any of the acknowledged objects or
lawful ends of the government." Congress could not erect a corporation to superintend the police of Philadelphia because Congress
could not regulate the police, but it could erect a corporation to
collect taxes, trade between the states or foreign countries or Indian
tribes because "it is incident to a general *sovereign* or *legislative
power* to *regulate* a thing, to employ all the means which relate to its
regulation to the *best* & greatest advantage."[26]

Jefferson's restrictive use of the "necessary and proper" clause was
wrong, Hamilton maintained. The constitutional right of exercising it
had to be "uniform & invariable—the same today as tomorrow," not
depending on "circumstances," as the secretary of state would have
it. The clause was intended by the convention "to give a liberal

latitude to the exercise of the specified powers." And so the practice of the government has been in such cases as the act establishing lighthouses, beacons, buoys and public piers. Hamilton added that "the means by which national exigencies are to be provided for, national inconveniences obviated, national prosperity promoted, are of such infinite variety, extent and complexity, that there must of necessity be great latitude of discretion in the selection & application of these means."[27]

The attorney general had enumerated the possibilities that might come under the enumerated powers to lay and collect taxes, regulate commerce, etc. Hamilton deemed the enumeration incomplete and controversial and, by adding his own corrections and additions, reduced Randolph's enumeration to an absurdity that was ineffective and presumptuous.

In his last few pages, Hamilton recapitulated his argument, showing the clear connection between the right to create the proposed bank and the delegated powers of Congress. The government must not be so restricted that it could not meet the demands put upon it. The wonder of Hamilton's argument is the clarity with which he foresaw the nation's future needs. Expansion, commerce, wealth, manufacturing and prosperity were part of that future. The country should not be deprived of its glorious destiny by its rulers' foolish fears of bigness. Hamilton stood alone on one side, with the three Virginians—Jefferson, Madison and Randolph—on the other. He believed that Washington shared his hopes.

While waiting for the president's signature or veto, there was a great deal of tension, particularly in New York City's financial community. Washington, who had received the bank bill from Congress on Monday, February 14, was having a difficult time deciding what to do. He asked Hamilton "to what precise period, by legal interpretation of the constitution can the president retain it in his possession, before it becomes a Law by the lapse of ten days." Hamilton answered immediately that he had ten days "exclusive of that on which the Bill was delivered to you, and Sundays. Hence in the present case if it is returned on Friday at any time while Congress are sitting, it will be in time."[28]

Washington, with only two days left to ruminate after the receipt of Hamilton's opinion, signed the bill. Hamilton's brilliant analysis convinced him.

In between his monumental report on the national bank and his successful defense of it, Hamilton delivered another major report on the establishment of a mint, which ranks among his major achievements.

A plan for the establishment of a mint, Hamilton told Congress on January 28, 1791, "involves a great variety of considerations intricate, nice and important. The general state of Debtor and Creditor; all the relations and consequences of *price*; the essential interests of trade and industry; the value of all property; the whole income both of the State and of individuals are liable to be seriously influenced, beneficially or otherwise, by the judicious or injudicious regulation of this interesting object."[29]

If it is such a difficult problem, Hamilton asked, why not leave things as they are? He answered that if this were done, the value of the property of the citizens of the United States would continue to "fluctuate with the fluctuations of a foreign Mint, and to change with the changes in the regulations of a foreign sovereign." If the United States had no coins of its own, it had to use those of other countries. English and French guineas, English crowns and shillings, French pistoles, Spanish doubloons and Portuguese johaines and moidores were among the potpourri of coins in general use. The Spanish milled dollar, depreciated by 5 percent of its original value, was employed in the country's financial transactions.

Hamilton pointed out that unequal values were allowed in different parts of the United States to coins of the same intrinsic worth. Such embarrassments and inconveniences made the late Confederation consider the establishment of a mint on several occasions, but now that "the favorable change in the situation of public affairs" had taken place, it would be carried into execution.[30]

Hamilton answered the six questions that he posed one by one. What ought to be the nature of the money unit of the United States; the proportion between gold and silver if there were to be coins of both metals; the proportion and composition of alloy in each kind; whether the government should defray the expense of the coinage; the number, denominations, sizes and devices of the coins; and, finally, whether foreign coins should be permitted, at what rate and for how long. After recommending the prevailing dollar as the standard of the present money unit because it was the practical decision, Hamilton declared that he favored a bimetallic standard. If "either were to be preferred it ought to be gold rather than silver," Hamilton wrote. Gold, because of its intrinsic superiority as a metal, its greater rarity or the prejudice of mankind, retained a preeminence in value over silver. But "to annul the use of either of the metals as money, is to abridge the quantity of circulating medium; and is liable to all the objections which arise from a comparison of the benefits of full, with the evils of a scanty circulation."[31]

The proportion to adopt between the two metals was of great importance because overvaluing either metal would result in the banishment of the undervalued one. After reviewing the ratio in other countries and even other times, Hamilton recommended 15:1, a proportion that was the commercial average and best agreed with that of the United States.

The use of alloy in coins, Hamilton explained to Congress, saved the expense of refining the metals and made them harder, which protected them from wearing out. Again, Hamilton advised using as models the coins most in circulation in the country, those of Spain, Portugal, England and France. The country should start with a small number of denominations of coins "till experience shall decide whether any other kinds are necessary." To start with, a ten-dollar gold piece, a one-dollar gold piece, a copper penny and a copper halfpenny would be sufficient. The pieces of small value "are a great accommodation and the means of a beneficial oeconomy to the Poor; by enabling them to purchase, in small portions, and at a more reasonable rate, the necessaries of which they stand in need," Hamilton wrote. If the poor could buy their necessities cheap, they could work for less, "the advantages of which need no comment."[32]

The devices on the coins "may be made the vehicles of useful impressions" and should be emblematical but simple. The fewer sharp points and angles, the less loss incurred in wearing. For the sake of expediency, the circulation of foreign coins should continue for one year after the mint started its operations, and it should be at the discretion of the president to continue the currency of the Spanish dollar.

For the organization of the mint, Hamilton suggested appointing a director, an assayer, a master coiner, a cashier, an auditor, several clerks and workmen and a porter. The annual expense was estimated at $15–20,000.

Debate on Hamilton's proposal was predictably factional. The gold dollar was eliminated and the amount of alloy in the silver pieces reduced. The idea of representing the heads of presidents on the coins was, one angry congressman said, too much like English coinage and insulting to the new bastion of democracy. The bill to establish the mint was passed with a few small changes, providing another impressive victory for Hamilton and his friends.

The victory became bittersweet when it was decided to place the mint under the State instead of the Treasury Department. Both Jefferson and Hamilton were concerned about the subject of the coinage and had had some correspondence about it shortly after they first became acquainted in the cabinet. Jefferson sent Hamilton a report of the National Assembly of France on the subject of *billion*, a mixture of one part silver and four parts copper. It would be more convenient than a copper cent, he said, but submitted it "to the better judgment of the Secretary of the Treasury," who, he hoped, "will consider the liberty taken as an advance towards [our] unreserved communications for reciprocal benefit."[33] Hamilton sent Jefferson a copy of his report on the mint before submitting it to the House of Representatives. Jefferson read it over "with a great deal of satisfaction." He agreed with bimetallism and the proportion established between the two metals and limited his criticism to some comments about the value of the dollar.

Though the success of his reports pleased Hamilton, there were political reversals that alarmed him. On January 19, Aaron Burr was elected by the New York State legislature to replace Philip Schuyler, whose senatorial term had expired. In one move, Hamilton lost a trusted advocate and gained, as he soon discovered, a relentless enemy. Burr hedged about opposing the bank outright but was outspoken in his concern about the activities of speculators. He noted that David Hume also had reservations about banks because, in the long run, the unnatural increase in the supply of money could create an inflationary market, which would prove harmful to the interests of a trading nation.[34]

The blow was not unexpected; warnings had come from New York friends and supporters. James Tillary, a New York City physician, wrote in January that "the head of Wild misrule in this City seems disposed to fall in with a few of those other powerful malcontents, in some of the Neighboring States, with a view to disturb the operations & happiness of the Union." The new alliance that Tillary deplored was that of the Livingstons with the Clintonians. Of Burr, the physician wrote, "He is avowedly your Enemy, & stands pledged to his party for a reign of Vindictive declamation against your measures. The Chancellor hates & would destroy you."

Tillary complained that the New York City Federalists lacked a leader. Schuyler's presence in the city would revive a drooping party and rouse the people, Tillary told Hamilton, whom he regarded as the real savior of the Federalists. "Long may you successfully fend off the Maddison's [*sic*] of the South & the Clintons of the North."[35]

Burr's election upset Robert Troup, too. "We are going headlong into the bitterest opposition to the Genl Government," he warned his friend Hamilton. "I pity you most sincerely, for I know that you have not a wish but what is combined with the solid honor & interests of America."[36]

William Duer also attributed Schuyler's defeat to the new coalition between Chancellor Livingston and Governor Clinton. The Federalist cause in the legislature "has a most gloomy Aspect," he wrote, and "there is so much Rottenness, that I know not who to trust."[37]

Hamilton wondered if the move to Philadelphia had not cost more than he had expected. Livingston's turnabout was probably due to his disappointment that the Washington administration had given no patronage either to him or to other members of his large and influential family. Hamilton could not have changed that, but had he been in New York he might have been able to keep the Federalists together and exercised some needed leadership.

Though Hamilton regarded Burr as an enemy at this time, there was no comparison in the importance of the two men. Hamilton was the most powerful man in the administration, second only to Washington. Burr was the junior senator from New York, with sharp doubts about his reception in the capital. "I have reason to believe that my election will be unpleasing to several Persons now in Philada," the new senator wrote to a friend. He meant Washington as well as Hamilton. Washington had lost respect for Burr during the Revolution while Burr was an aide to the commander in chief. Burr had been discovered by the general, surreptitiously reading his mail. There had been recriminations, and afterward Washington blocked Burr's rise in the army. Later on, Burr characterized Washington as formal and haughty, "entirely without independence of character, and without talent, and completely under the influence of Alexander Hamilton."[38]

The loss of his father-in-law's support in the Senate was a blow to Hamilton, and his replacement by Aaron Burr was a disaster. As William Seton, cashier of the Bank of North America, wrote in February 1791, "Your friends here lamented it [Burr's election], foreseeing the impediments it would throw in your way. Some say he [Aaron Burr] will act otherwise but what is bad in the bone will appear in the flesh. I anticipate, tho no politician, great opposition to evry salutary system."[39]

Hamilton had every reason to believe in the months that followed that Burr had joined the Virginia coalition of Jefferson, Madison and their friends who were planning to block the development of his financial system.

14

Of Manufacturing and Other Problems

Hamilton had the satisfaction of knowing that Congress accepted his financial program. But the principle upon which its success rested, that of a strong central government, was endangered on all sides. There was hardly an issue faced by the first administration that did not threaten national power. In this struggle, George Washington was Hamilton's staunchest ally. In their attitude toward the expansion of the West, Indian troubles and the need for trade treaties with European nations, Hamilton and Washington stood together; critics scornfully referred to Hamilton as Washington's prime minister.

Conversations with Beckwith continued to be the sole avenue of communication with Great Britain. The secrecy of the talks, coupled with the fact that America's spokesman was not the secretary of state, as would be expected, exposed the exchanges to a sinister interpretation. But Hamilton was effective, alternately threatening and cajoling the British agent while answering his questions and, in reality, manipulating him.

Beckwith stated at their January 19, 1791, meeting that he was disturbed by the House of Representatives' response to Washington's December 1790 message to that body, in which he recommended that American navigation be encouraged to "render our commerce and agriculture less dependent on foreign bottoms." The House of Representatives, with "a certain warmth of expression," Beckwith complained, had agreed, adding that the frequency of foreign wars made the dependence even more precarious and appointed James Madison chairman of a committee to deal with the problem.[1]

Hamilton replied patiently that "there is a Party which retaining the prejudices that were produced by the civil war, think nothing good can come from Great Britain, and that our obligations to France are never to be forgotten." There were those, also, who wanted to trade with England and thought that the only way to get a trade treaty with England would be to set up discriminatory duties that favored those countries that had made commercial treaties with the United States. They had learned from private letters, Hamilton hinted, that Great Britain would appoint a minister to the United States, probably Elliott. This would end the French party's assertion that "we are held in no consideration by the English Government." Then Hamilton assured Beckwith that nothing would occur during the congressional session "to the injury of your trade."[2]

The British were concerned about the situation in the West, where rampaging Indian tribes were killing American settlers and destroying their settlements. In the fall of 1790, expeditions against the Indian raiders, led by Gen. Josiah Harman and Maj. John F. Hamtramck, had both suffered humiliating defeats. Beckwith pointed out that these military activities might injure the profitable British-Indian fur trade. The Americans, Hamilton answered, were angered at the British and the traders, whom they suspected were arming and encouraging the Indians. To persuade Hamilton that the British were opposed to Indian violence, Beckwith introduced him to William Macomb, a Detroit fur trader.

"Impossible," Macomb said immediately. Indian violence would ruin trade, and the present Indian war would cause many bankruptcies in Detroit. Macomb was pessimistic about Indian relations after the failure of the American expedition. Since the Indians had lost only one man in the first action and nine in the second, "they will become infinitely more troublesome than formerly." If Harman had sent a message of peace instead of attacking, it would have been better. Hamilton agreed.[3]

In May, Beckwith brought a proposal to Hamilton that Lord Dorchester be asked to intervene in order to make peace between the United States and the Indians. The unofficial British representative said that he spoke "altogether as an individual," perceiving that the reestablishment of peace would advance American trading interests. Hamilton conceded that the end of Indian hostilities was to the government's interest, and dealing with the natives expensive and troublesome. But he could not submit the offer of mediation to the president's consideration because "the object of warfare are certain vagrant Indian tribes who cannot be considered to be on the footing which such a system as this would place them." It would be different if the United States were at war "with a great or respectable nation," Hamilton explained.[4]

Although England was not quite ready to send an official minister to America, during the winter of 1791, Lord Grenville discussed the subject informally with Colonel Smith, Vice-President John Adams's son-in-law, in London at the time. Hamilton repeated to Beckwith in July that Smith had been told of Elliott's declining the American appointment, but "it was the determination of the Administration to have a Minister here at a very early period." Grenville had also told Smith that Britain did not encourage Indian raids but hoped that the United States was not entertaining the idea of exterminating Indian nations, as Great Britain could not view this with indifference. Hamilton asked Beckwith whether this meant that England intended to take some part in the progress of the Indian business. America wanted peace with the Indians, Hamilton said, but only on "proper terms." The safety of the American settlers required attention.

During negotiations, an Indian chief had told Col. Timothy Pickering that British influence was being extended to promote peace, Hamilton informed Beckwith. The British agent reassured Hamilton that these pacific views were being extended by the British to all the tribes in the western territory.

The Indian problem came up again and again in cabinet meetings. Hamilton blamed some of the trouble on the American federal system, which left "the public plan of the union at the mercy of each State Government." A party from a Virginia county would come over the border into Pennsylvania and wantonly murder friendly Indians. The national government lacked the power to act; what happened depended upon the policies of the two states.

Rufus King described to Hamilton the serious Indian trouble in their own state's frontier settlements. "You are sensible that almost every person here is interested in our western lands; their value depends on the settlement of the frontiers, their settlement depends on Peace with the Indians." The legislature authorized Governor Clinton to draw money from the treasury to preserve the goodwill of the neighboring Indians, however possible.[5]

Washington, heavily invested in western land, was disturbed by the King letter, which Hamilton forwarded to him. The Six Nations had been assured by Colonel Pickering that they would be spoken to "by the Government of the United States *only*," the president wrote. "The interference of the States and the speculation of Individuals will be the bane of all our public measures."[6]

Although Hamilton conveyed to the president and his colleagues in the cabinet the protestations of the British that they were not arming and inciting the Indians, this was generally disbelieved. If it were true, it did not stop the Indian raids, nor did it stop an ill-fated American expedition under the command of Gen. Arthur St. Clair from setting out to avenge former defeats.

General St. Clair, at the head of an army of poorly trained, undisciplined troops, left Fort Washington, a post near Cincinnati, on a ninety-mile march into Indian territory. He was surprised and soundly beaten. Washington was handed the dispatches on December 9 while he and Mrs. Washington were entertaining their guests. It was a tale of terrorized, untrained soldiers ambushed by Indians who fired from the ground or from behind trees, seldom seen by the artillerymen. After three hours of seeing his men shot down and scalped, St. Clair, who was ill with gout and was being hauled about in a wagon, tried to organize a retreat. The Indians, "yelling and mad with victory," pursued the fleeing Americans. Fortunately, the Indians got tired of the pursuit after about four miles. The "greatest part of the men threw away their arms and accoutrments even after the pursuit . . . had ceased."[7]

By the time Washington was informed of the defeat, American diplomatic relations with England had become official. George Hammond, only twenty-eight years old but already an experienced diplomat, had been appointed the first British minister to the United States. He arrived in America in October but delayed presenting his credentials until he was assured by Jefferson that the United States was in the process of choosing a minister to go to England. He was presented to the president on November 11, 1791.

With the appearance of Hammond, Beckwith's secret mission was ended, but Hammond continued the policy of conversations with Hamilton, who was still regarded as a true friend of Great Britain.

As early as June 30, Hamilton knew that Hammond would be coming instead of Elliott. John Church, now a member of Parliament, told his brother-in-law that Hammond would be sent to America but cautioned him not to be too optimistic; Lord Hawkesbury, a member of the British cabinet, was anti-American and believed in the maintenance of the Navigation Act.

Hamilton was not overly concerned. The new government and his financial system had raised the United States in the estimation of Europe. America's credit was high. Holland had given the United States a loan on better terms than those awarded any European power, and subscriptions to the Bank of the United States had been filled in one day, which disappointed many applicants.

Before George Washington made a trip through the South in April and May of 1791, he submitted his itinerary to Hamilton, Jefferson and Knox. If anything serious arose during his absence, they would consult to decide whether he should be recalled to Philadelphia. If the problem could be legally and properly handled without him, he said, "I will approve and ratify the measures." The president presumed that Vice-President Adams would be in Boston, but if he was not, "I wish him also to be consulted."[8]

Washington had set a precedent for the management of his office during his absence that was logical and practical. A year earlier, during a bout with pneumonia, he had confided to Lafayette that "by having Mr. Jefferson at the head of the Department of State, Mr. Jay of the Judiciary, Hamilton of the Treasury and Knox of that of War, I feel myself supported by able coadjutors who harmonize extremely well together."[9] This statement of cabinet harmony was soon to become a mockery.

In early May, Madison and Jefferson set out on a trip through New York and New England for rest, recreation and scientific studies. Jefferson was particularly interested in the Hessian fly, a pest that infested these areas. The "botanical expedition" was of a month's duration and covered about 920 miles. The Virginians observed the flora and fauna; Jefferson took voluminous notes and ordered trees and shrubs for Monticello. It was a pleasant vacation, during which Madison and Jefferson cemented their friendship. After ample time to exchange ideas, Jefferson seemed to assume the leadership, and Madison became the leading disciple of Jeffersonianism.

The Federalists regarded the outing as a cover for devious political activity, centering on an alliance with the New York team of Livingston, Burr and Clinton. Robert Troup reported to Hamilton that there was every indication of "a passionate courtship" between the chancellor (Robert R. Livingston), Burr, Jefferson and Madison when the latter two were in town. Beckwith informed Grenville that it was "unreasonable to suppose" that the secretary of state and the congressman "failed to use the tour as a means of promoting their anti-British policy." At a dinner party, Pierrepont Edwards, Burr's uncle, ridiculed Jefferson and Madison's tour, "in which they scouted silently thro' the Country, shunning the Gentry, communing with & pitying the Shaysites and quarreling with the Eatables; nothing good enough for them." John Trumbull might write a satire about it. "They are supremely contemned by the Gentlemen of Connecticut."[10]

Many people commented on the expedition, but the chief actors left no record of any politicking. It is possible that the only accomplishments of the springtime jaunt were Madison's improved health and Jefferson's botanical notes. On the other hand, the episode may be regarded as the bucolic beginning of the American party system.

While Washington was in the South and Jefferson and Madison were enjoying the natural wonders of the North, Hamilton remained at his desk in Philadelphia, working very hard. He obtained Washington's approval for a Dutch loan and improved the organization of his own department. He sent out an order to the captains of the revenue cutters plying the coastal waters to use firmness coupled with tact in handling suspected smugglers. Officers should display "activity, vigilance & firmness" in pressing their objectives but had to keep in mind that "their Countrymen are Freemen & as such are impatient of every thing that bears the least mark of a domineering Spirit." Hamilton had not forgotten that several well-known patriots had been notorious smugglers during the colonial period.[11]

After Nicholas Eveleigh, comptroller of the Treasury, died in April, Hamilton proposed Oliver Wolcott, the auditor, as his replacement. He was an excellent and distinguished officer, Hamilton wrote, who had exhibited "moderation with firmness, liberality with exactness, indefatigable industry with an accurate & sound discernment, a thorough knowledge of business & a remarkable spirit of order and arrangement." In a private letter to Hamilton, from Mount Vernon, Washington agreed to the Wolcott appointment, which pleased the secretary immensely. He was willing to wait until Washington's arrival in Philadelphia for a decision on Wolcott's successor. "Nothing new here worth communicating except that all my Accounts from Europe, both private and official, concur in proving that the impressions now entertained of our government and its affairs (I may say) *throughout* that quarter of the Globe are of a nature the most flattering & pleasing," Hamilton wrote proudly to Washington.[12]

The summer of 1791 was a season of folly for the overworked secretary of the treasury. Betsey and the children were in Albany, as usual, to escape the heat and disease inevitable in the dirty, fly-ridden city. As early as mid-May, Philip Schuyler wrote: "I entreated Eliza to let me know when she would set out from Philadelphia to this place, that I might engage a good and discreet Master and an

Albany sloop to bring her to this place, and begged her to bring all the children and their nurse with her. I fear if she remains where she is until the hot weather commences that her health may be injured. Let me therefore entreat you to expedite her as soon as possible."[13] As a result, the Hamilton family left for the North earlier than usual. It was during their absence that Hamilton was entrapped into an affair whose aftermath concerned the nation.

While Washington was out of town, the rift between Jefferson and Hamilton widened. Jean Baptiste Ternant, the French Minister to the United States, informed Hamilton of a slave revolt in Haiti that had cost the plantation owners extensive property losses. The minister wanted $40,000 against the United States debt to France in order to send aid as soon as possible. Hamilton responded at once to the "calamitous event" and, that same day, came up with a plan to raise the money, thereby making a friend. The president was then informed by mail of the request and of Hamilton's prompt action. Washington's response, since he was himself a slave owner, was that Hamilton's "proceedings . . . meet my entire approbation."

Jefferson was very angry when he heard about the arrangements, believing it part of a plot by Hamilton to usurp his position as the proper negotiator with the French minister. And to compound the injury, while Washington and Jefferson were out of town, Hamilton had met with Ternant for four hours to discuss a new commercial treaty that King Louis had proposed. Hamilton considered the subject under discussion commerce, well within the bounds of his department. Jefferson suspected that Hamilton wanted to involve him and the president in a discussion with France in order to propose a similar commercial meeting with Hammond, Britain's minister. His wily fellow cabinet member, Jefferson wrote in his *Anas*, would then, by imposing an extravagant tariff, make it impossible to conclude an arrangement with Ternant and then turn around and propose "terms so favorable to Great Britain, as would attach us to that country by treaty."[14]

Jefferson and Hamilton were disturbed by the differences in their political philosophies. Jefferson had severely criticized a series of letters signed "Publicola," a defense of John Adams's *Discourses on Davila*, in which the vice-president attacked the French Revolution. It is now known that the author was young John Quincy Adams, Adams's oldest son, but at the time most people thought the author was the elder Adams.

Hamilton joined Jefferson in condemnation of Adams's writing, but his amplification of his statements was chilling to the pro-French secretary of state. "I own it is my own op[inio]n tho' I do not publish it in Dan & Bersheba, that the present govnt is not that which will answer the ends of society by giving stability & protection to its rights, and that it will probably be expedient to go into the British form. However, since we have undertaken the experiment, I am for giving it a fair course, whatever my expect[atio]ns may be." And "there are still . . . other stages of improvement, which . . . ought to be tried before we give up the republican form altogether."[15]

Jefferson described Hamilton at this time as "a singular character of acute understanding, disinterested, honest, and honorable in all private transactions, amiable in society, and duly valuing virtue in private life, yet so bewitched by the British example, as to be under thorough conviction that corruption was essential to the government of the nation."[16]

Hamilton recorded his impression of Jefferson in a letter to General C. C. Pinckney in 1792. He was a gentleman whom the secretary of the treasury "once very much esteemed" but who did not "permit me to retain that sentiment for him." He is "certainly a man of sublimated and paradoxical imagination, entertaining and propagating opinions inconsistent with dignified and orderly government."[17]

Jefferson and Hamilton were miles apart in their thinking, and now Madison, who had been Hamilton's ally and friend, was closely tied to the ideas of his fellow Virginian. The Jefferson-Madison coalition, however, lacked a newspaper to reflect their wisdom. To remedy this omission, they induced Philip Freneau, a classmate of Madison who was planning to start a newspaper in New Jersey, to accept a clerkship in the State Department and start his embryo newspaper in Philadelphia. Antiadministration from its first issue, the *National Gazette* appeared on October 31, 1791. During its two-year life span, Madison published in its pages a large number of intelligent articles highly critical of Washington and Hamilton. The way was being cleared for an all-out attack on Hamilton, but before the war against him got started, he presented his last major report, the "Report on Manufactures."

To promote industry in a nation committed ideologically as well as practically to agriculture required the kind of imagination and indifference to conventional thinking that made Alexander Hamilton so detested by his enemies and admired by his friends. But he had to overcome the eighteenth-century libertarian's conviction that the individual's right to own his land was the American dream. Hamilton was going to recommend the development of industry side by side with the romantic ideal of the rural life and, further, propose government interference in the project.

Hamilton had been directed by the House of Representatives, on January 15, 1790, to prepare a report on the subject of manufacture, "particularly the means of promoting such as will tend to render the United States independent of foreign nations for military and other supplies." His delay of almost a year was due to the pressing need to organize the Treasury Department, the chore of accumulating the necessary data and the need to develop the best way to present the subject to a potentially hostile audience.

In preparation, Hamilton sent out a circular letter to existing societies for the encouragement of manufactures to obtain data. Tench Coxe, secretary of the Philadelphia society, Loyalist turned patriot during the Revolution, merchant, delegate to the Annapolis convention and member of the Continental Congress in 1777 and 1778, sent an encouraging response. "Our success in Manufactures thus far has exceedingly increased our Reputation as an energetic and sensible people," he wrote. There were, however, certain threats to success. He proposed that duties on cotton, hemp and other raw materials necessary for labor-saving machines be abolished. Capitalists were needed to provide money for these expensive machines. Their shortcomings at the present time, Coxe summed up, were lack of workmen, machines "& Secrets in the Useful Arts."[18]

Hamilton, impressed with Coxe's analysis of the problems of manufacturing, got him appointed assistant secretary of the treasury in May 1790, and deputized him to collect information and write a preliminary report on American manufactures. Coxe's draft was carefully researched and thoughtful. He pointed out that those parts of the Union in which "manufactures have most strikingly encreased have recovered in the greatest degree from the injuries of the late war, and those States, which have given the most liberal encouragement to this branch of trade, are now among the most flourishing." To meet a shortage of available labor, he suggested some of the work be done by women and children. In time, he predicted, European workers would come to the United States, realizing its many advantages. European capital would be attracted by the promise of large profits. The government would have to help by such devices as protective duties and prohibition of rival articles.[19]

A significant phase of Coxe's plan was a system of internal improvements. There should be "the earliest & most efficient exertions of government" in supplying post roads, the improvement of inland navigation and a series of canals. The House was "humbly" requested to set apart a sizable amount of land "of good quality and advantageously situated" to reward the first "introducers or establishers of new and useful manufactures." Government aid was also needed to make possible the development of labor-saving machines, an enterprise that "has hitherto appeared too novel for individuals."[20]

Once Hamilton received Coxe's draft, he started to work on his own. A few months later, he asked Coxe for his draft, "as I am about to review the whole and give it its final form. I want to see the papers in their original state as there are some minute things which have been altered perhaps not for the better—& on a revision may be reinstated."[21]

Upon reviewing the manuscript, Hamilton was not satisfied. The fault was in his lack of information. In late June, he sent out another Treasury circular to the newly appointed supervisors of the revenue. He wanted "accurate information" on the manufactures in each district: the respective times of their first establishment; the degree of maturity they had obtained; quantities periodically made; prices at which they were sold; respective qualities; impediments, if any, under which they worked; encouragements, if any, from the laws of the state; and whether they were carried on by societies, companies or individuals. To balance his report, Hamilton also sought information on agriculture "to form as accurate an Idea as can be obtained of the yield of the product in proportion to the value of cultivated lands in different parts of the United States." The request included a caution to his correspondents to keep the knowledge to themselves "as whatever comes from the Treasury is apt to be suspected of having reference to some scheme of taxation . . . *in truth* it has not the remotest reference to any such purpose."[22]

As commanded, letters arrived from August through November. Some of them represented considerable effort, but the reporters were untrained in economic research, with the result that the information was haphazard and undigested. The data that Hamilton really wanted—on the comparative costs and profits of agriculture and manufacturing—could not be developed from this raw material.

The importance to the country of manufacturing had been pointed out by Hamilton as early as 1775 and 1776 in his polemics *The Farmer Refuted* and *A Full Vindication*. So when the secretary of the treasury sat down to work on Coxe's draft and his research materials, he was comfortable with his subject. His task was to promote the development of manufacturing without offending the agrarians. His other major task was to convince the House of Representatives that the government should support the development of manufacturing. The United States was in the situation of a country precluded from commerce. It could obtain the needed manufactured supplies but had to experience "numerous and very injurious impediments," not only from England but from the "regulations of several countries with which we have the most extensive intercourse." Hence, the United States could not "exchange with Europe on equal terms" and was exposed "to a state of impoverishment, compared with the opulence to which their political and natural advantages authorise them to aspire."[23]

Hamilton's report asserted that manufacturing as well as agriculture provided productive labor. Agricultural labor was periodical, seasonal, "while that occupied in many Manufacturies is constant and regular extending through the year, embracing in some instances night as well as day." However, Hamilton backed away from a conclusion favoring industry over agriculture by stating that "the one, as well as the other, occasions a positive augmentation of the total produce and revenue of the Society."[24]

Hamilton enumerated the contributions of manufacturing establishments: the division of labor, the use and development of machinery, additional employment of classes of the community usually not engaged in business such as women and children, promotion of immigration and the creation of a demand for the surplus produce of the soil. The multiplication of manufactures, Hamilton said, created a demand for articles that were unknown or produced in small quantities. "The bowels as well as the surface of the earth are ransacked for articles which were before neglected. Animals, Plants, and Minerals acquire a utility and a value which were before unexplored."[25]

Hamilton shaped economic principles to meet the needs of the young country, but he also understood man's reluctance to change. "Experience teaches us that men are often so much governed by what they are accustomed to see and practise, that the simplest and most obvious improvement, in the most ordinary occupations, are adopted with hesitation, reluctance and by slow gradations," he observed. Therefore *the government* of the United States had to encourage industry.

Hamilton suggested bounties as the best method for the government to promote manufactures. Although there was a prejudice against bounties because it appeared that public money was being given away without an immediate consideration, public money could not be better spent than to acquire "an new and useful branch of industry." A bounty was no different from any other form of encouragement. The constitutional right to use bounties was clearly stated in the power delegated to Congress "to lay and collect taxes, duties, imposts, and excises, to pay the Debts and provide for the *Common defense and the general welfare.*" (Italics are Hamilton's.)

A recent commentator claims that the secretary of the treasury did not support development of manufactures and preferred bounties to protective tariffs because "the tariff directly involved both government revenues and merchants importing manufactures."[26]

Hamilton's recommendations in the area of internal improvements were less direct and explicit than Tench Coxe's. The secretary of the treasury was also certain that roads, canals and inland waterways were essential for facilitating transportation of commodities, but he seemed to fear that these activities would be usurped by state and local governments. "It were to be wished that there was no doubt of the power of the national Government to lend its direct aid on a comprehensive plan," Hamilton said. Internal improvements could be developed "with more efficiency by the whole than by any part or parts of the Union." If undertaken by these smaller units, there would be danger of collision with local interests; "jealousies, in matters of this kind are as apt to exist as they are apt to be erroneous."

Nevertheless, Hamilton did urge his friends to encourage the cause of internal improvements. Nathaneal Hazard wrote to him in October 1791 that he was going to Hartford to attend the assembly and would "press Turn Pike Roads & the National Manufactures in Jersey upon my Connecticut acquaintances."[27]

At the close of his report, Hamilton pleaded that government support was essential for a young nation, "a community situated like that of the United States" whose "patriotic individuals" did not have great wealth. "In what can it [the public purse] be so useful, as in prompting and improving the efforts of industry."[28]

Hamilton had the president's blessing; it was Washington's own remarks that had caused the House of Representatives to order the report on manufactures to be prepared. In a letter to Jefferson in 1789, the planter president had commented that "the greatest and most important object of internal concern, which at present occupy the public mind, are manufactures and inland navigation." Hamilton's emphasis on bounties for promoting manufactures may have

stemmed from Washington's suggestions in a private letter from
Mount Vernon for bounties on hemp and cotton, two commodities
that he raised on his own land."[29]

Madison, on the other hand, was opposed to the concept of
bounties and, although not against industrial development, firmly
resisted Hamilton's assertion that the national government had the
constitutional right to tax for this purpose. Such broad power frightened him. "If not only the *means*, but the *objects* are unlimited, the
parchment had better be thrown into the fire at once," he said to
Henry Lee.[30]

Hamilton's carefully constructed plan for an American system was
misunderstood by his opponents. Their reaction was that Hamilton
was trying to change their beautiful agrarian utopia into an ugly
industrial wasteland. Jefferson opposed the "Report on Manufactures"
on principle. To Hamilton's disgust, the report was tabled by Congress. He then focused on a practical experiment that he hoped
would demonstrate to his fellow countrymen the possibilities contained in his report.

During the period that Hamilton was collecting his data, he was
involved in an advisory capacity in a unique manufacturing venture
sponsored by The Society for Establishing Useful Manufactures,
known as the SEUM. In April 1791, Hamilton sent a copy of Tench
Coxe's *Plan for a Manufacturing Society* to William Duer with the
comment that it was an idea that "we have often conversed on. . . . I
feel persuaded that it will equally promote the interests of the Adventurers & of the public & will have an excellent effect on the
Debt."[31]

The opportunity to participate in a pilot project that would show
the public the potential contribution of manufacturing to the financial well-being of the nation was irresistible to Hamilton. He ignored
any awkwardness of his position as a member of the administration.
Uninterested in personal financial gain, he lent all the aid he could to
promote the project. He believed sincerely that through the success of the SEUM, Congress would become enlightened about
manufacturing.

From August 9 to August 11, the original subscribers to the stock
of the SEUM—William Duer, four other New Yorkers and Matthew
McConnell of Philadelphia—met in Brunswick, New Jersey. Hamilton, who was also present, was given power of attorney and delegated to engage as many artisans and workmen for the project and on
such terms "as shall appear to you reasonable, for the purpose of

Carrying on a Manufactory of cotton its various branches and printing the same." The subscribers would reimburse him for any expenses but made no mention then or later of any pecuniary or other material compensation.[32]

At that meeting, the prospectus for the society, written either by Hamilton or Coxe or in collaboration, was adopted. The reason for the choice of New Jersey as the site of the enterprise was explained. It was thickly populated; provisions were cheap and abundant; and, without external commerce and large tracts of empty land, there would not be interests hostile to the development of manufacturing. The capitalization of the society was set at $500,000, but no subscriber had to pay until an act of incorporation was obtained.

As soon as the society had the necessary means to operate, skilled workmen from Europe and the appropriate machines were to be procured. Workmen "of secondary merit" could either be found in the United States or be quickly trained. As soon as an act of incorporation was obtained, the society would request permission to institute an annual lottery for five years for the sum of $100,000 per year, the profits from which would be used toward "indemnifying for the first unproductive efforts" and also invested in land. The plant buildings would occupy some of the land; the rest would be divided into town lots, which would provide a source of income for the company.

The plan provided for thirteen directors, including a governor and deputy governor. Each stockholder would have a number of votes in proportion to the number of shares held, probably one vote per share, but neither the United States nor any state that might hold stock would be permitted to have more than a hundred votes.

Hamilton began to search for personnel. On August 17, he hired Thomas Marshall, an English immigrant who had once been apprenticed to Sir Richard Arkwright, the inventor of the "water frame" spinning machine. A few days later he made a contract with William Hall, an English or Irish artisan who had migrated to the United States, to superintend "the business of printing, staining and bleaching of Cottons and Linnens" and "to construct or direct the construction of all such machines as are in use" for the yet unincorporated society. Hamilton also paid William Pearce, an inventor just arrived from Belfast, $100 toward providing "certain machines & models of machines to be delivered to the said Alexander Hamilton." Another immigrant, Joseph Mort, skilled in the manufacture of textiles, received a contract from Hamilton with the title of assistant in the manufactory.[33]

The SEUM's newly appointed experts were not always congenial, nor did they always agree on decisions to be made. At the end of August, Hamilton received a letter from William Hall that warned of dissension. Hall and Mort had been sent by the secretary of the treasury to look at sites for the SEUM's factory. They traveled up the Delaware River to a point about ninety-four miles from Philadelphia, where they saw several good sites. They then explored the Raritan valley; having run out of money, they returned to New York for funds and then proposed to go up the Passaic River. In the course of their travels, they called on Thomas Marshall. "He seems to understand the theory of the Business," Hall wrote, "but I am very doubtful if He is much acquainted with practice. . . . His machines won't work." Hamilton, reading Hall's report, had a great deal to worry about.

In early September, Hamilton heard good news from Hall and Mort. They had found a wonderful site at Passaic Falls (Paterson, New Jersey); "one of the finest situations in the world," for the factory, which "far exceeds our expectation. We are very desirous you shou'd see it," Hall wrote.[34]

Despite grumblings from other manufacturers about preferential treatment, the New Jersey legislature granted the SEUM a charter, which was signed on November 22, 1791, by Gov. William Paterson. In repayment for his cooperation and goodwill, the directors of the SEUM decided to name their new town for him. At its first post-charter meeting, William Duer was elected governor, an error in judgment that was unopposed by Hamilton. The secretary of the treasury was unable to attend but had sent his recommendations for the leading positions, which were all accepted.

It was only after several sessions that the Passaic River site was chosen for the new town of Paterson. Three of the SEUM directors were instructed to purchase the land. Philip Schuyler, experienced in judging waterworks, accompanied them; thus, Hamilton was represented by proxy.

It seemed certain that plans for a large manufactory of cotton goods would be carried to fruition, but the seeds of failure were present in the scheme from the very beginning. A financial panic in the spring of 1792, blamed on William Duer, was only one of the major disasters that befell the SEUM.

William Duer was regarded by most of his contemporaries as a kind of financial wizard with a flair for the calculated risk. The range of his financial interests was extensive: banks, government stocks, western lands, manufacturing and other ventures. No scheme was too complex or risky if he saw the chance of a good profit. His friends and his wife tried to restrain him, but in vain. He persisted until his affairs were in such a tangle that he could not extricate himself.

In the fall and winter of 1791 and 1792, Duer and his partner Macomb, having bought a quantity of United States bank stock and government bonds, started to buy Bank of New York stock in order to take advantage of the bank's precarious future. The possibility that a branch of the Bank of the United States would be established in New York City would mean a major loss for the Bank of New York. In early 1792, Duer, Macomb and other New York financiers proposed chartering three new banks in the city, but then, after causing the planned-for investment hysteria, reduced their demands to a legislative petition to charter the Million Bank at a capitalization of $1.8 million. The purpose of the scheme was to lower the price of Bank of New York stock, thereby allowing them to buy it cheaply until they controlled the bank and could ensure themselves financing for future speculative adventures.[35]

During the past summer, a period of excessive speculation in government and bank stocks, Hamilton had become suspicious of Duer. Rufus King assured him that Duer had not been "particularly engaged in raising the Bk certificates. So far as I can learn his conduct has been as correct as any Buyers and sellers could be."

Duer and Macomb were thwarted by overconfidence and Antifederalist counterspeculation. The price of securities stopped rising by the end of January; in a month, Duer ran out of money. Unable to meet the demands of his creditors, he went bankrupt, and by March 23, 1792, the governor of the SEUM was in jail, where he would stay until a short time before his death in 1799.

Earlier, on March 12, Duer wrote despairingly to his faithful friend, the secretary of the treasury, that unless he arrived in Philadelphia that very day, a suit would be brought against him by the Treasury Department for having skipped payment on his account. "For Heavens Sake Use for once your influence to defer this till my Arrival when it will not be necessary." If the suit was brought, he declared, "My Ruin is complete."[36]

The plea had come too late for him to act, Hamilton answered two days later. Wolcott's instructions, ordering Duer to pay up at once or face a lawsuit, had already been sent out. Duer had to be contented with the secretary's statement that he had "experienced all the bitterness of Soul on your account which a warm attachment can inspire."[37]

Hamilton received a colorful account of "our friend Duer's failure" from Robert Troup. Duer was in a state of almost complete insanity, Troup said. The poor man owed about half a million dollars and had neither money nor stock to pay his creditors, only a tract of land in Maine upon which his supporters were trying to float a loan. If this failed, "I fear his reputation will be eternally blasted, & that his person will be endangered," for widows, orphans, mechanics had lost money. The loan would be floated in Philadelphia, Troup continued. "If your friends in Philadelphia view the subject in the light we do here, they will suppose that Duer's total bankruptcy will affect the public interest by bringing the funding system into odium." He cautioned, "This letter is for your eyes only . . . give us your advice at the earliest opportunity."[38]

Duer was more rational than his friends gave him credit for. He thanked Hamilton for "the consolation" he offered and promised to "strictly *follow the Line you mark out*." He asked Hamilton for "a mature and candid opinion" on what constituted "a fair Creditor." Hamilton replied: "I am of the opinion that those friends, who have lent you their Money or security from personal confidence in your honor, and without being interested in the operation in which you may have been engaged, ought to be taken care of absolutely and preferably to all other Creditors as your situation does not permit delay." After those persons, the obligations to public institutions should be met, particularly the manufacturing society. "Adieu, my unfortunate friend," Hamilton wrote. "God bless you & extricate you with reputation. . . . Be honorable, calm and firm." On the same day this letter was written, March 23, 1791, Duer was arrested and taken to debtor's prsion.[39]

"I sincerely regret Duer's misfortunes and the consequences to him and to the very many who are and will be affected by them," John Jay wrote to Hamilton. Brockholst Livingston and others were profiting from the situation, Troup complained, "preying upon the vitals of public credit by every artifice & combination that can be devised to depress Stocks."[40]

Hamilton was associated in people's minds with Duer's failure both personally and officially. Philip Schuyler advised his son-in-law to give no opinions on the Duer bankruptcy, even if asked. It was good counsel, for manipulation of the market was continuing, even with Duer out of the way. The Livingston clan was still in action. Hamilton replied to Schuyler that " 'tis time there should be a line of separation between honest Men & knaves, between respectable stockholders and dealers in the funds, and mere unprincipled Gamblers. Public infamy must restrain what the laws cannot. Neglect must attend those who manifest that they have no principle but to get money."[41]

The Duer bankruptcy was followed in mid-April by the collapse of Macomb's company. William Seton asked Hamilton to go into the market for him on that day in force. "If it is known that I should do so," he argued, "in all probability" the city would be saved from ruin. Hamilton's answer was equivocal and disappointing to the bank officer. "I have found it best to eke out my aid," he explained. It is best "to keep up men's spirits by *appearing often*."

Hamilton did not abandon Duer, though he could not get to New York to see him. "Indeed I can hardly flatter myself that my advice could be of any real importance to you," he wrote rather unconvincingly. The truth was that Duer's financial collapse had been embarrassing to the secretary of the treasury and, most assuredly, a major cause of the failure of the SEUM.[42]

As soon as Nicholas Low, one of the SEUM's directors, learned that "poor Duer" had stopped payment on the funds, he called an informal meeting of the directors. The result was more consternation, he informed Hamilton who could not attend, because it was discovered that John Dewhurst, who like Alexander Macomb was closely associated with the Duer empire, was also sure to go bankrupt. Furthermore, Duer was being obstinate about giving up his governorship and directorship of the SEUM. Low thought it ridiculous, even dishonorable, for the society to allow him to remain. As expected, Dewhurst's failure occurred, which cost the manufacturing society the $50,000 entrusted to him to procure materials and workmen from abroad.

Despite all these blows to his favored project, Hamilton was undaunted. To Archibald Mercer as deputy governor, the secretary submitted an outline of the steps to be taken to save the SEUM. Since the place and land were already selected, the buildings should be started and a few essential workmen from Europe hired. The only retrenchment suggested was to confine the business to cotton manufacturing and postpone the lottery. If a loan was needed, Hamilton promised to cooperate in trying to procure one on favorable terms. "Nothing scarcely can be so injurious to the affairs of the Society as a much longer suspension of operation," he warned.[43]

The board of directors approved all of Hamilton's suggestions. Continuing his interest in the SEUM, in June 1792, Hamilton suggested that the necessary buildings be erected near the Great Falls for a mill to manufacture cotton goods. The next month he drafted a resolution to build fifty houses for SEUM workers who met the qualifications of good character and as married men. After attending meetings in early July, Hamilton described the building that should be constructed near the falls and also advised that Boudinot apply for a loan of not more than $30,000, in addition to the $10,000 already borrowed. He offered to help by writing Seton, the Bank of New York's cashier. "Pray, my friends, let nothing slumber," he said.[44]

Pierre L'Enfant, hired at Hamilton's request as the superintendent of building, understood the secretary's feelings about the project. He wrote with Gallic flair in August 1792 to assure Hamilton that "your favorit Child will be carefully nursed and bread up to your satisfaction without Involving the parents into Extravagant or useless Expence. My sole Embition being to deliver it worthy of its father and capable of doing honor to his Country."[45]

As for the proposal that Samuel Ogden, a brother-in-law of Gouverneur Morris and ironmonger in Morris's manufactury, be appointed the superintendent of the SEUM, Hamilton wrote that to choose Ogden would be "fatal" to the society. He is "one of the most opinionated men I ever knew" and would drive L'Enfant, whom he says knows nothing about waterworks although he is a civil engineer, to abandoning the project. All the people who head the various branches of the manufactory dislike him and he does not know how to direct the labor force."[46]

Nicholas Low was elected governor of the SEUM at the October 12, 1792, meeting; the following January, Hamilton prepared a plan for a lottery to raise money for the society. He worked out an intricate scheme that would yield the $30,000 needed. The New York legislature refused to endorse the scheme, and the tickets did not sell in New England. The drawings never took place, but a substitute scheme devised in November 1795, which limited the lottery to about $7,000, was carried out in the summer and fall of 1796. The lottery was a failure, and the expenses exceeded the intake.[47]

The SEUM sustained losses of every kind and continued to be ill fated throughout Hamilton's life. From 1792, when Duer and the others went bankrupt, through all the problems, Hamilton was the rock upon which the SEUM supporters leaned. He could not let the dream go. Powerless to force Congress to reconsider his "Report on Manufactures," the SEUM had become the practical embodiment of Hamiltonianism.

The hopelessness of the society's position was dramatically apparent by early 1795, when only three directors appeared at the first quarterly meeting; in August of the same year, United States stock had to be sold to pay debts. In November, Hamilton was elected a director, but there is no record that he attended any meetings in that role.

Ironically, the SEUM had a revival during the War of 1812, "flourishing beyond the most sanguine expectations." The stockholders prospered later on from their real estate holdings and power leases until the city of Paterson bought them out in 1945.[48]

How much should Hamilton be blamed for the failure of the SEUM? He was overconfident, lacking necessary experience, an absentee partner and, most telling, torn between his interest in the manufactury and his position as secretary of the treasury. As a recent critic said: "Hamilton's ties to manufacturers were first strained then severed by conflicts between their interests and his program."[49] As an employer, Hamilton also left much to be desired. He was taken in by some of those he hired, and L'Enfant, as well as others, proved to be poor choices.

The SEUM must be regarded as an integral part of Hamilton's manufacturing program. It included such elements as the development of cotton manufacturing, which imported the raw material from the South, a part of the American system; the importation and development of machinery, which would raise American manufacturing to a position where it would be capable of competing with European goods and lure skilled foreign workers to the United States, thus enlarging the labor force. Perhaps, Hamilton chose the wrong battlefield. He accepted the burial of his "Report on Manufactures" by Congress and then persisted in buttressing the doomed manufacturing company over a period of years during which expectations of success lessened drastically.

Hamilton was still enormously popular with New York City financiers, who supported Hamiltonianism with unabated enthusiasm. As a token of their appreciation, they financed a portrait of him to be painted by John Trumbull. It was an excellent likeness, one of Trumbull's best works, and was first displayed in the old City Hall in New York City.

But at the very time that Hamilton seemed to be at the crest of his influence, his opponents were preparing for all-out war. It was to be fought in the cabinet and in the press.

15

The Cabinet Split

THE FORCES OPPOSING FEDERALISM and Hamiltonianism, almost identical ideologies at this time, were the forces of Republicanism, which were developing and strengthening under the leadership of Jefferson and Madison. To Hamilton, however, it appeared that the opposition to his policies was directed at him personally. His newest enemy was Aaron Burr.

Burr was still thought of as a man without a party. Although he had dealt a major blow to Federalism by defeating Schuyler, as the junior senator from New York had worked to delay the acceptance of the Bank of New York and had participated in the Jefferson-Madison botany trip, he had many Federalist friends. When the Federalists sought a candidate to oppose Gov. George Clinton's reelection in April 1792, he became a serious possibility.

Robert Yates, the defeated Federalist candidate in the close election of three years earlier, decided in February 1792 not to run again. Isaac Ledyard, aware of Hamilton's grudge against Burr for taking his father-in-law's senatorial seat, tried to persuade the powerful secretary of the treasury of the considerable pro-Burr sympathy in New York and that his candidacy would attract many of Yates's old friends. In his letter of February 1, Ledyard revealed that Yates preferred Burr, and, in Ledyard's opinion, no one else could defeat Clinton. "If B. finally succeeds & you not have the merit of it, it will be an event extremely disagreeable to me," Ledyard warned. Burr had "a sincere regard" for the safety and well-being of the United States, Ledyard said, and "an entire confidence in the wisdom & integrity of your designs & a real personal friendship, which he does not seem to suppose you doubt of, or that you ever will unless it may arise from medling Interveners."[1]

James Watson, a New York City merchant and a director of the Bank of the United States, wrote to Hamilton in the same vein. If Burr's bid for the office of governor was denied Federal support, "will it not make him an enemy, if he is not one now, or increase his enmity if he now has any?" Watson asked. If they refused him and he failed, he would return to the Senate "embittered against the government & its ablest advocates," a regrettable circumstance *"in the present irritable State of the Legislature & Body Politic."* If, however, he had their support and he failed, "he will be bound to us by the ties of interest and gratitude." In a final effort to persuade, Watson tried to turn Burr's propensity for straddling the fence into an asset. "The cautious distance observed by this gentleman towards all parties, however exceptionable in a politician may be a real merit in a Governor."[2]

Hamilton was unmoved. Burr was established in his mind as a man without principles, as well as without a party. He preferred "to increase an hostility which he knew would be unrelenting rather than risk the interests of the state."[3] The secretary met the challenge by proposing a most acceptable candidate—John Jay, chief justice of the Supreme Court.

At a meeting of merchants held on February 9 at Farmers Hall, Hanover Square, in New York City, Jay was given their support. A week later he accepted the offer and became the Federalist candidate for governor of New York. Stephen Van Rensselaer, twenty-five years old, patroon and brother-in-law of Alexander Hamilton, became the candidate for lieutenant governor. Hamilton had proved his power and had intensified enmity with his rival.

Burr wanted to be governor of New York. At that time, the power and patronage that went with the office were greater than those of United States senator. Burr also needed the money for his large, demanding family. A word from Hamilton would, "In all probability, have made Aaron Burr Governor of New York," an early biographer wrote.[4]

Jay's entrance into the field meant that Burr was faced with the popular incumbent and the chief justice, who now had the support of the Federalists and the Yates people. On March 15, a month after Jay entered the race, Burr withdrew. Matthew Davis, Burr's friend and earliest biographer, said the senator withdrew because he had "the kindest feelings" toward Jay "who was a most amiable man" and so wished to remain neutral.[5]

Hamilton's involvement in the Jay candidacy was widely acknowl-

edged. A popular campaign jingle used by the Clintonians pilloried
Jay as "a tool, a blockhead, sour, perverse." If he should get in, the
state would tumble,

> Be sold to Congress for a trifle,
> For Hamilton to strip and rifle.[6]

Robert Troup wrote to Hamilton that "he abandoned all ideas of
Burr" and would do "everything in my power to promote Jay's elec-
tion." He then added mysteriously that he knew a secret about Burr's
election that he could not write but would tell him when he saw him.
"I have reason to suspect we have both been abused," he wrote.[7]
Whatever it was, Troup was now back in Hamilton's camp.

The Clinton-Jay campaign was heated and innovative. For the first
time, an election was openly concerned with class differences. The
small farmers spoke out against the landowners; the mechanics and
shopkeepers against businessmen and lawyers. Nonetheless, the election would have gone to Jay if the returns from Otsego, Tioga and
Clinton counties had not been invalidated. Stripped of those winning
ballots, the Federalist candidate was deprived of his victory. Even
then, Clinton won by a slim margin of 150 votes.

The canvassers asked the advice of their senators, Aaron Burr and
Rufus King. The issue was whether the technicalities involved
should disenfranchise the voters of three counties or whether there
should be a recount. It was a conflict between a strict interpretation
of the law and justice.

Hamilton was kept informed of all the developments. When Jay
appeared in New York City on July 11, Rufus King told Hamilton,
"The concourse was immense & Mr. Jay had been recd with the
ringing of Bells, firing of cannons, huzzaings & clapping of hands."
The shout was for "Jay & Liberty" when the chief justice addressed
his enthusiastic supporters, but he was circumspect, speaking of the
need for "a great degree of delicacy and reserve."[8]

Burr, torn between his loyalty to the Antifederalists who had sent
him to the Senate and his reluctance to lose Federalist support, gathered opinions from a large range of notables, including James Monroe and Attorney General Edmund Randolph. With a display of some
erudition and some double-talk, Burr decided that the letter of the
law should be upheld, thereby placing himself firmly in the Antifederalist camp.

Rufus King advised that the returns be recounted, but the issue
was finally settled on party grounds. The state assembly, predomi-

nantly Clintonites, voted thirty-five to twenty-two to uphold the ruling of the canvassers and thus gave their governor another term. King wrote to Hamilton, fearing that Jay and his more radical supporters would demand an appeal to the people, "a dreadful alternative," for it might set a precedent if disputes should arise in the succession of the presidency, and then "how are we to place confidence in the security of our Government?"[9]

Hamilton wanted Jay to be governor, but not if it meant that "a ferment may be raised which may not be allayed when you wish it. . . . Some folks are talking of Conventions and the Bayonet. But the case will justify neither a resort to first principles nor to violence." The canvassers had the final authority, and the decision should not be reversed by means unknown to the Constitution or laws. "The precedent may suit us today; but tomorrow we may rue its abuse." If a convention was called, it might "produce more than is intended. Such weapons are not to be played with." To placate King, Hamilton wrote that since he was out of reach of the "contagion," he was "very cool and reasonable; if I were with you I should probably not escape the contagion."[10]

Jefferson was extremely critical of Clinton's role in the disputed election. The New York governor could not be defended "as a just and disinterested man" if he took office, and it looked as if he would, the secretary of state wrote to Madison. "I really apprehend that the cause of republicanism will suffer and its votaries be thrown into schism by embarrassing it in support of this man."[11] But Clinton kept his office, continued to be one of the most popular men in the country and eventually became Jefferson's vice-president.

Troup, no longer a Burrite, embraced Jay's cause with blind enthusiasm. It was he who presented the resolution for those who opposed the canvassers' decision and called themselves the "Friends of Liberty." His object, Troup said, was to impress upon the public mind "the deep corruption of Clinton and his party," but, he assured Hamilton, "we shall not endanger the political ship . . . but . . . do not forget that allowances should be made for the keen anguish we suffer from the wound we have received." Hamilton read his prodigal friend's letter, took it for what it was worth and wrote on it, "Filed. No answer necessary."[12]

Burr, who had considered Clinton an enemy, was surprised when the governor nominated him to the state supreme court. Burr declined, preferring to retain his seat in the Senate. The second national election was soon to take place. If Washington ran, a second term was assured, but the Republican party had hopes for the vice-presidential office. Burr was still regarded as less objectionable to the Federalists than any of their other opponents, though Hamilton did not share his colleagues' feelings.

But Washington had to be convinced to run for a second term. Aware that his cabinet was unanimously opposed to his retirement, Washington turned to Madison for help. On May 5, 1792, at the chief executive's bidding, Madison called on him. Washington reminded his friend of his intention to leave public life at the end of his four years; now he wanted advice "on the *mode* and *time*" most proper for making known his decision.

Retirement might have hazardous effects for the nation, Madison objected, but Washington pleaded declining health, fatigue and vexation. He also deplored party division between his secretaries of state and the treasury and the open attacks upon himself in the newspapers.

A few days later a reluctant Madison gave as his opinion that the president should make a direct address to the public. Washington was silent, until suddenly he asked Madison for ideas for his annual address to Congress. Madison surmised that the president had changed his mind about retirement. Then Washington sent him a letter asking for a draft of a Farewell Address. Madison acceded but begged the president for "one more sacrifice," echoing a strong appeal from Jefferson.[13]

Hamilton, the success of whose program depended on Washington's staying in office, was insistent that the president stand for reelection. It was accepted by everyone that "your declining would be . . . the greatest evil that could befall the country at the present juncture, and as critically hazardous to your own reputation." The affairs of the national government were not yet firmly established, he warned, and its enemies stood ready to undo Washington's work.[14]

With some trepidation, Hamilton told Washington that some people thought that the reason he was refusing to run again was the possibility of division among the electors and "less unanimity in their suffrages." Hamilton argued that "the dread of public indignation will be likely to restrain the undisposed few," but if there were one or two votes against you, "of what moment can it be?" After an administration of four years in a new government originally opposed by a large proportion of the citizens "and obliged to run counter to many prejudices in devising the arduous arrangements, requisite to public Credit and public order, these few adverse votes would demonstrate only their authors malevolence and not any diminution of the nation's affection and confidence." Hamilton assured his chief that his sentiments were purely a regard for the public welfare and a reflection of his own "affectionate personal attachment."[15]

Sophisticated enough to realize that his well-wishers often had interests beyond what was best for him, Washington continued to ask, almost pleadingly, whether any other person was preferred in Philadelphia or what was the feeling about him in the South. All were for his continuance, Jefferson reassured him. Washington sighed and succumbed painfully to the inevitability of another care-ridden stint in public service. The factions, so deplored by him, looked to the vice-presidency for a contest in which to test their embryo political organization.

At that time, the Constitution provided that the individual who received the second highest number of votes in the electoral college would be the vice-president. Therefore, the winner of second place might be of a different political persuasion than the winner and could, theoretically, emerge as the leader of the opposition. Hamilton wanted, above all, to keep a Federalist in the second office. His game plan was directed against Jefferson, who he believed was the secret threat held by the Antifederalists.

John Adams was as unlike Alexander Hamilton as two members of the same party could be. A crusty New Englander, paunchy, acid, straitlaced, of little charm, Adams did not care for the flashy West Indian prodigy of doubtful origins whose good looks, aristocratic manners, flair with the ladies and influence over the president offended him. But John Adams was the incumbent and a Federalist and much more acceptable to Hamilton than, for instance, his archenemy George Clinton, who was being talked about as Adams's chief opponent.

Irritated by the vice-president's reluctance to promote his own career, Hamilton wrote to him toward the end of June that Clinton would be his competitor in the next election and that the *National Gazette* was preparing something very like a serious design to subvert the government. But Adams, who was spending the summer at Quincy, showed no inclination to return to Philadelphia until late in the season. Hamilton tried again to persuade him that his appearance in the capital would make an immense difference in this chance for success against Clinton.

Adams had every intention of not arriving in Philadelphia until the ballots were counted. His determination was increased because of

Abigail's failing health and his own many complaints, including poor eyes, diseased teeth and a hand tremor. To try to stir up the stubborn New Englander, Hamilton pushed Samuel Otis, the secretary of the Senate, to beg for the vice-president's return. Even Adams's second son. Thomas Boylston, was enlisted in the mail campaign.

Adams resisted his colleagues' appeals. He had lost several teeth during the summer due to pyorrhea and was sensitive about his appearance. Prone to pessimism, Adams was certain that he would lose the election. When he finally left Quincy in November, without Abigail, who was too ill to travel, his cold, wintry trip was made even more miserable by news along the way that he had a poor chance of reelection. In New York, his son Charles, just starting to practice law in the city, informed him that the Republicans planned to elect Clinton vice-president and to have him remain as governor of New York also, to prove that the national government was inferior to the state governments.

Aaron Burr, who had been gathering support quietly, was emerging as a rival candidate to New York's governor. Pierrepont Edwards, Burr's uncle, a New Haven lawyer, was promoting him in Connecticut; Alexander Dallas, a Philadelphia attorney, was rallying Pennsylvania votes.

Hamilton made it very clear that Burr was to be stopped at any cost. Clinton's success would be "unfortunate," he said, but the governor was, nonetheless, "a man of property" and "in private life, as far as I know, of probity." Burr, however, was unprincipled publicly and privately. He knew nothing but ambition and hoped to climb, however possible, to the top of the tree. "Embarrassed as I understand, in his circumstances, with an extravagant family—bold, enterprising and intriguing, I am mistaken if it be not his object to play the game of confusion." Hamilton stated his opposition in a letter of September 21, 1792, in as extreme a form as possible. "I feel it a religious duty to oppose his career," he vowed. A week later Hamilton restated his position. "In a word, we have an embryo Caesar in the United States, 'tis Burr."[16]

Hamilton informed Washington of Burr's candidacy and of his support in Connecticut and Pennsylvania, but he asserted that he was not convinced that the Burr movement was anything more than a diversion in favor of Clinton, the official position Hamilton wanted others to think he held.

The secretary of the treasury offered another interpretation of the Republican bid for the vice-presidency to Charles Cotesworth Pinckney of South Carolina, the only southern state friendly to Hamiltonianism. " 'Tis suspected by some that the plan is only to divide the votes of the N & Middle States to let in Mr. Jefferson by the votes of the South," he wrote. This also would be "a serious misfortune" to the government. The secretary of state "is certainly a man of sublimated and paradoxical imagination—entertaining & propagating notions inconsistent with dignified and orderly Government." He was unlike Adams, who, whatever objections one might have had to some of his theoretical opinions, was a "firm, honest, independent politician."[17]

To John Steele, a representative from North Carolina, Hamilton predicted in mid-October that Adams would have a nearly unanimous vote in the eastern states, lose New York, win Jersey and Pennsylvania and some votes in Delaware and Maryland. He would have none in Virginia or Georgia. His opposition would be Clinton, and, of late, "there have been symptoms of Col. Burr's canvassing for it." Again, Hamilton suggested "some say" one or both of them "will be played off as a diversion in favor of Mr. Jefferson." He would choose Adams over Jefferson because of the latter's ideas, which were "notoriously incompatible with regular and firm government."[18]

Hamilton was not well informed about activity in the Republican camp. Melancton Smith and Marcus Willet sent a letter to Madison and Monroe via messenger, informing them that Burr was the new favorite among Republican electors. But the Virginia Republicans, Monroe, Madison, Jefferson and Patrick Henry, burst the bubble. Monroe felt that Burr was too new a face, and his party position was too confused. "To place this gent'n, or any of his standing in the chair of the present incumbent, wou'd not be well thought of in America," he said to his fellow Virginians. Consequently, Monroe and Madison wrote a joint letter to Smith and Willett, saying that "the object of the Republican interest" in Virginia was Clinton, who "seems likely to unite a greater number of electoral votes than any other." To switch to Burr or anyone else "would hazard more on one side than can be hoped on the other."[19]

At a meeting in Philadelphia on October 16, the Pennsylvania and New York Republicans unanimously agreed to support Clinton for the second office in the country and to "drop all thoughts of Mr. Burr." The New York senator resigned himself to the inevitable, later saying that he withdrew with the promise of some southern commitment for the 1796 election.[20]

Washington was elected unanimously with 132 first ballots. The votes for the others were: 74 for Adams; 50 for Clinton; 4 for Jefferson, from Kentucky; and 1 for Aaron Burr, from a South Carolina elector.

The American party system began to emerge in this election. Clinton's strong showing demonstrated that the opponents of a powerful central government, the supporters of the French connection, the critics of the elite and the British were becoming a force to be reckoned with. The election also revealed the appearance of a new national figure, Aaron Burr, though his party affiliation seemed unresolved.

For the moment, the results of the election pleased Hamilton. "The success of the Vice President is as great a source of satisfaction as that of Mr. Clinton would have been of mortification and pain to me," he told John Jay. The chief justice rejoiced with him but issued a warning. "The increasing Industry and arts of the Antis, render Perseverance, union and constant effort necessary."[21]

Until their rift over the bank bill, Hamilton and Jefferson had dined at each other's houses and had had an amicable relationship. After that, their friendship diminished quickly, until there was left only a masked dislike. The secretary of the treasury recognized that Jefferson's opposition was not confined to cabinet meetings and that he was turning the Virginians against him, particularly his former friend Madison. The *National Gazette*, sponsored by Jefferson, became the chief weapon against the Hamiltonian program. Freneau, its editor, published anti-Hamilton diatribes enthusiastically.

Hamilton replied in his own organ, Fenno's *Gazette of the United States*, handling his own defense by publishing a deluge of articles under many different pseudonyms. The paper war between the two secretaries titillated while it amazed the public and disturbed the president, who looked on with increasing pain as his two favorite sons quarreled publicly.

There were serious differences between the two men. Hamilton believed in a strong, vigorous executive; firmness and leadership were to be encouraged. The separation of powers provided for in the Constitution meant that the executive was free to operate without constant, petty surveillance by Congress. Once given power by the legislature to handle a problem, it should be left to the executive branch to do it. Hamilton needed this free range to implement his economic program. Instead, he was being harassed by the House of Representatives. Hamilton was committed to commerce and industry, and its need for monetary expansion. He visualized the development of a powerful America that covered the continent. He had an almost Hobbesian view of man as base, greedy, motivated by self-interest and corruptible. And yet he himself was an attractive, engaging, amiable man, known for his wit and his ability to enjoy the pleasures of life.

Jefferson, who had a broad vision of man's perfectability if he were allowed to live in a free society, feared more than anything else an excess of power in the hands of one individual. It was better for the legislative branch to curb the executive, and better if the national government was weak; the many state governments preserved the people's freedom. The slave-owning planter regarded education as the means by which all men could rise together to achieve the happiness spoken of in the Declaration of Independence.

Washington, a soldier who avoided political theorizing, stood on the basic virtues of honor, fairmindedness and integrity. The Hamilton-Jefferson conflict was a personal grief to him, for he was fond of both contenders.

The first series of polemics from Hamilton's pen was written under the name of T.L. in the summer of 1792 and published in the *Gazette of the United States*. It was an open secret that the *Gazette*'s editor, John Fenno, received financial help from his patrons and he also did government printing.

T.L. opened the paper war with a query: Was Freneau, the editor of the *National Gazette*, being paid a salary from the government for "translation or for publications, the design of which is to vilify those to whom the voice of the people has committed the administration of our public affairs—to oppose the measures of government, and, by false insinuations, to disturb the public peace?" Hamilton was referring to Freneau's appointment to the post of translator for the State Department at $250 a year.[22]

Freneau replied in his newspaper by attacking Fenno as "a vile sycophant, who, obtaining emoluments from government, far more lucrative than his own," attempted to "poison the people by propogating and disseminating principles and sentiments utterly subversive of the true republican interests of this country."

Freneau described himself as a "French translator to the State Department and the editor of a free newspaper." Hamilton seized on this in T.L. #2. What induced our rulers to hire a man to abuse them? It did not seem easy to account for this branch of the national expense, considering that this "free newspaper" was always "free to defame, but never free to praise." When the treasury accounts were published, T.L. said, "then, perhaps, the mystery will be explained."[23]

Before the third T.L. appeared, Hamilton published two lengthy pieces as "An American." Protected by anonymity, the secretary of the treasury linked Freneau and Jefferson, describing how Jefferson's party benefited from Freneau's editorship. Freneau came to Philadelphia, at once editor of the *National Gazette* and clerk for foreign languages in the Department of State; "an experiment somewhat new in the history of political maneuvres in this country." Thus, Mr. Freneau "is the faithful and devoted servant of the head of a party, from which he receives the boon." The paper is "an exact copy of the politics of his employer, foreign and domestic." Hamilton then asked whether Freneau's services were equal to the compensation he received, since Jefferson himself was well acquainted with the French language, and the editor knew no other.

After listing Jefferson's areas of opposition to the administration, Hamilton, as "An American," abandoned all restraint. "If to National Union, national respectability, Public order and Public credit they are willing to substitute National disunion, national insignificance, Public disorder and discredit—then let them unite their acclamations and plaudits in favor of Mr. Jefferson."[24]

Stung by the fury of "An American's" assault on him and on his patron, Thomas Jefferson, Freneau printed an affidavit, stating that there had been no negotiation between him and the secretary of state over the establishment of the *National Gazette* and that he had never been directed, controlled or influenced in any way, "either by the Secretary of State, or any of his frends," and the editor alone was responsible for every line in his newspaper.[25]

Freneau also explained that the position of clerk of foreign languages was not a new post and had been held by John Pintard of New York at the same salary. And why shouldn't an editor of a newspaper have the job, and why should the secretary of state do his own translating? Should the secretary of the treasury "be obliged to perform every laborious duty in his own office?"[26]

"This is not the way to exculpate yourself before a judicious public," Hamilton chided in "An American" #2 on August 11. Hamilton repeated his accusations and presented the evidence. Jefferson did not negotiate with the editor about the founding of the paper because he "had too considerable a part of his political Education amidst the intrigues of a European Court" to hazard a direct personal commitment in such a case. He knew how to arrange the desired results without saying: "Sir, I mean to *hire* you for the purpose." As for Pintard, he was a holdover from the old government and "he was not the Printer of a Gazette."[27]

On the same day, August 11, T.L. #3 appeared, reiterating the assertion that despite double-talk denials, Freneau received pay in both characters. As an employee of the government, then, he was guilty of ingratitude, for as an editor, "his attacks upon the Government are frequent and licentious."[28]

"An American" made a last appearance a week later to answer Freneau's demand that "An American" come forward. Personal charges from an anonymous writer deserved no answer and would have none, Freneau said. They were not personal charges, Hamilton replied. They were facts. And he reminded Freneau that he had answered the charges, "even under the solemnities of an oath."

Hamilton deliberately began his attacks on Jefferson with an account of his dealings with Freneau, hoping to arouse interest and a scandal. In a letter to Jonathan Dayton, a member of the House of Representatives from New Jersey, he wrote that "some skirmishing" had begun in the *Gazette of the United States* respecting Mr. Freneau's receiving a salary from the government; would the representative please forward without delay "the particulars of all the Steps taken by Mr. Madison" and, if possible, an affidavit from his informant? Neither Dayton nor Elias, and not Elisha Boudinot, who received similar letters, were informed that Hamilton was T.L. and "An American," but the secretary added a postscript, saying that the queries were "perfectly confidential" and that his name "is to be kept out of sight."

Elisha Boudinot reported that Judge William Bradford, his nephew, had had the story from Francis Childs, the editor of New York's *Daily Advertiser*, for whom Freneau had worked before he came to Philadelphia. When Freneau received the letter from Jefferson asking him to start a newspaper in Philadelphia, he felt that his independence was being trifled with and wrote an insulting answer to Jefferson, which he showed to Childs. Childs persuaded Freneau not to send the letter. Boudinot suggested to Hamilton that he get into conversation with Childs on the subject. In the meantime, Boudinot promised to follow other leads.[29]

Dayton replied to Hamilton, stating that Jefferson's proposals to Freneau in regard to the clerkship and Madison's negotiations about the establishment of the newspaper were "undeniable truths." Although he would not reveal to the world his informant's name, Dayton told Hamilton it was Childs.[30] Hamilton's relentless pursuit of the Jefferson-Freneau connection can be understood only in terms of the terrible pressures that he felt as a result of Jefferson's machinations and regret over the loss of Madison's friendship, for which he blamed Jefferson.

In a long, revealing letter to Edward Carrington, a Virginia Federalist, Hamilton poured out his feelings and gave his version of the cabinet break. He would not have undertaken the Treasury job if he had known that he would lack Madison's support in the House of Representatives. Madison and Jefferson now headed a faction hostile to him and to the administration, and were activated by views that he judged "subversive of the principles of good government and dangerous to the Union, peace and happiness of the country." The two Virginians were his archenemies, but Jefferson was by far the most personally malignant. Jefferson wanted to be president, had expected to be in charge of the country's finances and so resented Hamilton's position; he was "a man of profound ambition and violent passions."

Hamilton was a proud man, used to flattery and praise. Jefferson's cool, understated style annoyed him. Hamilton was a man of vigor and action, while Jefferson was inclined to be cautious and contemplative. It was not Jefferson's way to engage in open encounters. Hence, the secretary of state handled his discomfort over his constant disagreements with the secretary of the treasury by offering to resign and by complaining to the president.

In a letter to Washington in late May 1792, Jefferson summed up the newspaper criticism of the administration and added his own comments. Washington replied that in his recent travels in Maryland and Virginia, he had spoken to many people and found them "contented and happy." He also defended Hamilton's financial program.

But Jefferson's critique disturbed Washington. At the end of July, still at Mount Vernon, he wrote "a private and confidental" letter to Hamilton, listing "a variety of matters," twenty-one of them, about which he was concerned. The letter was an almost verbatim reproduction of Jefferson's account of the nation's ills in his May letter.

Hamilton, defensive, replied a few weeks later with a long refutation that occupied thirty printed pages in his collected papers. He excused himself for "some severity" in some of his comments, but, he said, "I have not fortitude enough always to hear with calmness calumnies which necessarily include me as a principal Agent in the measures censured, of the falsehood of which I have the most unqualified consciousness & I cannot be entirely patient under charges which impeach the integrity of my public motives or conduct. . . . I merit them in no degree."[31]

The allegation that a monarchy or aristocracy was being introduced into the country was disposed of with "a flat denial." He said: "People so enlightened and so diversified as the people of this Country can surely never be brought to it, but from convulsions and disorders, in consequence of the acts of popular demagogues." A person who wanted to subvert the republican system did so by "flattering the prejudices of the people," causing civil unrest, and then, tired of anarchy, the people "take shelter in the arms of monarchy." The sort of person who would try to do this would be

a man unprincipled in private life, desperate in his fortune, bold in his temper, possessed of considerable talents, having the advantage of military habits—despotic in his ordinary demeanour—known to have scoffed in private at the principles of liberty—when such a man is seen to mount the hobby horse of popularity—to join in the cry of danger to liberty— to take every opportunity of embarrassing the General Government & bringing it under suspicion—to flatter and fall in with all the nonsense of the zealots of the day—It may justly be suspected that his object is to throw things into confusion that he may "ride the storm and direct the whirlwind."[32]

This description was a portrait of Aaron Burr by Alexander Hamilton. Its placement in the letter reflected his growing obsession with Burr.

What Washington wanted, above all, was peace among his cabinet members. He admired both Jefferson and Hamilton, and he refused to accept the obvious truth that two such opposite minds could never be united.

In answer to a letter from Washington in which he admitted to the internal dissension in the cabinet and its disagreeable effect on the administration, Jefferson replied at great length, exonerating himself and, with some bitterness, exposing his position on Hamilton. When he first came to New York, he was duped by the secretary of the treasury and "made a tool for forwarding his schemes," Jefferson declared. "Of all the errors of my life, this has occasioned me the deepest regret." He disapproved of Hamilton's financial system as "averse to liberty" and "calculated to undermine and demolish the republic, by creating an influence of his department over the members of the legislature." This was proved to him, Jefferson said, when he observed that those who voted for the Hamilton plan profited by it.

The "Report on Manufactures" was no less threatening to friends of the Constitution, Jefferson added. The assumption that the general government could exercise all powers for the *general welfare* would lead to a situation in which, having corrupted a sufficient number of the legislators, "that corps under the command of the Secretary of the Treasury, would step by step subvert the principles of the constitution which he [Hamilton] has so often declared to be a thing of nothing which must be changed."

In the area of foreign affairs, Jefferson accused, Hamilton had thwarted every principle. The secretary of state had wanted to give some "satisfactory distinctions" to France and to meet England with some restrictions that might have lessened their severities against American commerce. But Hamilton, "by his cabals with members of the legislature," had forced acceptance of his own system, which was the reverse. He also, on his own authority, had spoken to the ministers of two nations.

It was Hamilton who wrote the diatribes against him in Fenno's paper, Jefferson informed Washington, "for neither the stile, matter, nor venom of the pieces alluded to can leave a doubt of the author." "In the presence of heaven," Jefferson declared, he never directly or indirectly influenced what went into Freneau's newspaper, nor did he have any interest in its merits or demerits. "But is not the dignity & even the decency of govment committed, when one of its principal ministers enlists himself as an anonymous writer or paragraphist" for any newspaper? There should be a free press to criticize the government, and the government should neither know it nor notice its sycophants or censors.

Jefferson reminded the president of his wish to retire from office. "I shall count the days and hours still between me and it," he said. In the meantime, he would wind up the business of his office and avoid any new enterprises. Until he became a private citizen he would avoid any newspaper contests, lest he be charged with misapplying that time "now belonging to those who employ me which should be wholly devoted to their service."[33]

Hamilton, harried on all fronts about his program, defended it fiercely in the pages of the United States Gazette. On one day, September 11, Hamilton articles appeared under the bylines of "Amicus," "Civis," and "Fact." The sheer quantity of his writings during the summer months was astounding. In between newspaper writing and Treasury Department work, he wrote to friends and kept up a steady correspondence with Washington at Mount Vernon on public matters and on the cabinet rift. He wanted Washington on his side as passionately as did Jefferson. "It is my most anxious wish, as far as may depend on me, to smooth the path of your administration, and to render it prosperous and happy. And if any prospect shall open of healing or terminating the differences which exist, I shall most cheerfully embrace it; though I consider myself as the deeply injured party," Hamilton wrote.

As "Amicus," Hamilton replied to accusations that he was a monarchist and a defamer of Washington. To the old charge that he had advocated monarchy at the constitutional convention, he pointed out that he was the only delegate from New York who had signed the Constitution. "Fact No 1" denied that the secretary of the treasury had said that "public debts are public blessings." The words had been taken out of context. "The *funding* of the existing debt of the United States would render it a national blessing," was the correct statement. And the "invigoration of industry in the United States proves the prediction correct.[34]

On September 15, Alexander Hamilton Catullus, replying to "Aristides," stated: "Mr. Jefferson is the *Institutor and Patron of the National Gazette*." Catullus #2 reiterated Jefferson's rejection of the Constitution and his opposition to the administration program, not only to the activities of the Treasury Department but to "almost all important measures." In the same paper, Hamilton included Jefferson's note to Thomas Paine, which was published in the introduction to the American edition of *The Rights of Man*. "I am extremely pleased . . . that something at length is to be publicly said against the *political heresies* which have sprung up among us. I have no doubt our citizens will *rally* a second time round the *standard* of common sense." The text was Jefferson's; the italics were Hamilton's.[35]

Jefferson protested that he had had no idea that Paine would publish any part of his letter. His note was meant only as a graceful compliment. Hamilton answered that "the imputation of levity was preferred to that of malice." But anyone deceived by such artifices "must be little read in the history of those arts, which in all countries, and at all times have served to disguise the machinations of factions and intriguing men."[36]

Goaded by the thought of Washington's twenty-one questions, which he knew were Jefferson-inspired, Hamilton could not contain himself. With self-righteous ire, he contrasted himself with the sainted Jefferson. The *Gazette's* main object had been to hunt him down, he charged, "for the unpardonable sin" of having been "the steady invariable and decided friend of broad national principles of government." Mr. Jefferson had hitherto been distinguished as a quiet, modest, retiring philosopher—as the plain, simple, unambitious republican. Now it was time for the artful disguise to be unveiled. "When the vizor of stoicism is plucked from the brow of the Epicurean; when the plain garb of Quaker simplicity is stripped from the concealed voluptuary—when Caesar *coyly refusing* the proffered diadem is seen to be Caesar *rejecting* the trappings but tenaciously grasping the substance of imperial domination."

Hamilton was referring to an old scandal about Jefferson's attempted seduction of Betsey Walker, the wife of an old friend and neighbor. Hamilton knew about it but did not leak it to the press until 1802, when he revealed it to the editor of the *Gazette of the United States*. Jefferson did not know until 1802 that Hamilton referred to the Walker affair but was apprehensive that Hamilton's thrust referred to his relationship with Sally Hemings, a slave from Monticello, fearing that the scandal was about to become public knowledge.[37]

Hamilton continued to make many appearances in the press as "Metellus," "A Plain Honest Man" and "Catullus." The harder Jefferson's friends defended him, the more defiantly Hamilton countered them. No reconciliation, not even a working one, between Washington's opposing warriors was possible. If he had refused reelection, Washington realized, he would have left the country to the mercies of uncontrolled factions.

Hamilton wrote for his newspaper, cutting and thrusting. Jefferson worked quietly and secretly on a series of resolutions, to be presented in the House of Representatives by William Branch Giles, that would force the secretary of the treasury to resign. The plan was to time the Giles presentation so close to the adjournment of Congress that Hamilton would be trapped. Jefferson reckoned without the secretary of the treasury's powerful mind and tremendous endurance.

16

A Sea of Troubles

Attacking Hamilton's administration of the Treasury Department as corrupt and illegal, thus striking at his most sensitive spot, was a diabolical scheme that appealed to his enemies. It satisfied their desire for revenge and compensated them for having been victims of his anonymous barbs. On a higher level, the anti-Hamilton conspiracy believed that to rid the country of Hamilton was to end the rule of wealth and privilege and to return the republic to its real mission, which was to serve the needs of the people.

The setting for Hamilton's fall was to be, appropriately, the House of Representatives, with William Branch Giles and James Madison as executioners. Jefferson, as usual, stayed in the background; Giles was known to be his spokesman in the House. The basis of the charge against the secretary of the treasury was his handling of the funds from two congressional loans granted in August 1790. One law provided for a $12-million loan whose proceeds were to be used for the payment of interest and installments of the foreign debt. The second, a $2-million loan, was to be used to purchase the domestic debt. Hamilton, the Republicans said, had exceeded his authority by using part of the $12 million to pay the domestic debt. The money for the loans had been floated in Amsterdam and Antwerp, which also figured in the charges.

The first challenge was made by the congressional Republicans in late December 1792 after reading Hamilton's *Report on the Redemption of the Public Debt*, in which he proposed that the entire government debt to the Bank of the United States be paid by floating a new foreign loan. The Republicans, seeing a chink in the Hamilton armor, immediately called for information on the government loans. In a week, the secretary presented his *Report on Foreign Loans*, which was rejected by the House as unacceptable. On January 23,

1793, the anti-Hamilton faction pushed through the Giles Resolutions, which demanded a series of intricate reports from the secretary of the treasury.

Giles's address in the House was exhaustive and impassioned. The resolutions had grown out of "the embarrassments I have met with in attempting to comprehend" the secretary's reports, he complained. Giles then presented extensive charts and figures to support his queries. Giles insisted that "candor" required him to state that "impressions resulting from my inquiries into this subject" had been "by no means favorable to the arrangements made by the gentleman at the head of the Treasury Department." It could be, he suggested, that the House had been careless in that "we have been legislating for some years without competent official knowledge of the state of the Treasury, or revenues . . . and I conceive it is now time that this information be officially laid before the House."[1]

The Giles Resolutions, adopted on January 23, ordered Hamilton to deliver a staggering amount of information to the House. This included: accountings between the United States and the Bank of the United States; the balance of all unapplied revenues and loans; an account of all monies that came into the sinking fund; names of the persons by whom the respective payments had been made in France, Spain and Holland.

On the same day, the Senate adopted resolutions similar to those proposed to the House by Giles, asking the secretary of the treasury for several additional reports. As Fisher Ames said, "It was not intended by the leaders to stop at any temperate limit. . . . They thirst for vengeance. The Secretary of the Treasury is one whom they would immolate."[2]

Hamilton had been prepared for action against him; when it came, he was determined not to let the Republicans achieve his impeachment. The Republican congressmen and Jefferson, their instigator, should not succeed in adjourning Congress before he was able to answer them. Otherwise, the public would assume that he was guilty of Giles's charges. Hamilton undertook the Herculean task of assembling the required reports. He stayed at home, working through the days and nights, attending only to those official duties that could not be postponed.

George Cabot, senator from Massachusetts and a director of the Bank of the United States, visited him one day. He found the besieged secretary in the midst of a short break from his work, at play with his children. He was stretched out on the floor, laughing and joking while engaged in a game of marbles. However, Cabot could not help noticing that his friend's hair was uncombed and his face was haggard, betraying his exhaustion from late nights and grueling work.[3]

On February 4, Hamilton's *Report on the Balance of all Unapplied Revenues at the end of the year 1792 etc.* was communicated to the House. "I have lost no time in preparing it," Hamilton wrote wryly. "I cannot but resolve to treat the subject with a freedom which is due to truth, and to the consciousness of pure zeal for the public interest." The report was lucid and complete, as were those that followed.[4]

Hamilton, harassed as he was, wrote a private letter to Madrid, to William Short, a co-commissioner with William Carmichael, working on problems between Spain and the United States. Short, Hamilton wrote, would not suffer from the congressional investigation, no matter what happened. "The spirit of party has grown to maturity sooner in this country than perhaps was to have been counted upon," he observed. That an investigation against him was begun was all he allowed himself to say; he did not want questions about the foreign loans "to cross the Atlantic and be made an ill use of, to the prejudice of our country." The letter to Short was an "antidote" to be used or not, as he saw fit.[5]

Hamilton's answers were received from February 4 to February 19, but his accusers were still not satisfied. Giles introduced an additional set of resolutions, emphasizing Hamilton's handling of the Treasury. The nine original resolutions were in Jefferson's hand writing. He proposed that Congress reorganize the Department of the Treasury by making the office of treasurer of the United States "a separate department independent of the Secretary of the Treasury." The ninth and last resolution called for Hamilton's removal from office by the President of the United States because he had been guilty of "maladministration in the duties of his office."[6]

Giles softened the language of Jefferson's version and reduced the charges to six. Giles and Madison voted for all of them, but only three others joined them. The resolutions failed, and on March 22 Congress went home.

Hamilton's friends rejoiced with him that he had escaped his oppressors. At a large party given by Judge James Duane, an old friend recited a poem of Alexander Pope, written in memory of his friend, Secretary Craggs. The entire assemblage agreed that it was a perfect sketch of Hamilton's character.

Statesman yet Friend to truth, of Soul Sincere
In action Faithfull, and in Honour Clear!
Who broke no promise, served no Private end,
Who gained no Title, and lost no Friend,
Enobled by Himself, by all approved
Praised, wept, and Honoured, by the Muse he loved.[7]

William Seton wrote to Hamilton that "the infamous manner of the attack" of the Republicans "gave us all uneasiness & particularly from it being so near the close of the Session." Elisha Boudinot referred to Hamilton's "fiery ordeal," while Edward Carrington realistically commented that since Hamilton inevitably exposed himself to such attacks, his consolation must be that "do as they will with the further progress of your systems, they have proceeded far enough to widen the solidity of the principles on which they are laid . . . if they continue on their natural course they will at last be your most certain vindicators."[8]

Hamilton was relieved, but he did not deceive himself that the opposition had folded its tent and stolen away. A meeting of the commissioners of the sinking fund had been called by Jefferson, clue enough that the Republicans were still seeking ways and means to get at Hamilton.[9]

Americans were excited and supportive when they heard of the outbreak of the French Revolution in 1789. Lafayette's symbolic gesture, sending the prison key of the Bastille to George Washington at Mount Vernon, enchanted them. The American press was almost uniformly favorable to the French people's struggle against their aristocratic oppressors. Parades, a "civic feast" in Boston, the wearing of the revolutionary French cockade, liberty caps, were some of the ways of identifying with the revolution. The "Marseillaise" could be heard in taverns and at parties. When war broke out in Europe, with France lined up against almost all the European powers including Britain, American sympathy was with "Gallia's free band." The French mania lasted several years, and it was not until the excesses of the revolutionists, culminating in the king's execution, and the realization that England's entrance into the war would affect their trade that some grew less enthusiastic.

But the Francophiles had an answer to all objections. The aristocrats got no better than they gave. The atrocities were exaggerated. Playing on American bigotry, Republican apologists countered accusations of religious persecution with the argument that, in reality, Frenchmen were being liberated from the influence of papist priests who had always tried to keep the public in ignorance.[10]

At first, Hamilton accepted the French Revolution with reservations. He told Jefferson that the new "free government" would benefit the United States by giving real significance to the Franco-American commercial treaty. However, as time went on, Hamilton's doubts appeared to be justified. Gouverneur Morris, the American minister to France from 1792–94, conveyed his own disillusionment in letters to the secretary of state. He questioned the motives of the French leaders and deplored the waning probability of the establishment of a stable society. Morris's reports convinced Hamilton and Washington but confirmed the contention of the pro-French faction that Morris was a royalist and friend of the aristos. In 1791, Morris wrote that the people were becoming uncontrollable; the Reign of Terror bore out his words.[11]

After King Louis XVI was deposed in 1792 and royalty "abolished," Hamilton had to deal with the problem of payment of the French debt to a government that, in his opinion, was temporary. Was Ternant, the French minister sent by the king, still the bona fide representative of his government? Would there be a royalist government in exile? Hamilton's doubts were resolved, for better or for worse, with the arrival in the United States of Edmond Charles Genet, whose astonishing behavior was to preoccupy the Washington administration. The unprecedented spectacle of the French minister's dramatic landing at Charleston, South Carolina, and his triumphant progress to Philadelphia was one of the most unusual episodes in American diplomatic history.

Genet was only thirty years old when the Girondists sent him to the United States, but he had already had an impressive diplomatic career. He had been, for seven years, chief of a bureau at Versailles under Vergennes and as secretary to the French embassy had served a year in London, two in Vienna and one in Berlin. For five years he had been chargé in Russia and the year before his appointment to the United States, minister to Holland.

Meade Minnigerode, Genet's first biographer to see the family papers, revealed why Genet was considered for the American post. The problem of what to do with King Louis after his arrest, to execute him or not, was being debated. Danton, who represented the extreme position, said that since all Europe was united against France, the best answer was a king's head thrown in hostile faces. But the moderates, who were still in power, hesitated. Genet produced his answer quite informally at a small dinner given by Madame Roland. The discussion turned to America's role in the inception of the Revolution and, consequently, to her responsibility for the disposition of the king. Banish him to America, Genet offered. Since Americans were indebted to him for their liberty, they should receive him with open arms.

Soon afterward, Genet was asked by M. Lebrun to go to America and carry Capet (Louis XVI) and his family with him. Genet gave a cautious assent. Brissot, present at the interview, asked Genet what he would do with the royal family. Genet answered that since Capet loved agriculture, he would make him an American planter. This was the genesis of the Genet appointment. But King Louis was tried before the convention and found guilty of conspiring with the enemies of France, and on January 16, 1793, a majority voted unconditionally for death.

On the morning of January 21, King Louis XVI was beheaded. When Genet set out for America, part of his mission was obsolete, but the rumor about his original purpose, to carry the royal family across the sea, persisted. When he left Paris on the night of the execution, his carriage was stopped, and he was forced to go under escort to the nearest committee of vigilance, where his coach and baggage were thoroughly searched for the Dauphin, now King Louis XVII to the Royalists. The child was not found, but the belief that it was an impostor and not the little prince who remained imprisoned in the Temple and died there remains an intriguing mystery. The list of royal impostors who later claimed to be the lost dauphin is long, and many of the claimants lived in America.[12]

The events in Europe, particularly the war between republican France and monarchist Europe, had repercussions in the United States that forced the Washington administration to take a stand on several issues. The cabinet was divided; Hamilton was alert to Jefferson's every move. He tried to keep Washington's ear and, with a kind of righteous innocence, spoke to the foreign ministers, unconscious of any limitations upon him because he was secretary of the treasury and not secretary of state.

In February 1793, while his successor was en route to America, Ternant asked for the equivalent of three million livres against the United States debt to France, to be used to procure provisions within the United States to send to France. All of the cabinet except for the secretary of the treasury agreed. Hamilton dissented, saying that the supply should not exceed the $318,000 still in arrears; France had all the major powers against her, and the outcome for America's former ally looked doubtful. The rest of the cabinet overrode Hamilton, who had to disburse $444,500 in six equal installments.[13]

When news of the French king's death reached the United States, the Federalists were horrified, but, Jefferson wrote, the Republicans were pleased to discover there was "not the open condemnation from the monocrats I expected." The execution would demonstrate that monarchs were "amenable to punishment like other criminals," and the act would be advantageous to the republic by doing away with "the inviolability of the King's person."[14]

The execution of the French king was treated with cruel humor by some of the American newspapers. A pun that circulated—"*Louis Capet* has lost his *Caput*" (head)—offended the Federalists and shocked all Americans who deplored regicide or remembered the king's support against Britain during the Revolution. Hugh Henry Brackenridge, one of the radically pro-French editors, remarked, "From my use of the pun it may seem that I think lightly of his fate. I certainly do. It affects me no more than the execution of another malefactor."[15]

In March 1793, Jefferson noted that a connection between Ternant and Hamilton seemed to be springing up. With Genet on his way to replace him, Ternant "openly hoisted the flag of monarchy" by going into mourning for King Louis and, said Jefferson, "stopped visiting me thinking this a necessary accompaniment to his pious duty."[16] Ternant, who had served in America during the Revolution, decided to remain, fearing that a return to France might result in his being sent to join the king.

Hamilton took a position on the European war even before news of French-British hostilities reached America and before the president knew about it. In a conversation with George Hammond in early spring, the secretary expressed his commitment to American neutrality by agreeing to the justice of British freedom to capture contraband going to France in American ships. Hammond had made it clear that the British had no intention of honoring the principle of free ships making free goods. Hamilton accepted this, assuring the British minister that "he would be responsible for the concurrence of all the members of this Administration," revealing his deep-seated conviction that without a navy, the United States was pathetically weak on the high seas. Further, the financial stability of the country and, even more important, the success of the Hamilton system depended on British trade. Since 90 percent of American imports came from England and more than half of these were carried in American bottoms, to lose the revenue on the duty on these, the largest source of annual income for the Treasury, would be disastrous. It was clear to Hamilton that war with England could not be permitted.

By April 9, before George Washington left Mount Vernon for

Philadelphia to deal with the new international crisis, Hamilton had written two letters to Chief Justice John Jay, asking his opinion on whether Genet should be received "*absolutely* or with *qualifications*" and on the need for a declaration of neutrality. Jay urged caution. "It is happy for us that we have a President who will do nothing rashly."[17]

At the same time, Hamilton wrote to Washington that war had been declared by France against England, Russia and Holland. So far, he added, the *Commercial Intelligencer* indicated that the British government had displayed "unexceptionable conduct" toward American vessels. "This information is received here with Very great satisfaction as favourable to a continuance of peace—the desire of which may be said to be universal and ardent."[18]

In less than a week, Washington, alarmed by the news of war, started back to the capital, adamant that the United States maintain "a strict neutrality between the powers at war." He wanted steps taken immediately to stop privateering, and he wanted his cabinet to consider the situation seriously. Carrington, whose advice Hamilton solicited, wrote from Virginia that his part of the country wanted neutrality. "If we took any other position, we would do France no service, having no Navy, and would involve ourselves in distress."[19]

Washington presented each member of his cabinet with a series of questions as the agenda for a consultation on the Franco-British war. They were to meet at his house at nine on the morning of April 19 with the results of their "reflections." Jefferson observed that although the questions were in the president's handwriting, their style, "language, and the chain of argument" denoted Hamilton's work and reflected his doubts alone. As further proof, Edmund Randolph told Jefferson that the day before the date of the questions, Hamilton had gone over the reasoning of the queries with him, and he recognized them as soon as he saw them.[20]

The cabinet members agreed unanimously on the need for a proclamation of neutrality and that Genet should be received. Jefferson and Randolph wanted him received absolutely; Hamilton and Knox wanted him received with reservations.

The president issued the proclamation on April 22, 1793, avoiding the use of the word "neutrality." He declared that the United States, in view of the state of war existing among many of the European nations, would be friendly and impartial to all. American citizens were not to commit hostilities against any of the warring powers. Here, too, the president used caution by omitting the provocative word "privateers." Violators of the president's order would be punished.

Genet had made a tremendous stir in Charleston, where he landed, committing all kinds of outrageous acts, such as arming and sending to sea four privateers: the *Republican*, the *Sans-Culotte*, the *Anti-George* and the *Citizen Genet*. He would have to answer for these high-handed deeds when he reached Philadelphia, but in the meantime, he was enjoying a triumphal journey through an admiring South.

John Steele, a leading North Carolina Federalist, informed the secretary of the treasury on April 30 that Genet was leaving for Salisbury, North Carolina, and would then proceed to the capital by way of Richmond. He expected to take eighteen to twenty days to reach Philadelphia, including a stopover in Mount Vernon, where he hoped to see the president. Steele described the Frenchman as having "a good person, fine, ruddy complection, quite active and seems always in a bustle, more like a busy man than a man of business," very French in his manners, very outspoken about his mission and enthusiastic about his affectionate treatment by the Americans he had encountered so far.[21]

By the beginning of May, Hamilton and Knox had resolved the remaining Washington questions. In their opinion, France was waging an offensive war. Therefore, the guarantee of assistance in the Treaty of Alliance between the United States and France did not fit this case, even if the French West Indies were attacked by Great Britain. And since the treaty had been made with King Louis XVI, it would be best to delay any discussion of obligations. However, the debt to France should be paid.[22]

Jefferson was disgusted with this stand. The country, with "all the old Spirit of 1776," was enthusiastic about the French cause, he argued. When a French frigate arrived in Philadelphia with a British prize, "thousands of the yeomanry" crowded the wharves, shouting in exultation. "H[amilton] is panic-struck, if we refuse our breech to every kick which Great Britain may choose to give it," he told Madison. "He is for proclaiming at once the most abject principles." He complained that the votes in the cabinet were usually two and a half to one and a half. The split half was Randolph, whom Jefferson found to be vacillating.[23]

Madison agreed that Hamilton's reasoning was entirely self-serving and was disgusted with the neutrality proclamation, which gave an "anglified complexion" to the government.[24]

The French cause had gripped the country's imagination and stirred up hatred against the Federalists, who were accused of manipulating the public and exercising too much power. Secret political clubs dedicated to the defense of France were popping up in major cities all over the Union. Called Democratic societies, they bore an uncomfortable resemblance to the French Jacobin clubs, or so thought the Federalists. Their significance was more than transient; these societies became the breeding ground for a Republican party constitutency. The impact was nationwide; the local clubs were loosely connected through correspondence.

The first of these Democratic-Republican societies was the German Republican Society, founded in the nation's capital. Two Virginia clubs followed quickly, and in June, the most influential of the societies was established in Philadelphia and named the Democratic Society of Pennsylvania. The new society had such well-known, distinguished members as Charles Biddle, Dr. George Logan and Alexander J. Dallas. According to a circular letter issued by the Pennsylvania club, if France was defeated, "the successful European monarchies would not permit this country, the only remaining depository of liberty . . . to enjoy in peace the honors of an independent nation and the happiness of a republican government." There were domestic dangers also. "The seeds of luxury appear to have given root in our domestic soil; and the jealous eye of patriotism already regards the spirit of freedom and equality as eclipsed by the pride of wealth, and the arrogance of power."[25] Genet, who proudly took credit for founding the Philadelphia society, used these clubs to further his cause.

Genet arrived in Philadelphia on May 16. Here he would, finally, have to present his credentials to the president. An experienced diplomat, he knew that his progress through the South, in which he had behaved like visiting royalty, was irregular. But the Philadelphia Republicans had no interest in protocol. They planned an elaborate reception at Gray's Ferry, to be attended by a huge crowd. Genet avoided the demonstration by arriving in town early, thus displaying some common sense for the first time since arriving in America.

Hamilton had prepared a newspaper piece, which he never finished and never published, advising the citizens of Philadelphia to refrain from public demonstrations on M. Genet's arrival. It would be indiscreet because of American neutrality; because M. de Ternant, the retiring minister, a veteran of the American Revolution, had never received such a distinction; and because of the death of

Louis XVI, our benefactor, whose guilt had not been established. It was a feeble remonstrance and would have been ignored or laughed at.

On May 18, a celebration was given by the French citizens for the new minister at Oeller's tavern. And on June 1, American supporters of Genet gave a four-dollar-per-plate dinner, also at Oeller's, for two hundred guests. Jefferson was absent, but Genet was told that the secretary of state had composed the toasts. One was obviously aimed at Washington. "May republican simplicity be the sole ornament of the Magistrate of any elective government," it proposed.

Many years later, John Adams wrote to Jefferson: "You never felt the Terrorism excited by Genet in 1793," he told his old friend. He recalled "ten thousand People" in the streets of Philadelphia who, day after day, "threatened to drag Washington out of his House," and either effect a revolution in the government or compel it to fight for France against Great Britain.[26]

Hamilton was less perturbed by the mobs and the threatened violence than by the knotty problem of the French debt. Was the United States obligated to accede to the French republic's request, carried by Genet, to give all the money owed at this time in return for France's gesture of reciprocity, in the form of "drawing henceforth from the United States the greatest part of the substance & stores necessary for the armies, fleets & colonies of the French Republic"? Genet wrote: "Now what advantage more sensible can we offer to you than that of discharging your debt to us with your own productions, without exporting your cash, without recurring to the burthensome operations of Bankers."[27]

Hamilton wanted to reply to this with a negative and no explanations. Jefferson told Washington that to decline in this way would have "a very dry and unpleasant aspect indeed." If the installment due this year could be advanced without danger to the state, "I think it very material myself to keep alive the friendly sentiments of that country [France] as far as can be done without risking war or double payment." At the least, Jefferson recommended giving reasons for not changing the form of the debt.[28]

Washington was exceedingly hurt by the furor surrounding the French minister and the attacks on the administration and on him personally in the Republican press. Jefferson observed to Madison that the president was not well physically, subject to low-grade fevers that were affecting his looks most remarkably. As to the attacks in the press, "I think he feels these things more than any other person I ever met with." This sensitivity was to be expected, since Washington was surrounded by "satellites and sycophants." Jefferson added that "naked he would have been sanctimoniously reverenced, but enveloped in the *rags of royalty, they can hardly be torn off without laceration.*"[29]

Hamilton discussed the French debt and Genet's behavior with George Hammond in a series of confidential and secret conversations, but obviously, the secretary of the treasury wanted the British to know what the French were doing. Hamilton was informally treating Great Britain as an ally and evading Washington and Jefferson. He wanted to spare the president from having to take a position between his opposing secretaries.

Genet delivered his credentials to the president on June 13. He was ever present with his demands to Jefferson, or proceeding without him and precipitating cabinet crises. A major danger caused by the developing pro-French sentiment was the desire of individual Americans to aid France for profit, as well as for ideology. Though privateering was often lucrative, inevitably it would lead to friction between Great Britain and the United States. Genet did not limit his efforts to causing trouble on the high seas; he also tried to recruit Americans to attack Spanish possessions on the Gulf of Mexico.

On July 5, Genet appeared at the secretary of state's office and guilelessly read his instructions to recruit Americans from Kentucky for an expedition against New Orleans. Jefferson explained that these men would be hanged if they engaged in hostilities against Spain, a nation friendly to the United States. Hamilton, when he heard of this, hurried to give Washington chapter and verse for forbidding such action. He quoted Vattel's *Law of Nations*: "The equipping, manning and commissioning of Vessels of War, the enlisting, levying or raising of men for military service, whether by land or sea . . . are among the highest and most important exercises of sovereignty."[30]

The neutrality proclamation was unpopular among the Antifederalists. Madison called it "a most unfortunate error," which displayed ingratitude to France, indifference to the cause of liberty and thus was "wounding" to people's feelings. Furthermore, it was unconstitutional. The disposition of matters involving war and peace belonged to the legislative, not the executive, department.[31]

When Madison's constitutional interpretation reached Hamilton's ears, he picked up his pen and, as "Pacificus," wrote a series of articles defending neutrality. It was the president's right to issue the proclamation, "Pacificus" said, because it was merely an executive act. "If the legislature have the right to make war on the one hand— it is on the other, the duty of the Executive to preserve Peace 'till war is declared." France was fighting an offensive war, thus dismissing the charge of America's failure to live up to her treaty obligations. Gratitude was a personal emotion. Among nations, "the prominent motive is" the interest or advantages of the nations.[32]

Jefferson, whose pattern was to let others do his work for him, wrote to Madison that since Hamilton's Pacificus papers were not being answered, he feared his doctrine would be accepted. "For God's sake, my dear Sir, take up your pen. Select the most striking heresies, and cut him to pieces in the face of the public." Madison wrote some answers under the pseudonym "Helvedius" but lost interest and stopped.

Overbearing, single-minded Citizen Genet finally wore out Jefferson's patience. His conduct is "indefensible by the most furious Jacobin," Jefferson complained to Monroe. He was afraid that Hamilton's demand for a full appeal to the people about this persistent French gadfly would result in "a dissolution of friendship" between France and the United States. He deplored particularly Washington's suggestion—planted by Hamilton, he was certain—that customs house officials in all the ports be directed to watch for any arming or equipping of vessels and to report anything suspicious to the government. Washington was so stirred up that he considered calling Congress back into session, a move that even Hamilton discouraged.

Instead, Washington called a cabinet meeting for August 1, 1793, to decide what to do about Genet. The Frenchman's entire correspondence with the secretary of state was read, and it was decided to send a letter to Gouverneur Morris, the American minister in Paris, describing Genet's difficult behavior and asking for his recall. It was suggested that the Genet-Jefferson correspondence be made public. Hamilton made a speech in favor of the proposal and the next day made a forty-five minute reprise in its favor. Jefferson opposed the move. Then, unfortunately, Knox mentioned a scurrilous newspaper piece against Washington in which the president was placed on a guillotine.

Washington, exceedingly short-tempered that morning, went into a rage, denouncing "that *rascal Freneau*" who sent him three papers a day so that he would not miss any slander written against him.[33]

There were periodic meetings over Genet's recall but no resolution taken. Hamilton turned out a series signed "No Jacobin," in which he defended neutrality and explained what it meant for a nation to be neutral—no privateering for either side. "No Jacobin" exposed Genet's outrageous acts, particularly his interference in the politics of the United States by placing himself at the head of an American political club and, most outrageous of all, threatening to appeal to the people to support France, going over the president's head.

The cabinet ministers' tempers became as short as the president's as the European war and Genet's antics continued. At the end of June, Hamilton warned Washington that, "after mature reflection," he had decided to resign his office at the end of the term. He would delay only long enough to present some of his final plans to Congress "necessary to the full development of my original plan, and, as I suppose, of some consequence to my reputation." He also wanted to answer his accusers more fully while he was still in office.[34]

The attacks against Hamilton in the press were vicious. The French called him immune to gratitude, capable only of "dry sophistry," supporter of "the hellish combination of European tyrants" who want to destroy "the infant liberty of France; entangled by his aristocratic friends; the *Arnold* of his country." Randolph, when he returned from a summer in Virginia, told Jefferson that the people of Virginia were loyal to the government. All their opposition was "directed against the Secretary of the Treasury *personally* not against his measures."[35]

Hamilton's friends tried to dissuade him from yielding to "the envy, malice and ambition" of those who assailed him. "Stand fast and you cannot fail," Edward Carrington advised. "Resign, under pressure of the present opposition, and you fail irretrievably."[36]

Jefferson was going through a similar period of self-searching. "The motion of my blood no longer keeps time with the tumult of the world," he wrote poetically. He informed the president on July 31 that he planned to retire at the end of September. Washington called on the secretary of state at his country home on the banks of the Schuylkill. The president complained that he had not resigned because his friends had dissuaded him, and now he was being deserted by those upon whom he depended. Hamilton also was determined to leave at the end of the next congressional session, and it increased his difficulty that the two of them were leaving at different times. Before he left, Washington asked Jefferson to consider delaying his retirement for another quarter, "for that like a man going to the gallows, he was willing to put it off as long as he could." The next day Jefferson agreed to remain until the end of December.[37] On December 31, 1793, he left public life, or so he seemed to think at the time.

One of the most notorious examples of Genet's meddling was the case of the *Little Sarah*, an English ship captured by the French and taken to Philadelphia, where she was fitted out as a privateer with fourteen cannon. Her name was changed to the *Petit Democrate*, and she was ready to sail under the French flag. Washington was at Mount Vernon on July 8, 1793, when the problem developed; Genet refused to delay the ship's sailing until the president returned to Philadelphia and gave his opinion. Pennsylvania's Governor Mifflin, who knew that two of the *Sarah*'s cannon had been purchased in Philadelphia and that there were American citizens in the crew, sent Alexander Dallas, his secretary of state, to negotiate with Genet. The French minister would make no promise to keep the privateer from sailing until Washington's return. Further, if the president objected, he would go over his head to the American people.

At a hastily called cabinet meeting, Hamilton, supported as usual by Knox, wanted a party of militia stationed nearby to stop the privateer from sailing by firing on her if necessary. Firm action might preserve peace with France. If their minister was not checked, he could cause a rupture between the United States and France or cause one for us with his nation's enemies. The equipping of armed vessels in a neutral country, without that nation's approval, was clandestine and if discovered, expected to be suppressed.[38]

Jefferson opposed Hamilton's plan because he relied on Genet's word that the brig would not sail until Washington's return. Sending armed soldiers, Jefferson asserted, might well make the *Little Sarah* set sail and consequently cause bloodshed, even precipitate hostilities with France. In a burst of stirring prose, he said: "I would not gratify the combination of kings with the spectacle of the only two republics in earth destroying each other for two cannon; nor would I, for an infinitely greater cause, add this country to that combination, turn the scale of contrast, and let it be from our hands, that the hopes of man received their last stab."[39]

The rhetoric on both sides was expended in vain. While the cabinet deliberated, the new French commerce destroyer quietly set sail for Chester and then the open seas, where she became a menace to British commerce.

In the end, Genet, who had determined to force a reluctant United States to go to war with France's enemies, almost became a victim of the fanatical Jacobins who had come to power while he was in America. The new French regime was impatient of the Girondist foreign policy and interested only in the immediacy of the war against England. Robespierre's foreign minister denounced Genet for going beyond his instructions and ordered him home. Fauchet, the new French minister, arrived in the United States with orders to arrest Genet and send him back to France. Genet sought asylum in the United States.

It was Hamilton who suggested that Genet be permitted to stay, which offer was gratefully accepted. Eventually, he married Cornelia Clinton, the New York governor's daughter, and became a citizen of the United States. He died at the age of seventy, having outlived his opponent, Alexander Hamilton, by thirty years.

In September, Hamilton came down with yellow fever during an epidemic that started in Philadelphia in August 1793 and swept through the capital for two or three months. It was not until the early twentieth century that the *Aedes* mosquito was discovered to be the carrier of the yellow fever virus. In 1793 there were two schools of thought on the fever's cause: one attributed it to a miasma from the marshes and stagnant water; the other held that it had been brought from the West Indies. Jefferson blamed its origin on "the filth of Water Street," the area where the first cases were discovered. By the end of the epidemic, which exhausted itself in November, at least 5,000 people had died.

Hamilton became ill in September, and by the sixth, Jefferson reported to Madison there were two physicians in attendance at his house. He puts himself in danger "by his excessive alarm," said the secretary of state unsympathetically. "He had been miserable several days before from a firm persuasion he should catch it. . . . His friends, who have not seen him, suspect it is only an autumnal fever he has."[40]

Hamilton and his wife both succumbed to the disease, and the secretary's choice of treatment developed into a political issue. Ned Stevens, Hamilton's boyhood friend, now practicing medicine in Philadelphia, attended the Hamiltons. He used what was called "the West Indies treatment," consisting of frequent cold baths. Dr. Benjamin Rush, a Republican and close friend of Jefferson, used the "depleting treatment," which included drastic bloodletting and severe purges of jalap and calomel.[41]

Giving as his motives "humanity and friendship to the Philadelphia citizenry," Hamilton published an account of his yellow fever cure. Dr. Stevens, who had dealt with many yellow fever epidemics in the West Indies, Hamilton explained, used a method quite different from that of local physicians. If his method were adopted, "many lives will be saved, and much ill prevented." Dr. John Redman, president of the Philadelphia College of Physicians, approached Stevens after reading Hamilton's letter. The West Indian physician gave Redman an account of his method of treatment, which was published in the *Federal Gazette* and other papers.

Dr. Rush, exhausted by round-the-clock ministrations to yellow fever patients, took the newspaper account of the Stevens method of treatment as a personal criticism, especially since the *Federal Gazette*, which also published Rush's method and advertisements, supported the Stevens cure. On September 13 the *Gazette* announced Hamilton's recovery from yellow fever, adding, "This is a strong confirmation of the goodness of the plan by Doctor Stevens, and ought to recommend it to the serious consideration of our Medical Gentlemen."

Rush thought Stevens's regimen quackery, believing that Hamilton opposed his treatment because he was a friend of Madison and Jefferson. He declared on Ocober 2 that "Colonel Hamilton's remedies are now as unpopular in our city as his funding system is in Virginia or North Carolina."[42] However, Hamilton had the last word. In 1797, when Dr. Rush was proposed for a professorship at Columbia University's medical school, Hamilton, who was on the selection committee, vetoed Rush because of his method of treating yellow fever.

The Hamilton children had been sent to their grandparents at Albany to escape contagion. After Alexander and Betsey recovered from the disease, they traveled north for a reunion with the family and to convalesce. The trip was exhausting and frustrating. They were stopped at almost every town along the way "as infectious." At one tavern, fugitives from Philadelphia who were staying there insisted that the Hamiltons be turned away. The landlord refused, and after some recriminations the Hamiltons were put up for the night.[43] By the time they arrived at Greenbush, the ferry stop across the river from Albany, Alexander and Betsey were at the end of their endurance.

When he arrived in Albany, Hamilton discovered that his father-in-law had agreed to "conditions" before his children could be admitted into the city. The Albany Common Council had ordered that persons from Philadelphia, no matter whether they arrived by ship or ferry, were to be examined before allowed to enter. Abraham Yates, Jr., the mayor of Albany, wrote to Schuyler about the concern occasioned by Colonel Hamilton's arrival. "The fears of the Citizens are up, beyond conception, because of the idea that the Colonel's carriages, baggage

& servants may be infected and spread the disease." He reminded Schuyler of his promise, made previous to his son-in-law's arrival, that he would, at his own expense, have the Hamilton clothing destroyed, that the Hamiltons would come in an open chair without servants or carriages and that the Schuylers would be quarantined with a guard, which they would pay for, stationed near their house to enforce the quarantine. The Common Council, Yates stated, requested that all these stipulations be carried out. "Nothing but this can quiet the Citizens nor prevent effective measures to enforce the resolutions entered into by the Board."[44]

Schuyler replied that Colonel Hamilton would comply with the demands that were reasonable but claimed the right of citizenship that could not be violated. He and his wife had submitted to an examination by city physicians and had been certified free from infection. The hysteria had reached a preposterous level.

Once in Albany, Hamilton took up his own defense. He explained that he and his wife had been given a clean bill of health by their own physicians, had sustained a difficult journey with no ill effects and brought with them no clothing that had been on them while ill except perhaps for some washed linen. Since they had left from their summer residence outside Philadelphia, they had been away from the city for more than three weeks. It would be "absolutely inadmissible," he declared, to be under the eyes of a guard or to submit the family of General Schuyler to being cut off from town. It was understandable that the city magistrates wanted to protect their citizens from contagion, but they had to consider "the rules of reason, moderation & humanity." In a final word, Hamilton declared that he regarded all stipulations made by General Schuyler at an end.[45]

Abraham Yates answered stiffly, resting on his dignity and the rights of the Common Council to make rulings, but he released the general from his agreement. The law could not be relaxed in favor of any man, he pontificated. But under the circumstances, he preferred to close the "irksome correspondence" with the thought that originally the council "intended solely for your Accommodation."[46]

By October 23, his health restored, Hamilton was back in his summer home outside Philadelphia to find a letter from Washington, asking if the president had the right to convene Congress at a place other than the capital. Jefferson had already answered in the negative; he found nothing in the Constitution to support it. Madison had said yes, pointing out that "place" had been omitted in the Constitution to avoid convening where there might be local partialities. Hamilton, after a lengthy analysis of the problem, concluded that a removal of the seat of government to Germantown would be suitable until it was safe to return to Philadelphia.

About a week later, Hamilton became ill again, fortunately not a recurrence of yellow fever. The children remained in Albany with the Schuylers, who convinced the Hamiltons that it would be best for them to stay, rather than risk exposure to another outbreak of yellow fever. Schuyler made reference to the children's staying until spring, which should be proper "should you find yourself under the necessity of adhering to the resolution you mentioned to me when home." He meant Hamilton's decision to resign.[47]

Hamilton was devoted to his children and hated to be parted from them. He wrote to his daughter Angelica, then nine years old, that he was pleased that she was beginning to study French. He advised her that the best way to behave was "with so much politeness, good manners and circumspection, as never to have any occasion to make any apology."

During the summer an affectionate letter from Angelica Church crossed the ocean. She wrote to Alexander that she was in despair being separated from those she loved in America. "Yet were I in America, would ambition give an hour to *Betsey* and to me," she asked. "Can a mind engaged by Glory taste of peace and ease?" With the thought of resignation in mind, Hamilton had written to the Churches that he and Betsey might go to England. "I have no ideas for such happiness, but when will you come and receive the tears of joy and of affection?" Angelica asked.

Although Angelica regretted her separation from her family, her life in London was a glittering one. All the prominent Americans who came to England visited the rich, hospitable Churches, so she always had the latest news. She wrote to her sister Betsey that she had seen copies of Fenno's *Gazette* while visiting the American ambassador and was "very much edified" to read about "my Brother as he deserves, and as I and all who *dare* to know him think." Later in the same day she wrote again, saying that she had received a letter from the Hamiltons. "My love to Alexander the good, and the amiable," she told Betsey.[48]

Jefferson resigned at the close of 1793 but left his spokesman in the House, William Branch Giles, to continue the feud with Hamilton. Giles once more accused the secretary of the treasury of exceeding his authority. Hamilton, who was expecting this assault, asked that the House make a formal inquiry into his activities, which they did. Hamilton spent part of the winter preparing his answer and so stayed in the cabinet a year and a month after Jefferson resigned.

Exit Mr. Secretary of the Treasury

On New Year's Day, 1794, Washington appointed Attorney General Edmund Randolph as secretary of state to succeed Jefferson. The next day, the Virginian, whom his predecessor had found unpredictable and sometimes contentious, took the oath of office and wrote a conciliatory note to Hamilton. He hoped that any differences between them would be of men "who equally persue the object of their appointment, and that the public good will thereby be promted rather than injured."[1]

But in Congress, led by Madison and a strong Republican contingent, Jefferson's supporters were in full cry against the secretary of the treasury. Jefferson had presented his report on the treatment of American commerce by foreign countries, requested by the House, in February 1791, about two weeks before he retired. The extensive data had been collected and collated by Tench Coxe, Hamilton's assistant, who had given Jefferson his expert advice without any restraint due to loyalty to his chief.

Hamilton was not surprised by Coxe's treachery. William Heth, collector of Customs at Bermuda Hundred, Virginia, had warned the secretary of the treasury in June that Coxe had been working on undermining "*you*, in hopes of filling your place, through the Interests of———" [Jefferson]. Watch him closely, Heth advised, "& you will not be long in discovering the *perfidious* & *ungrateful friend*."[2]

The slant of the report was anti-British, the gist of it that while Britain imposed harsh restrictions on American trade, Spain, Portugal and France did not. Jefferson recommended a system of reciprocal favors and retaliation.

Madison embodied the essence of the report in seven resolutions that favored France and attacked Great Britain. Those nations that did not have a commercial treaty with the United States would have to pay higher tonnage taxes. Reciprocity would operate in port restrictions, and Congress would indemnify "citizens who sustained losses from foreign regulations which contravened the law of nations."[3]

Hamilton immediately met Madison's attack. William Smith of South Carolina, in a 15,000 word speech, reflected Hamilton's economic thinking. Through Smith's speech, Hamilton pointed out that Britain was the best customer of the United States, twice as good as any other. Britain was also the chief source of credit, essential for an infant nation. It was true that American ships were excluded from the British West Indies, whereas French regulations were more generous, but Britain, despite Jefferson's incorrect figures, was the better customer and supplied more goods. Emotional outpourings against the former mother country made poor sense. The United States needed patience to persuade Britain to agree to treaties, rather than lose our most important commercial contact.

The Federalist position in the debate was not a noble one. It presented the United States as a weak nation, ready to bow before superior strength in return for monetary benefits. The Anti-British contingent had strong stuff on their side. The British had shown their dedication to freedom, said one Republican, "by breaking our treaty, by withholding our posts, seizing our ships . . . inciting the Indians to murder us." Hamilton, behind the scenes, tried to keep the debate focused on the commercial issues, but tempers erupted on both sides. On February 3, 1794, Madison proposed a resolution for further restrictions on foreign manufactures and vessels, but it was put aside for six weeks.

Hamilton was overwhelmed with requests from all sides. In February, he wrote plaintively to John Adams as president of the Senate that "it is extremely to be desired that the two houses of the Legislature could fix upon a plan for regulating the returns which they would choose to have made to them periodically from the Treasury that the business might be prosecuted in formity to that plan. Congress would then have the information, which they may deem useful, and the Treasury could be prepared systematically to furnish it."[4]

Despite these official demands, Hamilton regularly ground out articles to support his positions. The *Americanus* series repeated the arguments of the William Smith speech: "If while Europe is exhausting itself in a destructive war; this country can maintain peace, the issue will open to as wide a field of advantages, which even imagination can with difficulty compass."[5]

While the French Revolution raged and its leaders changed periodically, the sympathies of Hamilton and his family were with the moderates. Angelica Church wrote to her sister, asking that she and "Alexander, the amiable" make "our country agreeable" to Messieurs Talleyrand and de Beaumetz. The two Frenchmen had been in self-exile in England since the fall of 1793, but Talleyrand was asked to leave in February 1794, after involvement in numerous plots culminating in accusations that he was stirring up an Irish rebellion. The émigrés were welcomed by the Hamiltons and, said Angelica, had written her "in raptures" over the Hamiltons' kindness and the secretary of the treasury's "abilities and manners."[6]

During his sojourn in America, Talleyrand made some interesting comments about Hamilton. One night, passing Hamilton's window, he saw his friend burning the midnight oil. With great admiration and, perhaps, puzzlement, he wrote: "I have seen a man who made the fortune of a nation, laboring all night to support his family." In his *Etudes sur la Republique*, he wrote: "I consider Napoleon, Fox, and Hamilton the three greatest men of our epoch, and if I had to choose between the three, I would give, without hesitation, the first place to Hamilton. He had divined Europe."[7]

Talleyrand and other émigrés provided almost the only source of personal descriptions of Hamilton in the nineties, at the height of his fame and influence. J. P. Brissot de Warville, a Girondist newspaperman, described Hamilton as "not tall," with firm features, a decided expression, a frank and martial manner. The Duke de Rochefoucauld-Liancourt called Hamilton "one of the most interesting men in America." He spoke of the secretary's "dignity and feeling, force and decision, delightful manners, great sweetness." In addition, he had "breadth of mind, clearness and facility of expression, information on all points, cheerfulness, excellence of character, and much amiability."[8]

Little of the softer side of Hamilton appears in surviving letters, which usually deal with finance, political discussion and economic problems. They reveal his energy, brilliance and drive to get things done. One of his greatest faults was his belief that he was right, particularly on the subject of good government. When he felt that his policies were being rejected, he became discontented and gloomy in the extreme.

The accomplishment of his program was Hamilton's first consideration, regardless of whether it gained or lost him popularity. His victories were always temporary. Having overthrown one dragon, two more sprang up in its place. As Christopher Gore said when he heard that Hamilton planned to resign: "Why should he [Hamilton] spend his health and his time and destroy the tranquillity of his mind for a people who really do not estimate his merits at a hundreth part of their value?" But Hamilton stayed in office in 1794 in order to defend himself against accusations. "I am just where I do not want to be," he told Angelica. "I know how I could be much happier . . . but circumstances enchain me."[9]

Among the gambits that the House used against Hamilton was an investigation into the authorities from the president to the secretary of the treasury respecting the making and disbursing of loans to France, the implication being that Hamilton had misappropriated the money directed by law to special purposes. Hamilton appealed to Washington, reminding him that he was always consulted and that nothing was done without his sanction, verbal when the president was in Philadelphia, in writing when he was out of town.

Hamilton admitted that he had applied to one purpose a loan designated by Congress for another purpose. His defense rested on two letters from Washington written while he was on his southern tour, containing what amounted to a blanket sanction for Hamilton's disbursements.

At first Washington did not remember the letters, not having kept copies, but after being shown them, he acknowledged them, though very chagrined. As he explained to Randolph, he did not want to be identified with any party. His opinions contained no systematic adherence to party, "but solely from my views of right," which fell "sometimes on one side sometimes on the other." Washington said directly, "I have no reason to suspect Col. Hamilton of any unkind disposition towards me—he has none on my part with relation to himself. . . . I never disclosed an idea concerning him which he might not hear, and which in many instances and particularly a late one he has not heard from my own mouth. . . . But I have reason to suspect others. . . . But I have said enough—perhaps too much."[10]

Washington replied to Hamilton officially, saying that from his "general recollection of the course of the proceedings, I do not doubt, that it was substantially as you have stated it in the annexed paper." It was a flabby, ambiguous endorsement of Hamilton's position. The secretary of the treasury was bitterly disappointed at the president's reserve.[11]

By March 1794, war with Great Britain was perilously close. The diplomatic bag brought a distressing report from Thomas Pinckney.

Lord Grenville had dismissed the American protest over the refusal of British troops to leave the western posts, declaring that for nine years the United States had flouted the terms of the peace treaty, which well nigh abrogated it. British orders limiting the freedom of neutral shipping, and the consequent seizure of a large number of American ships, increased anti-British feeling in the United States, as did the report of Lord Dorchester's speech to the western Indians, predicting that war between the United States and Great Britain was imminent and they could be the benefactors when the United States was defeated.

Even the Federalists were angered and expecting war. Hamilton was drawn into the crisis. To offset Madison's resolutions, Hamilton composed a series of alternatives, which he presented to Washington. In mid-March, Theodore Sedgwick introduced a program to the House that reflected these ideas.

The proposals called for auxiliary troops and new revenues to pay for them, an embargo and fortification of the principal ports. Hamilton did not want war and did not succumb to the growing hysteria, but he did not want the country to be caught unprepared. "The pains taken to preserve peace, include a proportional responsibility that equal pains be taken to be prepared for war," he said.[12]

The preparedness measures passed by Congress were milder than Hamilton's suggestions to the president. Congress did, however, seek Hamilton's advice on raising money for war. Money could be raised, Hamilton said, but not by foreign loans, since the prospective lenders would be our enemies, and not by domestic loans, the people were too poor. Therefore, it would have to be done by taxation of certain goods. He suggested excises on carriages, snuff, sugar and auction sales. Immediately, Madison charged that these taxes were aimed at the South and that the tax on carriages was a dual tax and therefore unconstitutional. When a tax on public securities and bank stocks was proposed, Massachusetts and the financial North balked. The Senate's effort to raise an army of 10,000 met rejection in the lower house. Madison said that "it was strangled more easily" than he had expected.[13]

During this period of congressional strife, Hamilton as "Americanus" wrote against war. France would be a disastrous ally, and domestic prosperity would be sacrificed.

In addition, there were internal problems that Hamilton thought dangerous to the Union. The western farmers, dissatisfied with the excise tax, were ready to erupt into armed revolt. Indian troubles and dissension between the British and French factions threatened the country. "I do not perceive that I could voluntarily quit my post at such a juncture," Hamilton wrote to Washington. If the president found his continuance in office "inconvenient or ineligible," Hamilton assured him that he would retire as scheduled, "with all the readiness naturally inspired by an impatient desire to relinquish a situation in which even a momentary stay is opposed by the strongest personal & family reasons & could only be produced by a sense of duty or Reputation."[14]

Washington responded: "On the contrary, I am pleased that you have determined to remain at your post until the clouds over our affairs, which have come on so fast of late shall be dispersed."[15]

Apparently the slight coolness between the president and the secretary of the treasury, which had developed over Hamilton's publication of the 1791 letter in which Washington had authorized him to use money obtained from the Netherlands for the Bank of the United States, had been forgotten. Hamilton had used this final resort to disprove the House charges against him for the management of the Treasury Department. It had embarrassed Washington, making him look pro-Federalist and a Hamiltonian. Hamilton was annoyed because Washington had not made a real effort to exonerate him from the charges and forgotten, conveniently, that the letter existed. Washington hated, above all, to lose his aura of Olympian superiority. Hamilton could not endure questioning of his probity in financial dealings. But their mutual respect and dependence overcame the temporary rift.

Washington and Hamilton, though both military men, were not willing to bow to a warlike solution to the problem with Great Britain. Washington preferred negotiation, also the Federalist solution, reached by a conference of Senators Rufus King, George Cabot, Caleb Strong and Oliver Ellsworth. On April 6, Secretary of State Edmund Randolph claimed credit as "among the first, if not the first," who suggested sending an envoy extraordinary to London, but the president did not act on the suggestion for ten days, perhaps hesitating over the choice of the envoy. Ellsworth, spokesman for the Federalist group, had proposed Hamilton's name to Washington as early as March 12. Washington replied that although there was no doubt in his own mind, his secretary of the treasury "did not possess the general confidence of the Country." When this reply was reported back to the Federalist caucus, King approached Senator Morris of Pennsylvania for support. Washington consulted Morris on

April 8 and listed the possibilities: John Adams, Hamilton, John Jay and Thomas Jefferson. Morris objected to Adams and Jefferson, and gave Hamilton as his first choice.[16]

The Republicans opposed Hamilton and wrote to Washington, telling him so. James Monroe informed the president that to appoint Hamilton would be injurious to the public interest and his own. Jefferson opposed the mission and deplored Hamilton as the missionary.

John Nicholas, a member of the Virginia house of representatives and Monroe's brother-in-law, was Hamilton's outspoken critic, reflecting the antagonism felt by many Republicans. He was astonished that a man of so many odious traits of character could be nominated envoy "when perhaps half America have determined it to be unsafe to trust power in the hands of this person . . . when at least half the legislatures are afraid to exert themselves in the most trying situations of their country lest his present powers should enable him to wrest them to purposes which he is supposed by them to entertain." Nicholas added, "Did it ever occur to you that the divisions of America might be ended by the sacrifice of this one man?"[17]

Though the Federalists wanted Hamilton, they had to be realistic; they settled on John Jay. Hamilton was used to keeping personal disappointment to himself. A trip to England, a longed-for reunion with Angelica, would have been a welcome change from the harassment at the Treasury. It would have been an added triumph for the penniless lad from the West Indies to arrive at the Court of St. James as a special envoy. But it was not to be.

King told Jay on April 12 that the new envoy would be either Hamilton or Jay. King said, "Hamilton might deserve the preference," but on the other hand, "for weight of character" at home and abroad, Jay had the advantage. Also, Hamilton was essential in his present job. Jay listened but did not comment, except to agree "to the propriety of Hamilton's appointment."[18]

Hamilton wrote to Washington on April 14, expounding at length on the "perilous" crisis in the country's affairs. Washington was exhorted to act and, if necessary, use his veto to object to laws "which he deems contrary to the public interest."[19] Finally, Hamilton got to the point. It was his conviction that Washington should nominate someone "who will have the confidence of those who think peace still within their reach." Speaking candidly, Hamilton advised that he be dropped from consideration for the post. "I assure you in the utmost sincerity that I shall be completely and intensely satisfied with the election of another."[20] Jay, he said, was the only man.

After receiving Hamilton's letter, Washington summoned Jay to a conversation "on an interesting subject." Jay was offered the envoyship. Later that same day, Hamilton, Strong, Cabot, Ellsworth and King pressed Jay to accept. He was the only man in whom they could confide. The situation of the country was "too interesting and critical" to permit him to hesitate. The next day, Jay conveyed his acceptance to Washington; wasting no time, the president forwarded it to the Senate for approval.

The Senate accepted Jay's appointment by a vote of twenty-six to eight. The most ardent opponent of the nomination was Aaron Burr. He pointed out that Thomas Pinckney, United States minister to Great Britain, was in London and capable of doing the job "at much less expense than by an envoy extraordinary to Great Britain" and "with equal facility and effect." Burr also opposed the precedent of allowing Supreme Court judges to hold another office that was "holden at the pleasure of the executive!" This was unconstitutional because it exposed them "to the influence of the executive" which was "mischievous and impolitic." Burr's resolution to exclude Jay and leave the mission in Pinckney's hands was defeated, seventeen to ten.

Jay was hurt by Burr's action; he considered the New York senator his friend. "*Mr Burr was among the few who opposed it,*" he told his wife in a letter that announced the Senate's approval of his nomination.[21] But Burr's vote was against Hamilton, not against Jay.

Denied the envoyship for himself, Hamilton proceeded to stage-manage the Jay mission. This required the cooperation of others, particularly the president. Hamilton met with Rufus King, George Cabot and Oliver Wolcott on the evening of April 21, 1794, to discuss Jay's orders. All agreed that the president might give instructions without consulting the Senate, that it would be best if he did so and that if a treaty were obtained, it should be signed subject to Senate approval. The Federalist leaders wanted included in a treaty: satisfaction for "the spoliations in our Commerce" and some rules to prevent it in the future; compensation for the capture of American vessels; evacuation of the posts in the Northwest and the resolution of problems connected with the Indians; the navigation of the Great Lakes and the West Indies.[22]

When Washington requested advice from his cabinet members, Hamilton gave him all these points and added others, such as indemnification "for our Negroes carried away during the Revolutionary war." He also suggested items to be included in a treaty of commerce. Jay's orders were issued under the signature of Secretary of State Edmund Randolph, but in a cover letter to the president,

Randolph wrote that the instructions had been "submitted to Mr Jay and Colo. Hamilton."[23]

Hammond thought Jay's appointment a promising portent for Anglo-American relations. As soon as he heard about it, he sought out Hamilton for a confidential conversation. He was taken aback when Hamilton entered into "a Pretty copious recital" of the injuries that American commerce had sustained from British cruisers. Hamilton announced that Jay would demand compensation for American vessels seized without proof that their cargo was French, for which action there was no appeal possible. Hamilton, said Hammond, spoke "with some degree of heat," remarking that when the people of Great Britain learned of the wrongs American commerce had suffered, "a very powerful party might be raised in that country in favour of this country." This new stern Hamilton, said Hammond, conceded only that Jay's instructions advised him to use the most conciliatory language and "evince the most sincere desire" on the part of the United States to settle all disputes "on an amicable and permanent principle."[24]

Before the chief justice left for London, the secretary of the treasury wrote, "I had wished to have found liesure [sic] to say many things to you but my occupations permit me to offer only a few loose observations." A stream of advice followed. "A treaty of Commerce ought not to be concluded without previous reference here for further instruction," Hamilton said pointedly.[25] Jay sailed for England in May 1794 with the good wishes of the Federalists, especially Hamilton, and the unconcealed hatred of the Democratic-Republicans.

Constitutionalists asked if there was a conflict of interest between Jay's position of chief justice and that of ambassador. Had he, in effect, resigned as chief justice? And most important, was not Congress's control of American commerce being usurped by the executive department? Some American westerners, remembering Jay as the man who had failed to uphold their right to navigation of the Mississippi during the peace talks, demonstrated against his appointment. He was burned in effigy and guillotined in Lexington, Kentucky.[26]

Jay was already in Europe when Hamilton expressed himself on the treaty between Denmark and Sweden for the maintenance of neutral navigation. Edmund Randolph had informed him in June that Jay was instructed, if expedient, to sound out those nations' ministers at the court of London about the treaty. It might be to the country's advantage, Randolph suggested, to form a concert with those nations, and it was up to Jay, who was on the scene in London, to decide. "The Secretary of the Treasury is against the measure," Hamilton wrote; the two northern European countries were weak, "and the entanglements of a treaty with them might be found very inconvenient."[27]

Hammond was relieved to convey Hamilton's sentiments on this issue to his superiors in London. In July, Hamilton told Hammond that it was America's policy, even if there was "an open contest with Great Britain," to avoid entangling European connections. This was another example of Hamilton taking upon himself the secret direction of American foreign policy. Its effect on negotiations could have weakened Jay's hand by preventing him from using a possible United States-Denmark-Sweden alliance as a talking point. However, since Hamilton regarded Jay as his substitute and further believed that Washington encouraged this assumption, Hamilton was only using his judgment in evading an alliance with two feeble northern nations.

Though believing that Britain was more important to American development than revolution-torn France, Hamilton felt loyalties to his French friends, particularly to Lafayette, his former companion-in-arms. After the marquis's unsuccessful attempt to save King Louis XVI in August 1792, he fled to the Austrian Netherlands. The French government declared him a traitor, and he was captured and imprisoned in a series of places. Washington, who never forgot his fondness for the gallant youngster who came from across the sea to help the American cause, asked his cabinet in January 1794 whether he might "in a *private and unofficial* character" send a letter to the king of Prussia, asking for Lafayette's release on parole. Hamilton, Knox and Randolph thought such a letter proper. Thomas Pinckney, the minister to Great Britain, was asked to receive James Marshall of Virginia, who was delegated to deliver the letter into the king's hand, and to advise him how best to approach the king. The president and the cabinet, though worried about repercussions from France, overcame them because of their unfortunate friend's "present sufferings" and in consideration of his "eminent services" to the United States.[28]

Marshall went to Berlin but was unable to fulfill his assignment; Lafayette was no longer in Prussian hands. He had been moved to Olmutz in Moravia, then a part of Austria. By an act of Congress of March 27, 1794, Lafayette was granted $10,000 for his war service. Since Lafayette was still in prison, Hamilton attempted to make arrangements to convey the money for his use. Despite the goodwill of his American friends, Lafayette remained incarcerated in the Austrian fortress until he was liberated by Napoleon in 1797. In

1824, an elderly gentleman of sixty-seven, Lafayette visited the United States, where he was received with unprecedented affection and made the first honorary American citizen.

The letters from Jay to Hamilton during the summer of 1794 were very revealing. The chief justice had been asked to dine with Lord Grenville; Alexander Wedderburn, the lord chancellor; and Mr. Pitt. At times he was "the single foreigner" present. He was hopeful that he could achieve his ends by accommodating, rather than disputing. So far, he did not regret any step he had taken but wished to be able to say the same thing at the conclusion of his business. The Jays had been received with great friendliness by the Churches. Mrs. Church, Jay wrote to Hamilton, "looks as well as when you saw her, and thinks as much about America and her Friends in it as ever. She certainly is an amiable agreable [sic] Woman."[29]

By mid-August, Jay reported to Hamilton that things looked promising, but the issue was uncertain. The following month, Jay complained to Hamilton of the pro-French party's activities in the United States and of Monroe's speech to the French Assembly in Paris, in which he extolled United States friendship with France. Other complaints from the now thoroughly anglicized Jay blamed his inability to conclude the mission on such anti-British activities as the state of Virginia taking British property, refusing to pay debts due British creditors unless England made reparations for spoliations and evacuated the Northwest posts.[30]

"My task is done," Jay wrote to Hamilton on November 19, enclosing the treaty in his letter. "Whether *Finis coronat opus*, the President, Senate and Public will decide." Lord Grenville was anxious to get the treaty sent to America. "If this Treaty fails, I despair of another," its author wrote. It would be best, lest the public be misled, that it be ratified and published as soon as possible. Jay was so exhausted, he decided to stay in England until spring and not risk a winter sea trip. "I really think the good Disposition of this Country should be cherished," said Jay, unaware that he was sending to the United States a bombshell that would cause an explosion of violent hatred against the author of the treaty.[31]

It was not until August that John Jay saw a New York paper with the news that the inquiry into Hamilton's official conduct had had a happy result. The conclusion of Hamilton's ordeal took place on May 22, when Abraham Baldwin, a member of the House committee to examine the state of the Treasury Department, made the report requested by Hamilton. It concluded that no monies of the United

States were ever used by the secretary of the treasury for any purpose except for those of the government. "Master Giles must be much mortified. I congratulate you upon the report relative to your Department," Stephen Higginson, a Boston merchant, wrote. William Heth congratulated him on his "second, and complete triumph, over the invidious persecution of a base faction. . . . The more you probe, examine and investigate Hamilton's conduct; rely upon it, the *greater* he will appear."[32]

Vindication had occurred, but there were still pressing matters to resolve. The secretary of the treasury's excise tax on whiskey, a cornerstone of his funding program, was under violent attack in four frontier counties of western Pennsylvania—Washington, Allegheny, Fayette and Westmoreland, which became the center of the storm against the whiskey tax. The farmers of this area found it more practical to turn their excess grain into distilled liquor. A pack horse could manage only four bushels of grain, but when it was turned into whiskey, he could carry the equivalent of twenty-four bushels over the mountains to be sold; the money this brought was doubled when it reached the East. To these farmers, the tax seemed discriminatory and so justified their restraining the revenue agents who came to collect it, by force if necessary, and their talking about secession from the Union.

Hamilton had ignored these protests, arguing that the duty was uniform throughout the states and that its burden fell heaviest on the West because more whiskey was consumed there. Western Pennsylvanians, mostly Scotch-Irish, bitterly remembered the tax collectors of their home countries and hated the breed. And they were not afraid to act on their feelings.

Hamilton has been blamed for provoking the incident known as the Whiskey Rebellion in order to destroy his enemies by involving them in a situation that could be seen as treasonable. However, the secretary of the treasury responded to western discontent in March 1794 by recommending to Congress that the law be eased and certain concessions granted, but to no avail. The Republicans had assigned the role of villain to Hamilton and wanted to see the play unfold.

Congress adjourned on June 9, leaving the country in the hands of the executive department. Washington was perturbed about a number of incidents in the South. Kentucky had adopted a remonstrance to the president and Congress against their failure to keep the British from insulting and injuring them, and stating their right to free and undisturbed navigation of the Mississippi. On the Georgian frontier, there were complaints about Creek Indian raids. And in July, Elijah Clark, with a body of Georgians, invaded Creek territory for the purpose of setting up an independent state.

Hamilton was unable to attend the cabinet meeting that the president called to deal with these matters. His two-year-old son, John Church, was very ill and Betsey completely exhausted from caring for the child. An excursion into the country and a change of air might help his invalids, the sectreary told the president. Washington regretted the child's illness but hoped that his secretary would find time before he left to give his opinion in writing on the Kentucky and Georgia business. "I have considered the two subjects . . . as maturely as my situation permitted," Hamilton answered. Nothing could be done unless there was some indictable action. With regard to Georgia, he offered the following steps: military coercion by the governor of Georgia to prevent the establishment of another state; assistance to the Creek nation with the assurance that the United States would cooperate and, if they were invaded, would dispossess the intruders.[33]

The two invalids failed to recover sufficiently to return to Philadelphia. Betsey, who was having a difficult pregnancy; John, still ailing; and six-year-old James would go to Albany. Hamilton would accompany them as far as Fishkill and then return to the capital. Philip, aged twelve; Angelica, ten; and Alexander, eight years old, remained in Philadelphia with their father. At the end of July, Hamilton told Betsey that he was planning to send the two youngest children to stay with Mrs. Robert Morris or Mrs. William Bradford since they had no school. He was deeply concerned about "my beloved Johnny—What shall I hear of you? This question makes my heart sink."[34]

The very day that Hamilton returned to Philadelphia, he found a deposition taken from Col. Francis Mentges of the Pennsylvania militia that complicated his life further.

The events that took place in mid-July in Washington County were filled with violence and rebellion against the excise law. Armed men, said Mentges, had made repeated attacks on the house of Gen. John Neville, inspector of the revenue. Over a two-day period, about 700 men besieged the house; one of the attackers was killed and several persons on both sides wounded. The house, the adjoining barn and the stables were burned.

After the assault on his house, Neville took refuge in a thicket nearby, leaving Major Kirkpatrick and ten soldiers to continue the defense. Kirkpatrick surrendered. Neville, Maj. David Lenox, Isaac Craig and two others were taken prisoner and unceremoniously dragged to the insurgents' rendezvous. After being released, Neville and Lenox descended the Ohio in a boat to escape further violence.

Mentges reported that Hugh Brackenridge, an eccentric lawyer and playwright who vacillated between the two sides, told him about a meeting of some 140 people at the Mingo Creek Meeting House in Washington County for approval of the action against Neville and a pledge to "stand by each other until the Excise law was repealed." The proposal did not pass, but the meeting accepted a resolution to send delegates from the four western counties of Pennsylvania and neighboring Virginia counties to a convention on August 14 at Parkinson's Ferry on Mingo Creek to adopt suitable measures.[35]

The president and the cabinet met with Pennsylvania's Gov. Thomas Mifflin and other state officials. Washington said that the events "strike at the root of all law & order" and that "the most spirited and firm measures" had to be taken by the state and general government, or else "there was an end to our Constitution and laws."[36]

Hamilton argued that the government had to maintain its authority and insisted upon "the propriety of an immediate resort to Military force."[37]

"I am so engaged with my Western insurgents & other matters that I have scarcely a moment to spare," Hamilton wrote to Betsey. He was alarmed about John. "I feel every day more & more how dear the child is to me." The harassed secretary was also worried about Betsey, who was still feeling ill. The older children clung to their father, who was an amusing and indulgent companion. When he tried to send them to the country, they were unwilling to leave him. "It is a great satisfaction to have them with me," Hamilton told his wife.[38]

Terming the acts of the dissident whiskey farmers "treason," Hamilton, at the president's request, prepared a plan of action. He recommended that an imposing force of militia be called out to deter opposition and save bloodshed. Since the four opposing counties had about 16,000 males over sixteen, 7,000 of whom might be armed, and the neighboring counties of Virginia might add to this force, as might Pennsylvania men on this side of the Alleghenies, Hamilton proposed a force of 12,000—900 on foot and 3,000 mounted.

The first source of manpower had to be Pennsylvania, as provided by law, but since that state's forces would be inadequate, the militias of neighboring states should be asked to make up the difference. The troops would rendezvous on September 10 at Carlisle in Pennsylvania and Cumberland Fort in Virginia. First, however, the law prescribed that a proclamation be issued to the insurgents, ordering them to disperse and return to their homes within a given time.

Hamilton sent Washington a summary of events from the first intimations of the Whiskey Rebellion. The malcontents had held their initial meeting on July 27, 1791, at Ted Stone's Old Fort and subsequently developed resolutions calling for violence against the tax collectors.

In October 1791 and again in May 1792, Hamilton reminded Washington, Congress had passed acts revising the original excise act. The duty was reduced to a moderate rate, and the distiller was given the option of paying a monthly rather than an annual rate. This had not helped. In November 1792, a further revision of the laws had been proposed, but other business was so pressing that Congress had adjourned before acting. Opposition in the western counties had escalated. In Allegheny County, the inspector of the revenue was burned in effigy, and on Election Day, the office of the collector of Fayette was broken into. He was forced, at pistol point, to give up his commission and books and resign, or else his house would be destroyed. At the end of 1793, tension eased, and the principal distillers complied with the regulations. This had alarmed the dissidents, who reopened hostilities in January 1794 by burning the barns of two men suspected of being loyal to the government. Frequent meetings were held in the spring and early summer to fan the flames of opposition. New violence flared in June.

Since June was the month for receiving annual entries of stills, efforts were made to open offices in Westmoreland and Washington counties. The Westmoreland office was saved by the courage of John Wells and Philip Ragan, despite frequent attacks. Malcontents came again and again to the Washington County office and on June 6 broke into agent John Lynn's house. They seized Lynn, tarred and feathered him, tied him to a tree and left him. In the morning he extricated himself but was visited again by the mob, which pulled down part of his house and forced him to leave town. The Neville case concluded Hamilton's calendar of outrages. The object of all these activities was to compel repeal of the law that taxed whiskey.[39]

At this critical juncture, General Knox had to go to Maine to look after his land interests there. The president turned the War Department over to Hamilton until Knox returned to the capital on October 5.

Hamilton continued to worry about the baby who did not regain his strength. Betsey, although worn out, wanted to return to Philadelphia. Hamilton discouraged her. Not only was the climate better in Albany, but mother and child could not, in their condition, make the journey alone.

Hamilton was always fascinated by medicine and often advised his wife and children on treatment. "I think well of the lime water for Johnny," he wrote to Betsey,

but I count more on exercise and nourishment. If the child is worse, abandon laudanum gradually. Give it to him overnight but not in the morning and stop it. Instead try a cold bath. . . . As soon as you take him out of the bath give him two teaspoons of brandy with enough water to keep him from choking. . . . Try an infusion of the bark in tincture [an alcoholic solvent] about midday but if it disagrees with him discontinue it. . . . Tell the Doctor about my advice, but if Johnny is worse do not be easily persuaded from the course I advise.[40]

Bad news continued to come from Albany about "our dear sick angel." Betsey wanted to return to her husband, an idea that Hamilton stopped resisting. "Come by land," he advised, "and try to prevail on Dr. Stringer to accompany you, with the understanding that we would make him a handsome compensation. . . . If you need money, get it from your father or William Seton in New York. Everyone here is well."[41]

On August 21, Hamilton was overjoyed to hear that Johnny was fast recovering his health. He wrote to Betsey that he would meet her in Newark.

Plans were going ahead for action against the insurrectionists. Knox informed the governors of Pennsylvania, New Jersey, Maryland and Virginia that the corps would consist of 4,500 infantrymen, 500 cavalry and 200 artillery. Hamilton, in charge of military activities, arranged with contractors for army supplies.

Hamilton persuaded Washington to permit him to publish his April report on the troubles so that the public would be informed. To increase the impact, using the pseudonym "Tully," he wrote four letters about the western insurrection published in Dunlop and Claypoole's *American Daily Advertiser* between August 23 and September 2. The second letter concluded with the paraphrase: "How long, ye Catilines, will you abuse our patience?"[42]

Tully-Hamilton called on the virtuous and enlightened citizens "of a now happy country" not to succumb to "the spirit of indolence and procrastination natural to the human mind" and to allow forcible resistance by a sixtieth part of the community to overcome the will of the whole. "There is no road to *despotism* more sure or more to be dreaded than that which begins at *anarchy*." The Pennsylvania farmers who were resisting constitutional laws that were not extraordinarily oppressive were committing "treason against . . . everything that ought to be dear to a free, enlightened, and prudent people. . . . Not to subdue it, were to tolerate it."[43]

The last Tully letter answered an article signed "Franklin" that appeared on August 30 in the Philadelphia *Independent Gazette*, accusing congressmen who passed the excise tax on whiskey of being motivated only by their own feelings and interests, and warning of a coming civil war.

Hamilton replied that although war was a great evil, it was less of an evil than the destruction of government. Putting down insurgents was not fighting a civil war, which implied a clash between two sizable parts of a nation, not one-sixtieth against the whole. "Where did they get their better knowledge of the principles of liberty?" Tully asked. Were they to be yielded "the palm of discernment, of patriotism, or of courage"?[44]

The governors of the states providing men and supplies for the expedition responded to the president's call. Hamilton, wearing his secretary of war hat, sent out the marching orders.

He was in poor health during the latter part of the summer of 1794. Anxiety over his wife and small son, responsibility for the older children and the work of two departments overcame him. Hence, it was not until September 2 that the secretary submitted the list that Governor Mifflin had requested of local Pennsylvania officers who had not complied with the excise law. "I have contented myself in the first instance with indicating particular cases and the sources of information without a formal exhibition of evidence," he informed the president, because he did not know what use the governor wanted to make of the information. "But I stand ready to afford the aid of this Department in bringing forward testimony in any cases the Governor may specifically demand it."[45]

In September, Hamilton informed Governor Lee of Maryland that the spirit of insurrection was spreading. Reports of "some riotous proceedings" had filtered through from Hagerstown. Though the episode was minor, Washington was concerned because the state arsenal at Frederick had to be kept from falling into rebel hands. A few days later, Hamilton advised Governor Mifflin that the time had come for the state troops to assemble at Carlisle, where they would be met by the Jersey militia. Hamilton took over the military task with gusto. In a sense, the middle-aged secretary of the treasury was reliving his youth as Washington's aide during the Revolution, but this time he had the power he craved to make decisions.

Hamilton was not hopeful that there would be a peaceful termination to all these military preparations, and careful plans for action were being formulated. Governor Lee, heading the Virginia militia, would be the commander if Washington decided not to go out. The president would be governed by circumstances; he would go if "the thing puts on an appearance of magnitude," Hamilton told Rufus King. Although still "out of health," Hamilton said, "if permitted I shall at any rate go."[46]

He planned to leave at the end of September to reach one of the columns at its ultimate point of rendezvous. By that time Knox would be back, and Hamilton would make arrangements for administration of the Treasury Department.[47]

At 10:30 A.M. on September 30, Washington and Hamilton left Philadelphia to join the troops at Carlisle. Before leaving town, Hamilton wrote to his two eldest sons at school in Trenton that he was setting out for Carlisle the next day and that their mother would arrive in a few days to take them back to Philadelphia. The boys were not to be uneasy about him, he cautioned. There would be no fighting and no danger, "only an agreeable ride which will I hope do me good."[48]

But Colonel Hamilton hoped for action. A passion for military glory possessed him all his life. In Federalist 17, he listed the "allurements of ambition"; war was one of them, along with commerce, finance and negotiation. Gouverneur Morris said about him after his death that he could be safely trusted because he was "more covetous of glory than of wealth and power."[49]

The management of the Treasury Department was left to diligent Oliver Wolcott. Household responsibilities were left to Mrs. Hamilton. Freed from his job and his family, Hamilton turned to soldiering with a youthful vigor and enthusiasm.

Knox, back from Maine, resumed his duties in the War Department and indicated that if the president led the troops, he, Knox, would like to join him. Hamilton had no intention of returning to Philadelphia. On October 10, he wrote to Betsey that they were leaving Fort Cumberland. "We are very strong & the Insurgents are all submissive so you may be perfectly tranquil." She should continue to write, sending the letters in care of General Knox to be forwarded.[50]

Always deferring to the president's wishes, Hamilton handled supplies, equipment and clothing. There was quite a stir over two homicides by members of the troops. A man at a little Dutch village called Myers-Town, between Lebanon and Reading, inflamed the New Jersey militia by shouting for the whiskey boys. In the struggle to seize him, he grabbed a soldier's bayonet. He was inadvertently stabbed and died in half an hour. And when a detachment of twenty horsemen was sent out to take some local whiskey boys, a few tried to escape; in the pursuit a dragoon's pistol went off by mistake, shooting a man in the groin. Later, he died from the wound.

Hamilton sent Governor Mifflin the president's regrets for the deaths of the two Pennsylvania men. "It is a very precious and important idea that those who are called out in support & defence of the Laws, should not give occasion, or even pretext to impute to them infraction of the laws," Hamilton said. Mifflin was asked to assure his troops that, despite rumors, they were not ultimately to be employed against British soldiers or Indians. The sole purpose of the expedition was to suppress the insurrection in the western counties of the state; once that was accomplished, they would not be kept in service a moment longer.[51]

On October 11, President Washington, Hamilton, Governor Richard Howell of New Jersey and his secretary Bartholomew Dandridge met with David Redlick and William Findley, who represented the whiskey dissidents. Findley and Redlick maintained that most of the people were ready to submit to the laws.

Washington took a firm stand. Continuing with the military plans was painful and costly, the president said, but "the Support of the Laws" was "an object of the first magnitude . . . nothing short of the most unequivocal *proofs* of absolute submission" would stop the army's march into the western counties, in order to convince them that the government could and would enforce obedience.[52]

From Bedford, acting for Washington, Hamilton issued instructions to Gov. Henry Lee, the commander in chief, to move his army into the insurgent counties to attack and "as far as shall be in your power to subdue all persons whom you may find in arms." Of those in arms who were taken prisoner, the leaders were to be delivered to the civil magistrate; the rest disarmed, admonished and sent home. When the insurrection was subdued, the army should be retired, except for a detachment to be stationed in the disaffected counties to protect the "well-disposed Citizens" and revenue officers. A general pardon in the name of the president would be promised to all not arrested.[53]

The next day, October 21, Washington set out for Philadelphia to be there when the new Congress met, leaving Hamilton in his place.

While in Bedford, Hamilton wrote to Angelica Church, explaining his mission with the playful candor that he reserved for his sympathetic sister-in-law. He was on his way "to attack and subdue the wicked insurgents of the West," he wrote. She was not to take his being there as "proof that I continue a quixot. . . . 'Twas very important there should be no mistake in the management of the affair— and I *might* contribute to prevent one . . . the insurrection will do us a great deal of good and add to the solidity of every thing in this country."[54]

When the army started on its march, Hamilton accompanied it. Along the way, he kept the president informed by letter of their progress. He reported that the dissidents had met again at Parkinson's Ferry, had once again appointed commissioners to protest the advance of the army and reiterate their peaceful intentions. "But there is nothing which can occasion a question about the propriety of the army's proceeding to its ultimate destination," Hamilton insisted. So far they had not met any opposition.[55]

While on this military mission, Hamilton continued to use his influence in the Senate to put down this insurrection and any future one. It was, in a sense, his crusade to save the national government. He wrote to Rufus King that it was urgent for Congress to pass an act of outlawry that could be imposed on the leaders of the insurrection if they tried to escape. "The political putrefaction of Pennsylvania is greater than I had any idea of," he said. "Without vigour every where our tranquillity is likely to be of very short duration & the next storm will be infinitely worse than the present one."[56]

On November 3, Hamilton reported to Washington from Cherrys Mill: Though it was raining all the time, the right wing of the army continued well, but the left wing suffered from sickness. On the whole, the troops were behaving well. Part of the right wing was to go toward Budd's Ferry (in Westmoreland County), and a cavalry brigade would go to Washington County.

Hamilton, traveling through the dense forests of western Pennsylvania with the army, was reliving his Revolutionary War experience. Although he held no military rank, he mingled with the troops, daily encouraging them and entertaining them with stories of the war for independence. In Washington's letters to Hamilton, he conveyed the news that all of his family were well. He also conveyed some less pleasant news about articles in Benjamin Franklin Bache's Philadel-

phia *General Advertiser*, questioning the motives of the secretary of
the treasury's presence with the army. Hamilton was with the army,
said Bache, because the excise is "the child of his own heart tho' a
bastard in the soil that gave it birth," and "through his talents and his
influence" he means to "forward the views of his faction." It was
whispered that Hamilton was with the army "without invitation" and
that his action was a first step "towards a deep laid scheme . . . the
advancement of his private interests and the gratification of an ambition, laudable in itself, if pursued by proper means." Bache was hinting at Hamilton's presidential ambitions.

Hamilton told Washington that he knew what Bache was about
but was indifferent because "my presence in this quarter was in several respects not useless," and "it is long since I have learnt to hold
popular opinion of no value. I hope to derive from the esteem of the
discerning and an internal consciousness of zealous endeavours for
the public good the reward of these endeavours."

Winter was expected soon in the western country, so the mission
against the whiskey boys had to be completed. Governor Lee had
decided to seize all the dissidents worth the trouble and turn them
over to the judiciary, Hamilton wrote to Washington from the
southwestern part of Westmoreland County on November 8. It was
possible to keep a regiment of infantry and four troops of horse for
nine months if they could be provided with a suit of clothing. This
was necessary because many of the ringleaders and promoters of
the insurrection had fled.[57]

Although he planned to leave western Pennsylvania by the fifteenth, on that date Hamilton was in Washington County to see the
conclusion of the phantom insurrection. Twenty persons had been
arrested and were to be brought to Washington, Pennsylvania, to be
imprisoned there. "The bad spirit is evidently not subdued," the secretary wrote to Washington. A liberty pole had been erected about
sixteen and a half miles from army headquarters, which proved that
it would be necessary to have a military force in this county for some
time. Hamilton planned to leave for Pittsburgh the next day and on
the nineteenth for Philadelpahia.[58]

He did not want to return home without presiding over the trial
and punishment of the malefactors. He and the judiciary corps arrived on November 17. A general pardon had been issued to the rank-
and-file "traitors," except for those on a list of preferred enemies.
Some were in prison and some had escaped.

Hugh Henry Brackenridge was examined by Hamilton on November 18 and 19. In his own account, Brackenridge wrote that he thought Hamilton had a "predisposition" against him because it was better for his funding system that some leading individuals, rather than the mass of people, opposed the excise law. Brackenridge was on record in a letter to Tench Coxe as against the funding system. He went to the interrogation with the expectation that it would conclude with his arrest.

After Brackenridge gave his version of the rebellion, Hamilton observed that his prisoner had a tendency to excuse the principal actors. He reminded him that he was included in the general amnesty. Brackenridge said he knew that and went on with his account until Hamilton was called to dinner; the interrogation was postponed until the afternoon.

At three o'clock the meeting was resumed. Brackenridge went on with an account of the Mingo Creek meeting that did not satisfy the secretary.

"Mr. Brackenridge, you must know we have testimony extremely unfavorable to you of speeches made at this meeting, in particular your ridiculing of the Executive." Hamilton referred to Brackenridge's implying that Washington was disposed to avoid war in the case of the British and Indians. "If Indians can have treaties, why cannot we have one or two?" he asked.

The examination recommenced the next morning on schedule. After Brackenridge finished his testimony, Hamilton commented on his own uneasy feelings and unfavorable impressions. "I now think it my duty to inform you, that not a single one [doubt] remains. . . . You are in no personal danger. You will not be troubled even by a simple inquisition by the judge." Much relieved, Brackenridge had different feelings "from those I had for a long time," he said.[59]

Not everyone fared as well as Hugh Henry Brackenridge. Hundreds were arrested, both offenders and witnesses. They were thrown into jail, held in unheated barns and outhouses and tied back to back in damp cellars. Some of the arresting officers treated the prisoners humanely. Others behaved cruelly. One captain drove his captives before him at a trot over muddy roads and through a river. He then held them in a wet stable and fed them dough and raw meat.[60]

The judiciary behaved much better. Neither Washington nor Hamilton wanted to create martyrs. On the contrary, they rejoiced that their point had been made without bloodshed. "The Judiciary is industrious in prosecuting the examinations of prisoners among whom there is a sufficient number of proper ones for examples & with sufficient evidence," Hamilton informed the president from Pittsburgh, where the legal proceedings were taking place. Col. Thomas Gaddis of Fayette, one of the most wanted public enemies, had just been brought in, which made a satisfactory conclusion to the campaign for Hamilton. "In five minutes, I set out for Philadelphia," he told the president. The army was also moving homeward, each state contingent taking the shortest route to its own headquarters.[61]

Hamilton's valedictory on the insurrection was not to blame the disturbances on opposition to his excise law on whiskey but on political meddling by the Mingo Creek Democratic Society. And in his sixth annual address to Congress on November 19, 1794, Washington attributed the rebellion in western Pennsylvania to "certain self created" societies, meaning the Democratic societies. A heated debate in Congress ensued during which Thomas Fitzsimmons, a congressman from Philadelphia, made a motion to reprobate the societies. Hamilton, who was behind the linking of the Mingo Creek Democratic Society and the insurrection, had communicated his information to Washington and Fitzsimmons. In a letter to the congressman he said he was willing for him use the information, which was "founded upon good proof and information recently received, though it would not be consistent with decorum to name me."[62]

Thomas Jefferson blamed Hamilton for the entire western scenario. "You will perceive his coloring on all the documents which have been published during his Mentorship to the commander-in-chief," he wrote to Madison. Washington's attack on the Democratic societies, said Jefferson, was an extraordinary act of boldness by the monocrats who managed to make the president their spokesman. According to the former secretary of state, the army was laughed at, not feared, and the western people's hatred of the excise law was universal.[63]

The insurrection in Pennsylvania was known in Europe. Several Dutch bankers wrote to Hamilton from Amsterdam that the manner of extinguishing the insurrection "must inspire new confidence in the Constitution" for the government's "firm, wise and moderate exercise of power to support the tranquillity, Credit and honor of the United States."[64]

Hamilton's return to Philadelphia was urgent for family reasons. Betsey had suffered a miscarriage or was in danger of one, and wanted her husband with her. When Hamilton reached home, he found his wife very ill. Betsey must have lost the baby, for there was no Hamilton child born until William Stephen on April 4, 1797.[65]

Installed once more in the Treasury Department, Hamilton's thoughts turned to retirement from public life. William Heth wrote: "I am sorry, my dear sir, as a Citizen of the U. States & a friend to our government to understand that you are preparing to retire. Your loss will be felt. But, as a private friend, I cannot but be pleased, at your endeavouring to find that contentment and happiness in private pursuits, which no public employment can possibly afford." And he added with understanding, referring to congressional harassment, "Your constitution must have recd a shock which will require time, much tranquillity of mind & cheerful company to restore."[66]

On December 1, the secretary of the treasury wrote formally to the president and to the speaker of the house that he intended to resign on January 31, 1795. He told Washington that he was giving him time to fill the vacancy, but to Frederick A. C. Muhlenberg, the speaker, he wrote with some condescension. His purpose in informing the House, he said, was to give them an opportunity, before he withdrew, "to institute any further proceeding which may be contemplated, if any there be, in consequence of the inquiry during the last session into the State of his Department."[67]

The House made no further demands on him, but Hamilton wrote his own valedictory. Unsolicited, he presented to Congress his final "Report on Public Credit," which, according to the editor of his papers, Harold Syrett, "is among the more significant and neglected of Hamilton's state papers." The report contained a plan to reduce the public debt, a measure that George Washington called for in his sixth annual message.

His report, Hamilton stated, was in answer to the president's request for a plan for redemption of the public debt and a consummation of *"whatsoever may remain unfinished of our System of Public Credit"* in order to prevent "that progressive accumulation *of Debt which must ultimately endanger* all Government."[68]

The secretary of the treasury recommended a series of ten proposals to achieve the extinguishment of the debt. In conclusion, Hamilton presented a defense of credit, which he called "the invigorating principle." It was necessary to every nation, but "to a young Country with Moderate pecuniary Capital and a very various industry" it was more necessary. Then as now, the most compelling arguments to Congress concerned national defense. Let any man "imagine the expence of a single campaign in a war with a great European power, and let him then pronounce Credit would not be indispensable. Let him decide whether it would be practicable at all to raise the necessary sum by taxes within the year. . . . He cannot but conclude that war without Credit would be more than a great calamity—would be ruin."[69]

The Hamiltonian proposals were incorporated by the House into fourteen resolutions. William P. Smith headed a committee to prepare a bill based on the resolutions. When it emerged from committee, Hamilton was saddened to note that among its detractors were several Federalists. The area of dispute centered on Hamilton's proposal to pay nonsubscribing creditors. This was "too nice" a refinement, James Hillhouse of Connecticut said, and impossible to carry into execution. Theodore Sedgwick, opposing Hillhouse's reasoning, understood that to fail to pay the nonsubscribers was "to violate, not by implication, but expressly, the solemn and pledged faith of the Government."[70]

Hamilton, even though he had retired from his post, was highly sensitive about the changes being proposed. The failure of the proposition concerning the unsubscribed debt caused him "chagrin and disgust. . . . I am tortured by the idea that the country should be so completely and so unnecessarily dishonored," he told Sedgwick. To Rufus King, he used the words "unnecessary, capricious & abominable assassination of the National honor." It "affects me more than I can express."[71]

He spilled out his intense feelings of betrayal to King in an unusual outburst, which revealed an obsession that intensified as he grew older and lost political power. "Am I then more of an American than those who drew their first breath on American Ground? Or what is it that torments me at a circumstance so calmly viewed by almost everybody else? Am I a fool—a Romantic quixot—or is there a constitutional defect in the American mind?" He exhorted King to "make a vigorous stand for the honor of your country. . . ." King had to reintroduce the provisions for payment of the unsubscribed debt in the Senate when the bill came up.[72]

Aaron Burr offered a number of amendments to the House bill when it reached the Senate. Hamilton wrote to Rufus King, asking him to "measure swords with the great Slayer of public faith—the hacknied *Veteran* in the violation of public engagements. . . . Unmask his false and horrid hypothesis. Display the immense difference between an able statesman and the *Man of Subtilties*."[73]

Hamilton left Philadelphia for New York soon after he wrote this letter. In New York, his agitation abated. The enthusiastic, affectionate welcome by his friends helped to restore him to a more reasonable frame of mind. He was able to bring himself to tell Rufus King that " 'tis better the thing should pass as it is than not at all." Somewhat resigned to his abdication of power, Hamilton observed wryly that Federalists who were not Hamiltonians would prevail. "But," he concluded, "I swear the Nation shall not be dishonored with impunity." Fisher Ames, insensitive to Hamilton's suffering over the measure, wrote fatuously that the bill was "the finale, the crown of federal measures. It can be regarded as a final congressional tribute to the Secretary of the Treasury, Alexander Hamilton."[74]

Washington viewed Hamilton's departure with regret and some apprehension. He wished him happiness in his retirement and offered his "sincere esteem and friendship." In a heartfelt tribute to almost twenty years of mutual service, the chief executive wrote, "In every relation, which you have borne to me, I have found that my confidence in your talents, exertions and integrity has been well placed." The austere president signed his letter with unusual informality, "your affectionate: Go Washington."

With Hamilton's departure from office, the Washington administration lost its prime policy maker. The halls of Congress had resounded with loud arguments over the issues of assumption, funding of the debt, the national bank and other phases of Hamilton's financial program. His insistence on the collection of the excise tax had precipitated the government's action against the whiskey boys, which became the first test of national strength. The national experience was now a closed chapter for Hamilton, who had to concentrate his efforts on the restoration of his fortune and the needs of his family.

18

A Not So Private Citizen

At the time of his retirement from the Treasury Department, Alexander Hamilton was a slim, well-proportioned, middle-sized man in his late thirties, with a graceful, elegant carriage. His complexion was delicate and fair. He wore his hair combed back from his forehead, powdered and tied in a cue. He had a musical voice that complemented his frank, impulsive manner. For everyday dress, he wore a blue coat with gilt buttons, a white silk waistcoat, black silk knee breeches and white silk stockings. His appearance was courtly, dignified and in keeping with his reputation for brilliance. He was a famous and powerful man.

After leaving New York City, where Mayor Richard Varick presented Hamilton with the freedom of the city in recognition of his public service as secretary of the treasury, the Hamiltons enjoyed a long, restful visit with the Schuylers. By late spring, the former secretary planned to resume his law practice in New York City.

Hamilton had consistently and stubbornly, many of his friends thought, refused to profit by any investments in land or stock that might create the suspicion that he was using his office to enhance his fortune. Robert Troup, in charge of Hamilton's finances after he closed his law practice, wrote that when Hamilton started as secretary of the treasury, what little property he had was sold, and when he left office, "he was worth little, if anything more, than his household furniture." He had to sell some small holdings to settle his debts before he left Philadelphia. He revealed to Angelica Church that he was poorer than when he went into office; financial comfort would take five or six years "of more work than will be pleasant though much less than I have had for the last five years."[1]

Madison, who kept Jefferson, now in retirement at Monticello, informed of all the capital gossip, made cutting allusions to Hamilton's financial status. "Hamilton will probably go to New York with the word poverty for his label," he wrote in January. The next month Madison informed his friend that "it is pompously announced in the newspapers that poverty drives him [Hamilton] back to the bar for a livelihood."

It was difficult to accept the former secretary's resolution that he would neither seek nor accept any office. His name was mentioned for governor of the state. The Albany *Gazette* reported that it would be pleased to hear he was a candidate: "Our fellow citizens would universally unite their suffrages for so able a statesman as Mr. H.," particularly since Mr. Jay, being overseas, would not be available.

Hamilton was adamant. He instructed his father-in-law to place a paragraph in the newspaper denying his candidacy. This failed to stop speculation. A Boston paper, in February 1795, printed the statement that Hamilton was in nomination for governor, with Nicholas Cruger (his old employer) as his running mate for lieutenant governor. "The Hon. Mr. *Burr* will be set in opposition to Mr. H.," the article continued. "The contest it is expected will be warm."[2]

Jay, still in England negotiating the treaty, was Hamilton's choice for governor. The Federalists believed he would be a strong contender, and it was generally accepted that he had been cheated out of the office in 1792. But if the treaty proved unpopular, Jay might lose the election. Also, the Republicans had gained power in New York City since 1792. Their anti-French position was appealing because of British attacks on neutral shipping, which had hurt the maritime interests in the city. Some prominent Federalists such as Robert and Edward Livingston had left the party, and the suppression of the Whiskey Rebellion was unpopular in many areas. Still, Hamilton regarded Jay as a winner.

At a Federalist caucus, Jay was nominated as the candidate for governor. Stephen Van Rensselaer, Hamilton's brother-in-law, the husband of Margarita Schuyler, was nominated as the candidate for lieutenant governor.

Clinton, who had declared his unavailibility for reelection due to severe rheumatism, opened the field to other Antis. The leading contenders were Robert Yates, Aaron Burr and Robert R. Livingston. Yates outclassed Burr, and Suffolk County's William Floyd became Yates's running mate.

Hamilton took little part in the campaign. There was some anxiety among the Federalists that Jay would not get back to the United

States in time to take office if he were elected. However, he returned to New York on May 28, after the election but while the votes were still being counted. The results, announced on June 5, gave Jay the victory over Yates.

In the spring of 1795, Troup tried to entice Hamilton into a land speculation scheme on Lake Erie in the Western Reserve (now Ohio). What would be expected from him, Troup said, was advice in executing the plan. "The lands of the United States like the lands of individuals in my opinion are fair objects of speculation and I cannot attach any share of dishonor to this species of commerce," Troup asserted. "Why should you object to making a little money in a way that cannot be reproachful? Is it not time for you to think of putting yourself in a state of independence?" he asked. Troup offered to conceal Hamilton's name by acting as his trustee. "Let me make a gentleman of you," he said jestingly. "For such is the present insolence of the world that hardly any man is treated like a gentleman unless his fortune enables him to live at his ease."[3]

Hamilton declined Troup's offer, not because he saw any "indelicacy" in the proposal but because of the country's critical situation. He did not want to be rich, he said, and if he couldn't live in splendor in town, he would live in comfort in the country, "and I am content to do so." Though he had implicit confidence in his friend Troup, he would do nothing for his own gain under cover. "This may be too great refinement. I know it is pride. But this pride makes it part of my plan to *appear truly what I am*."[4]

Troup replied with good humor. "I sincerely hope that . . . you may by some fortunate & unexpected event" acquire perfect independence, "in spite of all your efforts to be poor," or else "your friends will have to bury you at their own expence."[5]

Hamilton had completed his defense of his financial system and had every reason to believe that President Washington was committed to it. The unfinished business that bothered him was the treaty that Jay was negotiating with Great Britain.

One of the last questions the president asked before his secretary of the treasury left office was what measures to take if the treaty did not arrive before the legislature adjourned. Hamilton had said that delaying adjournment would be impractical, but immediately after adjournment, notice could be given of another meeting shortly afterward, by which time the treaty would arrive. On reflection, Hamilton revised his ideas, which he communicated to Washington at the end of February. The secretary of state should write to each member of the Senate, announcing the expected arrival of the treaty. The letters should go by land and sea, using special land expresses and swift sailing vessels to reach even the remotest members. Six weeks' notice would be enough for a special session. The president could not reconvene the Senate without declaring that an "extraordinary *occasion exists*," Hamilton reminded Washington. Therefore, he had to wait until he saw the treaty before arranging for another session. Congress adjourned on March 3, and the first copy of the treaty, signed by Jay and Lord Grenville on November 19, 1794, arrived in the United States on March 7.

The treaty had a very rough crossing. The first copy and a duplicate were, in error, placed on the same British ship, which was attacked by a French privateer. In order to protect their contents, both copies were thrown into the sea. The copy carried in an American ship almost had the same fate. A French privateer stopped the American vessel but did not find the carefully hidden treaty. After a voyage of three months, the ship arrived with the surviving copy of the treaty, which was delivered to Washington.[6]

He read the treaty with great care but, upon reflection, was not in favor of it. He disliked the clauses giving Canadian fur traders access to the Northwest territory and the Mississippi, even though, in return, the western posts would be evacuated by the British troops in June 1796, a very distant date, Washington thought. Among other concessions, the one that irritated Washington particularly and became the focus of hostility against the treaty was contained in Article 12. This got the British to open the British West Indies to American trade, but only American ships of under seventy tons were to be allowed into British West Indian ports. The quid pro quo for this paltry gesture was that American ships would not carry, even for transshipment, any products indigenous to the West Indies. Among these, along with sugar and molasses, was cotton, becoming a major American export and one that Washington promoted.

On the positive side was the British acceptance that the United States would not be expected to do anything contrary to any former treaty obligations. This clause did not suit the pro-French party, however; Jay seemed to have accepted a very broad definition of contraband. The issue of the impressment of American seamen was not mentioned, nor was compensation for slave owners and other property owners whose possessions the British had taken from them during the Revolution.

Washington's behavior after receiving the treaty was somewhat bizarre. He had allowed Hamilton to mastermind Jay's instructions, but he did not turn to him to interpret the results, nor did he inform him of the contents. His new cabinet members, Pickering, Wolcott and Bradford, were also kept in the dark. Only Secretary of State Randolph shared the secret of the contents of the treaty. He and Washington had daily sessions, during which the president went over his objections with Randolph, who was sworn to maintain complete silence until the document was turned over to the Senate for ratification.

For three months the treaty remained under wraps while the president waited for Congress to reconvene on June 8. In the meantime, he worried about inevitable factional furor. The pro-French party would have good reason to hate the treaty and would no doubt enlist the support of many others who would be hurt by Jay's concessions to England. On the other hand, rejection of the treaty threatened an even more dangerous consequence, a second war with England.

John Jay returned to New York in May to find that he had been elected governor of his state. He also found waiting for him a cordial and urgent letter from Randolph, which welcomed back the special envoy to his native country, "an event, for which I have been anxious on account of the approaching discussion of the treaty." The secretary of state also sent Jay seven questions to answer "as soon as your fatigue will suffer you to take up a pen."[7]

The hint that his presence in the capital would help the fight for ratification in the Senate was ignored by Jay. Pleading ill health, he resigned his position as chief justice in a formal letter and received, in return, a formal acceptance.

On June 8, the Senate met behind closed doors to review the still-secret treaty. Hamilton knew its contents, perhaps from Jay himself, but more likely from Rufus King. On July 11, in answer to a letter from Senator King, Hamilton referred to the controversial Article 12 and gave his opinion on ratification. "Reflection has not mitigated the exceptionable point," he said, yet anything but "an absolute & simple ratification will put something in jeopardy." No time being fixed for ratification, Article 12 could be taken as intended by Britain as a privilege. The Senate could then take the position that it would not go along with the privilege until a modification was agreed upon between the two countries. "This course appears to me preferable to sending back the Treaty to open the negotiation anew."[8]

Rumors about the treaty were flying about the country as the Senate sat in closed session. In mid-June there was a report that the treaty had been rejected. "I have assured those I have seen that I was convinced any rumors of a decision must be premature," Hamilton told Rufus King. He feared, he said, that the stability of the nation would be endangered if the treaty was turned down.

Closeted in its chamber, the Senate was handling the issue of Article 12 in just the manner that Hamilton wished. On June 17, a resolution was offered to suspend that part of it which concerned trade with the West Indies. The Senate advised that the president, without delay, resume friendly negotiations with the king of England on this point. The Senate debated the proposal for a week and then agreed on it unanimously.

Among the most articulate opponents to ratification was Aaron Burr. On June 22, he moved to delay further discussion of the treaty and to renegotiate with Great Britain. He argued that if British fur traders and settlers were to be allowed access to the American West and the Mississippi River, then American citizens should have "the use of all rivers, ports and places within the Territories of His Brittanic Majesty in North America." The South enjoyed no concessions in the treaty, Burr pointed out, so they should get payment for their slaves and property carried away during the Revolution.[9]

Burr and the Republicans failed to sway the Senate. The treaty was not to anyone's taste, but as a way to avoid war with England, it was a necessity. Hence, the Senate gave the treaty the required affirmative vote on June 24, 1795. It was now up to the president to complete ratification. The Senate advised that the treaty contents should remain concealed from the public until he had made up his mind.

Washington decided to seek public opinion at this juncture but was frustrated by his former desire for secrecy. There was no extra copy available to send to the printer until Randolph could retrieve the one he had lent to the new French minister, Pierre Adet. In the meantime, Benjamin Franklin Bache was given a copy by Senator Mason of Virginia, which he printed in a pamphlet. On July 3, Bache published a second edition of his pamphlet, which also carried the motions against the treaty proposed by Aaron Burr and Henry Tazewell of Virginia. William Bradford told Hamilton that he feared such publications would excite disgust for the treaty.

The long silence on the subject of the treaty between the president and Hamilton was broken in early July when Washington sent his former secretary of the treasury a letter marked "private and perfectly confidential." Washington wanted from dispassionate, knowledgeable men genuine opinions of each article of the treaty and their judgment on the whole. He wanted both favorable and unfavorable reactions. Hamilton should tell him how the treaty would affect future treaties with other nations. If the removal of Article 12 from the treaty was accepted by England, should the treaty go back to the Senate, or could the president sign it without the offending section?[10]

Hamilton replied in three letters that analyzed each article carefully and then, usually, justified it. Any doubts about Jay's competence Hamilton concealed. Jay had been his own selection, and Jay's orders had been his own proposals. There could be no other conclusion to Hamilton's remarks on the treaty but the ones he wrote. "It is conceived therefore upon the whole to be the true interest of the U States to close the present Treaty with G Britain in the manner advised by the Senate."[11]

"I offer you my sincere thanks," Washington wrote to Hamilton. "I am really ashamed when I behold the trouble it has given you, to explore, and to explain so fully as you have done, the whole of them." Once again Washington asked whether the treaty would have to be resubmitted to the British government. Hamilton's answer, unfortunately, disagreed with the advice of the cabinet members. Hamilton said that resubmission would be necessary. The president asked that Hamilton convey his ideas to Randolph. As requested, Hamilton wrote an explanatory letter to Randolph, who arranged a personal interview while Hamilton was in the capital to plead the carriage tax case.

The treaty had indeed caused a paroxysm of fever, as Washington put it. The people were inveighing against it. At noon on Saturday, July 18, a meeting was held at Federal Hall in New York City to discuss the Jay Treaty. The evening before, at the Tontine hall, Hamilton and Rufus King had met with a group of merchants to prepare the strategy for the next day's encounter. One contemporary newspaper reported that when Hamilton urged a full discussion of the treaty before citizens formed their decisions, he could not be heard "on account of hissings, coughings, hootings—which entirely prevented his proceeding."[12]

The hysteria of the day precipitated a quarrel that involved him in a challenge to a duel. His opponent was James Nicholson, an officer of the Democratic Society of New York, a rude, uneducated man and one who welcomed Genet. The confrontation was the second between the two men. Six or eight weeks before, Nicholson had remarked to Josiah Ogden Hoffman, a Hamiltonian and a lawyer, that he had authentic information that Hamilton had invested £100,000 in British funds while secretary of the treasury, which was being held for him in a London bank. Hoffman, angered, demanded immediate proof. Nicholson replied that he would present proofs at any time that he was called upon by Hamilton to do so. There was no action taken.

On the eighteenth, however, Hamilton interfered in a quarrel between Nicholson and Hoffman. Nicholson taunted the former secretary, calling him an "abettor of Tories" and saying that he would not respond to the insult, just as he had not on the previous occasion. Hamilton promptly challenged Nicholson to a duel.[13]

Two days later, Nicholson received a formal challenge. Paulus Hook was designated as the place for the meeting; eleven o'clock on Monday, July 27, the time. Col. Nicholas Fish, who delivered the note, would be his second. Nicholson replied the same day that he would not decline the invitation. However, the public nature of the affair and "the unusual visit of your friend" had made his family suspicious. Therefore, he requested an earlier date for their interview, no later than the following day.

Hamilton replied the same day. It would not be possible to fix an earlier date because of the needs of third persons "which affect my justice and reputation." Nicholson acceded to the date but was still afraid that procrastination might bring the business to the public ear.

Nicholson made another attempt to have the duel take place immediately. At 5:30 A.M. Wednesday, July 22, he sent a note to Hamilton saying that an acquaintance had tried the night before to warn Mrs. Nicholson of the forthcoming duel, and again the family had been alarmed. Hamilton replied that Nicholson should be able to quiet the family. As to the place for the rendezvous, he wanted it outside the state, which "cannot need explanation." The penalty in New York State, if one of the duelists was killed, was death.

Nicholson wrote that day that he had to be resigned to Hamilton's choice of date. However, should his business be closed earlier and the meeting could take place sooner, "you will be pleased to give me notice & I will immediately attend you."[14]

The duel never took place. The seconds, Nicholas Fish and Rufus King for Hamilton and DeWitt Clinton and Brockholst Livingston for Nicholson, found a way to avoid the interview. They asked Hamilton to submit a draft of an apology that would be acceptable to him. His draft of a statement for Nicholson to make was a reasonable declaration of general misunderstanding, which saved face for Nicholson and gave satisfaction to Hamilton. On Sunday evening, July 26, Nicholson made the required declaration in the presence of all the seconds. The statement was shown to Hamilton for his approval, and the seconds then issued a declaration that the controversy between the two men "has been settled in a satisfactory and honorable way to both the parties."[15]

Before Nicholson had agreed to a retraction, Hamilton had appointed Robert Troup executor of his will. "After a life of labour, I leave my family on the benevolence of others, if my course shall happen to be terminated here." John Barker Church was his chief creditor, for £5,000, which did not worry him a great deal for he did not doubt "the friendship and generosity of his brother-in-law."

The debt that concerned him most was to the unknown holders of two drafts drawn upon Hamilton by his father, one for $500 and one for $200. For some strange reason, Hamilton felt it necessary to make a statement about James Hamilton. "Though as I am informed a man of respectable connections in Scotland he became bankrupt in the West Indies and is now indigent. I have pressed him to come to me but his great age & infirmity have deterred him from the change of climate."

At the close of his letter to Troup, Hamilton referred to another skeleton in his closet. In his leather trunk, Troup would find a bundle inscribed: "JR To be forwarded to Oliver Wolcott Junr Esq. I entreat that this may be early done by a careful hand. This trunk contains all my interesting papers." JR was James Reynolds, and the letters the notorious Reynolds-Hamilton correspondence. Under his statement, at a much later time, Betsey Hamilton wrote, "to be retained by myself."[16]

The challenge to a duel with Nicholson had a sequel. On July 18, 1795, when a heated political discussion between Peter Livingston and Josiah Ogden Hoffman developed into a personal altercation, Hamilton entered the fray. He said that "if the parties were to contend in a personal Way he was ready that he would fight the whole party one by one." Edward Livingston was rebuffed when he tried to speak to him. Again Hamilton declared that he "was ready to fight the whole 'Detestable faction' one by one." Maturin Livingston, who had just arrived, accepted Hamilton's challenge and offered to meet him in half an hour wherever he chose. Hamilton answered that he already had an affair on his hands, meaning his dispute with Nicholson, but when it was settled he would call on him.

After the Hamilton-Nicholson matter was adjusted, Hamilton ignored the second challenge. But Maturin Livingston did not. In January 1796, Hamilton wrote to Livingston that he had been informed that, in the presence of several witnesses, Livingston had insinuated that Hamilton had acted "with want of spirit" on the occasion of their July 18, 1795, encounter. He wanted an explicit explanation. Livingston's answer was mild and conciliatory.

"It is still in your power at this time to satisfy what is due to delicacy by a disavowal of the exceptionable sentiment," Hamilton insisted, but the affair developed no further.[17]

Hamilton, dissatisfied with the way the public was receiving the Jay Treaty, launched a staggering one-man newspaper campaign of articles in defense of the agreement. These essays, thirty-eight of them, called "Defences" and signed "Camillus," were originally conceived of as another Publius venture to be undertaken by three authors: Hamilton, Rufus King and Jay. As in the Federalist papers, Jay dropped out, this time without contributing at all. Rufus King wrote numbers twenty-three through thirty, and thirty-four and thirty-five. The burden, as usual, was on Hamilton, who also wrote four essays in favor of the Jay treaty under the pseudonym "Philo Camillus." The Camillus group was published at intervals from July 22, 1795, to January 9, 1796, first in *The Argus* or Greenleaf's *Daily Advertiser*, an antiadministration paper, and then starting with No. XXII in *The Herald* (New York). In a comprehensive, thorough manner, Hamilton defended the treaty, supported its constitutionality, dissected each of its articles and answered attacks on it that had appeared in Republican papers.

In the Defence No. 1, Hamilton described Camillus as an ancient Roman who saved Rome from her enemies but never had the love of her people. Camillus achieved the agreement of the multitude to his measures, although "contrary to their inclinations," and they hated him for it. This first "Defence" recognized that the treaty would encounter "misconception, jealousy, and unreasonable dislike," while its "intrinsic merits" would be ignored.[18]

Washington liked Camillus as soon as he read the first Defence. He wrote to Hamilton, not knowing that Hamilton was Camillus, that, judging from the first number, the subject would be handled "in a clear, distinct and satisfactory manner." This work had to be disseminated widely, else "the opposition presses will spread their poison," and when Congress assembled, the delegates would have the impression that their constituents all opposed the treaty.[19]

Sometimes an alarmist, Hamilton overreacted and visualized riots throughout the country against the Jay Treaty. He wrote to Oliver Wolcott of suspicion that "the Jacobins" were planning violence against certain individuals," one of them, he believed, being himself. Wolcott should persuade Secretary of War Timothy Pickering to keep the military in the forts available. Wolcott agreed to see Pickering but was not concerned about dangerous riots; he was excited about quite another matter.

"I dare not *write* & hardly dare *think* of what I *know* & believe respecting a certain character; whose situation gives him a decided influence," Wolcott wrote cryptically to Hamilton. In a letter of July 30, he said, "I shall take immediate measures with two of my colleagues [Pickering and Bradford], this very day . . . we Will if possible . . . *save* our Country." At the end of this strange letter, Wolcott suggested that Hamilton, King or Jay come to Philadelphia the following week.

Wolcott's secret weapon was a letter that compromised Randolph. On March 28, 1795, a diplomatic bag from Jean Fauchet, the French minister to America, was taken from a French ship after its capture by a British man-of-war and sent to George Hammond to use at his discretion. While the battle over the Jay Treaty was raging and George Washington was away from the capital, on July 26, Hammond called on Wolcott and read him a translation of parts of Fauchet's Dispatch No 10. The dispatch seemed to say that Randolph, in return for money, promised to promote a pro-French policy. Two days after hearing the startling report, Wolcott showed the dispatch to Secretary of War Pickering who, fluent in French, made his own translation. On the following day, the attorney general was shown the papers. The three men decided to call the president back to Philadelphia.

Upon Washington's return on August 11, he was shown Pickering's translation of the damning dispatch. Washington read the document in great despair. Randolph, whom he had known since he was a child and who was closer to him than any other member of the cabinet, might have betrayed him. The possibility of bribery was particularly disturbing to the president.[20]

In Washington's mind, Randolph's guilt became tied to ratification of the treaty. Both the British and the Federalists had the intercepted dispatches. If Washington did not ratify, the damning papers would be published. The president would be accused of accepting the pro-French bias of his secretary of state who was, possibly, a traitor. Accordingly, the next morning, Washington informed his cabinet that he would sign the treaty and that Hammond should be informed of his decision as soon as possible.

Washington watched Randolph carefully and waited patiently until the treaty was on its way to England. Then, on August 19, he called his cabinet together at his house and handed Randolph the fatal papers, asking him to read them and make what explanation he wished. Randolph, who read French fluently, perused the letter without emotion.

"If I may be permitted to retain this letter a short time, I shall be able to explain in a satisfactory manner everything in it which has reference to me," he said evenly.

"Very well, retain it," Washington answered. Randolph made no explanation but resigned his office. To Pickering, and probably to Washington, this was a confession of guilt. However, Randolph published a pamphlet called *A Vindication of Mr. Randolph's Resignation* in which he declared that, once it became apparent to him that the president's confidence had been withdrawn "without a word or distant hint being previously dropped," he had no choice but to resign.[21]

Hamilton was relieved by Randolph's fall from grace. The Virginian was too close to the president. Having seen the intercepted letter, he wrote to Washington, "I read it with regret, but without much surprise for I never had confidence in Mr. Randolph." In a private letter written on October 29, Washington confided to Hamilton that Randolph had intended to insert letters from the president in all the newspapers to show that Washington's final decision to ratify the treaty "was the result of party advice; and that that party was under British influence." Washington had authorized the former secretary of state to publish "every private letter I ever wrote, and every word I ever uttered to him, if *he* thought they wd contribute to his vindication." But Randolph had also gathered all the official papers that would serve his purpose.[22]

Washington then unburdened the rest of his troubles. He could not fill the vacant cabinet offices; everyone had refused. The Algerian question was pressing. There were many problems in the executive department. "Aid me I pray you with your sentiments on these points & such others as may have occurred to you relative to my communications to Congress." Hamilton was back in the president's confidence; it was very satisfying. Private and confidential letters from the presidential residence to the Hamilton office became frequent.[23]

By mid-November, Pickering was still acting secretary of state. He finally agreed to accept the office and fill his regular office of secretary of war as well, but as soon as a replacement could be found for either post, he would keep the remaining job.

Concerned about public reaction to the Randolph letter to Fauchet, which was to be published, Pickering asked Hamilton to correct his translation of it. "I am sorry to propose this labour for you," he wrote, but the letter would soon be published and Hamilton was "implicated in every page: I therefore wish the translation may be exact."[24]

Hamilton agreed to correct the Pickering version. Both men were disappointed; the version printed in Fenno's *Gazette* was a translation by George Taylor, Jr., the chief clerk of the State Department, who had made it at Randolph's request. Pickering was critical of it because Taylor, who lacked "a *comprehensive* view" of the subject, very likely mistook the meaning of some of the passages.

The president denounced Randolph for impudently and falsely declaring that he had always been opposed to the commercial part of Jay's treaty. "But if you have seen his performance, I shall have you to judge of it, without any comment of mine," he told Hamilton.

Hamilton attempted to soothe the president and, at the same time, condemn Randolph. "It does not surprise me," he declared. "I consider it as amounting to a confession of guilt and am persuaded this will be the universal opinion." Randolph's attempts against Washington were "base," but would do him no good with the public. "It contains its own antidote." The result, Hamilton calculated, would be a general movement in favor of the government's position on the treaty.[25]

The controversy continued, and Hamilton continued to turn out copy in defense of the treaty.

Throughout the fall of 1795, Washington and Hamilton also dealt with a delicate problem concerning the presence in the United States of the imprisoned Marquis de Lafayette's young son, George Washington Motier Lafayette, and his tutor. Young Lafayette was traveling incognito in order to protect his mother from danger. The two Frenchmen arrived in Boston the last day of August. Lafayette immediately wrote an affectionate, respectful letter to Washington. M. Felix Frestel, the tutor, wrote a practical one, asking for an audience with the president and advice on what his charge might expect in America.

Touched as he was by his namesake's pathetic circumstances as an exile, the president explained to George Cabot, the senator from Massachusetts, that it would be imprudent to allow Lafayette to come to Philadelphia "where all the foreign characters (particularly that of his own nation) are residents, until it is seen what opinions will be excited by his arrival." Washington suggested that he enter Harvard University as a student for a while. Washington would carry all expenses.

Cabot replied that the young man would not be qualified for attendance at Harvard because his preparation was so different from that of American college students. Cabot thought it best for young Lafayette to continue to study privately. The decision was made to send the Frenchmen to New York. Cabot gave the refugees a letter to Hamilton.

By October 16, "GW Fayette" and Frestel were in New York and under Hamilton's care. Hamilton found young Fayette a modest lad with very good manners who expressed himself intelligently and with propriety. In Hamilton's opinion, the president would not displease France, or even his political enemies, if he displayed friendship to the young Frenchman. "The Youth of this person joined to the standing of his father make the way easy." Also, it was possible that the marquis would soon regain the esteem of his own country. Hamilton referred to the attempt in the House of Commons to direct the king to intervene for Lafayette's freedom. The motion was defeated, which pleased George III, who could not forget Lafayette's assistance in losing him the American colonies.[26]

In late October, Washington ordered Hamilton to send young Fayette and his tutor to him without delay. "To be in the place of a father and a friend to him, I am resolved, under any circumstances." A few weeks later the Frenchmen were still not in Philadelphia. Hamilton had started to have second thoughts. He had consulted others, whose judgment he respected, who believed that it could be a mistake for the president to give public protection to Fayette during the crisis over the Jay Treaty. It might be used as proof that Washington favored the anti-Revolutionists of France.

For the next couple of months, Washington and Hamilton corresponded about young Lafayette. They were torn between what was best for the administration and their concern for the son of their unfortunate friend. Washington, who had strong fatherly feelings, was tempted to ignore politics and welcome the Frenchman and his tutor into his family.[27]

By the end of November, Fayette felt thoroughly rejected by

Washington and pleaded for just one interview, after which he and
Frestel would go wherever prescribed. Hamilton still quoted the misgivings of his "more judicious friends." Washington fretted that he
hardly knew how to reconcile his feelings with a desire to see the
youth just long enough to tell him "from my own mouth" that he
would be his friend and supporter. A month later, Washington asked
if Fayette had received the undercover letter he had sent via Hamilton. Fayette had not acknowledged it. "His sensibility is hurt,"
Washington guessed. If the lad needed money, Washington was
ready to furnish it.[28]

Hamilton resolved the situation somewhat by arranging that
young Lafayette and his tutor stay with the Hamiltons. The Frenchman had grown thin and appeared melancholy, dejected over not
having been received by the president, particularly after a letter
from his mother had arrived with a message to be carried to
Washington.

Washington's ambivalence was complicated by the introduction of
another international character into the scenario. Justus Erich Bollmann, a young Hanoverian physician who had almost succeeded in
arranging Lafayette's release from the fortress of Olmutz, arrived in
America, hoping to find government employment. Bollmann came
with Francis Huger of South Carolina from England, where they had
been sponsored by the Churches. Dutifully, Hamilton wrote to Washington that he had not left Bollmann "unapprised of the difficulties in
his way," but that Bollmann had decided to go to Philadelphia.

Continuing his policy of avoiding offense to the French government, Washington sent Pickering to deal with Bollmann. The secretary of state told Bollmann that the president was interested in a new
effort to relieve Lafayette and would like him to write a letter, presenting his ideas on the subject. Bollmann's suggestion was to choose
an agent to negotiate who would be a friend of Lafayette's, fluent in
German and connected with the ruling family. Bollmann had described himself.

Throughout the early winter of 1796, Washington wrote intermit-
tently to Hamilton about his uneasiness over young Fayette, now
living in Ramapo, New Jersey, with his tutor. Washington finally
named April 1 for a visit. Then, on March 4, Edward Livingston
introduced a resolution into the House of Representatives, establishing a committee to inquire whether Lafayette's son was in the United
States and what measures should be taken for his support. Livingston
sent young Fayette a copy of the resolution and an invitation to

Philadelphia, so that the legislature could take him under its protection and show its gratitude to his father.

Young Lafayette responded cautiously to Livingston and, including a copy of Livingston's letter, wrote to Washington that he would do whatever the president wished. Proceed immediately to Philadelphia where a room in his house was ready for the young man, Washington answered.

Washington wrote to Hamilton that Bollmann "it is to be feared will be found a troublesome guest among us." Washington agreed to write to the emperor of Austria, "as a private person," his own and America's wishes for Lafayette's liberation, "conditioned on his repairing hither."[29]

In September 1797, Lafayette, with his wife and daughters who had joined him in captivity, were released from Olmutz and settled in Holstein. As soon as he heard the news, young Fayette wanted to join them. Washington advised him to wait for authentication of the report, but Fayette pleaded eagerness to see his family and fear of a winter passage. If the cost of the voyage required "greater pecuniary means" than young Lafayette possessed, Washington told Hamilton, "furnish them, and draw upon me for the amount & it shall be paid at sight."[30] George Washington Lafayette was reunited with his family in Holstein in February 1798.

Accusations against Washington, whose popularity dropped precipitously during the controversy over the Jay Treaty, became particularly ugly in October 1795, when an article addressed to Oliver Wolcott by "A Calm Observer" appeared in the Philadelphia *Aurora*. It asserted that the president, with the connivance of Hamilton, overdrew his annual $25,000 salary. By the time of his second inauguration, he had received $1,037 more than he was entitled to. Furthermore, an act of Congress of March 1793 provided that the president be paid his salary quarterly. Yet from March 1793 to July 4, 1793, the president was paid $4,750 more than he was entitled to. At the rate he was going, "A Calm Observer" noted, Washington would be receiving $44,000 a year instead of $25,000.

Wolcott answered the charges promptly. The advances, he explained, were made to defray the expenses of the president's household and were applied for in his name by his private secretary. The blame in no way rested on the president but on the Treasury Department, which, in his opinion, had done nothing contrary to law, and Congress had seen all the accounts.[31]

Hamilton wrote to Washington that he would publish an explanation with his own name affixed to the piece, should he think it "proper." Wolcott supplied the required data, and Hamilton wrote an explanation, which was printed in the *Daily Advertiser*, in which he vented his anger on "all the anonymous slanders by which I have been so long and so implacably persecuted." The president might not have known about the advances; they were all made to his secretary, Tobias Lear. "I am wholly answerable." There had never been any secrecy about the transactions. The documents were sent to Congress, and the members understood and acquiesced. Therefore, said Hamilton, he left "to a candid public, the decision on the charges."[32]

Almost a year had elapsed since Hamilton's resignation, but he had not relinquished his influence in the cabinet. He received bulletins from his successor, Oliver Wolcott, and from the others and gave advice freely. Answers to questions were treated with great care in long letters, carefully argued. In the case of the Jay Treaty, Hamilton expected his interpretations to find their way into written reports of cabinet members and so to the president. In the search for new cabinet members, Hamilton was consulted. For attorney general he thought Samuel Dexter or Christopher Gore would be suitable.

"But the embarrassment is extreme as to Secretary of State," since I am now able to tell you that Rufus King will not accept, Washington was informed by Hamilton. And "a first rate character is not attainable. A second rate must be taken with good dispositions & barley decent qualifications. . . . 'Tis a sad omen for Government." In January 1796, Washington solved his problem by appointing Timothy Pickering as permanent secretary of state and James McHenry, Hamilton's friend since the Revolution, as secretary of war.

The president's annual message, delivered on December 18, 1795, rested heavily on the Hamilton draft. The president had asked for suggestions of subjects to be covered and supplied Hamilton with the papers needed to prepare the message.

Hamilton's connection with the administration and his reputation as a lawyer resulted in an invitation from Attorney General William Bradford to be his auxiliary in the carriage tax suit, which was to be heard by the Supreme Court. "I consider the question as the greatest one that ever came before that Court," Bradford told Hamilton; it was most important that the act be supported unanimously by the justices on sound grounds. Washington, who backed the tax, agreed to Hamilton's involvement.

Bradford cajoled Hamilton into accepting. "We will all be rejoiced to see you," he said. And since no one understood the question better than Hamilton, it would be a proper occasion for his debut in the Supreme Court. The fee would be whatever he wished. Besides, "ought you not to have a little parental concern on this occasion & to take care that no injustice can be done to your own begettings?"[33]

The attorney general referred to Hamilton's proposal in the New York assembly for a tax on carriages. This case concerned the constitutionality of a tax on carriages, which included coaches, chariots and other four-wheeled pleasure vehicles. Madison had been against such a tax as unconstitutional, being a direct tax, not apportioned according to representation. Accordingly, using the tax as a political issue with which to oppose the administration, Daniel Hylton of Virginia brought suit, stating that his object in contesting the law was "merely to ascertain a constitutional point."

Hamilton accepted Bradford's invitation. The case was heard by the Supreme Court in February 1796. Charles Lee, who became attorney general after Bradford's death, appeared with Hamilton. Their opponents were Jared Ingersoll, attorney general of Pennsylvania, and Alexander Campbell, attorney of the Virginia District.

Hamilton's appearance in the court caused a great deal of public interest. Judge Iredell wrote that though he was in ill health, he spoke with astonishing ability and was listened to with the profoundest attention. His three-hour speech was thought to be impressive, eloquent and clear. Madison told Jefferson that Hamilton's speech did little but "raise a fog around the subject." On the other hand, the Boston *Centinel* reported that Hamilton's eloquence, candor and knowledge of the law "has drawn applause from many who had been in the habit of reviling him."[34]

The gist of Hamilton's argument was that a duty on carriages was as much within the government's authorization as a duty on land or buildings. To try to levy such a tax according to representation would be absurd; a state with a large population might have relatively few carriages. There was no reliable distinction, legal or economic, between direct and indirect taxes. It was enough that the carriage tax was uniform like other duties, imports and excises. Where the Constitution made a distinction between taxes (direct and to be apportioned) and excises (indirect, to be uniform), it was "fair to seek the meaning of terms in the Statutory language of that country from which our jurisprudence is derived."[35]

The Supreme Court, which rendered its decision on *Hylton* v. *United States* on March 8, 1796, upheld the congressional tax on carriages. The justices accepted Hamilton's argument that it was an excise and therefore needed only to meet the constitutional test of uniformity. This important case marked the first time the Supreme Court passed on the constitutionality of an act of Congress. Hamilton received a fee of $500 for his services.

The Senate approved Jay's treaty on June 24, 1795; the United States Senate ratified it on August 14, 1795; and the British ratified it on October 28 of the same year. Washington proclaimed it on February 29, 1796, but he did not send it to the House of Representatives until March 1, 1796. Holding the power of the purse, Congress had to vote appropriations for the three commissions provided for in the treaty.

The anti-treaty members had powerful leadership, including James Madison and Edward Livingston. Madison took a fairly reasonable position, but Livingston proposed a resolution that the President of the United States be requested to send the House a copy of Jay's instructions, given to him before he went to London to negotiate. The resolution passed by a vote of sixty-two to thirty-seven. Washington asked Wolcott to see the former secretary of the treasury, if he was still in Philadelphia, and ask him what position he thought the president should take. Hamilton had already told Wolcott that if Livingston's motion succeeded, it should not be complied with. It would be fatal to the government's negotiator if either house of Congress could, as a matter of course, call for all communications, no matter how confidential. Since this would be another precedent-setting decision, Hamilton drafted an answer for the president, "a hasty and crude outline of what has struck me as an eligible course." His first reaction was that too easy compliance would be mischievous, but too peremptory a refusal might cause just criticism.[36]

Since the matter was still in debate in the House, Hamilton wrote to his close friend and ally William Loughton Smith, who had often been his spokesman in the House, providing him with some cogent arguments against the Livingston resolution and Madison's position.

By the time Hamilton had a reply for Washington to the House request, the resolution had been carried. Hamilton believed that the publication of the orders would do harm. Under no circumstances should the president send anything other than the commissions and Jay's correspondence. After the fullest reflection, Hamilton concluded, "after the usurpation attempted by the House of Representatives, to send none & to resist in totality."[37]

Hamilton's long, comprehensive reply arrived too late. Washington had already submitted a draft written by Timothy Pickering and revised by Charles Lee.

Washington was very grateful and very apologetic to Hamilton for "the trouble (much greater than I had any idea of giving) which you have taken to show the impropriety of that request." From the first moment he was resolved *"to resist the principle"* involved in the House of Representatives' call, the president said. The ideas and materials that he had collected from his department heads embraced most, if not all, the principles detailed in Hamilton's paper, and from them he had composed the draft he sent in. Although Washington did not use Hamilton's draft, Madison told Jefferson that "there is little doubt in my mind that the message came from New York."[38]

The troubles over the treaty were still not over. In mid-April, Hamilton heard that, in a private meeting, a majority of the House members had decided to refuse the appropriations needed to carry out the terms of the treaty. The solution, said Hamilton to Rufus King, was to enlist public opinion. 1) The president ought immediately to protest to the House and send a copy to the Senate. That body should approve the president's principles and pledge firm support for his execution of the treaty. 2) The merchants of the cities should meet and second the measures of the president and the Senate, and seek support from their fellow citizens by obtaining petitions signed throughout the United States. 3) The Senate should hold out against adjournment until the House provided for the treaty. 4) The president should communicate to the British, confidentially, his regrets for the delay and his continued resolution in behalf of the treaty. However, if the treaty was not carried out, the president would be forced "by regard to his character & the public good to *keep his post* until another House voted on the Treaty."[39]

Hamilton organized a successful campaign against the House rebels. Merchants and traders signed petitions in Philadelphia "with unexampled unanimity." Similar petitions were prepared and signed in Baltimore and Annapolis. Merchants in New York, alarmed over the possibility of the loss of British trade, did all they could to get signatures and petitions.

The Republicans were ready with counterpetitions. Congress should not surrender its constitutional check on the executive, they protested. The Federalists were accused of emulating Cromwell's forcible dissolution of the Long Parliament. Washington came in for much of the blame. "Shall the *people* or the *President* be sovereign of the United States?" a Republican paper asked.[40]

Hamilton was elated by his successful campaign. "The current is in our favor throughout the city," he wrote. But he knew only too well that the opposition was fighting just as bravely. He delivered a broadside to be distributed to the citizens who met in the Fields in New York City on April 22 in a show of support for the House of Representatives. He appealed to their regard for Washington and Jay, and tried to persuade them that his side stood for the Constitution and peace, as opposed to the overthrow of the Constitution and war. "If you prefer the former—reject the advice which will be given to you today."[41]

Philip Schuyler had been active in Albany on behalf of the cause. A petition was prepared and 500 copies printed for distribution by persons appointed to collect signatures. Among those who signed were "many decided Antifoederalists," Schuyler informed his son-in-law.[42]

On April 29, the House, sitting as a Committee of the Whole, voted on the necessary appropriations for the treaty with Great Britain. The vote was tied, forty-nine to forty-nine. Chairman Frederick C. Muhlenberg broke the tie, voting in favor of the resolution. The next day, the House approved an $80,000 appropriation to carry out the terms of the treaty.

The Federalists rejoiced. Washington was vindicated, and Hamilton had achieved a personal triumph. According to the most authoritative work on the subject, the terms of Jay's treaty were "the result of the powerful influence of Alexander Hamilton . . . more aptly the treaty might be called Hamilton's Treaty."[43]

At the time, Jay's treaty was denounced as a sellout to Great Britain and a humiliation to the United States. Washington was permanently injured by the bitter insults he sustained from its detractors. But from the long-term point of view, its advantages were those that Hamilton had emphasized in its defense. The United States had won her independence from the mother country. She needed to buy time to develop into a strong nation. Hamilton had accomplished this through Jay's treaty, albeit by a narrow edge.

19

An End and a Beginning

ALTHOUGH NOW OFFICIALLY AN OUTSIDER, Hamilton's identification with the Washington administration was complete. Condemnation of it was tantamount to rejection of his own work. Hence, Washington's decision to encapsulate his accomplishments while in office and to advise the nation on its future in a valedictory address deeply concerned his former secretary of the treasury.

Toward the close of his first administration, Washington, seeking escape from his presidential bonds, had made Madison his confidant. He had extracted from the reluctant little Virginian advice and a draft of a "valedictory address from me to the public; expressing in plain and modest terms . . . that I take my leave from them as a public man." But Washington had bowed to the tremendous pressure exerted on him to serve again.

The year 1796, so laden with anxiety, uncertainty and political abuse, brought Washington closer to Hamilton. The president turned to his former secretary of the treasury again and again for advice on the ratification of the Jay Treaty and other matters. Hamilton answered every request with affectionate concern, giving his time unstintingly to the composition of full and brilliant replies. There was a real sympathy between them during that dismal year. It was during this period of mutual understanding that Hamilton wrote the drafts of Washington's Farewell Address.

While Hamilton was in the national capital in February 1796 to plead *Hylton* v. *United States* before the Supreme Court, Washington asked him to "*re dress* a certain paper which you had prepared. As it is important that a thing of this kind should be done with great care and much at leisure touched & retouched, I submit a wish that as soon as you have given it the *body* you mean it to have that it may be sent to me."[1]

It was not until May 15 that the president sent Hamilton his first draft of the valedictory. His instructions were to "throw the *whole* into a different form" if Hamilton should think it best and to return the draft "with such amendments & corrections" as necessary, "curtailed, if too verbose; and relieved of all tautology. . . . My wish is, that the whole may appear in a plain stile, and be handed to the public in an honest; unaffected; simple garb."[2]

The Washington version was much longer than the Madison draft. Its tone was less formal and its contents more specific. It was, in a sense, a defense of his administration and of himself. Washington was much more emotional about the significance of his legacy to the nation in 1796 than he had been four years earlier.

The method that Hamilton used in preparing his version of the Farewell Address was described in papers he left behind. Sometime after May 15, when he received Washington's letter and draft, and before July 5, when he sent Washington his own major draft, the former secretary of the treasury prepared an abstract of points to form an address. There were twenty-three of them. The first eight paragraphs follow the Madison-Washington draft, as do the last six. The entire middle section is Hamilton's.

"It has been my object to render this act *importantly* and *lastingly* useful," Hamilton told Washington when he sent him the draft. It was "to embrace such reflections and sentiments as will wear well, progress in approbation with time, & redownd to future reputation." Now he would begin the second part of his task, which was digesting the first address. He would try to finish the process in a fortnight, but he saw some awkwardnesses in it and some ideas that would not wear well. "Nevertheless when you have both before you you can better judge," he said.[3]

Washington was favorably impressed with the Hamilton draft except for its length, which he felt would be excessive for newspaper publication. On August 10, Hamilton sent off his second version, which incorporated the Madison draft. It was less than half the length of his first effort, and Washington preferred it as "being more copious in material points; more dignified on the whole; and with less egotism." Since Hamilton wanted to revise it further, Washington sent it back with the urgent request that it be returned as soon as possible; he wanted to hand it to the public before he left Philadelphia. What editor should publish it? he asked Hamilton. Should it go to him with a note, or should his secretary Tobias Lear carry it in person? If a note would be preferable, "let me ask you to sketch such a note as you may judge applicable to the occasion."[4]

On September 2, Hamilton wrote that he was sending a corrected draft. "Had I had *health* enough," he would have recopied it all, Hamilton wrote, in which case he would have revised and abridged it. "But . . . I seem now to have regularly a period of ill health every summer." It would be best to send the address with Lear directly to the publisher so that he could make a careful examination of the proof sheet.

Washington did not wait until October to declare his decision to step down from office, as Hamilton had recommended. The president did not want to be accused of delaying until too late for the Republicans to launch a campaign. On September 15, Washington showed his valedictory to his cabinet. He then arranged for its publication in Claypoole's (Philadelphia) *American Daily Advertiser* on September 19.

Hamilton and Washington were the joint authors of the valedictory. It was a true marriage of minds, the peak of amity and understanding between the two men, the final expression of the great collaboration between the first President of the United States and the founder of its financial system.

The tone of the address was positive, but words of caution were woven into the fabric of the piece. The most often quoted passage in the address reads: " 'Tis our true policy to steer clear of permanent alliances with any portion of the foreign world—so far, I mean, as we are now at Liberty to do it:—for let me not be understood as capable of patronising infidelity to pre-existing engagements." In Hamilton's major draft, it reads: "Permanent alliance, intimate connection with any part of the foreign world is to be avoided—so far (I mean) as we are now at Liberty to do it:—for let me never be understood as patronising infidelity to pre-existing engagements—These must be observed in their true and genuine sense—But 'tis not necessary nor will it be prudent to extend them—'Tis our true policy as a general principle to avoid permanent or close alliance(s)—"[5] They were Washington's thoughts, but Hamilton developed them and gave them a timeless expression.

General approbation for the valedictory and grief at Washington's announcement of his retirement met the publication of the address. Almost all the newspapers in the United States and even some European publications printed it. There were also many pamphlet editions. The Assembly of New Jersey and the Senate of New York voted to include the address in their journals as a memorial to the president. To George Hough of Concord's *Courier of New Hampshire* goes the credit for headlining the valedictory as "Washington's Farewell Address," which became its historical designation.[6]

James McHenry, describing, soon after its publication, its enthusiastic reception said: "I sincerely believe that no nation ever felt a more ardent attachment to its chief . . . and 'tis certain that history cannot furnish an example such as you have given. Those men who have relinquished sovereign power, have done it under circumstances which tarnished more or less the glory of the act; but in the present case, there is no circumstance which does not serve to augment it."[7]

During the eight years that Hamilton lived after the delivery of the Farewell Address, there is no evidence that he claimed authorship of the paper or indicated any involvement in its composition. Accounts by friends that he had told them of his work on it surfaced only after the Hamilton family made such claims.

The major Hamilton draft, his abstract of points for a Farewell Address and the letters from Washington on the subject, were found by Nathaniel Pendleton, one of Hamilton's executors, in 1810. Having decided that these papers were highly controversial, he gathered them together, sealed them and gave them to Rufus King for safekeeping. Pendleton's motive, King wrote in 1825, "was to prevent them from falling into the hands of the General's [Hamilton's] family." Pendleton knew that Mrs. Hamilton wanted to prove that her husband, not Washington, had written the Farewell Address. Pendleton believed that Washington had written it and that public opinion should not be stirred up.

Betsey Hamilton's determination was soon known to other friends of her husband, and rumors started to fly. In 1811, Judge Richard Peters wrote to John Jay about "the unnecessary *Buzz*, that Hamilton wrote it. I do not believe he did more than *dress* it, & most likely interweave some good things. If I had it in his Hand-Writing [Hamilton's] I would burn it. . . . Hamilton has fame enough." Jay was disturbed that Washington's Farewell Address was found among Hamilton's papers and wrote a lengthy analysis of why Washington must have been the true author. Jay then revealed that Hamilton had visited him with Washington's draft in his hand, and they had discussed and considered it, paragraph by paragraph. "Some amendments were made during the interview but none of much importance," he said.[8]

Jay's statement was taken up eagerly by Peters, who urged Jay to stop the story now gaining ground that Hamilton was the author of the address. "You are the only one living acquainted with the true State of the Facts. Hamilton, if alive would clear up all Doubts—or rather none arise. If Gen. W.[ashington] were alive he would wish you to declare what you know." Jay replied that he had not read the draft, had only discussed it with Hamilton. "In affairs of this kind there cannot be too much Circumspection."[9]

Talk died down, but Mrs. Hamilton would not leave the matter alone. In March 1818, she asked Bushrod Washington for permission to see any communication and papers he had in his possession "between your Uncle President Washington and my Hamilton."[10] She received permission, and an invitation from Judge Washington to visit him and his wife at Mount Vernon. In July, she made her way to Mount Vernon with one of her sons and her daughter Liza. They had a friendly visit of several days, during which Mrs. Hamilton tactfully avoided any mention of the Farewell Address.

Bushrod Washington spent a good deal of time searching for the letters Betsey requested from a list of dates she had prepared. He gave her all that he could find. It was not until after the visit that Judge Peters told Bushrod Washington that it was being whispered by certain persons in New York and Philadelphia that the author of the valedictory was Hamilton.

Five years later, in 1823, the gossip still persisted. Jefferson wrote to Judge Johnson that when Washington's address was printed, Madison had recognized several passages from his draft; "several others, we were both satisfied, were from the pen of Hamilton, and others from that of the President himself." After reading Jefferson's letter, Madison agreed. Jefferson, by pure deduction, came very close to the truth.[11]

On May 20, 1825, James Alexander Hamilton, then thrity-seven years old, at his mother's earnest solicitation went to Rufus King's house in Jamaica to claim the Hamilton papers that King had retained since 1810. Pendleton had told James Hamilton that the papers in King's possession were "most conclusive evidence" of his father's authorship of the valedictory.

According to James Hamilton, King was told at their meeting that the contents of the packet would not be published. The Hamilton family wanted them only for safekeeping. King said that he would not part with the papers while he lived, and at his death they would go to his two sons, John and Charles. He refused to unseal the packet. James stayed overnight at the Jamaica estate, but King did not change his mind. James left the house and, a few days later, renewed his request in a letter to King.

James's younger brother John Church tried another tactic. He called on Nicholas Fish, the only living executor of his father's will. Surprised at King's obstinacy, Fish said that he would ask him for the papers.

On May 25, James Hamilton renewed his request to King, mentioning his mother's "painful anxiety" over the matter. King refused once more. He was the last person to desire to impair the admiration of our country for "the merits and services of your father," but things had to remain as they are now, and "I cannot take measures to change."[12]

The Hamilton brothers carried the correspondence with King to Fish, who thought that the papers should be delivered to him. John C. Hamilton and Fish went together to Jamaica, where they saw King, who refused their request. In a letter to James, written later, Rufus King said that he had been mortified when threatened with legal action by his two visitors. Since Rufus King was to sail for England on June 1 as minister plenipotentiary, he regarded the threat as an attempt to keep him from his mission.

King went to England, but Mrs. Hamilton did start a suit to recover the papers. The newspapers got the story and gave a political connotation to King's refusal. If published, the papers "would compromise" King's reputation and that of other leading Federalists," M. M. Noah wrote in the *National Advocate.*[13]

King, somewhat alarmed by the suit, asked his son Charles to appeal to Judge Washington, who possessed "the sole power" over Washington's private and confidential letters, to make a statement. John Marshall, whom Bushrod consulted, advised him to make no opposition to publication of any correspondence about the address. Judge Washington took Marshall's advice and adopted a very shrewd position. He told Charles King that he had not "the most remote right to interfere in the extraordinary suit instituted by Mrs. Hamilton." If Mrs. Hamilton wished to establish General Hamilton's claim to the authorship of the Farewell Address, "(the validity of which claim is by no means admitted), I shall throw no impediment in her way, but leave her to pursue her own course."[14]

On November 26, 1825, Rufus King wrote to his son Charles that he had not replied to Mrs. Hamilton's suit. But the following spring, when he was about to return home, King consulted Lord Eldon, lord chancellor of England. Lord Eldon advised him that the letters belonged to the writer and to his family, the position that the courts take at present.

On October 17, 1826, James A. Hamilton received a letter and a bundle of papers. John Duer, acting for King, wrote that the publication of Jay's letter of March 29, 1811, exonerated King from his trust since it established Washington's authorship. On the same day, Hamilton informed Duer that the suit in chancery against Rufus King had been discontinued. The relationship between the King and Hamilton families remained hostile.

Betsey Hamilton never gave an inch in her belief that her husband was the true author of the address. She made a definitive statement on August 7, 1840. General Hamilton had suggested the idea of a valedictory and had been requested by President Washington to prepare the address. He had written it in his office when there were no clients about and when his students were absent, in order to avoid interruption. At such times, the old lady recalled, he would summon her to sit with him "that he might read to me as he wrote" so that he could "discover how it sounded upon the ear. . . . Therefore, the whole address or a great part of it was written by him in my presence," Mrs. Hamilton stated. It had been sent to Washington, who had sent it back with approval of all but four or five lines on the subject of public schools. Hamilton had made the alteration and returned it to the president.

Mrs. Hamilton added another anecdote. Shortly after the publication of the valedictory, Hamilton and his wife were walking on Broadway. An old soldier stopped the former secretary of the treasury and asked him to buy a copy of Washington's Farewell Address. Hamilton did so and then said to his wife, "That man does not know that he has asked me to purchase my own work."[15]

Now that all the drafts of the Farewell Address are available, as well as the Washington-Hamilton letters, a judgment can be made on the authorship. Its ideas were a great collaboration, though its prose was mostly Hamilton's. And as John Marshall said in a letter to Bushrod Washington, "I can have no doubt that it was published in the name of Washington from a perfect conviction that the valuable sentiments it contains would do more good proceeding from him than from any other person."[16]

The election of 1796 was unique in American history. For the first time since the Constitution had been adopted, George Washington was not a candidate. Political parties, so dreaded by the Founding Fathers, were now well enough established for the Federalists and the Republicans to back their own candidates.

Jefferson, enjoying a bucolic retirement on his mountaintop, had not entered actively into public affairs since leaving the State Department. Madison had been the party standard bearer, constantly prodded by Jefferson to battle the Hamiltonians. While he remained silent and remote, Jefferson's bid for the presidency would be the strongest of any from his party.

Though Hamilton was the Federalist party leader, he was not the party's choice for office. John Adams, Washington's vice-president, was his logical successor, and Hamilton had handicaps that could not be overcome. His illegitimacy, his foreign birth, his aristocratic bent and suspicion of his monarchist tendencies and his sometimes arrogant manner stood in his way.

Hamilton's ambition made him yearn for the highest office in the country, but hard-headed good sense would keep him from seeking it publicly. He would have to be satisfied with the role of kingmaker, and so his agile mind sought for the candidate certain to beat Jefferson.

After Hamilton's death, John Adams said that the Federalists had agreed to Washington's resignation "because they thought it an Advance toward the election of Mr. Hamilton who was their ultimate object." Adams's jealousy of Hamilton's leadership of the Federalist party prompted his statement. The high Federalists in the eastern and middle states would have preferred him, but his financial system was hated in the South and would have lost him votes from that section.[17]

Hamilton had loyal friends who thought he deserved the presidency. He also had enemies who tried to discredit him and his party by forging letters purportedly from Hamilton that revealed his plans for running for the presidency.

Robert Cowper of Suffolk, Virginia, informed Hamilton of five counterfeit letters that concerned his alleged bid for the presidency. Only one of them, which was addressed to Cowper, was supposed to have come from Hamilton himself. It concluded: "In my next I will be more particular . . . my Countrymen are Solicitous that I should become a Candidate for office—this I should at least have been persuaded to do but wished first to Know the Sentiments of the Southern States—will you give me some information on the Subject you may rely on it I shall not be ungrateful."[18]

In another letter, received by Stephen Graham, the alleged author John E. Van Allen, a member of the House of Representatives from Rensselaer County, New York, supposedly had had a conversation with Hamilton about the coming election. Hamilton was quoted as saying that Washington would not run again, and

Jefferson will be thrust into his place this as you must be well aware Does not coincide with my System and must by Some means or other be averted, that Cool Casuistic Frenchified fellow will in a little time undo what I have been so many years labouring to accomplish. I have Come to the resolution of offering myself a Candidate for that place. I hold it . . . a principle that when the object we have in view is a good one, we may take any measure whatever to obtain it to this end. You may well imagine that the dollars I have heaped together whilst handling the governments Cash will not be without their use. You understand me: write to your Friends disclose my intentions and hint to them that they shall not loose by their attachment to me.[19]

There is no evidence that Hamilton took any action about these forged letters. Graham and Cowper brought suit against Dr. Richard H. Bradford, the supposed author of the letters. The outcome of the suit is unknown; in 1866, the court records were destroyed in a fire.

John Adams was the heir apparent to the presidency, though he never had the kind of support from his party that Jefferson enjoyed. But at that time, a succession seemed logical. Adams had been a loyal and responsible Federalist whenever he had to cast a deciding vote over a tie in the Senate. He was a firm patroit who had rendered distinguished service to the country. Outspoken, he had never hidden his political philosophy under various pseudonyms, as had his contemporaries. He was proud to be plain-spoken and plainly dressed. But to many, his writing, particularly if taken out of context, revealed a man who was too pro-British and a monarchist. However, the vice-president's greatest problem was that he was not a favorite with his party's leader. The question still remains whether Hamilton accepted Adams as the inevitable Federalist candidate or tried to replace him with Thomas Pinckney of South Carolina, author of the recently completed treaty with Spain, which guaranteed the United States freedom of the Mississippi River.

Adams was not sure at that time or later whether Hamilton's politicking during the campaign was to ensure that the two top places went to Federalists in order to defeat Jefferson or whether he was trying to exclude Adams. After the election Adams excused Hamilton and his friends, saying that they did not "I believe meditate, by surprise to bring in Pinckney . . . they honestly meant to bring in me, but they were frightened, with a belief that I should fail, and they, in their agony, thought it better to bring in Pinckney President rather than Jefferson should be Vice President."[20]

Washington, by delaying his farewell until September, had left barely two months for campaigning. John Adams retreated to Quincy where he waited out the election, neither advising his supporters nor participating in the campaign. Jefferson also stayed away from the political arena, declaring that he was content to plant his crops and escape the storm of political passion.

Hamilton set to work to win the election for his party. First, he analyzed the chances of the Federalists by estimating the probable distribution of votes. The thirty-nine votes from New England were securely Federalist. The southern states, Georgia, Tennessee and Kentucky, were strongly Jeffersonian. However, it was possible that Pinckney could take some of the votes. New Jersey, Delaware and New York would hold for the Federalist candidates, with Maryland wavering but probably staying in the Federalist camp. Pennsylvania was the pivotal state.

In the midst of this atmosphere of uncertainty, there was a Federalist flurry for Aaron Burr, stirred up by his friend Jonathan Dayton, a Federalist congressman from New Jersey. Dayton's argument to Theodore Sedgwick, a leading Massachusetts Federalist, a chief lieutenant of Hamilton serving as senator to complete Caleb Strong's term, was that neither Adams nor Pinckney could defeat Jefferson, and therefore the Federalists should support Burr, who was really independent of the Republicans. Sedgwick sent Hamilton the two Dayton letters that contained the "secret" information.

The first letter emphasized that Pennsylvania was unanimously opposed to Adams, as "his chance is a desperate one." Burr would have the votes of the southern states and some support in the middle and eastern states. The second letter contained a brief but direct proposal. If Adams could not defeat Jefferson, would it not be desirable to have "at the helm a man who is personally known to, as well as esteemed and respected by us both? I assure you that I think it possible for you & me with a little aid from a few others to effect this."[21]

Sedgwick was astonished by Dayton's proposal but answered him in a calm, reasonable letter. Adams and Pinckney would be elected, he said. As for Burr, the Republicans wanted his talents but had no confidence in his loyalty. This had been proved when the party favored Monroe over Burr for the ministry to France. Hamilton characterized the correspondence with a simple statement penciled on the back of the third Dayton letter: "Concerning Dayton's intrigue for Burr." On December 1, he referred to "the machination to cheat us into Mr. Burr" in a letter to Jeremiah Wadsworth. The idea went no further. Burr worked for Republican support, spending six weeks campaigning through Connecticut, Massachusetts, Vermont and Rhode Island.[22]

Hamilton understood only too well the hazards of the cumbersome system that the Constitution provided for the election of president and vice-president. Accurate planning could not be attempted, since each elector cast two votes without indicating which person was to be president or vice-president. Intricate maneuvering could result in unexpected results, and the votes of one or two electors could determine who would be president or who would hold second place.

The newspapers, particularly the Republican press, exaggerated the so-called rift in the Federalist party over Adams and Pinckney. Hamilton's letters in the beginning of November clearly supported Adams for president and Pinckney for vice-president. However, he feared that New England's enthusiasm for Adams would cause their electors to "withhold votes from Pinckney . . . a most unpleasant policy." It could prevent them from voting for Pinckney "& . . . some irregularity or accident may deprive us of *Adams* & let in Jefferson." An added worry was that Vermont's votes would be lost because her electors might not have been chosen legally. The most votes Adams could depend on, he predicted, was seventy-three. If Vermont's were removed, he would have sixty-nine. " 'Tis therefore a plain policy to support Mr. Pinckney equally with Mr. Adams."[23]

In New England, Hamilton's instructions were disregarded. The electors placed sectional feelings and pride in a native son above the Federalist party and dissipated some second votes, mostly to Ellsworth, rather than risk electing Pinckney president instead of Adams. Vermont, whose votes were admitted, dutifully delivered four for Adams and four for Pinckney. The only other states that followed Hamilton's plan were New York and New Jersey. The electors from the South voted solidly for Jefferson, rejected Adams and divided their second votes among the other candidates. South Carolina gave eight votes to Pinckney and eight votes to Jefferson.

The results of the election were not as Hamilton wished. Jefferson, not Pinckney, was elected vice-president. The final count for Adams was seventy-one, giving him the election by only one vote. Jefferson received sixty-eight votes, Pinckney fifty-nine and Burr thirty.[24]

An important aspect of the 1796 election was French interference, directed by Pierre Adet, the minister from France. Monroe in Paris had promised the Directory that the new president would be pro-French, and Adet plotted to bring that promise to fruition. Bache's

Aurora carried Adet's four diplomatic notes, cleverly planned to appear in November just before Election Day in Pennsylvania. The insolent decrees threatened the United States with France's displeasure if an unacceptable president was elected. Jefferson was openly advocated as the favorite of the French Republic.

Hamilton saw at once that this outrageous action would harm the Republicans more than it would help them and was annoyed that Secretary of State Pickering rushed into print with a harsh response. "I regret the Reply to *Adet* otherwise than through the channel of Congress," Hamilton wrote to Wolcott. "The sooner the Executive gets out of the news Papers the better." Hamilton advised Washington and Pickering to be moderate and diplomatic toward France's envoy. But he used the French writer's indiscretion to attack Jefferson with accusations of being a French agent.[25]

John Adams agreed with Hamilton. The French minister's proclamations, Adams wrote, were just "some electioneering nuts [thrown] among the apes."[26] His son, John Quincy, estimated that French interference cost Jefferson thirteen votes.[27]

Crusty John Adams left Abigail and Quincy the last week in November, before the election was decided. En route to Philadelphia, he visited his daughter and her family in Eastchester and his son Charles in New York City. He spent an evening with John Jay, recalling old times. Adams was beset with conflicting emotions as he waited to find out whether he was to be president. He wanted the job, he needed the job, but he dreaded its responsibilities. The new president would have "half the continent on his back besides all of France and England, old Tories and all Jacobins to carry . . . a devilish load."[28]

While he was waiting, Adams learned about the Pinckney intrigue. As the evidence accumulated, he speculated on Hamilton's motives and, perhaps, Jay's also. At first he decided to try to keep the friendship of the conspirators. "I believe their motives were what they [conceived] for public good," he wrote to Abigail. Then, unable to tolerate the idea of the treachery of Jay or of his Boston friends, Stephen Higginson and George Cabot, he decided to blame Hamilton alone.

Abigail, her wifely loyalty thoroughly aroused, called Hamilton "ambitious as Julius Caesar" and reminded her husband that she had detected his intriguing nature. Adams soon agreed with Abigail. Giving his feelings free range, he damned Hamilton as "proud-spirited, conceited . . . with as debauched morals as old Franklin . . . a hypocrite." Abigail wrote, "Oh I have read his heart in his wicked eyes many a time. The very devil is in them. They are lasciviousness itself."[29]

Jefferson wrote to Adams from Monticello on December 28 that he had never doubted his election. Subtly, he drove a wedge between the Federalist president-elect and the head of the Federalist party. "Indeed it is possible that you may be cheated of your succession by a trick worthy the subtlety of your arch-friend of New York who has been able to make of your real friends tools to defeat their and your just wishes," he said. Vowing a disinclination for "riding in the storm," Jefferson wished Adams an administration "filled with glory, and happiness to yourself and advantage to us."[30]

The new vice-president's true sentiments were conveyed to Madison a few days later. "If Mr. Adams can be induced to administer the government on its true principles, and relinquish his ties to an English constitution," his future elections should be secured. "He is perhaps the only sure barrier against Hamilton's getting in." After reading Hamilton's pamphlets, Jefferson called him "a dexterous balance master." He told Madison: "We both, I believe, join in wishing to see him softened."[31]

Hamilton, then, was faced with a new adminstration that hated and distrusted him. The rest of his life would be lived amid the hostility of political foes in his own party, as well as in the opposition. A shrewd man, he found ways and means to continue to wield power, but in a sense, he was being forced underground.

New York City politics was another area of intense interest to the former secretary of the treasury. In that election, James Watson, the Federalist candidate, lost the congressional seat to Edward Livingston. Hamilton, who had worked feverishly during the three-day election period, blamed the defeat on the "unacceptable" Watson, who was "more *disagreeable* that I had supposed to a large body of our friends." There had been a last-minute effort by some of these friends to ditch Watson and nominate Hamilton. At a meeting at A. Moore's on December 13, 1796, resolutions were adopted to draft Hamilton. Hamilton was not nominated. The picture for the Federalists in the rest of New York State and the nation looked good. Hamilton, the nationalist, was encouraged. He told Rufus King, "We are labouring hard to establish in this country principles more and more *national* and free from all *foreign ingredients*—so that we may be neither 'Greeks nor Trojans' but truly Americans."[32]

The change in adminstration was critical for Hamilton. The results were uncertain for the high Federalists. The Jeffersonians and the Adamites were talking about the lion and the lamb lying down together. "This is to be a united and vigorous adminstration. Skeptics like me quietly look forward to the event.—willing to hope but not prepared to believe," Hamilton wrote to Rufus King.

Scandal

SOMETIME IN EARLY SUMMER 1791, a young woman called at Hamilton's Philadelphia house and asked to speak to him privately. He received her in a room apart from the family. With an air of deep affliction, Maria Reynolds, for so she identified herself, complained that her husband James had long treated her cruelly and had abandoned her recently to live with another woman. She was completely without means, but since Hamilton was a fellow New Yorker and known for his generosity, she felt that she could ask him for financial assistance. Her wish was to be able to return to her friends.

In the course of her tale, Maria presented her credentials. She was the wife of James Reynolds, whose father had been in the commissary department during the Revolution, the daughter of Richard Lewis of Dutchess County and the sister-in-law of Mrs. G. Livingston of New York.

Hamilton agreed to help her but explained that he was occupied at the moment. If she would give him her address, he would bring or send her some money. She gave him the street and number of her lodging house. That evening, putting a bank bill in his pocket, Hamilton went to Mrs. Reynolds's boarding house. He was shown upstairs, where he was met by the young woman who conducted him to her bedroom. Hamilton took the money out of his pocket and gave it to her. "Some conversation ensued from which it was quickly apparent that other than pecuniary consolation would be acceptable," Hamilton reported at a later date.[1]

This was the start of an affair between twenty-three-year-old Maria Reynolds and the secretary of the treasury. Its development from the first casual encounter to a blackmail plot became common knowledge when circumstances forced Hamilton to make the history of the affair public.

The early stages of the relationship proceeded routinely. There were frequent meetings with Maria that summer, most of them at Hamilton's house while his wife and children were in Albany. At the same time, Hamilton was writing affectionate, concerned letters to Betsey, who was not too well, about their "darling" James, three years old, who was seriously ill. As usual, Hamilton gave copious medical advice.

"Take good care of my lamb," wrote the faithless husband to his wife. He was waiting with all the patience he could muster for her return, but she was not to precipitate it. He would wait until her health was fully restored. The subject of health dominated his letters to Betsey. "Never forget for a moment the delight you will give me by returning to my bosom in good health. Dear Betsey—beloved Betsey. Take care of yourself." She must not forget her vitriol, he cautioned. "I have a wish you would try the Cold bath, begin by degrees. Take the air too as much as possible and *gentle* exercise." She was not to precipitate her return, he cautioned. "Adieu my angel."[2]

On August 12, Hamilton wrote to Betsey that he could not understand why she had not heard from him. He had written several times. "For let me be ever so busy, I could not forbear to allow myself the only Converse which your distance from me permits."

Little James had a relapse in mid-August. Hamilton said he would no longer dissuade her from coming home but asked her to persuade the physician attending James to come with them. Betsey decided not to stay in Albany later than September 1, and Hamilton answered that he would be delighted to embrace her and his children. He would meet the family in Elizabethtown. "Think of me—dream of me—and love me my Betsey as I do you," wrote her husband.[3]

Hamilton was unable to meet Betsey in Elizabethtown but sent his clerk, John Meyer, in his place. The change in the weather had brought on his chronic kidney complaint. "I am not *ill*," he told Betsey, "though I might make myself so by the jolting of the carriage were I to undertake the journey."[4]

While Mrs. Hamilton and her children were still in Albany, Maria Reynolds told her lover that her husband wanted a reconciliation. What should she do? Perhaps a little relieved, Hamilton advised her to agree to it. Soon after, Maria reported that the reconciliation had taken place. She also told Hamilton that Reynolds had been involved in speculation and had information about persons in the Treasury that would be useful to him.

Displaying a puzzling guilelessness, Hamilton sent for Reynolds, who revealed that he had obtained a list of claims from someone in the Treasury Department, which he had used in his speculations. Hamilton swallowed the bait and asked Reynolds who the person was, hinting broadly of the secretary's friendship and good offices if he disclosed the name. Reynolds named William Duer, who, said Reynolds, had put together the list in New York while in the Treasury Department.

Hamilton was not impressed with the revelation, since Duer had resigned long before the government had moved to Philadelphia. But, Hamilton wrote, "It was the interest of my passions to appear to set value upon it, and to continue the expectation of friendship and good offices." Reynolds said that he was leaving for Virginia shortly but on his return would reveal how he could be served. He might have mentioned something about employment in public office, Hamilton recollected.

When Reynold returned from the South, he asked Hamilton for a job as a clerk in the Treasury Department, which was refused. Hamilton had had a negative report about Reynolds.

Although Betsey and the children were back in Philadelphia, Hamilton continued to see Mrs. Reynolds. He was already beginning to grow suspicious of collusion between husband and wife, but Maria gave every appearance of "a violent attachment" and displayed "agonizing distress" at any idea of her lover giving her up, Hamilton said. Despite his doubts, he remained "irresolute." His plan was to break off with her gradually, but Maria had other plans. She worked at keeping Hamilton's attention, encouraging his visits and sending letters "filled with those tender and pathetic effusions which would have been natural to a woman truly fond and neglected," Hamilton wrote.[5]

On December 5, 1781, a letter came from Maria saying that "Mr has rote to you this morning" and swore that if he did not get an answer, he would write to Mrs. Hamilton.

Reynolds's letter arrived as promised. It was a misspelled, ungrammatical piece that was transparently insincere, accusing Hamilton of depriving him "of everything that's near and dear to me." He had become aware that something was wrong when he came home and found his wife weeping. Then he had found a letter directed to Hamilton, copied it and put it back. The next evening he had watched Maria give the letter to a black man in Market Street and followed the messenger to Hamilton's door. When he returned home,

Reynolds confronted his wife, who threw herself on her knees, begged forgiveness and confessed everything. Her version of the original meeting was that when Hamilton brought Maria the money, he took advantage of "a poor Broken hearted woman."[6]

Now, Reynolds complained, his wife cared for no other man in the world but Hamilton. So Reynolds was determined to leave his wife and take his daughter with him. Then came the threat. If he couldn't see Hamilton at his house, Reynolds said, "call and see me for there is no person that knows anything yet."[7]

Hamilton asked Reynolds to come to his office instead. The wronged husband repeated his grievances, to which Hamilton replied that he neither admitted nor denied a connection with Maria Reynolds. It did not take an experienced lawyer like Hamilton long to know that the wretched man desired money. Reynolds should decide what he wanted and then write to Hamilton.

Two days later the answer came. The letter was another rambling, self-righteous effort that came to no conclusion but suggested another meeting, this time at George Tavern. Instead, Hamilton went to see Reynolds. Adopting a firm tone, he insisted that Reynolds declare explicitly what he wanted. Unable to take a stand face to face with the secretary, Reynolds said that he would explain in a letter. Before meeting Reynolds that day, Hamilton had written to an unknown correspondent that he was going to a rendezvous that might involve "a most serious plot against me." For various reasons, he had to know the truth and hazard the circumstances.[8]

On December 19, Reynolds finally exposed himself. He demanded $1,000 in return for which he would leave town with his daughter and disappear. Maria would be left with her lover "to do for as you thin[k] proper." Payment was made in two installments: $600 on December 22 and the remaining $400 on January 3, 1792. Reynolds signed receipts for both payments.

About a month after the first payment, Reynolds wrote to Hamilton, asking him to see his wife "as a friend." He was "Reconsiled" to live with her and only wanted her happiness. Openly venal now, he wrote, "So dont fail in Calling as soon as you can make it Conveanant and I rely on your befreinding me." Hamilton recalled that he did not see Maria again until he received several "importunate" letters from her, sometime between January 23 and March 18.[9]

Maria wrote several distraught letters, telling Hamilton that she had been ill and begging him to see her for the last time. She had been on the point of doing "the moast horrid acts. . . . In vain I try to

Call reason to aide me but alas ther is no Comfort for me." He should call sometime that night between eight o'clock and midnight, or if he would not come, "send me a Line oh my head I can write no more do something to Ease my heart or Els I no not what I shall do for so I cannot live. . . ." Hamilton did not come.[10]

Two days later, Maria tried again. She wrote that she had found out from her husband that he had not forbidden Hamilton's visits and that it was her lover who refused to come to her. "Believe me I scarce knew how to beleeve my senses and if my saturation was unsupportable before I heard this It was now more so. . . . I shal be misarable till I se you and if my dear freend has the Least Esteeme for the unhappy Maria whose greatest fault is Loveing him he will come as soon as he shall get this."[11]

Receiving no response, five days later she wrote again to Hamilton. "Let me not die with fear have pity on me my friend for I deserve it . . . this favor . . . will be all the happiness I ever Expect to have." Hamilton resisted. Both husband and wife wrote to Hamilton on Sunday evening, March 24. Reynolds wrote that his wife was "in a setivation little different from distraction." She had told him that Hamilton had visited her and also that she had written Hamilton a letter, revealing threats that her husband had made against him and his family. Reynolds denied that he meant any harm "but did it to humble her." Getting to business, he said that he would see Hamilton the next day, when "I shall Convince you that I would not wish to trifle with you And would much Rather add to the Happiness of all than to distress any."[12]

Maria's letter played her refrain. She was anguished, drinking "the bitter cup of affliction." Her only consolation would be to see him once more "and unbosom Myself to you." She would go to him wherever he wished. "Let me se you death now would be welcome."[13]

The blackmailing pattern started again. On April 3, Reynolds asked for a loan of $30 for family necessities. He enclosed a receipt for $90, which suggests that he had received $60 at some earlier date. On the seventeenth, playing the long-suffering husband, Reynolds complained that Maria had treated him "more Cruel than pen can paint out and ses She is determined never to be a wife to me any more." Reynolds extracted $30 more from Hamilton about a week after this letter.

Apparently Hamilton resumed seeing Maria at this time, for on May 2, Reynolds canceled visitation rights. Further, the visits to his house were made furtively. "Am I a person of Such a bad Carector that you would not wish to be seen in Coming in my house in the front way?" he asked. Hamilton commented later that Reynolds was planning "some deepe treason" against him; despite his caution, Jacob Clingman, the Reynoldses' friend and ally, occasionally caught a glimpse of Hamilton at the Reynoldses' house.[14]

With some feelings of relief, Hamilton stayed away from his amour. "What have I done that you Should thus Neglect me?" Maria wrote on June 2. She was going to be alone for a few days. "Let me beg of you to Come and if you never se me again . . . I will submit to it . . . for heaven sake keep me not in Suspence. Let me know your intention." As a backup came James's newest request. He needed $300 to subscribe to the Lancaster Turnpike Road. If he didn't have the money, he couldn't leave town. Hamilton refused the request and won silence for a few weeks. At that time, the demand was reduced to $50. Hamilton gave Reynolds the money.[15]

The last letters from James Reynolds were dated August 24 and August 30. James wrote that he had taken a boardinghouse but was unable to furnish it for lack of funds. Two hundred dollars would make it possible for him to take in "genteel boarders" and would be repaid "as soon as it is in my power."

When no answer came, Reynolds sent another letter to Hamilton dated August 30, the last piece of correspondence with the husband or wife that Hamilton cited in his pamphlet. He did not make the loan.

Hamilton's summing up of the miserable love affair, five years after its apparent end, was dryly cynical. It was "an amorous connection . . . detected or pretended to be detected by the husband, imposing on me the necessity of a pecuniary composition with him, and leaving me afterwards under a duress for fear of disclosure." Mrs. Reynolds fanned the fear of exposure by hints that Reynolds would become discontented with his role, treat her badly, assassinate her paramour and get his revenge by informing Mrs. Hamilton. Reynolds needed to be humored, for, said Hamilton perceptively, "it was very possible that the same man might be corrupt enough to compound for his wife's chastity and yet have sensibility enough to be restless in the situation and to hate the cause of it."[16]

The Hamilton-Reynolds affair would have been no more than a sordid exercise in adultery had James Reynolds not been involved in two separate illegal activities. When he was caught, he tried to force Hamilton to help him by threatening to "make disclosures injurious to the character of the Secretary of the Treasury."[17]

In 1790, acting as the agent of a New York City merchant, Reynolds went to Virginia and North Carolina to buy up the claims to arrears of pay from veterans of the Revolutionary War. Congress had passed an act that same year protecting the interests of former soldiers, which Hamilton had opposed and had tried to persuade Washington to veto. There were charges at the time that Hamilton had supplied the speculators with lists of names and the amount of money due them.

Reynolds's second experiment in speculation was the one that landed him in jail. He and Jacob Clingman, formerly a clerk for Republican congressman Frederick A. C. Muhlenberg of Pennsylvania, were accused of aiding and abetting John Delabar "to defraud the United States of a Sum of money valued near Four hundred dollars." Delabar committed perjury, alleging that Ephraim Goudenough of Massachusetts, a claimant against the United States, was deceased. Reynolds and Clingman posed as executors of the estate. Oliver Wolcott, secretary of the treasury, brought suit against Reynolds and Clingman on November 16, 1792, and they were both arrested.

While Reynolds was in prison, he threatened to "make disclosures injurious to the character of some head of a Department." Wolcott informed Hamilton, who advised him to take no step to liberate Reynolds while such a report existed and was unexplained. At the same time, Clingman told Wolcott that he and Reynolds had obtained from the Treasury lists of names and the money due certain creditors of the United States. After Wolcott promised to try to get them freed of the charges against them, the two prisoners agreed to give Wolcott the lists and reveal the person who had supplied them, and then refund the money to the Treasury or the proper owners.

After he was charged, Jacob Clingman went to Muhlenberg for assistance. The congressman agreed to help his former clerk but balked at aiding Reynolds. During the three weeks of negotiations, Clingman often dropped hints to Muhlenberg that Reynolds "had it in his power materially to injure the secretary of the treasury and . . . knew several very improper transactions of his." At first Muhlenberg paid no attention to the insinuations, but after a while he decided it was his duty to consult with friends. He spoke to Senator James Monroe and Representative Abraham Venable, both from Virginia.

The two Virginians went immediately to the prison to see Reynolds. Although he did not mention Hamilton's name, Reynolds left no doubt that it was he whom Reynolds claimed to have in his power

for "a long time past." Reynolds promised to give information about
Hamilton's misconduct after he was released from prison that evening. He was afraid to do so before, lest it prevent his discharge.
The case against Clingman and Reynolds was dismissed on December 12, and when the two inquisitors arrived to see Reynolds, they
were told that their informer had either "absconded or concealed
himself."[18]

Reluctant to lose the trail, that same evening Monroe and Venable
went to Reynolds's house, where they found Maria alone. She gave
them some information with great reluctance. At Colonel Hamilton's
request, she said, she had burned a considerable number of letters
from him to her husband, "touching business between them, to prevent their being made public." She believed that Mr. Clingman had
several anonymous letters from Mr. Hamilton to her husband. She
said that Hamilton had advised her to go to her friends. He would
give her financial assistance and would give "something clever" to
Reynolds to leave these parts, never to be seen again. This was not
from friendship, Maria offered, but from fear that her husband
"could tell something, that would make some of the heads of departments tremble." She also told them that Jeremiah Wadsworth had
been active in her behalf, partly through friendship for her and
partly through friendship for Hamilton. Wadsworth had visited her
yesterday and mentioned that two congressmen had visited her husband in jail. Mr. Wadsworth had said that Mr. Hamilton had enemies who would try to prove some speculations on him, but he
would be found "immaculate." Maria had answered him that she
doubted it. The two visitors saw in her possession two notes that
were anonymous but were endorsed "from Secretary Hamilton, esq."
by Reynolds; and one from Wadsworth, which offered Maria help.
Mrs. Reynolds denied having heard from Hamilton or having received any money from him lately.

On that same day, December 13, 1792, an exceedingly damaging
deposition against Hamilton was collected from Jacob Clingman. He
had seen Hamilton frequently at the Reynolds house in January and
February. In March, after Duer's failure, Reynolds confided he could
have made £1,500 with Hamilton's assistance had Duer held up
three days longer. Hamilton had made $30,000 by speculation and
had supplied Reynolds with money for him to speculate. Clingman
also deposed that he had occasionally lent Reynolds money and had
been told that repayment could always be obtained from Hamilton.
On one occasion, Clingman recalled, he had loaned Reynolds $200.

Then the two men had gone to Hamilton's house. Clingman had seen Reynolds go into the house and then come out with $100. A few days later, Clingman had received the balance, which, Reynolds said, Hamilton had given him after returning from the SEUM meeting in New Jersey.[19]

After Reynolds was jailed, Clingman had asked Maria why she did not go to Hamilton. Maria answered that she had seen Hamilton, who had sent her to Wolcott but told her not to say that he had sent her. Maria told Wolcott her story and was advised to get some respectable person to intercede, such as Mr. Muhlenberg. When Clingman had asked Mrs. Reynolds for Hamilton's letters to her husband so he could use them to gain her husband's liberty, she said that, at Hamilton's request, she had burned all of them in his handwriting or that bore his name. Finally, she admitted that she had not destroyed all of them and gave him several notes said to be from Hamilton, which he had then submitted to Muhlenberg.

Jeremiah Wadsworth was brought into the scenario because during the Revolution, Reynolds's father had served under him. Sometime in November or December 1792, Maria had presented herself at Wadsworth's house as James Reynolds's wife and asked him to apply to Hamilton, Wolcott or General Mifflin for her husband's release. Wadsworth had refused. Maria then "fell into a flood of tears" and told a long story about her application to Hamilton for money when she was in distress over her husband's absence "& that it ended in an amour" which had been discovered by her husband. Wadsworth agreed to see Wolcott and Mifflin.

The next morning, Wadsworth saw both men. Mifflin said that Mrs. Reynolds had already told him "the story of the amour." Wadsworth then saw Maria and told her he would interfere no longer; her husband had to be tried. Clingman had been present part of the time during this session. Maria called on Wadsworth again and begged him to deliver letters to Hamilton. Wadsworth saw Hamilton, who refused to receive the letters and wanted them destroyed. After Maria continued to bombard him with messages, Wadsworth went to her house and told her that Hamilton refused to correspond with her, and, as he had told her before, her husband had to be tried.[20]

According to Clingman, Maria Reynolds's account differed from Wadsworth's. She said that she had received money in a note from Hamilton during her husband's confinement and had burned the note.[21]

Reynolds was discharged from prison at eight or nine o'clock on Wednesday evening, December 12, 1792. Clingman said that about midnight, Reynolds sent a letter to Hamilton by a girl. Reynolds followed the girl, and Clingman followed Reynolds. After the girl went into Hamilton's house, Clingman joined Reynolds, and they walked back and forth in the street until the girl reappeared. She told Reynolds that he should see Hamilton between seven and eight in the morning. The next morning, Clingman observed Reynolds going into Hamilton's house. Since then, Clingman said he had not seen Reynolds and supposed he had gone out of the state.[22]

Hamilton knew nothing about the investigation of the congressional team until the three of them presented themselves at his office on the morning of December 15. Muhlenberg, the spokesman, observed to the secretary of the treasury that they *"had discovered a very improper connection"* (the italics are Hamilton's) between him and Mrs. Reynolds. Hamilton gave way to "very strong expressions of indignation." The trio immediately retreated, explaining that they did not accept the fact as established but wanted to inform Hamilton of information that there was "an improper pecuniary connection" between him and Mr. Reynolds. It was their duty to pursue it, and they had in their possession some suspicious documents. They had contemplated informing the president but thought it correct to tell Hamilton first and give him the chance to explain. They then showed Hamilton the notes written in his disguised hand, which he acknowledged as his. He agreed to answer them and to present written documents that would explain "the real nature of the business." A meeting was agreed on for that same evening at Hamilton's house.[23]

Hamilton then called on Wolcott and told him for the first time of his affair with Maria Reynolds and the visit of the congressmen. Wolcott was given the documents in the case and asked to be present at the evening interview. In a document written at Hamilton's request on July 12, 1797, Wolcott described the proceedings.

Monroe started the conference by reading certain notes from Hamilton and a narrative of conversations with Reynolds and Clingman. Hamilton then gave his explanation, backed up by a variety of written documents showing that the transactions in question had no connection with speculation in funds, claims on the United States or any public or official transactions. This was so evident that Representative Venable asked Hamilton to stop exhibiting further proofs, but the secretary persisted in order to clear up any doubts about his official conduct.

After Hamilton's explanation, Monroe, Muhlenberg and Venable acknowledged that the affair had no relation to official duties and regretted the trouble the explanation had caused.

Hamilton thought there had been a "full and unequivocal acknowledgment" of perfect satisfaction with his explanation. "Mr. Muhlenberg and Mr. Venable, in particular manifested a degree of sensibility on the occasion. Mr. Monroe was more cold but intirely explicit."[24]

The next morning, Hamilton wrote a memorandum of the substance of the meeting and sent a copy of it to each of his three accusers. It said that they regretted the trouble and uneasiness caused Hamilton and were perfectly satisfied with his explanation. There was nothing in the transaction to affect the secretary's "character as a public officer" or lessen public confidence in his integrity. The statement was followed a few days later with a request for copies of the papers themselves so that he could have his own copies made, in order to avoid a repetition of the episode.[25]

In time, Monroe sent copies, asking that they be returned after they were transcribed. That closed the incident, Hamilton thought, except for "some dark whispers" that Henry Lee told him about on May 6, 1793. "Was I with you I would talk an hour with doors bolted and windows shut, as my heart is much afflicted by some whispers which I have heard."[26]

It was overoptimistic of Hamilton to believe, if he did, that so juicy a scandal known to a number of friends and foes could be concealed for any length of time. He did not have very long to wait.

The stab in the back occurred on June 26 with the publication of Pamphlet No. V of James Thomson Callender's series of tracts. When published in book form, it was called *The History of the United States for 1796: Including a Variety of Interesting Particulars Relative to the Federal Government Previous to that Period*. Oliver Wolcott sent Hamilton a copy of the pamphlet on July 3. "You will see that the subject is but partially represented with a design to establish an opinion that you was concerned in speculation in the public funds," Wolcott wrote. "You will judge for yourself, but in my opinion it will be best to write nothing at least for the present. I think you may be certain that your character is not affected, in point of integrity & official conduct. The indignation against those who have basely published this scandal is, I believe, universal." Wolcott spoke too soon. On July 4, Pamphlet No. VI was published. Wolcott wrote to Hamilton: "I am astonished at the villainy of Monroe—a

more base, false, & malignant suggestion than is contained in his
Note of Jany 2 1793 was never entered." The note reported a meeting
with Clingman on January 2, 1793, held after Hamilton's December
15 defense. Clingman told Monroe that when Maria Reynolds heard
about Hamilton's explanation to the three members of Congress, she
was much shocked and wept copiously. She denied that she had had
a relationship with Hamilton and declared that it was a fabrication
of his with the assistance of her husband. Reynolds had been with
Hamilton the day after he left the jail, when he was supposed to be
in New Jersey.[27]

Callender defended Monroe in his pamphlet, asserting that he had
shown "the greatest lenity to Mr. Alexander Hamilton" who had
made "a volunteer acknowledgement of *seduction*." Monroe and the
others had also agreed to delay telling the president about his secretary of the treasury's actions if he promised "a guarded behavior in
future."

"Your own declaration to me at the time contradicts absolutely the
construction which the Editor of the pamphlet puts upon the affair,"
Hamilton reminded Monroe. Therefore, he wanted another statement from Monroe, similar to the first one to which all the legislators
subscribed. Though not attributing a "dishonourable infidelity" to
Monroe and the others privy to the episode, "yet the suspicion rests
on some Agent made use of by them."[28]

Hamilton published a letter in Fenno's *Gazette of the United
States* that drew protests about its accuracy from the principals.
Callender was brashly outspoken. He said that none of the members
had believed a single word that Hamilton had told them. Monroe
was now in New York, "where you can see him personally." As for
Hamilton's statement that he was going to place the matter before
the public, Callender said that the public had long known him "as an
eminent and able statesman. They will be hugely gratified by seeing
you exhibited in the novel character of a lover."[29]

Hamilton arranged to meet Monroe at his lodging, Thomas Knox's
house at 46 Wall Street, with David Gelston, New York City merchant and Republican politician, and John Church also present.
Gelston's account of the hour-long interview provides the only
description of what happened.

Hamilton appeared very agitated when he entered the room with
his brother-in-law. He immediately embarked on a wordy account of
the earlier meeting in Philadelphia until Monroe impatiently said
that the history was not necessary. Hamilton answered heatedly that
he was coming to the point directly.

Monroe explained that he had become involved in the business by accident. He had heard that there was a Mr. Reynolds from Virginia in jail, called to help him and discovered it was a Mr. Reynolds from New York. After the meeting with Hamilton and the other two men, Monroe insisted, he had sealed up his copy of the papers and sent or delivered them to a friend in Virginia (Jefferson). He knew nothing about the publication until he arrived in Philadelphia from Europe and was sorry that it had been done.

Hamilton said stiffly that he wanted an immediate answer to the letter he had written to him and the two others. Monroe, irritated, said if Hamilton would be quiet for a moment, he could explain that he and the others had not yet had time to arrange a meeting so that they could issue a joint answer, but they would do so when he returned to Philadelphia. However, if Hamilton wished to hear the facts as they appeared to him, Monroe would relate them. Hamilton said he would.

The packet of papers remained sealed with his friend in Virginia, Monroe repeated. Hamilton interjected that this was totally false, at which both men rose to their feet.

Monroe: "Do you say I represented falsely; you are a scoundrel."

Hamilton: "I will meet you like a Gentleman."

Monroe: "I am ready get your pistols."

Church and Gelston interceded, Church repeating over and over, "Gentlemen Gentlemen be moderate." Finally, everyone sat down, and the two antagonists seemed calmer. Monroe repeated that he was ignorant of and surprised at the publication of the papers.

Gelston proposed that the affair rest until Monroe returned to the capital, met with Venable and Muhlenberg and issued a joint letter. This was agreed upon. Before the meeting broke up, Church suggested that any unguarded expressions that had been made during the meeting should be buried as if they had never been said. Both Monroe and Hamilton accepted the proposal.[30]

Monroe and Muhlenberg, Venable being absent in Virginia, sent a satisfactory statement to Hamilton on July 17, but Hamilton was still upset by Monroe's meeting with Clingman.

Hamilton wrote to Monroe that he gave "credit and sanction to the suggestion that the defence set up by me was an imposition," and he wanted an explanation from Monroe on that point. Monroe's answer was unsatisfactory. He admitted to being surprised by Clingman's communication but had no opinion on it at the time. He reserved to himself the "liberty to form an opinion upon it at such future time as I found convenient," Monroe said.[31]

Hamilton was shaken by Monroe's unexpected reluctance to clear him. "It appears to me liable to this inference, that the information of *Clingman* had revived the suspicions which my explanation had removed," Hamilton wrote to Monroe. This would include the suspicion of fabricating the Reynolds letters and forging those of Mrs. Reynolds, since hers contradicted "the pretence" communicated by Clingman. "I therefore request you to say whether this inference is intended." Monroe answered on July 18, the same day, in a manner that demonstrated his intention to keep Hamilton on tenterhooks. He had not intended to convey his own opinion but "left it to stand on its own merits."[32]

There is some evidence that the Republicans wanted to keep the pot boiling to discredit the administration. While in Philadelphia, John Church learned that Madison and Giles and other Republicans were having frequent meetings, trying to persuade certain people that Hamilton was involved with Reynolds in speculation on certificates.[33]

Hamilton was in Philadelphia himself during mid-July and stayed there longer than his business required, hoping to resolve his quarrel with Monroe. Betsey was expecting a baby within the next few weeks, so Hamilton was anxious on her account. The furor over the Reynolds affair seemed to be making no impression on her at all. John Church told Hamilton that she handed him the Callender letter of July 10 with the attitude that "the whole Knot of those opposed to you" are scoundrels.[34]

Delaying his departure from Philadelphia from day to day while letters were exchanged between himself and Monroe without any satisfaction, finally Hamilton could stay no longer. He gave William Jackson, an old friend, a surveyor and inspector of the revenue for Philadelphia, a letter to deliver to Monroe. Monroe seemed to have accepted Clingman's "wretched tale" and so could only have "malignant and dishonorable motives," as the world would see when "the publication of the whole affair which I am about to make shall be seen."

Jackson tried to play the role of peacemaker. He delivered Hamilton's letter to Monroe, explaining that Mrs. Hamilton was in the last stages of pregnancy and her husband had to return to New York but would be back in Philadelphia in about a fortnight. Monroe read the letter and then told Jackson that he was going to Virginia at the end of the week but would return to Philadelphia shortly. Jackson reported to Hamilton that Monroe thought that the correspondence between them should be withdrawn and destroyed but did not want to make the suggestion. He did not intend to be Hamilton's accuser and thought that his letters had been respectful, whereas Hamilton's letters to him were not.

Jackson entreated "my dear Hamilton" to postpone any publication on the subject until Monroe returned. An acceptable statement from Monroe, Muhlenberg and Venable would be superior to entering into a detailed publication, "which although it might fully satisfy all impartial men (who by the way are already satisfied), would only furnish fresh *pabulum* for the virulent invective and abuse of faction to feed on." To bolster his position Jackson consulted James McHenry, who advised Jackson to visit Monroe again. After that meeting, Monroe said that he would write to Hamilton once more.

Monroe's position in his letter of July 25 was that Hamilton had adopted "a harsh stile." If he wanted to make a personal affair out of it, he should have been more explicit; but if he wanted to place the question on its true merits, "it is illy calculated to promote that end." Monroe repeated that he could not state that Clingman's communication had made no impression on his mind, but he did not want it understood that it had changed his opinion. However, Monroe retained the right to note Clingman's communication or any other.[35]

From New York, Hamilton answered that he was prepared "for any consequences" that his words might lead to, but the subject "is too disgusting to leave me any inclination to prolong the discussion of it." A public explanation "to which I am driven must decide . . . between us. Painful as the appeal will be in the principal point, it must completely answer my purpose."

Hamilton proceeded to strengthen his case by collecting data and assembling evidence. He wrote to Jeremiah Wadsworth, asking for samples of Maria Reynolds's handwriting. Hamilton sent Wadsworth samples of Maria's notes and asked him for an affidavit stating that he had received letters from Mrs. Reynolds, was acquainted with her handwriting and believed the letter to be in her handwriting.

Wadsworth replied that, unfortunately, he had no knowledge of Maria's handwriting, but he repeated an account of his meeting with her, which included her statement that her encounter with Hamilton "ended in an amour & was discovered by her husband." He was fully convinced, Wadsworth stated, that she, Reynolds and Clingman had combined "to swindle" Hamilton. Wadsworth also regretted that Hamilton found it necessary to publish anything, for the enemies would "invent new calumnies."[36]

Edward Jones, a clerk in the Treasury Department, furnished

Hamilton with information from Richard Folwell, a Philadelphia printer and publisher. Folwell had met Maria Reynolds a few days after she had first arrived in Philadelphia, when she appeared at his mother's house asking to stay there for a short time while she tried to reclaim her prodigal husband; he had deserted her and his creditors in New York. Mrs. Folwell had agreed to take her in, for her "innocent countenance appeared to show an innocent heart." Soon, however, she revealed herself as a seductress who prostituted herself to gull money from her victims. She told Folwell that her husband "frequently enjoined and insisted that she should insinuate herself on certain high and influential characters."[37]

Folwell last saw Maria a year or two after Reynolds dropped from view. She was then Mrs. Clingman. She contacted Richard Folwell to ask him to provide her with a clear character in East Nottingham, Cecil County, Maryland, where she and Clingman had been living at the home of one of Folwell's distant relatives. Folwell answered the notorious Mrs. Reynolds by telling her that her character was now even worse because Mr. Reynolds was alive in New York. Maria replied that her only fault was that she had married Clingman one half hour before she obtained her divorce, but Folwell refused to give her a good character.[38]

By the last day in July, Jackson had a change of heart. He advised Hamilton to go on with his publication, since Monroe seemed unwilling to grant the certificate.

Before leaving Philadelphia, Monroe wrote to Hamilton that he had no wish to do him a personal injury, but if his explanations did not satisfy, he could give no other "unless called on in such a way which always for the illustration of truth, I wish to avoid, but which I am ever ready to meet." On August 4, the day that his son William Stephen was born, Hamilton wrote to Monroe: "In my opinion the idea of a personal affair between us ought not to have found a place in your letters or it ought to have assumed a more positive shape." The option was up to Monroe, but if an advance was intended, Hamilton wrote, he would not decline. He authorized Major Jackson to be his second and to settle time and place.[39]

Jackson called on Monroe and told him that Hamilton regarded his last letter as an overture to a personal meeting. Monroe asked if the letter from Hamilton was a challenge. Jackson replied that the letter would explain. Monroe then told him that he would consult with a friend and give an answer.

The next day, August 6, 1797, Monroe wrote to Aaron Burr, enclosing the complete correspondence with Hamilton. If Hamilton meant his last letter as a challenge, then Burr would accept it, Monroe ordered. But if he thought that he was accepting Monroe's challenge, then the enclosed letter explained, because Monroe never meant to give him a challenge, "seeing no cause so to do." If there was to be a duel, Monroe told Burr, he needed a three-month delay. His publication had to be completed and his family affairs adjusted. The place for the encounter should be the Susquehanna. Since Burr had a child and family, Monroe would not expect him to participate but would call on Mr. Dawson. Burr should settle the disagreeable affair so there would be no further correspondence. "I am satisfied that he is pushed on by his party friends here, who to get rid of me wd be very willing to hazard him," Monroe wrote. "In truth I have no desire to persecute this man, tho' he justly merits it."[40]

Burr became the peacemaker, but before his answer to Monroe arrived, Dawson called on William Jackson as Monroe's representative. Each of the principals thought that he was the injured party; it was not clear who should be challenging whom. After speaking to Dawson several times, Jackson's advice to Hamilton was to await the effect of his publication. James McHenry, who had seen the letters, agreed.

Hamilton wrote to Monroe on August 9 that he would take no further steps toward a personal interview. A few days earlier, Monroe had written to Burr that he was not opposed to making a statement. And on August 13, Burr informed Monroe that he had reread the correspondence with Hamilton "& wish it all burnt. . . . If you and Muhlenberg really believe, as I do, and think you must that H is innocent of the charge of any concern in speculation with Reynolds, it is my opinion that it will be an act of magnanimity and Justice to say so in a joint certificate."

For the time being, hostilities were averted. But after Hamilton's pamphlet, which contained Monroe's letters, was printed, the Virginian considered reopening the matter. He wrote to Madison, asking if the part of Hamilton's pamphlet which referred to him presented grounds for resuming the controversy. Madison answered that all the ground had already been covered, and the case between them "seems to have been brought to a final close."[41]

In December, Monroe was still worrying about Hamilton's affront. Burr was sent another long letter of more or less the same substance as the previous letters. Once again, Monroe wanted Burr to act as his second and enclosed a letter for Burr to deliver to Hamilton.

And at Monroe's request, Dawson, Edward Livingston, Burr and others conferred. Dawson wrote that all of the gentlemen except Livingston agreed that "it wd be unwise, impolitic & unnecessary for you to take any further step in the business." Dawson repeated his earlier analysis of the dispute, which was that Hamilton's object was to distract the public mind from his guilt in another business.[42] Madison and Jefferson agreed with Dawson. No further correspondence has been found on the subject. Very likely, Monroe was more interested in the reception of his own pamphlet. On December 21, his vindication of his behavior as minister to France was published.

Hamilton, on his part, had occasional flareups of anger against Monroe. As late as January 1798, he drafted a challenge to Monroe but did not send it.

Burr, who took full credit for averting the interview, saved Hamilton for himself.

On August 25, 1797, Hamilton's pamphlet was published with the ponderous title: *Observations on Certain Documents Contained in No. V & VI of "The History of the United States for the Year 1796," in Which the Charge of Speculation Against Alexander Hamilton, Late Secretary of the Treasury, is Fully Refuted. Written by Himself.* The opening pages attributed the Callender attack to "the spirit of Jacobinism." Hamilton wrote: "It threatens more extensive and complicated mischiefs to the world than have hitherto flowed from the three great scourges of mankind, War PESTILENCE and Famine."

This spirit, Hamilton explained, accomplished its purpose by calumny, and "it is essential to its success that the influence of men of upright principles, disposed and able to resist its enterprises, shall be at all events destroyed." If any "little foible or folly" could be traced to such a person, it became "a two-edged sword, by which to wound the public character and stab the private felicity of the person. . . . Even the peace of an unoffending and amiable wife is a welcome repast to their insatiate fury against the husband."[43]

The story of the events was presented in the pamphlet. In addition, various parts of the action were analyzed to demonstrate Hamilton's innocence. Of the paltry sums that Reynolds demanded of him Hamilton wrote: "What a scale of speculation is this for the head of a public treasury. . . . He must have been a clumsy knave, if he did not secure enough of this excess of twenty-five or thirty millions, to have taken away all inducement to risk his character in such bad hands and in so huckstering a way." Hamilton also pointed out that no accusation was made against him until Clingman and Reynolds were under prosecution by the treasury "for an infamous crime."[44]

In answer to Clingman's allegation that Mrs. Reynolds "denied her amorous connection with me" and said it was a contrivance between her husband and the secretary of the treasury to cover up, Hamilton explained that Maria Reynolds's own letters contradicted her. "The variety of shapes which this woman could assume was endless," her lover said. Hamilton referred to his reputation as a philanderer, saying there were those who felt that he had no dread of the disclosure of an amorous connection since he had "nothing to lose" as to his "reputation for chastity concerning which the world had fixed a previous opinion. I shall not enter into the question what was the previous opinion entertained of me in this particular," Hamilton wrote, "nor how well founded." However, he pointed out, "There is a wide difference between vague rumours and suspicions and the evidence of a positive fact." The truth was, Hamilton asserted, he dreaded extremely a disclosure.[45]

The disappearance of Reynolds after his release from jail could have many explanations other than, "as was imputed, a method of his getting rid of a dangerous witness," Hamilton said. Reynolds might have been guilty of other offenses against the Treasury Department, or his creditors may have been after him.

Hamilton concluded his defense by repeating that his desire to destroy the slander completely had led him to the copious examination of it. Anyone reading the Reynolds letters had to be convinced "there is nothing worse in the affair than an irregular and indelicate amour. . . . I have paid pretty severely for the folly and can never recollect it without disgust and self condemnation."[46]

Hamilton's pamphlet created a sensation among the members of both parties, but to the Republicans it was a source of barely contained glee. Madison, writing to Jefferson, called the publication "a curious specimen of the ingenuous folly of its author."[47]

James Callender wrote to Hamilton on October 29, 1797, asking to inspect the papers that Hamilton said he had lodged with William Bingham "that I may judge what credit is due to them." If he found them genuine, the presumptuous editor wrote, "I shall be as ready to confess my conviction to the public, as I was to declare my former opinion."[48] Hamilton never answered him.

The Reynolds pamphlet papers pose a mystery. In 1799, Bingham denied ever having possessed them when James McHenry asked for them at Hamilton's request. But in 1801, he wrote to Hamilton that the papers he had deposited with him "have long lain dormant in my Possession." He was going to Europe and wanted to return them.[49] The letters, as far as can be determined, were never seen by anyone.

John Adams, who was a master of invective and was angry at Hamilton for thwarting him, spared no words to describe Hamilton's prurience. He talked of "the profligacy of his life; his fornications, adulteries and his incests." His ambitions, Adams said, came from "a superabundance of secretions" that he "could not find whores enough to draw off."[50] But there is no evidence of Hamilton's amours other than the self-confessed one with Maria Reynolds. Burr's papers are littered with passionate notes from sundry mistresses, but Hamilton's papers contain none. Burr, who died a bachelor, estranged from Madame Jumel and without living issue, had only Matthew L. Davis to comb his literary remains. Hamilton's widow and sons removed all that might be damaging to his reputation.

Only the titillating correspondence with Angelica Church, Hamilton's sister-in-law, remains to be analyzed by a biographer. Angelica's letters contrast so pointedly with Betsey's spare, pedestrian ones that it often occurs to the reader that Hamilton married the wrong sister. Together, Alexander and Angelica might have conquered the world. Perhaps not. Betsey's may have been the unquestioning, leveling influence that her flamboyant husband needed.

While the Churches were in England, Angelica and Hamilton wrote to each other frequently. His letters to her have a sense of freedom and interest absent from his brief, dutiful letters to his wife. In October 1791, he chided Angelica for her intimacy with "amiable" princes, French émigrés, whom the Churches were entertaining. "But I pray you don't let your Vanity make you forget that such folks are but men and that it is very possible that they not be half as worthy of the good will of a fine woman as . . . a Secretary of the Treasury." He was not, however, "in a violent fit of dudgeon" with her. "You are as much in my good graces as ever . . . you must be a very naughty girl indeed before you can lose the place you have in my affection."[51]

In February 1796, the Churches decided to move to New York City. Hamilton was delegated to find them a house. Angelica complained to him that he had not described the house and lot he was arranging to buy for them. She was troubling him, Angelica wrote, but "I was asking from one who promised me his love and attention if I returned to America." In June 1796, Hamilton wrote that he and Betsey wished that Mr. Church would not delay his departure any longer. "Life is too short to warrant procrasti[nation] of the most favourite and precious objects." The letter was signed, "Yrs as much as you desire, AH." The Churches did not arrive in New York until May 1797, at which time they rented the governor's private mansion on Broadway.[52]

The Schuylers rallied around Hamilton no matter what he did. Betsey ignored the implications of the pamphlet and reacted only to the part of it that revealed the vicious attacks on her husband's honor. Philip Schuyler never ceased to admire his famous son-in-law. Angelica had written earlier that her father "speaks of you with so much pride and satisfaction, that if I did not [love] you as he does, I should be a little jealous of his attachment."[53]

Julian Boyd, editor of the Jefferson papers, accepts Callender's accusation that the Maria Reynolds letters were forged and that the affair never occurred. Hamilton had a gift for polemical and political writing, but Boyd's assertion that he could easily compose a body of spurious love letters in a day or two is hard to accept. The Maria Reynolds letters present a picture of an uneducated, overwrought, dependent woman torn by love. She was a weak woman who submitted to the pressures of several men—her husband, her lover and her future husband. And she must have been flattered by the attentions of an attractive, powerful man.

Granted that the summer the affair started, Hamilton was lonely, overworked and vulnerable, but the liaison continued off and on after his wife and family returned to Philadelphia. Did the dark-eyed young woman, abandoned by her husband, with a young child whom her husband threatened to take away from her remind him of his mother? Rachel Lavien was married to an abusive husband who drove her away and kept her child.

Sordid, shabby, most of all unfortunate, the Reynolds affair brought only grief to everyone concerned. The pamphlet moved the Republicans to laughter and the Federalists to frustration. Jefferson, Madison and Monroe were certain that there was some truth to Callender's accusation that Hamilton had helped his friends to lists of soldiers' and officers' arrears of payments. Any hope, no matter how ephemeral, that Hamilton had of one day becoming President of the United States perished after the publication of the Reynolds pamphlet. Hamilton was permanently relegated to the role of deus ex machina. He started as soon as John Adams took office.

Hamilton v. Adams

"**I** WISH YOU JOY of your President," Angelica Church wrote from London, expressing precisely the feelings of the Hamilton faction of the Federalist party about John Adams. A rapprochment between the two parties, based on the friendship and understanding of President Adams and Vice-President Jefferson, caused some alarm. The "*Lion* & the *Lamb* are to lie down together," or so the Jacobins and Adams's personal friends said, Hamilton reported disapprovingly to Rufus King. Philip Schuyler agreed that there was cause for trepidation. Adams's farewell to the Senate and inauguration speech left "very unfavorable impressions in my mind," he said.[1]

The suspicions of Hamilton and his supporters that the Republican leaders were planning a stop-Hamilton movement were well founded. Jefferson regarded Adams as "the only sure barrier against Hamilton," but he also knew that it would not be easy to promote amicable relations with the president; there would be "machinations" to produce misunderstandings between the two executives, proceeding from the Hamiltonians "by whom Adams is surrounded" and who were "only a little less hostile to him than me."[2]

Jefferson hoped that Adams would recognize his experience in foreign affairs and give him an active role in the government. In this he was to be disappointed. Crusty John Adams was inclined to be egotistical and self-willed. He did not want to be eclipsed by Jefferson or Hamilton. But Adams was surprisingly unaware for a long time that his cabinet was infiltrated by Hamiltonians who maintained close ties to the former secretary of the treasury. Adams continued in office Secretary of State Timothy Pickering, Secretary of the Treasury Oliver Wolcott and Secretary of War James McHenry, Hamiltonians all.

After his resignation from the cabinet, Hamilton had corresponded with and advised President Washington and his cabinet on all phases of government. He saw no reason not to continue after the new president took office. Indeed, he was encouraged to do so. After Adams's inauguration, Pickering wrote to Hamilton: "I beg you to continue to communicate to me your ideas on public affairs, especially at the present interesting period." Hamilton's influence on Franco-American relations was not limited to his series of polemics signed "Americus" and titled *The Warning*, published in the Philadelphia *Gazette of the United States*. He had a direct line to the executive office, unbeknownst to the president.

During the latter part of the Washington presidency, Hamilton had made outspoken statements on the proper position to take on French depredations against American shipping. He was in agreement with Washington's statement that the conduct of France toward the United States was "outrageous beyond conception. . . . The sooner you can give me your "sen [timents] . . . the more pleasing they will be," Washington had said.[3] Hamilton proposed a three-man commission, composed of Madison, Charles Cotesworth Pinckney and perhaps a third person from a northern state, such as Mr. Cabot. This mission would duplicate the earlier mission to England, which would soothe French pride and give the opposition party representation, a most important consideration if the mission failed. Its purpose would be to adjust mutual compensation amicably and "remodify the *political* and *commercial relations* of the two Countries."[4]

The election of Adams made Hamilton even more certain that his plan for a commission was a good one. He believed that the French government's resentment against the United States was very much "levelled at the actual President." The change of person might "furnish a bridge to retreat over." Hamilton proposed the same three members for the commission. Madison would be most influential with the French, he commented, yet "I would not trust him alone lest his Gallicism should work amiss."[5]

The situation with France became very tense when, on March 14, ten days after his inauguration, Adams learned that the Directory had rejected Gen. Charles Cotesworth Pinckney, Monroe's replacement as minister to France. Rufus King speculated to Hamilton whether this French action resulted from news of the election of Adams or Napoleon Bonaparte's astonishing victories over the Austrians at Rivoli and in Mantua.

On March 25, Adams issued a call for Congress to convene in a special session on May 15 to deal with French anti-American policy. During the interim, Hamilton bombarded his cabinet friends with advice and counsel. He still wanted a commission to be sent to France. He also advocated a day of prayer so that Americans could consider themselves the defenders of their country against "Atheism, conquest and anarchy." The European war could force Americans to defend "our fire sides & our altars." In addition, Hamilton recommended strong defensive measures: an embargo, a naval force, warships for convoys to our trade, a provisional army of 25,000 to be ready in case of war. "We shall best guarantee ourselves against calamity by preparing for the worst," he wrote.[6]

Pickering welcomed Hamilton's ideas and reported back to him that the president had already decided to convene Congress and consider some of the other measures. However, a commission was not feasible at this time. The Directory would not receive one until the redressment of "griefs" against the American government. But Hamilton did not change his mind. He wrote to Wolcott, advocating the commission and arguing that though the Directory would not receive a minister from America, this did not exclude "an extraordinary Messenger." The fact that the enemies of the government wanted such a commission was a strong reason for pursuing it. Friends of the government were beginning to suspect that the administration wanted war with France. "My Opinion is to exhaust the expedients of Negotiation & at the same time to prepare *vigorously* for the worst," Hamilton said. He also wrote to McHenry, rehearsing all the arguments he had made to the others. "I write you this letter on your fidelity," he told the secretary of war. "No *mortal* must see it or know its contents."[7]

Hamilton's suggestion to send Madison to France was opposed by his friends in the cabinet who felt that Madison was not to be trusted. If Madison was balanced by Pinckney and Cabot, his intrigues could not operate as they imagined, Hamilton answered. All in all, Hamilton thought that the French threat was good for the United States, but he was upset that his influential friends opposed him on these public issues. McHenry tried to explain Wolcott's "unpleasant feelings." He wrote: "Where opinions clash, and where superiority is made too apparent something a little like envy will come into play especially should a suspicion take place that pains are used to gain proselites."[8]

This was a tactful warning to Hamilton not to press too hard, but

McHenry wanted Hamilton's help in composing a report for Adams on defenses necessary at this time. Hamilton responded with a detailed draft in which all of the president's questions were answered. McHenry used the Hamilton draft in its entirety in his reply to Adams.

The temporary disagreement on the commission to France did not stop any of the cabinet members from consulting Hamilton again and again. Hamilton seemed to have all the information at his fingertips, and despite his law work and poor health, he answered his correspondents.

Jefferson just about disappeared as a rival influence in the administration after his letter to his Italian friend, Philip Mazzei, was published in the United States. The letter, which was one year old at this time, criticized Washington and the Federalist foreign policy with France. The timing of its publication, May 2, shortly before the special meeting of Congress, served to arouse the American people against Jefferson's "treachery" and make them, at least momentarily, pro-Federalist.

When Adams addressed the special session of the fifth congress, he limited his speech to the French problem, criticizing the Directory for refusing to receive Pinckney and thus dishonoring America. He would try to heal the wound by a fresh negotiation, he said, but at the same time he asked for an increase in the army and navy so as to defend American neutrality. Hamilton's ideas were represented in the speech through his memoranda to cabinet members.

The speech caused division. Jefferson and his party saw at once that the brief meeting of minds at the time of the inauguration was over. They suspected Hamilton's influence. The Senate, where the Federalists had a majority, accepted the president's proposals. The House, Republican-dominated, debated for two weeks. The representatives supported the president's position, but their statement on France was milder than his.

Adams met unexpected opposition from his cabinet, which did not want a bipartisan commission for the French mission. Adams's proposal of Elbridge Gerry of Massachusetts, acceptable to the Republicans, was met with so much resentment that he backed down. Instead, he came up with Francis Dana, chief justice of the Massachusetts supreme court. Pinckney, persona non grata to the French, was to head the mission; the third member chosen was John Marshall, a Virginia Federalist, cousin to Jefferson and his political enemy. The Senate confirmed the nominations.

Several weeks later, Dana, pleading poor health, declined the appointment. Adams then displayed his stubborn, independent spirit by appointing Gerry without consulting his cabinet. This was unprecedented and offensive to them, and justified their qualms about consulting party chief Alexander Hamilton. The Gerry appointment pleased the Republicans, particularly the vice-president, who begged him to accept. He did and was confirmed by the Senate.

Responsibility for getting the defense program accepted was placed in the hands of William Loughton Smith of South Carolina, Hamilton's chief spokesman. In April, Hamilton sent him a long paper on "the course of Conduct proper in our present situation." The ten resolutions Smith introduced on June 5 embodied the Hamilton document. In a letter to Smith during the debate, Hamilton outlined his ideas on how revenue could be raised to pay for the frigates and cutters needed for defense. He proposed taxes on buildings, a stamp tax and a tax on salt but was not optimistic that Congress would approve. "Our country will be first ruined and then we shall begin to Think of defending ourselves," he said.[9] Republican resistance to the proposals was so strong that Congress discussed no other subject for several weeks. The bill that emerged was very weak. Republican fear of war with France dominated the response. But despite the mildness of the defense bill, some military preparation took place: an increase in the army and navy; a loan for expenses; and, later, provision for salt and stamp taxes.

Their mission accomplished, Congress went home to escape Philadelphia's tropical heat and seasonal yellow fever outbreak. There was an epidemic that year which the Federalists said started from a French ship *The Marseilles* and the Republicans said spread from the British *Arethusa*. The Academy of Medicine effected a truce when it published its "proofs of the domestic origin of our late epidemic."[10]

On June 19, John Adams and his family returned to Quincy, Massachusetts. The next day, John Marshall left from Philadelphia on the French mission, followed, a few days later, by Elbridge Gerry, who departed from Boston. Pinckney, who was still abroad, would meet them.

The French Directory was very hostile to the American Federalist government. John Quincy Adams, the American minister to Prussia, wrote to his father very discouraging warnings from his Berlin observation post. President Adams foresaw that his commissioners to France might be refused an audience or be ordered to leave without accomplishing their object. On January 24, 1798, he asked his cabinet for advice on steps to take if such an event occurred. Should there be an immediate declaration of war, an embargo and "above all what will policy dictate to be said to England?" James McHenry rushed a copy of Adams's queries to Hamilton. "Will you assist me or rather your country" with opinions on this? he requested.[11]

Hamilton obliged with pages of advice that were relayed to Adams, almost word for word, under McHenry's signature. There was nothing to be gained by a formal war with France, Hamilton said. If negotiations failed, the government should increase the navy, allow privateering against the French, suspend treaties with France and raise an army of 30,000. It would be best to avoid alliance with England. Mr. King should sound out England in regard to cooperation of her naval force. "All on this side of the Mississippi must be *ours* including both Floridas." In addition, the president should declare a day of fasting and prayer.[12]

Adams sent a message to Congress on March 5; he had received the first dispatches from the envoys extraordinary, and they were being deciphered. The dispatches reported a French resolution closing French ports to all neutral ships that touched at an English port. There was no hope of being officially received by the French government. Adams addressed Congress on March 19, urging members to adopt promptly "such measures as the ample resources of the country can afford, for the protection of our seafaring and commercial citizens." The Senate, on the following day, voted to ask the president for the instructions given to the commissioners and their dispatches. Hamilton advised Pickering that it was essential to comply with the Senate's request; otherwise, there would be a loss of confidence and "criticism will ensue which will be difficult to repel."[13]

Pickering agreed and asked Hamilton again what should be said to the British government. The U. S. brig *Sophia*, a dispatch boat, was about to sail and could still be diverted to England with instructions. Hamilton received Pickering's letter too late to return a detailed reply, but he did state that he opposed an alliance with Great Britain. Her self-interest would ensure cooperation, and a treaty would accomplish no more but would entangle us with her, and public opinion was not yet ready for it. "If *Spain* would cede Louisiana to the U States I would accept it" absolutely, if possible, or temporarily, to be restored later.[14]

Once again Hamilton took up his pen to support his position. He wrote a series called *The Stand*, consisting of seven numbers published in *The Commercial Advertiser* (New York) under the pseudonym "Titus Manlius," designed to inflame the nation against France. "Honest men of all parties will unite to maintain and defend the honor and the sovereignty of this country." The crisis demanded it. " 'Tis folly to dissemble. The despots of France are waging war against us. . . . All amicable means have in vain been tried toward accommodation." We had to "resist with energy," and for that we needed "a respectable naval force" and "a respectable army."[15]

After Congress failed to legislate an increased army and an embargo, Hamilton's pieces became more inflammatory. In *The Stand No III*, published April 7, 1798, he wrote: "It is not necessary to heighten the picture by sketching the horrid group of proscriptions and murders which have made of France a den of pillage and slaughter; blacking with eternal opprobrium the very name of man. . . . France swelled to a gigantic size and aping ancient Rome, except in her Virtues, plainly meditates the controul of mankind."[16]

Support for Hamilton's position came with the publication of the first set of dispatches sent from France by the United States envoys. When the full picture emerged of the rejection and humiliation the American envoys had suffered in the anterooms of the French Directors, there was a surge of anger and a passion for revenge. After a period of being largely ignored, the trio had been approached by agents of Talleyrand, designated in the president's report to Congress as X, Y and Z, insinuating that, for $250,000 paid discreetly to the Directors and Talleyrand, negotiations might be started.

Pickering sent Hamilton a copy of the dispatches, including a quotation from Jefferson saying that the Directory was not implicated in the villain, "or at least that these [the dispatches] offer no proof against them." Bache's Republican paper, the *Aurora*, called Talleyrand notoriously antirepublican and "an intimate friend of Mr. Hamilton, Mr. King and other great federalists"; it was only because of their determined hostility against France, that Talleyrand discovered in them while in this country, that the Government of France "consider us only as objects of plunder."[17]

However, most Americans were outraged by the cynical demand for money. The slogan "Millions for defense but not one cent of tribute" became the rallying cry. Hamilton, in *The Stand*, fanned the flames. "Informal agents probably panders and mistresses" had been appointed by the French government "to intrigue with our envoys. . . . At so hideous a compound of corruption and extortion, at demands so exorbitant and degrading, there is not a spark of virtuous indignation in an American breast which will not kindle into a flame." And yet, Hamilton did not propose a declaration of war against France. Instead, "our true policy" should be "calm defiance" and preparedness.

After the dispatches were made public, Hamilton, as Titus Manlius, answered Jefferson's defense of the Directory. "The high-priest" of the French faction in this country, he wrote, suggested that there was no proof of the Directory's involvement. "The recourse to so pitiful an evasion betrays in its author a systematic design to excuse France . . . and to prepare the way for implicit subjection to her will." In a direct thrust at his American foes, Hamilton wrote that "France places absolute dependence" on the Gallic faction and "counts upon their devotion to her as an encouragement to the hard conditions they attempt to impose."[18]

Jefferson was very anxious about Hamilton's lust for power. He regarded him as a war hawk and worried that he would be named senator in place of John Sloss Hobart, who had filled the vacancy when Philip Schuyler resigned and was now himself resigning. The vice-president believed that Jay, after reelection as governor of New York, would announce his selection of Hamilton. But Hamilton refused the job. "There may arrive a crisis when I may conceive myself bound once more to sacrifice the interest of my family to public call. But I must defer the change as long as possible," he told Jay.[19]

The war fever that followed the publication of the XYZ dispatches brought Adams sudden, unexpected popularity. It also caused a wave of patriotic fervor that soon showed its ugly side. The Federalists saw their chance to stamp out Jacobinism by suppressing the opposition's right to criticize the government. French aliens in the United States, many of them royalist refugees themselves victims of the Directory, were terrorized. The black cockade, an anti-French badge, was sported all over the United States by Federalists. The president made belligerent noises in his speeches but stopped short of asking for war.

The Alien and Sedition laws, which Congress passed in June and July of 1798, were designed to give the president special powers over aliens, meaning the French, and over any political opposition, particularly by the press. These measures were uniformly approved by the Federalists.

Hamilton did not propose these measures, as Adams stated in 1809, and was as innocent of influencing Congress to pass them as the president claimed to be. Adams wrote: "Nor did I adopt his

[Hamilton's] idea of an alien or sedition law. I recommended no such thing in my speech. Congress, however, adopted both these measures. I knew there was need enough of both, and therefore I consented to them."[20]

Hamilton's opposition to the Sedition law is substantiated only by his objection to a harsh bill introduced into the Senate by James Lloyd of Maryland on June 26, 1798. Hamilton warned Wolcott that the bill seemed "highly exceptionable" and might spark a civil war. The more moderate bill, which the Senate eventually passed, did not elicit any objections from Hamilton. Earlier in June, Hamilton spoke to Pickering in defense of Frenchmen "whose situations would expose them too much if sent away & whose demeanour among us has been unexceptionable. . . . Let us not be cruel and violent."[21]

Although war with France seemed inevitable after the outburst of patriotism over the XYZ affair, there were mitigating circumstances that delayed it. John Marshall arrived in New York harbor on the *Alexander Hamilton* after a fifty-three-day voyage from Bordeaux and stayed in New York for a few days before going on to Philadelphia. Jefferson observed that while in New York, no doubt Marshall received "more than hints from Hamilton as to the tone required to be assumed." When Marshall reached the capital, there were parades and dinners in his honor.

After consulting with him, Adams decided to postpone a request for war and to allow negotiations in France to continue. After he spoke to Congress, the legislature granted the president the power to appoint officers for an additional army of 10,000 and, on July 16, voted a further increase of the military establishment to be known as the provisional army. This 50,000-man provisional army was to be a reserve force not to be called until a real war began. Adams, who favored the development of a strong navy, was not too pleased with these additions.

As usual, Hamilton had been way ahead of the others. As early as May 19, 1798, he had written to George Washington at Mount Vernon about the probability of the United States having to enter into a "very serious struggle with France." Hamilton had a plan. The former president, using health as the reason for his travels, should make a circuit through Virginia and North Carolina. In the course of the public dinners that would be given for him, he could express his support of the government. At the end of this cajoling letter, Hamilton got to the point. In the event of an open rupture with France, the nation would recall him to lead its armies, he told Washington. "You will be compelled to make the sacrifice. All your past labour may demand to give efficacy this further, this very great sacrifice."[22] Subtly and cleverly, Hamilton laid the groundwork for his own ambitions.

Washington rose to the bait. No, he would not make a tour of the southern states. His health had never been better, and their enemies would turn the journey to their own advantage, so that "the reception might not be such as you supposed." As to open war, the ex-president doubted France would attempt to do more than they had done. If such a crisis arose, however, and the country called him, he would have no choice. He could declare "to *you*" that he might not serve the nation any better than other commanders. Then came the words for which Hamilton waited. Washington asked him "whether you would be disposed to take an active part, if Arms are to be resorted to."[23]

Hamilton's answer to Washington rolled off his pen. "The suggestion in my last was an undigested thought begotten by my anxiety," he said. "It is a great satisfaction to me to ascertain what I had anticipated in hope, that you are not determined in an *adequate emergency* against affording once more your military services." Then he revealed his position. "If I am invited *to a station in which the service I may render may be proportioned to the service I am to make*—I am willing to go into the army." If Washington commanded, Hamilton said, he would be most useful as inspector general. "This I would accept." Then, planting another idea in the former president's mind, he observed that he would take it for granted that "your choice would regulate the Executive. With decision & care in selection an excellent army may be formed."[24]

At the end of May, Congress authorized Adams to raise a provisional army of no more than 10,000 and to appoint a commander for it. About a month later, Adams wrote to Washington, asking him what to do. Should he "call out the old Generals or appoint a young Sett? We must have your Name, if you, in any case permit Us to Use it." Adams did not wait for his predecessor's reply. On July 2, he nominated him lieutenant general and commander in chief of all the armies raised. The Senate approved the nomination the next day.[25]

Washington replied graciously that in the case of an actual invasion by a formidable force, he would assist in repelling it. Once the Washington nomination was confirmed, Adams took no chance that the old gentleman would change his mind. He sent Secretary of War James McHenry to Mount Vernon to deliver the appointment by hand.

The sixty-six-year-old ex-president, "uncommonly majestic," still

commanding in his face and figure, received McHenry with customary reserve. He would accept the commission with certain
reservations. He would not take an active part in the preparations
and must not be called into the field until there was a state of war,
and it was most important that he be consulted about the selection of
the generals to serve directly under his command. He was an old
man, Washington told McHenry, so the second in command would
be in charge, pending actual hostilities.[26]

Hamilton wanted to be inspector general and second in command
with an intensity that he seldom allowed himself to feel. He expected
Adams to be reluctant to elevate him to a rank second only to Washington's; therefore, Adams had to be coerced through Washington
and through the three disloyal cabinet members.

The other two major contenders for the top post were Gen.
Charles Cotesworth Pinckney, still abroad on the French mission,
and Gen. Henry Knox, who had served as secretary of war until 1794,
a resident of Boston and often away, looking after his property in
Maine. During the period of the three-way struggle, President
Adams was at home in Quincy, while the pro-Hamilton cabinet
members, McHenry and Pickering, were in Philadelphia, conniving
with their choice.

On July 14, in a confidential letter, Washington repeated to Hamilton what he had told McHenry at Mount Vernon. He had to have two
major generals and an inspector general with the rank of major general. "I have given the following as my sentiments respecting the
characters fit & proper to be employed. They were Alexr Hamilton,
Inspector, Chas C. Pinckney and Henry Knox."[27]

The president sent the names to the Senate just as Washington had
proposed them, and they were approved in that order. Hamilton was
named inspector general. A week later, on July 25, McHenry sent
Hamilton his appointment and commission. But the problem remained
that Knox outranked Pinckney, and both Knox and Pinckney outranked Hamilton. Washington had written to Pickering that if
France should invade any part of the United States, it would be
south of Maryland so that Pinckney would certainly not be accepting
a junior position. If he rejected the appointment, it would "sow the
seeds of discontent" at so important a crisis. If such an invasion
occurred, Pinckney should be engaged in repelling it. Under the circumstances, Pickering hoped that Hamilton would still be willing to
come forward "if not at the height of my wishes and of those of your
friends, certainly in a situation in which you can render invaluable

services, and as certainly obtain a large share of honor and military fame."[28]

Hamilton replied that he had considered being second to Knox, if "thought indispensable," but did not feel it necessary in the case of Pinckney. Though willing to leave the question of relative ranks to future settlement, he was not satisfied with the principle that every officer of higher rank in the Revolutionary War should be over him. "Few have made so many sacrifices as myself . . . if . . . I am to be degraded below my just claim in public opinion—ought I to acquiesce?"[29]

The absence of a decision on the relative rank of the major generals was noted by all. John Jay wrote to Hamilton that "doubts on such a point ought not to remain." Hamilton did not need prodding to take up "the delicate subject." After accepting his appointment, he approached Washington. A great majority of the Federalists were of the opinion that had the former president declined the command, "it ought to devolve on me."[30]

John Adams did not want Hamilton at all, and certainly not in a prominent position. For three days running, he asked Pickering's advice about which one of the three should have top billing. Three times Pickering answered, Colonel Hamilton. Adams said nothing in answer until the third day. "O no! It is not his turn by a great deal," he commented. "It was from these occurences that I first learned Mr. Adams's extreme aversion to or hatred of your father," Pickering told James Hamilton.[31]

It was the president's prerogative to settle the ranking of the generals. From Peacefield in Quincy, he rejected McHenry's request to call to his aid Inspector General Hamilton and General Knox. To do this would present difficulties, the president wrote, "unless the rank were settled." General Knox was entitled to the rank next to Washington and Pinckney next, and if it was agreed that the order should be Knox, Pinckney and Hamilton, "then the call into service can be made." Otherwise, there would be a long delay and much confusion. The five New England states "will not submit to the humiliation that has been meditated for them," Adams said.[32]

When McHenry received a letter from Henry Knox saying that he wanted to serve his country and would regret having to refuse because of "unsurmountable obstacles" which would bring "public degradation," the secretary of war wrote to Hamilton, enclosing a copy of the Knox letter. "What is to be said to General Knox?" he asked. Hamilton replied that he was sorry to give Knox pain, but the preference given to him was important to the "public in its *present* and *future* consequence." Hamilton enclosed a draft of a letter that McHenry might send to Knox. When Adams received a copy, he refused to send it, saying that it did not reflect his feelings. "The power & authority is in the President," he reminded McHenry. If it were referred to General Washington or to discussion among the gentlemen involved, it would come to Adams at last "after much altercation & exasperation of passions & I shall then determine it exactly as I should now—Knox, Pinckney & Hamilton."

In a private letter, Pickering reviewed the strength of Hamilton's position. The president seemed to have forgotten that General Washington "made your appointment the *sine qua non* of his accepting the chief command." General Knox's proposal to use Revolutionary rule of rank to determine precedence plainly had been proposed by General Knox for his own benefit. And as to the president's notion that the New England states would be offended if Hamilton preceded Knox, "It was among the New England members of Congress that I heard you, and you only, mentioned as the Commander in Chief."[33]

McHenry informed Washington on August 25 that Adams wanted to alter the relative grade of the three major generals, putting Hamilton last; then he relayed the information to Hamilton. "My mind is made up," Hamilton declared on September 8. He would not keep his commission if he were not number one. "I do not, I cannot blame you for your determination," McHenry answered. Pickering, Wolcott and Stoddert would all communicate with the president, he promised. "You will not hear from me, relative to the commands of the President, 'till the result is known to me."[34]

Washington wrote to Hamilton from Mount Vernon, asking that he suspend a final decision until further word. The ex-president then wrote to Adams, reminding him of the arrangement made through Secretary of War McHenry. The generals stood Hamilton, Pinckney, Knox, and so the names were sent to the Senate and so was the expectation "of all those with whom I conversed. But you have been pleased to order the last to be first, and the first to be last. . . . I have no hesitation in declaring, that if the Public is to be deprived of the Services at Col. Hamilton in the Military line, that the Post he was destined to fill will not be easily supplied." With respect, Washington requested that he be informed "whether your determination to reverse the order of the three Major Generals is final."[35]

Even before Washington's letter arrived, Adams had relented. In a letter to Wolcott dated September 24, which was never sent, Adams wrote that, although disagreeing that Hamilton should have the second in command, he was persuaded to issue commissions to the three contenders all dated on the same day, "in hopes that under the Auspices of General Washington the Gentlemen may come to some amiable settlement of the dispute."

"The sun begins to shine," McHenry wrote to Hamilton. Then, having delivered the good tidings, he ordered, "Burn this letter." Five days later, Wolcott wrote to Hamilton privately, criticizing the secretary of war for hesitating to announce to the public Hamilton's appointment to the rank of first major general. He hoped that Knox would retire, due to his embarrassed pecuniary situation.

From his Quincy retreat, Adams informed Washington that he had signed the commissions and dated all of them on the same day. If the gentlemen could not agree among themselves, the ex-president had to deal with it as commander in chief. If, however, "anyone should be so obstinate to appeal to me from the Judgment of the Commander-in-Chief," Adams said, "there is no doubt . . . that by the present Constitution of the United States, the President has the Authority to determine the Rank of officers."[36]

On October 12, McHenry was still hesitating and consulted the other cabinet members. Pickering, Wolcott and Stoddert advised that, since Adams had agreed to Washington's arrangement of rank, the secretary of war should transmit the commissions to the major generals, sparing the president any further communications on the subject.

Thus prodded, McHenry informed Hamilton officially of his position as second in command, requesting him to come as soon as possible to Trenton, where the government had moved to escape the yellow fever epidemic in Philadelphia, or to Philadelphia, no later than November 10. Hamilton agreed to reach the capital about the first of November.

Knox, as Wolcott had predicted, declined his appointment on the grounds that he could not be expected to consent to his own degradation. When Pinckney, in France during the controversy, arrived in New York City on October 12, he did not disembark; a yellow fever epidemic was raging. But within four hours after the ship anchored, friends came aboard with the news of his appointment and his rank below Hamilton. "I declared then, and still declare," Pinckney told the secretary of war, "it was with the greatest pleasure I saw his name at the head of the list. . . . I knew that his talents in war were great, that he had a genius capable of forming an extensive military plan, and a spirit courageous and enterprising, equal to the execution of it. . . . I . . . would with pleasure serve under him."[37] The battle of the generals had been won by Alexander Hamilton.

In addition to his regular army duties, Hamilton had been designated by Governor Jay and the president to undertake the fortification and defense of New York. The state legislature appropriated $150,000 for constructions and fortifications on Governor's Island, Bedloe's Island, Oyster Island and Paulus Hook. Among the members of New York City's military committee was Aaron Burr, who, as a member of the state assembly, had been instrumental in passing the bill for the fortifications, although he had been overlooked for a military appointment.

His position established, Hamilton now turned to another problem. Although James McHenry was a good friend to Hamilton, he had shown himself to be indecisive and timid. Fearing such incompetence, General Hamilton informed Washington that he would aid the secretary of war as fully as permitted. "But every day brings fresh room to apprehend" that the War Department "cannot prosper in the present *Very well disposed* but *very unqualified* hands."[38]

By mid-November, the top brass gathered in Philadelphia to consult with each other and with the administration. Hamilton arrived on the tenth to meet McHenry so that the two of them could escort Washington, who also arrived that day, to his lodgings in Eighth Street. Pinckney joined the others a few days later. Adams was still in Quincy.

Hamilton told Betsey that he would not be able to leave Philadelphia in less than a fortnight. "The delay will be to me irksome. I discover more and more that I am spoiled for a military man."[39] In the meantime, there were issues to be discussed: military appointments, recruiting and provisioning the troops, military stores and equipment. Washington delivered queries on these subjects to be answered by Generals Hamilton and Pinckney.

Hamilton's amazing organizing ability was now directed toward creating a 50,000-man army, fortifications, arsenals, a commissariat and supplies of all kinds. Much of the work was tedious and demanding, but with his ability to overcome the drudgery of detail, Hamilton worked on all phases of the task. Drafting bills and taking over many of the jobs that should have been done by the secretary of war added to his burden.

While waiting for his appointment, Hamilton had flirted with the idea of supporting Francisco de Miranda's scheme to free the

Spanish-American colonies. Over the years, Miranda had written letters full of quixotic plans to Hamilton, who had been a sympathetic listener but had always made clear that he could not participate "unless patronised by the Government of this Country." In the summer of 1798, on the eve of his elevation to high military command, Hamilton wrote to Miranda in London that by winter 1799, "an effectual cooperation by the U States may take place. In this case I shall be happy in my official station to be an instrument of so good a work." The British fleet, an American army, "a Government for the liberated territory agreeable to both the Cooperators" was the way Hamilton saw it. "We are raising an army of about Twelve thousand men," Hamilton informed Miranda. Displaying caution, he enclosed his letter to Miranda in a dispatch to Rufus King. The American minister to England was to read the letter to Miranda and decide whether it should be delivered.

General Hamilton was attracted to his scheme. The United States government would furnish the entire land force, he wrote to King, and "the command in this case would very naturally fall upon me." The Latin American colonies, once free, would provide a tremendous source of trade for the United States. We would have cooperation from Great Britain "the moment *we are* ready," King assured Hamilton.[40]

Hamilton died before the revolutions in the Spanish-American colonies began. Miranda led an unsuccessful expedition to the Venezuelan coast in 1806, two years after Hamilton's death, and then returned to Venezeula in 1810 after the revolution began. Following a short reign as dictator and a series of misfortunes, he finally angered Bolívar by surrendering to the Spanish in 1812. He died in a Spanish dungeon four years later.

War activity engrossed the newly appointed first major general, but the French political scene was changing. On the last of July, due to the efforts of Talleyrand, the Directory repealed its hostile restrictions on American shipping. After the French Foreign Minister was informed how the XYZ affair had inflamed the American people, he recommended a more conciliatory policy.

Hamilton, virtually in command of the army, served the congressional hawks well. The high Federalists, particularly the New Englanders, favored war. "I feel that war with all its calamities would be less Injurious to my country, than a peace which might be followed, and probably would be with the reintroduction of the pernicious and destructive principles which prevail in France," Philip

Schuyler wrote, expressing the party viewpoint. What he meant was that a war would halt the triumph of the Republicans, who would not be able to hold their dovish position without appearing to be "internal foes."[41]

During the fall of 1798, the president remained at Quincy because of his wife's precarious health. Isolated from Philadelphia, he had time to reflect on Hamiltonian power and its increase since he had been forced to appoint the party chief to high military rank. Hamilton stood for war, so Adams had to stand for peace. Elbridge Gerry, friend of France, had returned to the United States and gained the president's ear. William Vans Murray's letters from abroad pointed out that war with France was not inevitable. The president wrote to Pickering, asking that he obtain the cabinet's advice for his second annual message to Congress, to be given in December. Should he ask for a declaration of war against France or make further overtures to France for peaceful negotiations? Rather than a declaration of war, Adams favored a new mission, wich such commissioners as, perhaps, Patrick Henry and William Vans Murray, both of whom would be acceptable to the French.

The Hamilton Federalists were dismayed when they heard of the president's new approach. With Hamilton's assistance, the cabinet started to prepare a bellicose address for Adams. The army contingent, Washington, Hamilton, C. C. Pinckney and others in command positions, met in Trenton to discuss ways and means to sidetrack Adams.

When Adams returned to Philadelphia on November 25, the cabinet members all advised different methods to continue America's anti-French position. Oliver Wolcott, coached by Hamilton, was the most reasonable. He conceded that a declaration of war was "inexpedient and ought not to be recommended," but it would be equally inexpedient to send another American minister to negotiate unless France made the first move by sending an envoy to the United States. The Hamiltonian strategy was to continue the war preparations and avoid another peace effort.

The Adams message, delivered on December 8, was indecisive, too weak to please the Federalist hawks and too strong for the Jeffersonian doves. Harrison Gray Otis, chairman of the House committee on defense, wrote to Hamilton, asking his opinion on policy for extending internal defense measures. He also asked about the proper size and strength of the army, whether the president under the present act could trade with any part of the French dominions that might withdraw from France and whether the president should be authorized to capture any of the French West Indies in retaliation for the depredation to American trade. Hamilton's reply was predictable. "Any reduction of military power would argue to our enemy that we are either very narrow in our resources or that our jealousy of his designs are abated." The act respecting the militia should be renewed. If negotiations between the United States and France were not in progress by August 1 or had failed, Congress should empower the president to declare a state of war with France. Since France might attempt to take the Floridas and Louisiana, the president should be ready to deal with "so dangerous an enterprise" and, "by taking possession of those countries for ourselves," obviate their falling into foreign hands. The United States had to keep "the key of the Western country. I have been long in the habit of considering the acquisition of those countries as essential to the permanency of the union." Also, France's pursuit of a universal empire could be further halted by detaching South America from Spain.[42]

Adams was horrified by Hamilton's grandiose schemes. "This man is stark mad or I am," he said. Such a system would produce "an instantaneous insurrection of the whole nation from Georgia to New Hampshire."[43]

Adams had a direct line to European affairs through his sons, John Quincy, minister to Prussia, Thomas Boylston, his brother's secretary and aide, and their friends, sources that he quietly tapped. On January 15, 1799, John Adams was entertaining a roomful of guests at his weekly Tuesday night reception when his steward appeared with the news that his son, Thomas Boylston, awaited him upstairs. After a joyful reunion, they talked on into the morning about serious matters. William Vans Murray, the United States minister to Holland, had been holding secret meetings with Pichon, a member of the French foreign office, and had come to the conclusion that the French would negotiate because it was in their self-interest. American policy to develop military and naval power had been successful. It was now time to act from the new position of strength and reach a settlement with France. As a result of this information, Adams asked Timothy Pickering to draft a new treaty and sent pro-French Elbridge Gerry's diplomatic correspondence to Congress.

While the president was privately preparing for peace, Hamilton was continuing to raise and develop an army. There was some difficulty about his pay. He wrote to McHenry that he had given up most of his income from his law practice and now was in "perfect uncer-

tainty whether or when I am to derive from the scanty compensations of the office even a partial retribution for so serious a loss. . . .
Were I rich I should be proud to be silent on such a subject. . . . But
. . . dependant as I am for the maintenance of a wife and six children
on my professional exertions, now so seriously abridged—I . . . ask
you to define my situation." The secretary of war replied immediately that Hamilton would be paid from November 1798, when he
first came to Philadelphia.[44]

There was a rumor at this time that France might send Lafayette
to the United States as an ambassador. Hamilton hastened to advise
his friend against accepting the post. "It would be very difficult for
you here to steer a course which would not place you in a party and
remove you from the broad ground which you now occupy in the
hearts of all." Both Hamilton and Robert Liston, the British minister
to the United States, were relieved that Lafayette did not come.

Hamilton's health suffered from the pressures of overwork. He
complained of a cold that confined him to his bed off and on, and
which left him feeling debilitated for months. His poor health troubled him a great deal; his correspondence at this time mentioned it
often and it was given as an explanation for delaying answers to
requests by McHenry, Pickering and even Washington.

The West Indies, an area of particular interest to Hamilton, was
the center of an undeclared naval war between the United States and
France. French privateers attacked American merchant vessels that
plied their trade in the Caribbean. By 1798, losses in American shipping had become so great that insurance costs for a voyage from an
American coastal port to Jamaica cost almost half the value of the
ship and its cargo.[45]

Saint Domingue, which had produced more sugar than all the
British West Indies before the slave revolt in 1793 drove the French
planters from the island, became an important issue during the quasi-
war. Toussaint L'Ouverture, a black former slave who had led the rebellion, ruled most of the island. By the end of August 1798, the British
had signed a secret agreement with Toussaint to evacuate the island
in return for the black leader's promise not to support a revolt in
Jamaica and to open his ports to the British. The French retained
the fiction that Toussaint was a general in command and that Saint
Domingue was still a French colony.

The United States position on Saint Domingue was complicated by
conflicting interests. The southerners feared that its freedom from
France and recognition by the United States might inspire the Amer-

ican slaves to revolt. The Federalists, on the other hand, favored taking the French West Indies and holding them until France paid for her spoliation of American shipping.

Hamilton advised Pickering in February 1799 that the United States should not be committed to Saint Domingue's independence. "No guarantee no formal treaty—nothing that can rise up in Judgment." Let Toussaint be assured "verbally but not explicitly" that if he declared independence, there would be commercial intercourse as long as he protected our vessels and property.[46]

Hamilton's boyhood friend, Dr. Edward Stevens, was appointed consul general of the United States to Saint Domingue on February 20, 1799. Pickering asked Hamilton to frame his instructions. Hamilton, still complaining about illness, jotted down a few ideas: No regular system of liberty would suit the island yet; the best form of government would be military, with a feudal system. He proposed a strong single executive who would hold his place for life.

Hamilton and his Ultra-Federalists, as Adams called them, were profoundly disturbed by the president's secret move to solve the French crisis by sending William Vans Murray to France as minister plenipotentiary. Theodore Sedgwick was against it even if Murray were "the ablest negotiator in Christendom," but, he told Hamilton, Murray was "feeble and guarded, credulous & unimpressive." Madison was given the astounding news by Jefferson, who commented that the appointment had been kept secret from the congressional Federalists, "as appeared by their dismay." They were divided between those who opposed it and those who did not know what to do.[47]

Hamilton observed that the president's step would "astonish, if any thing from that quarter could astonish." Murray was not strong enough for "so immensely important a mission," he advised Sedgwick.

The Senate committee to consider Murray's nomination, headed by Sedgwick, decided to consult with Adams, although it was against the principle of separation of powers. They planned to urge him to select a commission instead of an individual negotiator. The action had to be taken since they were dealing with "the wild & irregular starts of a vain jealous and half frantic mind" and Adams's "total ignorance of human nature."[48]

Adams, after his meeting with the congressional committee, still insisted that the Senate approve or reject his nomination. If rejected, he might name other commissioners. His action was "wholly *his own act*," Pickering wrote to Hamilton. By the end of February, Adams

capitulated and presented the Senate with the names of three commissioners—Oliver Ellsworth, Patrick Henry and Murray—with the
stipulation that the two America-based nominees not embark for Europe until France sent formal assurance to the United States that
the commissioners would have a proper reception. The Senate approved the nominations on February 27, less than a week before
adjournment.

Patrick Henry, pleading age and debility, refused the appointment. Adams replaced him with Gov. William R. Davie of South
Carolina, a Federalist. Since the Senate was no longer in session, the
appointment was not approved until December 1799.

Adams's motivation for appointing Murray surreptitiously, in defiance of the powerful Ultra-Federalist bloc of his own party, is puzzling. The election of 1800 was near enough for the president to
weigh the effect of his action on his chances for a second term.
Adams liked recognition and believed he had earned it after his
many years of dedicated public service. However, he preferred to
follow his own principles, no matter what the cost. Convinced that
war with France was wrong, he took the necessary steps to avoid
it.

Although he stayed in New York, the spring of 1799 was filled with
war duties for Hamilton, who made the decisions for McHenry as
well as solving his own problems. Hamilton's observations on the
nature of the military man were often incisive. "Nothing is more
necessary than to stimulate the vanity of soldiers." To this end, smart
dress was essential. "Otherwise the soldier is exposed to ridicule and
humiliation. If the articles promised to him are defective in quality
or appearance, he becomes dissatisfied," a bar to discipline. The government was no longer as poor as it was during the Revolutionary
War, so the military could be properly taken care of. McHenry replied with respect and humor. Cockades and loops had always been
furnished to the soldiers under the direction of his office. "If you are
of the opinion that the public ought to . . . furnish loops, cockades,
and materials to cock the hats, I shall take measures accordingly."[49]

Hamilton took a severe stand in the court-martial of Sgt. Richard
Hunt, charged with desertion. On Hamilton's orders he was brought
before a court-martial and tried in New York City on April 16, 1799.
He was found guilty and sentenced to death. Since desertion was a
problem at the time, Hamilton felt that an example had to be made.
If this culprit escaped, Hamilton warned McHenry, "it will have a
most malignant aspect towards the Service." The president had to be
impressed with the realization that "Severity is indispensable."[50]

Opposition to the war program took various forms. The direct tax on land and houses, levied to pay the costs of the armed forces, was hated fervently by the Pennsylvania German farmers in Bucks, Northampton and Montgomery counties. John Fries, a fifty-year-old auctioneer and a veteran of the Whiskey Rebellion, organized a small force of about fifty armed riders who harassed the assessors.

The day after eighteen activists were arrested and jailed in Bethlehem, Pennsylvania, about 140 armed men, with Fries at their head, rode up to the jail. Intimidated, the federal marshall released the captives.[51]

The president issued a proclamation, declaring the existence of an insurrection, and invoked a recent law that empowered him to call out the volunteers. Hamilton acted at once, deploying troops to the Pennsylvania counties. He wrote privately to McHenry the day he sent out the troops: "Beware, my dear Sir, of magnifying a riot into an insurrection, by employing in the first instance an inadequate force. 'Tis better far to err on the other side. Whenever the Government appears in arms it ought to appear like *Hercules*, and inspire respect by the display of strength."[52] The rebellion was almost instantaneously quashed, and Fries and the other leaders arrested.

Hamilton kept troops stationed on "the insurgent scene" in impressive numbers. The Fries affair strengthened Republican uneasiness that the army was becoming a tool of the Federalists and a threat to freedom for the opposition. John Randolph, in a speech delivered on the floor of the House of Representatives, termed the army "a handfull of ragamuffins," for which statement he was attacked by two marine officers while attending a play on the same evening as the speech.[53]

Despite Republican opposition, the business of developing the army burdened Hamilton, although he was beginning to realize that the threat of a French invasion was receding and with it his hopes for an American empire to be wrested from France and Spain. Hamilton's interest in James Wilkinson was tied to this ambition. He knew that there were rumors about Wilkinson's ties with Spain; he also knew that the general was very powerful in the Natchez area and all through the West. Wilkinson's promotion would conciliate the inhabitants and "render them auxiliary in case of need to our military operations," Hamilton told Adams. In communicating with Wilkinson, Hamilton had been direct about the southwestern country. He called it "a treasure worth cherishing."[54]

No effort on the part of his dissenting cabinet could persuade Adams to give up his peace mission to France. Hamilton met with him several times to dissuade him but was unsuccessful. In 1809, Adams wrote an account of one such meeting. "I received him with great civility, as I always had done from my first knowledge of him." Hamilton, the president reported, talked about European politics, emphasizing that Pitt was determined to restore the French monarchy and that the British nation was united behind him. Adams's answers did not stop Hamilton. He repeated his arguments "with such agitation and violent action, that I really pitied him, instead of being displeased." However the president thought him entirely wrong.[55]

Abigail Adams, in a letter to her sister, Mary Cranch, described the meeting in much the same vein. "Genll Hamilton made no secret of his opinion," Mrs. Adams wrote. He told the president that "the Stateholder would be reinstated before Christmas and Louis 18th upon the Throne of France."[56]

Hamilton found the internal situation of the United States very threatening in the fall of 1799. The Kentucky and Virginia Resolutions, written to protest the Alien and Sedition Acts by Jefferson and Madison respectively, were nothing other than "an attempt to change the Government" by uniting the state legislatures in direct resistance to certain laws of the Union, Hamilton said.

To extend the influence and promote the popularity of the government, he proposed the extension of the judiciary; improvement of roads and turnpikes; a society with funds for the advancement of new inventions, discoveries and agriculture and the arts. A million dollars could easily be raised by increasing rates on some indirect taxes. Among other innovations were the increase of the navy, the establishment of a military academy, the opening of canals and promotion of inland navigation to aid military transportation, commerce and agriculture.

To lessen state power, Hamilton suggested an amendment that would provide a way of subdividing large states. "Great States will always feel a rivalship with the common head" and would try and perhaps succeed in machinating against it. It would probably be "inexpedient & even dangerous to propose at this time an amendment of this kind." Laws were needed to restrain and punish incendiary and seditious practices. The federal courts should protect the reputations of officers of the general government. Renegade aliens who conducted incendiary presses in the United States should be sent away. Hamilton was referring to such foreign-born Republican pressmen as Callender, John D. Buck and Thomas Cooper.[57]

During this period of the quasi-war, George Washington placed complete confidence in his second in command. "I wish you at all times, and upon all occasions, to communicate interesting occurrences with your opinion thereon . . . with the utmost unreservedness, to me," Washington wrote to Hamilton from Mount Vernon in February 1799. The two men were closely linked in everyone's mind. In May, the Society of the Cincinnati, at the sixth triennial general meeting, elected Gen. George Washington president general and Gen. Alexander Hamilton vice-president general.

A project very close to the hearts of Washington and Hamilton was the founding of a military academy. Washington had first broached the subject to Hamilton in May 1783, when he recommended academies for instruction in the military arts, particularly engineering and artillery. Ten years later, Washington again proposed an academy for teaching gunnery and engineering, and, in 1796, Hamilton included the need for an academy in his draft of Washington's eighth annual address to Congress, which the president then incorporated into his congressional speech in December 1796. Nothing concrete developed from this suggestion.

In November 1799, Hamilton wrote to McHenry that he had always thought a military academy "of primary importance." He supplied a detailed blueprint encompassing five schools: a fundamental school; a school of engineers and artillery; a school of cavalry; a school of infantry; and a school of the navy.

"The site of the Academy ought to be on navigable water" for naval exercises, and it should be near "founderies of Cannon and manufactures of small arms," Hamilton wrote. McHenry submitted the Hamilton plan almost verbatim in his report to the president on a military academy in January 1800. A copy of Hamilton's letter to McHenry went to Washington. Hamilton apologized that his other duties had kept him from completing the task until very lately. "Any alterations in the plan which you may do me the honor to suggest will receive the most careful attention," he told the commander in chief.[58]

Washington answered that he had always considered a military academy of primary importance to the country and had recommended one at every opportunity when president. "But I never undertook to go into a *detail* of the organization of such an Academy," leaving the task to experts in science. For the same reason, he would not make any observations on Hamilton's plan. "I sincerely hope that the subject will meet with due attention and that the reasons for its establishment, which you have so clearly pointed out in your letter to the Secretary, will prevail upon the Legislature to place it upon a permanent and respectable footing."[59]

This was Washington's last letter to Hamilton. On the morning of the day he wrote it, Washington went out to inspect his farms. Though snow, hail and a freezing rain pelted him, he stayed out until three o'clock in the afternoon. The next day, he admitted to a sore throat but refused to listen to Tobias Lear, his secretary, who wanted him to stay home. In the afternoon, the sky having cleared, Washington walked around his lawn, pointing out trees he wanted cut down. His voice was hoarse and became more so as time went on. In the evening, Washington, his wife and Lear sat together in the parlor, reading newspapers. In a hoarse voice, Washington read some amusing bits out loud until Martha went to bed. Then, at Washington's request, Lear read aloud excerpts from debates in the Virginia assembly. The ex-president became very agitated when he heard that Madison supported Monroe for the Senate. He calmed himself and decided to retire, refusing Lear's suggestion that he take some medicine for his cold.

At about three o'clock in the morning, Washington awakened his wife, saying that he was very ill. His breathing was labored, and Martha wanted to send for help, but Washington refused. By morning, Washington was so much worse that the doctors were sent for. The medical team, consisting of Drs. James Craik, Elisha Dick and Gustavus Brown, applied all the customary measures. Bleeding, blistering and purging no doubt further weakened the patient, who was diagnosed as suffering from acute tonsillitis, called quinsy. The youngest physician in attendance, Dr. Dick, suggested a tracheotomy to enable Washington to breathe, but he was overruled.

As the day progressed, the patient's suffering increased. His throat closed, and breathing was labored. Moving from his bed to a seat by the fire did not relieve him. He had to be helped back to bed. The agony persisted, and the doctors could do nothing. Washington bore the pain of the illness and the treatment with a hero's composure. Toward the end he said to Dr. Craik, "I die hard but I am not afraid to go." Between ten and eleven o'clock on December 14, he died. The cause of death was probably either a streptococcal infection or diphtheria. Neither was curable at the time.

Hamilton was in Philadelphia standing with Theodore Sedgwick when Washington's death was announced. Overcome with emotion, he burst into tears, exclaiming, "America has lost her Saviour—I a father."[60]

Hamilton's natural father had died in the West Indies just six months earlier. Every effort by Hamilton to persuade him to come to America had been met with a distant coldness. He was willing to accept his son's money, wrote occasionally in answer to Alexander's letters but preferred to keep his distance. His last letter to his son, written in 1793, pleaded ill health and the dangers of travel during the war. After the end of hostilities he would take the first vessel bound for Philadelphia. The letter lacked conviction. The disreputable failure who had deserted his son either preferred not to face his guilt or was genuinely indifferent.

Hamilton's grief at Washington's death has been criticized as excessive by some historians, which betrays a failure to appreciate the importance of their friendship of over twenty years. "Perhaps no friend of his [Washington's] has more cause to lament, on personal account, than my self," Hamilton wrote to Charles C. Pinckney. "The public misfortune is one which all the friends of our Government will view in the same light. I will not dwell on the subject. My Imagination is gloomy, my heart sad."[61]

In a condolence note to Martha Washington, written four months after her husband's death, Hamilton again claimed that his was a special loss because of "the numerous and distinguished marks of friendship" he had received. "I cannot say in how many ways the continuance of that confidence and friendship was necessary to me in future relations."[62] That was the rub. With Washington gone, Hamilton's prop was removed. Hamilton had relied on Washington to back him up with his great influence and prestige. Hamilton's was the keener intellect, but Washington's was the greater presence.

With Washington gone, what would happen to the inspector general and to the new army? Hamilton was the nominal head of the army, but it seemed to him most unlikely that Adams would appoint him commander in chief.

The army was only one small part of the nation's problems. In a letter to Rufus King written in January 1800, Hamilton pinpointed its enemies. Adams was perverse and capricious. The Virginia Republicans, Madison and Jefferson among them, were developing a dangerous combination with Aaron Burr's New York Republicans. "The irreparable loss of an inestimable man removes a control which was felt and was very salutary," was Hamilton's epitaph on George Washington and his two decades of leadership.

Hamilton v. Jefferson

W<small>HEN THE GREAT PARTNERSHIP</small> of Washington and Hamilton was dissolved so unexpectedly, Hamilton was forced to carry on alone. His position was not clear, although McHenry assumed that the command of the army devolved now on General Hamilton. In his letter to Hamilton deploring Washington's death, General Wilkinson said that it had to be a consolation to all "to find the chief command in Hands so able to administer the functions of the Station."[1]

Once the first shock and grief were over, Hamilton reflected on how much the great man's death would alter his own destiny. Tobias Lear's letter announcing Washington's death had missed him between New York and Philadelphia, so it was not until January 2, 1800, that he answered it. "I have been much indebted to the kindness of the General and he was an Aegis very essential to me," he wrote to Washington's private secretary.[2] Washington had been his patron; he had chosen him to be secretary of the treasury and later major general. He had been Hamilton's protection from the attacks of the Republicans and from the dislike of John Adams. Without him, Hamilton was likely to become the victim of all his enemies.

There was a practical consideration that worried Hamilton. He and Washington had exchanged a multitude of private letters over the years. "In whose hands are his papers gone?" Hamilton asked Lear. "Our very confidential situation will not permit this to be a point of indifference to me." Lear, who had never liked Hamilton and had resented his close relationship with Washington, answered with some hostility. "No one living beside yourself knows as well as I do, the loss which *you* have sustained by the General's death." Commenting on Hamilton's use of the word "aegis," Lear said, "I know at the same time, that no one, under these circumstances, could find a greater resource in himself than you can."[3]

On his deathbed, Washington had asked his private secretary to arrange his papers, Lear told Hamilton. His confidential communications with the general "have never passed under the eye of any person but him and myself." They were kept separate from the mass of papers, and when they will be delivered to Judge Bushrod Washington, "I . . . shall tell him how sacred their contents are and have no doubt but in his hands they will be a sacred deposit."[4]

As for Hamilton's private life, his family concerns were primary in his thoughts. Angelica Church, who returned to the United States with her husband and children in May 1797, lived near the Hamiltons in New York City, and the two families were very close. When Hamilton wrote to Angelica, his letters were not only affectionate but had a sparkle reserved only for her. From Albany, where he was staying with the Schuylers, Hamilton sent his "Dr sister" a particularly charming note. Her father's reception of him was more than usually cordial, he wrote, and its "pleasure was heightened" by dining

in the presence of a lady for whom I have a particular friendship. I was placed directly in front of her and was much occupied with her during the whole dinner. She did not appear to her usual advantage, and yet she was very interesting. The eloquence of silence is not a common attribute of hers. . . . Though I am fond of hearing her speak, her silence was so well placed that I did not attempt to make her break it. You will conjecture that I must have been myself dumb with admiration. Perhaps so, and yet this was not the reason for my forbearing to invite a conversation with her.

The letter referred to a portrait of Angelica Church and her son Philip, painted in London by John Trumbull in 1784, which hung in the Schuyler dining room.[5]

The friendship between Angelica Church and her brother-in-law was noted, mostly with disapproval, by Hamilton's colleagues. Robert Troup was particularly sour about the elegant hostess at whose balls he observed his friend's behavior. "Though not yet in the field of Mars he maintains an unequalled reputation for *gallantry*—such at least is the opinion entertained of him by the ladies. When I have more leisure, I will give you the history of the Ghost of Baron [Ciominie?] & Mrs. Church as published by our Gallant General," he told Rufus King.[6]

Harrison Gray Otis told an anecdote about Hamilton and Angelica often repeated through the years. The episode took place at Breck's, where Otis dined with Hamilton; Christopher G. Champlin, a con-

gressman from Rhode Island, and his wife; Angelica Church, Miss
Schuyler; and others. Mrs. Church, said Otis, was "the mirror of
affectation, but as she affects to be extremely affable and free from
ceremony, this foible is rather amusing than offensive." Miss Schuyler (a younger sister) was characterized as "a young wild flirt from
Albany, full of glee & apparently desirious of matrimony." After dinner, Angelica dropped her shoe bow, which was picked up by Miss
Schuyler. She put it in Hamilton's buttonhole saying, "There brother
I have made you a Knight." Angelica asked, "But of what order he
can't be a Knight of the garter in this country." Miss Schuyler replied: "True sister but *he would be if you would let him.*"[7]

At that same dinner party, Champlin complained to Otis that
Hamilton was casting "some liquorish looks at his *cara sposa*" and
commented that the former secretary "appears to him very trifling in
his conversation with ladies."[8]

Except for his letters to John Laurens when they were both young
men, only Angelica Church received light-hearted, witty letters from
Hamilton, with a sincerity about them lacking in the heavy-handed,
dutiful expressions of love to the "wife of my bosom." He wrote to
Mrs. Church: "I am more and more the fool of affection and friendship. In a little time I shall not be able to stir from the sides of my
family & friends. . . . Adieu Dr. sister."[9]

By 1800, Hamilton was the father of seven children. The youngest,
a second daughter, Elizabeth, was born on November 20, 1799. The
few letters that have survived between Hamilton and his eldest son
Philip reveal a loving, sympathetic relationship. He was the firstborn
and the best loved. His portrait, painted at age twenty, depicts a
handsome young man who resembled his father, with lively eyes and
an intelligent face. Philip Hamilton followed in his father's footsteps,
attending Columbia College, from which he graduated with high
honors in 1800, and then going on to study law.

In a letter written to his father early in his career at Columbia,
Philip reported on a speech that he had delivered to Dr. William S.
Johnson, president of the college. "He has no objection to my speak-
ing," Philip said, "but he has blotted out that sentence which appears
to be the best and most animated in it; which is, you may recollect:
'*Americans you have fought the battles of mankind; you have en-
kindled that same fire of freedom which is now,*' &c." Obviously,
Hamilton had been consulted about the speech.[10]

A set of rules that Hamilton composed for Philip's guidance after
he graduated from Columbia provides insight into the father's val-

ues. Philip was to rise no later than six o'clock from April to October; the rest of the year he could sleep an hour longer. If he should rise earlier, "he will deserve commendation." Throughout the year, he should go to bed by ten. From the time he was dressed in the morning until nine, excluding breakfasttime, he should read law. From nine to dinnertime, he should go to the office, where he should write and read law. After dinner, he should read law until five o'clock. For two hours, until seven, he could do whatever he pleased. From noon on Saturday, he could study whatever he pleased. On Sunday morning, he had to attend church and spend the rest of the day "in innocent recreations. He must not depart from any of these rules without my permission," Hamilton said.

Eighteen hundred was an election year and critical for the two young American parties. The Republicans had decided that it was time for them to take power because the Federalist party was divided. The Adamites were loyal to the difficult, sometimes erratic incumbent, but the Hamiltonians were disgusted with him and his independence of the wishes of the faction, and especially its leader.

President Adams's bold stroke in sending a commission, headed by William Vans Murray, to deal with France displeased the high Federalists, who regarded it as a bid by Adams for personal glory. The party, in fact, had lost an effective issue. Had the danger of war been a real one at election time, the Federalists could have played on patriotism and turned the country against the Francophile Republicans. But the seeming French willingness to negotiate made the expensive temporary army appear unnecessary, the Alien and Sedition laws menacing. There were rumors that Hamilton's army existed to oppose the people when the public observed the prosecution of Republican editors.

Hamilton's hope for military fame faded in early 1800. Instead of fighting glorious battles, his job was to oversee the dissolution of the temporary army. Even for this purpose, Adams withheld from Hamilton an appointment to replace Washington as commander in chief. There were rumors that Gen. Henry Lee would be given the post. Lee, a Virginia Federalist, was dismayed. "You may have seen in some opposition papers paragraphs placing me as yr. rival. I must assure you (tho I know it is not necessary) that such insinuations are entirely groundless," he wrote to Hamilton on February 20, 1800. Hamilton replied that "these miscreants" could not impair the friendship and confidence he felt for Lee. However, he added, "I am not insensible of the Injustice which I from time to time experience. . . .

Perhaps my sensibility is the effect of an exaggerated Estimate of my service to the U. States. . . . In no event however will any displeasure I may feel be at war with the public Interest. This in my eyes is sacred."[11]

At the end of February, Hamilton sent out feelers to Theodore Sedgwick about when Congress would adjourn and what, if anything, the Congressional Federalists would do about the election. Would his presence in Philadelphia be required? "Unless for indispensable reasons I had rather not come." Hamilton was inundated with work, and ill health was chronic.

The mantle of political intrigue was settling firmly on the shoulders of Aaron Burr during the spring of 1800. "Mr. Hamilton will have at this election a most powerful opponent in Colonel Burr," Matthew Davis wrote to Albert Gallatin late in March. Burr was organizing all the Republican interests, displaying a skill at management that was "most astonishing." He was "more dreaded by his enemies than any other character."[12]

New York would be the pivotal state in the coming election. Her twelve votes had gone to Adams in 1796, but during the past four years changing sentiment had made the outcome impossible to guess. As alarmed Federalists were informing Hamilton, Burr meant to turn the tide for Jefferson and himself.

In order to win, the Republicans had to gain seats in both legislative houses in Albany, and Burr planned to achieve this by getting New York City votes. His first coup was to force the Federalists to reveal their candidates for the city election before he announced his ticket, which had been chosen already. It was a strong one that included important personalities and war heroes who together would unify the Republican party.

Hamilton, on the other hand, had serious problems with his list. The first requirement was loyalty to Hamilton, which was difficult for many potential candidates because it had leaked out that he was supporting Gen. Charles C. Pinckney for the presidency, not the incumbent.

Although he was in New York on April 15, Hamilton did not attend the small Federalist meeting that gathered to choose the ticket. After much internal dissension, the Federalists decided on Jacob Morton for Congress. The list of assemblymen was remarkable only for the absence of distinguished names. The Republican list, which Burr now released, offered Dr. Samuel L. Mitchill for Congress and such other luminaries as former governor George Clinton, Gen. Horatio Gates and Brockholst Livingston. At first, the three outstanding Republican candidates refused to run, but Burr persuaded them. However, Clinton told his friends that his name was being used "without his authority or permission" and refused to campaign actively, lest it be construed that he supported Jefferson. Clinton made clear that his interest in the campaign was wholly for Burr.[13]

During the period before the election, Burr was tireless. He enlisted the aid of the members of Tammany Hall, who divided the city into districts. Ward meetings were held to study reports on voters in each district and to plan strategy. A finance committee assessed contributions, particularly from the wealthy. The new Republican bank, The Manhattan Company, which Burr had conjured into existence under the pretense that it would bring fresh water into New York City, promised needed funds and, perhaps, helped to purchase land to add to the number of qualified voters. Burr even opened his home to campaign workers, who camped out on mattresses and worked long hours.[14]

On Election Day, Burr visited all the polling places when they opened and met Hamilton on horseback at some of them. When the polls closed on the evening of May 1, both parties waited eagerly for the results. The next night, Hamilton's greatest fears were realized. The Republicans had made a clean sweep, although the margin of victory was less than 500 votes. Dr. Mitchill and all the Republicans won, and Aaron Burr, who had run from Orange County, considered safe for a Republican, had been elected, too. "The Victory is complete," Burr wrote to Jefferson, and the manner of it highly profitable."[15]

In a terse note to Theodore Sedgwick shortly after the debacle, Hamilton predicted correctly that the presidential electors from New York would be Antifederalists all. The urgency of the situation required that Adams and Pinckney be supported equally, Hamilton insisted. " 'Tis the only thing that can possibly save us from the fangs of *Jefferson*."

Convinced that the end justified the means, Hamilton suggested a questionable move to Gov. John Jay. He proposed that the state legislature be called together to choose electors by the people in districts, which would ensure "a Majority of Votes in the U. States for Foederal Candidates." To justify his proposal, Hamilton said "that scruples of delicacy and propriety . . . ought to yield to the extraordinary nature of crisis." This was a *"legal* and *constitutional* act," necessary to prevent an *Atheist* in religion and a *Fanatic* in politics from getting possession of the helm of the State."

At the time he received Hamilton's disturbing suggestion, Jay read of a letter in a Philadelphia newspaper, reporting that, at a party meeting in New York, it had been suggested that the governor immediately call the old Federalist-dominated legislature together to give him power to choose the electors for president and vice-president. Upset by this, Jay filed the Hamilton letter with a note: "Proposing a measure for party purposes wh. I think it wd. not become me to adopt."[16] Hamilton's extremism would lose him some of his oldest supporters.

In 1800, each state decided for itself when it would hold its election. New York selected her twelve electors, all Republican, in May, but in a number of states the elections took place so late that on December 20 the results were still not known in Kentucky, Georgia and Tennessee.

With this in mind, Hamilton had many months to influence the election for Pinckney. He wrote letters, spoke to friends and acquaintances, and made an extended swing through New England. As time went on, Hamilton's dislike for Adams grew, and his determination to stop him because unrestrained by his usual good sense. His power at the seat of government was ebbing away. Just two days after a congressional caucus of Federalists chose an Adams-Pinckney ticket, Secretary of War James McHenry resigned. A week later, the secretary of state handed in his resignation. Adams had demanded both of them.

McHenry informed Hamilton that he would stay on until the first of June. On the heels of that disaster, news reached Hamilton that Pickering had been dismissed after refusing the opportunity to hand in his resignation. Adams had written that he required a change in the Department of State for diverse reasons. "You are hereby discharged from any further service as Secretary of State."[17]

Sedgwick commiserated with Hamilton. "Every tormenting passion rankles in the bosom of that weak & frantic old man," he wrote to Hamilton, "but I have good reason for believing that Pickering and McHenry have been sacrificed as peace offerings." He referred to a conviction held by many anti-Adamites that the president had made a bargain with Jefferson. The arrangement, according to rumor, was that Adams would make certain changes in the cabinet, and, in return, Jefferson would delay his presidential bid until 1804. For the most part, it was denied. The Federalist *New Jersey Gazette* of Trenton did carry an article called *Correct Information* on June 2, 1800, saying that "many federalists are positively secured from removal, and many others selected for promotion—Mr. Hamilton will be secretary of State if he chooses."[18]

Hamilton was against a second term for Adams under any circumstances. He congratulated McHenry on his release "from the fetter" of the Adams administration. "But my friend we are not to be discouraged. A new and more dangerous Aera has commenced. . . . Property, Liberty and even life are at stake. The friends of good principles, must be more closely linked."[19]

McHenry disclosed the details of the cabinet purge, which had its genesis in the disagreement over the mission to France. He, Wolcott and Pickering had opposed it, while Stoddert and Lee had sided with the president. Adams had become obsessed with his reelection; the acts of his administration were "to be made subservient to electioneering purposes." Increasingly, he distrusted those near him who did not feed his hopes. "At times he would speak in such a manner of certain men and things, as to persuade one that he was actually insane," McHenry wrote.[20]

On April 5, after the congressional caucus decided that Adams and Pinckney would run for president without giving preference to either, Adams asked to see McHenry. He accused his secretary of war of having biased General Washington to place Hamilton before Knox in the list of major generals and of praising Hamilton in his report to Congress. He then ordered McHenry to resign, which he did the next morning.

About two months later, McHenry sent Adams a memorandum of his recollection of the conversation preceding the resignation. Hamilton figured prominently in the dialogue. The president said, " . . . (with great warmth) Hamilton has been opposing me in New York. He has caused the loss of the election." In a lengthy tirade, Adams called Hamilton "an intriguant—the greatest intriguant in the World —a man devoid of every moral principle—a Bastard, and as much a foreigner as Gallatin. Mr. Jefferson is an infinitely better man; a wiser one, I am sure, and if President will act wisely. . . . I . . . would rather be Vice President under him, or even Minister Resident at the Hague, than indebted to such a being as Hamilton for the Presidency. . . . You are subservient to Hamilton who ruled Washington, and would still rule if he could."[21]

McHenry asked Hamilton to keep the contents of his memo secret. Hamilton, angered by some of the personal comments, asked "Dear Mac" to reconsider. "Such a paper Shewn confidentially would be very important," he pleaded. "The man [Adams] is more mad than I ever thought him and I shall soon be led to say as wicked as he is mad," Hamilton stated.[22]

Pickering's resignation was even more precipitous. Adams asked him on a Saturday to resign and to name the day by Monday morning. Pickering answered that important matters would make his services useful until the close of the present quarter and he did not feel it his duty to resign. In an hour, a peremptory discharge was received; by Monday evening, Pickering left the office. The only Hamiltonian left in the administration was Oliver Wolcott, who, Pickering said, was being retained because the president was afraid to upset the affairs of the Treasury Department.

Hamilton had already made up his mind that he would never support Adams, "even if though the consequence should be the election of *Jefferson*. If we must have an *enemy* at the head of the Government, let it be one whom we can oppose and for whom we are not responsible, who will not involve our party in the disgrace of his foolish and bad measures." The Philadelphia *Aurora* said that there were three parties in the Senate now: the Republicans, the Federalists and the Pickeronians. The last "consists of those who have leagued with *Hamilton*."[23]

From June 7 to June 30, Hamilton made a swing through four New England states, Massachusetts, New Hampshire, Connecticut and Rhode Island, allegedly to review the brigade stationed at Oxford, Massachusetts, and to disband them. It was to be a farewell to the men and to his army career. It also enabled him to support Pinckney's candidacy against the president. As Adams told his son, Thomas Boylston, General Hamilton's New England tour was "to choose electors who will give a unanimous vote for Gen. Pinckney. ... My information is from Gentlemen of the best & first character in more than one state." President and Mrs. Adams both believed that the Essex Junto, a right-wing Federalist group mostly from Essex County in eastern Massachusetts, was opposed to an Adams presidency. Although Adams blamed the group for actively thwarting him in 1796 and again in 1800, he was wrong.

Actually, the members of the so-called Essex Junto, insofar as they were active at all in 1796, were active in Adams's behalf. The aim was to prevent "the election of a French President," not to prevent the election of John Adams. Adams, who had recently returned from ten years in Europe and did not understand contemporary Massachusetts politics, practiced guilt by association. Since the Hamiltonians were against him, he assumed that the Essexmen, some of whom were close to Hamilton and supporters of his economic system, had to be against his presidency. Adams also held it against Cabot for urging him to give first place in the battle of the generals to Hamilton, not Knox, seeing this as a conspiracy to destroy him. The Essexmen, he raged, had "crammed Hamilton down my throat."[24]

The term "Essex Junto" may have been original with Adams, whose excesses of violent anger disturbed his fellow Federalists while they amused his enemies. He seemed haunted by the idea of an Essex Junto plot. The Junto, he raged, working closely with Alexander Hamilton, was planning to destroy the Adams family.

Despite John Adams's allegations, the members of the so-called Essex Junto involved in the election of 1800 were actively supporting the president, except for Pickering, who belonged to the group headed by Hamilton committed to the election of Pinckney.

On June 7, Hamilton left New York for Oxford by way of Stratford, Connecticut, and New Haven. When he reached Oxford, he stayed there for three days of military pomp and nostalgia. He reviewed the brigade and gave a public dinner for the brigade officers and some members of the permanent army. At an appropriate moment, Hamilton proposed a toast to the memory of Washington. There was not a dry eye in the assembly.

At seven in the morning, the brigade formed into a hollow square. Hamilton delivered a farewell address to the troops, emulating his "aegis," George Washington. A Boston newspaper called the speech "an affectionate acknowledgement of the patriotism and spirit" of the officers and men who took the field at the first signal of danger. After their retirement to private life, Hamilton predicted, this spirit would stay alive, and if their country called them again, they would be ready to "make new sacrifices to its defence."[25]

His military duties accomplished, Hamilton left for Boston. On Thursday evening, a banquet was given in his honor at Concert Hall to pay him high respect for his service, talents and patriotism. A Boston paper reported that the company was "the most respectable ever assembled in this town on a similar occasion." The toast to General Hamilton said: "So long as our Constitution shall last, or public credit be supported, may we respect the supporter of the one and the founder of the other."[26]

The next day, Hamilton left Boston for Portsmouth, New Hampshire. Hamilton's Boston-Portsmouth trip was much publicized because of contradictory reports of his reception in Newburyport and Portsmouth. An Adams Federalist from Newburyport wrote that when General Hamilton stopped there overnight, he had no attention paid to him, public or private. The same treatment was given him in Portsmouth. The Hamilton faction of the Federalist party called this report "one of the most contemptible purilities ever brooded in the brain pan of Jacobinism." On the contrary, "A Portsmouth Federalist" said, Hamilton was welcomed everywhere with respect and cordial friendship.

Back in Boston on June 23, he set out for Dedham the next day. Dr. Nathaniel Ames, brother of Fisher Ames, wrote in his diary, "A. Hamilton, the high Adulr. run after a tiptoe thro' Dedham." This colorful entry was contradicted by Fisher Ames's report to Rufus King that Hamilton had spoken in most companies while in Dedham "without reserve. You know he is the most frank of men." By June 26, Hamilton was in Newport. He discussed the coming election with Gov. Arthur Fenner.

Governor Fenner was surprised at Hamilton's bold approach during his Newport visit. "He was an entire stranger," Fenner wrote. Hamilton had begun immediately to discuss the election, saying that all New England would vote for Adams and Pinckney, but in the South a number would vote for Jefferson and Pinckney, so that Pinckney would win.

Being strongly anti-British, Fenner gave no encouragement. Fenner liked Adams better now than before because of his policies and would, under no circumstances, support Pinckney. If he were an elector, the governor said, he would give all the votes to Jefferson in preference to Pinckney, "for the British yoke I abhorred." If Hamilton had been disturbed by Fenner's words, he remained "very sanguine."[27]

Hamilton maintained his equanimity, but he was not deceived. All New York electors would be for Jefferson and Burr, the four eastern states would be federal, but Rhode Island was in question. Governor Fenner would go as far as he could to promote Jefferson, he told Charles Carroll of Carrollton. Under the circumstances, said Hamilton, it would be best for the middle states not to support Adams, "seeing his success desperate," and adhere to Pinckney. Maryland was not too deeply pledged to the support of Mr. Adams. "His administration has already very materially disgraced and sunk the government." There were basic defects in his character which would grow. Dr. Franklin had described Adams as "always honest, *sometimes* great, but *often* mad." Hamilton added, "As to the first trait . . . as far as a man excessively *vain* and *jealous* and ignobly attached to *place* can be."[28]

Unless Pinckney was elected, Hamilton realized that he would be nothing more than a fallen leader and once again an outsider. He had to bring the matter to a head.

"I have serious thoughts of writing to the *President* to tell him that I have heard of his having repeatedly mentioned the existence of a British faction in this Country & alluded to me as one of that faction —requesting that he will inform me of the truth of this information & if true what have been the grounds of the suggestion," Hamilton said to Wolcott. "The inquiry I propose may furnish an antidote and vindicate character. What think you of the idea? For my part I can set Malice at Defiance."[29]

Wolcott, who found it disgusting that the president was being praised for his pursuit of peace with France when the last mission was only "a game of diplomacy" intended "to gain popularity at home," approved of Hamilton's plan to challenge the president.[30] On the first of August, Hamilton sent his letter to the president.

In a direct, almost impertinent style, Hamilton confronted Adams with the accusation that he had, "on different occasions," alluded to the existence of a British faction in the United States that included a number of influential Federalists. "You have sometimes named me," at other times plainly alluded to him as one of them, he said. Adams was requested to reveal his grounds for these assertions.

Two days later, not having received an answer from the president to his "respectful letter," Hamilton gave serious thought to publishing it. He was particularly angry that the Adamsites had accused him of undue influence on the Treasury Department, the press and members of the Adams administration. He resented also the allegation that his opposition to Adams was based on "pique and disappointment."[31]

There was still no response from Adams in mid-August. Hamilton started to collect material for his forthcoming letter of criticism. Some of Hamilton's supporters were worried about this latest project. The contents "might be converted to a new proof that you are a *dangerous man*" and "will give the enemy an advantage to which he has no claim," George Cabot wrote. Two days later, he wrote again, adding, "*I don't think however we can discard Mr Adams as a candidate at this late period without total disarrangement & defeat in this quarter.*" Cabot admitted to the "apparent absurdity" of supporting a man unworthy of trust, but the Massachusetts Federalists agreed to vote for Adams and Pinckney together.[32]

Fisher Ames was even more direct. They would elect Jefferson if they rejected Adams, he asserted. "I am therefore clear that *you* ought not with your name, nor if practicable in any way that will be traced to *you*, to execute your purpose of exposing the reasons for a change of the executive," he wrote.[33]

Hamilton's support of Pinckney had already aroused his enemies to vicious attacks against him. A letter appeared in the Boston *Independent Chronicle and Universal Advertiser* at the end of July that referred to Hamilton's pretensions to the presidency and his vanity and ignorance in thinking that the people of the eastern states would not care about his "descent from a dubious father, in an English island."[34]

Usually reticent about his past, Hamilton now complained to his old friend William Jackson about this most ungenerous persecution and gave him a much censored and carefully gilded account of his origins. He claimed James Hamilton, son of the Laird of Grange, as his father. Because of "too generous and too easy a temper," Hamilton explained, he had failed in business and had been supported by his friends in Scotland and for several years before his death "by me." His faults had been "too much pride and too large a portion of indolence." Otherwise, his character was "without reproach and his manners those of a Gentleman." He described his mother as a victim of her ambitious mother, who had married her handsome young daughter, endowed with "a snug fortune," to a Danish fortune hunter named Lavine. The marriage had been unhappy and had ended in divorce. His mother had gone to St. Kitts, where she had met his father. They had been married, "followed by many years cohabitation and several children." History had turned up only Alexander and his unsuccessful brother. "But unluckily it turned out that the divorce was not absolute but qualified, and thence the second marriage was not lawful." Thus, at his mother's death, her property had gone to his half-brother Lavine, who later died in South Carolina. The explanation was neat and credible. Neither then nor later did this statement or any other explanation satisfy Hamilton or anyone else. His illegitimacy remained a psychological hazard for him.[35]

This letter was never sent to William Jackson. Instead, Hamilton enclosed it in a letter to James McHenry, with a postscript that said, "I have concluded to send the inclosed to you instead of Major Jackson." McHenry was a warm, loyal, affectionate friend. "I sincerely believe that there is not one of your friends who have paid the least attention to the insinuations attempted to be cast upon the legitimacy of your birth, or would care or respect you less were all your enemies say or impute on this head true," he responded.[36]

Hamilton wrote the letter exposing Adams so dreaded by the New England Federalists. It was addressed to Col. Aaron Ogden and would be sent to the newspapers. To a letter from Wolcott trying to persuade Hamilton not to publish under his signature, Hamilton replied, "Anonymous publications can now effect nothing." He sent Wolcott a first draft, which he wished to be sent to individuals in the New England states to promote Pinckney's election and to vindicate Pickering, McHenry, Wolcott and himself. He asked Wolcott to look it over. Wolcott received it and made a few notes. His verdict was that "the Style & temper is excellent." However, he reminded Hamilton, the party was opposed to publication with his signature. "I am of opinion with you, that anonimous publications do no good."[37]

Hamilton's *Letter on the Public Conduct and Character of John Adams* revealed for a second time—the first being the Reynolds pamphlet—that his judgment was faulty when he had to deal with personal abuse. As soon as a clash of personalities occurred, he lost his sense of proportion. Adams had done him an injury, refused to admit it or to acknowledge Hamilton's protest. The unfortunate John Adams letter resulted.

The Adams letter was supposed to be privately printed, with a limited circulation among Federalists. Matthew L. Davis, Burr's general factotum, said that Hamilton planned to circulate the printed copies in South Carolina a few days before the election, so that Pinckney would get more electoral votes than the president, becoming the next president and Adams the vice-president.

"Colonel Burr ascertained the contents of this pamphlet and that it was in the press," Davis wrote. Burr knew that its immediate publication would be a disadvantage to the Federalists, so he arranged to get a copy made as soon as the printing was done. Then he, Davis, John Swartwout and Robert Swartwout met at Burr's house, where they read the pamphlet and made extracts for the press. Davis delivered the extracts to William Duane, editor of the *Aurora*, and Charles Holt, editor of the *Bee*, a New London publication; they were published immediately.[38]

The publication of the letter "rent the federal party in twain," the Burr henchman reported with satisfaction. Hamilton was forced to publish the entire pamphlet in the *Daily Gazette*, with the explanation that "by some unknown means" extracts had reached the public, and therefore the whole would be presented.[39]

There is no contemporary corroboration of the Matthew Davis story that Burr obtained the extracts. Others, including editors, knew that the work was in process. John Lang, editor of the New York *Gazette*, wrote that Hamilton, who had to go to Albany at publication time, had left a letter with a friend, directing that if extracts of the letter appeared in opposition newspapers, then the letter should be placed in publication. That letter was never found.[40]

Hamilton was silent on the subject. The Davis account could very likely be true. William Shaw, Adams's private secretary, reflected the president's sentiment when he wrote to William S. Smith, Adams's son-in-law, that Hamilton's pamphlet had to be made public. "It seems [Hamilton] has treacherous friends as well as others," he wrote with some satisfaction.[41]

"Not denying to Mr. Adams patriotism and integrity, and even talents of a certain kind, I should be deficient in candor, were I to conceal the conviction, that he does not possess the talents adapted to the *Administration* of Government, and that there are great and intrinsic defects in his character, which unfit him for the office of Chief Magistrate," Hamilton wrote in his *Letter*. Adams's career was then reviewed, particularly in the light of the way it appeared to Alexander Hamilton.

The tone of the letter was often sarcastic, always provocative. Its conclusion, Hamilton admitted, was "temporising. But the Foederal Stomach would not bear a stronger dose." The many answers to it in the press, Hamilton told McHenry, might require an answer, reinforced by new facts that McHenry might possess. He also asked Pickering for "new anecdotes" that he could use in another piece. Apparently Hamilton was unmoved by the furor his letter aroused. Once he took action, he never looked back or regretted it.

Robert Troup wrote that Hamilton was only momentarily "confused" when he got the news that Burr had stolen the letter and published extracts from it. When Troup commented to Hamilton that publication would do harm to him personally and the federal cause generally, Hamilton answered that he had "well considered it and had no doubt it would be productive of good."[42]

In Albany, the Federalists lamented that the letter would be injurious, and in New York there was even stronger disapprobation. "Not a man in the whole circle of our friends but condemns it," Troup told Rufus King. General Hamilton's usefulness would be much lessened thereafter.[43]

Hamilton's blatant preference for Pinckney was now known to all, as well as his effort to control the South Carolina vote. There was nothing to do but watch the returns, which came in from the various states at different times. "There seems to be too much probability that Jefferson or Burr will be President," Hamilton wrote as early as August. By the end of the year, the possibility of a tie between the two Republicans was generally recognized. The leading Federalists approached Hamilton with a proposal to support Aaron Burr. Should they send for Burr and try to make an agreement with him? Theodore Sedgwick informed Hamilton that there was a tie in Georgia and that ties were expected in Kentucky and Tennessee. Sedgwick preferred Jefferson, but many of his friends differed with him, for if Burr were chosen, he would have to "throw himself into the hands of the Federal party." On December 18, James Gunn reported accurately that there were seventy-three votes each for Jefferson and Burr. "It is probable that the Federalists will have to choose among the Rotten Apples," he said. Gouverneur Morris also reported to Hamilton that many wanted Burr, although he felt that it was the intention of the citizens to elect Jefferson, and it was proper to do so. Those who pretended to know Burr's views thought he would bargain with the Federalists, Morris observed, "of such *Bargain* I shall know."[44]

Hamilton answered with variations on the same theme. Burr was unreliable, his private circumstances "render disorder a necessary resource. For heaven's sake, let not the Foederal party be responsible for the elevation of this Man." To Morris, Hamilton wrote succinctly. "Jefferson, I suspect, will not dare much. Burr will dare every thing, in the sanguine hope of effecting every thing." Let them get Jefferson's assurances on the important issues, Hamilton suggested— public credit, the navy and neutrality.[45]

Hamilton surprised himself with the fervor of his preference for Jefferson. "If there be a man in the world I ought to hate it is Jefferson," he observed to Morris. "With *Burr* I have always been personally well." Burr in high office frightened Hamilton. He would try "to reform the government *a la Buonaparte*. He is as unprincipled and dangerous a man as any country can boast—as true to Catiline as ever met in midnight conclave."[46]

Some Federalists were making overtures to Burr as the reality of the tie crystallized at the beginning of 1801. Both their candidates defeated, something had to be retrieved from the debacle. Burr, considered by many a man of all parties, was their preference. Hamilton stood firm against them. It would be signing the "death warrant" of the Federalist party, he said. Burr was "a profligate, a bankrupt, who, laughing at democracy, has played the whole game of flawed Jacobinism." Confidential letters flowed copiously from Hamilton's pen, addressed to leading Federalists around the country.

What were Burr's plans in this dilemma? At a time when a tie seemed improbable, Burr had written to Maryland congressman Samuel Smith that should he have "equal votes with Jefferson . . . every man who knows me ought to know that I should utterly disclaim all competition. . . . I now constitute you my proxy to declare these sentiments if the occasion shall require." As late as December 23, Burr vowed loyalty to a Jefferson administration, declaring his "whole time and attention shall be increasingly employed" in this because of his "sense of duty and most devoted personal attachment."[47]

Certainty of the tie, however, changed the situation. Now, when Samuel Smith tried to get a final statement from Burr that he would relinquish any pretension to the presidency, he failed. Instead, Burr, when in Trenton, complained about the impertinence of one gentleman who asked him "whether if I were chosen President I would . . . resign. . . . I was made a Candidate against my wish; God knows, never contemplating or willing the result which appeared."[48]

On January 2, the ballot count eliminated any uncertainty. Jefferson and Burr tied, with seventy-three votes each. Adams received sixty-five votes, and Pinckney had sixty-four. However, the victorious Republicans were greatly troubled because the decision of which man was to be president rested in Federalist hands. Jefferson could not be elected "against the will of the federal party," James Bayard declared. The House of Representatives would decide the issue, and the winner would need the votes of nine states. At this moment, said Bayard, there was a Federalist inclination in favor of Burr.

The Federalists held a caucus in Washington on January 9, 1801, to organize the defeat of Jefferson, even, an extremist said, to prevent the election of any president. But the Marylanders would not cooperate, so no "decisive measures" were decided upon. Hamilton looked on any Federalist game to prevent an election and so leave the executive power in the hands of a future president of the Senate "with distaste." It would be "a most dangerous and unbecoming policy. . . . The present is a crisis which demands the exertions of men who have an interest in public order."[49]

Hamilton never changed his conviction that Burr was an evil genius, only using the Federalists for his own aggrandizement. The hope that if elected he would divorce himself from the Antifederalists was "a perfect farce." If elected, he would "add the unprincipled of our party & he will laugh at the rest." If the Federalist party supported Burr for president, Hamilton declared, he would consider himself *"an isolated man"* and could not continue to be a member of a party that "degraded itself & the country."[50] He was no apologist for Jefferson; he had, perhaps, been the first to unfold the true character of Jefferson, but "he is as likely as any man I know to temporize." Burr, on the other hand, said Hamilton, was "far more *cunning* than *wise*, far more *dexterous* than *able*." He would attempt usurpation. Therefore, it would be best for the Antifederalists to take their own man and for the Federalists "to remain *free, united* and without *stain*. . . . If the Federalists substitute Burr, they adopt him and become answerable for him."[51]

Burr took a strange stance. He neither promoted his own candidacy nor removed himself from the contest. In early February, while the decision was being made in Washington, Burr attended his eighteen-year-old only child's wedding. Theodosia Burr, a brilliant and gifted young woman, married Joseph Alston of South Carolina in Albany. Burr, a delegate to the state legislature, remained in that city, attending the session. In mid-February, a secret letter came from Albert Gallatin, urging Burr to come to Washington to secure the votes of three congressmen who could tip the scales in his favor and break the deadlock—James Linn of New Jersey, Samuel Smith of Maryland and Edward Livingston of New York.

Peter Townsend and John Swartwout, the two friends with whom Burr consulted, urged him "to get into the first conveyance you can procure—lose not a moment—hasten to Washington and secure the prize." Burr prepared to leave for the capital. "But at the critical moment, his heart failed him," Townsend told Benjamin Betterton Howell, a merchant; "he remained at Albany and wrote letters." Burr proposed nothing more drastic than to make an overt move "in case of usurpation" by the president pro tem of the Senate or in any other way. If such a desperate situation arose, Burr told Gallatin, he would go to Washington. Otherwise, he would be there just before the inauguration.[52]

From Wednesday February 11 to Thursday February 17, the House of Representatives cast ballot after ballot to achieve nine states or more for one of the candidates. Tension grew in Washington as crowds poured into the city to witness either an inauguration or a usurpation.

On the first ballot, Jefferson had only eight states; the Maryland and Vermont delegations were divided, and James Bayard, who had Delaware's only vote, was pro-Burr. Finally, when it became obvious that the Republicans would not shift to Burr and that legislative usurpation would be dangerous for the nation, the Federalists concurred. The Burrites in Maryland and Vermont cast blank ballots. Bayard and South Carolina, rejecting Jefferson to the last, did the same. On the thirty-sixth ballot, the House of Representatives elected Thomas Jefferson president and Aaron Burr vice-president.

Hamilton cannot be credited with the Jefferson victory. It was the solidarity of the Republicans, who refused to desert Jefferson and stood firmly against the Federalist assault. Although Hamilton had the satisfaction of seeing the less dangerous Republican win the presidency, he was now the quasi-leader of a deposed and divided party. He had, in this election, incurred the enmity of Burr and, more threatening to his political future, of the Adams Federalists as well.

The national election over, Hamilton switched his full attention to the state gubernatorial election. In February, the Republican members of the state legislature reconfirmed their nomination of George Clinton, a veteran of six terms, for governor. The Federalists, at a caucus held in Albany on January 28, 1801, had chosen Stephen Van Rensselaer, Hamilton's brother-in-law, for governor and, on February 3, James Watson, a New York City lawyer, for lieutenant governor. Burr, said Hamilton to his wife, "as a proof of his conversion to Federalism, has within a fortnight taken a very active part against Rensselaer in favor of Clinton." No secret Federalist was he, Hamilton told James Bayard, but "resolved to adhere to & cultivate his old party, who lately more than ever have shewn the cloven foot of Rank Jacobinism."[53]

Hamilton, who had gone up to Albany on February 22 to attend court there, stayed about a month. His business was finished by mid-March, but his sister-in-law Peggy (Mrs. Stephen Van Rensselaer) was gravely ill. She asked Hamilton to stay, as did the Schuylers. Peggy died on March 14 at the Manor House.

On the way home from Albany, Hamilton narrowly escaped death at sea. While his ship was anchored in Haverstraw Bay for the night, a fire started in the forecastle. The pilot, risking suffocation, plunged among the flames and doused it out with buckets of water. "Five minutes more would probably have rendered it impracticable to save the vessel," Hamilton told Philip Schuyler. "Had you perished, my calamity would have been complete," Schuyler answered. Then he cautioned his son-in-law about his health. "Unremitted exertions of the mind, and without bodily exercise, will injure if not destroy the machine."[54]

Hamilton campaigned for his brother-in-law and the other Federalist candidates, "making eloquent impressive speeches," according to Robert Troup. Aaron Burr reported that the general worked day and night "with the most intemperate and outrageous zeal, but I think wholly without effect." The vice-president was correct. Hamilton's harangues at ward committees were often received with hostility. At one of the pools, he was repeatedly called a thief by the people; at another, a rascal and a villian. The gubernatorial election took place on April 28, 29 and 30. George Clinton won by a majority of nearly 4,000 votes, and all the Federalist candidates for the Assembly were defeated.[55]

Hamilton was "supremely disgusted" with the affairs of the state and of the nation. He was convinced that Jefferson and his party were without the talent and virtue necessary to run the government. The ultimate result, he predicted, would be ruin. Nothing short of such "a general convulsion will again call him into public life." He devoted himself to his law practice and, said Troup proudly to Rufus King, "I have at length succeeded in making him somewhat mercenary. I have known him latterly to dun his clients for money."[56]

"I am anxious to hear from Philip. Naughty young man," Hamilton wrote to Betsey on October 25, 1801, about their beloved nineteen-year-old son. Less than a month later, Philip was killed in a duel with George I. Eacker, a Republican lawyer.

On Friday evening, November 20, both men were at the Park Theatre in New York City. Philip Hamilton and his friend Stephen Price, also a recent Columbia graduate, stood near Eacker's box, shouting insulting comments about the lawyer's Fourth of July speech in which he was critical of the Federalist party and particularly of Hamilton's military and financial policies. Insults were bandied back and forth after the play. An attempt later that evening to settle the dispute was unsuccessful, and Price challenged Eacker to a duel to take place on November 22. The duel took place as arranged, without injury to either party. A Mr. Lawrence, Eacker's second, and David Samuel Jones, Hamilton's second, tried to avoid another encounter. The plan was to persuade Eacker to apologize to young Hamilton, after which Philip would reciprocate. Eacker refused to apologize. Later in the evening of November 22, Philip Hamilton sent a challenge to Eacker, which was accepted. The meeting was to take place at Powles Hook, New Jersey, on the afternoon of November 23.

When Hamilton learned of the approaching encounter, he ordered his son to reserve his fire until Eacker had shot, and after that to discharge his pistol into the air. Hamilton hoped for a successful negotiation, but when he found that his son had left for New Jersey, he called on Dr. Hosack, the family physician, to inform him that his professional services might be required. The distraught father was so overcome by anxiety that he fainted.

While Hamilton slowly recovered at Hosack's house, the doctor was summoned to Greenwich, where Philip had been taken after he was wounded. Hamilton, in sufficient control now, went to his son's bedside. He determined the nature of the wound, looked at Philip's face, felt his pulse and then, turning from the bed, took Dr. Hosack's hand, "which he pressed with all the agony of grief," and said, "Doctor, I despair."

Thomas Rathbone, a Columbia classmate of Philip who visited him that evening, described the scene for his sister. "On a bed without curtains lay poor Phil, pale and languid, his rolling, distorted eye balls darting forth the flashes of delirium—on one side of him on the same bed lay his agonized father—on the other his distracted mother."

The body rested at the Church home until burial. Angelica told her brother that Hamilton's conduct "was extraordinary during his trial," and Betsey too was "a little composed." But at the funeral, Hamilton was so overcome with grief that he was "with difficulty, supported to the grave of his hopes."[57]

The tragedy shattered Hamilton. Philip, the golden child, died to defend his father's honor, becoming a symbolic sacrifice to the gods for his father's public humiliation of the family. Hamilton was unable to attend to business until early December, when he forced himself to resume work to take care of his large, young family.

Philip Schuyler tried to comfort his grieving children. He begged "dear Hamilton" to come to Albany and to bring Betsey with him. Condolence letters poured in from all over the country. Dr. Benjamin Rush wrote from Philadelphia, "You do not weep alone. Many, many tears have been shed in our city upon your account." John Dickinson, the Quaker author of *Letters from a Farmer in Pennsylvania*, wrote from Wilmington, Delaware, that "with heart-felt love" he did "most deeply" sympathize "with thee and thy family in your present affliction."

It was not until the end of March that Hamilton was able to answer the letters of sympathy. "'Til very lately the subject has been so extremely painful to me, that I have been under a necessity of flying from it as much as possible," he wrote to John Dickinson. Time and effort and occupation were restoring some tranquillity of mind to

Hamilton. The magnitude of his loss had not diminished. Philip was "that highest as well as the eldest hope" of his family. A woeful consolation remained for him. His son was now "out of the reach of the reductions and calamities of a world, full of vice, free of danger —of least value in proportion as it is best known."[58]

The Hamilton family sustained an additional tragedy as a result of Philip's death. Seventeen-year-old Angelica, the second child, a beautiful, intelligent young woman, was so overwhelmed with grief by her brother's death that she went into shock and never recovered. Although she lived until she was seventy-three, her mind was gone, and she spoke often of her brother Philip as if he were still alive.

Philip's tragic death occurred when Hamilton's fame and influence were almost in eclipse. His political career seemed to be over and the Hamiltonian system in disrepute. Work was a panacea of sorts. But even while enduring the darkest days, Hamilton was enough of a political animal to respond to Jefferson's first annual address delivered on December 7, 1801. Using the pseudonym "Lucius Crassus," Hamilton wrote eighteen articles which were published in *The New-York Evening Post* from the winter of 1801 to April 8, 1802. The newspaper was founded by Hamilton, who believed that New York needed a Federalist daily. Editor William Coleman, chosen by Hamilton, became his spokesman and devoted friend.

Hamilton did not write for the paper but provided Coleman with information. Hamilton would set up an appointment, usually at a late hour in the evening. "He always keeps himself minutely informed on all political matters. As soon as I see him, he begins in a deliberate manner to dictate, and I try to note down in short hand. When he stops my article is completed," Coleman said.[59]

The Examination papers were an exception. Hamilton, as Lucius Crassus, wrote the refutation to Jefferson's message with the care and thought that he applied to his earlier efforts, but something was missing. The fire was out. Only an occasional jab hit home, such as his statement that the president's message should "add much to the popularity of our chief magistrate," but at the same time, it should "alarm all who are anxious for the safety of Government, for the respectability and welfare of our nation." It makes "a most prodigal sacrifice of constitutional energy, of sound principle and of public interest."

Time and space were given to the Tripolitan war, the internal revenue, the national debt and the naturalization process. The strongest attack was reserved for Jefferson's attempt to modify the

judiciary system. John Adams and the Federalist Congress, disturbed
by the defeat of the Federalist party, had made a desperate attempt
to keep one branch of the government under the domination of the
party by appointing the "midnight judges." Among the president's
appointments was that of John Marshall to the post of Chief Justice
of the Supreme Court. Jefferson's hatred of his cousin and the power
of the judiciary, and his efforts to destroy them both, colored his
presidency.

Hamilton called Jefferson's attempts to unmake the courts and
judges, just created, unwise and imprudent. "Who does not see what
is the ultimate object?—ill-fated Constitution which Americans had
fondly hoped would continue for ages, the guardian of public liberty,
the source of national prosperity."[60]

The most objectionable feature in Jefferson's message was his
proposal to abolish all restrictions on the naturalization of aliens,
which had been imposed by the hated Alien and Sedition laws. Hamilton, an immigrant himself, wrote: "The impolicy of admitting foreigners to an immediate and unrelieved participation in the right of
suffrage, or in the sovereignty of a Republic, is as much a received
axiom as any thing in the science of politics, and it is verified by the
experience of all ages." Aliens needed time to lose their foreign ways
and acquire American attachments. A residence of at least five years
ought to be required. To admit foreigners to instantaneous citizenship would be "nothing less, than to admit the Grecian horse into the
Citadel of our Liberty and Sovereignty."[61] In this Hamilton had his
way. The fourteen-year residency requirement was dropped and replaced in April 1802 with a five-year requirement, which is still in
force.

The Examination papers, often repetitive, always somewhat labored, lacked Hamilton's familiar passionate style. They were also
handicapped by his loss of position. No longer a member of the
administration or its kingmaker, his sources had dried up. The little
lion, weakened by grief for his lost Absalom, had lost his fierceness.

Hamilton diagnosed his own case poignantly to Gouverneur Morris. "Mine is an odd destiny. Perhaps no man in the U States has
sacrificed or done more for the present Constitution than myself—
and contrary to all my anticipations of its fate, as you know from the
very beginning I am still labouring to prop the frail and worthless
fabric. Yet I have the murmurs of its friends no less than the curses of
its foes for my rewards. What can I do better than withdraw from
the scene? Every day proves to me more and more that this American
world was not made for me."[62]

"Your *Talents* if not your *Birth* entitle you to the rank of an American citizen," Morris fired back. But it was little consolation. Hamilton was besieged with a new demon. Jefferson was undesirable, though not as great an evil as another. Aaron Burr, Hamilton's final adversary, was taking first place on his enemies' list.

23

Hamilton v. Burr

Hamilton had become obsessed with Burr. Having worked to defeat him for the presidency, he supported the proposed constitutional amendment that would designate separately the candidates for president and vice-president. With Burr in mind, he suggested that without such a constitutional safeguard there was "all possible scope for intrigue."

Hamilton's response to the episode of the "strange apparition" at the birthday feast showed signs of growing paranoia. In celebration of Washington's birthday, on February 22, 1802, the Federalist members of Congress met at Stelle's Hotel in the capital. According to Troup, Burr came to the dinner uninvited, asked whether he was "an intruder" and, when told that he was not, stayed. He offered a toast—"*The union of all honest men*"—which was interpreted by the Federalists "as an offer on his part to coalesce." The episode became known and "created heart burnings with some of Burr's party."[1] Burr's henchman, John P. Van Ness, dismissed the mysterious appearance as accidental and momentary, though he did admit to the toast.

Hamilton could not take the matter lightly. He wrote to James Bayard with great emotion about "*the apparition & the toast.*" The eagerness of the party to recover lost power might link the Federalists with Burr. "I dread more from this, than from all the contrivances of the bloated and senseless junto of Virginia," he said. If Burr were raised to the presidency by the Federalists, it "will be the worst kind of political suicide." Hamilton would secede from the party and be a passive spectator, joined by many of the Federalists.[2]

There is no evidence that Burr was plotting either to take over the Federalist party or to start a third party, as Hamilton suggested.

Bayard tried to calm Hamilton. The toast, he conceded, has been indiscreet. Hamilton professed to be relieved by Bayard's words, but he was not. Philip's death was changing him from a man ruled almost entirely by his head to one who questioned reason. The Republicans, he alleged, understood that men were for the most part governed by the impulse of passion. "They are courting the strangest & most active passion of the human heart—VANITY!"[3]

Suddenly religion appeared to Hamilton to be the panacea for the ills of the country. The Christian Constitutional Society he proposed in a letter to Bayard was the product of Hamilton's anguish. In 1802, he was a statesman without portfolio, haunted by his son's death and his own fall from power.

The dual objectives of this society were support of the Christian religion and of the Constitution of the United States. In a brief outline, Hamilton described its organization. It would have a national directing council, consisting of a president and twelve members; subdirecting councils in each of the states, consisting of a vice-president and twelve members; and within each state as many local societies as practical. Annual membership dues would finance newspapers and pamphlets to disseminate information. The clubs would meet weekly to discuss the contents of the newspapers, keeping in touch with other branches of the society through committees of correspondence, and would act "in concert to promote the election of *fit men.*" The society would also promote and manage charitable institutions and, in cities, provide relief for immigrants, as well as academies to teach workers mechanics and the elements of chemistry. Hamilton observed to Bayard that the Jacobins had always concentrated on the cities. During the time that the House of Representatives was resolving the Jefferson-Burr tie, the Jacobins were organized in several cities "to cut off the leading Federalists & seize the Government," in case there was no election.[4]

In Bayard's reply to Hamilton's proposal, there was surprise and some distaste, It was a plan of "great ingenuity" but probably "not applicable to the state of things in this country," he said tactfully. He recommended patience; the Jeffersonians would soon demonstrate "the soundness of our doctrines and the imbecility" of theirs.[5]

Hamilton's despair had been aggravated by the growing popularity of the Republicans in New York City. In a speech in the Second District on April 21, 1802, Hamilton criticized the Jefferson administration as being weak, disorganized, impolitic and unconstitutional. Pessimism about the future of the country permeated his thinking. War was likely, and our treasury was bare. The only hope was to support a Federalist congressional candidate. A Republican account of the speech stated that General Hamilton had appeared again on the election ground to harangue "the merchants of the Coffee House . . . who view the little General as a god."6

As the Jefferson administration developed its program, Hamilton grew more concerned. "No army, no navy, not by arms but by embargoes, prohibition of trade etc—as little government as possible within" were "pernicious dreams," he told Rufus King.

The incurable schism between "the chief and his heir apparent" was not helping the Federalists because they were not staying neutral in the quarrel, Hamilton complained. The Jefferson-Burr break had been exacerbated by James Cheetham's barrage against Burr, which had opened with a letter to President Jefferson of December 10, 1801, accusing Burr of plotting Jefferson's defeat during the tie.

Hamilton regarded the rift at the seat of power as a danger to the health of his party. Unfortunately, important Federalists "like the enterprising and adventurous character" of Burr. They were ready to link themselves to the vice-president, "professing to have no other object than to make use of him; while he [Burr] knows that he is making use of them."7

There were "no satisfactory symptoms of a revolution of opinion in the *mass*," Hamilton wrote to Rufus King, "informe in gens cui lumen ademptum." This quotation from Virgil's *Aeneid*, meaning, "dreadful monster, shapeless, huge, blind," is the only sentence in Hamilton's writings that can have prompted Henry Adams's oft-quoted, damaging statement. Adams wrote in his *History of the United States during the First Administration of Thomas Jefferson* that Hamilton had declared at a dinner in New York City: "Your people, sir—your people is a great beast."8

In the spring of 1802, Burr took a leave of absence from the Senate to go to Charleston, South Carolina, to be with his daughter Theodosia when her child was born. Joseph Alston, his son-in-law, was a wealthy planter, lawyer and member of the South Carolina legislature.

Burr's southern tour was a triumphal journey. In Raleigh, North Carolina, a bipartisan group welcomed him with a six-gun salute, symbolizing the six states that had supported him in the House of Representatives at the time of the tie. At other places along the route, he was entertained by private individuals who often invited Federalist friends to meet him. Burr arrived in time to be present when his grandson was born on May 22; soon after, he returned to New York with Theodosia and the baby, so that they might escape the intense heat.

About ten days after the arrival of Aaron Burr Alston, Betsey Hamilton gave birth to a son who was named Philip, after the brother who had died in the duel just nine months earlier.

The Hamiltons were living at The Grange, the country house they had built in Harlem Heights, named after Hamilton's father's family estate in Ayrshire, Scotland, and the St. Croix plantation owned by James Lytton.

The thirty-five-acre plot of land upon which the house was built occupied what is now 140th to 147th streets, from Edgecombe Avenue to Hamilton Place, in New York City. The property was on a ridge, with a view of the city and the Hudson River. While it was being built, the Hamilton family stayed in the renovated Scheiffelin farmhouse, located on the northwestern corner of the estate.

The two-story white clapboard house was spacious and solidly built. It was a square building, with four chimneys and verandas on either side of it. The grounds were secluded and beautiful. A dense grove of trees ensured privacy, and the gradual descent of the meadowland was halted by a ravine through which a stream ran.

Judge James Kent provided the only description available of Hamilton as the lord of the manor. Hamilton and Kent drove out to the Grange, an eight-mile trip, on Saturday April 21, 1804. During the night there was a terrible storm, so violent that it was almost a hurricane. The house, situated on top of a hill, was so exposed to the elements that Kent said his room on the second floor "rocked like a cradle." He commented that Hamilton had "never appeared so friendly and amiable" as he did that stormy night. He treated me "with minute attention that I did not suppose he knew how to bestow." Hamilton "in his domestic state," Kent added, was "a plain, modest and affectionate father and husband."[9]

Philip Schuyler had taken a great interest in the building of the house. His letters were filled with advice about construction and materials. "Your father advises that the Ice House be shingled and with cedar Shingles in preference," Hamilton wrote to his wife in October 1801. "I am taking measures to have some additional trees for you." True to his promise, tulip trees were planted in a row along the outer fence of the garden, with hemlocks between them.[10]

The Grange was an appropriate and attractive home for the many Hamilton children. It was also a symbol of success and permanence for the disinherited West Indian. But for a busy lawyer, it was too inaccessible. Hamilton's office was in the city at 12 Garden Street; he rented a house at 54 Cedar Street, where he stayed during the week. In early May 1804, Hamilton wrote to Betsey from the city that Jerome Bonaparte and his wife "will dine with you. We shall be 16 in number if [Gouverneur] Morris will come. Let the waggon as well as the Coach come in on Saturday." Morris's diary revealed that he dined at General Hamilton's with the Bonaparte family. Jerome Bonaparte, Napoleon's youngest brother, was, at that time, married to Elizabeth Patterson of Baltimore. The young man was serving in the French navy and, while stationed in the West Indies, had paid a visit to Baltimore. He met Elizabeth there and, aged nineteen, married her on Christmas Eve 1803, without his brother's consent. In 1805, when he returned to France, Napoleon had the marriage annulled. Later, Jerome married Princess Catherine of Württemberg, was made king of Westphalia by Napoleon and led a division in the Battle of Waterloo.[11]

"A disappointed politician you know is very apt to take refuge in a Garden," Hamilton commented to his friend Richard Peters, a Philadelphia lawyer. That explained retirement from public life but did not mean that, like the plantation-owning presidents and statesmen, he could sit under a fig tree. Hamilton's law practice became increasingly active and demanding. Hamilton, as a lawyer, was praised for his learning, brilliance, power of analysis, painstaking preparation of cases and impressive delivery. By this time, he served as counsel, no longer as an attorney. A counsel argued cases in court and handled pleadings. The courts of the day were constantly in session, and a busy counsel like Hamilton was terribly overworked. Though his health was often impaired, his mind remained quick and sharp. Perhaps the greatest accolade was awarded to Hamilton by Chancellor James Kent: "The selfish principle, that infirmity too often of great as well as of little minds, seemed never to have reached him. . . . He was a most faithful friend to the cause of civil liberty throughout the world."[12]

In this context the case of the *People* v. *Croswell*, which involved liberty of the press, must be examined. Harry Croswell, a printer and editor of Hudson, New York, was charged with "wilfully traducing and vilifying Thomas Jefferson." During the summer of 1802, several articles against the president appeared in the *Wasp*, a four-page weekly printed by Croswell. No. 4 of the *Wasp* (August 12, 1802) attacked Jefferson's record before he was president and also his conduct in office as "in direct hostility to common sense and the constitution." No. 7 of the *Wasp* (September 9, 1802) repeated the charge that Jefferson, while vice-president, had approved of James Thomas Callender's *The Prospect Before Us*, an attack on the Adams administration and other Federalists, and had helped to finance its publication by sending money to Callender on two occasions.

The case against Croswell, which had both political and legal angles, was prosecuted with vigor by the Republicans. Croswell was represented by a team of leading upstate lawyers: William Van Ness, Elisha Williams and Jacob Van Rensselaer.

Even in its early stages, the Federalists tried to get Hamilton involved in the Croswell case. Philip Schuyler was approached to enlist Hamilton's aid. Schuyler wrote to Betsey that a dozen Federalists had entreated him to "write to your General." They wanted Hamilton to attend the hearing of Croswell's case at Claverack. Though Hamilton was not able to make it, he did write to William Rawle of Philadelphia for information about an earlier case that might be used as a precedent.

At Claverack, Croswell was tried before Chief Justice Morgan Lewis and convicted. Judge Lewis, who subscribed to the English law of libel as stated by Lord Mansfield, instructed the jury not to judge the truth or the intention of the publication, only the fact of the libels. The jury brought in a verdict of guilty after staying out all night.

The significance of the case emerged as the arguments progressed. Although Croswell himself was not important, the question of freedom of the press and the emerging paper war between the two parties over the matter could not be ignored. In a complete turnabout, the Federalist press, supporters of the Sedition Act just a few years before, were shouting for freedom of the press. The Republicans were mocking the Federalist reversal and accusing their opponents of hypocrisy.

Croswell's attorneys made a motion for a new trial, based on the assertion that the jury had been misdirected by the judge. The cause was heard at bar, and the argument took place at Albany during the February term of the Supreme Court.[13] Justices Morgan Lewis, James Kent, Brockholst Livingston and Smith Johnson sat. Ambrose Spencer and George Caine were the attorneys for the people; Alexander Hamilton, Van Ness and Richard Harrison appeared for Croswell.

Hamilton was said to have spoken for six hours in a marathon presentation lavishly praised for its eloquence and brilliance. Judge

Kent commented that a reporter tried to take a complete transcript but was so excited by Hamilton's words that he threw down his pen, unable to follow him. What has survived of the great speech substantiates Judge Kent's praise. "He was, at times, highly impassioned and pathetic. His whole soul was enlisted in the cause. . . . The aspect of the times was portentous, and he was persuaded that if he could overthrow the high-toned doctrine contained in the charge of the judge [Lewis] it would be a great gain to the liberties of the country." Never before had Kent heard Hamilton command "Higher reverence for his principles, nor equal admiration for his eloquence."[14]

Hamilton's speech drew tears from his own eyes and from every eye in the numerous audience. Ambrose Spencer's words, spoken after his antagonist's death, must be noted. "Alexander Hamilton was the greatest man this country ever produced. . . . He argued cases before me . . . Webster has done the same. In power of reasoning, Hamilton was the equal of Webster; and more than this can be said of no man. In creative power Hamilton was infinitely Webster's superior."[15]

There were two parts of the main question in this cause, Hamilton asserted. The first was, Could the truth be given in evidence? The other, Was the jury to judge of the intent of the law? The liberty of the press, Hamilton said, "consists in publishing the truth, from good motives and for justifiable ends, though it reflect on government, on magistrates, or individuals." If this was not done, "the voice of the people would be raised in vain" against "the inroads of tyranny!" However, Hamilton did not advocate "unbridled license" for the press. Pointing to a portrait of Washington that hung on the wall, he said: "I know the best of men are not exempt from the attacks of slander though it pleased God to bless us with the first of characters, and though it has pleased God to take him from us, and this band of calumniators, I say, that falsehood eternally repeated would have affected even his name."[16]

The jury had to decide on the intent—"they must in certain cases be permitted to judge of the law, and pronounce on the combined matter of law and fact." The independence of our judges was not so well secured as in England. The power of the jury had to be upheld. It was difficult to define libel. Hamilton's definition then was this: "I would call it a slanderous or ridiculous writing, picture or sign, with a malicious or mischievous design or intent towards government, magistrates or individuals." Hamilton contended that no act was criminal, abstracted and divested of its content. Therefore, nothing could be libel independent of circumstances. "*Truth* is a material ingredient in the evidence of intent."[17]

Kent noted that Hamilton then entered into "a terrible and impressive Philippic upon the *Starr Chamber*, which was a most abitrary Court & is the polluted Source from whence the Prosecutors Doctrine is derived." Hamilton played on American hatred of that dread institution of English tyranny, which, he said, "bore down the liberties of the people and inflicted the most sanguinary punishments. It is impossible to read its sentences without feeling indignation against it."[18]

Hamilton concluded his arguments with irony. No man more than he truly revered Lord Mansfield's character, which the attorney general "has taken vast paines to celebrate." I only "conceived his sentiments were not fit for a republic." He was the parent of the doctrines of the other side. These were not the doctrines of the common law, nor of this country, and "in proof of this a new trial we trust will be granted."[19]

The case was argued in the building in which the state legislature met. The senators and assemblymen deserted their halls to listen to the proceedings, especially interested because a bill to change the libel law was before the legislature.

The decision was not favorable to Hamilton's side. The court was divided on the motion for a new trial. The public prosecutor was, therefore, entitled to move for judgment on the verdict, but he did not act. Croswell was not sentenced. Hamilton had a belated, posthumous victory. The state legislature, after a few failures, passed a bill on April 6, 1805, incorporating the Hamiltonian principles. The jury was given the right to determine the law, and the truth was to be admitted in evidence but was not to be regarded as a justification unless it was proved that it "was published with good motives and for justifiable ends." The statute, Elisha Williams wrote, "laid down the rule suggested by the immortal Hamilton: its verbiage was a maxim taken from the brief which he held in his hand." The substance of Hamilton's position on libel was incorporated in the New York constitution of 1821 and is still in effect as Article 1, Section 8 of the present Constitution.[20]

By an ironic twist, one of Hamilton's schemes became the crowning achievement of Jefferson's administration. As early as 1792, Hamilton believed that in addition to free navigation of the Mississippi River for the United States, "a Seaport communicating with the Mississippi" was an acquisition "essential to the security and improvement of all the other advantages." If such a port could not be effected by negotiation, "the necessity of obtaining it by any means must at some period ultimately lead to a rupture between the United States and Spain."[21]

The purchase of New Orleans, the seaport on the Mississippi, and of the vast Louisiana territory from Napoleon, who had obtained the area from Spain, fulfilled Hamilton's prediction. But the Federalists were very unhappy. This additional territory meant more states; even worse, more slave states. The power of New England and the Northeast would decline proportionally.

Hamilton had to reconcile his approval of the purchase of the Louisiana territory with his need to criticize the purchaser and his terms of purchase. On June 30, 1803, news of the cession of Louisiana to the United States reached New York. In Hamilton's editorial in the New-York *Evening Post* of July 5, 1803, he stated his position. "In future the navigation of the Mississippi will be ours unmolested," he declared. The purchase was an important acquisition, "essential to the peace and prosperity of our Western country, and as opening a free and valuable market to our commercial states." Having conceded its value to the United States, Hamilton challenged "the éclat" to the Jefferson presidency that the purchase "will, doubtless give." The acquisition "has been solely owing to a fortuitous concurrence of unforseen and unexpected circumstances, and not to any wise or vigorous measures on the part of the American government."[22]

By 1803, Hamilton was already taking a back seat in national politics. His triumphs at this time were legal, rather than political. As Rufus King put it, Hamilton was at the head of his profession and making a handsome income. He was living at the Grange and commuting into the city every day. "I don't perceive that he meddles or feels much concerning Politics. He had formed very divided opinions about our System as well as our administration, and as the one or the other has the voice of the country, he has nothing to do but to prophesy."[23]

Catharine Schuyler, Hamilton's mother-in-law, died in March 1803. Betsey went to Albany to comfort her bereaved father, while Hamilton stayed home with the children. "I am here with my two little boys *John* & William who will be my bed fellows tonight," he wrote to his wife. John was eleven years old and William six. The rest of the children were well, he added.[24]

General Schuyler was aging rapidly and suffering from many ills. Hamilton, to whom Schuyler had been unfailingly kind, tried to persuade the old man to join them at the Grange. But Schuyler's growing feebleness made the trip impossible. "We live in a world full of evil," Hamilton wrote to Betsey, in Albany trying to console her father. "In the later period of life misfortunes seem to thicken round us; and our duty and our peace require that we should accustom ourselves to meet disasters with Christian fortitude."[25]

At this period in his life, Hamilton appeared to have become mellower and more resigned. Though only in his late forties, the dashing young soldier and statesman had turned into a middle-aged, sedate family man of uncertain health. "Wife children and *hobby* are the only things upon which I have permitted my thoughts to run," he told Betsey. His "hobby" was the Grange.

The New York gubernatorial election of 1804 changed Hamilton's resolve to cultivate his garden and ignore the outside world. He viewed this election as of far more importance than a routine struggle for power. It was "a question of the preservation or dissolution of the union," Hamilton said. The Federalists were too weak to elect one of their own party, but they were in a position to swing the vote to the Republican whom they favored. Hamilton's role was once again to oppose Burr, whose nomination was expected and to prevent his election to the office of governor.

On February 10, 1804, Hamilton made a speech to an informal meeting of Federalists, giving eight reasons why it would be more desirable to elect John Lansing governor of New York rather than Aaron Burr. Oddly, Hamilton was supporting Lansing, who had been his opponent in the Poughkeepsie convention and, recently, in the *People* v. *Levi Weeks*, an important court case. Hamilton accused Burr of ultra ambition, talent and intrigue that would attract "such foederalists as from personal good will or interested motives may give him support." Dislike of Jefferson and jealousy of Virginia's ambition had led to support for a dismemberment of the Union. "It would probably suit Mr. Burr's views to promote this result to be the chief of the Northern portion—And placed at the head of the State of New York no man would be more likely to succeed." Lansing's personal character, Hamilton asserted, would afford some security against pernicious extremes and also would hasten the breakup of the much divided Republican party. His election might lead to "a recasting of parties," by which the Federalists would gain. Burr, however, better than anyone else might unite and direct them and "infuse rotteness" in New England, the only remaining sound part of the country.[26]

The speech convinced Republicans that Burr and Hamilton were not working together, as had been charged. It also revealed serious fissures in the Federalist party.

Five days after Hamilton's speech, the Republican members of the New York State legislature, by a large vote, nominated Lansing to succeed Gov. George Clinton. A few days later, dissenting Republicans met in Albany and New York to nominate Aaron Burr, who already knew that he would not be renominated for vice-president, for governor. Oliver Phelps received the nomination for lieutenant governor and would run against John Broome, the regular Republican candidate for the office.

Hamilton's greatest fears were realized. "It is an axiom with me that he [Aaron Burr] will be the most dangerous chief that *Jacobinism* can have," he told a friend. And Burr's opponent was not John Lansing, who declined the nomination, but Morgan Lewis, chief justice of New York, Robert R. Livingston's brother-in-law, the choice of "the families," as the *Morning Chronicle* put it. "Burr's prospect has extremely brightened," Hamilton commented. The Federalists as a body could not be diverted from Burr to Lewis "by any efforts of leading characters," Hamilton complained to Rufus King. Lansing might have outrun Burr, but not Morgan Lewis. Hamilton and others reconsidered running a Federalist candidate to keep the party from supporting Burr. If such an attempt was to be made, Rufus King should be the candidate, Hamilton told him. To detach the Federalists from Burr, they had to believe that the party was running a candidate about whom they were in earnest and with chance of success.

After considering Hamilton's proposal, King turned it down, leaving the ground to the two Republican candidates. "New York seems to be in danger of republican division," Jefferson wrote calmly. His official position was to steer clear of the New York election since both candidates were Republicans. But several newspapers quoted the president as saying to Oliver Phelps that the Burrites were not part of "the real Republican interest." Jefferson and Hamilton were in agreement in their mistrust and dislike of Burr.[27]

The New York gubernatorial campaign was bitter, concentrating on personalities and alleged scandals, rather than political issues. The loyal Burrites welcomed their chief on his return from Washington, eager to launch a victorious battle. Burr, who coveted the prize, ignored custom and participated actively in his own cause, distributing broadsides and making speeches.

Amidst the mudslinging, there was clear recognition that the struggle for power was between the powerful Clinton-Livingston machine and the Burrites. Another, more subtle undercurrent did not quite surface but was more dangerous than any mere political campaign. It became known to history as the New England Confederacy.

In pre-Civil War times, the issue of secession was still an open one. The government under the Constitution was only fifteen years old. All sections of the Union, except for New England, had already threatened secession—the South during the quasi-war with France, and the West often, before open navigation of the Mississippi was assured by the Louisiana Purchase. Jefferson's election and the ascendancy of Virginia, which meant southern domination and a strong French connection, had alarmed many prominent New Englanders.

Jefferson's antijudiciary acts caused consternation among the Federalists. The acquisition of Louisiana congealed their fear. William Plumer, the senator from New Hampshire, expressed his colleagues' apprehension. "If the President could *purchase* new states without the consent of the old, what was to prevent him from *selling* an old state without its consent?" The states derived from the purchase, he predicted, would be "so many satellites moving round & subordinate to Virginia." New England would become only a "cypher." Christopher Gore commented to Rufus King pessimistically that Jefferson would depend on the West and the South, and "leave the Eastern States to perish . . . in poverty and disgrace."[28]

Secession fever seized many of the Federalist legislators during the term of the Eighth Congress. Federalist power had suffered blow upon blow in quick succession: the Louisiana Purchase, the Twelfth Amendment and the Pickering case. Most depressing of all, it was clear that Hamilton had lost the power to influence the course of national affairs. Pickering, now a senator from Massachusetts, turned to the extremist solution, New England secession.

The secessionist plot was spawned by Samuel Hunt, a New Hampshire congressman who had lived abroad for some time and had distinguished connections, such as his uncle, Governor Caleb Strong of Massachusetts. Roger Griswold, a Connecticut congressman, and Pickering rallied to the movement and remained loyal even after it went underground in 1804 and did not emerge for two decades. In its first stages, William Plumer, Oliver Wolcott and Uriah Tracy, a senator from Connecticut, favored it.

Plumer recollected a walk with Timothy Pickering around the

northern and eastern edges of Washington. After much hesitation, Pickering said that he thought the United States was too large and its interests too varied for the Union to continue long. New England, New York and perhaps Pennsylvania "might and ought to form a separate government," he suggested. Plumer asked whether "the division of the states was not the object which General Washington pathetically warned the people to oppose." Plumer answered, "Yes, the fear of it was a ghost, that, for a long time, haunted the imagination of that old gentleman."[29]

Since New York was essential to the success of the plot, Burr was viewed as the leader who could and would lead the conspiracy. Burr would detach New York and then New England from the Union, forming a northern confederacy with him at its helm.

In March 1804, Pickering wrote to Rufus King that if a separation were necessary, five New England states, New York and New Jersey could form a permanent union, with New York at the center. Roger Griswold wrote in the same vein to Oliver Wolcott. On April 4, when Griswold visited Burr in New York, Burr made no clear commitment to the secessionist movement. He conceded that New England had been spurned by the administration and that "the Northern States must be governed by Virginia, or govern Virginia, and that there was no middle mode." Further than that, the wily New Yorker refused to go. A toast given at Boston at a public dinner on April 24 summed up the feelings of the Federalists. "Aaron's Rod: may it blossom in New-York; and may federalists be still and applaud, while the greater serpent swallows the less."[30]

Hamilton's fixed opposition to Burr was a disappointment to the conspirators. He showed no inclination to be "the Joshua of the chosen people" and lead the dissident north out of the Union to the chosen land. The secessionist plot had nothing to offer the founder of the Federalist party. Burr was cast in the leading role, which could not be tolerated. And second place would probably go to Timothy Pickering.

Personal motives aside, Hamilton abhorred the plot. Separation was not the cure for the ills of the Republic. Therefore, Hamilton opposed Burr and the northern separatists, and worked to keep his wing of the Federalist party from voting for the American Catiline.

On April 25, when New Yorkers went to the polls to choose a new governor, the odds favored Morgan Lewis. The city, the Burrite stronghold, gave its leader a beggarly hundred-vote majority. In the rest of the state, except for the western district, there was little support for the vice-president. "The election is lost by a great majority; *tant mieux*," Burr wrote to his daughter Theodosia. But when the votes were tallied, the score was humiliating to Burr. Lewis won the election by 30,289 votes to 22,139, the largest victory achieved by any New York gubernatorial candidate. Jeffersonianism was secure in this powerful state. For the secessionist Federalists, there was left only hope that a meeting scheduled to take place in Boston in the fall of 1804 would obtain Hamilton's support.

An Affair of Honor

AT ELEVEN O'CLOCK on Monday morning, June 18, 1804, William P. Van Ness called at Hamilton's office. He brought a note from Aaron Burr and an enclosure that was a letter, dated April 23, 1804, written by Charles D. Cooper to Philip Schuyler. After Hamilton read both communications, he observed to Van Ness that he did not think the publication in question authorized Burr to call upon him and that the languages and references in it were so general that he could not give Burr a specific answer. If Burr would refer to any *"particular expressions,"* he would either acknowledge or deny them. Van Ness, a devoted Burrite, answered that he did not think Burr was ready to be specific but that the publication of Cooper's letter obviously alluded to words of Hamilton's that were derogatory to Burr's character and reputation. Hence, the laws of honor justified Burr in making inquiries from the author of those expressions. Hamilton disagreed with Van Ness and said he needed time to study the publication. He promised to send an answer to Van Ness's office later that day.[1]

Burr's note was curt but explosive. "I send for your perusal a letter signed Ch. D. Cooper which, though apparently published some time ago, has but recently come to my knowledge. Mr. Van Ness . . . will point out to you that Clause of the letter to which I particularly request your attention. You might perceive, Sir, the necessity of a prompt and unqualified acknowledgement or denial of the use of any expressions which could warrant the assertions of Dr. Cooper." The enclosed letter referred to defamatory comments made by Hamilton about Burr at a private dinner given at his house in Albany by Judge John Taylor sometime before April 12, 1804. Dr. Charles D. Cooper, Taylor's son-in-law who was present, wrote about the dinner conversation to Andrew Brown, a resident of Berne, a small town nineteen miles west of Albany. The letter mentioned that Hamilton was decidedly against Burr, had spoken of him "as a dangerous man, and who ought not to be trusted." A sentiment, Cooper wrote, that had also been expressed by Judge Kent, another guest. Cooper's letter to Brown had been entrusted to John J. Deitz. Somehow the letter had been stolen and broken open, and subsequently an anonymous handbill had been published, containing Cooper's remarks. Philip Schuyler wrote to Samuel Stringer, chairman of the Federal Republican Committee, saying that he had seen Cooper's letter and that his facts concerning the political views of Hamilton, Stephen Van Rensselaer and James Kent were inaccurate.

It was the April 23, 1804, letter from Dr. Cooper to Philip Schuyler that sparked Burr's action against Hamilton. In it, Cooper repeated the statements of his letter to Brown and added: "It is sufficient for me, on this occasion, to substantiate what I have asserted. I have made it an invariable rule of my life, to be circumspect in relating what I may have heard from others; and in this affair, I feel happy to think, that I have been unusually cautious—for really sir, I could detail to you a still more despicable opinion which *General Hamilton* has expressed of *Mr. Burr*." The last eighteen words drove Burr to make "an immediate investigation" of Hamilton's meaning.[2]

For some time, Van Ness quoted Burr as saying, he had wanted an explanation of language Hamilton had used "highly injurious to his reputation." But there was nothing "sufficiently authentic" to justify it. The "more despicable opinion" phrase, Burr and his friends agreed, justified a note to Hamilton.

At 1:30 P.M., on June 18, Hamilton called at Van Ness's house. A variety of engagements for that day and the following had made it impossible for him to give Burr's note the necessary deliberation. On Wednesday, he would return his answer. On Wednesday morning, Van Ness and Hamilton met in court. Again, Hamilton asked for a brief delay but promised an answer by afternoon. Van Ness waited until eight o'clock in the evening and then went out. When he returned, he found Hamilton's reply.

Hamilton's first letter was reasonable, although not conciliatory, saying that the offending phrase "*still more despicable* admits of infinite shades, from very light to very dark." Dr. Cooper had never mentioned "whom, when, or where. . . . How am I to judge of the degree intended? Or how shall I annex any precise ideas to language so indefinite? Between Gentlemen, *despicable* and *more despicable* are not worth the pains of distinction. . . . How could you be sure, that even this opinion had exceeded the bounds which you would yourself deem admissible between political opponents." Hamilton would be ready to avow any precise opinion he was charged with having made about any gentleman. But on a basis so vague, he could not be expected to enter into an explanation. "I trust on more reflection, you will see the matter in the same light with me. If not, I can only regret the circumstance, and must abide the consequences." Hamilton noted that he had not seen Dr. Cooper's publication until after the receipt of Burr's letter.[3] The last statement is difficult to understand, since the letter had been addressed to Philip Schuyler and two months had elapsed since it had first been sent to him.

Inflamed by his recent defeat, the blame for which he laid at Hamilton's door, Burr was in no mood to accept anything from his nemesis but complete capitulation. He knew his adversary. They had each other's measure from encounters in the political arena and in the law courts. When Burr wrote his answer to Hamilton on Thursday, June 21, he had murder in his heart.

Hamilton's response lacked "sincerity and delicacy which you profess to Value," Burr accused Hamilton. The meaning of "more despicable" is "derogatory to my honor. . . . Political opposition can never absolve Gentlemen from the necessity of a rigid adherence to the laws of honor and the rules of decorum. I neither claim such priviledge nor indulge it in others. . . . Your letter has furnished me with new reasons for requiring a definite reply."[4]

Hamilton intuitively understood Burr's wish for a confrontation. He read Burr's letter and said that it "seemed to close the door to all further reply." Had Burr asked him to state what had given rise to Dr. Cooper's inference, he would have done so frankly, and "it would not have been found to exceed the limits justifiable among political opponents." If Burr would reopen the discussion along these lines, Hamilton said that he would consider the last letter as undelivered. Otherwise, he could make no reply, and Burr had to pursue whatever course he wished.[5] Van Ness, that same afternoon, reported Hamilton's answer to Richmond Hill, Burr's house in Greenwich.

After his discussion with Van Ness, Hamilton visited Nathaniel Pendleton and showed him the correspondence with Burr. Contrary to his earlier decision, he gave Pendleton a letter for Van Ness and went to the Grange. The brief note refused Burr's request for "a direct avowal or disavowal. . . . If you mean any thing different admitting of greater latitude it is requisite you should explain." This letter crossed with one of Burr's, so that Van Ness did not deliver Burr's letter of June 22 until he had seen Hamilton's reply to him.[6]

While Hamilton spent the weekend at the Grange, Pendleton had several conversations with Van Ness, during which he tried to clarify Hamilton's position. He reiterated Hamilton's request that Burr write a letter asking him to state whether Dr. Cooper had alluded to any particular instance of dishonorable conduct. When Hamilton returned to his office on Monday morning, he received Burr's June 22 letter.

On June 25, Pendleton for the first time questioned Hamilton on what had been alluded to in the conversation at Judge Taylor's dinner table. Hamilton was hazy on details and could remember only imperfectly what had been said. It seemed to him that he had commented on Burr's political principles and what the results would be if he were elected governor. There had been no reference that Hamilton could recollect "to any particular instance of past conduct or to private character."[7]

The two spokesmen traveled back and forth on June 25, carrying messages, but no real progress was made. Both Hamilton and Burr were locked into their positions. Correspondence between the principals was at an end. All communication was now between the chosen intermediaries. Burr wanted a blanket disavowal from Hamilton that he had not intended in his various conversations to convey impressions derogatory to Burr's honor. Hamilton maintained that his remarks had been political, not personal.

A letter from Burr to Van Ness on this date (June 25) suggests that Burr had decided on a meeting with Hamilton. "If it should be asked whether there is no alternative, most certainly there is, but more will now be required than would have been asked first."

The next day, June 26, Van Ness met with Burr, who summed up Hamilton's proposal as "mere evasion." In a letter to Pendleton, Burr's position was again set forth and a meeting with Hamilton's second requested. Hamilton, upon seeing this latest letter, instructed Pendleton to write that Burr had "extended the ground of the inquiry" and was aiming at "nothing less than an inquisition" into his confidential and other conversations throughout the period of his acquaintance with Burr. He could not consent to be questioned about "rumours." In the position Burr had assumed, Hamilton declared that he could "discover nothing short of predetermined Hos[t]ility."[8]

Van Ness's letter to Pendleton on June 27 was so rambling and repetitious that the challenge contained in it was almost obscured. Hamilton read the letter and accepted the invitation. Since he was in the midst of a circuit court session, he asked that he be allowed to continue his services to his clients to save them from having to seek other lawyers who would not have the time to prepare their cases. He also wanted time to arrange his personal affairs.

The awful decision made, Hamilton prepared for "this last critical scene, if such it shall be." With remarkable self-control, he concealed the impending duel from his family. Although he disapproved of dueling and had so suffered the loss of his dearest child, he could not evade the challenge.

Analyses of Hamilton's motives in allowing Burr to force him to give his life as a forfeit abound in history and fiction. Hamilton explained it most honestly himself in his heartbreaking letter to Betsey written on the Fourth of July. "If it had been possible for me to have avoided the interview, my love for you and my precious children would have been alone a decisive motive. But it was not possible without sacrifices which would have rendered me unworthy of your esteem. I need not tell you of the pangs I feel, from the idea of quitting you and exposing you to the anguish which I know you would feel. Nor could I dwell on the topic lest it should unman me."[9]

On that same day, Hamilton attended the annual Fourth of July dinner at Fraunces Tavern given by the Society of the Cincinnati. Observers said that Hamilton, the president of the organization, was cheerful and gregarious. He sang "The Drum" very well and with apparent pleasure.

Burr was also present at the dinner. He was silent and did not mix much with the company. Except when he spoke, turning on his "precious smile," he looked like "a disappointed and mortified man." When Hamilton sang, however, he lifted his head and listened.[10]

Hamilton had confided the news to several friends other than his seconds. Rufus King was blamed later for not having taken more heroic measures to try to stop the duel. He explained that since Hamilton had refused to discuss "the question of duel or no duel," he left New York the Friday before the meeting took place to visit relatives in upstate New York with Egbert Benson, who was also aware of the impending interview. The travelers stopped off at Jay's country house, where the three of them commiserated about the matter but saw no possibility of changing Hamilton's mind. John B. Church lent Hamilton the pistols used in the duel, so he, too, must have had some idea of what was coming. Church was a veteran of the dueling ground having been engaged in a duel with Burr earlier over Burr's involvement with the Holland Land Company, in which there had been no physical damage to either man, only to Burr's coat, which had been ripped by Church's bullet.[11]

Burr, however, told no one. His letters to Theodosia were light-hearted, gossipy, filled only with concern for his little grandson, Aaron Burr Alston. He made one veiled reference to the duel in his letter to Theodosia of July 1, when he talked of the unseasonably cold weather and the comfort of the fire in his library. "I am sitting near it and enjoying it," he wrote, "if that would be applicable to anything done in solitude. . . . Let us, therefore, drop the subject lest it lead to another one in which I have imposed silence on myself."

The closing of the circuit court session on Friday, July 6, released Hamilton so that final arrangements could be made, Hamilton would be ready at any time after Sunday, Pendleton informed Van Ness. On Monday, the particulars were arranged.

The Hamiltons gave a dinner party on Saturday, which Hamilton attended, summoning all his emotional resources to appear in his normal guise. After the party, he and John Trumbull were alone. "You are going to Boston. You will see the principal men there. Tell them from ME, at MY request, for God's sake, to cease these conversations and threatenings about a separation of the Union. It must hang together as long as it can be made to," he said to Trumbull.[12]

Early Sunday morning, before the heat of the day, Hamilton strolled with Betsey around their property. On their return, he read the morning service of the Episcopal church to his assembled family. The rest of the day all the Hamiltons were together, and at dusk the father gathered all his children around him under a tree and "laid with them upon the grass until the stars shone down from the heavens."[13]

On Monday, Hamilton returned to New York City, leaving his wife and children unsuspecting. His behavior at the office was cheerful and composed, his law clerk, Judah Hammond, said. Hamilton spent Monday afternoon at Oliver Wolcott's house. "He was uncommonly cheerful and gay," Wolcott attested.[14]

The last visit Hamilton made was to his college friend, Robert Troup. "The whole tenor of his deportment manifested such composure and cheerfulness of mind, as to leave me without any suspicion of the rencontre that was impending; his manner having an air of peculiar earnestness and solicitude," Troup wrote.[15]

Alone in his city dwelling, Hamilton attended to the melancholy

chores of arranging his financial affairs and writing his will. Even
more painful was the soul-searching statement on the impending
duel that Hamilton labored over between June 28 and July 10. He
had wanted to avoid this interview for religious and moral reasons,
for love of his wife and children, for obligations to his family and his
creditors and because he had no "ill will" to Burr, other than political
opposition that proceeded from pure and upright measures. But the
duel could not be avoided. "There were *intrinsick* difficulties in the
thing, and *artificial* embarrassments, from the manner of proceeding
on the part of Col. Burr." Hamilton exonerated Burr from blame.
Probably the animadversions of Hamilton's that he had heard "bore
very hard on him" and "were enlarged by falsehoods. . . . I hope the
grounds of his proceeding have such as ought to satisfy his own
conscience."

Hamilton concluded that since he might have injured Burr, however much he did not believe so, "I have resolved . . . to *reserve* and
throw away my first fire, and *I have thoughts* even of *reserving* my
second fire."[16] The memory of Philip's death must have been with
him constantly as he fulfilled these sad tasks.

A letter of farewell to Betsey, written at ten o'clock on Tuesday
evening, asked her to look after his cousin, Ann Mitchell, "to whom
as a friend I am under the greatest obligations." He had invited her
to this country and intended to "render the Evening of her days
comfortable." His scruples as a Christian, Hamilton told his wife,
decided him to expose his own life, rather than bear the guilt of
taking Burr's. "Heaven can preserve me (and I humbly hope will)
but in the contrary event, I charge you to remember that you are a
Christian."[17]

There was one last letter to write that night. It was to be Hamilton's final political statement and his posthumous effort to save the
Union. The letter was written to Theodore Sedgwick, who had asked
Hamilton for his views on Federalist politics. Hamilton had been
working on a complete, serious response. Due to "much avocation,
some indifferent health, and a growing distaste to Politics," the letter
was not finished. However, he wanted to express one sentiment. Referring to the project to establish a northern confederacy, Hamilton
wrote, "Dismemberment of our Empire will be a clear sacrifice of
great positive advantages, without any counterbalancing good." It
would not relieve "our real disease, which is *democracy*, the poison
of which by a subdivision will only be the more concentrated in each
part, and consequently the more virulent."[18]

Burr, at Richmond Hill, had written his will, put his papers in order and composed separate letters to Theodosia and to her husband, Joseph Alston. "I have called out General Hamilton and we meet tomorrow morning. Van Ness will give you the details," Burr told Alston. If he should fall, "yet I shall live in you and your son. I commit to you all that is most dear to me—my reputation and my daughter." Alston should encourage Theodosia to cultivate her mind and study Latin, English and natural philosophy, so she could pass it on to ABA.[19]

Theodosia, the deepest and purest love of Burr's dissolute life, was not told about the duel in her letter. Burr only gave her instructions about the disposal of his property "if I should die this year." All his private letters and papers were put in her charge. She was requested "to burn all such as, if by accident made public, would injure any person. This is more particularly applicable to the letters of my female correspondents." The letter concluded with words that are among the most affecting a father had ever written to a beloved child. "I am indebted to you, my dearest Theodosia, for a very great portion of the happiness which I have enjoyed in this life. You have completely satisfied all that my heart and affections had hoped or even wished. With a little more perseverance, determination and industry, you will obtain all that my ambition or vanity had fondly imagined. Let your son have occasion to be proud he had a mother. Adieu. Adieu."[20]

One can but speculate on why Burr and Hamilton made such elaborate arrangements for the eventuality of death before this meeting. Dueling was a familiar phenomenon to both. Burr's most recent encounter, although never publicly revealed, occurred not long before July 11, 1804. Family sources divulged that Samuel Bradhurst, a Hamiltonian and a relative of Burr by marriage, heard somehow of the impending duel. He went to Richmond Hill and forced himself on Burr with the purpose of arranging a reconciliation between the two antagonists. Burr received him with such obvious distaste that the outcome of the visit was a challenge by one of the men. Where and when the confrontation took place is unknown, but it was probably at Weehawken. Burr was untouched, but Bradhurst was wounded in the arm or shoulder.[21]

Before dawn on July 11, Hamilton, Pendleton and Dr. David Hosack embarked from Horatio Street, Greenwich, for the dueling ground across the Hudson River at Weehawken, New Jersey. The spot was a popular place for such encounters because of its accessibility to the river and its privacy. It was a grassy ledge that hung about twenty feet above the Hudson, about two yards wide by twelve yards long, adequate to the needs of the duelists. A beach at water level had two landing places with a clump of bushes between them so that the two opponents could not see each other's arrival and departure. A natural flight of steps up to the promontory started at the edge of the beach. It was impossible to see what was going on above from the beach and equally impossible to see down to the ledge from the Palisades, which were so steep that they could not be scaled by foot.[22]

After traveling in the barge for three miles, Hamilton and his party arrived at the south landing place at about seven. Burr and Van Ness, already there as planned, had cleared the underbrush. Hamilton's opponent, who had started from the foot of Charlton Street and been rowed across the Hudson to the northside landing, was elegantly dressed in black cotton pantaloons, half-boots and a coat of bombazine. Hamilton and Burr greeted each other formally and waited quietly for their seconds to prepare the scene for the encounter.

Pendleton's version of the rules for the duel had been accepted earlier. The distance between the parties was to be ten yards and the pistols used not to exceed eleven inches in the barrel. The seconds would determine by lot the choice of positions and who would give the word. Once the opponents were at their stations, the second designated to give the word would ask if they were ready. Once answered in the affirmative, he would say, "Present," after which the parties were free to present and fire at will. If one party fired before the other, the opposite second would say, "One, two, three, fire; and he shall fire or loose his fire. A snap or flash was to be considered a fire."[23]

As arranged, the seconds measured the ten full paces and cast lots for the positions, both of which went to Pendleton for Hamilton. For some reason, Pendleton chose the upper end of the ledge, which faced the river and exposed Hamilton to the morning sun and the reflection from the Hudson. Burr's position, facing the Palisades, was more advantageous.

The pistols provided by John Church were loaded by the seconds in the presence of the adversaries, who were then directed to take their positions. After the rules were repeated, Burr and Hamilton were asked if they were prepared. Both answered in the affirmative; the word "present" was spoken. "Both of the parties took aim & fired in succession, the Intervening is not expressed as the seconds do not precisely agree on the point," was the statement made in the joint report on the duel issued by William P. Van Ness and Nathaniel Pendleton on July 17, 1804.[24] Both agreed that Burr's fire took effect, and Hamilton fell almost instantly. Burr then moved spontaneously toward Hamilton in what seemed to Pendleton a gesture "expressing regret" but, urged by Van Ness, said nothing and withdrew reluctantly from the field, lest he be seen by the surgeon and bargemen who approached. He was hustled into his waiting barge and quickly rowed away from the scene.[25]

Dr. Hosack, waiting below, was summoned as soon as Pendleton saw that Hamilton had been struck. Pendleton described the general as receiving Burr's fire in his right side; then, raising himself on his toes, Hamilton turned a little to the left, at which time his own pistol went off, and he fell on his face. Hosack found Hamilton ashen with the look of death upon him, supported in Pendleton's arms. He had just strength enough to say: "This is a mortal wound, Doctor," before he fainted and appeared lifeless.

Hosack stripped off the wounded man's clothes; he soon saw that the ball had gone through a vital part. No pulse could be felt. He did not seem to be breathing, nor could Hosack find a heartbeat. The doctor thought he was "irrevocably gone."

The only chance for Hamilton's survival was to get him on the water as soon as possible. The two lifted the wounded man and carried him out of the woods to the water's edge, where the bargemen helped to get him into the boat. Immediately, they put off. Hosack, still unable to find any symptoms of revival, rubbed Hamilton's lips and temple with hartshorne (spirits of ammonia). He applied it to his neck, breast and even tried to pour some into his mouth. When they were about fifty yards from shore, Hosack noticed that Hamilton was beginning to breathe. In a little while, the injured man sighed and his respiration improved. His eyes barely open, unable to focus, Hamilton said, "My vision is indistinct." Gradually, his pulse became stronger and his respiration more regular. He could see again. Hosack examined the wound to check the bleeding.

His sight returned, Hamilton noticed the case of pistols lying in the boat. Observing that the pistol he had used was on its side, he cautioned: "Take care of that pistol; it is undischarged, and still cocked; it may go off and do harm—Pendleton knows"—he tried to turn his head toward his second—"that I did not intend to fire at him." "Yes," said Pendleton, "I have already made Dr. Hosack acquainted with your determination as to that." Apparently relieved, Hamilton closed his eyes and spoke no more, except to answer Hosack's questions about his condition.

Lying in the open boat in the heat of the July sun, Hamilton did not complain but took an interest in his progress. Once or twice he asked Hosack about his pulse. His lower extremities had lost all feeling, Hamilton reported. Hosack tried to change the position of the patient's limbs, but to no purpose. They had lost all sensibility. Hamilton told Hosack that he would not long survive.

As the boat approached the shore, Hamilton's thoughts turned to his family. "Let Mrs. Hamilton be immediately sent for—let the event be gradually broken to her; but give her hopes," he urged.

William Bayard, who had been told by Hamilton's servant of the expedition across the river and had guessed its purpose, was standing on the wharf in a state of great agitation. When the boat came closer and he saw only Hosack and Pendleton sitting up on the stern sheets, he became distraught. Hosack called to him to have a cot prepared and Bayard saw Hamilton lying in the bottom of the boat. He raised his eyes to heaven and burst into tears.

Only Hamilton retained his composure as his friends carried him as tenderly as possible to the house. The Bayard family, on seeing him in such a state, dissolved into such an outburst of emotion that they were hardly able to help the victim.

The shock and pain of the removal from the boat made Hamilton more languid. Hosack revived him with a little weak wine and water. His friends then undressed him, put him to bed and darkened the room. The pain in his back increased, so Hosack gave him frequent doses of laudanum and applied tepid, moist dressings to the area nearest the wound. Because Hamilton had a delicate stomach, Hosack avoided some remedies usually used. Hamilton's sufferings increased; they were almost intolerable, even after a large dose of laudanum.

Both Hosack and Dr. Wright Post, a prominent New York physician and member of Columbia College's medical faculty who had been called into consultation, agreed that there was no hope. Gen. Antoine-Venance Gabriel Rey, the French consul, invited the surgeons of French frigates anchored in New York harbor, experienced with gunshot wounds, to help. Hosack described the wound, the direction of the ball and the symptoms. One of the Frenchmen went to Hamilton's bedside, but all agreed that nothing could be done to save him.

Immediately after Hamilton's arrival at Bayard's house, a message had been sent to Benjamin Moore, Episcopal Bishop of New York and president of Columbia College, requesting him to administer holy communion to Hamilton. Moore went to Hamilton but, needing time to resolve his doubts about whether he could perform the office under the circumstances of the duel, refused him. At one o'clock, Moore was again called to Hamilton's bedside. "My dear Sir," Hamilton said, "you perceive my unfortunate situation and no doubt have been made acquainted with the circumstances which led to it." Again he expressed his desire to receive communion. Moore spoke of his reservations, which the dying man recognized and accepted. Moore asked Hamilton if, were he to regain his health, "Will you never be engaged in a similar transaction? and will you employ all your influence in society to discountenance this barbarous custom?" Hamilton answered, "That, sir, is my deliberate intention." Moore then asked, "Are you disposed to live in love and charity with all men?" Hamilton lifted up his hands and answered, "I have no ill will against Col. Burr. I met him with a fixed resolution to do him no harm—I forgive all that happened." Communion was then administered.[26]

After Hamilton fell, Burr went to Richmond Hill with Van Ness and a servant. He betrayed no sign that a tragedy had just taken place. About two hours after his return from Weehawken, he saw his broker on business without displaying any agitation; he seemed cheerful and good humored. That night, he welcomed a Connecticut cousin who arrived unexpectedly, offering him a bed for the night. In the morning, after breakfast, the young man strolled down Broadway. He was shocked when, near Wall Street, a friend rushed up to him, saying that Colonel Burr had killed General Hamilton.[27]

Hamilton spent a fitful night. The next morning, his symptoms were aggravated, but the pain had diminished. His mind "retained all its usual strength and composure." His overwhelming concern was for his distracted wife and children. Dr. Hosack, at his bedside constantly, said that Hamilton spoke again and again of "My beloved wife and children." On Wednesday, the day of the duel, Betsey was kept ignorant of the cause of her husband's illness; no one dared tell her the truth. Hamilton's fortitude failed only once. When all seven of his children were brought to his bedside, he could not speak. He opened his eyes, gave them one look and then closed his eyes again, unable to bear to see them there. They had to be led away before he dared to reopen his eyes. Betsey's grief, when she learned that her husband had fallen in a duel, was so passionate that she could not be contained. She was calmed only by Hamilton's exhortations. *"Remember, my Eliza, you are a Christian,"* he said again and again in a firm voice, "but in a pathetic and impressive manner."[28]

Angelica Church, Oliver Wolcott and Dr. John Mason stood in the shadows of the large square room where Hamilton lay dying. Dr. Hosack and Bishop Moore stayed at his bedside, while Betsey fanned his face.

At two o'clock in the afternoon, Alexander Hamilton died "without a struggle and almost without a groan."[29]

Instantly, the cloak of martyrdom fell on the dead man's shoulders. The nation wept for its fallen hero. In the mourning city of New York only Hamilton's murderer was unmoved by the tragedy. Burr was unrepentant, while fully aware that Hamilton's death had dealt a potentially fatal blow to his own future.

The day before, using the formal third person, Burr had sent a note to Dr. Hosack, inquiring about Hamilton and speaking of "the hopes which are entertained of his recovery." The vice-president's genuine feelings were conveyed to Charles Biddle, a Philadelphia friend. The general "had long indulged himself in illiberal freedom with my character . . . my own fault has been in bearing so much so long."[30]

The true facts about what had happened at Weehawken had been suppressed, Burr said. Hamilton's assertions that he did not mean to injure him were lies. For example, when the parties had taken their places on the dueling ground, their pistols in their hands, cocked, and Pendleton asked if the antagonists were ready, Hamilton had said, "Stop, in certain States of the light one requires glasses." He had then pointed his pistol in different directions to try the light and, putting on his spectacles, had repeated the experiment several times. He had kept on his glasses and said he was ready. When the signal was given, he had taken aim at his opponent and fired very promptly. His adversary had fired two or three seconds later, and Hamilton fell instantly, exclaiming, "I am a dead man." On the ground, Hamilton was a good deal agitated and looked "oppressed with the horrors of conscious guilt." Burr insisted to Biddle that the episode of the glasses had delayed the actual firing. He had Van Ness send a more detailed letter about it to Biddle.[31]

Burr's fears that he was to become a scapegoat were soon realized. The duel was regarded by the people of New York and New Jersey as nothing less than premeditated murder. Burr was hounded out of the city and forced to travel south.

Months later, he resumed his office as president of the Senate, but after the trial of Samuel Chase, which he staged in an imperial style, he retired from office. The rest of Burr's long life was filled with adventure and tragedy. He was tried for treason after a mysterious western adventure. After he was exonerated, he starved and plotted in European exile, until, finally, he returned to the United States. His beloved grandson died, and his adored daughter was lost at sea. For twenty years he practiced law successfully but in comparative obscurity in New York City. Eccentric John Randolph of Roanoke predicted Burr's future a few months after Hamilton's death. He had "fallen like Lucifer, never to rise again." His was "an irreparable defeat."[32]

Dr. Hosack was asked by some of Hamilton's friends to perform an autopsy, which he did in the presence of Dr. Post and two other gentlemen. The ball had struck the second or third false rib, fractured it in about the middle and then passed through the liver and diaphragm, where it probably lodged in the first or second lumbar vertebra. The vertebra in which the ball was lodged had been splintered. About a pint of clotted blood, probably from the liver, was found in the cavity of the belly.

Hamilton's spine had probably been fractured; had he lived, he might have been a paraplegic. With the knowledge and skill of modern medicine, his life might have been saved. However, from Hosack's sketchy description, it is impossible to say exactly what killed Hamilton.[33]

The Common Council of New York City, in recognition that its first citizen had met an untimely, tragic death, decided to give him a solemn and impressive funeral. Business would be suspended for the day so that the citizenry could participate in the mournful occasion.

Hamilton's body rested at the home of the Churches, and at noon on July 14, the procession formed to carry the martyred hero to Trinity Church for burial. The Society of the Cincinnati was in charge of the funeral ceremonies.

The military, under Lieut. Col. Morton, stood at attention as the bier was carried out of the Church house. The entire line presented arms, and the officers saluted while the large band played military music. The soldiers then marched in front of the bier in open column and inverted order, the left in front with arms reversed and the band playing a dead march. First came the artillery, then the 6th Regiment of militia, flank companies, the Cincinnati Society and a train of clergy. The coffin followed, carried by Gen. Matthew Clarkson,

Oliver Wolcott, Richard Harison, Abijah Hammond, Josiah Ogden Hoffman, Richard Varick, William Bayard and Judge Lawrence. On top of the coffin was the general's hat and sword. Hamilton's gray horse, dressed in mourning, the general's boots and spurs reversed, was led by two black servants dressed in white and wearing white turbans, trimmed with black. Hamilton's children and relatives followed. Then, in order, came the physicians; Gouverneur Morris, the funeral orator, in his carriage; the lawyers in deep mourning; the lieutenant governor in his carriage; the officials of New York City; foreign officials; the president, professors and students of Columbia; the Tammany Society; and, lastly, citizens in general.

All along the funeral route the streets were lined with people. The doors and windows held weeping women; on housetops stood spectators, some of whom had come from all over the nation to see the funeral. While the procession marched slowly along the route, there was a regular discharge of guns from the Battery, fired by a regiment of artillery. In the harbor, the ships' flags hung at half-mast. A British warship, anchored at Sandy Hook, fired salutes for forty-eight minutes and wore mourning, as did two French frigates.

When the military parade arrived at Trinity Church, it wheeled backward to form a lane. The soldiers upended their muskets and rested their cheeks on them in proper mourning stance. Through the avenue of soldiers the clergy and the Society of the Cincinnati, followed by the coffin, Hamilton's relations and the rest of the retinue, entered the church. The band, drums muffled, played a solemn tune.

A stage had been erected in the portico of Trinity Church on which Gouverneur Morris and four of Hamilton's sons were seated. Gouverneur Morris rose to deliver the funeral oration. Speaking extemporaneously, he said: "Far from attempting to excite your emotions, I must try to repress my own, and yet I fear that instead of the language of a public speaker, you will hear only the lamentations of a bewailing friend. But I will struggle with my bursting heart, to portray that Heroic Spirit which has flown to the mansions of bliss." He could hear the sobs of the dead man's sons by his side.

He capsulized Hamilton's achievements: his gallantry during the Revolution, his service to the Republic and his brilliance as a lawyer. He exhorted the members of the luminati and the legal profession to honor and emulate him. To his fellow citizens, he said, "*I charge you to protect his Fame.* . . . Let it be the test by which to examine those who solicit your favour. Disregarding professions, view their conduct, and on doubtful occasion ask, Would Hamilton have done this thing?" Of the circumstances of Hamilton's death, Morris cautioned, "I cannot, I must not dwell. It might excite emotions too strong for your better judgment."[34]

The oration over, Hamilton's corpse was carried to its grave. Bishop Moore read the burial service as the troops, which had entered the churchyard, formed an extensive hollow square and fired three volleys over the grave.

Dr. John Mason, in a funeral oration delivered to the New York State Society of the Cincinnati, said: "Five years have not elapsed since your tears flowed for the Father of your Country, and you are again assembled to shed them over her eldest son."[35]

Alexander Hamilton, the unknown, penniless lad who came to America to seek fame, distinction and honor, who, more than any one else, got the United States Constitution adopted, who established the financial system of the infant Republic, could have wished for no better epitaph.

Notes

CHAPTER 1   THE PRICE OF ILLEGITIMACY

1. Morris, Anne Cary, ed., *The Diary and Letters of Gouverneur Morris*, 2 vols., 2:8.
2. Ramsing, H. U., "Alexander Hamilton og hans modrene Slaegt. Tidsbilleder fra Dansk Vest-Indiens Barndom," in *Personalhistorisk Tidsskrift*, translated from Danish, microfilm, New York Public Library; Mitchell, Broadus, *Alexander Hamilton, Youth to Maturity 1755–1788*, p. 8.
3. Mitchell, *Hamilton, Youth to Maturity*, p. 11.
4. Ramsing microfilm.
5. Atherton, Gertrude, *Adventures of a Novelist*, pp. 352–53; Irving, Washington, *Life of Washington*, 4 vols., 1:66–67.
6. Flexner, James Thomas, *George Washington: The Forge of Experience* (1732–1775), p. 270.
7. Ramsing microfilm.
8. Syrett, Harold C., *The Papers of Alexander Hamilton*, 26 vols., 1:1–3.
9. Hamilton, John Church, *History of the Republic of the United States as traced in the Writings of Alexander Hamilton*, 7 vols., 1:42.
10. Mitchell, Broadus, "The Man Who Discovered Hamilton," p. 105.
11. Larson, Harold, "Alexander Hamilton; the Fact and Fiction of His Early Years," p. 147.
12. Hamilton, J. C., *History*, 1:44–47.
13. Syrett, *Hamilton Papers*, 1:4–5.
14. Ibid., pp. 10–12.
15. Ibid., pp. 17–18.
16. Ibid.
17. Ibid., p. 24.
18. Ibid., pp. 23–24.
19. Ibid., p. 25.
20. Ibid., pp. 27–29.
21. Mitchell, *Hamilton, Youth to Maturity*, p. 485.
22. Syrett, *Hamilton Papers*, 1:6–7.
23. Ibid., pp. 34–38.
24. Miller, John C., *Alexander Hamilton: Portrait in Paradox*, p. 7.
25. Atherton, *Adventures of a Novelist*, p. 317.
26. Hamilton, Allan McLane, *The Intimate Life of Alexander Hamilton*, p. 29.

CHAPTER 2   EDUCATION FOR A REVOLUTIONARY

1. Schachner, Nathan, ed., "Alexander Hamilton viewed by his Friends. The Narratives of Robert Troup and Hercules Mulligan," pp. 209–11.
2. Syrett, *Hamilton Papers*, 1:43–44.
3. Ibid., p. 41.
4. Schachner, ed., "Troup and Mulligan Narratives," p. 209.
5. Ibid.
6. Mitchell, *Hamilton, Youth to Maturity*, p. 503.
7. Schachner, ed., "Troup and Mulligan Narratives," p. 213.
8. Ibid.
9. Hamilton, J. C., *History*, 1:22–23; Oliver, Frederick Scott, *Alexander Hamilton: An Essay on Union*, p. 28.
10. Lodge, H. C., *The Works of Alexander Hamilton*, 12 vols., 1:7.
11. Ibid., p. 15.

12. Ibid.
13. Hamilton, Alexander, *The Farmer Refuted*; Morris, Richard B., ed., *Alexander Hamilton and the Founding of the Nation*, pp. 9-10.
14. Morris, *Hamilton and the Nation*, pp. 11, 15.
15. Ibid.
16. Ibid.
17. Lodge, *Hamilton Works*, 1:541.
18. Schachner, ed., "Troup and Mulligan Narratives," pp. 218-19.
19. Ibid.
20. Lodge, *Hamilton Works*, 1:184-85, 196.
21. Oliver, *Hamilton*, pp. 29-33.
22. Schachner, ed., "Troup and Mulligan Narratives," p. 210.
23. All quotes from Alexander Hamilton to John Jay, November 26, 1775, Syrett, *Hamilton Papers*, 1:176-78.
24. Ibid., p. 181.
25. Schachner, ed., "Troup and Mulligan Narratives," pp. 214, 210.
26. Syrett, *Hamilton Papers*, 1:183-85.
27. Ibid., p. 185.
28. Ibid., pp. 186-87.
29. Schachner, ed., "Troup and Mulligan Narratives," p. 211.
30. Mitchell, *Alexander Hamilton, Youth to Maturity*, p. 26.
31. Morris, Richard B., *Seven Who Shaped Our Destiny*, p. 238.

CHAPTER 3   THE LITTLE LION

1. Syrett, *Hamilton Papers*, 1:199-201.
2. Ibid., pp. 209-10.
3. Ibid., pp. 219-22.
4. Ibid., pp. 242-44, 233-34.
5. Ibid., pp. 253-54.
6. Nevins, Allan, *The American States During and After the Revolution*, pp. 161-64.
7. Syrett, *Hamilton Papers*, 1:244-45.
8. Force, Peter, *American Archives: Fourth Series*, 6 vols., 5:1043.
9. Kline, Mary-Jo, ed., *Alexander Hamilton: A Biography in His Own Words*, p. 54.
10. Ibid., p. 55.
11. Syrett, *Hamilton Papers*, 1:274-77.
12. Ibid., pp. 281-83.
13. Ibid., pp. 285-86.
14. Ibid., pp. 289-90.
15. Ibid., pp. 302-304.
16. Ibid., pp. 306-309.
17. Ibid., pp. 310-12.
18. Ibid., pp. 314-16.
19. Ibid., pp. 320-21.
20. Rush, Benjamin, *Autobiography*, ed. George W. Corner, pp. 132-33.
21. Butterfield, L. H., ed., *Adams Family Correspondence*, 2 vols., 11:349; Butterfield, L. H., ed., *Diary and Autobiography of John Adams*, 4 vols., 2:264-65.
22. Syrett, *Hamilton Papers*, 1:327-28.
23. *Adams Family Correspondence*, 2:349; John Adams, *Diary*, 2:264-65.
24. Syrett, *Hamilton Papers*, 1:331, 333.
25. Ibid., p. 348.
26. Ibid., p. 351.
27. Ibid., p. 353.
28. Ibid., p. 355.
29. Ibid., p. 357.
30. Ibid., p. 360.
31. Ibid., pp. 360-62.
32. Ibid., pp. 362-63.
33. Ibid., p. 369.

34. Ibid., pp. 371–72.
35. Freeman, Douglas Southall, *George Washington*, 6 vols., 2:571–78.
36. Syrett, *Hamilton Papers*, 1:435.
37. Ibid., pp. 439–44.
38. Jacobs, James R., *Tarnished Warrior; Major General James Wilkinson*, p. 48.
39. Miller, *Triumph and Freedom: 1775–1783*, p. 166.
40. Kline, *Hamilton*, pp. 62–63.
41. Syrett, *Hamilton Papers*, 1:414–21, 497–501.
42. Ibid., p. 506.
43. Mitchell, *Hamilton, Youth to Maturity*, p. 166; Schachner, Nathan, *Alexander Hamilton*, p. 84.
44. Freeman, *Washington*, 4:34–36.
45. Syrett, *Hamilton Papers*, 1:510–14.
46. Ibid., pp. 507–509, 517–21.
47. Ibid., pp. 522–23.
48. Ibid., pp. 602–604.
49. Parmet, Herbert S., and Hecht, Marie B., *Aaron Burr: Portrait of An Ambitious Man*, pp. 37–38.

CHAPTER 4 THE FORTUNES OF LOVE AND WAR

1. Mitchell, *Hamilton, Youth to Maturity*, p. 172.
2. Lodge, *Hamilton Works*, 1:204–209.
3. Syrett, *Hamilton Papers*, 11:108–109.
4. Ibid., pp. 125–26.
5. Ibid., pp. 148, 188.
6. Ibid., p. 222.
7. Ibid., pp. 315, 313.
8. Hamilton, Allan McLane, *Intimate Life*, p. 245.
9. Flexner, James Thomas, *Young Hamilton*, p. 212.
10. Syrett, *Hamilton Papers*, 2:17–19.
11. Ibid., pp. 34–38.
12. Flexner, *Young Hamilton*, p. 215.
13. Ibid.
14. Syrett, *Hamilton Papers*, 2:230–31.
15. Ford, Henry Jones, *Alexander Hamilton*, p. 100.
16. Syrett, *Hamilton Papers*, 2:270.
17. Desmond, Alice, *Hamilton's Wife*, p. 97.
18. Hamilton, Allan McLane, *Intimate Life*, pp. 126–27.
19. Syrett, *Hamilton Papers*, 2:305–307, 309–10.
20. Ibid., p. 350.
21. Ibid., pp. 347–48.
22. Ibid., pp. 350–51.
23. Ibid., p. 353.
24. Ibid., pp. 397–98.
25. Ibid., p. 387.
26. Ibid., p. 423.
27. Ibid., p. 428.
28. Ibid., p. 442.
29. Ibid., p. 440.
30. Parmet and Hecht, *Burr*, p. 38.
31. Ibid.
32. Van Doren, Carl C., *Secret History of the American Revolution*, p. 200.
33. Syrett, *Hamilton Papers*, 2:466.
34. Ibid., p. 467.
35. Ibid., p. 468.
36. Ibid., p. 469.
37. Van Doren, *Secret History*, p. 367.
38. Ibid.

39. Syrett, *Hamilton Papers*, 2:470.
40. Ibid., p. 456.
41. Ibid., p. 494.
42. Hamilton, Allan McLane, *Intimate Life*, p. 139.
43. Desmond, *Hamilton's Wife*, p. 97.
44. Syrett, *Hamilton Papers*, 2:539.
45. Ibid., pp. 549–50.
46. Ibid., pp. 563–68.
47. Ibid., pp. 575–77.
48. Ibid., pp. 594–95.
49. Ibid., pp. 592, 594–95.
50. Ibid., pp. 601–602.
51. Ibid., pp. 636–38.
52. Ibid., p. 675.
53. Ibid., p. 676.
54. Miller, *Triumph and Freedom*, p. 599.
55. Syrett, *Hamilton Papers*, 2:677–78.
56. Hamilton, J. C., *History*, 1:271.
57. Ibid.
58. Mitchell, *Hamilton, Youth to Maturity*, p. 259.

CHAPTER 5   REHEARSAL FOR GREATNESS

1. Syrett, *Hamilton Papers*, 2:472–73.
2. Kline, *Hamilton*, pp. 84–86.
3. Syrett, *Hamilton Papers*, 3:5.
4. Goebel, Julius, Jr., *The Law Practice of Alexander Hamilton*, 2 vols., 1:47–48.
5. Ibid.
6. Ford, *Hamilton*, pp. 134–35.
7. Syrett, *Hamilton Papers*, 3:99.
8. Ibid., p. 117.
9. Ibid., pp. 132–44.
10. Ibid.
11. Ibid., pp. 150–51.
12. Ibid., p. 160.
13. Ibid., pp. 183–84.
14. Hamilton, J. C., *History*, 2:318.
15. Syrett, *Hamilton Papers*, 3:191–93.
16. Schmucker, Samuel M., *The Life and Times of Alexander Hamilton*, p. 123.
17. Kline, *Hamilton*, p. 123.
18. Syrett, *Hamilton Papers*, 3:238.
19. Flexner, *Young Hamilton*, p. 330.
20. Kohn, Richard H., "The Inside Story of the Newburgh Conspiracy: America and the Coup d'Etat," p. 192.
21. Syrett, *Hamilton Papers*, 3:253–55.
22. Ibid., p. 279.
23. Kline, *Hamilton*, pp. 126–27.
24. Hamilton, J. C., *History*, 2:493; Syrett, *Hamilton Papers*, p. 491.
25. Syrett, *Hamilton Papers*, pp. 277–79.
26. Kohn, R. H., *Newburgh Conspiracy*, p. 209.
27. Ibid., p. 210.
28. Hamilton, J. C., *History*, 2:499–500.
29. Syrett, *Hamilton Papers*, 3:317–21.
30. Ibid., pp. 329–31.
31. Ibid., p. 377.
32. Ibid., pp. 397–98.
33. Kline, *Hamilton*, pp. 133–35.
34. Syrett, *Hamilton Papers*, 3:408–409.
35. Ibid., p. 413.

CHAPTER 6   A PRIVATE INTERVAL

1. Kline, *Hamilton*, pp. 140–41.
2. McDonald, Forrest, *E Pluribus Unum: The Formation of the American Republic 1776–1790*, p. 39.
3. Goebel, J., *Hamilton's Law Practice*, 1:290–91.
4. Morris, *Hamilton and the Founding of the Nation*, p. 23.
5. Syrett, *Hamilton Papers*, 3:483–97.
6. Ibid., pp. 512–14.
7. Ibid., pp. 528–29.
8. Kline, *Hamilton*, pp. 144–45.
9. Goebel, *Law Practice*, 1:406.
10. Ibid., p. 369.
11. Ibid., p. 374.
12. Morris, *Hamilton and the Founding of the Nation*, p. 219.
13. Kent, William, *Memoirs and Letters of James Kent*, p. 20.
14. Ibid., pp. 31–32; Davis, Matthew L., ed., 2 vols., 2:22.
15. Parmet and Hecht, *Burr*, pp. 59–60.
16. Desmond, *Hamilton's Wife*, p. 133.
17. Kline, *Hamilton*, pp. 157–58.
18. Morris, *Hamilton and the Founding of the Nation*, p. 132.
19. Syrett, *Hamilton Papers*, 3:520.
20. Kline, *Hamilton*, p. 147.
21. Ibid.
22. Parmet and Hecht, *Burr*, p. 61; Flick, Alexander, ed., *History of the State of New York*, pp. 250–51.
23. Hamilton, Allan McLane, *Intimate History*, pp. 268, 225.
24. Syrett, *Hamilton Papers*, 3:599, 506.
25. Ibid., pp. 617–18.
26. Parton, James, *The Life and Times of Aaron Burr*, 2 vols., 1:169.
27. Kline, *Hamilton*, pp. 150–51.
28. Ibid., pp. 152–53.
29. McDonald, *E Pluribus Unum*, p. 56.

CHAPTER 7   A NECESSARY INTERLUDE

1. Nevins, *American States*, p. 281.
2. Schachner, *Hamilton*, pp. 187–88.
3. Kline, *Hamilton*, pp. 153–54.
4. Nevins, *American States*, pp. 286–87.
5. Brant, Irving, *James Madison, The Nationalist 1780–1787*, p. 381.
6. Hendrickson, Robert, *Hamilton I 1757–1789*, p. 443.
7. Morris, *Hamilton and the Founding of the Nation*, p. 89.
8. Schachner, ed., "Troup and Mulligan Narratives," p. 216.
9. Syrett, *Hamilton Papers*, 4:3–12; Kline, *Hamilton*, p. 161.
10. Syrett, *Hamilton Papers*, 4:3–12.
11. Ibid., pp. 31–32.
12. Ibid., p. 39.
13. Kline, *Hamilton*, pp. 164–65.
14. Spaulding, E. W., *His Excellency George Clinton*, pp. 142–48.
15. Fox, Dixon Ryan, *Yankees and Yorkers*, p. 172.
16. Ibid.
17. Syrett, *Hamilton Papers*, 4:115–18.
18. Ibid., pp. 126–41.
19. Mitchell, *Hamilton, Youth to Maturity*, pp. 374–79.
20. Syrett, *Hamilton Papers*, 4:101.
21. Hamilton, Allan McLane, *Intimate Life*, pp. 265–66.
22. Hamilton, J. C., *History*, 2:362.

CHAPTER 8   "AN ASSEMBLY OF DEMIGODS"

1. Beard, Charles A., *An Economic Interpretation of the Constitution of the United States*, p. 114.
2. Madison, James, *Notes on Debates in the Federal Convention of 1787 Reported by James Madison*, p. 129.
3. Rossiter, Clinton, *1787*, p. 120.
4. Madison, *Convention Notes*, p. 28.
5. Ibid., vii; Cappon, Lester, ed., *The Adams-Jefferson Letters*, p. 196.
6. Farrand, Max, ed., *Records of the Federal Convention of 1787*, 3 vols., 2:368.
7. Morris, *Hamilton and the Founding of the Nation*, p. 149.
8. Madison, *Notes*, p. 132.
9. Ibid., pp. 134, 136, 137.
10. Morris, *Hamilton and the Founding of the Nation*, pp. 154–55.
11. Wood, Gordon S., *The Creation of the American Republic 1776–1787*, p. 552.
12. Lycan, Gilbert L., *Alexander Hamilton & American Foreign Policy*, p. 13.
13. Madison, *Notes*, pp. 152–54, 163.
14. Ibid., p. 170.
15. Ibid., pp. 172, 173.
16. Syrett, *Hamilton Papers*, 4:216–17; United States Constitution Article 1; Section 6.
17. Syrett, *Hamilton Papers*, 4:196.
18. Farrand, *Records*, 2:470–73.
19. Madison, *Notes*, p. 216.
20. Bowen, Catherine Drinker, *Miracle at Philadelphia*, p. 115; Farrand, *Records*, 3: 369.
21. Syrett, *Hamilton Papers*, 4:223–25.
22. Ibid., pp. 229–32, 248–53.
23. Ibid., pp. 226–28, 233–34.
24. Madison, *Notes*, p. 438.
25. Syrett, *Hamilton Papers*, 4:235.
26. Ibid., p. 236.
27. Ibid., pp. 240–42.
28. Madison, *Notes*, p. 589; Morris, *Hamilton and the Founding of the Nation*, p. 158.
29. Madison, *Notes*, p. 590.
30. Ibid., pp. 609–10.
31. Ibid., pp. 610–14.
32. Ibid., p. 654.
33. Ibid.
34. Ibid., p. 659.

CHAPTER 9   HAMILTON AS "PUBLIUS"

1. Bowen, *Miracle at Philadelphia*, pp. 311–12.
2. Cooke, Jacob E., "Alexander Hamilton's Authorship of the 'Caesar' Letters" in *William and Mary Quarterly*, p. 85.
3. Syrett, *Hamilton Papers*, 4:280–81, 284–85.
4. Ibid., pp. 306, 284–85.
5. Plutarch, *The Lives of the Noble Grecians and Romans*, p. 127.
6. De Pauw, Linda, *The Eleventh Pillar*, p. 72.
7. Ford, Paul Leicester, *Essays on the Constitution of the United States, Published during its discussion by the People 1787–1788*, p. 245.
8. Ibid.
9. Cooke, "Authorship of 'Caesar' Letters," p. 85.
10. Syrett, *Hamilton Papers*, 4:287–301.
11. Ibid.
12. Cooke, Jacob E., ed., *The Federalist*, xxviii.
13. Ibid., pp. 6–7.
14. Ibid., pp. 35, 219.

15. Wood, *Creation of the Republic*, p. 499.
16. Cooke, *Federalist*, pp. 97–98.
17. Ibid., p. 482.
18. Ibid., p. 525.
19. Konefsky, Samuel J., *John Marshall and Alexander Hamilton: Architects of the American Constitution*, p. 63; Cooke, *Federalist*, p. 581.
20. Konefsky, *Marshall and Hamilton*, p. 20.
21. Cooke, *Federalist*, p. 578.
22. Ibid., pp. 578–81.
23. Crane, Elaine F., "Publius in the Provinces: Where Was *The Federalist* Reprinted Outside of New York City?" in *William and Mary Quarterly*, pp. 589–90.
24. Pancake, John S., *Thomas Jefferson and Alexander Hamilton*, p. 132.
25. Syrett, *Hamilton Papers*, 4:332.
26. Crane, "Publius in the Provinces," p. 591.
27. Syrett, *Hamilton Papers*, 4:207.

CHAPTER 10 "THE POLITICAL PORCUPINE"

1. De Pauw, *Eleventh Pillar*, p. 86.
2. Syrett, *Hamilton Papers*, 4:649–52.
3. De Pauw, *Eleventh Pillar*, p. 85.
4. Ibid., pp. 145, 149.
5. Ibid., p. 89.
6. Ibid., p. 134.
7. Dangerfield, George, *Chancellor Robert L. Livingston of New York, 1746–1813*, pp. 218–19.
8. De Pauw, *Eleventh Pillar*, p. 139.
9. Ibid., p. 185; Syrett, *Hamilton Papers*, 4:684.
10. Syrett, *Hamilton Papers*, 4:694–50.
11. Ibid., 5:2.
12. Ibid., pp. 5–6.
13. Ibid., p. 9.
14. Aly, Bower, *The Rhetoric of Alexander Hamilton*, p. 134; Dangerfield, *Chancellor Livingston*, p. 226.
15. De Pauw, *Eleventh Pillar*, pp. 193, 195.
16. Mitchell, *Hamilton, Youth to Maturity*, p. 439.
17. The Poughkeepsie Country Journal, June 31, 1788.
18. Kline, *Hamilton*, pp. 194, 195.
19. Aly, *Hamilton's Rhetoric*, p. 143.
20. Kline, *Hamilton*, p. 195.
21. Ibid., p. 196.
22. Ibid., p. 197.
23. Syrett, *Hamilton Papers*, 5:35.
24. De Pauw, *Eleventh Pillar*, p. 202.
25. Syrett, *Hamilton Papers*, 5:67–74.
26. Ibid., pp. 80–86.
27. Aly, *Hamilton's Rhetoric*, p. 162.
28. Ibid., p. 163.
29. Mitchell, *Hamilton, Youth to Maturity*, p. 452.
30. Syrett, *Hamilton Papers*, 5:104.
31. Kline, *Hamilton*, p. 200.
32. Syrett, *Hamilton Papers*, 5:114–25.
33. Ibid., pp. 140–41.
34. De Pauw, *Eleventh Pillar*, pp. 216, 217.
35. Aly, *Hamilton's Rhetoric*, pp. 124–25; Syrett, *Hamilton Papers*, 5:147–48.
36. Syrett, *Hamilton Papers*, pp. 91–92.
37. Ibid., pp. 156–58.
38. Aly, *Hamilton's Rhetoric*, p. 176.
39. Kline, *Hamilton*, p. 204.

40. Ibid., pp. 205–206.
41. Syrett, *Hamilton Papers*, 5:171–78.
42. Ibid., p. 187.
43. De Pauw, *Eleventh Pillar*, pp. 238–39.
44. Brooks, Robin, "Alexander Hamilton, Melancton Smith and the Ratification of the Constitution in New York" in *William and Mary Quarterly*, p. 352.
45. Ibid., p. 354.
46. Syrett, *Hamilton Papers*, 5:184–85.

CHAPTER 11   FEDERALIST POLITICS

1. Spaulding, E. Wilder, *New York in the Critical Period*, pp. 270–71.
2. Syrett, *Hamilton Papers*, 5:201.
3. Flexner, James Thomas, *George Washington and the New Nation* (1783–1793), p. 16.
4. Freeman, *Washington*, 6:148.
5. Hamilton, J. C., *History*, 3:551.
6. Syrett, *Hamilton Papers*, 5:22–221.
7. Ibid., pp. 225, 226.
8. Ibid., p. 231.
9. Ibid., pp. 335–37.
10. Ibid., pp. 247–49.
11. Freeman, *Washington*, 6:154–55.
12. Hamilton, J. C., *History*, 3:568.
13. Smith, Page, *John Adams* (2 vols.), 2:742.
14. Ibid., p. 760.
15. Syrett, *Hamilton Papers*, 5:252.
16. Ibid., pp. 263–64, 266–68.
17. Ibid., pp. 269–74, 270–72.
18. Ibid., pp. 277–78.
19. Ibid., pp. 291–93.
20. Ibid., pp. 298, 299.
21. Mitchell, Broadus, *Alexander Hamilton: The National Adventure 1788–1804*, p. 560.
22. Spaulding, *Clinton*, p. 189; Syrett, *Hamilton Papers*, 5:310–14; Kline, *Hamilton*, p. 217.
23. Syrett, *Hamilton Papers*, 5:359–62, 336.
24. Freeman, *Washington*, 6:195.
25. Hamilton, J. C., *History*, 4:29–30.
26. Syrett, *Hamilton Papers*, 5:335.
27. Lamb, Mrs. Martha J., and Harrison, Mrs. Burton, *History of the City of New York*, 3 vols., 2:339–40.
28. Maclay, William, *Journals of William Maclay, Senator from Pennsylvania 1789–1791*, ed. Edgar S. Maclay, p. 100.

CHAPTER 12   MR. SECRETARY OF THE TREASURY I

1. Hamilton, J. C., *History*, 4:30–31.
2. Schachner, ed., "Troup and Mulligan Narratives," pp. 223–25.
3. Ketcham, Ralph, *James Madison*, p. 287.
4. Syrett, *Hamilton Papers*, 5:425–27.
5. Ibid., pp. 439, 507.
6. Ibid., 6:50.
7. Mitchell, *Hamilton National Adventure*, p. 43.
8. Cooke, Jacob E., ed., *The Reports of Alexander Hamilton*, pp. 81, 12.
9. Ibid., p. 34.
10. Ibid., p. 39.
11. Mitchell, *Hamilton National Adventure*, p. 111.
12. Kline, *Hamilton*, p. 229.

13. Hamilton, J. C., *History*, 4:757.

14. Brant, Irving, *James Madison: Father of the Constitution 1787–1800*, p. 298; Ford, *Hamilton*, p. 236.

15. Syrett, *Hamilton Papers*, 6:290–93.

16. Fitzpatrick, J. C., *Writings of Washington*, 39 vols., 21:52, 30; Meyer, Freeman W., "A Note on the Origins of the Hamiltonian System," in *William and Mary Quarterly*, pp. 579–81.

17. Padover, Saul, ed., *The Complete Jefferson*, pp. 1209–1210.

18. Cooke, Jacob E., "The Compromise of 1790," in *William and Mary Quarterly*, p. 526.

19. Ibid., p. 530.

20. Ibid., pp. 538–39.

21. Note: Jacob E. Cooke in his essay "The Compromise of 1790" exploded the myth of the importance of the bargain between Jefferson and Hamilton. Later an exchange between Cooke and Kenneth R. Bowling (*The William and Mary Quarterly*, Third Series, Vol. 28, No. 4) developed into an absorbing battle of wits. But Cooke proved conclusively that "the bargain worked out by Jefferson, Madison and Hamilton was not consummated" and that the crucial battles for assumption took place in the Congress.

22. Brant, *Madison Father of the Constitution*, p. 302.

23. Syrett, *Hamilton Papers*, 6:346–47.

24. Ibid., pp. 333–35.

25. Ibid., pp. 335–37.

CHAPTER 13   MR. SECRETARY OF THE TREASURY II

1. Syrett, *Hamilton Papers*, 6:545.

2. Kline, *Hamilton*, p. 234.

3. Lycan, *Hamilton Foreign Policy*, p. 122.

4. Ibid., p. 123.

5. Syrett, *Hamilton Papers*, 7:47.

6. Ibid., p. 48.

7. Ibid., pp. 136–37.

8. Cooke, *Hamilton Papers*, p. 50.

9. Ibid., p. 53.

10. Ibid., p. 54.

11. Ibid., pp. 56–57.

12. Ibid., p. 58.

13. Ibid., p. 64.

14. Ibid., pp. 72, 73.

15. Ibid., p. 81.

16. Maclay, *Journals*, p. 345.

17. Ketcham, *Madison*, p. 320.

18. 2, *Annals of Congress*, 1950.

19. Ketcham, *Madison*, p. 320.

20. Syrett, *Hamilton Papers*, 7:50.

21. Commager, *Documents*, p. 159.

22. Padover, *Complete Jefferson*, p. 345.

23. Ibid., p. 346.

24. Syrett, *Hamilton Papers*, 7:62; Mitchell, *Hamilton National Adventure*, p. 99.

25. Syrett, *Hamilton Papers*, 7:97.

26. Ibid., p. 101.

27. Ibid., p. 105.

28. Ibid., p. 135.

29. Ibid., 7:570.

30. Ibid., p. 571.

31. Ibid., p. 578.

32. Ibid., p. 601.

33. Ibid., pp. 389–90.
34. Aaron Burr to Theodore Sedgwick, February 3, 1791, Sedgwick Papers, Massachusetts Historical Society.
35. Syrett, *Hamilton Papers*, 7:614–16.
36. Ibid., p. 445.
37. Ibid., pp. 442–44.
38. Parmet and Hecht, *Burr*, p. 66; Anonymous to Mr. Bird, Litchfield Historical Society, Litchfield, Connecticut; Seward, Frederick W., ed., *Autobiography of William Seward*, 3 vols., 1:98.
39. Syrett, *Hamilton Papers*, 8:4–5.

CHAPTER 14   OF MANUFACTURING AND OTHER PROBLEMS

1. Syrett, *Hamilton Papers*, 7:442.
2. Ibid.
3. Ibid., pp. 608–12.
4. Ibid., 8:342.
5. Ibid., p. 212.
6. Ibid., pp. 241–42.
7. Freeman, *Washington*, 6:336.
8. Syrett, *Hamilton Papers*, 8:243.
9. Flexner, *Washington and New Nation*, p. 245.
10. Parmet & Hecht, *Burr*, p. 69; Bemis, Samuel Flagg, *Jay's Treaty*, p. 15; Hamilton, J. C., *History*, 4:506.
11. Kline, *Hamilton*, p. 247.
12. Syrett, *Hamilton Papers*, 7:291–94, 493–94.
13. Ibid., p. 344.
14. Padover, *Complete Jefferson*, p. 1219.
15. Kline, *Hamilton*, p. 254.
16. Padover, *Complete Jefferson*, p. 1211.
17. Morris, *Hamilton and Founding of Nation*, p. 524.
18. Syrett, *Hamilton Papers*, 26:521–22.
19. Ibid., p. 635.
20. Ibid., pp. 632–37.
21. Ibid., pp. 603, 605.
22. Ibid., 9:37.
23. Cooke, *Hamilton Reports*, pp. 137–38.
24. Ibid., pp. 121, 127.
25. Ibid., pp. 128, 136.
26. Nelson, John R., Jr., "Alexander Hamilton and American Manufacturing," in *Journal of American History*, p. 991.
27. Ibid., p. 993; Syrett, *Hamilton Papers*, 9:366.
28. Cooke, *Hamilton Reports*, p. 205.
29. Syrett, *Hamilton Papers*, 9:384.
30. Brant, *Madison Father of Constitution*, pp. 787–800, 348.
31. Syrett, *Hamilton Papers*, 8:301.
32. Ibid., 9:24.
33. Ibid., pp. 73, 80, 91.
34. Ibid., p. 171.
35. McDonald, Forrest, *The Presidency of George Washington*, p. 87.
36. Syrett, *Hamilton Papers*, 9:126.
37. Ibid., p. 132.
38. Ibid., pp. 155–58.
39. Ibid., pp. 170–72.
40. Ibid., p. 173; 26:655.
41. Davis, *Essays*, 1:282; Syrett, *Hamilton Papers*, 11:219.
42. Syrett, *Hamilton Papers*, p. 325.
43. Ibid., p. 281.
44. Ibid., p. 611; 12:27.

45. Ibid., p. 262.
46. Ibid., p. 538.
47. Ibid., 13:518.
48. Mitchell, *Hamilton and National Experience*, p. 626.
49. Nelson, *Hamilton and American Manufacturing*, p. 194.

CHAPTER 15   THE CABINET SPLIT

1. Syrett, *Hamilton Papers*, 11:2.
2. Ibid., p. 6.
3. Parmet and Hecht, *Burr*, p. 75.
4. Parton, *Burr*, 1:212.
5. Davis, *Burr Memoirs*, 1:332.
6. Spaulding, *Clinton*, p. 201.
7. Syrett, *Hamilton Papers*, 11:155.
8. Ibid., p. 211.
9. Ibid., 12:21.
10. Ibid., 11:588; 12:100.
11. Spaulding, *Clinton*, p. 201.
12. Syrett, *Hamilton Papers*, 11:155.
13. Brant, *Madison Father of the Constitution*, p. 356.
14. Syrett, *Hamilton Papers*, 12:137, 138.
15. Ibid., p. 139.
16. Ibid., pp. 408, 480.
17. Ibid., p. 544.
18. Ibid., pp. 568–69.
19. Parmet and Hecht, *Burr*, p. 84; James Monroe and James Madison to M. Willett, October 19, 1792, Monroe Papers, vol. 2, Library of Congress.
20. Parmet and Hecht, *Burr*, p. 84.
21. Syrett, *Hamilton Papers*, 13:338, 385.
22. Ibid., 12:107.
23. Ibid.
24. Ibid., p. 102.
25. Ibid., p. 188.
26. Ibid.
27. Ibid., p. 192.
28. Ibid., p. 194.
29. Ibid., p. 211.
30. Ibid., p. 275.
31. Ibid., p. 229.
32. Ibid., p. 252.
33. Lipscomb, Andrew A., and Bergh, Albert Ellery, *The Writings of Thomas Jefferson*, 20 vols., 8:394–408.
34. Syrett, *Hamilton Papers*, 12:355, 161.
35. Ibid., pp. 399, 502.
36. Ibid., p. 524.
37. Brodie, Fawn, *Thomas Jefferson*, p. 76.

CHAPTER 16   A SEA OF TROUBLES

1. Syrett, *Hamilton Papers*, 13:532–38.
2. Hamilton, J. C., *History*, 5:212.
3. Ibid., p. 208.
4. Syrett, *Hamilton Papers*, 13:543.
5. Ibid., 14:7.
6. Ibid., 13:541.
7. Ibid., 14:186.
8. Ibid., pp. 193, 247.
9. Ibid., p. 276.

10. Stewart, Donald H., *The Opposition Press of the Federalist Period*, p. 122.
11. Lycan, *Hamilton Foreign Policy*, p. 104.
12. Account from Minnigerode, Meade, *Jefferson Friend of France*, pp. 125–35.
13. Syrett, *Hamilton Papers*, 14:141.
14. Ibid., p. 145; Lipscomb and Bergh, *Jefferson Writings*, 9:34, 45.
15. Brackenridge, Hugh Henry, *Incidents of the Insurrection*, p. 52.
16. Lipscomb and Bergh, *Jefferson Writings*, 9:35.
17. Syrett, *Hamilton Papers*, 14:307.
18. Ibid., p. 296.
19. Ibid., pp. 316, 352.
20. Ibid., p. 236.
21. Ibid., p. 359.
22. Ibid., p. 395.
23. Lipscomb and Bergh, *Jefferson Writings*, 9:77.
24. Peterson, Merrill D., *James Madison, A Biography in His Own Words*, p. 196.
25. Hacker, Louis M., *Alexander Hamilton in the American Tradition*, p. 209.
26. *Adams-Jefferson Letters*, p. 346.
27. Syrett, *Hamilton Papers*, 14:515.
28. Lipscomb and Bergh, *Jefferson Writings*, 9:116–17.
29. Ibid., p. 120.
30. Padover, *Complete Jefferson*, p. 1248.
31. Hamilton, J. C., *History*, 5:283.
32. Syrett, *Hamilton Papers*, 15:36, 81.
33. Padover, *Complete Jefferson*, p. 1256.
34. Syrett, *Hamilton Papers*, 15:12.
35. Hamilton, J. C., *History*, 5:311; Lipscomb and Bergh, *Jefferson Writings*, 9:169.
36. Syrett, *Hamilton Papers*, 15:77, 79.
37. Lipscomb and Bergh, *Jefferson Writings*, 9:117, 176; Padover, *Complete Jefferson*, p. 1260.
38. Syrett, *Hamilton Papers*, 15:77, 79.
39. Padover, *Complete Jefferson*, p. 1251.
40. Syrett, *Hamilton Papers*, 15:325.
41. *Autobiography of Benjamin Rush*, p. 98.
42. Syrett, *Hamilton Papers*, 15:332.
43. Ibid., p. 356.
44. Ibid., p. 345.
45. Ibid., p. 348.
46. Ibid.
47. Ibid., p. 399.
48. Hamilton, Allan McLane, *Intimate Life*, p. 66.

CHAPTER 17   EXIT MR. SECRETARY OF THE TREASURY

1. Syrett, *Hamilton Papers*, 15:604.
2. Ibid., p. 544.
3. Brant, *Madison Father of the Constitution*, p. 389.
4. Syrett, *Hamilton Papers*, 16:9–10.
5. Ibid., pp. 12, 19.
6. Hamilton, Allan McLane, *Intimate Life*, pp. 258, 288.
7. Ibid., p. 255.
8. Ibid., p. 37.
9. Syrett, *Hamilton Papers*, 15:592.
10. Conway, Moncure Daniel, *Edmund Randolph*, p. 206.
11. Syrett, *Hamilton Papers*, 16:249.
12. Ibid., p. 236.
13. Lycan, *Hamilton Foreign Policy*, p. 217.
14. Syrett, *Hamilton Papers*, 16:434.
15. Ibid., p. 441.
16. Ibid., p. 261.

17. Hamilton, J. C., *History*, 5:163.
18. King, Charles R., ed., *The Life and Correspondence of Rufus King*, 6 vols., 1:559.
19. Syrett, *Hamilton Papers*, 16:265.
20. Ibid., p. 278.
21. Davis, *Burr Memoirs*, 1:408.
22. Syrett, *Hamilton Papers*, 16:319.
23. Ibid., p. 323.
24. Ibid., pp. 285, 286.
25. Ibid., p. 284.
26. Stewart, *Opposition Press*, p. 190.
27. Syrett, *Hamilton Papers*, 16:578.
28. Ibid., p. 638.
29. Ibid., pp. 608–609.
30. Ibid., 17:222.
31. Ibid., p. 390.
32. Ibid., 16:570.
33. Ibid., p. 600.
34. Ibid., pp. 615, 626.
35. Ibid., 17:3–7.
36. Ibid., p. 91.
37. Ibid., p. 12.
38. Ibid., p. 15.
39. Ibid., pp. 24–58.
40. Ibid., pp. 84–85.
41. Ibid., p. 102.
42. Ibid., p. 160.
43. Ibid., pp. 150, 160.
44. Ibid., p. 180.
45. Ibid., p. 202.
46. Ibid., p. 241.
47. Ibid., pp. 254–55.
48. Ibid., p. 288.
49. Stourzh, Gerald, *Alexander Hamilton and the Idea of Republican Government*, p. 202.
50. Syrett, *Hamilton Papers*, 17:315.
51. Ibid., p. 318.
52. Ibid., p. 321.
53. Ibid., pp. 331–36.
54. Ibid., p. 340.
55. Ibid., pp. 346–47.
56. Ibid., pp. 348–49.
57. Ibid., p. 361.
58. Ibid., p. 373.
59. Brackenridge, *Incidents of the Insurrection*, pp. 189–201.
60. Ibid., p. 202.
61. Syrett, *Hamilton Papers*, 17:296.
62. Ibid., p. 394.
63. Lipscomb and Bergh, *Jefferson Writings*, 9:296.
64. Syrett, *Hamilton Papers*, 18:24.
65. Ibid., 17:428.
66. Ibid., p. 571.
67. Ibid., p. 405.
68. Ibid., 18:58.
69. Ibid., p. 126.
70. Ibid., p. 56.
71. Ibid.
72. Ibid., pp. 278–79.
73. Ibid., p. 279.

74. Ibid., p. 284.

CHAPTER 18   A NOT SO PRIVATE CITIZEN

1. Hamilton, J. C., *History*, 6:213; Syrett, *Hamilton Papers*, 18:288.
2. Syrett, *Hamilton Papers*, pp. 18–19.
3. Ibid., p. 310.
4. Ibid., p. 329.
5. Ibid., p. 343.
6. Flexner, James Thomas, *George Washington: Anguish and Farewell 1793–1799*, p. 204.
7. Conway, *Randolph*, p. 234.
8. Syrett, *Hamilton Papers*, 18:371.
9. Parmet and Hecht, *Burr*, p. 105.
10. Syrett, *Hamilton Papers*, 18:400.
11. Ibid., p. 453.
12. Ibid., p. 486.
13. Ibid., p. 471.
14. Ibid., pp. 471, 473, 474, 491.
15. Ibid., p. 503.
16. Ibid., p. 507.
17. Ibid., 20:42, 44.
18. Plutarch, *Lives*, p. 161; Syrett, *Hamilton Papers*, 18:479.
19. Syrett, *Hamilton Papers*, p. 524.
20. Flexner, *Washington: Anguish and Farewell*, p. 226.
21. Conway, *Randolph*, pp. 286, 287.
22. Syrett, *Hamilton Papers*, 19:356.
23. Ibid., p. 363.
24. Ibid., p. 438.
25. Ibid., p. 514.
26. Ibid., 18:376.
27. Ibid., p. 455.
28. Ibid., pp. 460, 512.
29. Ibid., 20:165.
30. Ibid., 21:298.
31. Ibid., p. 351.
32. Ibid., pp. 401, 420, 423.
33. Ibid., p. 396.
34. Warren, Charles, *The Supreme Court in United States History*, 2 vols., 1:148, 149.
35. Mitchell, *Hamilton National Adventure*, p. 381.
36. Syrett, *Hamilton Papers*, 20:65–66, 69.
37. Ibid., p. 85.
38. Ibid., pp. 103, 105, 66.
39. Ibid., p. 115.
40. Stewart, *Opposition Press*, p. 226.
41. Syrett, *Hamilton Papers*, 20:132.
42. Ibid., p. 139.
43. Bemis, *Jay's Treaty*, p. 373.

CHAPTER 19   AN END AND A BEGINNING

1. Syrett, *Hamilton Papers*, 22:173.
2. Ibid., p. 174.
3. Ibid., p. 264.
4. Ibid., pp. 307, 308.
5. Paltsits, Victor Hugo, *Washington's Farewell Address*, pp. 156, 197.
6. Ibid., pp. 341, 67.
7. Ibid., p. 262.
8. Ibid., pp. 263, 271.

9. Ibid., p. 277.
10. Ibid., p. 279.
11. Ibid., p. 82.
12. King, *Correspondence*, 6:617.
13. Paltsits, *Washington's Farewell Address*, p. 86.
14. Ibid., p. 286.
15. Syrett, *Hamilton Papers*, 20:173.
16. Paltsits, *Washington's Farewell Address*, p. 285.
17. Mitchell, *Hamilton National Adventure*, p. 394. Note: Hamilton was eligible for the presidency although he was not born in the United States. The Constitution provides that any person who was a citizen of the United States at the time of the adoption of the Constitution was eligible to be president.
18. Syrett, *Hamilton Papers*, 20:115.
19. Ibid., p. 119.
20. Hamilton, J. C., *History*, 6:576.
21. Syrett, *Hamilton Papers*, 20:404.
22. Ibid., p. 407; Parmet and Hecht, *Burr*, p. 109.
23. Syrett, *Hamilton Papers*, 20:418.
24. Dauer, Manning J., *The Adams Federalists*, p. 106.
25. Syrett, *Hamilton Papers*, 20:380.
26. Smith, *John Adams*, 2:899.
27. Miller, *Hamilton*, p. 450.
28. Smith, *John Adams*, 2:905.
29. Ibid., p. 908.
30. Lipscomb and Bergh, *Jefferson Writings*, 9:357.
31. Ibid., p. 360.
32. Syrett, *Hamilton Papers*, 20:446.

CHAPTER 20   SCANDAL

1. Hamilton, Alexander, *Observations on Certain Documents contained in No. V and VI of "The History of the United States for the Year 1796," in which the charge of speculation against Alexander Hamilton late Secretary of the Treasury, is fully refuted*, p. 17.
2. Syrett, *Hamilton Papers*, 19:26.
3. Ibid., p. 87.
4. Ibid., p. 172.
5. Ibid., 11:252.
6. Ibid., 10:376.
7. Ibid.
8. Ibid., p. 390.
9. Ibid., pp. 396, 519.
10. Hamilton, *Observations*, p. xvi.
11. Ibid., p. xvii.
12. Ibid., p. xix.
13. Ibid., xx.
14. Ibid., xxiii; Syrett, *Hamilton Papers*, 21:254.
15. Hamilton, *Observations*, p. xxiv.
16. Syrett, *Hamilton Papers*, 21:255–56.
17. Ibid., p. 128.
18. Ibid., p. 270.
19. Ibid., p. 273.
20. Ibid., pp. 193–94.
21. Ibid., pp. 271–75.
22. Ibid., p. 275.
23. Ibid., p. 258.
24. Hamilton, *Observations*, p. 27.
25. Ibid., p. xxxv.
26. Ibid., p. xxxvi; Syrett, *Hamilton Papers*, 21:132.

27. Ibid., p. 136.
28. Ibid., p. 148.
29. Ibid., p. 156.
30. Ibid., p. 162.
31. Ibid., p. 173.
32. Ibid., p. 174.
33. Ibid., p. 163.
34. Ibid.
35. Ibid., p. 184.
36. Ibid., p. 194.
37. Hamilton, Allan McLane, *Intimate Life*, pp. 473, 474.
38. Ibid.
39. Syrett, *Hamilton Papers*, 21:193, 200.
40. Ibid., p. 202.
41. Ibid., p. 317.
42. Ibid., p. 319.
43. Ibid., p. 239.
44. Ibid., pp. 245, 247.
45. Ibid., pp. 263, 264.
46. Ibid., p. 267.
47. Ibid., p. 139.
48. Ibid., p. 305.
49. Ibid., p. 143.
50. Brodie, *Jefferson*, p. 318.
51. Syrett, *Hamilton Papers*, 9:266.
52. Ibid., 20:56, 233.
53. Ibid., 6:245.

CHAPTER 21   HAMILTON V. ADAMS

1. Syrett, *Hamilton Papers*, 20:516; 544.
2. Lipscomb and Bergh, *Jefferson Writings*, 9:359, 381–82.
3. Syrett, *Hamilton Papers*, 20:477.
4. Ibid., p. 481.
5. Ibid., p. 522.
6. Ibid., p. 546.
7. Ibid., pp. 549, 568.
8. Ibid., p. 481.
9. Ibid., 21:339.
10. De Conde, Alexander, *The Quasi-War: The Politics and Diplomacy of the Undeclared War with France 1797–1801*, p. 35.
11. Syrett, *Hamilton Papers*, 21:339.
12. Ibid., p. 345.
13. Ibid., p. 369.
14. Ibid., p. 380.
15. Ibid., pp. 385–86.
16. Ibid., p. 408.
17. Ibid., p. 409.
18. Ibid., p. 447.
19. Ibid.
20. *A Correspondence of the Late President Adams, originally published in the Boston Patriot*, p. 68.
21. Syrett, *Hamilton Papers*, 21:522, 495.
22. Ibid., p. 468.
23. Ibid., pp. 471, 472.
24. Ibid., p. 479.
25. Ibid., p. 535.
26. Hecht, Marie B., *Beyond the Presidency*, p. 4.
27. Syrett, *Hamilton Papers*, 22:19.
28. Ibid., p. 23.

29. Ibid., p. 24.
30. Ibid., p. 37.
31. Hamilton, Allan McLane, *Intimate Life*, p. 324.
32. Syrett, *Hamilton Papers*, 22:7.
33. Ibid., p. 160.
34. Ibid., pp. 166, 179.
35. Ibid., p. 15.
36. Ibid.
37. Ibid., p. 202.
38. Ibid., p. 221.
39. Ibid., p. 336.
40. Ibid., pp. 154, 156.
41. Ibid., p. 57.
42. Ibid., pp. 382, 394, 441.
43. De Conde, *Quasi-War*, p. 171.
44. Syrett, *Hamilton Papers*, 22:407–409.
45. De Conde, *Quasi-War*, p. 125.
46. Syrett, *Hamilton Papers*, 22:475.
47. Ibid., p. 489; Lipscomb and Bergh, *Jefferson Writings*, 10:112.
48. Syrett, *Hamilton Papers*, 22:495.
49. Ibid., 23:123, 133.
50. Ibid., p. 152.
51. De Conde, *Quasi-War*, p. 197.
52. Syrett, *Hamilton Papers*, 22:553.
53. Stewart, *Opposition Press*, p. 443; Miller, John C., *The Federalist Era*, p. 249.
54. Syrett, *Hamilton Papers*, 23:547.
55. *Adams Correspondence in Boston Patriot*, pp. 29–30.
56. Syrett, *Hamilton Papers*, 23:547.
57. Ibid., pp. 599–604.
58. Ibid., 14:70, 79.
59. Ibid., p. 100.
60. Hamilton, J. C., *History*, 7:354.
61. Syrett, *Hamilton Papers*, 24:116.
62. Ibid., p. 184.

CHAPTER 22 HAMILTON V. JEFFERSON

1. Syrett, *Hamilton Papers*, 24:118.
2. Ibid., p. 155.
3. Ibid.
4. Ibid., p. 199.
5. Ibid., p. 212.
6. Schachner, *Hamilton*, p. 390.
7. Ibid., p. 392.
8. Ibid.
9. Syrett, *Hamilton Papers*, 24:212.
10. Ibid., 21:53.
11. Ibid., 24:238, 299.
12. Adams, Henry, *Life of Albert Gallatin*, p. 233.
13. Ibid., pp. 236–37; Parmet and Hecht, *Burr*, p. 148.
14. Parmet and Hecht, *Burr*, p. 150.
15. Ibid., p. 151.
16. Syrett, *Hamilton Papers*, 24:466.
17. Ibid., p. 483.
18. Ibid., p. 486.
19. Ibid., p. 490.
20. Ibid., p. 509.
21. Ibid., p. 557.
22. Ibid., p. 573.

23. Ibid., p. 483.
24. Fischer, David, "The Myth of the Essex Junto," in *William and Mary Quarterly*, material from article.
25. Syrett, *Hamilton Papers*, 24:578.
26. Ibid., p. 581.
27. Ibid., p. 596.
28. Ibid., 25:2.
29. Ibid., p. 5.
30. Ibid., p. 6.
31. Ibid., pp. 54, 55.
32. Ibid., p. 77.
33. Ibid.
34. Ibid., p. 91.
35. Ibid., pp. 88–91.
36. Ibid., p. 111.
37. Ibid., p. 126.
38. Davis, *Memoirs of Burr*, 2:65.
39. Ibid., p. 161.
40. Ibid., p. 176.
41. Ibid., p. 177.
42. King, *Correspondence*, 3:330–33.
43. Ibid.
44. Syrett, *Hamilton Papers*, 25:260, 262, 266.
45. Ibid., p. 274.
46. Ibid., pp. 56, 275.
47. Parmet and Hecht, *Burr*, pp. 158, 160.
48. Ibid., p. 161.
49. Syrett, *Hamilton Papers*, 25:302, 304.
50. Ibid., pp. 314–15, 319.
51. Ibid., p. 322.
52. Parmet and Hecht, *Burr*, pp. 164–65; Journal of Benjamin Betterton Howell, New-York Historical Society (unpublished manuscript).
53. Syrett, *Hamilton Papers*, 25:340, 341.
54. Ibid., pp. 371, 374.
55. Davis, *Burr Memoirs*, 2:149; Syrett, *Hamilton Papers*, 25:378.
56. Syrett, *Hamilton Papers*, pp. 376, 388.
57. Ibid., pp. 436–37.
58. Ibid., p. 584.
59. Ibid., p. 452.
60. Ibid., p. 489.
61. Ibid., pp. 494, 497.
62. Ibid., p. 544.

CHAPTER 23   HAMILTON V. BURR

1. Syrett, *Hamilton Papers*, 25:560.
2. Ibid., pp. 588, 589.
3. Ibid., pp. 601, 605.
4. Ibid., p. 608.
5. Ibid., p. 613.
6. Ibid., pp. 612, 610.
7. Ibid., 26:14.
8. Virgil, *Aeneid*, Book 3, line 659; Syrett, *Hamilton Papers*, 26:13; Adams, Henry, *History of the United States during the First Administration of Thomas Jefferson*, 9 vols., 1:85.
9. Syrett, *Hamilton Papers*, 25:41.
10. Ibid., pp. 422, 481.
11. Ibid., 26:231.
12. Hamilton, Allan McLane, *Intimate Life*, p. 199.
13. Goebel, *Law Practice*, 1:793.

14. Hamilton, J. C., *History*, 7:726; Kent, *Memoirs*, 325–26.
15. Hamilton, J. C., *History*, 7:725.
16. Goebel, *Law Practice*, 1:809, 810.
17. Ibid., p. 813.
18. Ibid., pp. 836, 820.
19. Ibid., p. 832.
20. Hamilton, J. C., *History*, 7:736; Goebel, *Law Practice*, 1:848.
21. Syrett, *Hamilton Papers*, 12:1.
22. Ibid., 26:129.
23. King, *Correspondence*, 4:326.
24. Syrett, *Hamilton Papers*, 26:95.
25. Ibid., p. 94.
26. Ibid., pp. 188, 189, 190.
27. *American Citizen* (New York), April 24, 1804, New-York Historical Society.
28. Turner, Lynn, *William Plumer of New Hampshire 1759–1850*, pp. 112, 115; King, *Correspondence*, 4:334–35.
29. Plumer, William, Jr., *The Life of William Plumer*, p. 300.
30. King, *Correspondence*, 4:365–66; New York *Evening Post*, April 30, 1804, New-York Historical Society.

CHAPTER 24   AN AFFAIR OF HONOR

1. Syrett, *Hamilton Papers*, 26:242.
2. Ibid., pp. 242–46.
3. Ibid., p. 248.
4. Ibid., p. 250.
5. Ibid., p. 251.
6. Ibid., p. 254.
7. Ibid., p. 261.
8. Ibid., pp. 270–71.
9. Syrett, Harold C., and Cooke, Jean G., eds., *Interview in Weehawken*, p. 111.
10. *American Citizen*, August 8, 1804, New-York Historical Society.
11. Parmet and Hecht, *Burr*, p. 210.
12. Syrett, *Hamilton Papers*, 26:310; Hamilton, J. C., *History*, 7:822–23.
13. Hamilton, J. C., *History*, 7:823.
14. Syrett, *Hamilton Papers*, 26:311.
15. Ibid.
16. Ibid., pp. 278–80.
17. Ibid., p. 308.
18. Ibid., p. 309.
19. Parmet and Hecht, *Burr*, p. 208.
20. Ibid.
21. Ibid.
22. Wilson, James G., ed., *Memorial History of the City of New York*, 4 vols., 3:181.
23. Syrett, *Hamilton Papers*, 26:307.
24. Spannenberger, Philip, "Burr-Hamilton Duellers Discovery" in *Guns and Ammo*, December 1976. The United States Bicentennial Society decided to reproduce the Church pistols. After dismantling them, it was discovered that there had been hidden single-set triggers, which, if used by Hamilton, would have given him a considerable advantage over Burr. A gun expert, who experimented with them, said that, contrary to the assertion that the set trigger could be activated simply by pulling it forward with his trigger finger, it would not have been so simple. Two hands would have been necessary for leverage. From this distance of time and with no witnesses to what happened, this becomes only another point of controversy over the details of the duel.
25. Syrett and Cooke, *Interview in Weehawken*, p. 142.
26. Ibid., p. 146.
27. Parmet and Hecht, *Burr*, p. 213.
28. Syrett and Cooke, *Interview in Weehawken*, p. 164.

29. Syrett, *Hamilton Papers*, 26:316.
30. Biddle, Charles, *Autobiography*, p. 405.
31. Syrett, *Hamilton Papers*, 26:404.
32. Parmet and Hecht, *Burr*, p. 221.
33. Interview with Dr. Sidney Lenke.
34. Coleman, William, *A Collection of the Facts and Documents Relative to the Death of Major-General Alexander Hamilton*, pp. 37–48.
35. Coleman, *Collection*, p. 255.

Bibliography

PRINTED PRIMARY SOURCES

Adams, Charles Francis, ed., *Letters of Mrs. Adams*. Boston: Wilkins, Carter and Company, 1848.

——, ed. *The Works of John Adams*. 10 vols. Boston: Little, Brown, 1856.

——, ed. *Memoirs of John Quincy Adams Comprising Portions of His Diary from 1795–1848*. 12 vols. Philadelphia: Lippincott, 1874.

Adams, Henry, ed. *Documents Relating to New-England Federalism, 1800–1815*. Boston: Little, Brown, 1877.

Ames, Seth, ed. *Works of Fisher Ames*. 2 vols. Boston: Little, Brown, 1854.

Annals of Congress, 1789–1804.

Biddle, Charles. *Autobiography*. Privately Published. Philadelphia, 1883.

Boudinot, Jane J. *Life, Public Services, Addresses and Letters of Elias Boudinot*. 2 vols. Boston: Houghton Mifflin, 1896.

Boyd, Julian, ed. *The Papers of Thomas Jefferson*. 18 vols. Princeton: Princeton University Press, 1950–72.

Brackenridge, Hugh H. *Incidents of the Insurrection*. Edited by Daniel Marder. New Haven, Conn.: College and University Press, 1972.

Butterfield, Lyman H., ed. *Diary and Autobiography of John Adams*. 4 vols. Cambridge, Mass.: Harvard University, 1961.

Callender, James Thomson. *The History of the United States for 1796. . . .* Philadelphia: Snowden and McCorkle, 1797.

Cappon, Leslie, ed. *The Adams-Jefferson Letters*. New York: Simon and Schuster, 1971.

Coleman, William, ed. *A Collection of the Facts and Documents Relative to the Death of Major-General Alexander Hamilton*. Boston: Houghton Mifflin, 1904.

Cooke, Jacob E., ed. *The Federalist*. Middletown, Conn.: Wesleyan University Press, 1961.

——, ed. *The Reports of Alexander Hamilton*. New York: Harper & Row, 1964.

A Correspondence of the Late President Adams, originally published in the "Boston Patriot." Boston: Everett and Munroe, 1809.

Davis, Matthew L. *Memoirs of Aaron Burr*. 2 vols. New York: Harper & Brothers, 1838.

Farrand, Max, ed. *Records of the Federal Convention of 1787*. 3 vols. New Haven: Yale University Press, 1911.

Fitzpatrick, J. C., ed. *The Writings of Washington*. 39 vols. Washington, D.C.: George Washington Bicentennial Commission, Houghton Mifflin and Company, 1884.

Gibbs, George. *Memoirs of Administrations of Washington and Adams*. 2 vols. New York: W. Van Norden, 1846.

Hamilton, Alexander. *Works*. Edited by J. C. Hamilton. 7 vols. New York: J.F. Trow, 1850–51.

———. *Works*. Edited by Henry Cabot Lodge. 12 vols. New York: Putnam, 1904.

———. *The Papers of Alexander Hamilton*. Edited by Harold C. Syrett. 26 vols. New York: Columbia University Press, 1961–79.

Hamilton, John Church. *History of the Republic of the United States as traced in the Writings of Alexander Hamilton*. 7 vols. New York: Appleton, 1857–64.

Hamilton, James A. *Reminiscences*. New York: Scribner's, 1869.

Jay, John. *Correspondence and Public Papers*. Edited by H. P. Johnston. 4 vols. New York and London: G. P. Putnam's Sons, 1890–93.

Kent, James. *Memoirs and Letters*. Edited by William Kent. Boston: Little, Brown, 1898.

King, Rufus. *Life and Correspondence*. Edited by Charles R. King. 6 vols. New York: G. P. Putnam's Sons, 1894.

Koch, Adrienne, and Peden, William, eds. *Selected Writings of John and John Quincy Adams*. New York: Alfred A. Knopf, 1946.

Lipscomb, Andrew A., and Bergh, Albert Ellery. *The Writings of Thomas Jefferson*. 20 vols. Washington, D.C.: The Thomas Jefferson Memorial Association, 1903.

Maclay, William. *Journal*. Edited by Edgar S. Maclay. New York: Albert and Charles Boni, 1927.

Madison, James. *Notes of Debates in the Federal Convention of 1787*. New York: W. W. Norton & Co., 1969.

———. *Writings*. Edited by Gaillard Hunt. 9 vols. New York: G. P. Putnam's Sons, 1900–1910.

Monroe, James. *A View of the Conduct of the Executive in the Foreign Affairs of the United States*. Philadelphia: Benjamin Franklin Bache, 1797.

Morris, Gouverneur. *The Diary and Letters*. 2 vols. New York: Scribner's, 1888.

Padover, Saul, ed. *The Complete Jefferson*. New York: Duell, Sloan & Pearce, 1943.

Paine, Thomas. *The Complete Writings*. Edited by P. S. Foner. 2 vols. New York: The Citadel Press, 1945.

Roosevelt, Theodore. *Letters*. Edited by Elting E. Morison. 8 vols. Cambridge, Mass.: Harvard University Press, 1954.

Rush, Benjamin. *Autobiography*. Edited by George W. Corner. Princeton: Princeton University Press, 1948.

Schachner, Nathan, ed. "Alexander Hamilton Viewed by His Friends. The Narratives of Robert Troup and Hercules Mulligan." *William and Mary Quarterly*, 3d Series, Vol. IV.

Seward, Frederick W. *Autobiography of William Seward*. 3 vols. New York, 1877–91.

Van Buren, Martin. *Autobiography*. *Annual Report* of the American Historical Association for the year 1918 (Vol. 11). Washington, D. C.: Government Printing Office, 1920.

Webb, Samuel Blachly. *Correspondence and Journals*. Edited by W. C. Ford. 3 vols. New York: Wickersham Press, 1893–94.

BOOKS AND PERIODICALS

Adair, Douglas. "A Note on Certain of Hamilton's Pseudonyms." *William and Mary Quarterly*, 3rd Series, Vol. XII (1955).

Adams, Henry. *Life of Albert Gallatin*. New York: Peter Smith, 1943.

Aly, Bower. *The Rhetoric of Alexander Hamilton*. New York: Russell & Russell, 1965.

Ammon, Harry. *James Monroe*. New York: McGraw Hill, 1971.

Atherton, Gertrude. *Adventures of a Novelist*. New York: Liveright, 1932.

———. *A Few of Hamilton's Letters*. New York: Macmillan, 1903.

———. *The Conqueror*. New York: Macmillan, 1902.

———. "The Hunt for Hamilton's Mother." 175 *North American Review* (1902).

Beard, Charles A. *Economic Origins of Jeffersonian Democracy*. New York: Macmillan, 1915.

———. *An Economic Interpretation of the Constitution of the United States*. New York: Macmillan, 1948.

Bemis, Samuel F. *Jay's Treaty*. New Haven: Connecticut, Yale University Press, 1962.

Bolles, A. S. *The Financial History of the United States*. 2 vols. New York, 1879.

Bowen, Catherine Drinker. *Miracle at Philadelphia*. Boston: Little, Brown, 1966.

Bowers, Claude. *Jefferson and Hamilton*. Boston: Houghton Mifflin, 1941.

Bowling, Kenneth R. "Dinner at Jefferson's." *William and Mary Quarterly*, 3d Series, Vol. XXVIII (October 1971).

Bowman, A. H. "Jefferson, Hamilton and American Foreign Policy." *Political Science Quarterly* 71 (1956).

Boyd, Julian P. *Number 7, Alexander Hamilton's Secret Attempts to Control American Foreign Policy*. Princeton: Princeton University Press, 1964.

Brant, Irving. *James Madison*. 5 vols. Indianapolis: Bobbs Merrill, 1941–53.

Brigham, Clarence S. *History and Bibliography of American Newspapers 1690–1820*. 2 vols. Worcester, Mass.: American Antiquarian Society, 1947.

Brodie, Fawn M. *Thomas Jefferson*. New York: W. W. Norton & Co., 1974.

Brooks, Robin. "Alexander Hamilton, Melancton Smith and the Ratification of the Constitution in New York." *William and Mary Quarterly*, 3d Series, Vol. XXIV, No. 3 (July 1967).

Bryce, James. *The American Commonwealth*. New York: Macmillan, 1907.

Charles, Joseph. *The Origins of the American Party System*. New York: Harper & Brothers, 1961.

Conway, Moncure D. *Omitted Chapters of History Disclosed in the Life and Papers of Edmund Randolph*. New York: G. P. Putnam Sons, 1889.

Cooke, Jacob E. "The Compromise of 1790." *William and Mary Quarterly*, 3d Series, Vol. XXVII, No. 4 (October 1970).

———. "Alexander Hamilton's Authorship of the 'Caesar' Letters." *William and Mary Quarterly*, 3d Series, Vol. XVII, No. 1 (January 1960).

Crane, Elaine F. "Publius in the Provinces: Where Was the *Federalist* Reprinted Outside of New York City?" *William and Mary Quarterly*, 3d Series, Vol. XXI (October, 1964).

Dangerfield, George. *Chancellor Robert R. Livingston of New York, 1746–1813*. New York: Harcourt Brace, 1960.

Daniels, Jonathan. *Ordeal of Ambition: Jefferson, Hamilton, Burr*. New York: Doubleday, 1970.

Dauer, Manning J. *The Adams Federalists*. Baltimore: Johns Hopkins University Press, 1953.

Davis, Joseph S. *Essays in the Earlier History of American Corporations*. 2 vols. Cambridge, Mass.: Harvard University Press, 1917.

De Conde, Alexander. *Entangling Alliances: Politics and Diplomacy under George Washington*. Durham, N.C.: Duke University Press, 1958.

———. *The Quasi-War*. New York: Charles Scribner's Sons, 1966.

De Pauw, Linda G. *The Eleventh Pillar: New York and the Federal Constitution*. Ithaca, N.Y.: Cornell University Press, 1966.

Dictionary of American Biography. 20 Vols. New York: Scribner's, 1928–36.

Domett, Henry W. *History of the Bank of New York 1784–1884*. Compiled from official records and other sources at the request of the Directors, 1884.

Dunbar, C. F. "Some Precedents Followed by Alexander Hamilton." *Quarterly Journal of Economics* III (1888–89).

Dunbar, Louise. *A Study of 'Monarchical' Tendencies in the United States from 1776–1801*. Urbana, Ill., 1922.

Fischer, David. "The Myth of the Essex Junto." *William and Mary Quarterly*, 3d series, Vol. XXI, No. 2 (April 1964).

Flexner, James Thomas. *George Washington: Anguish and Farewell, 1793–1799*. Boston: Little, Brown, 1972.

———. *George Washington and the New Nation, 1783–1793*. Boston: Little, Brown, 1970.

———. *George Washington: The Forge of Experience 1732–1775*. Boston: Little, Brown, 1965.

———. *Young Hamilton*. Boston: Little, Brown, 1976.

Flick, Alexander C., ed. *History of the State of New York* 10 vols. New York: Columbia University Press, 1933.

Force, Peter. *American Archives: Fourth Series*. 6 vols. Washington, 1837–53.

Ford, Henry Jones. *Alexander Hamilton*. New York: Scribner's, 1920.

Ford, Paul Leicester. *Essays on the Constitution of the United States Published during its Discussion by the People 1787–1788*. Brooklyn: Historical Printing Club, 1892.

Fox, Dixon Ryan. *The Decline of Aristocracy in the Politics of New York 1801–1840*. New York: Harper & Row, 1965.

———. *Yankees and Yorkers*. Port Washington N.Y.: Ira J. Friedman Inc., 1963.

Freeman, Douglas Southall. *George Washington*. 6 vols. New York: Charles Scribner's Sons, 1954.

Freud, Anna. *Ego and the Mechanics of Defense*. New York: International Universities Press, 1946.

Goebel, Julius, Jr. *The Law Practice of Alexander Hamilton*. 2 vols. New York: Columbia University Press, 1964–69.

Hacker, Louis M. *Alexander Hamilton in the American Tradition*. New York: McGraw Hill, 1957.

Hamilton, Allan McLane. *The Intimate Life of Alexander Hamilton.* New York: Charles Scribner's Sons, 1911.

Hammond, Bray. *Banks and Politics in America.* Princeton: Princeton University Press, 1957.

Hecht, Marie B. *Beyond the Presidency.* New York: Macmillan, 1976.

Hendrickson, Robert *Hamilton I (1757–1789).* New York: Mason/Charter, 1976.

———. *Hamilton II* (1789–1804). New York: Mason/Charter, 1976.

Hofstadter, Richard. *The Idea of a Party System.* Berkeley: University of California Press, 1970.

Irving, Washington. *Life of George Washington.* 4 vols. New York: G. P. Putnam & Co., 1856.

Jacobs, James R. *Tarnished Warrior: Major General James Wilkinson.* New York: Macmillan, 1938.

Kenyon, Cecilia. "Alexander Hamilton: Rousseau of the Right." *Political Science Quarterly,* LXXIII (1958).

Ketcham, Ralph. *James Madison.* New York: Macmillan, 1971.

Kirk, Russell. *The Conservative Mind.* Chicago: Henry Regnery Company, 1953.

Kline, Jo-Ann, ed. *The Founding Fathers: Alexander Hamilton A Biography in his own Words.* New York: Newsweek, 1973.

Koch, Adrienne. *Power, Morals and the Founding Fathers.* Ithaca, N.Y.: Cornell University Press, 1961.

Kohn, Richard H. "The Inside Story of the Newburgh Conspiracy: America and the Coup d'Etat." *William and Mary Quarterly,* 3d Series, Vol. XXVI (1970).

Konefsky, Samuel J. *John Marshall and Alexander Hamilton: Architects of the American Constitution.* New York: Macmillan, 1964.

Kurtz, Stephen G. *The Presidency of John Adams.* Philadelphia: University of Pennsylvania Press, 1957.

Lamb, Mrs. Martha J., and Harrison, Mrs. Burton. *History of the City of New York.* 3 vols. New York: A. S. Barnes, 1896.

Larson, Harold. "Alexander Hamilton; the Fact and Fiction of His Early Years." *William and Mary Quarterly,* 3d Series, no. 9:139–151.

Leary, Lewis. *That Rascal Freneau.* New Brunswick, N.J.: Rutgers University Press, 1941.

Lifton, Robert Jay, ed. *Explorations in Psychohistory.* New York: Simon and Schuster, 1974.

Lodge, Henry Cabot. *Alexander Hamilton.* Boston: Houghton Mifflin, 1909.

Lossing, B. J. *The Life and Times of Philip Schuyler.* New York: Sheldar and Co., 1872.

Lycan, Gilbert L. *Alexander Hamilton & American Foreign Policy.* Norman, Okla.: University of Oklahoma Press, 1969.

McDonald, Forrest. *E Pluribus Unum: The Formation of the American Republic 1776–1790.* Boston: Houghton Mifflin, 1965.

———. *The Presidency of George Washington.* New York: W. W. Norton, 1974.

———. *Alexander Hamilton.* New York: W. W. Norton, 1979.

Main, Jackson T. *The Anti Federalists.* Chapel Hill, N.C.: University of North Carolina Press, 1961.

Malone, Dumas. *Jefferson and the Rights of Man.* Boston: Little, Brown, 1951.

———. *Jefferson and the Ordeal of Liberty.* Boston: Little, Brown, 1962.

———. *Jefferson, The President, First Term.* Boston: Little, Brown, 1970.

Marshall, John. *The Life of George Washington.* 5 vols. Philadelphia: C. P. Wayne, 1804–1807.

Meyer, Freeman W. "A Note on the Origins of the 'Hamiltonian System.'" *William and Mary Quarterly,* 3d Series, Vol. XXI, No. 4 (October 1964).

Miller, John C. *The Federalist Era 1789–1801.* New York: Harper & Brothers, 1960.

———. *Alexander Hamilton: Portrait in Paradox.* New York: Harper & Row, 1959.

———. *Triumph and Freedom.* Boston: Little, Brown, 1948.

Minnigerode, Meade. *Jefferson Friend of France 1793: The Career of Edmond Charles Genet 1763–1834.* New York: G. P. Putnam's Sons, 1928.

Mitchell, Broadus. *Alexander Hamilton, Youth to Maturity 1755–1788.* New York: Macmillan, 1957.

———. *Alexander Hamilton, The National Adventure 1788–1804.* New York: Macmillan, 1962.

———. "The Man Who Discovered Hamilton." 69 *New Jersey Historical Society* Proceedings.

———. *Heritage from Hamilton.* New York: Columbia University Press, 1957.

Morris, Richard B., ed, *Alexander Hamilton and the Founding of the Nation.* New York: The Dial Press, 1957.

———. *Seven Who Shaped Our Destiny.* New York: Harper & Row, 1975.

Morse, John T., Jr. *The Life of Alexander Hamilton.* 2 vols. Boston: Little, Brown, 1882.

Mostellen, Frederick, and Wallace, David L. *Inference and Disputed Authorship: The Federalist.* Reading, Mass., 1964.

Nelson, John R., Jr. "Alexander Hamilton and American Manufacturing." *Journal of American History.* Vol. CXV (March, 1979).

Nevins, Allan. *The American States During and After the Revolution.* New York: 1924.

———. *History of the Bank of New York and Trust Company 1784–1934.* Privately Printed. New York, March 1934.

Nichols, Roy F. *The Invention of the American Political Parties.* New York: Macmillan, 1967.

Oliver, Frederick Scott. *Alexander Hamilton: An Essay on American Union.* New York: G. P. Putnam's Sons, 1923.

Paltsits, Victor Hugo. *Washington's Farewell Address.* New York: New York Public Library, 1935.

Panagopoulus, E. P. *Alexander Hamilton's Pay Book.* Detroit, 1961.

Pancake, John S. *Thomas Jefferson and Alexander Hamilton.* Woodbury, N.Y.: Barron's, 1974.

Parmet, Herbert S., and Hecht, Marie B. *Aaron Burr: Portrait of an Ambitious Man.* New York: Macmillan, 1967.

Parton, James. *The Life and Times of Aaron Burr.* 2 vols. Boston: Houghton Mifflin, 1882.

————. *Life of Thomas Jefferson*. Boston: James R. Osgood & Company, 1874.

Perkins, Bradford. *The First Rapprochement: England and the United States 1795–1805*. Berkeley: University of California Press, 1967.

Peterson, Merrill D., ed. *James Madison: A Biography in His Own Words*. New York: Newsweek, 1974.

Pickering, Octavius, and Upham, C. W. *The Life of Timothy Pickering*. 4 vols. Boston: Little, Brown, 1867–73.

Plumer, William, Jr. *Life of William Plumer*. Boston: Phillips Sampson, 1856.

Plutarch, *The Lives of the Noble Greeks and Romans*. New York: The Modern Library, N.D.

Pomerantz, Sidney J. *New York An American City 1783–1803.*: A *Study of Urban Life*. Port Washington, N.Y.: Ira J. Friedman Inc., 1965.

Ramsung, H. U. "Alexander Hamilton og hans modrene Slaegt. Tidsbilleder fra Dansk Vest-Indiens Barndom," in *Personalhistorisk Tidsskrift*. Translated from Danish microfilm. New York Public Library.

Rossiter, Clinton. *Alexander Hamilton and the Constitution*. New York: Harcourt Brace and World, 1964.

————. *1787*. New York: Macmillan, 1966.

Schachner, Nathan. *Alexander Hamilton*. New York: Appleton, 1946.

————. *Thomas Jefferson*. New York: Appleton-Century-Crofts, 1951.

Shaw, Peter. *The Character of John Adams*. Published for The Institute of Early American History and Culture Williamsburg, Virginia. Chapel Hill, N.C.: University of North Carolina Press, 1976.

Smertenko, Johan J. *Alexander Hamilton*. New York: Greenberg, 1932.

Smith, James M. "Alexander Hamilton, The Alien Law and Seditious Libels," *Review of Politics* XVl (1954).

————. *Freedom's Fetters: The Alien and Sedition Laws and American Civil Liberties*. Ithaca, N.Y.: Cornell University Press, 1956.

Smith, Page. *John Adams*. 2 vols. New York: Doubleday, 1962.

Smucker, Samuel M. *The Life and Times of Alexander Hamilton*. Philadelphia: J. W. Bradley, 1857.

Spannaus, Nancy B. and White, Christopher. *The Political Economy of the American Revolution*. New York: Campaign Publications, 1977.

Spaulding, E. Wilder. *New York in the Critical Period*. New York: Columbia University Press, 1932.

————. *His Excellency George Clinton*. New York: Macmillan, 1938.

Steiner, Bernard. *The Life and Correspondence of James McHenry*. Cleveland: Burrows Bros., 1907.

Stewart, Donald H. *The Opposition Press of the Federalist Period*. Albany: State University of New York Press, 1969.

Stourzh, Gerald. *Alexander Hamilton and the Idea of Republican Government*. Stanford: Stanford University Press, 1970.

Syrett, Harold C., and Cooke, Jean G. *Interview in Weehawken The Burr-Hamilton Duel*. Middletown, Conn.: Wesleyan University Press, 1960.

Thomas, Milton Halsey. "Hamilton's Unfought Duel of 1795." *The Pennsylvania Magazine of History and Biography* LXXVIII (July 1954).

Turner, Lynn. *William Plumer of New Hampshire 1759–1850*. Chapel Hill, N.C.: University of North Carolina Press, 1962.

454

Vandenberg, Arthur H. *The Greatest American: Alexander Hamilton*. New York: G. P. Putnam's Sons, 1921.

——. *If Hamilton Were Here Today*. New York: G. P. Putnam's Sons, 1923.

Van Doren, Carl C. *Secret History of the American Revolution*. New York: Viking, 1941.

Warren, Charles. *The Supreme Court in United States History*. 2 vols. Boston: Little, Brown, 1926.

Warshow, Robert I. *Alexander Hamilton First American Business Man*. Garden City, N.Y.: Garden City Publishing Company, 1931.

White, Leonard D. *The Federalists: A Study in Administrative History*. New York: Macmillan, 1956.

Wilson, James G., ed. *Memorial History of the City of New York*. 4 vols. New York: New York History Co., 1892–93.

Wiltse, C. M. *The Jeffersonian Tradition in American Democracy*. Chapel Hill, N.C.: University of North Carolina Press, 1935.

Wood, Gordon S. *The Creation of the American Republic 1776–1787*. Institute of Early American History and Culture, Williamsburg, Virginia. Chapel Hill, N.C.: University of North Carolina Press, 1969.

Young, Alfred. *The Jeffersonian Republicans of New York: The Origins 1763–1797*. Chapel Hill, N.C.: University of North Carolina Press, 1967.

Index